Selves

Selves

An Essay in Revisionary Metaphysics

GALEN STRAWSON

CLARENDON PRESS · OXFORD

OXFORD

UNIVERSITY PRESS

Great Clarendon Street, Oxford OX2 6DP

Oxford University Press is a department of the University of Oxford.
It furthers the University's objective of excellence in research, scholarship,
and education by publishing worldwide in

Oxford New York

Auckland Cape Town Dar es Salaam Hong Kong Karachi
Kuala Lumpur Madrid Melbourne Mexico City Nairobi
New Delhi Shanghai Taipei Toronto

With offices in

Argentina Austria Brazil Chile Czech Republic France Greece
Guatemala Hungary Italy Japan Poland Portugal Singapore
South Korea Switzerland Thailand Turkey Ukraine Vietnam

Oxford is a registered trade mark of Oxford University Press
in the UK and in certain other countries

Published in the United States
by Oxford University Press Inc., New York

© Galen Strawson 2009

The moral rights of the author have been asserted
Database right Oxford University Press (maker)

First published 2009

British Library Cataloguing in Publication Data

Data available

Library of Congress Cataloging in Publication Data

Strawson, Galen.
Selves : an essay in revisionary metaphysics / Galen Strawson.
p. cm.
Includes bibliographical references (p.   ) and index.
ISBN 978–0–19–825006–7
1. Self (Philosophy) 2. Self. 3. Ontology. 4. Phenomenology. 5. Metaphysics. I. Title.
BD450.S7775 2009
126—dc22   2009009572

Typeset by Laserwords Private Limited, Chennai, India
Printed in Great Britain
on acid-free paper byPrinted in Great Britain
on acid-free paper by
CPI Antony Rowe, Chippenham

ISBN 978–0–19–825006–7

1 3 5 7 9 10 8 6 4 2

To E, T, G, H, and I

CONTENTS

DETAILED CONTENTS

PREFACE

> Truth in philosophy, though not to be despaired of, is so complex and many-sided, so multi-faced, that any individual philosopher's work, if it is to have any unity and coherence, must at best emphasize some aspects of the truth, to the neglect of others which may strike another philosopher with more force.
>
> (P. F Strawson, 1985: viii)

This book is a work of psychology (the more philosophical division), and many of the claims in it are open to, and I believe deserve, empirical investigation. It has, however, no obvious audience, because it freely mixes philosophy of mind, phenomenology, history of philosophy, and general metaphysics, and philosophers tend—more than ever before—to stay inside their areas of specialization. It's not for the sake of this book that I wish this weren't so; specialization is good and necessary, in philosophy as in other disciplines, but philosophers need generalism as one of their specialisms. Chremes is a busybody, in Terence's play *The Self-Tormentor*, but he's very well-intentioned, and his famous remark in defence of his inquisitiveness—*homo sum: nihil humani a me alienum puto*—transfers well from the human to the philosophical case: *philosophus sum—nihil philosophici a me alienum puto*.

Selves is longer than it might have been, and I've listed some short cuts below. One reason for its length is that it includes material additional to the main argument, although relevant to the overall subject (pages 117–60, for example, or 221–249). A second is that passages that take account of historical figures grew into the book after the main ideas were in place. A third is increasing uncertainty about what time is. A fourth, Pascalian reason is that I haven't had enough time to make it shorter; ideas can be unwilling to settle into their best form (as 8.6 in particular shows), and too much of this book has been written in the gaps between doing too many other things. A fifth reason is that I make a number of points more than once; but I'd have preserved most of the repetition (repetition with variation) even if I'd had more time. I'd like to invoke l'Abbé Terrasson, as Kant does in his introduction to the *Critique of Pure Reason*, arguing that 'if the size of a volume be measured not by the number of its pages but by the time required for mastering it, it can be said of many a book, that it would be much shorter if it were not so short' (Axviii), but I've used the Terrasson defence once too often. I think, though, that repeated exposure to unfamiliar ideas can have a useful protreptic function, freeing thought (sometimes years later) by diminishing initial incredulity.

Much of the book falls short of argument in the strict sense. I'm not trying to argue other people into my view by starting from their premises, let alone premises we share. My main aim is to give useful expression to, and develop further in certain respects, views that others are already interested in or already disposed to find sympathetic. I'm not as pessimistic as Bradley writing to William James

Please do not think I want to lead you into a discussion. I have always myself found such things useless. One may, where an objection is not a mere mistake, profit by it when one reconsiders the matter as a whole, but otherwise I fancy never. So do not trouble yourself to reply to what I say   (1897: 307)

but when it comes to those to whom one's thinking is unsympathetic, one can define success as making things that seem obviously wrong to them seem a little less obviously wrong. Perhaps this book will gradually undermine certain natural views of the self, in some, in a lasting way, even though its specific conclusions are utterly rejected (its aims are, in a certain sense, indirect). Many, though, will find that their sympathies lie more with my sceptical and sometimes truculent imaginary interlocutor, who first appears on page 9.

Philosophers from the further past feature constantly in this book because their ideas lie in the vanguard of thought. If the history of philosophy is some sort of separate academic corral, then I'm not doing history of philosophy when I discuss Descartes, any more than I am when I discuss Dennett, Dainton or Damasio. The older philosophers regularly express ideas and formulate problems with greater clarity, directness, or insight than their most read twentieth and twenty-first century descendants. Their lack of certain present-day assumptions shows how questionable—blinding—some of those assumptions are, even as it increases one's appreciation of others. Philosophers of mind who think that recent science—or indeed philosophy—has radically changed the map of their discipline, rather than providing various forms of expression and concrete illustrative support for long existing hypotheses, don't know much about their subject.

Short cuts   Readers primarily interested in the metaphysics of the self can reduce 425 pages to 197, reading the introduction (1–18), the definition of self-consciousness (102–3), and the definition of 'sesmet' (208), before skipping to page 249. If another 50 pages are allowed, I would add [1] pages 19–31, a discussion of those who think the self is just the body or the whole human being, and those who, intent on stressing the importance of the body, have overshot and forgotten the mind; [2] pages 72–93, a discussion of the necessary singleness of the (sense of the) self, which connects with some of the present-day discussion of the topic of personal identity; [3] pages 109–117, an examination of the idea that self-consciousness requires some sort of sense of oneself as a mental entity; [4] pages 176–81, a challenge to the ancient view, endorsed by Ryle as 'the systematic elusiveness of "I" ', that the mind can no more apprehend itself directly than the eye can see itself directly; and [5] pages 217–21, a proposal about the sources of our natural belief in a persisting self. There's a more or less self-standing passage on my Mamertian understanding of Descartes, on pages 338–49, and a continuing and overlapping thread of reflection on Kant's views on the self on pages 48–52, 188–9, 45–7, 169–73, and 379–85.

There are a large number of internal cross-references in this book. They began as markers for my own use, and I've left them because they may be helpful to those who want to read individual parts or sections. The logical symbolism that begins on p. 320 has the same origin, and may again be helpful to some. I've tried to make sure at every point that one doesn't have to understand the symbolism at all in order to understand what I'm saying.

History   I began *Selves* in 1995, when I was invited to give a lecture on the topic of the self in the 1996 Wolfson College lecture series 'From Soul to Self'. Its origins lie earlier, though, in puzzlement about self-consciousness, which dated from the time I arrived as a postgraduate student at Oxford in October 1974. Five years later, Gareth Evans asked why my DPhil thesis about free will was taking so long. I gave him my tangled work on self-consciousness, which was part of the thesis. The next time I met him, early in 1980, he said he understood why.[1]

The first class I gave on the self was a graduate seminar at New York University in the fall of 1997. By the end of that academic year, in which I held, most happily, a British Academy/Leverhulme Trust Senior Research Fellowship, the basic structure of the book was in place, together with a good deal of the content. I presented some of the ideas in a seminar at the University of Oxford in the academic year 1998–1999, and again at Rutgers University in the autumn of 2000.

In January 2001 I moved from a tutorial fellowship at Jesus College, Oxford to a professorship at the University of Reading, and had no further opportunity to try my thoughts in a graduate seminar until I took up an appointment at City University of New York Graduate Center in 2004, which I held jointly with my post at Reading. After giving classes on Hume's, Kant's, and William James's views on the self (among other things) in 2004 and 2005, I presented the central material of this book in the fall of 2006. A term of research leave from the UK Arts and Humanities Research Council then enabled me to submit a full draft to Oxford University Press in June 2007. Throughout this time I kept coming across historical precedents and pertinent things written by others, and gathering apposite quotations. I also learned more about the Phenomenological tradition in philosophy through my time as a visiting professor at the Center for Subjectivity Research at the University of Copenhagen in 2003, and my friendship with Dan Zahavi, the director of the Center.

Parts of the book have appeared in earlier versions in other places (most were parts of the book before they were anything else). The basic structure, set out in Part 2, derives from ' "The Self" ' (1997) and was taken a little further in 'The Self and the Sesmet' (1999). 3.5 is a direct development of section 9.3 of *Freedom and Belief* (1986). 3.7–3.19 were written in 1995, and appeared in abridged form as 'Self, Body and Experience' (1999). 4.4 was first aired in 'The Self and the Sesmet'. 4.6 expanded into, and was then cut down

---

[1] Shortly before Evans died in August 1980 I received my paper back from him with a kind note explaining that he was no longer able to comment on it in any detail. The work he saw survives in chapter 9 of *Freedom and Belief* and in Appendix E, 'The sense of the self'.

from, 'Mental ballistics: the involuntariness of spontaneity' (2003). The first draft of Part 5 was laid out in ' "The Self" '. 6.3 expands section 5.10 of *Mental Reality* (1994), and 6.6–6.9 draw on chapters 3 and 4 of *Mental Reality*, and the development of those chapters in 'Real materialism' (2003) and 'Realistic monism: why physicalism entails panpsychism' (2006). 6.10–6.15 began as parts of 'The Self and the Sesmet', and a large part of 6.15 appeared as 'The identity of the categorical and the dispositional' (2008). Sections of Part 7 appeared in 'Panpsychism? Reply to commentators, with a celebration of Descartes' (2006). The theme running through sections 7.4 and 8.8–8.10 began as 'What is the relation between an experience, the subject of an experience, and the content of the experience?' (2003), a paper which underwent substantial correction when it was republished in *Real Materialism and Other Essays*. Three shorter and as yet unpublished books, *Life in Time*, *Locke on personal identity* and *The Evident Connexion: Mind, Self and David Hume*, broke away from this book by becoming too large, leaving various traces behind.

Acknowledgements   Barry Dainton and Sam Coleman read the whole of this book. I'm extremely grateful to them for their comments. No one else has read much of it, but I've benefited from many observations made by many people, many of whom I can no longer identify. As far as known sources are concerned, let me first thank the members of my graduate classes—at New York University in 1997, Oxford in 1998 and 1999, Rutgers University in 2000, and the CUNY Graduate Center in 2004–2006—for their scepticism and help, in particular David Auerbach, Chris North, Peter Langland-Hassan, Myrto Mylopoulos, Doug Parvin, Daniel Shargel, Adam Swenson, and Rosemary Twomey.

For particular points here and there, I'm grateful to—among others—Jesus Aguilar, Torin Alter, Harvey Brown, Fred Beiser, Jeremy Butterfield, Darragh Byrne, Quassim Cassam, Desmond Clarke, Jonathan Dancy, Shaun Gallagher, Jonardon Ganeri, Don Garrett, Max de Gaynesford, Brie Gertler, Maureen Dunne, Philip Goff, Mark Greenberg, Alan Hollinghurst, Trenton Merricks, Mark Johnston, James Ladyman, Michael Lockwood, Bill Lyons, Brian McLaughlin, Christia Mercer, Peter Momtchiloff, Michelle Montague, Adrian Moore, Martine Nida-Rümelin, Ben Olsen, Doug Parvin, Charlie Pelling, Antonia Phillips, Wlodek Rabinowicz, John Richardson, Dan Robinson, David Rosenthal, Simon Saunders, Julia Simon, Barry C. Smith, Paul Snowdon, Jim Stone, P. F. Strawson, Udo Thiel, Keith Turansky, Bas van Fraassen, Peter van Inwagen, Dan Zahavi, and Dean Zimmerman.

More institutionally, I thank the British Academy and the Leverhulme Trust for the year I spent as a British Academy/Leverhulme Senior Research Fellow in 1997–8; the Danish National Research Foundation, sponsor of the Center for Subjectivity Research at the University of Copenhagen during the time I was there; and the UK Arts and Humanities Reasearch Council for giving me a term of Research Leave in 2007, which enabled me to submit the typescript to the Oxford University Press. I also thank all the various universities that have allowed me to practise my profession. Fichte may exaggerate temporally, in his Rectoral Address given in Berlin in 1811, when he says that 'the University is the visible representation of the immortality of our race ... the most holy thing that the human race possesses', but he seems otherwise accurate.

The book would not exist without the editorship of the increasingly legendary Peter Momtchiloff of Talulah Gosh, Heavenly, the Would-be-Goods, and the Oxford University Press. I am greatly indebted to Jean van Altena's copyediting, Angela Anstey-Holroyd's proof reading, and Tessa Eaton's production.

Finally, I'm grateful to the copyright holders for permission to reprint the passages from Richard Hughes's *A High Wind in Jamaica* and Elizabeth Bishop's 'In the Waiting Room' in the appendices to Part 4.

Conventions

Simple numerals inside brackets refer to pages of this book; references of the form '6.6' refer to sections of this book. When I cite a work I give the date of first publication, or occasionally the date of composition, while the page reference is to the edition listed in the bibliography. I make an exception to this rule when citing Hume's *Treatise* (1739–40), Locke's *Essay* (1689–1700), and Kant's *Critique of Pure Reason* (1781–7). I refer to these as '*Treatise*', '*Essay*' and '*Critique*', respectively, and in the case of the *Critique* I often simply give the page reference number in the standard form (e.g. A235/B288). I usually cite standard editions of texts, but the translations are sometimes different from those found in the standard edition. In quoting Descartes, for example, I cite the Cottingham, Stoothoof, Murdoch, and Kenny edition, but draw also on Desmond Clarke's translations and my own. My translations of Kant are a mixture of Kemp Smith, Pluhar, and myself, helped (especially) by Frederick Beiser, Maren Meinhardt, Michael Rosen and Ralph Walker.

Part 1

Introduction

Self has turned out to mean so many things, to mean them so ambiguously, and to be so wavering in its application, that we do not feel encouraged.

(F. H. Bradley 1893: 101)

1.1 The plan

I think one has to travel a long road in order to work out the best thing to say about the self. One may have a good unreflective hold on the matter, but one has to go down a long road and cross complicated regions of doubt before one can acquire genuine philosophical tenancy, and there may be more than one road, and the place of arrival may be a region, not a single point or peak.

This book has eight parts, of which this introduction is the first. In Part 2 I propose that if one wants to enquire into the existence and nature of the self (Is there such a thing? What is it like if it exists?), then it's wise, and perhaps necessary, to start with an investigation of the experience of there being such a thing: an investigation of the general form of the experience of there being such a thing. It seems a good idea to approach the metaphysics or ontology of the self, which addresses the questions just raised, through the phenomenology of the self. Metaphysics (or ontology) is the general study of how things are or can be or must be. It's a matter for scientists and mathematicians as well as philosophers, and I take it to include physics as an evolving part. Phenomenology is the study of a particular part of how things are or can be or must be. It's the general study of the character of experience in all its sensory and cognitive richness.[1]

There's a distinctive kind of experience which I'll call 'SELF-experience'. (I explain the small capitals in the next paragraph.) SELF-experience is not just experience of what is in fact oneself. Nor is it just expressly self-conscious experience of what is in fact

---

[1] I'll use a capital letter—'Phenomenology'—to mark the distinctive tradition in phenomenology that is generally held to have been initiated by Husserl. In recent analytic philosophy the word 'phenomenology' has been used to denote the phenomena of consciousness or experience themselves, rather than their study, and I will also sometimes use it in this way.

oneself, i.e. experience of oneself conceived of specifically as oneself. In the ordinary human case it's experience of oneself as being an 'inner' subject of experience or locus of consciousness—inner relative to the human being that one is considered as a whole.[2] More generally, it's experience of oneself as something which is not the same thing as a human being considered as a whole; experience of oneself as a specifically mental presence of some sort, a mental someone or something. One might say that it's experience of oneself as having nothing more than mental being, inasmuch as it doesn't involve any positive or express figuration of oneself as something that has any existence beyond one's mental being; but it certainly needn't positively exclude the idea that one has existence that goes beyond one's mental being.

I use terms written in small capitals, like 'SELF', to designate mental elements of any sort that need to be mentioned in giving a full description of the character of experience because they contribute to it. I'll call them 'experience-determining mental elements', or 'experience-structuring mental elements', understanding 'structuring' in a wide sense according to which any contribution to the character of experience is a contribution to its structure. Concepts are obvious examples of experience-determining mental elements, in so far as they feature in people's thoughts, and much of what I have to say can be understood by taking the terms written in small capitals to denote concepts. The term is too narrow for all my purposes, though, and it's helpful to have the more general terms available. 'Experience-determining mental element' and 'experience-structuring mental element' apply to moods and emotional dispositions as well as concepts, and also to more general cognitive formations for which words like 'conception' and 'sense' (in the cognitive use of the term) seem more appropriate. They also apply to determinants of the experiential character of experience that are neither moods nor cognitive formations, allowing us to say that RED-experience and PAIN-experience (and SQUARE-experience) can occur in creatures—newborn babies, for example—that cannot plausibly be said to have the concepts RED and PAIN (or SQUARE).[3]

SELF-experience, then, is experience informed or shaped by—involving the deployment of—a certain complex experience-determining mental element: the idea or sense or feeling of the self. SELF-experience can exist whether or not selves do, just as PINK-ELEPHANT-experience can exist whether or not pink elephants do.

Let me repeat this: SELF-experience exists, as a form of experience, whether or not selves do. 'SELF-experience' is a strictly phenomenological term. It's a name for an aspect of our experience of how things are that exists whether or not things are that way in fact. SELF-experience may turn out to be illusory in so far as it purports to be experience of an existing entity properly called a self, but its phenomenological reality—its reality as a form of experience, a way of conceiving or apprehending things—is not in doubt.

---

[2] I'll restrict my attention to the human case except when I say otherwise.

[3] One problem with the word 'concept' is that the recent intense focus on 'externalist' conceptions of concepts obscures the 'internalist' use of the word to mean an experience-structuring mental element. Those who are unsure of the point of the small capitals can ignore them.

Many analytic philosophers take phenomenology to be restricted to feelings, sensations, images, non-cognitive mental phenomena. There is, however, more to the overall character of our experience; we can't hope to give a full description of it just by referring to such things. There is cognitive phenomenology in every sense in which there is sensory phenomenology (2.8), and 'SELF-experience' is, through and through, a cognitive-phenomenological term. It's a term for a certain kind of essentially cognitively informed experience: experience informed by the notion—concept, conception, idea, posit, mental element, cognitively loaded feeling—SELF.

The central task of phenomenology, when it comes to the problem of the self, is to analyse the complex, cognitive experience-determining element SELF that is active in SELF-experience and that gives it its distinctive character. Once one has determined the content of this experience-structuring element, one can go on to ask the ontological question 'Is there anything in reality to which it applies?'. What is perhaps peculiar about the present project is the proposal that one can and should identify the content of SELF by a partly—largely—phenomenological method. It may be thought that this can't be the right way to proceed—to move from phenomenology to ontology. I defend it in 2.12.

Right or wrong, the decision to begin with phenomenology, and in particular with cognitive phenomenology—which is not restricted to the business of characterizing actual occurrent experience, because it also studies the mental structures that lie behind ways of experiencing things—sets up a framework for the book, and most of Part 2 is devoted to an attempt to characterize the ordinary human form of SELF-experience. Such SELF-experience, I propose, figures the self as a (1) subject of experience that is a (2) single, (3) persisting, (4) mental (5) thing (in some solid sense of 'thing' that needs discussion) that is (6) an agent that has a certain (7) personality and is (8) not the same thing as a human being considered as a whole. I take it that the ordinary human form of SELF-experience is richer than the minimal form of genuine SELF-experience, and propose that genuine SELF-experience can exist in the absence of (3), (6), (7), and a suitably generalized version of (8), i.e. one that isn't restricted to human beings.

In Part 3 I take up this proposal about the minimal form of SELF-experience in order to consider the relation between SELF-experience and self-consciousness. Does self-consciousness require or presuppose SELF-experience? I present the case for answering No, while acknowledging that the two things go naturally together. Then I put the case for Yes, and tentatively endorse it.

I then ask the converse question: Does SELF-experience require or presuppose self-consciousness? If the answer is Yes, then all the grounds or conditions of self-consciousness are also grounds or conditions of SELF-experience, and the absorbing and time-honoured task of trying to work out the grounds or conditions of self-consciousness becomes part of the task of giving a general account of SELF-experience. That would be neat, but there are grounds for thinking that the best answer to the second question is No. There is nevertheless a natural understanding of what SELF-experience is that delivers the answer Yes, and on this basis I go ahead with the task of considering the grounds or conditions of self-consciousness. On the whole Part 3 is more metaphysics than phenomenology, but metaphysical and phenomenological concerns sometimes run close.

In Part 4 I defend the proposal about the minimal case of genuine SELF-experience made in Part 2 and drawn on in Part 3. I argue that any genuine form of SELF-experience must involve some sense or conception of the self as a *subject of experience* that is a *single mental thing*, in a sense that requires further characterization, but need not involve anything more. (I take expressions like 'conception of the self' and 'sense of the self' to be similar to 'SELF-experience', in that they do not imply that there are any such things as selves.)

At this point I have a detailed phenomenological proposal about the irreducible core of SELF-experience and can turn to the metaphysical question: Are there such things as selves? Is there anything to which the term 'SELF' applies? There is still a lot of preparatory work to do, however, and in Part 5 I continue with phenomenology. I consider certain aspects of the way in which we experience time—aspects that may be active in conditioning our beliefs about the nature of the self.

Unmixed metaphysics begins in Part 6. I raise some general metaphysical questions that need comment before addressing the particular question of the self: questions about the nature of objects or 'individual substances', about the notion of the subject of experience, and about the content of any tenable version of the doctrine of materialism or physicalism (I take 'materialism' and 'physicalism' to be interchangeable) in the philosophy of mind.

Finally, in Parts 7 and 8, I take on the metaphysics of the self directly. In the rest of this introduction I will try to give some idea of how things turn out, and then make a few more general comments about a project of this kind.

1.2 I

I exist and I know that I exist; Descartes was right that one can know this. 'The question is, what is this "I" that I know?' (Descartes 1641: 1.18). I answer: I am a human being, a product of evolution by natural selection, a living organism, an animal, a man, a physical object—a wholly physical object. I'll take all this for granted, although I'll later raise questions about the notion of a physical object. I'll assume the truth of materialism, or, more precisely, the view that everything that concretely exists (which includes everything mental) is physical.[4]

I should admit, though, that I don't fully know the nature of the physical. No one does. Nearly all of us take it that the physical is essentially spatiotemporal, for example, but no one expert in these matters claims to know for certain what space and time are, or even whether they are (as we standardly conceive them) really fundamental features of reality. Many are sure they're not, and doubts of the same order arise about the spacetime of relativity theory. And even if our best theories are right about

---

[4] By 'concrete' I mean not abstract, in the metaphysical or ontological sense of 'abstract'. Numbers, propositions, and so on are abstract entities, given this use, while even the most abstract of thoughts are wholly concrete phenomena.

the nature of spacetime, the overall nature of the physical remains in many respects profoundly obscure to us—a point made vivid by the fact that although the experiential-qualitative or 'what-it's-likeness' character of conscious experience is itself a wholly physical phenomenon, if materialism is true, our most general science of the physical, i.e. physics, provides no resources for its description, for the positive acknowledgement of its reality. This leads some 'materialists' to question the existence of the what-it's-likeness character of conscious experience, which I'll call 'experience' for short. No serious materialist can do this, however, no *real materialist*, as I will say. However much they learn about experience, real materialists preserve untouched the realism about the qualitative character of experience (colour experience, pain experience, etc.) that is common to all human beings before they encounter philosophy (see 6.6–6.9 below).

So even if I know—take for granted—that I'm a wholly physical thing, much remains unknown. I am, nevertheless, an animal, a human being, a physical thing. What else am I? I'm a subject of experience, and I know I am. This is part of what I know with certainty in knowing I exist. There is, furthermore, a fundamental sense in which I know what sort of thing a subject of experience is just in being one and in being self-conscious. This is so even though there may be philosophical and scientific truths about what it is to be a subject of experience that I don't know.

I am a subject of experience, then. Am I also a self? Only if selves exist. Do they? It depends what one means by 'self'. I'm going to make a case for understanding the word 'self' in a rather demanding way before arguing that the right answer to the question whether selves exist is Yes. But most, I suspect, will judge that my Yes amounts to a No, because they won't be prepared to take the word 'self' in the way I do.

Perhaps I'd do better to argue that the answer is No. In many ways my position puts me closer to the No-sayers than the Yes-sayers, and in saying Yes I'm likely to lose the sympathy of both sides. Each will object that I concede too much to the other. The pro-selfers will say that the selves I claim to exist don't really deserve the name, and that by using 'self' in this way I'm obscuring the fact that there are other things that do deserve the name. The anti-selfers will agree with the pro-selfers that the selves I claim to exist don't deserve the name, and say that by using 'self' in this way I'm obscuring the fact that nothing deserves the name.

Does this matter? Not much, I think. If this introduction leads you to think that my real answer to the question whether selves exist is No, then you can read everything else in that light. But I'm going to argue that selves exist, 'inner' subjects of experience that are not identical with human beings.

1.3 'I'

If I am a human being, say human being H, and if the 'am' I have just used is the 'am' of identity, as it certainly seems to be,[5] then I = H. And if I am a self, say self

---

[5] The 'am' in 'I am undone', 'I am English', or 'I am here' is not the 'am' of identity.

S, and if this 'am' is again the 'am' of identity, as it certainly seems to be, then I = S. It follows, by the logic of the identity relation, that S = H—that the self that I am is just (just is) the human being that I am. So selves are just human beings. They're not items distinct from, in the sense of non-identical with, human beings considered as a whole.

Some analytic philosophers think that this conclusion is inevitable, if one is going to talk of selves at all. Many infer that it's better not to: it's enough to talk of human beings; talk of selves is superfluous and intensely misleading.[6]

I disagree. I agree that I'm a human being, and I think that I'm a self, but I don't think that the self that I am is the human being that I am. I don't reject the logic of the identity relation; that would be silly. I reject the assumption that 'I' is univocal in the thought or speech of any given individual. The reference of 'I' standardly shifts between two different things in my thought and speech and in the thought and speech of others. Sometimes 'I' is used with the intention to refer to a human being considered as a whole, sometimes it's used with the intention to refer to a self—two things that have quite different identity conditions (if selves exist), and that stand (I'll argue) in a straightforward part–whole relation.

To say this is not to assume that selves exist. It's simply to report a fact about how the word 'I' is used. If it turns out that the best thing to say about selves is that there aren't any, then the best thing to say about 'I' may well be that it is univocal after all; that the apparent doubleness of reference of 'I' is just the echo in language of a metaphysical illusion; that 'I' is not in fact used to refer to selves as distinct from human beings even when its users intend to be making some such reference, expressly or not, and believe that they're doing so. On this view, the semantic intentions of 'I'-users sometimes incorporate a mistake about how things are. (It certainly doesn't follow—see pp. 103, 150–1—that 'I' can fail to refer.)

I disagree. I argue that we do at different times successfully use 'I' to refer to different things, to human beings considered as a whole and to selves. Sometimes, I think, uses of 'I' can be taken either way. Sometimes they can be taken to refer to both things at once. It's all pretty relaxed.

Some think that the univocity of 'I', and the fact that it refers to a human being considered as a whole when it occurs in a human being's thought or speech, can be established a priori from considerations about the essential nature (in particular, the public nature) of language. From this they argue to the non-existence of selves considered as distinct from human beings considered as a whole. I reject this idea in 2.2. My view may seem inelegant in its abandonment of the univocity of 'I', but the elegance of a theoretical view is a matter not just of its form, but also of its adequacy to the reality it is supposed to be about. If the reality is complex in a certain way, the theory must be too.

---

[6] See, paradigmatically, Kenny 1988, 1999, quoted on p. 21 below.

The claim, then, is that there's a fully correct use of 'I' in which it is true to say that I'm not a human being, i.e. a human being considered as a whole. Perhaps Cicero had something like this in mind when he said (in a legal or forensic context) that 'the mind of a person is that person'.[7] One might call it the Ciceronian use.

1.4 The brief

Whatever the best account of 'I', 'self' is a further matter. No one thinks we should stop using the word 'I', but many philosophers think that talking of the self does no good and a considerable amount of harm. They think we should stop, especially in philosophy and psychology, and try to get everyone else to stop, if only because the notion of a self is so hopelessly unclear.[8]

This proposal is unrealistic. People will always talk of the self, both in and out of theoretical contexts, and there are good reasons for this. The idea of the self is compelling, and I think, as remarked, that there is a fundamental sense in which we're right to think and talk in terms of the self, although we may not be right about why we're right. I have therefore decided to take on the self, the putative self, along with its close accomplice, the word 'self', as a lawyer takes on a client. I'm sorry to report that my client is regularly charged with being a confusion or an illusion—with non-existence, no less. My brief is to establish my client's innocence and good standing—its reality; to show that there is such a thing as the self.

It's true that the phrase 'the self', incorporating the definite article 'the', is very misleading in some contexts and directly question-begging in others. For this reason I'll often speak of selves, or *a* self, rather than of *the* self. But 'the self' will often be the most convenient expression, and when it is I'll use it freely.

I'm going to argue the case within a materialist framework, as remarked. Some may think this a disappointing constriction of scope, but it won't prevent me from considering other non-materialist options, and the constriction is not what some may suppose. Materialism as I understand it—real, realistic materialism—bears little resemblance to what many have recently taken it to be. All materialists were real or realistic materialists until about eighty years ago, and I use the word 'materialism' in the traditional sense. The idea that materialism involves the denial of the existence of experience (consciousness) is very new. Materialism is, in fact, compatible with panpsychism, a view to which I am sympathetic but will put aside for the purposes of this book.[9]

---

[7] *Mens cuiusque is est quisque* (54–51 BCE: vi. 26).   [8] See e.g. Kenny 1988, 1999; Olson 1998.

[9] See e.g. G. Strawson 1994: §3.9, 2006b. It's worth noting that panpsychism doesn't involve the highly implausible view that tables and chairs are subjects of experience; and that even when one has put aside panpsychism, it's unclear that any remotely realistic version of materialism can avoid the view that experientiality is one of the fundamental properties of the physical (see G. Strawson 2006a).

1.5 'My inmost self'

A self is certainly—essentially—a subject of experience, and it's certainly—essentially—not the same thing as a human being considered as a whole. I take these two claims to be true by definition. Some say that the only thing that is legitimately called 'the subject of experience' is the human being considered as a whole. One must reject this view if one holds that there are such things as selves. A self is some sort of inner conscious presence that is not the same thing as a human being considered as a whole, if it is anything at all. It's the kind of thing human beings have had in mind, over thousands of years, in talking of 'my inmost self'; 'my self, my inward self I mean'; the 'living, central, ... inmost I'; the 'secret self ... enclosed within'. It's part of what Hindus have argued about for at least three millennia, and Buddhists for almost as long: 'my self, that which I most intimately am'.[10]

SELF-experience is experience of there being such a thing as this. It's experience *as of* there being there being such a thing as the self, whether or not there are such things. SELF-experience exists on a view like Dennett's, for example, according to which selves don't really exist in the straightforward sense I've committed myself to defending, but are, rather, useful fictions or abstractions that help us to organize our experience when we think about ourselves and our lives.[11]

It's a mistake to think that this form of experience, this sense of self, is a peculiarly modern or 'Western' phenomenon, or a product of the Romantic movement or of an unusually leisured or intellectual life. It is, for one thing, and as just remarked, something that has been explicitly discussed in the Eastern tradition of thought for thousands of years. But that is a vanishingly small point next to the point that SELF-experience, as understood here, is as old as humanity, fundamental to the daily experience of all normal human beings.[12]

If you doubt this, I haven't yet managed to convey what I have in mind. SELF-experience is something extremely basic. It begins in early childhood. It's vivid in one's coming to consciousness of the fact that one's thoughts are unobservable by others and of the fundamental respect in which one is 'alone in one's head'. It's universal in ordinary human beings, in the sense in which I'm concerned with it. It's not subject to significant cultural variation. There is, furthermore, no conflict between the fact that SELF-experience presents the self as a specifically mental presence or entity and the fact that SELF-experience is fundamentally grounded, in all ordinary human beings, in the experience of embodiment.

SELF-experience is not something that is less available or natural in (say) traditional African societies. Mbiti considers the replacement, in such societies, of the Cartesian 'I think, therefore I am' with 'I am because we are, and since we are, therefore I am' (1969: 106). Senghor suggests replacing or complementing 'I think, therefore I am'

---

[10]   St Paul, Romans 7: 22; Spenser *c*.1594: xlv.3; Clough (1862); Traherne (1637–74); McGinn 1999: 172. Clough and Traherne are quoted by Kenny (1989: 86).

[11]   See Dennett 1991: 426–7.   [12]   It's arguable (see 3.5) that it's a necessary consequence of self-consciousness.

with 'I think, I dance the other; I am'.[13] These proposals have a clear and vivid point, but the sense in which they're accurate doesn't conflict with the present claim that SELF-experience is universal in ordinary human beings. To think that it might be somehow less prevalent or less strong in such societies is to show that one hasn't understood what I have in mind when I talk of SELF-experience. One is thinking instead in terms of some more theoretically and culturally encumbered notion of SELF-experience.

When Henry James writes, of an early book, 'I think of ... the masterpiece in question ... as the work of quite another person than myself ... a rich relation, say, who ... suffers me still to claim a shy fourth cousinship' (1915: 562–3), he knows perfectly well that he's the same human being as the author of that book, but he doesn't feel he's the same person or self as the author of that book. This feeling is common when people consider their past, and perhaps also their future: one of the ways in which people tend to figure themselves to themselves, quite independently of whether or not they have any religious beliefs, is as something whose persistence conditions—identity conditions, existence conditions—are not necessarily the same as the persistence conditions of the whole human being that they are. This way of figuring oneself presupposes—involves—the fundamental phenomenon of SELF-experience.

1.6 Transience

In the end, my brief for the self leads me to conclude that there are many short-lived or transient selves, if there are any at all. This is the Transience View of the self. Many will think it disappointing or absurd. Some will think it equivalent to saying that selves don't exist, because they take it to be true by definition that selves persist for a long period of time (e.g. a lifetime) if they exist at all. They'll think me a poor advocate, pretending to defend the self while doing it down.

—Right. And there's a much simpler and much more plausible way for materialists to uphold the claim that selves exist. Each normal human being contains some complex persisting brain structure, call it 'Q', which is not the same thing as the whole human being and which can be roughly characterized as follows: Q is that which supports the consciousness and personality of a human being. Imagine a human being losing limbs, body, reduced by a life-saving surgical *tour de force* to a head or just a brain or even something less than a brain, without any fundamental disruption of Q or of psychological life or character. In this case a subject of experience plainly persists. This fact alone justifies one, when faced with an undamaged human being, in talking of a persisting self distinct from the whole human being.[14] And the argument from surgery is unnecessary. It's enough simply to equate the self

---

[13] 1964: 73; see also Wiredu 1998: 98.

[14] Those who identify selves with the human being considered as a whole can agree that the brain alone, or Q alone, is the self, in the case in which the brain, or Q, is all that is left after radical surgery, but deny that this shows that there is a self distinct from a human being, on the ground that the brain, or Q, is in this case the whole human being.

with Q, the self-organ, as it were. Q is simply part of the brain, a brain structure, and there can be no objection to thinking of it as a persisting thing like a hand or an eye although it isn't a single part of the brain in any simple physiological sense, in the way that the amygdala is. One might call this the 'brain-system' view of the self. It states that the self is whatever anterior-insula/precuneus/medial-prefrontal-cortex/reticular-activating-system/etc.-involving thing in the brain supports the consciousness and personality of a human being and is still there when the human being is in dreamless sleep.

If you're a materialist and favour a persisting self, this is probably the view for you. Selves can certainly be said to exist and persist when defined in this way, as surely as hearts do. Why don't I accept it? It's written into my brief that if the self's claim to exist is to be sufficiently vindicated, then it must be shown to qualify as a *thing* or *individually existing entity* or *object* in some robust sense that remains to be determined. It must be shown to qualify as an object in fundamental metaphysics, by which I mean (at least) metaphysics that gives no special weight to the ordinary categories of thought. More precisely, it must qualify as an object *if* and in so far as fundamental metaphysics recognizes the existence of such things at all. Perversely or not, I find that this raises a difficulty for the brain-system view: there's a doubt about whether brain structures of the sort just proposed can pass this test.

   I won't be able to explain this properly until Part 6. For the moment let me note that I find common ground here with Peter van Inwagen, who agrees that selves understood as brain structures can't be said to be objects.[15]

1.7 Thing, object

—Brain-system selves are going to pass any reasonable version of your object test, but that doesn't matter, because the test is already a mistake. You say you want to show that there is such a thing as the self, and that you use words like 'thing', 'entity', and 'object' advisedly, but you're already way off track. You've been grossly misled by the word 'self'—by the fact that it is grammatically substantival, a noun.

This objection is venerable, but it ignores my brief, which is precisely to defend my client's claim to be a individual thing or entity or object (assuming that fundamental metaphysics recognizes the existence of such things). I may fail to produce a convincing defence, but this is my brief. Only a defence that shows my sadly maligned client to be a thing or object of some sort (given that there are such things) will count as a defence that shows it to exist. My client has expressly requested this, in view of the enormous weight of prejudice against it. The request amounts, in an older and potentially highly misleading vocabulary, to the—non-negotiable—requirement that the self be shown to be an *individual substance* or *substantial individual* of some sort.

---

[15]   van Inwagen 1990a: §15; he holds the same view about hearts. He holds, in fact, that hearts and brain-system selves can't even be said to exist—since only objects can be said to exist—and his reasons are of great interest.

—Of course there are objects and substances.

When metaphysics gets serious, large uncertainties arise about whether the traditional notions of object or individual substance have application to concrete reality—especially given the assumption that there is or can be a plurality of such things. Formidable doubts are raised by Nāgārjuna and Nietzsche among others. There are Spinoza's related doubts, echoed in present-day physics and cosmology, about whether more than one concrete thing can possibly qualify as a substance. According to traditional definitions, an individual substance is (i) a bearer of attributes that is in some manner over and above its attributes. It is (ii) something that can exist by itself without dependence on other beings (or at least without dependence on other created beings). It is (iii) a subject of predication that is not itself 'predicable' of anything, i.e. a possessor of properties that is not itself a property of something else.[16] With Descartes, Spinoza, and others, I think that the first of these traditional requirements is provably mistaken. I suspect that realistic adherence to the view that there is a plurality of individual substances requires one to abandon the second, and that the third depends on an untenable metaphysical framework. I discuss this in Part 6, where I endorse a fourth traditional definition of substance, favoured by Leibniz among others, according to which activity is the fundamental essential property of a substance.

Suppose that the result of imposing this *object* condition on the self is that I can't find a sufficiently worthy candidate for selfhood. Suppose I can't even show that a view that takes the self to be an object or substance of some sort is better than a view according to which it's best seen as a property of some other thing like a human being or a brain. Suppose, in Kant's words, that I find it 'quite impossible to determine the manner in which I [i.e. the self or soul] exist, whether it be as substance [object] or as accident [property]'.[17] In that case I may have to conclude that my client is guilty as charged: non-existent. I may have to conclude that the SELF-*phenomena*—i.e. all the undoubtedly real phenomena that lead us to talk in terms of the self, whether or not there is such a thing—simply don't provide adequate grounds for the claim that selves exist. I may have to fall back on a weaker brief or resign the case altogether.

For the moment, though, the brief is to show that selves exist, and that they're things or objects or 'substances' of some sort, and hence, given materialism, physical objects. One possibility is that there are in fact no better candidates for the title of 'physical object' than selves—even if there are others that are as good.

1.8 Object, physical

This last suggestion is likely to strike many as obviously false, but this reaction may stem in part from a failure to think through what it is for something to be physical, on a

[16] See e.g. Kant 1783: §46; Descartes 1644: 1.210; Aristotle *Categories* 2ª11–12.
[17] 1781–7: B420. From this point on all references to the *Critique of Pure Reason* will be in the standard 'A/B' form, referring either to the 1st 1781 (A) edn. or the 2nd 1787 (B) edn. or to both.

genuine or realistic materialist view, and, equally, from a failure to think through what it is for something to be a thing or object. I think one has to solve for three inadequately conceived quantities—*self, object, physical*—simultaneously, using each to get leverage on the others. Most of the work on the notions *object* and *physical* takes place in Part 6, and both emerge with values—meanings—considerably different from those normally assigned to them. As for *self*, it is the constant subject of this book.

One simple point rehearsed in Part 6 is that all physical objects are literally processes, even if—or even though—not all processes are objects. If it's a 'category mistake' to say that things are processes, don't blame me; blame the collision of ordinary thought and language with the world. Another simple point is that the most basic acquaintance with physics shows physical objects—from stones to brains—to be almost inconceivably insubstantial relative to our everyday conception of them, 'mere' collocations of patterns of energy, fabulously diaphanous process entities whose existence involves a constant interchange with the quantum vacuum, given which it is literally correct to say that they're partly constituted by the vacuum (see e.g. 6.9). This is a fact about the world that it's very useful to bear in mind, both when we ask whether selves exist and are objects and in many other philosophical contexts.

In saying that the self is a thing or object, then, I'm not saying it isn't a process, because I think it is a process. And in saying that it's a process, I'm not saying that it isn't an object, because I think it is an object, or, rather, at least as good a candidate for being an object as anything else. In saying that it's a process that is an object, I am, rather, doubting the metaphysics that says that a process requires an object or 'substance' distinct from itself in which to occur. I hope that the work on *object* and *physical* in Part 6 will lessen the felt oddity of the claim that selves are physical things or objects, especially when it throws out the traditional distinction between an object and its properties in 6.15 and focuses on the notion of unity—activity-unity—as the fundamental criterion of objecthood. If all goes well, the discussion of *self* in Parts 7 and 8 will complete the process. (Note that anyone who thinks that selves can be morally responsible entities is likely to want to say that they are objects; events, properties, and suchlike don't seem to be promising candidates for this status.)

1.9 The strong brief and the weak

A sense of oddity may persist, so let me distinguish the strong brief from the weak. The strong brief is committed to showing that selves are concrete physical things of a certain specific sort, and indeed that they qualify as objects (if objects exist at all). It's on the terms of the strong brief that I conclude in Parts 7 and 8 that there's a fundamental sense in which human selves can't be supposed to have long-term diachronic continuity, so that there are many transient selves in the case of an individual human being if there are any at all.

The trouble with the brain-system view just sketched, according to the argument, is that brain-system selves fail the object test. This conclusion, however, may be cogently questioned—the object test's conditions on objecthood may be held to be too stringent—and the weak brief is more accommodating. It's committed to real, realistic materialism, like the strong brief, but it's more relaxed about the object requirement and aims to make the best possible case for the self on the assumption that selves must be allowed to have some sort of long-term existence if they're going to be said to exist at all. The main business of this book remains the prosecution of the strong brief.

This conclusion that selves are transient entities may not only look disappointing or absurd; it may also look like one of those philosophical views which can perhaps be defended and made consistent and even shown to have certain theoretical advantages and affordances, but which are ultimately tiresome because they're too far removed from what we feel and what we want. I hope things won't turn out this way. I think the view that there are transient selves can be made compelling and shown to be natural even to those who feel it to be incessantly contradicted by the character of their experience.

1.10 Science and philosophy

Natural science and philosophy have the same goal. Both seek to give true accounts, or, failing that, the best accounts possible, of how things are, although the methods they employ are generally very different. Philosophy usually works at finding good ways of characterizing how things are without engaging in much empirical or a posteriori investigation of the world.[18] It's one of the great sciences of reality (many unobvious truths about reality can be established a priori), but it's unlike natural science in this methodological respect.

This book is a work of philosophy that sometimes looks to science for instruction. It aims to set out some ordinary and widely agreed facts in a way that illuminates their nature in spite of being initially off-putting. The off-puttingness is a problem, for nothing is so difficult in philosophy, as Hare remarks, as to 'get people to be sympathetic enough to what one is saying to understand what it is' (1981: 65). Philosophers tend to read adversarially, not to say contrasuggestibly, and when it comes to the topic of the self, the prospects of being understood are perhaps uniquely poor. Still, William James is onside. He also proposes that there are many short-lived selves, in his great book *The Principles of Psychology*, and I'm happy to be on the same side as James.[19] I hope also to receive the blessing of certain Buddhists, who do not deny the existence of the selves for which I will argue. I hope also to show that there's something right about the account of the self famously set out for inspection—but not finally endorsed—by Hume in his *Treatise* (251–62, 164–71). If this discourages you, let me add that pursuit of the idea that human selves are transient (if they exist) is a good way to articulate thought about the notion of the self even if it's not in the end the best thing to say.

---

[18] Mental self-examination is the main form of original empirical research undertaken by philosophers ('empirical' does not imply 'publicly observable').

[19] Cf. James 1890: 1. 360–3, 371, 400–1, discussed on pp. 351–4 below.

1.11 Philosophy and temperament

Is my view of the metaphysics of the self influenced by the particular character of my SELF-experience? Looking around, I think it may be. This may be a problem, but it may not be. One possibility, after all, is that SELF-experience like mine assists insight into features of the world that remain obscure to others. Another possibility, of course, is that SELF-experience like mine makes it harder to see the truth about selves—if there are such things.

So be it. Either way there's a fact of the matter about how things are in reality, and people with one sort of emotional-intellectual temperament may be in a better position to get at some parts of it than people with another. Just as the practice of meditation can lead to an appreciation of facts about mental reality that can't normally be attained by other means, so too, natural, uncultivated differences of temperament, of general 'existential' style, may give some people advantages over others when it comes to understanding how things are in one area of enquiry or another. It's an old thought that philosophical positions are covert expressions of differing human temperaments,[20] not only in relatively obvious cases (e.g. disagreement about the relative merits of consequentialism and deontology) but also in apparently entirely non-evaluative disputes (about the relative merits of realism and 'anti-realism', say, or the regularity theory of causation), and although its importance can be exaggerated, it's a thought that strikes with particular force when one comes to the problem of the self. So we should note it before we pass on. It doesn't of course have the incoherent consequence that reality itself is 'perspectival' or 'relative' in any way. How things are is how things are.

1.12 Temperament and time

In Part 5 I consider some differences in the way people experience or claim to experience the process of consciousness, because there are reasons for thinking that these differences may influence their attitudes to questions about the self. I also briefly consider some more fundamental differences of existential style that are likely to be influential when it comes to the problem of the self, distinguishing between Endurantist (or Diachronic) and Impermanentist (or Episodic) forms of life, on the one hand, and Narrative, and non-Narrative forms of life, on the other. If one is *Endurantist*—briefly—the idea that one was there in the (further) past and will be there in the (further) future is integral to one's overall SELF-experience, one's experience of oneself when one is apprehending oneself specifically as a self rather than as a human being considered as a whole. If one is *Impermanentist*, by contrast, one has little sense that the self that one now experiences oneself to be was there in the past and will be there in the further future, although one is fully aware

---

[20] '... systems of philosophy reduce themselves to a few main types, which ... under the technical verbiage ... are just so many visions, *modes of feeling the whole push* ..., forced on one by one's total character and experience' (James 1909: 639; my emphasis).

that one has long-term continuity as a human being. To be *Narrative* is—roughly—to have a tendency to apprehend one's life as constituting a story or having a story-like development of some sort, and also, perhaps, to have some sort of investment in this way of apprehending it. To be *non-Narrative* is to have no such tendency or investment.

The Endurantist/Impermanentist distinction and the Narrative/non-Narrative distinction don't coincide (see pp. 221–2), but Endurantists are often Narratives, and Impermanentists are often non-Narratives. I take myself to be Impermanentist and strongly non-Narrative. My general sense is that the Endurantist and Narrative outlooks are more common in human beings than the Impermanentist and non-Narrative outlooks, but I'm not sure about this (the Endurantist and Narrative outlooks may just be more visible, better documented, more common among writers, more of a cultural norm or default).

The most interesting expressions and consequences of these differences are moral and emotional—ethical in the largest sense. As such they lie beyond the scope of this book. For the moment, the Endurantist/Impermanentist and Narrative/non-Narrative differences are of concern only in so far as they're likely to affect attitudes to the strictly metaphysical problem of the self. Narratives and Endurantists will presumably be more strongly disposed to believe in the existence of a persisting inner entity appropriately called the self, for they experience the presence of such a thing—they experience themselves as such a thing.

1.13 Human difference

Differences between Endurantists, Impermanentists, Narratives, and non-Narratives complicate things when one theorizes about the self, but in a potentially valuable way. Other complications have no such virtue. One such complication is that the present project risks being self-undermining, especially in its phenomenological phase. Philosophical reflection on the nature of SELF-experience may disrupt the natural tissue of pre-reflective experience, misting or knocking out the very thing it's trying to examine. One may also accumulate bias as one reflects, slanting oneself unconsciously to find only what one wants to find, or even artificially generating what one wants to find. In the attempt to avoid these dangers, one may well overcompensate, overestimating the weight of apparently negative data, or even artificially and unconsciously generating such data.

Another possibility, of course, is that concentrated reflection on the nature of SELF-experience may transform the thing that it is trying to examine in a valuable way, rather than merely obscuring it. Philosophical reflection on some feature of experience may well not leave everything as it is, but it doesn't necessarily fail in its task, or destroy its object, if it changes what it sets out to examine. Its target in the present case is SELF-experience in general, not just ordinary pre-reflective SELF-experience, and whatever changes it induces are themselves potentially valuable data. One important possibility is that reflection on SELF-experience may alter pre-reflective SELF-experience precisely because it increases insight into how things actually are, so far as the existence of selves is concerned. This is one of the aims of some meditative practices, and it may be one of the effects of reading a book like this.

These difficulties arise principally in private study. They're compounded when one moves out into public discussion. Consider, for example, the difference between those who believe that there's a sense in which it's possible or even necessary to create oneself or one's self, like Mary McCarthy

I suppose everyone continues to be interested in the quest for the self, but what you feel when you're older, I think, is that you really must make the self. It is absolutely useless to look for it, you won't find it.   (1963: 37)

or Thomas Szasz

people often say that this or that person has not yet found himself. But the self is not something one finds; it is something one creates.   (1973: 49)

or Germaine Greer

human beings have an inalienable right to invent themselves; when that right is pre-empted it is called brain-washing.   (*The Times*, 1 February 1986)

—and those like myself to whom the idea that one should or could do any such thing seems absurd, those who agree with Gadamer that

the self that we are does not possess itself; one could say that it 'happens'.[21]

There seems to be a positive correlation between this difference and the difference between those who believe (roughly) that having particular thoughts is a kind of intentional action and those to whom it seems clear that it's something that just happens (see 4.6). This temperamental difference bears directly on people's views about whether or not selves are necessarily agents.

A third potentially relevant difference is that between those who claim to experience themselves *in foro interno* as a kind of fractious parliament—those who judge, in Eric Erikson's words, that

various selves ... make up our composite Self. There are constant and often shocklike transitions between these selves   (1968: 217)

or, in Mary Midgley's, that

[Dr Jekyll] was partly right: we *are* each not only one but also many .... Some of us have to hold a meeting every time we want to do something only slightly difficult, in order to find the self who is capable of undertaking it   (1984: 122–3)

—and those, like myself, for whom the idea of any such experience of separate interests is unimaginable and bewildering (see p. 84ff.).

---

[21] 1962: 55. I am not sure of the import of Gadamer's phrase in context.

Fourth, there's the difference between those, Like Thomas Nagel, who record experience of the 'objective self, ... the self that seems incapable of being anyone in particular'—

The picture is this. Essentially I have no particular point of view at all, but apprehend the world as centerless. As it happens, I ordinarily view the world from a certain vantage point, using the eyes, the person, the daily life of TN as a kind of window. But the experiences and the perspective of TN with which I am directly presented are not the point of view of the true self, for the true self has no point of view   (1986: 61)

—and those who are incapable of developing any clear feeling for what he is talking about.

Finally by way of example, there's the difference between those who have a sense of themselves as having a particular personality with a particular 'taste' or flavour, and those who have no such sense: the difference between Gerard Manley Hopkins, who talks of

my self-being, my consciousness and feeling of myself, that taste of myself, of *I* and *me* above and in all things, which is more distinctive than the taste of ale or alum, more distinctive than the smell of walnutleaf or camphor, and is incommunicable by any means to another man ... .   (1880: 123)

and Iris Murdoch, reported here by her husband John Bayley:

Iris once told me that the question of identity had always puzzled her. She thought she herself hardly possessed such a thing, whatever it was. I said that she must know what it was like to be oneself, even to revel in the consciousness of oneself, as a secret and separate person .... She smiled, looked amused, uncomprehending.   (1998: 51–2)

Plainly differences of this kind may be reflected in different approaches to the question of the self. I'm concerned with them partly because my outlook may regularly put me in the minority in debates in which the influence of such 'existential' or temperamental factors is not usually—or sufficiently—acknowledged. Perhaps I'm wrong about this, but it is in any case useful and important, when confronted with apparently factual disagreements about the nature of selves, to be alert to the question whether and how such temperamental differences may be in play.

To acknowledge the influence of these factors is, again, not to endorse any sort of relativism or perspectivalism about truth, although the differences may put some people in a better position than others, when it comes to getting at different aspects of the truth of whatever matter is in question.

The complicating effect of these temperamental differences is compounded by the great variety of emphases that govern theoretical approaches to the question of the self in philosophy and psychology. The word 'self' attracts a remarkable number of different qualifying adjectives, and this is a source of considerable difficulty when one first begins to read what others have written on the question. As far as I can see, the confusion simply has to be lived through. There is no quick way to acclimatize oneself to all the tensions and incompatibilities between the many approaches to the question. It takes patience to accommodate oneself to the autobiographical self, the cognitive self, the conceptual self, the contextualized self, the core self, the dialogic self, the ecological self, the embodied self, the emergent self, the empirical self, the existential self, the extended self, the fictional self, the full-grown self, the interpersonal self, the inviolable self, the material self, the metaself, the narrative self, the nuclear self, the philosophical self, the physical self, the private self, the proto-self, the representational self, the rock-bottom essential self, the semiotic self, the social self, the transparent self, the true self, the verbal self, and the working self—to name only a few.[22]

I haven't chosen to write about any of these presumed entities—or not under these names—but I'm not sure I object to any of them. Theorists love incompatibilities, but I don't think there's any inevitable conflict between my approach and approaches that view the self as fundamentally and essentially 'socially constituted'. Nor is there anything in my view that conflicts with Feuerbachian, Wundtian, or Gibsonian ('ecological') approaches to self and SELF-experience that stress the primordial role of the body in our sense of self (23). My interests and emphases are often orthogonal to the interests of those who are mainly concerned with social, interpersonal, or ecological issues, but orthogonality isn't opposition or conflict. It seems to me that it's possible to navigate coherently among the strikingly disparate theoretical approaches to questions about the self, and develop one's own line fruitfully in the light of one's knowledge of the others, without losing one's way. The terminological chaos—the theoretical biodiversity—is daunting, especially at first, but it's also potentially enlightening; and if one takes one's time and approaches the problem in a sufficiently dialectical spirit, I think one can see that there is in spite of everything a deep consensus about which part of reality is being talked about when the self is talked about.

Let me say finally that the word 'self', used as a count noun with the plural 'selves', sounds uncomfortable to many, including me. I'm going to use it partly for this reason, in fact, but it can for most purposes be replaced by 'subjects of experience that are not the same thing as a human being considered as a whole'. The question is whether there are such things, in the human case.

---

[22] See among others Butterworth 1995, 1998; Cole 1997; Damasio 1994, 1999; Dennett 1991; Gallagher and Marcel 1999; Gazzaniga 1998a; Gibson 1993; James 1890; Legerstee 1998; Neisser 1988, 1999; Pickering 1999; Sheets-Johnstone 1999; Sorabji 2006; Stern 1985.

Part 2

Phenomenology:
the local question

... the feeling that corresponds to the pronoun *I*.

(Priestley 1777: 284)

2.1 Three illusions?

Some say that human life is founded on three illusions—the illusion of free will, the illusion of love, and the illusion of the self. This is a rather sweeping remark, if only because individuals vary greatly in their preoccupations and change their views as they grow older, but it has a certain force. It's not just a 'Western' view.

Of the three supposed illusions, love—romantic love—is probably the most common target of scepticism, but it may be in better shape than the other two. A thing may be rare but real. In many, cynicism is a mixture of fear and ignorance. Romantic love is naturalistically respectable. There's nothing in the theory of evolution that rules it out.

I hold out no hope for free will as ordinarily understood. There are many senses of the word 'free', and in some of these senses we can certainly be said to have free will, but it's an illusion in the strong form in which many suppose it to exist.[1]

The self is the most difficult of the three. This is partly because it's so much less clear what we're talking about when we talk about the self. But it's not as if language is a special agent of confusion. The problem is not, in the older Wittgenstein's phrase, that the 'seas of language' run particularly high in the case of the self (1953: §194). Or rather, they do, but the swell lies in the character of our experience considered independently of the attempt to express it in language. Wittgenstein thought that we can make high seas subside in philosophy by examining the behaviour of the words we use to express what puzzles us. This procedure may work in some cases, but it doesn't get us far when

---

[1] See e.g. G. Strawson 1994.

it comes to the problem of the self. 'The I, the I', wrote young Wittgenstein, 'is what is deeply mysterious' (1916: 80). It's not clear that the older man would have wished to correct the younger on this point.

It's true that the use of the word 'self' is unnatural in many speech contexts. Some think that we can conclude from this that it's an illusion to think that there are such things as selves, an illusion that arises from an improper use of language. This, however, is very implausible. People are not that stupid. The problem of the self doesn't arise from an unnatural use of language that arises from nowhere. On the contrary: use of the word 'self' arises from a powerful, prior, and independent sense that there is such a thing as the self. The word may be unusual in ordinary speech, and it may have no obvious direct translation in some languages, but all languages have words or phrases that lend themselves naturally to playing the role that 'self' plays in English, however murky that role may be, and such words and phrases certainly mean something to most people.[2] They have a natural use in religious, philosophical, and psychological contexts, and these are very natural contexts for human beings.

2.2 A bad argument

'So be it', says a philosopher:

the fact remains that the 'problem of the self' can be solved by brisk attention to a few facts about language. For consider: if there really is such a thing as the self, one thing that's certain is that it's what we refer to when we use the word 'I'. So we must start by considering the behaviour of 'I' in some detail. To find out about the real or legitimate import or content of philosophically loaded words like 'I', and so about the nature of the things we use them to think and talk about, we must begin by paying close attention to the way in which we use these words in ordinary, everyday communication with each other. Plainly this procedure won't help much in the case of words for natural kinds, like 'gold' and 'proton', whose nature is a matter for investigation by science; but it's vital in the case of all other words that raise philosophical problems.

So to begin. We certainly use the word 'I' to refer to ourselves considered as human beings, embodied human beings taken as a whole, things that essentially have both mental properties and large-scale bodily properties. And even if there is some special use of the word 'I' to refer to the putative self, this use doesn't ordinarily stand out as distinct from use of the word 'I' to refer to the whole human being. When we're talking to other people we never think 'Aha! Now they're using "I" with the special *inner-self* reference', or 'Now they're using "I" with the standard *whole-human-being* reference'. Nor do we ever think this about ourselves when we're talking. It's *no* part of ordinary thought that 'I' has two meanings—that 'I' can have two different referents as used by a given single person either at a single time or at different times (I put aside cases of dissociative identity disorder). We have no reason to doubt that it's univocal whenever it's used—no reason to think that it's ambiguous or indefinite in some way.

This is good news, because it follows that the so-called 'problem of the self' has a quick and complete solution. It doesn't require any high or heavy metaphysical exertions, because

---

[2] For the case of the ancient Greeks, see Sorabji 2006: 5.

it's certain, as just remarked, that use of 'I' to refer (or apparently refer) to the putative self doesn't stand out as distinct from use of 'I' to refer to the human being in ordinary talk, and it follows from this that we don't in fact draw this distinction in ordinary thought unwarped by philosophy. More strongly, it follows that we can't legitimately draw it, and that we're talking a kind of nonsense when we think we do. But if this is so—and it is so—then we can prove that *my # self*, the putative inner self, is either nothing at all, or is simply *myself*, the living, embodied, publicly observable whole human being. For we've already established that the term—'I'—that allegedly refers to the putative former thing, 'the self', undoubtedly refers to the latter thing, the whole human being. But that means that either the self is the whole human being, or it's nothing at all. There is, by the logic of identity, no other possibility. So the self, considered as something distinct from the human being, 'is a mythical entity', in Kenny's phrase. 'It is', he says, 'a philosophical muddle to allow the typographical space which differentiates "my self" from "myself" to generate the illusion of a mysterious entity distinct from … the human being …. Grammatical error … is the essence of the theory of the self …. "The self" is a piece of philosopher's nonsense consisting in a misunderstanding of the reflexive pronoun.' The end.[3]

I think this argument is worthless—a *reductio ad absurdum* of the principles on which it relies. The appeal to ordinary, everyday, public language use, in the attempt to solve a philosophical problem, is perhaps nowhere more inappropriate than in the case of the problem of the self, precisely because ordinary, public language use reflects the public, third-personal perspective on things. Suppose it's true that the referring term 'I' is rarely used in ordinary communication in such a way as to reflect any distinction between the putative self and the whole human being. What does this prove? All it proves is that the public, third-personal (non-first-personal) perspective on things is built into the everyday public use of language. And what does this fact about the everyday public use of language prove regarding the nature of reality and the scope of intelligible thought about it? Absolutely nothing. It may be true that the best thing to say, in the end, is that there's no such thing as the self, considered as something distinct from the human being, but this is certainly not the right way to try to show that it's true. Even if referring terms like 'I' were *never* used in ordinary communication, as opposed to private thought, in a way that indicated awareness or acceptance of a distinction between the self and the whole embodied human being, this would have no consequences for the question whether or not there are such things as selves.

Some hold that the force or content of the word 'I' in private thought can't possibly differ from the force or content of its use in public communication. They hold, further, and for various reasons, some of which were mentioned above, that the reference of 'I' in public communication can only be to the whole human being. Suppose, again, that they're right about this. Even so, there are no easy or guaranteed inferences from facts about ordinary public language use to facts about how we fundamentally—or really—think about things. Facts about ordinary everyday public language use and its typical interpretation can't immediately prove that the ordinary everyday belief or

---

[3] Kenny 1988: 4, 1989: 87, 1999: 39–40.

feeling that there is such a thing as the self involves an illusion. Metaphysics is not that easy. And when we think in private, nothing stops us from doing what we (or vast numbers of us) naturally do: which is to think of ourselves, using 'I' inasmuch as we use language at all, as, primarily or fundamentally, inner conscious entities that are not identical with the embodied human beings that we are, considered as a whole. Consistent and thoughtful materialists do this as much as anyone else; it doesn't involve any belief that anything non-physical exists (2.7). Clubbable assertions about ordinary public language use can't break in on our 'sessions of sweet silent thought'[4] to tell us that we're not really doing what we think we're doing, not really thinking what we think we're thinking. To suppose that they can is to make the great Wittgensteinian (or 'Wittgensteinian') mistake about the nature of language and thought and metaphysics, the career-swallowing mistake that makes it look (for example) as if a word like 'pain' can't be what it so simply and obviously is—a word for a publicly unobservable or 'private' sensation, a word that picks out and means the private sensation considered just as such, i.e. entirely independently of any of its behavioural or other publicly observable causes and effects.[5]

So I reject the basic presupposition or procedure of the argument from the public use of language. It's arguable that it fails even on its own terms, that the distinction between 'I' the (inner) self and 'I' the human being is in fact clearly marked in ordinary thought and talk. People sometimes naturally and sincerely report their experiences to each other by saying things like 'I felt completely detached from my body', or 'I felt I was floating out of my body, and looking down on it from above'. Experiences of this sort are particularly vivid and common in adolescence, occurring spontaneously in about 1 in 300 individuals. It doesn't matter that the floatings and detachings don't actually happen. What matters is that there are experiences of this sort, and that statements of this kind are natural forms of talk about real experiences in which the intended reference of 'I' is not to the whole human being and is understood not to be to the whole human being.[6] There is plainly no difficulty—no problem of communication stemming specifically from the use of 'I'—in using language in this way to describe one's experiences to others. Defenders of the argument from the public use of language may dismiss these cases as marginal and 'degenerate', misleading and 'parasitic', but this is to beg the question.

It may be that when we listen to another person's report of an out-of-body experience, we most naturally take the report to be about the whole human being in front of us, or at the other end of the telephone connection, in spite of its express content. Perhaps we nearly always apprehend or construe each other primarily or solely in this way—as human beings considered as a whole—when we communicate with each other. The fact remains that the distinction between the use of 'I' to refer to the self or 'inner someone' and the use of 'I' to refer to the embodied human being is sometimes clearly marked in ordinary thought and talk.

---

[4] Shakespeare, Sonnet 30.   [5] See e.g. G. Strawson 1994: ch. 8, esp. 219–25.
[6] I consider this in more detail in 7.2. The way we experience ourselves in dreams is also important—see p. 30.

I propose, then, that there are two natural uses of 'I': the *inner-self use* and the *human-being-considered-as-a-whole use*. If there is any parasitism, it's arguable that the latter is parasitic on the former, rather than the other way round. It's arguable, in other words, that the central or fundamental way in which we, or many of us, experience/conceive ourselves, much of the time, is precisely as an inner entity, an inner presence that is not the same thing as the whole human being.[7] This applies as much to sex addicts, manual labourers, athletes, and supermodels as to the rest of us—people may be more rather than less likely to experience themselves in this way if they are, for whatever reason, preoccupied with their bodies. To see that this point is correct, one needs to be truly shot of Wittgensteinian or 'Wittgensteinian' reflexes, capable of taking the actual semantic intentions of thinkers and speakers properly into account; one must understand that language and thought just don't operate in the way Wittgensteinians say they do and must.

Many present-day philosophers and psychologists—following and perhaps overextending Wittgenstein, Heidegger, Merleau-Ponty, Gibson, and others—have come to find this hard to see, or rather remember. Many of them think that it's precisely claims like these that give philosophy a bad name and direction, an ivory-tower problem, and skew it away from the truth of the everyday consciousness of real fleshly human beings incessantly engaged in practical intercourse with the world and each other. But it is these philosophers, I think, who are up in the blind tower. They are of course right—following Platner, Herbart, Feuerbach, Wundt, Nietzsche, James, Peirce, Bradley, the Phenomenologists, and many others who preceded them (I omit Descartes because he is so widely misunderstood that his inclusion would be misleading)—about the profoundly environmentally embedded, embodied, 'enactive', 'ecological', or (for short) *EEE* aspects of our experiential predicament as organic and social beings situated in a physical world, but they're victims of theoretical overreaction. The EEE character of our existence must be thoroughly recognized, but there must be equal recognition of the entirely compatible fact that one of the most important things about human life is the respect in which one experiences oneself as an inner entity distinct from the whole human being. Nietzsche shows penetration when he writes that

I am body entirely, and nothing else; and 'soul' is only a word for something about the body. The body is a great intelligence .... Your little intelligence, my brother, which you call 'spirit', is ... an instrument of your body. ... You say 'I' and you are proud of this word. But greater than this—although you will not believe in it—is your body and its great intelligence, which does not say 'I' but performs 'I' .... Behind your thoughts and feelings, my brother, stands a mighty commander, an unknown sage—he is called Self. He lives in your body, he is your body ....
(1883–5: 61–2)

---

[7] Fichte doesn't disagree when he says that 'the majority of men could sooner be brought to believe themselves a piece of lava in the moon than to take themselves for a *self*', for he has something very special in mind (1794–1802: 162).

for reasons that have become increasingly apparent in the century since he wrote. He follows Feuerbach, writing forty years earlier in the sophisticated tradition of German materialism that followed German idealism:

whereas the old philosophy started by saying, 'I am an abstract and merely a thinking being, to whose essence the body does not belong', the new philosophy, on the other hand, begins by saying, 'I am a real sensuous being and, indeed, the body in its totality is my self (*Ich*), my essence itself'.   (1843: 54)

Neither, though, questions the present claim that we regularly figure or experience ourselves primarily as inner conscious entities or selves. Their remarks take their point precisely from the fact that it is true.

2.3 Experience of mind

Why—how—do we come to experience ourselves in this way, given the EEE aspects of our existence? Part of the answer seems plain. It's a consequence of something which has become hard for many to see in recent analytic philosophy of mind: the way in which awareness of ourselves as mentally propertied is, to varying degrees, constantly present when it comes to our overall apprehension of ourselves. It's not just that we're often expressly taken up with our own conscious thoughts, living with ourselves principally in our inward mental scene, incessantly presented to ourselves as things engaged in mental business, even while aware of our external surroundings. This point needs new emphasis, in the current climate of discussion, but the further and larger point is that awareness of our own conscious mental goings-on is very often—arguably always—present, to varying degrees, even when we're thoroughly and directly taken up with our bodies, or, generally, with things in the world other than our own mental goings-on.

It's instructive to watch people in the street. Hurlburt *et al.* made random samplings of the character of people's experience as they went about their daily life, by activating beepers that they carried with them: 'it was striking that the great majority of subjects at the time of the beep were focused on some inner event or events, with no direct awareness of outside events at that moment'.[8] Such inturned thoughts may be almost exclusively concerned with external-world matters; they may, for example, be rehearsals of past events or anticipations of future events. The present point is that their occurrence involves an experienced contrast between one's inner mental goings-on, on the one hand, and one's external surroundings, of which one usually remains more or less aware, on the other hand. The experience of this contrast is rarely in the focus of attention. It is in other words rarely 'thetic', in the Phenomenological (Sartrean) sense of the term (the words 'thematic' or 'positional' are used in the same way). It is none the less there.

---

[8] See Hurlburt, Happé and Frith 1994: 387. For more experimental evidence see also Baars 1996; Hurlburt and Schwitzgebel 2007.

Plainly we can be the subjects of conscious mental goings-on without being expressly aware of them considered specifically as such; our attention can be intensely focused outward. But even then we have a constant background awareness of our own conscious mental goings-on (its quality is such that it's usually inadequate to say that it's merely background awareness) and a constant tendency to flip back, however briefly, to some more salient, not wholly background apprehension of ourselves as minded or conscious. (It isn't as if there isn't enough mental space—or time—for this. Conscious apprehension is extremely fast and rich. 'Thought', as Hobbes says, 'is quick' (1651: I. iii).) What is the 'lifeworld', the *Lebenswelt*? There's a fundamental sense in which it's an 'inner' (or mental) world—even when one is preoccupied with the outer world, sailing a yacht, climbing a mountain, using a hammer, jogging, or running for one's life.[9] Silent thoughts hit people in a roaring football crowd, and they're aware of this happening (and of the strange detachment—but unarguable reality—of the 'place' in which this thought is present), not just of the content of the thought. What is the shepherd on the hill thinking about, or the woman at the loom, or the child lying awake in the dark? I can see a man collecting garbage from the side of the road with tongs. He's not locked exclusively on the details of his immediate task and surroundings and bodily feelings. It's not as if there is nothing more to the content of his current experience than the external environment which he directly perceives, plus awareness of his bodily state. There are many things going on in his (conscious) mind, and he's not only aware of their content. He's also aware, however non-thetically, of himself as minded. This is not just the view of a dreaming philosopher.

Which stand out most for us, in daily life: our mental features or our bodily features? Most of us find that our moods and emotional feelings are a great deal more present to our attention than our bodies, most of the time.[10] These mental conditions profoundly colour our experience of outer things, and we're not so fiercely world-focused as to be generally unaware of this fact. Why is it important for philosophers to stress the EEE aspects of existence? Precisely because of the regularly dominant position of mental as opposed to non-mental[11] features in our overall experience of ourselves.

It's not a fatal philosophical aberration, then, as some have supposed, to focus on the mind as opposed to the body, when considering the human condition; it's not an aberration at all. Even if it were an aberration, it wouldn't be a distinctively philosophical aberration. It would, rather, be an aberration intrinsic to the human condition. We are, in a sense, strangely—astonishingly—rarefied creatures. We don't make any mistake in being this way or in experiencing ourselves in this way. We are what we

---

[9] Moments of crisis can precipitate extraordinary innerness. For an extreme example of this, see Oliver Sacks's description of his mental state after an encounter with a bull on a mountain in Norway (1984: ch. 1).

[10] Their causes may lie in our bodies in such a way that representationalists as different as Descartes and Tye want to say that they are about our bodies, but that is a separate point.

[11] I use 'non-mental' where many would use 'physical' for reasons set out in 6.6; see also G. Strawson 1994: 57–8. Briefly, materialists hold that everything is physical, so if they admit the existence of the mental, the only relevant distinction available to them is between the mental physical and the non-mental physical.

are. Our mentality is a huge, absorbing, and utterly all-pervasive fact about us. It's a natural object of attention for us. We're constantly aware of it even when we're not focusing on it. We live constantly at or over the edge of express awareness of our own mental goings-on considered specifically as such. Those who think that in normal human experience the external world wholly occupies the field of consciousness in such a way that we normally have no sort of awareness of the phenomenon of our awareness, those who think that the sensations and feelings that give us experience of the world are like invisible glass, so that we are generally wholly unaware of them, utterly falsify the extraordinarily rich, rapid, nuanced, complexly inflected, interdipping flow of everyday experience. In their fury to be 'anti-Cartesian' (or something) they completely forget what it is like to live an ordinary human life. They forget the profound and constant innerness of so much of everyday experience, its felt hiddenness and privacy. They forget that inner mental goings-on *experienced as such* are constantly present in all our engagement with the world, however little they're dwelt on—as we move around thinking of this or that, swim, play a fast sport, argue with someone, or take a bath.

There's no conflict between this point and 'direct realism' about the perception of objects in the world. Direct realism states, correctly, that when one sees a desk in normal conditions, one is in 'direct perceptual contact' with the desk, and not merely in indirect perceptual contact with it, via some mental representation of it. There is, of course, and necessarily, a conscious mental representation of the desk involved in one's seeing the desk. No conscious mental representation, no seeing. Seeing is a conscious mental thing (although we can also give sense to a notion of unconscious seeing). But having the right sort of conscious mental representation just is seeing the desk. It's what being in direct visual perceptual contact with the desk is. You don't see the desk 'through' the mental representation. Having the conscious mental representation, in the normal veridical perceptual case, just is—again—seeing the desk. And there is, as direct realists insist, a fundamental respect in which one's sense experience is in the normal case entirely 'transparent' or 'diaphanous' for one, when one perceives the world: one's sense experience is not in any way taken into account as such.

This is particularly apparent when one considers vision (it's much less compelling in the case of the other senses, where awareness of the medium by which one perceives the world is often more patently present, although not in the focus of attention). But even in the case of vision it does not follow, and is not true, that one isn't aware of the sensory-qualitative character of the sensory experience, as Thomas Reid points out in 'Of Sensation' (1785: 2.16). One is always and necessarily aware of the sensory-qualitative character of the sensory experience. Otherwise one wouldn't see the desk! This said, one needn't have any significant awareness of the sensory experience *specifically as a process of sensory experience*.

But nor is this excluded: I can directly see—be in 'direct perceptual contact' with—the desk while also being clearly non-thetically aware of my awareness of the desk. Direct realism doesn't involve the false claim that one has to be entirely unaware of the occurrence of the process of experience, and many very ordinary everyday circumstances bring it to the fore for us. Awareness of awareness is built into simple things like changing positions to see something one can't see from where one is.

In general, our experience is saturated with experience of ourselves as experiencing. Aron Gurwitsch is very accurate when, speaking of perception, he says that

consciousness ... is consciousness of an object on the one hand and an inner awareness of itself on the other hand. Being confronted with an object, I am at once conscious of this object and aware of my being conscious of it. This awareness in no way means reflection: to know that I am dealing with the object which, for instance, I am just perceiving, I need not experience a second act bearing upon the perception and making it its object. In simply dealing with the object I am aware of this very dealing.   (1941: 330)

His closing formulation in this passage, 'I am aware of this very dealing', is less likely to mislead than the earlier 'I am ... aware of my being conscious of [the object]', because the phenomenon in question doesn't require any thought of oneself as such. This is indeed Gurwitsch's main point, which he has already made three pages earlier: 'the subject in his dealing with the object, aware as he is of this dealing, is nevertheless in no way aware of his ego, much less of his ego's involvement in his dealing' (1941: 327).

Switching focus, consider next the fact that awareness of one's own hidden, inner mental goings-on is one of the most salient, unremitting features of human communication. Bargaining, negotiating differences, making plans for cooperation, playing chess—these activities provide one vivid set of cases. Awareness of the possibility of concealment, deception, hypocrisy, both on one's own part and on the part of others, is integral to our communication and ancient in our phylogenesis.[12] Humans are full of hidden conscious intentions to keep secrets or omit details, both when they seek to cheat and betray and when they seek to surprise, or exercise tact, or avoid upsetting others. They're constantly thinking things that they decide to say or not say. All this feeds a pervasive and ever-present awareness of the privacy of mental life, a sense of privacy we must clearly recognize, and allow to be in certain fundamental respects accurate, even as we also recognize that many aspects of our mental lives are directly observable to others in our eyes, facial expressions, and larger scale observable behaviour.

This vast arena of concealment from others, good or bad, is only a tiny part of what feeds the sense of the innerness of mental life when communicating with others. When one describes a remembered scene, one is aware of a great deal that is present to one's mind—some of it in sketchy, fleeting, quasi-sensory form—but unavailable to one's interlocutor. There is conscious experience of selecting from material that comes to mind. One is routinely aware of things that one is not saying because one has to keep things short. There is, in conversation, the experience of one's thought wandering off the other's words, of something else coming vividly and privately to mind. There is the experience of realizing in a flash *in foro interno* what one wants to say in reply to someone while he or she is still speaking, and so on. All these things are real, concretely existing

---

[12] It is one of the fundamental grounds of our intelligence, for reasons well set out by Trivers (1985) and Frank (1988).

phenomena of which we are aware just as we're aware of phenomena in our external environment. We're built to be aware of many things going on around us, and this, unsurprisingly, includes our own mental goings-on. Heideggerian cobblers absorbed in their work, nails in mouth and hammers in hand, are bathed in the reality of their mental innerness.

Why has it become hard for some philosophers and psychologists to give these facts their proper weight? Many, as remarked, are so anxious to dissociate themselves from a view they call 'Cartesianism', when discussing the nature of mind, that they tend to throw out everything that is right about Cartesianism along with anything that is wrong; attraction or habituation to the idioms and ways of thinking of experimental psychology is also influential. But there's no conflict here. Our background awareness of our bodies is important, but this is wholly compatible with our regularly experiencing ourselves primarily or centrally as inner conscious presences who are not the same thing as human beings considered as a whole; and although background awareness of body is indeed experience of the body, this doesn't prevent it from feeding or grounding SELF-experience, a sense of self that presents the self primarily as a distinctively (and in some cases purely) mental entity. Background awareness of body is indispensable to a sense of the self in creatures like human beings, indispensable, in Damasio's words, to 'the feeling essence of our sense of self' (1999: 171), indispensable both to its development in each individual and to its continuing existence, but it doesn't follow that any such sense of the self must figure the self *as* embodied in any way. This, after all, is precisely Wundt's point, and Nietzsche's, and Dewey's, and Feuerbach's before them, and arguably Fichte's before Feuerbach, and Platner's in any case before Fichte.[13] Bradley has 'no doubt that the

---

[13]   Dewey inveighs famously against the 'spectatorial' conception of the knowing human subject (see e.g. 1929: 215). Fichte's argument is indirect: I cannot have self-awareness without awareness of an external world, and by implication a body for the world to act upon (see Beiser 2002: 309–13, 325–33); for Platner (1772), see Thiel (forthcoming). Wundt is worth quoting at some length:

> In this development (of consciousness) one particular group of percepts claims a prominent significance, namely, those of which the spring lies in ourselves. The images of feelings we get from our own body, and the representations of our own movements distinguish themselves from all others by forming a *permanent* group. As there are always some muscles in a state either of tension or of activity it follows that we never lack a sense, either dim or clear, of the positions or movements of our body. ... This permanent sense, moreover, has this particularity, that we are aware of our power at any moment voluntarily to arouse any one of its ingredients. We excite the sensations of movement immediately by such impulses of the will as shall arouse the movements themselves; and we excite the visual and tactile feelings of our body by the voluntary movement of our organs of sense. So we come to conceive this permanent mass of feeling as immediately or remotely subject to our will, and call it the *consciousness of ourself*. This self-consciousness is, at the outset, thoroughly sensational, ... only gradually the second-named of its characters, its subjection to our will, attains predominance. [As this happens] our self-consciousness begins both to widen itself and to narrow itself at the same time. It widens itself in that every mental act whatever comes to stand in relation to our will; and it narrows itself in that it concentrates itself more and more upon the inner activity of apperception, over against which our own body and all the representations connected with it appear as external objects, different from our proper self. This consciousness, contracted down to the process of apperception, we call our Ego [or self. But this] abstract ego ..., although suggested by the natural development of our consciousness, is never actually found therein. The most speculative of philosophers is incapable of disjoining his ego from those bodily feelings and images which form the incessant background of his awareness of himself. The notion of his ego as such is, like every notion, derived from sensibility, for the process of apperception itself comes to our knowledge chiefly through those feelings of tension which accompany it. (1874, quoted in James 1890:1.303n.)

inner core of feeling, resting mainly on what is called Coenaesthesia, is the foundation of the [sense of the] self'.[14] He follows James, who writes that 'the nucleus of the "*me*"' that the present thinking subject takes itself to be 'is always the bodily existence felt to be present at the time'; 'the "I" meaning' for the present thinking subject is 'nothing but the bodily life which it momentarily feels':

We feel the whole cubic mass of our body all the while, it gives us an unceasing sense of personal existence. Equally do we feel the inner 'nucleus of the spiritual self', either in the shape of yon physiological adjustments, or (adopting the universal psychological belief), in that of the pure activity of our thought taking place as such. ... The character of ... warmth and intimacy ... in the present self ... reduces itself to either of two things—something in the feeling which we have of the thought itself, as thinking, or else the feeling of the body's actual existence at the moment,—or finally to both.[15]

Nearly everyone, perhaps, agrees that background interoceptive or somatosensory awareness of one's body is the foundation of SELF-experience, whatever place they also rightly give, with James, to 'the feeling which we have of the thought itself, as thinking'. It's a further point that background awareness of one's mind, of one's experiential goings-on, is no less constant than background awareness of one's body—that background awareness that experiential goings-on are going on is as much part of the overall field of experience as background somatic awareness. The notion of background awareness is imprecise, but we can for the moment sufficiently define it as all awareness that is non-thetic, not in the focus of attention. It then seems plausible to say that there is never *less* background awareness of awareness or experience than there is background awareness of body. I suspect there is more; that background awareness of awareness predominates over background awareness of body.[16] Nothing hangs on this quantitative claim, however, for the constantly impinging phenomena of one's mental life are in any case far more salient in the constitution of one's sense that there is such a thing as the self than are the phenomena of bodily experience, and it is this sense of self that is of primary concern. When we're fascinated by the outer scene our awareness of ourselves and our mental lives may seem dim. The outer scene may seem to flood consciousness. But even in these cases we're likely to be as aware of ourselves as mentally aspected—our fascination is itself such a property, and we feel it—as we are of ourselves as embodied.[17] When we have sufficiently digested the

---

[14] 1893: 68. Coenaesthesia (pron. *seeneestheesia*) is 'the totality of internal sensations by which one perceives one's own body', 'the general sense of bodily existence; the sensation caused by the functioning of the internal organs'.

[15] 1890: 1.400, 1.341n., 1.333. Note that James uses 'thought' in the Cartesian way as a completely general word for conscious experience (1890: 1.224). In the first quotation I've put 'present thinking subject' in place of James's capitalized 'Thought' in accordance with his explicit terminological provision (1890: 1.338, 400–01; see further 7.6).

[16] C. O. Evans traces the sense of the self to 'unprojected consciousness' which 'can only be experienced as background', and consequently identifies this unprojected consciousness as the best candidate for the title 'self' (1970: 149).

[17] It depends what we're doing. If we watch athletics, we may tense up empathetically and may be to that extent more aware of the body. If we're walking by the sea or watching shooting stars, we're more likely to be aware of our mentality.

Platner–Wundt point that somatosensory awareness has a foundational role both in our acquisition of self-consciousness and in our continuing sense that there is a self, we need to register—or re-register—the obvious but fashion-occluded point that awareness of one's mind and mental goings-on is no less important.

Does it follow, from the fact that occurrent awareness is background, or non-thetic, that it isn't explicit in any way? The question doesn't arise, because the implicit/explicit distinction lacks application when 'awareness' is used specifically to refer to occurrent experience. It makes good sense to talk of implicit as opposed to explicit *understanding*, and the expression 'implicit awareness' also has currency, given the dispositional use of the term 'awareness', and invites a contrasting use of 'explicit'.[18] But there is, again, no such thing as implicit occurrent awareness, and I will use the adjective 'express' to do most of the work that is done by 'explicit'. The pertinent distinction is simply the one already noted: the undeniably real if soft-bordered distinction between focused, express, attentive, thetic awareness, on the one hand, and unfocused, more or less dim, non-attentive, non-thetic awareness on the other.

Dreams are also important, when it comes to understanding the naturalness of the sense of the self as a mental entity. When one dreams, one often has no particular sense (no sense at all) of oneself as embodied, although one's sense of one's presence in the dream scene is vivid. Such dream experience is part of our experience from infancy. It isn't necessary to appeal to it to make the present case, but I suspect it contributes profoundly to our overall susceptibility to experience of ourselves as being, in some sense, and most centrally, conscious presences that are not the same thing as a whole human being (an alternative is that the susceptibility is independently grounded, ease of dream disembodiment being just one manifestation of it). As Shear remarks, the experiential character of such dreams shows 'how discoordinated a basic aspect of our deeply held, naive commonsensical notions of self [is] from anything graspable in terms of body, personality, or, indeed, any identifiable empirical qualities at all'.[19]

To say that one central way (arguably the central way) in which we conceive of or experience ourselves is as an inner conscious entity that is not identical with the whole human being is not to say that we're ever right to do so, although I think we are. Nor is to think of oneself in this way to adopt any sort of dualist or immaterialist position; one can and does naturally think of oneself in this way even if one is an out-and-out materialist (37). Nor is it to deny that we also have a strong natural tendency to think of ourselves as human beings considered as a whole, 'Strawsonian' persons, essentially

---

[18] A person who is dreamlessly asleep can be aware of your intentions. One can even talk of unconscious awareness when considering things like blindsight (see e.g. Rosenthal 2005). The term 'peripheral awareness' is also useful, but the spatial character of the metaphor of peripherality is potentially very misleading when one is trying to give a general characterization of elements of awareness that are out of the focus of attention.

[19] Shear 1998: 678. This is not to say that one could dream in this way if one didn't have (or hadn't once had) normal experience of embodiment, or (as Shear stresses) that there is any sense in which one is or even could be independent of one's body. One possibility is that the experience of disembodiment in dreams might have something to do with the decoupling mechanism that ensures that we do not actually make the movements we make in dreams (this might be so in spite of the fact that this decoupling is necessary precisely when we are experiencing ourselves as embodied in our dreams).

unified, indissolubly mental-and-non-mental single things to which mental and bodily predicates are equally and equally fundamentally applicable.[20] Nor is it to deny that the primary way in which we ordinarily think of people other than ourselves is as Strawsonian persons. The point is simply this: whatever else is the case, the sense that there is such a thing as the self, and that it is not the same thing as the whole human being, is one of the fundamental structuring principles of our experience.

The central question of this book is whether this conviction has a defensible form. The current philosophical orthodoxy, I think, is that it does not. My aim is to defend the view that it does within a materialist framework. What unprejudiced investigation finds, I think, is that one's natural, powerful sense of the self coexists comfortably, in the normal course of things, with one's equally natural tendency to conceive of people (including oneself) in the Strawsonian way as nothing more than essentially unified single things that have both mental and bodily properties. The Strawsonian conception of persons is stamped deep into our ordinary apprehension of others and our normal use of language in communication, but it is not similarly stamped into the fundamental character of our private thought about ourselves—even though we standardly express our thought to ourselves in language. John Updike writes that 'our names are used for convenience by others but figure marginally in our own minds, which know ourselves as an entity too vast and vague to name' (2000: 76). The point can be transferred to 'I' in further response to those who think that the word 'I', as used by GS, say, refers only to whatever 'GS' refers to in general use.

2.4 The two uses of 'I'—preview

It's a merely phenomenological remark—to say that human beings naturally have a sense that there's such a thing as the self, and that it isn't the same thing as the whole human being. Nothing follows about whether this is reasonable or correct. I'm going to argue that it is reasonable, and indeed correct. At some point, therefore, I'll have to move on from the claim that a dual use of 'I' reflects the way we often think to the stronger claim that it reflects the way things are. The move comes in 7.2. I propose that the reference of the word 'I' can contract inwards or expand outwards in a certain way in normal use, and bears comparison in this respect with a phrase like 'the castle'. Sometimes 'the castle' is used to refer to the castle proper, sometimes it's used to refer to the ensemble of the castle and the grounds and buildings located within its outer walls. Similarly, when I think and talk about myself, my reference sometimes extends only to the self that I am, and sometimes it extends further out, to the human being that I am. Often my thought or semantic intention is unspecific as between the two.

This claim is not the same as Wittgenstein's suggestion that there are two legitimate uses of 'I': the use 'as object' and the use 'as subject' (1958: 65–9). It is, rather, the

---

[20] P. F. Strawson 1959: 101–10. These are also Cartesian persons, in fact, but current misunderstandings of Descartes make the point opaque.

proposal that there are two uses 'as subject': the use to refer to oneself considered as a whole human being and the use to refer to oneself considered as a self. Both are legitimate, because there really are two distinguishable things in question, or so I will argue. There's no such thing as the use merely 'as object' (see further 3.16).

Some may insist again that the referential force of 'I' in thought or talk always automatically and necessarily runs out to encompass the whole human being, even when 'I' is used with the specific intention to refer only to the self—even in the case in which someone says 'I was floating out of my body and looking down on it from above'. I've already argued that the a priori, 'logico-grammatical' defence of this claim, which appeals to considerations about the public nature of words and concepts, has no force; but by the end of 7.1 this will no longer be important. All that will be important is the metaphysical claim that there are as a matter of fact two kinds of objects to be found, selves and human beings considered as a whole, and the truth or falsity of this claim will not hang on any facts about language.

2.5 A structure for discussion

I've argued that we have, so far, no reason to doubt that the notion of a self is respectable, and that there is a real philosophical problem about the self rather than just a relatively uninteresting problem about why we think there is a problem. We have, in other words, so far, no reason to doubt that there is a real and difficult question of fact: Do selves exist? Clearly, though, we need to know what sort of things we're asking about before we can begin trying to find out whether or not they exist. We have to get the (apparently straightforwardly ontological) question into focus in this way before we can hope to make progress with it. I think the question requires a classically metaphysical approach, rather than a linguistic approach of the sort described in 2.2, but I also think that metaphysics must wait on phenomenology. A lot of recent discussion of the problem of the self by analytic philosophers has started from work in philosophical logic, in the large sense of the term,[21] and although this work has considerable intrinsic interest, I'm going to argue that a more phenomenological starting point is needed.

Why, after all, does there seem to be a problem about the self? The starting fact is this: many people believe—have no doubt—that there is such a thing as the self distinct from the human being considered as a whole. And if we ask why so many people believe in the self, conceived of as a distinct thing in this way, the answer is plain. They believe in it because they have a distinct sense or experience of there being such a thing in their own case, and they're quite sure that this experience is not delusory. They have what I call 'SELF-experience'.

It is, then, the phenomenon of SELF-experience—what Leibniz called 'the sense of I', what Priestley called 'the idea of self, or the feeling that corresponds to the

---

[21] See e.g. the essays collected in Cassam 1994.

pronoun *I*'[22]—that is the source of the philosophical problem of the self, and it invites—requires—careful phenomenological investigation for that reason alone. I believe that it is in fact the whole source of the problem of the self, in such a way that when we ask whether selves exist, what we're actually asking is whether anything like the sort of thing that is figured in SELF-experience exists or can exist. There is—I propose—nothing more at issue than this.

If this is right, the first thing one has to do, when addressing the problem of the self, is to produce an account of what sort of thing is figured in (and in that sense postulated by) SELF-experience. Then, and only then, can one usefully ask whether or not there exists such a thing as the self. Which is to say that phenomenology must precede metaphysics when it comes to the problem of the self. This book acquires its structure from this idea, which I'll defend further in 2.11. It won't matter much, however, if you're not convinced, if you think that the self is best treated as a theoretical posit that has no special answerability to or definitional connection with SELF-experience, a posit that must earn its place in one's philosophy in the way that other theoretical posits do, by being useful or even indispensable in an account of the nature of things. In that case you can read this book as dealing with two separate but connected matters, the phenomenology of the self and the metaphysics of the self, and you can assess the phenomenological and metaphysical claims without paying much attention to the way they're said to be related. In fact you can try skipping straight to Part 6, using the index and the references in the text when you need to understand a term introduced in the parts you have skipped (the intervening passages that it would be most helpful to read are 2.18–2.20, 3.5, 4.8, and 5.11).

I'll now set out the structure of the book in a little more detail. The proposal is that before we ask the basic ontological or factual or metaphysical question

I.1 Do selves exist?

and its inseparable companion

I.2 What is the nature of selves, if they exist?

we have to ask and answer the phenomenological question

II What sort of thing is figured in (and in that sense postulated by) SELF-experience?

We have to consider II in order to find out what I is asking.

For our purposes, II is best taken, at least in the first instance, as a question expressly about human beings: as the *local* phenomenological question

II.1 What sort of thing is figured in ordinary human SELF-experience?

But whatever the answer to this question is, it leads naturally to the *general* phenomenological question

II.2 What is the minimal form of genuine SELF-experience?

---

[22] Priestley 1777: 284 (*Disquisitions* X. V); Leibniz 1704: 236. Here Leibniz is characterizing, very precisely, what Locke has in mind when he speaks of 'consciousness' in his discussion of personal identity; see G. Strawson, in preparation, b. The '*Selbstgefühl*'—the feeling of self—was much discussed in eighteenth-century philosophy; see Thiel 2001, 2006. See also Frege 1918: 25–6, quoted on p. 98 below.

Or in other words (2)

II.2 What is the ineliminable core of the experience-determining/structuring element SELF?

This question is crucial, for my central contention on behalf of my client the self (whose very existence, I am sorry to say, has been brought into question in these proceedings) is that if there exists anything that has the properties that selves are figured as having in any (every) genuine form of SELF-experience, then that thing is a self. My task, accordingly, is to develop a decent sense of the possible forms, or core form, of SELF-experience, in order to set up the right conditions for a fruitful enquiry into the question of the nature and existence of the self.

The phenomenological questions II.1 and II.2 are central to the present project, and they naturally raise a further question in the philosophical mind, the *conditions* question, or *grounds* question

III What are the grounds or preconditions of SELF-experience?

And III in turn raises a battery of further questions, both empirical and a priori, including (or so it may seem)

IV What are the grounds or preconditions of self-consciousness?

Questions III and IV are questions of great interest, and I'll consider them in Part 3. I don't, however, think that one has to answer them in order to answer question I. One does have to answer question II, but one can gain sufficient purchase on the question of the nature of SELF-experience without knowing its grounds or preconditions.

Let me stress again that 'SELF-experience' is a phenomenological term, a name for a certain form of experience that doesn't imply that there actually are such things as selves (2). As for my use of the word 'self' without small capitals—it's like William James's when he writes that we must first try 'to settle for ourselves as definitely as we can, just how this central nucleus of the Self may *feel*, no matter whether it be a spiritual substance or only a delusive word' (1890: 1. 298). Here James uses the word 'self' freely and loosely as if it refers, while expressly allowing that it may in the end turn out to be only a delusive word. I do the same in describing the character of experience of there being such a thing as the self: I speak freely of how the self is figured or experienced without in any way ruling out the possibility that the final conclusion will be that there is really no such thing. It will sometimes be convenient to use the expression 'experience of (the) self' instead of 'SELF-experience', but if I turn the phrase round in this way and ostensibly refer to the thing, the self, rather than the experience-structuring mental element SELF, I will not be intending to activate the 'factive' or 'success' implications of the word 'experience' and thereby presuppose that there are such things as selves.

2.6 'Humanism'

—To ask the local phenomenological question is to assume that we can generalize about human SELF-experience, but this is far from clear. There are profound psychological differences between members of different cultures. Many influential anthropologists and sociologists doubt that we can make any such generalizations.

SELF-experience may have a different quality or tone in different cultures, but the basic phenomenon is universal. There are fundamental psychological similarities between human beings next to which differences in cultural experience are trifling. The aspects of ordinary human SELF-experience that are of concern in what follows are, I propose, fundamental in this way. They arise from features of our cognitive and epistemic situation that are universal in any ordinary human life—e.g. the silent experience of one's own private thought from childhood onwards. They're situated below any level of plausible cultural variation. Clifford Geertz's well-known claim that

the Western conception of the person as a bounded, unique, more or less integrated motivational universe, a dynamic centre of awareness, emotion, judgement, and action organised into a distinctive whole and set contrastively against other such wholes and against its social and natural background, is ... a rather peculiar idea within the context of the world's cultures

is as Melford Spiro says 'wildly overdrawn', and even if there were some interesting sense in which it were correct, it wouldn't constitute grounds for doubt about the present project, given the very basic nature of the features of SELF-experience that are in question.[23] Radical forms of cultural relativism rest on a massive underestimation of the genetic determinants of human nature and of the universal psychological consequences of certain universal human needs, together with a false view about the nature of human mental development. One might put the point by saying that the profound similarities between human bodies across all cultures (including of course all similarities of internal organs) are a perfect model for the profound similarities between human minds across all cultures. Reversing the analogy, one might take differences of external bodily appearance across cultures as a model for differences of internal psychological nature across cultures: the external differences are striking to our eyes, but superficial relative to all the profound similarities between us. When we examine the spectacular facts of cultural difference, and the dramatic and pervasive influence of culture on individual human psychology, we need to remember the extent of our common humanity.

For these reasons, and because I have a perhaps annoying Kantian confidence in the ability of philosophy to reach conclusions of extreme generality in this area, I expect my claims about ordinary human SELF-experience to apply, if true, to human beings generally. The function of this section is simply to mark the strong cultural relativists' objection, not to argue against it. That said, it's worth stressing that the deepest respects

---

[23] Geertz 1974: 126; Spiro 1993: 116. In a devastating criticism of the Geertzian position, Spiro shows that apparently significant differences in cultural conceptions of the self or person simply aren't matched by corresponding differences in SELF-experience (on the side of difference, see also Markus and Kitayama 1991; Nisbett 2003). If we did find a striking exception to the claim that the same fundamental spread of psychological styles is found in all human cultures, I would expect it to be grounded in genetic rather than cultural differences (it is conceivable that environmental conditions, which include cultural conditions, could strongly disadvantage and so breed out certain types of personality, especially in small or isolated human societies).

in which human beings can vary psychologically are fully on display within in any given culture; they're not differences that can be found only when one compares different cultures. (Psychopathology, of course, provides one arena of fundamental human difference, and I will consider it at various points.)

2.7 SELF-experience—second pass

I need to say more about SELF-experience—the experience that people have of themselves as being an 'inner' locus of consciousness, something that is essentially not the same thing as a human being considered as a whole; a specifically mental presence, a mental someone, a mental something that is a conscious subject. It's a particular way of experiencing oneself that comes to every normal human being in early childhood, and it is by definition experience that an experiencing being has of itself and only of itself.[24] One can be said to have experience of there being such a thing as the self in the case of someone other than oneself, but this isn't SELF-experience as defined here, although it may influence SELF-experience.[25]

The sense of oneself as an inner conscious presence, the early realization of the fact that one's thoughts are unobservable by others, the experience of the profound sense in which one is alone in one's head or mind, the experience of oneself as experiencing, as having a 'palpitating inward life'[26]—these aspects of SELF-experience are among the deepest facts about human existence. SELF-experience may be vivid when one is alone, thinking or watching sheep on a hilltop, but it can be just as strong in a room full of people. It's connected with (although it doesn't require) a feeling that nearly everyone has had at some time—the feeling that one's body is just a vehicle or vessel for the mental presence that is what one really or most essentially is, 'the most enduring and intimate part of the self, that which we most verily seem to be'.[27] This feeling may be open to criticism, but it is what it is, and it illustrates one aspect of SELF-experience. Theorists who are anxious to stress the EEE aspects of our experiential predicament as essentially embodied social and organic beings located in a physical environment risk losing sight of the respect in which SELF-experience is fundamental to human existence, although there is in fact no conflict between emphasizing the existence of SELF-experience and an EEE view of human beings. Emphasis on the former doesn't threaten the force and reach

---

[24] It doesn't require the special kind of experience recorded by Nagel (1986: ch. 4) or by Emily in Richard Hughes's book *A High Wind in Jamaica* (1929: ch. 6) or by Elizabeth Bishop in 'The Waiting Room' (1971)—see pp. 213–16. For this is by no means universal.

[25] Those who think that one can't be self-conscious without attributing consciousness to things other than oneself (wrongly, in my view—see 3.7) may equally think that one can't have SELF-experience without attributing SELF-experience to things other than oneself.

[26] James 1890: I. 299. Some of us feel, with Scipio Africanus, that we are never less alone than when by ourselves.

[27] James 1890: I. 296; see further pp. 296–8. When one is alone and thinking, one may also be walking, cycling, sailing, or running. Strenuous or complicated or otherwise salient physical activity—or pain—does not diminish the extent to which one's SELF-experience presents oneself to oneself as, specifically, an inner conscious presence. On the whole, it is more likely to increase it.

of the latter in any way; anyone inclined to object that the insistence on the reality of SELF-experience stems from a limited, 'Western', academic, deskbound, etc. perspective is almost certainly a 'Western', deskbound, etc. academic.

Some philosophers deny that they have any SELF-experience, any sense of themselves as a subject of experience or locus of consciousness that isn't the same thing as the human being considered as a whole.[28] This isn't because they've engaged in meditative practices of the kind that are designed to eliminate a sense of the self but rather, it seems, because they subscribe to deeply entrenched doctrines in philosophical metaphysics and philosophy of mind, philosophical logic, and in philosophical psychology—doctrines about personal identity, about the reference of the word 'I', about the fundamental importance of the body in shaping our experience, and so on—that they take to provide powerful grounds for resistance not only to the claim that there's such a thing as the self, the subject conceived of as something distinct from the human being considered as a whole, but also to the claim that SELF-experience exists. Trefil, though, is right about the phenomenology: 'no matter how my brain works ..., one single fact remains ... I am aware of a self that looks out at the world from somewhere inside my skull ... this is ... the central datum with which every theory of consciousness has to grapple' (1997: 181), as is Dawkins: 'each of us humans knows that the illusion of a single agent sitting somewhere in the middle of the brain is a powerful one' (1998: 283–4)—even as he says that this experience is illusory.

It's wrong to think that SELF-experience automatically incorporates some sort of belief in an immaterial soul, or in life after bodily death. It doesn't, even if it's often the basis of such a belief. Philosophical materialists who believe as I do that we're wholly physical beings who don't survive bodily death, and that complicated conscious experience of the sort with which we are familiar evolved by purely physical natural processes on a planet where no such experience previously existed, have SELF-experience as strongly as anyone else.

Let me add that nothing in the descriptive-phenomenological notion of SELF-experience conflicts with anything true in the 'structuralist' or 'post-modernist' doctrine of the 'disappearance (or dissolution) of the subject', or with the ancient view that the subject of consciousness can never catch itself in such a way as to take itself as the object of consciousness (see 4.4 below). Nor is it any part of the present claim that SELF-experience necessarily involves experience of oneself as some sort of coherent, stable, persisting inner conscious entity. SELF-experience is present in schizophrenia.

2.8 Cognitive phenomenology (cognitive experience)

Many analytic philosophers think that phenomenology is restricted to the study of non-cognitive mental goings-on: to merely sensory experiences (including mental images

---

[28] In debate, John Campbell and Tim Williamson vigorously denied that any human being has or has ever had SELF-experience as I characterize it here.

of certain sorts) and feelings (including mood feelings and emotional feelings) in so far as these things can be and are considered just in respect of their entirely non-cognitive felt character. I will say that phenomenology so understood is confined to *sense-feeling experience*, bringing under this heading all sensation-mood-emotion-image-feeling phenomena considered independently (sofar as they canbe) of any cognitive mental phenomena. Phenomenology, however, is the general study of the character of experience or 'what-it's likeness (5), and the character of experience is as much cognitive as it is sensory. There is more to the overall character of our experience than sense-feeling experience. There is also *cognitive experience*—the name is exact. Only analytic philosophers, perhaps, have ever doubted this—Husserl would have difficulty understanding why this section is necessary—but they've done so with some pride.

The most cursory attention to the character of complex emotional experiences shows the mistake. Experiences of this sort—experiences of morally problematic situations, for example—are vivid cases in which it's hopelessly implausible to suppose that the overall character or what-it's-likeness of one's experience is simply a matter of wholly non-cognitive, sense-feeling experiential content. Some philosophers, however, hold the line. They grant, no doubt, that morally and emotionally complex experiences standardly involve cognitive goings-on, entertainings of certain conceptual contents, and so on, but insist that the *phenomenological* component of such experiences is merely a matter of sense-feeling experiential content. These philosophers are, I think, beyond help.

Experiences of morally problematic situations are decisive, if one stops to think (or doesn't start to think), but I'm going to put such cases aside. They contain unnecessary distractions, now that the ground has been churned up to the point where thoughtful people can sincerely claim to doubt the existence of cognitive experience, and I'm going to argue for the existence of cognitive experience—cognitive-experiential mental content, cognitive-phenomenological mental content—independently of reference to morality or emotion. Note that this use of the expression 'mental content' ('content' for short) is the natural but currently occluded internalist use according to which the content of one's current experience can be exactly as it is even if—to take one example—there's no external world of the sort there seems to be. In the terms of a familiar thought-experiment: my 'brain-in-a-vat Twin' and I, in having experience that is *ex hypothesi* qualitatively indistinguishable, have experience that has exactly the same cognitive-phenomenological content, although mine is experience of things—concretely existing mountains, say—that his is not experience of.

Consider now, as a specific example of cognitive experience, the experience of consciously entertaining and understanding specific propositional contents. I'll call this form of cognitive experience 'propositional meaning-experience'. In fact almost all if not all our actual daily experience essentially involves cognitive-experiential content in a larger sense, whether we're birdwatching or cooking or climbing. It's integral to our seeing trees, chairs, and so on specifically as trees, chairs, and so on, integral to the fact that we are actually incapable (at least without special training) of treating our visual experience just as colour-patch experience. I doubt that we're able to have significant stretches of experience that lack cognitive-experiential content, unless, perhaps, we're in the final stages of Alzheimer's disease (we wouldn't be more accomplished hedonists if we were). Here, though, I'm going to put these points aside, in order to focus on the particular case of propositional meaning-experience. More narrowly still, I'm going to focus on the case of propositional meaning-experience involving linguistic representation, because it's a salient example and has been specifically resisted, in the wake of Ryle and Wittgenstein, among others.[29]

Consider, then, your reading and understanding this sentence and the next two. This comprehending reading—it's going on at this very moment—is part of the course of your experience. More specifically: your apprehension of the content of the sentences, including this one, is playing a large part in determining the overall character, the overall qualitative character, of this particular stretch of the course of your experience, although you're also aware of the page and the print, rain on the window, birdsong, traffic noise, or whatever it may be.

Note that the word 'qualitative' is redundant in the last sentence; it adds nothing to 'character'. I use it for emphasis, because one considerable difficulty that people have with the notion of cognitive experience is with the idea that it is, like sense-feeling experience, ultimately and wholly a matter—to repeat the pleonasm—of the *qualitative* character of experience. In order to stay clear about this, after a conventional training in analytic philosophy, one needs a firm grip on the distinction between (a) cognitive-experiential content and (b) cognitive content *tout court*. Once again, my brain-in-a-vat Twin, or, as a variation, my Twin on Perfect Twin Earth, where water is H_2O, but the Nelson Mandela I know is not to be found, suffices to illustrate the distinction. For although my Twin and I are cognitive-experientially identical in respect of as-of-Mandela thought-experiences, our as-of-Mandela thought-experiences have quite different cognitive content.

The best way to treat this issue in general terms, I think, is to pass beyond the familiar notion of a sensory modality and introduce the more general notion of an *experiential* modality, which we may define by saying that one experiential modality is distinguished from another by the fact that the experiential-qualitative character of experiences available in the first experiential modality is different in type from the experiential-qualitative character of experiences available in the second.[30] We can then say that all the sensory or sense-feeling modalities (however we count them) are experiential modalities, and ask whether, conversely, all experiential modalities are sensory or sense-feeling modalities?

The answer, I take it, is No. But, before developing this line of thought in more detail, I'm going to go back to the example of your comprehending (now) of this very sentence. The claim is that the cognitive-experiential content of your comprehending is

---

[29] In what follows I draw on G. Strawson 1994: 5–13, and 2005: §6. There's a brilliant discussion of certain aspects of propositional meaning-experience in James 1890: ch. 9. See also Ayers 1991 (vol. 1 ch. 31); Pitt 2004. I introduced the term 'cognitive phenomenology' in G. Strawson 1986 (see e.g. pp. 30, 55, 70, 96, 107–9) when discussing the complexities of what it is like to experience oneself as a free or truly responsible agent.

[30] 'Qualitative' has to be qualified by 'experiential', strictly speaking, because experiences also have non-experiential qualitative character, according to standard materialism: every non-relational property of a thing contributes to its qualitative character. Having made the point, I will usually bracket 'experiential' or follow common practice and omit it.

something that has to be adverted to in a full account of the (qualitative) character of your current experience, which includes its cognitive-experiential character. The point is obvious to unprejudiced reflection, but has become obscure in some philosophical fora.

One reason for this may be the fact that it's extremely hard to pin down the contribution to the overall character of your experience that is being made by your apprehension of the content of a sentence in such a way as to be able to take it as the object of reflective thought (it's far easier to do this in the case of the phenomenological character of an experience of green). In fact, when it comes to the attempt to figure to oneself the phenomenological character of understanding a sentence like 'Consider, then, your reading and understanding this very sentence', it seems that all one can usefully do is rethink the sentence as a whole, comprehendingly; and the trouble with doing this is that it seems to leave one with no mental room to stand back in such a way as to be able to take the experiential character of one's understanding of the sentence, redelivered to one by this rethinking, as the principal object of one's attention: one's mind is taken up with the sense of the thought in such a way that it is very hard to think about the character of the experience of having the thought.

True. But this doesn't put the reality of meaning-experience in doubt. Consider the experiential difference between the event of your hearing and understanding the sentence 'Hume's *Dialogues Concerning Natural Religion* is not a late work; he was working on it as early as 1749' and the event of your hearing and understanding the sentence 'This sentence is a sentence of English'. The difference is not just a matter of the different auditory experiences you have in the two cases. Nor is it, in the reading case, just a matter of the different shapes and/or silently entertained sounds of the words. It is also, and far more importantly, a matter of the difference between their cognitive-experiential content which is explicable principally by reference to the difference between the cognitive content of the two sentences.[31]

Suppose we want to give a truly compendious description—as complete a description as possible—of the overall character of the course of your experience, your lived experience, during a ten-second period of time during which (among many other things) you comprehendingly entertain the thought that no one could possibly have had different parents. The claim is this: we will not be able to give anything resembling a compendious description of the character of your experience over that time without citing the thought that no one could possibly have had different parents. And by 'the overall character of the course of your experience' I mean, of course, and again, and pleonastically, the overall *experiential*—*qualitative*—character of the course of your experience. We have to acknowledge the existence of cognitive-experiential qualitative content in addition to sense-feeling experiential qualitative content.

I use undramatic sentences to make the point, rather than sentences like 'They killed him in front of his children' or 'Here come the capybaras on their bikes'.[32] This is

---

[31] It's not as if we can reduce the experiential difference to the auditory/visual differences plus *non*-experiential differences in the ways in which exposure to the two sentences alters one's behavioural dispositional set (G. Strawson 1994: 8–9).

[32] Fenton 1972:.101.

important, for in talking of cognitive experience, and more particularly propositional meaning-experience, and in focusing on the linguistic case, I'm not concerned in any way with any of the imagistic or emotional or mood-tone experiences that can accompany the understanding of certain words (often in such a way that they can seem to be integral to the semantic understanding). My aim is to damp down all such accompaniments as far as possible, in order to highlight what is then left over, something that is equally real and definite although it can seem troublesomely intangible when we try to reflect on it: the experience that is standardly involved in the mere comprehending of words (read, thought, or heard), where this comprehending is considered completely independently of any imagistic or emotional accompaniments.

I don't know what more to do to avert misunderstanding on this point. Suppose I say 'This sentence has five words' or 'To study is to love, and there is no relief in love'.[33] Suppose you're attending. Your experience has a certain overall character between the time I start and the time I finish. It involves some sensory awareness of your surroundings and bodily state. It also involves hearing sounds like the sounds produced when someone with a voice like mine says 'This sentence has five words' or 'To study is to love, and there is no relief in love'. But there's more. There's the way your experience is specifically in virtue of the fact that you understand what is said.[34] Consider the difference between my saying 'I'm reading *War and Peace*' and my saying 'barath abalori trafalon'. The point is, again, obvious. It needs to be noted because many analytic philosophers in the last sixty years have denied it vehemently and sometimes, it must be said, rather scornfully.

Another way to make the point is to observe that one often reads or hears words or thinks thoughts that are extraordinarily interesting. They're experienced as interesting. Suppose, for example, you're interested in what you're reading now. Clearly, your being interested must be a response to something in the content of your experience. What is it in the content of your experience that it is a response to?

You may in fact be bored by what you're reading now, but you have at some time read a book or listened to words (perhaps on the radio) because the content conveyed by them was very interesting—fascinating. The question, again, is: Why did you continue to read or listen? What was it about the character of your experience that made you continue? Was it merely the sensory content of the visual or auditory goings-on? Obviously not. It was the cognitive-experiential content of your experience.[35]

---

[33] Halliday 1973.

[34] Slightly more precisely: there is the way your experience is specifically in virtue of the fact that you automatically (and involuntarily) experience the sounds you hear as representing that *p*, for some proposition *p*. For the point that misunderstanding is as much a matter of cognitive experience as understanding, see G. Strawson 1994: 7.

[35] Why not replace the cumbersome phrase '*cognitive-experiential* content of experience' by '*conceptual* content of experience'? Well, you'd then have to say that the conceptual content of your experience is identical to that of your philosophical Twins' experience, given that the cognitive-experiential content of your experience is *ex hypothesi* identical to theirs. So your Twins would have to have exactly the same *concepts* as you—GIRAFFE, BANANA, and so on. ... I think one can in fact make sense of such an 'internalist' notion of a concept or thought-element. It would, however, cause nothing but confusion, given the currently accepted understanding of what concepts are.

Perhaps you have various imagistic, bodily-feeling accompaniments as you listen or read, and you want them to continue. But what's causing them? (Perhaps your skin is prickling.) Is it merely the visual and acoustic properties of the marks or sounds? If so, then the same sounds or marks could presumably have the same effect on someone who is (somehow) just as familiar as you are with the sounds or marks considered just as such, but doesn't experience them as meaning anything in particular.

The difficulty is plain. If one wants to give anything like a full account of the qualitative character of our experience in merely sense-feeling terms, one has to be able to explain in those terms alone how the experience of looking at a piece of paper with a few marks on it, or of hearing three small sounds, can make someone collapse in a dead faint. One has to be able to look at a class of motionless children listening raptly to a story and give a full explanation of the exceptional physiological condition into which the story has put them by reference to nothing more than the spoken words considered simply as sounds.

It can't be done (all the examples make the same point). We need some notion like the notion introduced earlier—that of an experiential modality.[36] All the sense-feeling modalities (however we count them) can then be filed neatly under the general category *experiential modality*, while space is left for other possible experiential modalities, and, in particular, for the experiential modality of conscious thought, or, more generally, the experiential modality of cognitive experience.

How many experiential modalities are there? One can individuate them in different ways, according to one's theoretical purposes. When it comes to counting sensory modalities, the best thing to do for most purposes is to stick to general differences of experiential type of the kind we mark out by sorting experiences into tactile, aural, olfactory, gustatory, visual, visceral, vestibular, musculoskeletal, kinaesthetic, and so on. It's a difference of this general kind that's in question when it comes to the proposal that we need to add the general experiential modality of conscious thought to whatever set of experiential modalities we distinguish under the heading of sense feeling modalities. But one can if one likes cut much finer (there may be theoretical contexts in which it's useful to say that every qualitatively different colour experience involves a different experiential modality). Moods are an interesting case. Some may say that they're all of the same general type in being, distinctively, mood modalities. There may, however, be contexts in which it seems best to treat mood states that are as different as contentment and depression as distinct experiential modalities.

'The experiential modality of conscious thought'. Words like these trigger deep reflexes of suspicion, at least in members of my generation and its successor. To assert the existence of such a thing is still to make a radical claim in the context of current philosophical discussion of experience—especially given all the input from psychology and neuropsychology, which strongly constrains people to think that all experience *must* be somehow sensory, a matter of feeling.

What's the remedy? The most important thing, I think, is to get clear on the point that there isn't any difficulty at all, let alone any special difficulty, in the idea that

---

[36]   See G. Strawson 1994: 196; 2005: 264.

the particular form of the experiential modality of conscious thought that is found in creatures like ourselves is wholly a product of a process of evolution by natural selection, just as the particular forms of the sensory modalities that are found in creatures like ourselves are wholly a product of a process of evolution by natural selection. Any realistic materialist or naturalist who believes in the theory of evolution must believe that this has happened, because the existence of the experiential modality of conscious thought—of cognitive experience—is an evident fact. It's one of the first pieces of data that any credible naturalism must accommodate.

It may be that nothing like the fully developed human form of the experiential modality of conscious thought can evolve until sense-feeling modalities like ours are already well evolved (it's possible that cognitive experience is principally located in early sensory areas of the brain). It may be that the former grows out of the latter, or on top of them, in some way. Perhaps the former can't exist in nature independently of the latter. Perhaps the latter are in Kant's phrase 'always already' seeded with the former in some way.[37] Questions about these matters are as old as they are important. They are, however, questions of detail, relative to my present concern, and none of them touch the point that the existence of the experiential modality of conscious thought is an unbudgeable natural fact. *The mass of the moon is just over 1 per cent that of the earth.* Nor do they cast any doubt on the idea that the experiential modality of conscious thought is a distinct experiential modality, as distinct from each of the sensory modalities as they are from each other. The Buddha puts the point very clearly when he distinguishes six principal 'senses', seeing, hearing, smelling, tasting, touching, and thinking, the last of which is a matter of 'non-sensory mental activity'.[38]

So far I've focused on the case of occurrent linguistic propositional meaning-experience. It's a particularly luminous example of the general phenomenon of cognitive experience, although it can seem troublingly elusive when one tries to inspect it directly (evasive as target of thought, bright when acquired). It stands out vividly when we consider hearing and understanding a particular sentence at a particular time, or comprehendingly entertaining a particular thought, because the cognitive-experiential feature of the character of experience that then concerns us is in the spotlight, expressly figured in consciousness, even as it evades inspection by a distinct act of apprehension.[39]

---

[37] A346/B404. There are old and obvious reasons to be suspicious of the idea of pure or mere sensation, given the entanglement of sensation and cognition in perception. One can register this point while agreeing with Fodor's (1984) rejection of the idea that there is no theory-independent observation, and before one considers the 'conceptualist' view, advanced paradigmatically in McDowell 1994, that there is no non-conceptual content.

[38] S. Hamilton 2001: 53. I propose that 'experiential modality' ('mode of experiencing') is an exact translation of Buddha's word 'āyatana', which is usually translated by 'sense' in spite of the fact that one of the senses is then said to be a matter of non-sensory activity.

[39] By 'expressly figured' I don't mean that it's entertained through the medium of some quasi-acoustic or visual imagery, for although we do engage in a lot of such imagery, we can grasp cognitive-experiential content far faster than that, and wholly without imagery: 'thought is quick'. (I can't be sure that Hobbes had conscious rather than unconscious thought primarily in mind when he said this, but thought can in any case be incredibly rapid in its conscious representations of contents; for an illustration see G. Strawson 1994: 18–21.) Those who feel that remarks like these are precisely what philosophy had (so painfully and laboriously) to learn to distrust must give us a full account, using only sense-feeling terms, of the overall content or character of their experience right now as they read this.

Occurrent propositional meaning-experience (linguistic or not) is, however, only a small part of the overall subject matter of cognitive phenomenology as I understand it.

The main reason why this is so was given on page 38. Cognitive-experiential content pervades all experience. I don't suppose undamaged adult human beings are capable of being in experiential states that have no cognitive-experiential aspect. Here I have a different point in mind, which has to do with the definition of cognitive phenomenology as a discipline. Consider a representative human being whom I'll call 'Louis'. I take it, first, that any non-sense-feeling element of Louis's overall mental set—any concept that he possesses, for example—is a proper object of study for cognitive phenomenology just so long as it can inform or condition the cognitive-experiential character of his experience in some way; the domain of cognitive phenomenology as I understand it extends beyond the occurrent and experiential. I also take it that an experience-determining/structuring mental element may be crucially active in shaping the overall character of Louis's experience at some particular time, and be in that robust sense part of the content of his experience, i.e. (redundantly) part of the explicit content of his experience, in the wide sense of 'explicit' introduced on page 30, without being in the focus of attention in any way, and without being easily discernible, even on reflection, as a distinct element in that content.

When it comes to the study of SELF-experience, cognitive phenomenology deals principally in elements of the sorts just mentioned. Its task is to describe the general conception of what a self is that structures and animates actual, occurrent SELF-experience. It's concerned with the general conceptual framework of SELF-experience: with the complex non-sense-feeling experience-determining mental element SELF. One might say that it aims at a phenomenological deduction or extraction of the core content of the non-sense-feeling experience-structuring element SELF—of the *thought-element* SELF.[40]

I'm going to take it that this involves considering SELF-experience independently of any emotional or affective aspects that it may have, though without rigidly excluding reference to emotional experience.

---

[40] Why not simply use 'concept' instead of 'thought-element'? I use 'concept' sparingly for reasons already noted (2)—its recent use in philosophy has clogged it with associations that are irrelevant or misleading in the present context (associations with specifically linguistic phenomena, for example, and excessively externalist theories of mental content), and because it seems too narrow. It may never be wrong to say that to possess a certain thought-element or set of thought-elements is to have available a certain way of conceptualizing or conceiving things, a certain way of figuring or apprehending things, but the current notion of a thought-element retains a connection with experience that the currently favoured notion of a concept lacks, given (say) that *idiots savants* who find that answers just 'pop into their heads' can be said to have the concept of multiplication even if their minds are as experientially blank, mathematically, as pocket calculators. For a being B to have a thought-element in its general mental economy, then, is—among other things—for it to be capable of having experiences with a certain specific cognitive-experiential character. The phenomenological rule for judging whether B has a particular thought-element κ in its mental economy is simple. We start with a description of B. If, given this description of B, which may be very exiguous, e.g. 'B is self-conscious', we find we can't give an adequate specification of the overall nature or content of the experience that B is capable of having or disposed to have without making use of κ, then we may judge that B has κ in its mental economy. The rule is in a sense trivial, but it helps to state it explicitly and emphasize the connection with experience. (I don't place any conditions on thought-element possession that advert to dispositions to overt behaviour for reasons given in G. Strawson 1994, e.g. ch. 10.)

—This can't be right. SELF-experience, anything that is reasonably called SELF-experience, can't exist without having a certain affective or emotional character or import. If Louis loses all affect while remaining otherwise unchanged, then he no longer really has any SELF-experience, even though he is still fully self-conscious, aware of his private inner thought, and so on.

This clarifies what I mean by SELF-experience. On my terms, Louis still has SELF-experience, in having a sense of himself as a specifically mental presence, a mental someone, even if he's been deprived of a certain kind of self-concern that is almost universal in human beings (whether positively deprived, as in the case of a certain sort of spiritual development, or negatively, as in the case of clinically pathological 'depersonalization').

—Bracketing the affective aspects of experience is bound to produce distortions in any attempt to give a good general account of the basic structure of ordinary human SELF-experience.

The following discussion constitutes my defence of the claim that this isn't so. In human beings, the cognitive phenomenology of SELF-experience is bound up with the affective phenomenology of SELF-experience in deep and complicated ways which are of central concern to Buddhist practice, and the affective phenomenology of SELF-experience is in itself of the very greatest interest and importance. But deep similarities in the former are compatible with huge differences in the latter, whereas the reverse is not so. To this extent the cognitive phenomenology lies deeper than the affective phenomenology, and is worth separate study as far as possible.

—When we try to analyse the thought-element SELF, we are on your terms specifically concerned with something that structures experience, 'the lived character of experience', and we're concerned with it specifically in so far as it does this. That's the way you like to put it, and you call it phenomenology. But everyone's doing phenomenology, by this test. Kant is doing phenomenology when he attempts a 'metaphysics of experience', in the special Kantian sense of the term, and P. F. Strawson is doing the same when, following Kant, he puts forward a 'descriptive metaphysics'.

If so, good. There is, however, a further reason why I take myself to be doing phenomenology. It's because I try to lay out the structure of the thought-element SELF by using a distinctively phenomenological method; that is, by examining the form of experience I'm calling SELF-experience. The method isn't exclusive of other methods. In practising it one isn't debarred from using arguments that are transcendental in the Kantian sense: one may, for example, wish to argue that a form of experience couldn't possibly fit one phenomenological description unless it also fitted another, or couldn't exist at all unless some other condition obtained.

I'd prefer to speak simply of 'phenomenology' in what follows, rather than of 'cognitive phenomenology'. My experience, however, is that analytic philosophers tend to revert to thinking that phenomenology is concerned only with sense-feeling phenomena, so I will from time to time qualify it as 'cognitive'.

2.9 SELF-experience—third pass

Back now to the local phenomenological question: What is the nature of ordinary human SELF-experience—our ordinary, unreflective lived conception of the self? What is its basic form? How is it animated, conceptually speaking? In ordinary human SELF-experience, I propose, the self is figured as something that is

First and foremost, a subject of experience, a conscious feeler and thinker. I'll call this first experience-structuring mental element 'SUBJECT'.

Second, it's figured as a thing of some sort, in at least the sense that it's figured as something that has properties and is not itself merely a property of something else. Retaining the valuable vagueness of 'thing' I will call this experience-determining element 'THING'.

Third, it's figured as something mental. By this—*nb*—I mean only and simply that it's considered as something mentally propertied, something that has mental being, whatever else is true of it ('MENTAL').

Fourth and *fifth*, it's figured as something single ('SINGLE'), both when considered 'synchronically' or at any given particular time ('SINGLE$_s$') and when considered 'diachronically' as something with some sort of temporal extension ('SINGLE$_D$'). I'll use the simple form 'SINGLE' when there's no need to be more specific, and I'll standardly use 'PERSISTING' rather than 'SINGLE$_D$' to mark the fact that the self, in being figured as diachronically single, is standardly figured as something that has relatively long-term singleness or continuity through time ('relatively' is intentionally vague).

Sixth, it's figured as an agent, as an intentional agent ('AGENT').

Seventh, it's figured as something that has a certain character or personality ('PERSONALITY').

Eighth, it's figured as something distinct from, in the sense of not identical with, the organism considered as a whole, the whole human being ('DISTINCT').

This, I propose, is the basic framework of the ordinary human sense/experience/conception of the self. These are the eight key elements that structure the sense of the self in ordinary unreflective SELF-experience.

The proposal may be thought to be too strong in various ways (it's not clear that PERSONALITY should be included). There are various close interdependencies between the elements, and there is redundancy in the list (the first entails the third, for example). Nevertheless, it provides a base and a target. I don't think it omits anything essential, even if it includes things that aren't essential. I'm going to assume that this is so, but it won't matter much if I'm wrong, for a framework of this kind can be helpful in articulating thought about the self even if it isn't complete. If an omission is identified, it can simply be added to the existing framework and dealt with in turn.

Am I claiming that all these thought-elements are explicit or active (even if only in some minimal way) in any individual occurrent episode of ordinary human

SELF-experience? It doesn't take much to be a matter of explicit awareness, given the definition of 'explicit' on page 30, but I don't need to insist on the point. What is at issue is the general thought-elemental framework of SELF-experience as it might be elicited by asking people questions about how they experience things, getting them to spell out aspects of their experience that they don't normally pay attention to.[41] This is a wholly phenomenological enterprise, given the current understanding of phenomenology.

It may be suggested that the self is also

Ninth, figured as self-conscious ('SELF-CONSCIOUS')

in ordinary human SELF-experience. This, though, isn't obvious. Even if all genuine SELF-experience presupposes and involves a capacity for express self-consciousness of the sort with which we are familiar, it doesn't follow that an apprehension of the self *as* self-conscious is a necessary part of SELF-experience, either in general or in the ordinary human case. Very young children already have what I'm calling 'ordinary human SELF-experience', and although they are indeed self-conscious, it doesn't follow that they must be figuring themselves *as* self-conscious, in having SELF-experience—even if they are or must be exercising their capacity for self-consciousness in having SELF-experience. Note that we naturally think of infants as having or being selves before we think of them as being self-conscious. To this extent self-consciousness doesn't seem to be a necessary component of our ordinary notion of what a self is, although some philosophers choose to define the notion of the self in such a way that it does require self-consciousness.

It may be said that any exercise of self-consciousness must bring with it some grasp of the *concept* of self-consciousness. But even if this is so,[42] one can doubt the further step (it is a further step) of claiming that self-consciousness, in being necessary for SELF-experience, has the consequence that all ordinary human SELF-experience comports some sense or conception of the self as something self-conscious, and I'm going to omit SELF-CONSCIOUS from my base list. (I return to this question in Part 3.)

It may next—and relatedly—be proposed that in ordinary human SELF-experience the self is also

Tenth, figured as something that has SELF-experience.

Is there something in this? Might it be true that (a) having some sort of sense of oneself as a thing that has some sort of sense of itself as a self or inner mental presence, is itself part of (b) having a sense of oneself as a self or inner mental presence—either in every case or at least in the ordinary human case? Put this way the proposal seems

---

[41] The questions would have to be Socratically phrased so as not to pressure the respondents towards the expected answers (one reaction might be of the form 'I see now that I do in fact think of myself in this way').

[42] It may not seem compelling when one thinks of the dawning of self-consciousness in children, and is also likely to fail on definitions of self-consciousness that accord it to chimpanzees, bonobos, magpies, dolphins, elephants, and other non-human animals, on the ground that their behaviour in front of mirrors suggests that they grasp that they see themselves in the mirror (see e.g. Gallup et al. 2002).

rather strenuous, but it can be expressed more simply as the idea that ordinary human SELF-experience essentially figures the self as something that is (so to say) at home to itself, something that is, as a self or inner mental presence, in some way aware of itself as such.

There's something attractive about this idea, and I list it for that reason. Does it identify an essential feature of ordinary human SELF-experience? I don't know. It's an empirical proposal, like all the others, testable in principle by psychological research—although it wouldn't be easy to agree terms and sort out experimental protocols.

I've made ten proposals and endorsed eight. These provide the main framework for the discussion that follows, although I'll also consider questions raised by the ninth and tenth. I came up with the list by sitting and thinking. It hardly follows that it came to my mind untouched by philosophical theories about the self.[43] Nor does it show that it's independent of any peculiar biases I may have. It is, furthermore, designed to be a strong proposal that invites qualification and denial. I think, nevertheless, that it makes a good starting point.

2.10 A Kantian connection?

I was two years into this work before I realized that the list has a strong affinity with Kant's list in his discussion of the four 'Paralogisms of Pure Reason'. SUBJECT, THING, and AGENT connect with his discussion of *substance* in the first section of the Paralogisms, SINGLE$_s$ connects with his discussion of *simplicity* in the second, PERSISTING (SINGLE$_D$) connects with his discussion of *diachronic continuity* in the third (as well as his discussion of substance in the first), and MENTAL and DISTINCT connect with his discussion of Descartes's 'real distinction' between mind and body in the fourth. Only PERSONALITY makes no direct connection.[44]

—Plainly you find this affinity very satisfying, but it has a further and for you less welcome aspect. For when you claim that one should and perhaps must preface metaphysical considerations by phenomenological considerations, in examining the question of the nature of the self or soul, you recommend something reminiscent of the move that Kant criticizes so devastatingly in the Paralogisms section of *The Critique of Pure Reason*. Where do the 'rational psychologists' who are his targets go wrong? Their central error, according to Kant, is to take certain a priori or 'logical' features of the *I* (or self or soul or subject of experience) as proof that it has a certain ultimate ontological nature; but his argument also has a phenomenological strain. On this reading the rational psychologists' great mistake is to think that they can derive sound metaphysical conclusions about the ultimate ontological nature of the *I* or self or subject or 'soul' from certain very broadly speaking phenomenological or as one might say logico-phenomenological facts about the character of our *experience* of the *I* or self or subject—facts

---

[43] The list spreads out the elements I came up with in 1979, when relatively unmarked by philosophy (G. Strawson 1983: 48–50, 1986: 160, 323–9).
[44] The Third Paralogism discusses 'personality', but the word then referred simply to the issue of the diachronic identity of the mind or soul.

about how we figure the *I* or self or subject of experience in what Kant calls '*inner sense*, or *empirical apperception*'.[45]

Taken in this way, Kant's position is that the rational psychologists are quite right about how we figure ourselves as subjects in so far as we have a sense of ourselves as subjects in having experience (e.g. when we reflect). They're right, in particular, that one's figuring of oneself as a subject in inner sense presents the subject as being some sort of mental thing that can't possibly be a mere property of something else (cf. Kant's discussion of the First Paralogism), something that is as such single or simple at any given time (Second Paralogism), persists as single through time (Third Paralogism), and can exist independently of matter (Fourth Paralogism). They're also right to think that our experience/conception of ourselves as subjects of experience *necessarily* has this character; it may be that the experience of any possible genuinely self-conscious being necessarily has this character. They are, however, quite wrong to think that we can infer anything at all from this about whether simple (Second Paralogism) persisting (Third Paralogism) substantial (First Paralogism) non-material (Fourth Paralogism) selves or souls or subjects really exist as a matter of ultimate ontological fact. Phenomenology—even a priori phenomenology, transcendental-logical phenomenology as it were, i.e. phenomenology that is concerned with facts about the necessary character of experience—is one thing, metaphysics is another.

The proposal, then, is that Kant's argument has a legitimate logico-phenomenological reading. According to this reading, it criticizes a move from (1) features of the necessary character of the experience of the I or subject, not just a move from (2) features of the 'merely' or 'purely' logical character of the concept of the I or subject, to an ontological conclusion. (The first is a version of the second, in so far as the error is to mistake (2) for (1)). Consider the discussion of the First Paralogism, read in this way. Kant allows and indeed stresses the point that one inevitably figures oneself as thing-like or substance-like, rather than as somehow just a property or predicate of something else, in one's apprehension of oneself as a subject of experience. But he then insists that we can't rule out the metaphysical possibility that the subject-of-experience phenomenon is in fact only a predicate or property or accident of something else (e.g. B419–20). Take the discussion of the Second and Third Paralogisms in the same way. It's true, Kant says, that the self or subject necessarily presents as something single, both synchronically and diachronically, in the experience of being a subject that is available to cognitively sophisticated creatures like ourselves. But, he continues, its presenting as synchronically and diachronically single—even its necessarily presenting as synchronically and diachronically single—may arise from a reality that isn't in fact single but multiple in its ultimate substantial nature, both synchronically and diachronically considered.[46] As for the Fourth Paralogism: the mind or self, figured or apprehended specifically as such, does indeed appear to be irremediably different in its fundamental ontic character from non-mental physical reality (that's how it is for us phenomenologically), but it doesn't follow that it is in fact fundamentally different. We don't and can't know enough about the ultimate nature of reality—about the nature of that which underlies both mental appearances and non-mental appearances, in Kant's scheme of things—to be able to assert this; see e.g. B427–8.[47] Given all this, it's unwise for you to claim affinity with Kant.

---

[45] A107. The addition of 'logico-' to 'phenomenological' is meant to capture the idea that some of these claims purport to state facts about how we must experience or figure the subject of thoughts and other experiences, and not only about how we do experience or figure it.

[46] See A353, A363 and n. For a more detailed discussion of issues relating to the Second Paralogism see 8.5.

[47] On this central feature of the Fourth Paralogism see also A358–60, 379–80, B409. The basic point is found in Arnauld's (1641) set of objections to Descartes's *Meditations*, and indeed in every one of the seven sets of objections to

I agree that the fundamental form of Kant's claim is logico-transcendental. He argues that one can't establish that the subject is a simple substance by reference to certain formal or 'logical' features of subjecthood, such as the fact that a single experience must have a single subject if it is to occur at all. 'The logical exposition of thought in general', including of course the logical exposition of the notion of the subject of thought, is 'mistaken for a metaphysical determination of the object' (B409). He argues that the rational psychologists are wrong if they think otherwise. They're wrong, in particular, if they think they can establish that the subject is a simple substance in such a way as to be able to conclude that it is something immaterial, hence incorruptible, hence immortal.[48] That said, I also agree that Kant also puts things in a more phenomenological-sounding way, and I'll take the point a little way. I'll usually translate Kant's word 'denken' and its cognates by 'experience' and its cognates, rather than by 'think' and its cognates. This will sound uncomfortable to some, but the uncomfortableness may be helpful. We tend to take 'think' only in the narrower, non-Cartesian sense when reading Kant, and this can be misleading, especially in the present context.[49] Plainly, though, translating 'denken' by 'experience' requires us to take 'experience' widely, as something that includes cognitive experience (2.8), and not take it to refer only to non-cognitive sense-feeling experience, i.e. 'intuition' in Kant's terminology.

Kant certainly holds that we have some sort of experience of ourselves as subjects in 'empirical apperception' or 'inner sense' (he uses these two terms interchangeably). He allows that 'our experiencing subject … is represented by us as object of inner sense' (A357). He says that I encounter 'the representation of myself, as the experiencing subject, … in inner sense' (A371), that 'the experiencing *I* … is given to inner sense', and that it is 'represented through inner sense in time' (A379). 'The proposition *I experience*', he says, 'expresses the *perception of the self*' (A342–3; second emphasis mine); 'the proposition *I am simple* [*single*]', he says, 'must be regarded as a direct expression of apperception' (A355).

It may be objected that he understands apperception in a merely transcendental sense here, i.e. not as something that has any experiential aspect. He has, after all, just said that 'the formal proposition of apperception *I experience* … is not itself an experience, but [merely] the form of apperception' (A354); and he most certainly doesn't think that 'the *I experience*' is or involves any sort of determinate 'intuition of the subject as object' (B423). That is in fact his main point, from which it follows immediately, on his terms, that we can't possibly have any knowledge of the nature of the subject, e.g. knowledge of its persistence and natural incorruptibility, because all such knowledge requires the application of a concept to a genuine intuition. At the same time, he says that the *I experience* is 'the form of apperception', and he defines apperception as 'consciousness of oneself' that consists of 'the simple representation of the *I*' of experience (B68). It may be that

---

the *Meditations*, in Regius's objection to Descartes (Regius 1647), in Locke's *Essay* (1689–1700), in Priestley (1777), and many others.

[48]   It's important that this is their principal goal and, accordingly, Kant's principal target; see further 4.3.
[49]   The verb 'mind' also has the right kind of generality, in one old use — 'I mentate', 'I conscious-ize'.

this too can be interpreted as something that has no experiential aspect. It does never-theless seem clear that Kant thinks that our apprehension of the *I experience* has some experiential aspect for us, albeit of a certain uniquely indeterminate and 'empty' sort, an experiential aspect which is, indeed, the origin of the rational psychologists' mistake. It is a crucial part of the First Paralogism that 'everyone must necessarily regard himself as a substance' when considering himself as subject, and must regard all episodes of thought or conscious episodes 'as being only accidents of his existence'.[50]

Udo Thiel thinks that Kant is simply restating part of the First Paralogism argument when he claims that 'everyone must necessarily regard himself as a substance', but even if this is so (an alternative view is that the exposition ends in the previous sentence), Kant is endorsing the claim[51] in order to go straight on to his central point: that this representing of the subject as a substance, and even the fact that we are unable not to represent it in this way, proves nothing about the actual metaphysical substantiality of the subject, because it involves no sort of experience of the subject in the sense of an intuition of the subject. An intuition of the subject is strictly necessary, on Kant's view, if any knowledge of its metaphysical nature is to be possible.

He repeats the point in the corresponding passage in the B edition: 'I, who experiences, must[52] in *experiencing* always be considered as a subject, and as something that does not merely attach to experiencing like a predicate' (B407; my emphasis). It's possible to read 'must in experiencing always be considered as a subject' as a wholly non-phenomenological comment that isn't about how the thinker is bound to experience itself when having experience, but about how we as theorists must consider the *I* of experience when we consider experience. But this reading is strained, even if the grammatical passive encourages it. The literal translation of the opening of the passage just quoted is 'that [the] I, whom / that I experience / am conscious of / think', and Kant's next major comment on the First Paralogism in the B edition is that its minor premiss, 'an experiencing being, considered merely as such, cannot be thought otherwise than as subject', talks about a being only 'in so far as *it considers itself* as subject' (B411; my emphasis): 'an experiencing being, considered just as such, can't consider itself otherwise than as *subject*'.

—Kant says that in the proposition 'everyone must necessarily regard himself as substance', 'we *have not taken as our basis any experience; the inference is merely from the concept* of the relation which all thought has to the *I* as the common subject in which it inheres' (A349–50; my emphasis). This refutes your phenomenological reading.

---

[50] A349. The addition of 'a' in front of 'substance' is sufficiently justified in the next sentence: 'But what use am I to make of this concept of a substance?'

[51] Both the premisses of the First Paralogism are fine, on his view; the problem arises from the fact that the two premisses take the word 'subject' or 'substance' in different ways. This is what the 'paralogism' consists in.

[52] I read 'must' with Pluhar and every native speaker I've consulted. Kemp Smith's and Guyer and Wood's translations wrongly have 'can'. This seems to result indirectly from two things: (1) a mistaken reading of 'gelten' as 'to be valid' rather than 'to consider as' or 'to count as' (the whole sentence is 'Dass aber Ich, der ich denke, im Denken immer als S u b j e k t, und als etwas, was nicht bloss wie ein Prädikat, dem Denken anhängend, betrachtet werden kann, gelten müsse, ist ein apodiktischer und selbst I d e n t i s c h e r S a t z'); (2) a mistaken worry (which may lie behind (1)) that the 'must' reading is not compatible with Kant's famous but differently intentioned claim that 'It must be possible for the "I experience" to accompany all my representations' (B131).

No. The point is precisely that the rational psychologists are mistaking the character, or rather the import, of their *experience*. There is a certain sort of experience of the *I*, but what they think is given in that experience, for the purposes of reaching metaphysical conclusions, is not in fact given. They think that experience has provided their basis for the inference, but it has not actually done so. They have in *that* sense not taken any experience as basis for their inference. In other words, and again, there is no actual 'intuition of the subject as object' of a sort that allows knowledge claims about its ultimate metaphysical nature.[53]

I'll return to this part of Kant's *Critique* in 2.20 and 3.15, and again in 4.3 and 8.5. For the moment it's enough to note that nothing here constitutes an objection to the present project of moving from phenomenology to metaphysics. I can see why Walsh concludes his discussion of the Paralogisms section by saying that 'in future no philosopher will be able to base an argument that concludes that the self exists and has a particular nature on the bare fact of consciousness with any hope of succeeding' (1975: 183), but I'm not sure he's right. Kant's attack is wholly successful, given his opponents' metaphysical agenda, in particular their aim to establish our immortality; but if one shifts the metaphysical ground, things change. I think one needs to shift the ground, and I'll eventually propose that Kant's first two Paralogisms about the substantiality (thing-likeness) and simplicity (synchronic singleness) of the soul or self can be recast in such a way that they cease to be paralogisms and become sound arguments to robust metaphysical conclusions.

2.11 Phenomenology and metaphysics

Why begin with phenomenology, when trying to answer the metaphysical (ontological) question whether there are such things as selves? I've claimed that one should do this because the phenomenon of SELF-experience is the (whole) source of the problem of the self. The idea is not simply that it can be helpful to try to trace a felt philosophical problem back to its source in our experience in order to get a better understanding of what it is; it's also that SELF-experience is the source of the problem of the self in such a way that its character sets the terms of discussion in a constitutive manner. What we're actually asking, on this view, when we ask whether selves exist, is whether there exist things that are like the things figured in SELF-experience—be it ordinary human SELF-experience or at least some form of SELF-experience that we can recognize as genuine. If so, we have to address the cognitive-phenomenological question 'What sort of thing is or can be figured in genuine SELF-experience?' ('What is the content of the non-sense-feeling experiencing-determining mental element SELF?') before we can address the metaphysical question whether selves exist. We have to take on the phenomenological question before we can know what the metaphysical question comes to.

---

[53] Reimarus (1694–1768), Merian (1723–1807) and Eberhard (1739–1809) are among those who stress the character of our experience in this correction. For an outstanding discussion of Kant's views on these matters that doubts the validity of any such phenomenological interpretation, see Thiel, forthcoming.

This suggests the procedure sketched in 2.5. First, answer the local question about ordinary human SELF-experience: I've proposed that it has the eight central elements listed in the previous section. Next, raise the general phenomenological question 'What is the minimal form of genuine SELF-experience? Are there other possibilities, so far as SELF-experience is concerned?' On the assumption that the eight elements don't omit anything essential to genuine SELF-experience, this question about the minimal case amounts to the question 'Which, if any, of the eight elements can one dispense with while still having something that qualifies as genuine SELF-experience?' Once one has an answer to this question, one can begin to address the metaphysical or ontological question (I.1) 'Do selves exist?' For the content of this question will have been supplied and fixed by the answer to the phenomenological question. We will, in other words, have an answer to the question (I.2) 'If selves exist, what is their nature?' which allows us to set out to consider whether things with that nature actually exist.

Obviously one can approach the metaphysical question in other ways. One can posit the self as a theoretical entity, holding that the self is that thing, whatever its nature, which plays this or that role or has this or that function, and deny that it must have the properties attributed to it in SELF-experience and in particular in minimal SELF-experience. One may then set about trying to find out which concrete entity has the favoured role or function. One such suggestion starts from the observation that individual thoughts and other experiences involve disparate mental elements jointly constituting a certain sort of unity. It then asserts that the correct reference of the term 'the self' is simply whatever is central in the correct explanation of how this happens, i.e. whatever mechanism or entity turns out to solve the supposed 'binding problem' (presumably some bundle of neural mechanisms). But why should one accept this? It seems likely to have the consequence that the self is not even a subject of experience.

—I'm prepared to agree that the self-entity, if it exists, is something whose nature is represented in SELF-experience. But why should this tell me anything about its essence? Why couldn't we establish the nature of SELF-experience, and give a sharp phenomenological account of the way the self is figured in SELF-experience, without having established anything about the actual nature of the self. This could remain entirely hidden.

Many, perhaps, will agree with you, but I don't think that the term 'self' can be supposed to make a successful referential hit unconstrained by any aspect of the descriptive content of the SELF-experience-enshrined idea of the self. It can't (for example) turn out that a self isn't even a subject of experience, for in this case there is no longer a sufficient rationale for using the word 'self' rather than some other word.

—I disagree. It might indeed turn out to be, theoretically, the best thing to say. Like everyone else, you're just co-opting the term 'self' for your own purposes. Your use of the word, which links it analytically to the phenomenon you've chosen to call SELF-experience, and seeks to fix its meaning by studying the nature of that experience, doesn't have any kind of special—let alone unique—validity.

It's true that my proposal about how to use the word 'self' is one among others. I don't expect many to agree that it has, as I believe, a favoured status. At the same time, I think that when one backs off from all theoretical constructions and presuppositions in order to try to work out where to enter on the problem of the self, this is what one comes up with. The starting fact is that each of us is confronted with SELF-experience, i.e. with the SELF-phenomena, by which I mean all those phenomena that naturally lead people to think and talk in terms of the self; and the starting question, accordingly, is whether anything like the entity that seems to present in SELF-experience exists. The first task, therefore, is to see whether it is possible to give a reasonably determinate and sufficiently general account of the character of SELF-experience. I think this can be done. If it can't, then we should consider reverting to some other framework of discussion of the self.

This is a highly substantive proposal about procedure; I'll examine it further in the next section because it raises a number of potentially interesting methodological issues (those uninterested in such issues can skip to 2.13). Many, I think, will see nothing to recommend it, but one can engage with the various theses about the phenomenology and the metaphysics of the self put forward in this book without accepting the idea that the phenomenology of the self must set the agenda for, and therefore precede, the metaphysics of the self, and without worrying about most of the details of the structure that this approach imposes on the discussion. One can ignore the 'architectonic' and still engage the issues.

—This can't work. You say that the phenomenological study of SELF-experience sets the agenda for the metaphysical question whether selves exist, so that one must engage in phenomenology before starting on metaphysics; but if this programme is going to have any chance of succeeding, the phenomenological study of SELF-experience must proceed independently of any theoretical, metaphysical (philosophical, religious, psychological) views about what selves are. But how can it? Even if it can be theory-independent in the required way when it concerns itself with the local, human case—the idea, I suppose, is that it is in this case rooted in direct, theory-innocent experience—it's bound to lose this independence when it turns to the general case and looks for the minimal form of SELF-experience. At this point distinctively theoretical, metaphysical views are bound to be part of what governs one's judgements about whether some candidate for being SELF-experience is really genuine. So phenomenology can't really be prior to and independent of metaphysics at this crucial stage. What's more, theoretical-metaphysical views about selves are highly likely to be influencing one even when one is trying to delineate the human case. The project of making a completely theory-free start on the metaphysical problem of the self by beginning with phenomenology is a fantasy.

This objection has considerable force. Nevertheless, I think that the case for the eight proposed elements of ordinary human SELF-experience can be made without any significant reliance—covert or overt—on academic or religious or otherwise expressly theoretical views about the nature of the self. I also think that our judgements about whether there are any other forms of genuine SELF-experience can remain comfortably independent of any such theoretical view, and that judgements about the minimal form of SELF-experience can be sufficiently supported by reference to actual human cases without reliance on imaginary thought-experimental cases.

I'll defend these two claims by trying to provide detailed answers to the local and general questions in the rest of Part 2 and in Part 4, but neither of them is of central importance here, where the principal question is not whether phenomenology can proceed independently of metaphysics, but the converse: Can metaphysics proceed independently of phenomenology, when it comes to the problem of the self?

I've said No. Sound metaphysical enquiry into the existence and nature of selves must take its bearings from phenomenological investigation of the character of SELF-experience. This proposal will still seem very unnatural to many, but it may be of some interest even to those who think it implausible, and I will now try to articulate it further in the *Equivalence Thesis*.

Before beginning, note that there are philosophers who fully agree that the metaphysics of the self depends on the phenomenology of the self, in such a way that one can't do the former without doing the latter, but who don't favour the present proposal. They make the connection in a much simpler way. They take it that the existence of the experience of there being such a thing as the self just *is* the existence of the self. The phenomenological reality of occurrent SELF-experience guarantees the metaphysical reality of the self, and displays its nature, because it is identical with it. On this view, the self, considered as a metaphysical entity, is some kind of wholly phenomenologically constituted entity. The phenomenology of the self just is the metaphysics of the self.

I'll return to this idea in 8.5 (see also p. 176). For now, let me just note a possible connection with Fichte's famous and seemingly paradoxical claim that

the I exists only in so far as it is conscious of itself. ... The *self posits itself*, and by virtue of this mere self-assertion it *exists*; and conversely, the self *exists* and *posits* its own existence by virtue of merely existing.   (1794–1802: 97)

2.12 The Equivalence Thesis

According to the Equivalence Thesis

[E] The metaphysical question 'Do selves exist?' is equivalent to the question 'Is there anything that has the properties attributed to the putative self by any (every) genuine form of SELF-experience?'

Put slightly differently, selves exist if and only if there is something that has the properties denoted by those thought-elements that feature in every genuine form of SELF-experience.

This is a strong claim, and seems implausible at first. Nor is its import immediately obvious—it helps to split it in two. The first half is

[E1] If there are such things as selves, then they must have the properties attributed to the putative self in any (every) genuine form of SELF-experience.

They must, in other words, have the properties picked out by the thought-elements that feature in the description of any (every) genuine form of SELF-experience, whatever other properties they have or do not have. The second half is

[E2] If there exist things that have the properties attributed to the putative self in any (every) genuine form of SELF-experience, then those things are selves (whatever other properties they have or lack).

It's not just [E1] that they must have the properties to be selves. It's also [E2] that if they have them, then they're selves.[54]

   Clearly [E1] and [E2] can be challenged, [E1] as follows:

[C1] There is really no very good reason to think that if selves exist, then they will have the properties attributed to them in any (every) genuine form of SELF-experience. Perhaps a self, as it is in itself, is ineffable, or at least quite unlike any experience of it.

One might say that [C1] is Kantian in spirit.

   The challenge to [E2] will have the following general form:

[C2] There is something that has the properties attributed to the self in any genuine form of SELF-experience, but this thing doesn't qualify for the title 'self' because it doesn't have feature ϕ (e.g. it isn't an immaterial, $\pm$ immortal, $\pm$ whatever, substance).

Both these challenges are natural and cogent. The import of [E]—[E1] + [E2]—consists precisely in the fact that it rejects them. One has already made a mistake, according to [E], if one thinks that one has to try to meet challenges like [C1] and [C2] on the terms of debate that they bring with them. The dependence of the metaphysics of the self on the phenomenology of the self consists precisely in the fact that one doesn't have to do this.

   [E], then, imposes a strong and substantial constraint on metaphysical theorizing about the self. One might say that it attempts to reclaim the word 'self', reduced to uselessness by the long and colourful history of its use, for serious philosophical discussion. [E1] rules out metaphysical claims about selves that fail to respect the conditions on counting as a self revealed by the phenomenological investigation. It states a *necessary* condition on qualifying for the title 'self': nothing can be allowed to count as a self unless it possesses all the properties attributed to the self by all genuine forms of SELF-experience—whatever other properties it may or may not possess. [E2], by contrast, states a *sufficient* condition on qualifying for the title 'self'. It lays down that there is no further test to pass: nothing can fail to count as a self if it possesses all the properties that feature in all genuine forms of SELF-experience, whatever other properties it may possess or lack.

   To endorse [E], then, is to hold that one must have well-developed answers to phenomenological questions about SELF-experience before one can begin to answer

---

[54] I'm grateful to Rosemary Twomey for persuading me to simplify my original formulation of the Equivalence Thesis. Note that it doesn't rule out the possibility that there may be selves that aren't self-conscious and don't have SELF-experience.

metaphysical questions about the existence and nature of selves. [E] excludes two forms of metaphysical excess. Metaphysical miserliness is blocked by [E2], according to which we can't say, in the manner of [C2], 'Yes, there are things which have the properties attributed in SELF-experience, but it doesn't follow that they're selves, or that selves exist.' Metaphysical extravagance, of the sort exemplified by [C1], is blocked by [E1], according to which we can't answer the question 'Are there such things as selves?' by saying 'Yes there are, or may be, but we have (may have) no understanding of their fundamental nature.'

—You've gone too far. It follows from [E1] that the minimal form of SELF-experience can't possibly misportray the nature of selves. It can't credit selves with some property that they don't actually have. This can't be right; it can't be right to leave no room for the possibility that the minimal form of SELF-experience might involve—perhaps inevitably—some sort of mistake or illusion about the nature of selves.

I've gone as far I intended. It does follow from [E1] that the minimal form of SELF-experience can't misportray the nature of selves. This is precisely the idea—this is the constraint that [E1] places on any attempt to establish the nature and existence of selves. This is how [E] proposes to give (empirical) grounding or content to the question of the nature and existence of selves. It states that any property (thinghood, singleness, whatever) attributed to selves in the minimal form of SELF-experience must be a property of selves, and that if there are no things that have all the properties attributed to selves in the minimal form of SELF-experience, then there are no selves. This is how the phenomenology of SELF-experience sets and gives content to metaphysical questions about the existence and nature of selves.

Suppose it turns out that four of the eight experience-determining or experience-structuring elements that are claimed to be central to ordinary human SELF-experience aren't necessary components of any possible genuine form of SELF-experience. Suppose SUBJECT, THING, MENTAL, and SINGLE are not only necessary but also minimally sufficient—that PERSISTING, AGENT, PERSONALITY, and DISTINCT are not essential to SELF-experience (and are perhaps absent in SELF-experience in early childhood). What follows for the metaphysics of the self? Well, each of the eight elements figures the self as possessing a certain wholly non-phenomenological property, and if we now introduce italic equivalents of the names of the experience-determining elements to denote the corresponding non-phenomenological properties—*subject, thing, mental, single, persisting, agent, personality*, and *distinct*—we can put things as follows. If SUBJECT, THING, MENTAL, and SINGLE are indeed minimally sufficient for genuine SELF-experience, the fundamental question of fact about the existence of selves is

Are there any things that have the properties *subject, thing, mental,* and *single*?

If the answer is Yes, then there are such things as selves, according to [E], whatever other properties these things may have or lack (they may also have some or all of *persisting, agent, personality,* and *distinct*). If the answer is No, then there are no such things as selves, according to [E]—even if there are things (human beings, for example) that have a good selection of the eight properties.[55]

It may help to consider briefly some alternative versions of the Equivalence Thesis. Suppose we replace [E] by [E^{oh}], according to which the content of the thought-element SELF is grounded in *ordinary human* experience in such a way that

[E1^{oh}] If there are such things as selves, then they have the properties attributed to the putative self in ordinary human SELF-experience

and

[E2^{oh}] If there exist things that have the properties attributed to the putative self in ordinary human SELF-experience, then those things are selves

state the right constraints on any metaphysical claim about whether or not selves exist.

Some may prefer [E^{oh}] to [E]. I think there's no substitute for [E], according to which there are selves just so long as there are things that possess the properties attributed to the putative self in the minimal form of SELF-experience. That said, arguments for the minimal case of philosophically interesting phenomena (knowledge, perception, personal identity, and so on) are always dogged by difficulties, and the task that [E^{oh}] sets for metaphysics is at least free from the kinds of doubts that surround minimal-case arguments, even though it leaves plenty of room for disagreement about the nature of ordinary human SELF-experience.

[E^{oh}] states that nothing can count as a self unless it fulfils whatever characterization of selves is distillable from the phenomenology of the ordinary human case. That characterization is likely to be a rich one, relative to any characterization of the minimal case, and some may for this reason prefer the intermediate and more liberal [E^{h}], according to which

[E1^{h}] If there are such things as selves, then they have the properties attributed to the putative self by some (genuine) human form of SELF-experience

and

[E2^{h}] If there exist things that have the properties to the putative self attributed by some (genuine) form of human SELF-experience, then those things are selves.

[E^{h}] retains the idea that human SELF-experience must set the bounds on—ground—the content of the thought-element SELF in any investigation that we may carry out, while giving no special place to the ordinary or paradigm case.

It doesn't in so doing involve any kind of 'anti-realism'. It simply states that any things that are candidates for being selves must have the properties attributed to selves by some (genuine) human form of SELF-experience if they are to be rightly judged to be selves. This is as metaphysically realist as anyone could wish. [E] goes further, rejecting the idea

---

[55] In fact, things are somewhat more complicated, for reasons that begin to emerge in 2.17. Note the assumption that the thought-elements SUBJECT, THING, MENTAL, and SINGLE that are said to be active in SELF-experience do indeed have as their content the real, objective, wholly non-phenomenological properties *subject*, *thing*, *mental*, and *single* that are invoked when trying to answer the fundamental metaphysical question 'Does the self exist?'. This assumption may be questioned, and I defend it in 6.2.

that limits on human SELF-experience are *ipso facto* limits on what selves can be like. But we are human beings, and a human constraint remains, even though [E] admits non-human cases of SELF-experience, simply in so far as these must be cases that strike us as possible given our human outlook. Here we come up against a familiar boundary: we cannot think beyond the limits of human thought. I take this fact to be untroubling, and will say a little more in 2.14.

Consider finally [E^g], a generalized and adjustable variant of [E] that can be applied in any case in which we have a term 'X' that we take to be a candidate for having a reference. According to [E^g]

[E1^g] If there are such things as Xs, then (necessarily) they must have the properties attributed to them by the—or some—ordinary/actual human conception or apprehension of what Xs are

and

[E2^g] If there are things that have the properties attributed by the—or some—ordinary/actual human conception or apprehension of what *being (an) X* is, then (necessarily) those things are Xs.

[E^g] is wildly implausible overall, and anti-realist for some versions and some substitutions for '(being) (an) X', but there are versions that work for some cases. One gets tellingly different results if one substitutes in words like 'witch', 'gold', 'unicorn', 'person', 'physical object', 'red', 'square', 'pain', and so on.[56]

2.13 SELF and PERSON

What about 'person'? It's arguable that there are versions of [E1^g] and [E2^g] that come out true both for 'person' and 'self', and although the approach to the nature of selves in this book has little connection with most present-day philosophical approaches to the nature of persons, it's worth briefly comparing the two cases.

Locke defined a person as a 'thinking intelligent being ... capable of a law, and happiness, and misery, ... that has reason and reflection, and can consider itself as itself, the same thinking being in different times and places' (*Essay*, 2.27.9, 2.27.26), and it's widely thought that his definition is as good as any.[57] It treats persons as a 'functional

---

[56] Consider a few cases relative to actual conceptions. (1) *Witch*: arguable that [E1^g] and [E2^g] come out true, on the ground that we really have nothing else to appeal to in our judgements; but [E1^g] and [E2^g] may also be rejected, on the ground that it could turn out that the most impressive cases of those who were in the past judged to be witches were aliens in human form. (2) *Unicorn*: arguable that [E1^g] comes out true and [E2^g] false (the problem with [E2^g] is that if unicorns are essentially fictional animals, then even if animals just like unicorns were discovered on another planet, they would not really be unicorns, even though we would almost certainly call them 'unicorns' if we came across them). (3) *Gold, physical object*, and so on: most would judge that [E1^g] comes out false while [E2^g] is more debatable. (4) *Red*: this produces a spray of different results, depending on which account of the meaning of the word one subscribes to.

[57] I've integrated an essential part of Locke's definition of a person that occurs in §26 ('capable of a law, and happiness, and misery') into the famous passage from §9, which has caused much misunderstanding by being taken on its own. See e.g. G. Strawson, in preparation, *b*.

kind'. It states that to be a person is to possess certain capacities or functional abilities, including of course experiential capacities and abilities. It's not the case that only human beings can be persons—dolphins and Martians (never mind gods and angels) can count as persons just so long as they have the requisite capacities—and it doesn't matter at all what persons are made out of. Louis (a representative human being) qualifies as a person, on Locke's view, whether he has an immaterial soul or whether he is, as Parfit suggests, nothing but 'a body, and the occurrence of a series of thoughts, experiences, and other mental and physical events' (1995: 116). Louis qualifies as a person just so long as he has the requisite capacity properties, whatever else is or isn't true of him.

Locke's account is attractive, taken in this way, but its details aren't important here because the present question is the general methodological question 'How does one proceed, in order to arrive at a definition in the case of the concept PERSON?'.

The answer, most agree, is that the thing to do is to engage in a process of informed philosophical reflection that takes its start from the way the word 'person' operates—so richly—in ordinary human thought and talk. To accept this is not to accept that one must or should finish up accepting something like the common, explicit everyday view of what persons are. Far from it; one may finish up endorsing something like Parfit's 'Constitutive Reductionist' view, or concluding that there are no such things as persons,[58] and one's finishing point will have the force and point that it does precisely because one has started out from facts about the way 'person' operates in ordinary human thought and talk. To start by examining ordinary human thought and talk is not at all to limit oneself to 'descriptive' rather than 'revisionary' metaphysics, in P. F. Strawson's sense.

Suppose this is the right way to proceed in the case of PERSON. Can the process of arriving at a definition be the same in the case of SELF? It can't be quite the same. For although SELF is—I take it—also and essentially a notion of a functional kind, I don't think we can arrive at a satisfactory definition of it by a process of informed philosophical reflection on the way the word 'self' operates in thought and talk, ordinary or not. This is because it comes into play principally in contexts involving psychological, psychiatric, religious, and philosophical speculation, and its use in these contexts is invariably and heavily theory-driven (dogma-driven), and extremely diverse. It doesn't follow that its use in these special contexts is not interesting or telling or important, for it is all these things. It can't, however, anchor a process of philosophical investigation in anything like the way that enquiry into the ordinary grasp of the constantly used word 'person' seems to be able to do.

What should one do? Write off the notion of self as useless for serious theoretical purposes?[59] I've proposed an alternative: go back behind the noise of all the different theoretical uses of the word 'self' to the source of those uses in SELF-experience, which exists whether or not one has any familiarity with any such word as 'self' or any religious commitment. Try, as far as possible, to factor out the effects of special theoretical commitments—psychological, psychiatric, religious, or philosophical. Go

---

[58] See e.g. Stone 1998, 2005.   [59] This is Olson's choice (1998).

back to the basic cognitive-experiential structure of SELF-experience—already fully present in childhood—and start from there. It is there, if anywhere, that one will find the thought-element SELF that philosophy needs to consider when it asks if there are any such things as selves. That's the proposal.

2.14 Building and whittling—summary and preview

The local phenomenological question asks what sort of self is figured in (and in that sense postulated by) ordinary human SELF-experience. The general phenomenological question asks what sort of self is figured in (and in that sense postulated by) any genuine form of SELF-experience. If the answers to these questions go well, they give us—I claim—a good idea of what we're really asking when we ask whether selves exist. We can then try to give an answer, either with reference to ordinary human SELF-experience or with reference to the minimal form of SELF-experience, and commit to the flames all metaphysical speculations about selves that aren't subordinate to phenomenology in the way described. Those who doubt that the metaphysics of the self should be approached through the phenomenology of SELF-experience in this way can treat the Equivalence Thesis (which enshrines this approach) simply as setting a framework within which to articulate the general problem of the self.

In the next eight sections I'm going to try to answer the local phenomenological question in greater detail, arguing that SUBJECT, THING, MENTAL, SINGLE, PERSISTING, AGENT, DISTINCT, and perhaps PERSONALITY are all elements of ordinary human SELF-experience. I'll take up the general phenomenological question (about the minimal form of SELF-experience) in Part 4, after a more metaphysical interlude in Part 3, and argue that one can have genuine SELF-experience without figuring oneself, considered as a self, either as an agent, or as something that has a personality, or as something that persists through significant stretches of time (without AGENT, PERSONALITY, and PERSISTING). In the limiting case, I argue, one need not even figure oneself, considered as a self, as distinct from the entity that one is considered as a whole (as DISTINCT).

Whittling away at ordinary human SELF-experience in this way in Part 4, I conclude that the minimal form of SELF-experience is experience of the self, apprehended as it is in the present moment, as a subject of experience that is a single mental thing. It is, in other words, experience that involves only the elements SUBJECT, THING, MENTAL, and SINGLE (SINGLE$_s$). There is, however, more to it than that, because these elements must also compound in certain ways, to form elements like SINGLE-as-MENTAL, in a way that I'll begin to describe on page 65.

—I still don't see how can you justify giving such a central role to the project of working out the minimal form of SELF-experience. Even if this whittling method works well, in showing that one can have SELF-experience without PERSISTING, AGENT, PERSONALITY, and DISTINCT, it's quite unclear how it can deliver a proof that one has whittled away everything inessential. But it would be very weak to conclude that the four remaining elements are essential on the grounds that one cannot in one's armchair imagine SELF-experience that lacks them. What appears to be the minimal form of X from the human point of view—even the best possible human point of view—may not in fact be any such thing.

I have three replies to this. First, we have limits. We may not be able to prove that we have gone as far as it is possible to go in pursuit of the minimal form of X, when we think that we have done so. I don't, however, think this is a great problem. A priori or armchair grounds are sometimes the only ones we have when we're trying to reach a conclusion about whether certain things must feature in the description of the minimal case of some phenomenon, but they aren't always shaky. They can be extremely robust, and they can be known to be so. Philosophical wisdom doesn't always involve background doubt. Sometimes it consists in breaking through to confidence that one has the truth (although there's nothing one can do with this confidence when debating with others). Philosophy often begins by training one to doubt everything, but it also and *ipso facto* teaches one to doubt one's doubt (this being, by then, the more difficult lesson) and also to have no impulse, in certain cases, to move up to the third order and doubt one's doubting of one's initial doubt.

The second reply is that for some philosophical purposes (a), whatever appears to be the minimal case of X from the human point of view, is scarcely less interesting than (b), the actual minimal case of X as discerned from some all-knowing point of view—if indeed the two things differ. Even an out-and-out realist like myself can agree that (a) is more interesting and important than (b) in certain philosophical circumstances, and for certain substitutions for 'X', and it's arguable that this is so when X = SELF-experience—if indeed (a) and (b) differ in this case, which I doubt. Even if one's principal aim is merely descriptive phenomenology, or Strawsonian descriptive metaphysics, even if it is simply to feel out the structure of SELF-experience, the pursuit of (a) is a powerful form of investigation.

The third reply is that after having discarded PERSISTING, AGENT, PERSONALITY, and DISTINCT by running what I will call the Whittling Argument, one may be able to perform an independent check on the necessity of the elements that remain by running what I will call the Building Argument. Thus suppose that one takes as a working assumption the claim that self-consciousness is necessary for SELF-experience

[SELF-experience → self-consciousness]

where '→' represents the central 'if... then ...' or entailment relation, metaphysical necessity, not mere 'material implication'.[60] This entails that anything that is necessary for self-consciousness is also necessary for SELF-experience. It follows that if one can show that SUBJECT, THING, MENTAL, SINGLE, and the compounds that they form (e.g. SINGLE-as-MENTAL) are necessary for self-consciousness—if one can show that

[self-consciousness → SUBJECT, THING, SINGLE-as-MENTAL, etc.]

—one can thereby confirm that they're all necessary for SELF-experience. In this way one can hope to build up towards an account of the minimal form of SELF-experience by

---

[60]   Note that it does not follow from this claim that the self must be figured *as* self-conscious in genuine SELF-experience; see p. 47 and n. 54 above.

analysing the consequences of the fact that SELF-experience requires self-consciousness, rather than trying to give such an account merely by whittling away parts of the rich edifice of ordinary human SELF-experience by a process of phenomenological reflection.

I'll consider the prospects of the Building Argument in Part 3 and return to it in 4.9 after I've finished with the Whittling Argument. If things go improbably smoothly, the two procedures or forms of argument—whittling and building—will not only be genuinely independent but will meet in the middle. The Building Argument will show that the Whittling Argument can go no further, thereby confirming its validity. That is, perhaps, too much for hope for, but the structure of enquiry generated by this approach may prove helpful.

All this requires preparation. I need to enrich the description of ordinary human SELF-experience before I can try to whittle away at it. The central claim is by now familiar: we ordinarily figure the self in SELF-experience as a subject of experience, a conscious feeler and thinker; as a thing of some sort, in a sense to be further determined; as mental, essentially mentally propertied, in a sense to be further determined; as a single thing; as a persisting (single) thing; as an agent; as something that has a certain character or personality; and as something that is not the same thing as the human being considered as a whole. In the rest of Part 2 I'll consider each of these elements in turn. Some of what I say may seem too specific and complicated to be plausible as an account of our unreflective thought, but unreflective thought can be structured by highly complicated conceptions that can't be spelt out without considerable reflection—just as smooth and simple mechanical movements can depend on complex gearing. The concept of an object, for example, appears simple in so far as it features as an explicit element in our thought, but the most perspicuous analytic description of it is far from simple. Kant remarks similarly that 'the concept of "right", in its common-sense usage, contains all that the subtlest speculation can develop out of it, though in its ordinary and practical use we are not conscious of the manifold representations comprised in this thought' (A43/B61).

2.15 SUBJECT

The self is thought of—figured—as a subject of experience   This is obvious. It raises a large philosophical question—What is a subject of experience?—but this question can be put aside for the moment.[61] The ordinary unreflective notion of the subject of experience is all that is needed now, and each of us has a very good general grasp of what a subject of experience is just in being one and being self-conscious.[62] The generality of

---

[61] Many, including myself, think it enough to say that a subject of experience is an entity which is of such a kind that there is, for it, 'something it is like' to be it. I consider this question further in 6.3.

[62] 'Very good' doesn't entail 'complete', and St Augustine is right when he says that 'we know what ... consciousness (*animus*) is by considering our own, for we have consciousness' (*c.*410: 8.6.9). Some, overexposed to certain strains

this grasp—the fact that it can be (is) a grasp of what is essential to being a subject of experience however much subjects of experience can differ from each other—is certainly not put in question by the fact that it's based on experience of one's own case.[63] It need not be articulable in language by those who have it. It doesn't require any view—materialist, idealist, dualist, whatever—about the ultimate substantial nature of subjects of experience. It's available to young children, and it lies at the centre of ordinary human SELF-experience, and indeed of any SELF-experience at all, whether or not we can give it clear verbal expression. It's plausible that no sane self-conscious subject of experience can fail to have a good grasp of what a subject of experience is. It doesn't matter, however, if this isn't so.

Selves aren't the only things that are thought of as subjects of experience. We also say that human beings and other animals considered as a whole are subjects of experience. In fact, the use of the expression 'subject of experience' to refer (only) to the whole creature has become automatic for many analytic philosophers, who may not now easily see or remember that it is neither mandatory nor particularly natural. This change of use was good in its time, a corrective to overspiritualized pictures of The Subject. Since then it has worked too much in the other direction, and has obscured a number of simple and important truths, so that another correction is needed. But the dominance of the whole-creature use never overrode the phenomenological fact that human beings (analytic philosophers or not) have a deep tendency to think that the subject of experience properly speaking is something—some sort of inner mental entity or presence, a self—distinct from, not identical with, the human being considered as a whole.

It may be that this mentalistic tendency is stronger when one considers oneself than when one considers another person. It may be that it comes most strongly to some when they're alone and thinking (here is the self, myself, here am I, the mental person present in awareness, the hidden thing, the subject of experience). However that may be, a vivid sense that it is the self alone that is the subject of experience is an essential constituent of our ordinary sense or conception of the self. This is obvious, but it does seem to have been occluded for some.

Part of the work of this book is to show that the mentalistic attitude to the notion of the subject is neither mistaken nor otherwise pernicious. I don't, however, want to be thought to be begging the question in any way, so I'm going to use the terms 'subject of experience' and 'SUBJECT' in a strictly neutral way that neither favours nor excludes either (i) the wide or *thick* whole-creature understanding common in analytic

---

of Wittgensteinianism, have to fight their way back to the fact that moves of this sort are philosophically correct—essential—when considering the nature of knowledge of mental phenomena.

[63] Another striking Wittgensteinian or 'Wittgensteinian' mistake lies here—the mistake of thinking that one can't coherently think that other creatures may be in mental states radically unlike one's own if one's overall conception of what mental states are is based partly on one's private experience of being in them. In fact, this isn't true even if one's conception of what mental states are is based wholly on one's private experience of being in them. (In its extreme form, the Wittgensteinian/'Wittgensteinian' mistake is to think that one can't in this 'solipsistic' case even coherently think that anyone other than oneself is in mental states at all.)

philosophy and experimental psychology or (ii) the *traditional* understanding according to which 'subject of experience' refers to some kind of 'inner' mental entity, something that is not the same thing as the whole human being.

2.16 THING

The self is figured as a thing of some sort   In a way, this is the least clear of all the claims, and some may find it particularly unpalatable. But what's the alternative? The self is not figured in ordinary human SELF-experience as a mere state or property, or as a mere event or series of events, or, given the ordinary understanding of the word 'process', as some sort of mere process.[64] To that extent, I propose, there is nothing else for it to be figured as, other than as a thing or entity of some sort. As Nozick says, the self 'has a particular character, that of an entity' (1989: 148). It isn't apprehended as being a thing in the way a stone or a chair is, but it is none the less apprehended as a thing of some kind. This is especially clear when we bring to the front the idea that a thing or object is something that has properties but is not itself just a property of something else. For the self is, centrally, experienced as something that can undergo experiences, have thoughts, decide things, perform actions, and, most simply, be in some experiential state or other—sad, say. None of these things can be true of states, properties, events, or processes as ordinarily conceived.

One can make the point by linking THING to SUBJECT: the fundamental sense in which the self presents as a thing of some sort is integral to the way in which it presents as a subject of experience. It presents as a thing specifically in so far as it presents as a subject, whether or not it also presents as a thing in some other way. That is, SELF-experience (the thought-element SELF) not only involves the elements THING and SUBJECT. It also involves the compound element

THING-as-SUBJECT.

It's specifically in so far as it is figured as a subject of experience that the self is figured as a thing of some sort. Or at least: it's figured/experienced as a thing of some sort in being figured/experienced as a subject, even if it's also figured as a thing for some other reason. (There's an important connection here with Kant's first Paralogism, which I consider further in 4.3.)

I'm going to argue that SELF involves a number of such compound elements, both double (e.g. SINGLE-as-MENTAL) and triple (e.g. SINGLE-as-THING-as-MENTAL). Such claims may at first look implausibly strong and overcomplicated, but I think they turn out to be routine and unsurprising, even trivial. They may also look cumbersome, but they seem to be exactly what's in question when SELF-experience is in question. They're what we find when we try to expose the structure of the simple-seeming phenomenon of SELF-experience.

---

[64] These uses of the word 'mere' will come into question in Part 6, along with the ordinary understanding of words like 'process'.

What more can be said about experience of the self as a thing? Consider Berkeley's characterization of the self as a 'thinking, active principle' (1713: 116). This seems helpful, for a thinking principle manages to sound like a thing of some sort, in this old use of the word 'principle' to mean something concrete and active, without sounding anything like a chair or a dog. (One may take 'active' in its basic sense, the sense in which a volcano is active although incapable of intentional action.)

The general idea behind the present use of the term 'thing' is probably much the same as the idea behind the philosophical use of the word 'substance' as a count noun with a plural. I'll use the word 'substance' sparingly, because I reject most of the traditional understandings of it, as remarked (11), but it has a place here, and provides a bridge to the point that—in Locke's words—'powers … make a great part of our … ideas of substances' (*Essay*, 2.22.10), a point that we can re-express by saying that the idea that something possesses a certain sort of causal nature is fundamental to the idea of its being a thing. If we then consider our idea or experience of the self, it seems clear that we think of the self as having the causal profile typical of a thing—both in the way it can affect things and in the way it can be affected. Attributing causal powers and natures to things doesn't distinguish them from everything else, because we also attribute causal powers to events and properties, but the observation seems worthwhile.

—I don't see this. I agree with Shoemaker: 'when one is introspectively aware of one's thoughts, feelings, beliefs, and desires, one isn't presented to oneself as a flesh and blood person, and one does not seem to be presented to one as an object at all'   (1984: 102).

I also agree with Shoemaker, given what he means by 'presented as an object', and we both agree with a host of Phenomenologists. I take his claim to be fully compatible with what I mean by saying that the self is experienced as a thing of some sort. Plainly I need to say more about what I mean by the experience of something as a thing. I'm going to defer this until 4.3, however, when I argue that a sense of the self as a thing is necessary to any genuine form of SELF-experience.

Fichte uses the striking term *Tathandlung*, 'deed-activity', for the I or self as it is and is experienced (1794–1802: 97), and this may seem strongly at odds—designedly so—with any conception of the self as a thing. But this isn't so, given what I have in mind. Fichte's *Tathandlung* doesn't seem to be a particularly natural characterization of the ordinary human experience/conception of what the self is, in fact, but we can put this point aside here,[65] for the more important point is that a *Tathandlung*, like a 'thinking active principle', falls comfortably into the category *thing* as I understand it. I'll explain this in 6.10–6.12, when I come to consider the non-phenomenological, metaphysical question of what a thing or object is.

Since I'm piling up puzzlements, I may as well add that I take it that the sense in which the self is figured as a thing is entirely compatible with a sense in which it is not

[65] It might be said that Fichte's description was phenomenologically very apt in so far as we can be said to have a kind of 'bare-flow' experience of the self, where this is considered independently of any experience-structuring conception of the self. See further 7.5.

figured as a 'thing among things', in Sartre's and Merleau-Ponty's phrase—as simply one object among other objects.[66]

2.17 MENTAL

The self is figured as (something) mental   This third claim looks rather unhelpful. On the one hand it seems trivial, on the other hand it seems unclear—if only because the extension of the general notion of the mental is unclear.

There's certainly a respect in which it's trivial that MENTAL is one of the elements of SELF-experience (one of the essential components of SELF), for SELF-experience was initially characterized as experience of oneself specifically as a mental phenomenon, a mental presence, a mental something (a mental something that is not identical with the whole human being). It also follows immediately from the claim that SUBJECT is one of the essential elements of SELF. Fine. One of the great things about trivial—truistic—truths is that they're true. It's often important to stress them in philosophy.

What about the charge of unclarity? What is it, exactly, to experience X as mental, or as mentally propertied, or as having mental being? Well, what is it for something to *be* something mental, or to be mentally propertied, or to have mental being? If we can answer the second question, we ought to be able to make progress with the first.

That seems simple enough, but it turns out that there is an extraordinary amount of disagreement about the answer to the second question among philosophers, which threatens to carry over into disagreement about the answer to the first. This problem, however, can be put aside. The general notion of the mental appears unclear to some when it's put under philosophical pressure, but this doesn't matter when one is characterizing ordinary thought, as here. Nor will it matter much when we put aside phenomenology for metaphysics, for although philosophers quarrel about which properties are mental and which aren't, there's a vast central group of properties whose claim is not in serious dispute. There are experiential mental properties like feeling happy or sleepy, experiencing pain, seeing green, thinking about justice, imagining disaster, and so on. There are also non-experiential mental properties, 'dispositional' mental properties (mental properties you can be said to have even when you're dreamlessly asleep) like knowing Arabic or the perfect squares up to 100×100, believing there are Moonies on the moon, liking walnuts, and so on. Dispositional mental properties also include traits of character like being kind, diffident, irritable, and witty, and to these one may add further capacity properties like the capacity to plan, reason, imagine, think, feel: in brief, all mental properties standardly acknowledged by ordinary thought. With this in place, one doesn't need to consider any of the large metaphysical questions about

---

[66] See e.g. Merleau-Ponty 1945 and van Fraassen 2004.

the nature of the mental and the non-mental and the relation between them. These questions will arise again in 6.5–6.9, but are not at issue here. The general notion of the mental is sufficiently anchored by the examples in the last paragraph, and with this background we can turn to the claim that the self is ordinarily figured as something mental.

Consider two claims: 'X is figured as (something) mental' and 'X is figured as mentally propertied, or as having mental being'. A human being considered as a whole is ordinarily figured as something that has mental properties or mental being, but it isn't ordinarily figured as 'something mental', and is certainly not ordinarily figured as a 'mental thing'. A self, by contrast, is ordinarily figured not only as something that has mental properties, or mental being, but also as 'something mental', in some sense, and indeed as a 'mental thing', in some sense.

In due course I'm going to argue for the claim that a self is ordinarily figured as a mental thing; I will then do my best to block likely misunderstandings (the claim is entirely compatible with materialism, for example). For the moment, though, the claim under consideration is simply the happily trivial claim that the self is figured as mentally propertied or as having mental being. 'Figured as mental' means only 'figured as mentally propertied or as having mental being', and applies to the whole human being just as much as it does to the putative self. In terms of thought-elements: to deploy the element MENTAL with respect to X is simply to figure or apprehend X as being mentally propertied or as having mental being. The opening summary of this section, 'The self is figured as (something) mental', can be replaced by the more perspicuous 'The self is figured as mentally propertied or as having mental being', although I hope eventually to justify the heading as it stands.

Given this replacement, the claim that the self is figured as something mental is obviously true, but there are a number of further things to say. The first is that I take it that something may be figured or experienced as mental (mentally propertied) by a creature—e.g. a young child—that doesn't have a fully-fledged concept of the mental (whatever exactly that is). For something to be figured as mental is for it to feature in experience in a way that simply does not require possession of anything like the fully-fledged concept. In the same way, things can be experienced as coloured, and as red and green, by a neonate that doesn't have the concept COLOUR by most people's lights (or even, perhaps, RED or GREEN, though this is disputable).

The next question is whether there's anything special about the way a self is figured as mental. Well, we can say this. A whole human being is figured as having mental being, just as a self is; but a self, in being figured as having mental being, is not normally also figured as also having non-mental being, and is certainly not figured as essentially having non-mental being; whereas a whole human being is ordinarily figured as also having non-mental being, and indeed as essentially having non-mental being. One might say that a self is experienced as something *essentially and especially mental* in its nature in a way that a whole human being is not. This may seem vague, but I think it serves to distinguish the way in which the self is experienced as having mental being from the way in which the whole human being is, while in no way ruling out the possibility that the self also (and even essentially) has non-mental being as a matter of metaphysical fact.

We may add this: the self is figured as something *merely* mental, or wholly mental, in so far as, and to the extent that, it is expressly figured as something that has mental being and is not, in being so figured, also figured as something that has non-mental being. Note, though, that this figuring is wholly undogmatic, metaphysically. It's not as if the self is expressly and positively and with metaphysical aforethought figured as *immaterial*, in not being expressly figured as having non-mental being. Like all ordinary human beings I figure the self as something especially and essentially mental, but if you ask me whether I think that the self is merely mental (or indeed immaterial), metaphysically speaking, I'll reply 'Not at all. I take it that the self is wholly a brain phenomenon. There's a clear sense in which I naturally and unreflectively experience the self as a specifically mental presence, just as mentally propertied; but I certainly don't think that it has no non-mental being at all—now that you've raised the question and moved the discussion on to the scientific or metaphysical plane.'[67]

—It may be true that selves are not ordinarily thought of as having non-mental being, but they're not ordinarily explicitly thought of as not having non-mental being either. Some seem to hold that a self or soul is some sort of purely mental entity, metaphysically speaking, and others might find the idea that a self has non-mental properties or non-mental being fairly peculiar, if they were presented with it, but the question is simply not considered in the ordinary course of things.

Right. This is another way of distinguishing the way in which the self is figured as mental from the way in which the whole human being is, since the whole human being is obviously expressly figured as also having non-mental being. One might say that the self is ordinarily taken to be an entity that is by its nature not only essentially engaged in mental business, but also, in some fundamental sense, *exclusively* engaged in mental business, and is to that extent not also engaged in non-mental business—even if most of its mental business concerns the non-mental world (I'm not denying anything that EEE enthusiasts are rightly enthusiastic about). This is the principal idea, and ordinary thought enquires no further.

Like many I have, vaguely, a sense that the self is (that *I* am) wholly situated in my head—a couple of inches behind the eyes, say, and perhaps a bit further up. There is, however, no tension between this natural picture of spatiotemporal, cerebral location and the fact that the self is figured as an entity that is essentially and in some sense exclusively engaged in mental business. This figuring of the self doesn't involve a metaphysical view of it as definitely having mental being in some way in which it definitely doesn't have non-mental being; it's just not theoretical in that way. One might say that for a self to be figured specifically as mental is for there to be a positive sense of it as mentally propertied, or as having mental being, in a context

---

[67] Here I put aside my 'pure panpsychist' tendencies (see e.g. G. Strawson 2006b: §15).

of thought in which the question of whether or not it might also have non-mental being is simply not in play; in which there is no resort to a conception of it as having non-mental being.

It may seem that I'm trying to introduce extra content into the thought-element MENTAL, in making these points about the special character of the way in which the self is experienced as MENTAL. But this isn't so. Let me put the point another way. I've ruled that to deploy the element MENTAL with respect to X is simply to figure or apprehend X as being mentally propertied or as having mental being. This ruling makes it obvious that MENTAL is an essential component of SELF, and this is just as well, perhaps, because the notion of the mental keeps throwing out heavy metaphysical grapples that are irrelevant to the present phenomenological concerns.[68] By the same token, though, the claim that MENTAL is an essential component of SELF is not now very illuminating, since it's equally true that we deploy MENTAL in our experience of ourselves as whole human beings. Our attention is therefore led on to the seemingly stronger claim that the self is ordinarily figured as *something mental*, as a *mental thing* of some sort. This last claim can't now be expressed by saying that ordinary human SELF-experience involves MENTAL (since to deploy MENTAL in SELF-experience is simply to figure or apprehend the self as mentally propertied or as having mental being), so it needs to be expressed in some other way.

One way to do so, I propose, is to say that SELF-experience ordinarily involves not only THING and MENTAL but also the compound thought-element

THING-as-MENTAL.

The self, in other words, is experienced as being a thing of some sort *specifically in so far as it is being figured as mentally propertied*, and so without resort to any other way of figuring it. I will argue further for this claim in 4.3. Here I will simply make a few initial remarks.

It's obvious that people also naturally talk and think of themselves as things that essentially possess non-mental properties as well as mental properties ('I have black hair', 'I weigh 110 pounds'). This, though, is fully compatible with the present claim. Nor does it undermine it indirectly; for even if it were true that we very often think of ourselves as things that essentially possess non-mental properties, it would be no less true that we very often experience ourselves as fundamentally or primarily mental things. This experience is not confined to ivory towers. It happens all the time, in battles, streets, and factories, behind the plough or wheel, during sex or even lunch (this is not a failure of sensuality; it's one of its expressions). A great theme of recent philosophy has been that such experience involves an illusion, however natural it may be; but even if it did involve an illusion, that wouldn't diminish its phenomenological reality (which is what is at present in question) in any way. Nor is there any good reason for materialists to think that it involves an illusion simply because they're materialists. That said, it's

---

[68] They're a particular danger for analytic philosophers primed by long discussions of behaviourism, functionalism, radical externalism, and 'representationalism'.

worth recalling the point that in figuring the self as especially or exclusively involved in mental business, people don't thereby explicitly or expressly figure the self as *not* having any sort of non-mental being. On the whole, the question of non-mental being simply doesn't arise.

—Isn't there going to be a tension between this claim and the claim that SELF involves THING-AS-MENTAL? Doesn't deployment of the thought-element THING-AS-MENTAL involve some sort of focus on the self's being a thing mentally considered of a sort that positively excludes any idea of it as a thing non-mentally considered?

No. It's no part of the logic of the x-*as*-Y construction I have introduced that 'x-as-Y' entails 'NOT: X-as-NON-Y' or positively excludes 'x-as-NON-Y'. 'THING-as-MENTAL' doesn't entail (or even favour) 'NOT: THING-as-NON-MENTAL' or exclude (or disfavour) 'THING-as-NON-MENTAL'.

It may now be objected, from the other side of the debate, that I'm underestimating the naturalness of belief in an immaterial soul. This is not so. It's true that I've stressed the point that the basic experience of having or being a self needn't involve any kind of express or positive belief in an entity, such as an 'immaterial soul', that has no non-mental being. At the same time I've tried to make it clear that SELF-experience contains elements that make beliefs of this kind come extremely naturally to human beings, quite independently of any other psychological needs that such beliefs may serve. Phenomenologically speaking, the self can very easily seem to exist in a sphere of being that is quite other than the sphere of being described by physics or experienced by our senses, and this is just one aspect of something much more pervasive—the fact that mental phenomena in general, conscious or experiential mental phenomena in particular, can easily seem to exist in a sphere of being quite distinct from the sphere of non-mental phenomena.

This, after all, is what gives rise to the supposed 'mind–body' or 'conscious-ness–matter' problem. And whether or not we're exercised by that problem, it's arguable that our tendency to experience mental phenomena and non-mental phenom-ena as if they existed in different spheres of being is an inevitable consequence of our basic sensory-intellectual constitution.[69] Things are not as they seem if materialism is true; for if materialism is true, then mental phenomena and non-mental phenomena, and in particular experiential (i.e. conscious) phenomena and non-experiential phenomena, do after all belong wholly to the same single sphere of being, i.e the physical sphere, and the fact that we lack a conception of the nature of the physical that provides us with any decent sense of understanding how this can be so doesn't change the fact that it is so.

Does the problem of the self contain the mind–body problem as a part, so that we can't hope to solve the former without solving the latter? No. We don't need to make any progress with the mind–body problem—if this means providing some kind of intuitively or theoretically illuminating account of the relation between the

[69] See e.g. McGinn 1989, and many others.

phenomena of conscious experience and the phenomena of the brain-as-characterized-by-neurophysiology-and-physics—in order to address the central problem of the self: the question whether selves exist.

I'll return to these metaphysical questions in Part 6. For the moment I'm still concerned with the phenomenological question of how the self is ordinarily figured in human SELF-experience, rather with the question of what, if anything, it is. In the last two sections I've proposed that the self is experienced as a *thing* of some sort, and as something *mental*, and also as something that is a *mental thing*, in some sense. I hope to give further content to these proposals in the next section, when considering the claim that it's thought of as single.

2.18 SINGLE: three starting thoughts

The self is figured as single   To think of the self as a thing is already to think of it as single in some way, for it is to think of it as *a* thing. What more can be said? I'll introduce three thoughts and discuss the second and third in some detail. My principal aim in this section is to characterize ordinary human SELF-experience, in order to be able to answer the local phenomenological question; but I also hope to do quite a lot of work towards characterizing the nature of any genuine form of SELF-experience (thereby answering part of the general phenomenological question).

First thought. In so far as a self is experienced as single, it's not experienced as merely a single assemblage or collectivity. It's not figured as having singularity only in the sense in which a group or bundle of things can be said to be a single group or bundle: it's not figured merely as 'bundle-single', as one might say. It's figured as single in the way in which a single marble is figured as single when compared with a single group of marbles: it's figured as 'single-marble-single', as one might say. Developing the point made on page 66 about the fundamental causal component in our idea of a thing, one might say that a self is figured as something that has the kind of unity of internal causal connectedness that a single marble has, as compared with the much weaker unity of internal causal connectedness found in a single pile of marbles. A marble, of course, is made of atoms, and is a collection of things from the point of view of an atom, and an atom is a collection of things from the point of view of an electron or a quark or string, and perhaps the series continues. This is the point of the term 'single-marble-single', which compresses the complex comparative adjective 'single in the way in which a marble is single when compared with a single pile of marbles'. I'll always mean single-marble-single as opposed to bundle-single unless I say otherwise.

Second thought. There's a fundamental sense in which the self is apprehended as having singleness in a way that is independent of any singleness it may have, or appear to have, when considered in its non-mental being, whatever that may be, or may be considered to be. In this sense it's taken to be *single specifically as mental*, specifically in so far as it has mental being. It is, essentially, apprehended as mental, and there's no resort to a conception of it as non-mental as a source of grounds for the conception of it as single. In the present terms, then, SELF-experience involves the thought-element

SINGLE-as-MENTAL

at least in the ordinary human case. This may seem obscure, at least to professional philosophers, but consider the statement 'X is a single physical thing', where 'physical' is used to mean roughly 'non-mental' in the way that is still standard in philosophy, although it's ruled out for genuine or realistic materialists (283–4). Such a statement comes naturally both to philosophical thought and to ordinary non-philosophical thought, and one might express the present point by saying that the statement 'X is a single mental thing' is no more problematic for ordinary non-philosophical thought than 'X is a single physical thing' is for ordinary thought, philosophical or not, whatever difficulties philosophical thought may be pleased to find in it.[70]

Another way to put the point is to say that the self's *principle of unity* is ordinarily—and however implicitly—taken to be mental rather than non-mental. What does this mean? Well, it's arguable that everything that is conceived of as a single thing or object—electron, atom, neuron, sofa, nation-state—is conceived of as a single thing only relative to some principle of unity according to which it *counts* as a single thing. An atom, for example, counts as a single thing relative to one principle of unity, while it counts as many things relative to principles of unity that recognize the existence of subatomic particles, strings, loops, preons, field quanta, or what have you. Some go on from this point to the claim that there are no ultimate facts of the matter about which phenomena are things or objects and which aren't—the claim that all 'principles of objectual unity', as one might call them, are ultimately interest-relative, or subjective, or 'perspectival' in character. This, however, is a distinct and further claim. In itself, the view that everything that is taken to be a single thing is so taken relative to some principle of objectual unity is compatible with the view that there are right answers to questions about which things are genuinely single objects and which aren't. It leaves open the possibility that certain principles of objectual unity are fundamental and fully objective.

This issue is important, and I address it directly in 6.10 when I raise the general question 'What is a thing or object?'. For the moment it can be put aside, because the claim now under consideration (the phenomenological claim that the self is figured as single specifically as mental) remains in place whatever position one takes on the question of what objects are, and it amounts—at the very least—to this: the self is of course figured as something mental, and is also figured as single, and there is no resort to a conception of it as *non*-mental when it is figured as single. The negative formulation preserves the point that the fact that the self is figured as single specifically in so far as it is figured as mental may not be expressly entertained in any way.

---

[70] We move easily in philosophy from 'X has a physical property' to 'X is a physical object', using 'physical' to mean 'non-mental' in a way that is natural although unavailable to genuine or realistic materialists, but we reject any move from 'X has a mental property' to 'X is a mental object'. Many reasons may be given for this (I consider some of them in 6.4) but it's not clear that any of them are good.

This leads straight to a closely related claim. The self is not only taken to be something single specifically in so far as it is apprehended as something mental; it's also taken to be single specifically as a subject of experience. In the present terms: SELF-experience ordinarily involves the thought-element

SINGLE-as-SUBJECT.

One might put this by saying that there is in SELF-experience no resort to a conception of the self as something other than a subject of experience as a source of grounds for the conception of it as single.[71] More particularly, there is no resort to a conception of the self as something other than a subject of experience considered just as such, i.e. just in respect of its being and activity as thinker or experiencer, and hence as something mental. There is no resort to a conception of it as a single brain or single brain-part, for example, or as a single human being. It's specifically as figured as subject-of-experience-considered-just-as-such that it is figured as single. I'll try to put this in other ways in what follows.

The force of the 'considered just as such' is 'considered just in respect of being a locus of consciousness, and hence just in respect of its mental being, without regard to any other properties that it may have'. And this may be expressed by saying that it is figured as

SINGLE-as-SUBJECT-as-MENTAL.

It is specifically as subject-figured-specifically-as-mental that the self is figured as single; a point to which I will return.

The proposal so far is that SELF-experience not only involves SINGLE; it also involves SINGLE-as-MENTAL, and SINGLE-as-SUBJECT, and indeed SINGLE-as-SUBJECT-as-MENTAL. What do these closely related and arguably obvious claims come to? I'll say more about them after introducing the third main thought about singleness.

This is that the self is standardly figured as single (single-marble-single) both when it is considered *synchronically*, or as a thing existing at a given moment in time, and when it is considered *diachronically*, i.e. as a thing that persists through time. In 2.9 I marked this distinction by saying that ordinary SELF-experience involves the thought-elements (experience-structuring elements) SINGLE$_s$ and SINGLE$_D$, but I'll use the term 'SINGLE' without temporal restriction when this distinction is not importantly at issue.

It may be said that to figure the self as single is necessarily to figure it both as synchronically and as diachronically single, for it is simply to figure it as a single thing full stop, a single thing for however long it lasts. True, but two points need to be made. The first is that it may be possible for a subject of experience to figure itself (itself figured as a self) as diachronically single although it never has any sense of itself as something that exists for more than few seconds. Second, and more dramatically, it may be possible for a subject of experience to figure itself-figured-as-a-self as single only in the present, with no significant sense of existence beyond the present. That is, it may be possible for

---

[71] Cf. P. F. Strawson 1966: 164–5. Note that this claim is compatible with the view that experience of oneself as non-mentally single is a necessary condition of both self-consciousness and SELF-experience.

a subject to figure itself-figured-as-a-self as synchronically single without also figuring itself-figured-as-a-self as diachronically single.

2.19 SINGLE: synchronic and diachronic

'Synchronic' needs to be stretched a little, though, if it is to have phenomenological reality. I'm going to take it that to figure the self as something synchronically single is to figure it as single in the present of lived experience, or, as I will say, the *lived present of experience*. This stretches the meaning of 'synchronic' somewhat, because the lived present of experience—Husserl's *lebendige Gegenwart*, that which is experienced as the present of consciousness, the 'conscious Now'—has, at least in the normal human case, an intrinsically temporal, essentially duration-involving, phenomenological character.

To figure or experience the self as synchronically single, then, is not just to figure it abstractly as it is at a phenomenologically invisible instant in time, an indefinitely thin time slice, although one may perfectly well do this. It is to figure/experience it as single during the lived present of experience. The notion of the lived present of experience is obviously related to the notion of the *specious present*, and this is a matter I'll take up in 5.9. Can we say how long it is? Dainton tentatively estimates the maximum duration of the specious present to be half a second or less (2000: 171), and I'm happy to transfer that estimate to the lived present of experience. I choose to use a different term because my notion of the lived present of experience differs from at least some current notions of the specious present. For example, I take the notion of the lived present of experience to be, so far, a strictly phenomenological notion, in the following sense: it does nothing more than pick out a feature of the character of experience. The notion of the specious present, by contrast, seems to be used in such a way that the temporal reference it contains has both a phenomenological and a non-phenomenological application. Thus, if a particular specious-present experience is taken to cover about a third of a second's worth of events in the world, it is also thought to occupy a period of time that is objectively about a third of a second long. I think this is a potential source of error, as I'll explain in 5.9.

So much for the special definition of 'synchronic'. 'Diachronic' is directly opposed to 'synchronic', applying to any considering of the self that is a considering of it as existing in or for a period of time that extends beyond the lived present of experience. Combining the notions of synchronicity and diachronicity with the notion of singleness, we get

SINGLE$_s$: to figure the self as something synchronically single is to figure it as something single or unified when considering it as something existing in the lived present of experience.

SINGLE$_D$: to figure the self as diachronically single is to figure it as something single or unified when considering it as something that lasts longer than the lived present of experience.

On these terms one can figure the self as diachronically single or unified even if one never figures it as something that lasts more than a second or two, but my main concern, when it comes to diachronic singleness, will not be with such short-term diachronic singleness, but with relatively long-term singleness or continuity, long-term persistence: hours, days, weeks, months, years (as on page 46, the vagueness of 'relatively long-term' is intentional). So I'll generally use the longer-duration-implying word 'PERSISTING'

PERSISTING: to figure the self as something persisting is to figure it as diachronically single or unified when considering it as something existing for some relatively long period of time

in place of 'SINGLE$_D$'. It's clear that the self is ordinarily thought of as something persisting in this sense. In fact it's usually taken to be something that lasts a lifetime, although many people, including Proust, find it natural to talk of their 'earlier selves' as if these were different people from the people they are now.

A self, then, is standardly figured as something that is synchronically single: it is figured as something that is single at any given time, e.g. during the lived present of experience. It is also standardly figured as something single (single-marble-single) through time, something persisting, something that continues to exist not only beyond the lived present of experience but also for much longer periods of time—days, years, lifetimes.

It may be objected that something can be said to persist even if it divides into several parts, and that it would be better to convert the 'P' of 'PERSISTING' into a subscript and use 'SINGLE$_P$' instead of PERSISTING, in order to keep the singleness element vivid. Nevertheless, I'm going to stick to 'PERSISTING', and take it that diachronic continuity and diachronic singleness entail each other when it comes to the self.

It's very hard to be precise about the temporality of experience, whether one considers it objectively or subjectively, and the synchronic/diachronic distinction I've just presented may be problematic in various ways. I think, though, that it's enough for my present purposes, and I'm now going to return to the claim that ordinary human SELF-experience figures the self as single-as-mental, as single specifically as something mental—after first introducing a small technical device.

I will use 'I*' to represent: that which I experience myself to be when I'm apprehending myself specifically as a self, i.e. as a subject of experience that isn't the same thing as the whole human being that I am, something whose persistence conditions or identity conditions are not necessarily the same as the persistence conditions of the whole human being that I also am. I'll use plain 'I' when I'm not considering myself specifically as a self, and also when I have no need to draw attention to the mental-self pole or aspect of my experience of myself.[72] 'I*' comes with a large family of cognate forms—'me*', 'my*', 'mine*', 'myself*', 'one*', 'oneself*', 'you*' 'themselves*', and so on, and the ontological presumption built into these terms is that they succeed in making genuine reference to something that is a good candidate for the title 'self' (a subject of experience that is distinct from a whole human being). This exactly mirrors the ontological presumption built into SELF-experience. It doesn't matter if the presumption is incorrect: 'I*' and its

---

[72] For the legitimacy of this notion of an aspect or pole, see the argument for the non-univocal reference of 'I' in 2.4 and 7.2. I take it that 'I' routinely shifts between two referents—the self and the whole human being—in the mouths of ordinary human speakers, and perhaps (see 7.2) between three.

cognates can function in phenomenological contexts to convey the content of a form of experience that incorporates the presumption even if the presumption is indefensible (there can be SELF-experience even if there is no such thing as the self).

To return now to the question of singleness. What do I mean by saying that the self is taken to be single specifically as something mental? In a sense I think it's obvious, but I'll try to explain it further.

Suppose first, contrary to fact and for the sake of argument, that it's normal for those who think that the self exists to figure it expressly as something that has non-mental being as well as mental being. Few give the matter much thought, but this supposition doesn't beg any questions. On the contrary, it makes things more difficult for me. Suppose, also, that the self is naturally thought of as having singleness when considered in its non-mental being—being identified with the brain-as-it-appears-to-physics-or-neurophysiology, say, or some part of the brain-as-it-appears-to-physics-or-neurophysiology, or with a unit of immaterial soul-substance conceived of as a support of mental goings-on that is not itself wholly and purely mental in nature. (This supposition also makes things more difficult for me.) My claim is then this: even if one supposes all these things, the fact remains that the self is apprehended as being something single independently of any thought of it as something that is single in its non-mental being. In that clear negative sense, at least, if not also in a stronger sense, it's apprehended as something that is single in its mental being.

I take it that this clearly holds in the synchronic case, and probably also in the diachronic case. As for the former, the claim, again, is that the self is not only figured as synchronically single, and as something that is mentally propertied or has mental being; it's also figured as synchronically single-as-mental. As for the latter, it seems that the self is not only figured as diachronically single, and as something that is mentally propertied; it's also figured as diachronically single independently of any thought of it as something that is (diachronically) single in its non-mental being, and it is in that sense figured as single$_D$ (persisting) specifically in so far as it is something that is mentally propertied. The diachronic case is less clear than the synchronic case, but I'm going to take it, nevertheless, that human SELF-experience ordinarily involves the thought-elements

SINGLE$_S$-as-MENTAL

and

SINGLE$_D$-as-MENTAL

and indeed

SINGLE$_P$-as-MENTAL

i.e.

PERSISTING-as-MENTAL.

It may be said that the ordinary human sense of the diachronic singleness of the self depends essentially on some kind of idea of its non-mental persistence, in so far as it's standardly allowed that the self may sometimes be unconscious or non-conscious.

Non-conscious does not, however, entail *non-mental*, on most ordinary understandings of the mental, and ordinary human SELF-experience is in any case wholly uncommitted on this point.

These claims can be probed by thought-experiments that move between phenomenology and metaphysics. Suppose someone convinces you, perhaps by hypnosis, that your current mental life with all its familiar characteristics, including your current sense of yourself as a single self, depends on the activity of three spatially separated brains in three different bodies (two of them immobile, perhaps, or entirely lacking ordinary human form). Will this immediately annihilate your natural sense of your singleness as a self? Surely not. Your fundamental sense of your singleness as a self or mental presence is as it is, and it is powerful. It won't be touched by this sort of theoretical information. Your thought is likely to be 'Wow, I've got three brains (I, the single thing or person that I am)'.[73] Your overall SELF-experience will continue unchanged. It doesn't depend on your believing that you have a single brain or body in a way that would render it vulnerable to upset by this revelation, although one might find it rather unnerving. This holds both for the synchronic and for the diachronic case.

The same goes if we suppose, somewhat more moderately, that you discover that there are three separate brains in your single body collaborating to produce your experience. Or suppose you learn for the first time that millions of separate neurons collaborate to produce your experience at any given time, including your sense of yourself* as single. This will not override the experience of the singleness of the self. Nor will confirmation of the fact that there is no neatly single persisting brain structure in us that is the seat of the self or SELF-experience. This too holds for both the synchronic and the diachronic case.[74]

What does this show? It shows, I think, the strong and straightforward sense in which one figures oneself* as single considered specifically as something mentally propertied, however else one may or may not figure oneself. And since (as remarked on p. 74) one essentially figures oneself as a subject of experience, in figuring oneself as single qua something mental in this way, we may add to the list of thought-elements by recording the point that ordinary human SELF-experience involves the thought-element

SINGLE$_s$-as-SUBJECT

—and also, no doubt, the thought-element

SINGLE$_p$-as-SUBJECT

i.e. the thought-element

PERSISTING-as-SUBJECT

—about which I will have more to say.

---

[73] Kant makes a closely related point (A353 and A354).

[74] Suppose one learns that brain structures that regularly serve as part of the 'brain-system self' (10) have other functions at other times (perhaps as a result of neuromodulation). Suppose that this makes vivid for one the idea that the self is in some sense merely a functional and transient unity. This, too, will not disrupt the experience of oneself* as single that concerns me here.

On pages 64–5 I committed myself to a neutral use of the term 'SUBJECT', neutral between an inner-entity use and a whole-human-being use, and it follows from this decision that the complex thought-elements just listed don't incorporate a very strong claim. For one can be naturally said to consider oneself as single, as subject, both at a time and through time, even when one considers oneself as subject of experience *qua* whole human being. Given the neutral use of 'SUBJECT', SINGLE$_s$-as-SUBJECT and SINGLE$_p$-as-SUBJECT, which compound into plain SINGLE-as-SUBJECT, fail to represent the fact that to figure oneself as subject of experience, in figuring oneself as single mentally considered, is to figure oneself as subject of experience in the traditional, inner, mental sense of 'subject of experience'. (The present argument moves in a small area.) The neutral use of 'SUBJECT' is well worth preserving, though, and the fact just recorded can be easily expressed in the present scheme by saying that ordinary human SELF-experience involves the compound thought-element

SINGLE-as-SUBJECT-as-MENTAL

—as already observed.

This, I claim, is a—in fact, the—fundamental element in ordinary SELF-experience, whether or not it is a necessary element of any genuine form of SELF-experience.[75] It's nothing odd or complicated, although it may look it as stated here; it's an integral element of something that ordinarily feels simple to us—the everyday sense of the mental self.

Let me re-express the claim one more time. It is as figured as *subject* figured specifically or merely as *mental* that the self is figured as *single*, where to figure something specifically as mental is (at least) to figure it as having mental being in a context of thought in which the idea that it might also have non-mental being is simply not in play (in which there is no resort to a conception of it as having non-mental being). This is hardly a controversial claim—it's comfortably close to trivial.

Note that it's part of the logic of the present '-as-' construction that 'x-as-y-as-z' entails 'x-as-z', so that we can derive 'SINGLE-as-MENTAL' from 'SINGLE-as-SUBJECT-as-MENTAL'. And we can test claims of the form '*a* is figured as x-*as*-y-*as*-z' by seeing if '*a* is figured as x-*as*-z' stands up—or is objectionable—on independent grounds.[76]

Note also that the reasoning applied above to SINGLE-as-SUBJECT applies equally to THING-as-SUBJECT, the element canvassed on page 65 above. If ordinary human SELF-experience involves THING-as-SUBJECT—I argue the case further in 4.3—then it does so in the traditional inner mentalistic sense of 'SUBJECT'. This means that it's not enough, on the present terms, to say that ordinary human SELF-experience figures the self as a thing of some sort when it figures it as a subject (THING-as-SUBJECT), for 'SUBJECT' is

---

[75] I think that it is in the synchronic case, but not in the (relatively long-term) diachronic case. See 4.8.

[76] One can devise a different '-as-' construction (to represent conscious modes of presentation in thought, say) for which it is not true that to deploy the thought-element F-as-G-as-H is *ipso facto* to deploy the thought-element F-as-H. The present construction, however, rests on something like the following idea: if a grasp of x as F embeds (as it were) a grasp of x as G, and if the grasp of x as G embeds a grasp of it as H, then the grasp of x as F embeds a grasp of it as H. Or, to put it the other way round: if a grasp of x as G is built into a particular grasp of x as F, and a grasp of x as H is built into that grasp of it as G, then a grasp of x as H is built into that grasp of it as F.

neutral between the whole-creature and inner mentalistic conceptions of the subject. Full explicitness requires one to say that when ordinary human SELF-experience figures the self as a thing of some sort, in figuring it as a subject, it does so when it considers it, as subject, specifically as something that has mental being:

THING-as-SUBJECT-as-MENTAL.

Removing the middle term, it figures the self as a thing of some sort when considering it specifically as something having mental being—

THING-as-MENTAL

—rather than in some other way, e.g. as a brain or part of a brain thought of as a lump of matter in a standard way, or as a unit of 'soul stuff', where soul stuff is not thought of as being, in itself, something essentially mental in nature.

The remaining elements of ordinary human SELF-experience also compound in this way to produce

AGENT-as-SUBJECT-as-MENTAL
PERSONALITY-as-SUBJECT-as-MENTAL
DISTINCT-as-SUBJECT-as-MENTAL,

trivially so, in the case of DISTINCT. One could say that '-as-SUBJECT-as-MENTAL' is the core element of SELF-experience, the core conception to which all the other elements attach. It captures the most basic idea of what a self is, and is a necessary part of any SELF-experience, not just ordinary human SELF-experience. To be concerned with SINGLE$_s$-as-MENTAL and SINGLE$_p$-as-MENTAL is always to be concerned with SINGLE$_s$-as-SUBJECT-as-MENTAL and SINGLE$_p$-as-SUBJECT-as-MENTAL.

—The terminology may or may not be tolerable, but (to get back to SINGLE) your three-body story is no good, because you simply help yourself to the fact that you still experience yourself in the way an ordinary single-bodied being does. What one discovers, according to your story, is that one's actual mental life, with its fundamental character of being the experience of a single-bodied creature, depends on three brains in three bodies, so it's hardly surprising (to say the least) that one has a continuing sense of oneself as single when considering oneself as a self.

I intended nothing different; but one can also, it seems, imagine a three-bodied creature that naturally experiences itself as three-bodied, and as receiving sensory information from all three bodies (perhaps via different sense modalities, perhaps not), while still naturally and automatically thinking of itself as 'I', and still having a strong sense of itself* as single. It's not as if such three-bodied experience is in and of itself likely to make a sense of the singleness of the self less likely. On the contrary. It's likely to make the sense of the singleness of the self particularly vivid. The character of an ordinary human being's experience of himself* or herself* as single is no doubt profoundly and essentially shaped by the experience of having a single body and a single spatiotemporal location at any given time, but it doesn't follow, and isn't true, or so I will argue in 3.8–3.9, that any possible experience of oneself* as single depends essentially on experience of having a single body.

So much for the synchronic case; now for the diachronic case. Suppose you experience your mental life as something that has strong, long-term diachronic singleness or unity. And suppose you then discover, or become convinced, that your mental life depends for its existence on the successive existence of a series of numerically distinct brains or neuronal entities. Will this annihilate your sense of the self as a single thing persisting through time? It would be extraordinary if it did, for, by hypothesis, everything else will be the same for you, experientially, as it was before you made this discovery. It seems that confrontation with the fact of one's non-mental serial multiplicity will have no more force to undermine one's sense of one's singleness considered as a self in the diachronic case than in the synchronic case.[77]

In a famous footnote Kant asks us to imagine an 'elastic ball that strikes another similar ball in a straight line' and

communicates to the latter its entire motion and therefore its entire state (if we take account only of positions in space). If, in analogy with such bodies, we postulate substances such that the one communicates mental contents to the other together with consciousness of them, we can conceive a whole series of substances of which the first transmits its state to the second, the second its own state together with that of the preceding substance to the third, and [so on]. The last substance would then be conscious of all the states of the previously changed substances as being its own states, because they would have been transferred to it together with consciousness of them.   (A363–4)

One can gloss his point in an explicitly phenomenological way by saying that no experience of seamless continuity of consciousness, or of the long-term diachronic singleness or persistence of the self, however vivid and seemingly self-authenticating, can possibly establish that the self or *I* is in fact a persisting diachronically continuous thing or substance, metaphysically speaking. Certainly the 'representation *I*' is a 'permanent appearance that we encounter in the soul', permanent in the sense that it is always to be found, as he goes on to say. We are, however, 'unable to prove that this *I*, a mere thought, may not be in the same state of flux as the other thoughts which, by means of it, are linked up with one another' (A364). This is surely true, given Kant's terms of discussion (here as elsewhere he follows Hume), and the present claim—that even if one became convinced that the existence of the self did *not* involve the existence of a diachronically continuous substance, there is no reason to suppose that this would somehow undermine one's experience of the self as diachronically single—is wholly compatible with Kant's. (The converse is also plainly true: even if I experience myself as constantly changing, or constantly new, even if I have, with John Updike, 'the persistent sensation, in my life ..., that I am just beginning' (1989: 239), this does not prove that my experiences are not in fact states of a single, persisting individual substance.)

---

[77] The series might or might not be overlapping: one can vary its description. One could have alternating 'deciduous' brain hemispheres. Today hemisphere A is the sole site of neural activity, but it will soon grow connections to and transmit all its information to the newly matured hemisphere B, at which point it will wither and seed a new hemisphere C. (The actual rate of replacement of atoms in the human brain is not known; one estimate is that they remain for an average of about two to three weeks.)

I hope this sufficiently illustrates the sense in which the self is experienced as something single, as single-as-mental. Even if one takes it for granted that the self has non-mental being, and that it has singleness considered in its non-mental being, and even if this is vivid for one (in a way that would be most unusual), still one's sense of it as something single appears to be entirely independent of any belief that it is single—either synchronically or diachronically—in its non-mental being.

Consider the converse of this idea: that experiences which occur in a single body or brain (or single substance of some other sort) can fail to seem anything like the experiences of a single self or experiencer, both when apprehended 'from the inside' (i.e. from the point of view of the subject of any of the experiences in question) and when apprehended 'from the outside' (i.e. by someone who is not the subject of any of the experiences, but who has access to the contents of the experiences, as in a novel). Is this possible? The question has both a diachronic and a synchronic aspect, and one can consider each of these aspects from two perspectives—from the outside and from the inside. I'll begin with the diachronic case and the view from outside.

Imagine, then, that a series of self-conscious experiences or 'I-thoughts' occurs in the same brain, one at a time. None of them ever involves any awareness of any experience earlier than itself, or any anticipation of any experience later than itself, and no two of them ever stand in any of the relations—of connectedness of content, general temperamental coherence, and so on—in which pairs of thoughts so often stand when they are the thoughts of a being that we naturally think of as a single subject. In this case it may be said that we, considering things from the outside, lack any mentally or experientially grounded reason for saying that there is a single subject persisting through time. Some may want to say that there is none the less a single subject or experiencer, simply because a single persisting brain is the locus of all the thoughts. But why should the fact of non-mental diachronic singleness trump the rather natural judgement that there's no plausible candidate for a diachronically single self in this case? The fact of non-mental multiplicity in the three-bodies case has no power to defeat the natural judgement that the self or mental someone is itself something single. Why should the fact of non-mental singleness in this case defeat the arguably natural judgement that there is no single self or mental someone in this case—that there are distinct or multiple subjects or mental someones?

Turning now to the view from the inside in the diachronic case, it seems that it hardly allows for the question whether there is one self or many selves to arise. We have to imagine the occurrence of something like the following rather protracted thought: 'A single persisting brain is the non-mental being of I* who am thinking now, and there have been many past thoughts and experiences of which I know nothing occurring in this brain, and there will be many future thoughts and experiences occurring in this brain of which I know nothing. But I*—I* who am now thinking—am definitely a single persisting thing, because this brain is.' The transition is hardly compelling.

One can also appeal to the phenomena of dissociative identity disorder in support of the idea that occurrence in the same brain is not a sufficient condition of seeming from the inside to belong to the same self. The present argument doesn't require this, however, and the case I'm considering is more extreme than any case of dissociative identity disorder. For one thing, it appears to exclude all relations of psychological continuity and psychological connectedness as defined by Parfit,[78] and these are relations that typically persist in a complex fashion in cases of dissociative identity disorder, in which they not only link the various personalities, during their periods of tenure, to their own past appearances, but also link some of the personalities to each other.

Let us now consider the views from the outside and the inside in the synchronic case. Imagine that a single brain is the site of experiential phenomena that are just like the experiential phenomena taking place simultaneously in the brains of three different people, of whom the first is thinking exclusively about Vienna, the second exclusively about menhirs, and the third exclusively about DNA. Here it is rather natural to judge that there are three subjects of experience, both when considering things from the outside and when considering things—in so far as one can—from the inside; so that if one counts the whole brain non-mentally considered as the non-mental being of each of the three apparently distinct thought-thinking selves, then one has multiplicity of selves in spite of non-mental singleness.[79]

—The judgement that there are three subjects of experience may seem natural in this case, but it can be cogently challenged. It's extremely difficult to draw clear conclusions about the number of subjects of experience associated with a single brain from facts about the contents of the experiences occurring in that brain. As far as the diachronic case is concerned, it's not clear that there's any neat lower bound on the connectedness of the successive thoughts and experiences of a single subject of experience: it's not clear that there's any point at which we can say with certainty 'These experiences are too unconnected and disordered to count as the experiences of a single subject of experience'.[80] As far as the synchronic case is concerned, it may be a fact about human beings that they can only genuinely entertain one conscious thought at a time, but it hardly follows that it's an a priori truth about all conscious thinking. Perhaps beings different from ourselves can pay attention to three thoughts at once in something like the way in which we can be aware of colour, sound, and smell at once.

I agree, but the point stands. Even if we had very good reasons, in a particular case, for taking the site of all this mental activity to be something that was a single thing non-mentally considered (a body, for example, or a brain or part of a brain), that in itself would not give us good grounds for thinking that there was only a single self involved.

---

[78] See e.g. Parfit 1984: 205–6. A person picked out at time t_1, and tagged, for ease of reference, with the name 'P$_1$', is said to be (directly) psychologically *connected* to a person picked out twenty years ago at time t_{20}, and tagged 'P$_{20}$', in such a way as to leave it open that P$_1$ is the same person as P$_{20}$, if—to take the case of memory—P$_1$ can now remember having some of the experiences that P$_{20}$ had twenty years ago. P$_1$ is psychologically *continuous* with P$_{20}$ if there exists an overlapping chain of such direct connections (if, for example, P$_1$ is psychologically connected to a person picked out at t_2 and tagged 'P$_2$', P$_2$ is psychologically connected to a person picked out at t_3 and tagged 'P$_3$', and so on back to P$_{20}$). Clearly P$_1$ can be psychologically continuous with P$_{20}$ even if it is not psychologically connected to P$_{20}$, and conversely.

[79] Obviously the argument doesn't work if three brain areas B1, B2, and B3 that are entirely distinct non-mentally considered are the sites of the three thoughts T1, T2, and T3 respectively, and if B1–B3 respectively are taken to constitute the subjects of experience thinking T1–T3 respectively. There are many possible versions of this story.

[80] See van Inwagen 1990a: 196–202.

And—to return now to the main point—as far as ordinary human SELF-experience is concerned, the fundamental fact is that the self is experienced as single entirely independently of any thought about any non-mental being that it may or may not have. It's experienced as single when consideration of its nature is confined—as it almost invariably is—to consideration of it simply as something that has mental being, a mental presence or mental someone.

2.20 SINGLE: my name is Legion?

—Perhaps human SELF-experience does standardly figure the self as something single, and as something single considered specifically as something mental. Some, however, sincerely claim to experience the self as fragmentary or multiple, and many of us have had experiences that give us—so we feel—some understanding of what they mean. You've left no room for this phenomenon, although it's part of ordinary experience.

I'm not at all sure that it is part of ordinary experience, and whatever these experiences of multiplicity amount to, they don't touch the fundamental sense in which one experiences oneself as single in experiencing oneself as a self. The reasons for this are very general, and to set them out is not only to show, in answer to the local phenomenological question, that ordinary human SELF-experience does figure the self as single. It's also to show the fundamental sense in which any genuine form of SELF-experience must figure the self as single, thereby answering part of the general phenomenological question in advance of the main discussion of it in Part 4. Even if the experience of multiplicity could somehow affect PERSISTING/SINGLE$_D$, it couldn't affect SINGLE$_s$; or so I'll argue.

Can one experience oneself* (oneself apprehended as a self) as synchronically multiple, multiple in the lived present of experience, in the having of the present experience? One may be under stress, and subject to rapidly changing moods. One may feel oneself pulled in different directions by different desires. Human thought-processes are sometimes extraordinarily rapid and tumultuous, disparate contents tumbling over one another,[81] and a madman may try to speak truly when he says, biblically, 'my name is Legion' (Mark 5: 9). But the question remains. What exactly is being claimed, when it's said that one may consciously experience oneself* as synchronically multiple in the having of one's present experience?

Two possibilities come to mind: either one's sense is that there are many selves or subjects present, or one's sense is merely that one* is complex (and no doubt conflicted) in a certain way. But in the second case, the experience of complexity that is claimed to justify the description 'multiple' depends on the self's already being experienced as single. 'Multiple' is a characterization that is applied to something that must have already presented as single in a way that defeats the characterization 'multiple' in order for the characterization 'multiple' to be applied at all.

---

[81] I find that this is often accompanied by a quasi-spatial experience of each content whooshing off in a direction different from the one before.

What about the first case, in which the experience is that there are many selves present? Well, we're bound to ask who has the experience that there are many selves present; and to ask the question is to realize that any actual experience that has this character must have the character of being experience from one single mental point of view (the word 'mental' is not redundant here, because the three-bodied person on page 80 who has sensory experience of being three-bodied may have three sensory points of view while still having only one mental 'point of view'). Even if a single brain is the site of many distinct experiences that there are many selves present, each such experience must have the character of being experience from a single point of view. This is the trivial aspect of the claim that experience of oneself* as synchronically multiple is not really possible. For one's experience must not only be that there are many selves or subjects present; it must also be that one* is—literally—all those many selves. But then, presumably, one's experience must be that one is, in having the thought 'I am multiple', literally having many thoughts of the form 'I am multiple' simultaneously, in such a way that the distinctness of each of them is experientially apparent even while its being one's own thought is also apparent and even while the content of one's current thought is still nothing but 'I am multiple'. ...

This sounds comfortably impossible to me, but some may not be satisfied. They may still be attracted by the idea that the self can be experienced as multiple, and can indeed be multiple. So perhaps we should try to imagine that 'the self is multiple' could be an accurate representation of how things are.

Suppose we encounter a subject who sincerely claims to have—to live—such an experience/conception of the self. What are we to think? Considering the case from the outside, with maximum metaphysical sympathy, we must suppose that this subject who speaks is, in effect, and at best, acting as a spokesman for other selves or subjects of experience. But these other selves must indeed be genuinely distinct from the spokesman if what the spokesman says is to be literally true; which leaves the spokesman single after all. This is so even if there are indeed many selves and they all speak—literally—with one voice.

If we try to consider things from the inside—to suppose that the 'I am multiple' description of SELF-experience is genuinely conceived to be true by whatever spokesman-subject we are dealing with (perhaps all of them at once), and is not offered simply as a metaphorical way of expressing a sense of complexity or confusion—it's equally hard to make literal sense of the supposition. It seems that success is failure. For success—which we may conditionally describe as genuinely conceiving of oneself* as many selves—must set up any other selves as genuinely separate from the one that is doing this conceiving; which leaves it single. Even if there really are many selves, and they all conceive of themselves as many selves, each of them must in so doing set up any other selves as genuinely separate from itself as it is doing the conceiving; which leaves it single.

The metaphor of numerical multiplicity comes naturally to some people in some circumstances, but it is only a metaphor for a certain sort of complexity, and it can easily mislead. When the mind races and tumbles, one may experience oneself as a largely helpless spectator of the pandemonium, and many suppose that this is a case in which there may be experience of multiplicity of self. But there's a more fundamental respect in which experience of chaotic disparateness of contents reinforces a sense of singleness rather than diminishing it: when things are mentally chaotic, the chaos is happening to me, and it's only relative to some basic sense of singleness that it appears as chaos.[82]

What about normal, non-pathological experience of conflict of desire? Can't this give a genuine sense that one* is multiple? I don't think so. I think, in fact, and again, and on the contrary, that it depends essentially on experience of oneself* as single. One can't experience conflict—one can't be pulled both ways—unless one experiences both desires as one's own (Shall I marry X or Y? Shall I have another helping of stewed plums or not?). Suppose one 'identifies' with one of the desires, as we say, and feels the other to be alien. This doesn't help. For in this case the identification presents one to oneself as a single being who is harassed by an impulse that seems external to one. No sense of multiplicity is involved in this. The picture of two or more selves in conflict may seem to some to have a certain vivid truth, but it is, I think, stagey and superficial.

Earlier I imagined someone saying that experience of oneself* as fragmentary or multiple was part of ordinary experience, however rare, but I have no idea what it might be like. When Erik Erikson says, in a passage quoted in part in 1.13, that 'various selves ... make up our composite Self. There are constant and often shocklike transitions between these selves .... It takes ... a healthy personality for the 'I' to be able to speak out of all these conditions in such a way that at any moment it can testify to a reasonably coherent Self' (1968: 217), his words bear no relation to anything in my experience, or anything I can imagine. The same goes for Mary Midgley's words, also quoted in part in 1.13, when she proposes that the fictional Dr Jekyll 'was partly right: we *are* each not only one but also many. ... Some of us have to hold a meeting every time we want to do something only slightly difficult, in order to find the self who is capable of undertaking it. ... We spend a lot of time and ingenuity on developing ways of organizing the inner crowd, securing consent among it, and arranging for it to act as a whole. ...' (1984: 122–3). I find it hard to believe that anyone really has such experience, unless perhaps they're schizophrenic. Reassuringly, Midgley goes on to say that others 'do not feel like this at all, hear such descriptions with amazement, and are inclined to regard those who give them as dotty'.

Suppose that a creature has three spatially separated bodies, and, as far as possible, experiences itself* as inhabiting each of them in something like the immediate way in which one experiences oneself* as inhabiting one's actual body. And suppose that information from the three bodies is experienced in such a way that it's correct to say that there is only one subject or centre of consciousness enjoying some sort of experience of triple embodiment. What can this be like? It isn't *ipso facto* a case in which the self is experienced as synchronically multiple, even if such a case is possible, for experience from the three bodies is, precisely, integrated in such a way that it's correct to say that

---

[82] Experience of mental chaos can also prompt a sense that there is no self there at all.

there's only one centre of consciousness. If we suppose instead that there are three subjects or centres of consciousness, each enjoying some sort of experience of triple embodiment, there is, again, no reason to say that any one of them is experiencing itself* as synchronically multiple, multiple within the space of any single experience. Once again the basic point is trivial or 'logical'. One can see three—or a dozen—different scenes simultaneously on a bank of television monitors, but one must do so from a single point of view, the singleness of the point of view being integral to the character of the experience.

One might re-express the point by saying that what is the case and what seems to be the case are not independent in this instance, because the seeming-to-be-the-case is a central part of the what-is-the-case that is in question. It may at first seem coherent to say 'Of course it is logically impossible for one point of view to *be* many points of view, but it doesn't follow that one point of view can't *seem*—from the inside—to be many points of view'. And there are various superficial senses in which one point of view can seem to be many: one can look at several different monitors showing different scenes, or desire two profoundly incompatible things, or even, perhaps, experience the world via three different bodies. But these senses in which there is multiplicity are only superficial: just as genuinely seeming to be in pain is being in pain, so too a single point of view's genuinely and *per impossibile* seeming-from-the-inside to be many points of view would have to be—again *per impossibile*—its being many points of view. Nothing can really count as a single point of view's genuinely seeming, from the inside, to be many points of view.

Could two or more subjects somehow have the same thought numerically speaking? Plainly not. If two or more subjects really do have experiences, it follows immediately that there are two or more experiences, which must be numerically distinct even if they're qualitatively identical. Couldn't the two subjects be 'Siamese twins in the brain', sharing parts of the brain in such a way that numerically the same thought-elements GRASS, GREEN, and LONG feature in both of their experiences when they think that the grass is long and green? To the extent that we allow this, we have to think of the shared thought-elements as in themselves non-experiential sources or bases of the two experiences, just as a single tree is the source of both your and my experience of it, for the two experiences themselves are necessarily numerically distinct, in belonging to numerically distinct subjects. Couldn't one be a perfect mind-reader in such a way that one has exactly the same experiences as the person whose mind one is reading? Once again there are *ipso facto* two numerically distinct experiences. The point is trivial or 'logical'.[83]

'That the *I* of apperception, and therefore the *I* in every experience, is *one*, and cannot be resolved into a plurality of subjects' is, as Kant says, 'something that lies already in the concept of experience, and is therefore an analytic proposition.'[84] But we can go beyond this 'logical' or 'transcendental' point (the point that a thought like *the grass is long and*

---

[83] The case in which a person A 'fissions' into two people B and C in such a way that both B and C may reasonably be said to have had the experiences that A had is not relevant.

[84] B407. As before I'm using 'experience' instead of 'thought' or 'act of thought'.

green involves elements, GRASS, GREEN and LONG, that cannot possibly be distributed among several subjects if the thought is to occur at all), whether or not Kant will accompany us. As in 2.10 (50) we can take 'apperception' to have a straightforwardly experiential empirical application in addition to its transcendental, non-experiential application, an empirical application in which it is synonymous with 'inner sense', and then stress the equally and at present more important (logico-) phenomenological point that the subject cannot but *experience* itself as single or simple in so far as it apprehends itself as subject of experience in ordinary empirical consciousness: the point that there's an absolutely fundamental sense in which one's consciousness of oneself as subject of experience must have the character of being consciousness of something single or simple.

Taken phenomenologically or logico-phenomenologically in this way, the Kantian criticism of the 'rational psychologists' in the Paralogisms section of the *Critique of Pure Reason* derives its force precisely from this point. 'The *perception of the self* ... [that] the proposition *I experience* ... expresses', in Kant's words, does indeed necessarily involve some sort of figuring of the self as something single or simple, although this 'inner perception is nothing more than the mere apperception *I experience*' (A342–3; first emphasis mine), and so has no content deriving properly from 'intuition', and is to that extent entirely 'empty' (A355). Kant's further point is then that absolutely nothing about the ultimate ontological nature of the self or subject, in particular its singleness or simplicity, can be deduced from this fact.

It's easy for Kant to show that this is so, given his understanding of the terms of debate (one can accept the point even if one doesn't think that his text contains any such phenomenological elements). For the unity of a thought is, as he says, a collective unity involving several elements (e.g. GRASS, GREEN, and LONG) and may for all we know be substantially grounded in or realized by a 'collective unity of different substances acting together' (A353; we outside the Kantian frame may well suppose that these different substances are neurons or atoms or subatomic particles). We can't possibly hope to show a priori that its unity requires a metaphysically simple subject in the sense that the rational psychologists require in order to establish the indivisibility, hence incorruptibility, hence immortality, of the soul. Nevertheless, the fact remains that 'the subjective *I* can never be ... divided and distributed', and it is this I 'that we presuppose in all [self-conscious] experience'.[85] Read phenomenologically: self-conscious beings like ourselves necessarily presuppose—necessarily experience as the form of apperception or inner sense—what he later strikingly calls the 'qualitative' unity or simplicity or singularity of themselves as thinkers—the 'merely logical qualitative unity of self-consciousness in thought in general, which has to be present whether the subject be composite or not' so far as its ultimate ontological nature is concerned.[86]

---

[85] A354. Here Kant claims that we're obliged to base our attempt to achieve a general understanding of the notion of a subject of experience (a thinking being) on our own experience.

[86] B413. Suppose one walks into a church filled with a pure, single note. Suppose that it's being produced by five flutes, and that one can't tell, by considering its qualitative character, that this is so. (See, though, the remark about 'qualitative unity' on p. 382.)

There is, then, a fundamental sense in which experience of oneself as (synchronically) single is inevitable, when one apprehends oneself as mental subject, and given that one is self-conscious. In Kantian terms again, 'the proposition *I am simple [single]* must be regarded as a direct expression of apperception' (A355), apperception being 'consciousness of oneself' that consists of 'the simple representation of the *I*' of thought/experience (B68). It's an essential component of consciousness of oneself as a self or subject, and 'through the *I*, I always entertain the thought of an absolute but logical unity (simplicity) of the subject'.[87]

I've laboured the point, for although it's trivial in one sense, it's deep in another, and invites rumination even at the price of repetition. It is, after all, the foundation of what Kant calls 'the Achilles of all dialectical inferences in the pure doctrine of the soul' (A351), and by 'the Achilles' he means the most powerful one (the Second Paralogism), not the one with the Achilles heel. There's a fundamental sense in which the subject synchronically considered must present or be figured in experience as single in so far as it presents or is figured in experience (in inner sense) at all. This is, so far, a merely phenomenological claim, but there's also—so I will argue—a fundamental sense in which the subject must actually *be* single, and this is a straightforwardly ontological claim. I'll defend the ontological claim later, in 6.12 and 8.4–8.5. Here it's enough to say that it isn't the claim that is made by Kant's opponents, the rational psychologists, in their pursuit of immortality.

This conclusion isn't put in question by what Husserl calls the '*splitting of the I*' in transcendental-phenomenological reflection (1931: 35). Husserl is up to something quite different. Nor is it put in question by a thought-experiment of Parfit's in which he imagines being able to 'divide his mind' in order to do two separate calculations in two separate streams of consciousness, and then reunite it, and notes that 'in each of my two streams of consciousness I would believe that I was now, in my other stream, having thoughts and sensations of which, in this stream, I was unaware' (1984: 246–8). We may wonder what my experience of the division process would be like after several divisions and reunions, or indeed after years of splitting and reuniting. Would I by then experience myself* (myself considered as a self or subject) as double? Not in any sense that threatens the present claim. For my (*ex hypothesi* correct) belief in my doubleness as subject would have no experiential force in the moment-to-moment course of lived consciousness. I

---

[87] A356. It is, I think, important to note that the transcendental point about the necessary unity of the subject is as valid for beings that have no empirical self-consciousness as for those that do. A dog chasing a rabbit through undergrowth must be integrating all the complex elements of the scene, and must have 'transcendental unity of consciousness' in that sense. Kant, though, is not concerned with beings that lack empirical self-consciousness, and it seems plausible that the necessary unity acquires a clear phenomenological correlate only in a self-conscious being. Against that one may set Damasio's suggestion that *all* conscious experience incorporates some sort of sense of self, however muted and merely felt and transient: it is, he proposes, a non-verbal, implicit form of awareness, a 'feeling-image' whose content, in so far as it can be expressed in propositional form, is 'that there is an individual *subject* ..., that the images of any given object that are now being processed are formed in our *individual* perspective, that we are the *owners* of the thought process, and that we can *act* on the contents of the thought process' (Damasio 1999: 125, my emphasis; bringing this suggestion to the present discussion, one might connect the words italicized with, respectively, SUBJECT, SINGLE, SUBJECT again, and AGENT). The following at least seems plausible: that in whatever respect there is a felt sense of self in animals that have conscious experience but are not self-conscious in the way that we are, there is also a felt sense of the self as single.

would not live my subjectivity as double, for the basic phenomenological character of my experience of calculation would still, on each side of the divide, be similar to the experience that an ordinary person would have if he shared out the calculations with a friend or twin. The division of consciousness is experienced by me as something I bring about, I in my singleness, and it presents as a division only relative to the continuing sense of the singleness of the self or subject that informs my undivided state as much as ever, and also informs each stream of consciousness when I'm divided. If I ever think, when divided, that I am now, in my other stream, having thoughts and sensations of which, in this stream, I am unaware, I am, precisely, thinking of myself as single. If I split permanently, and couldn't put myself back together again, I suspect that any sense of doubleness would decrease, rather than increase.[88]

It seems to me, then, that in whatever sense one may come to think of oneself as double, this won't be something that is part of SELF-experience in the present understanding of the term. This is not to say that Parfitian division couldn't change SELF-experience in any significant way; it's only to say that it couldn't give rise to SELF-experience lacking the fundamental experience of the self as synchronically single. Similar arguments apply to cases of dissociative identity disorder. I conclude that there's a fundamental and immovable sense in which one can't experience the self as multiple in the synchronic case: SELF experience necessarily involves SINGLE$_s$. This is something that was, perhaps, obvious all along. It may be, though, that it started out as obvious, ceased to seem so under philosophical pressure, and was then recovered as obvious, and this is one of the best kinds of philosophical movement.

I've been considering the synchronic case. Let me now consider the (long-term) diachronic case. For when people think of themselves specifically as selves, they standardly conceive of the self as something that has long-term diachronic singleness or persistence. I think they may be wrong to do so, but the present question is simply whether someone whose SELF-experience includes a sense of the self as something that has long-term diachronic continuity can figure the self as something diachronically multiple?

Suppose that when one thinks of oneself as a self, say S_1, one has, acutely, the Proustian sense that one is a different self from *one's earlier self* S_0, and then, later, feels that the self one then experiences oneself to be, say S_2, is different from S_1; and so on. At first this sounds reasonably sensible, as a description of the content of one's experience; but it's not really intelligible. The problem is that the word 'different' is ambiguous between 'qualitatively different' and 'numerically different'. The qualitative sense helps the description of the Proustian experience sound intelligible, but it's the numerical sense that is needed, and the numerical sense tips the description into unintelligibility.

---

[88] Although the splitting is voluntarily undertaken, one can imagine that a powerful tendency to deny or discount the reality of the other locus of consciousness, of the sort found in 'split-brain' patients in experimental conditions, might persist.

If qualitative difference is all that is in question, then what is being described, in a dramatic idiom, is simply a sense of oneself as changing radically through time while remaining the same single self. If numerical difference is in question—contradiction. For the claim is then that one—i.e. S_1—experiences oneself as a numerically different self from *the self one was*—S_0. But to say that one experiences S_0 as the self one was is to say that one experiences oneself, S_1, as having been that self, S_0, which is to say that one does not after all experience oneself as numerically different from S_0, and so does not after all experience oneself as diachronically multiple after all. Any illusion of coherence is created by the formulations italicized above (*one's earlier self, the self one was*). Simply put: if one thinks or feels anything like 'First I'm one self, then I'm another', the thought or feeling presupposes that one is diachronically single.

What one can choose to say, of course, is that there's a single persisting human body occupied successively by different selves. This eases the way to talk of past selves as if they were somehow *oneself* although at the same time *not oneself*. But it doesn't give a self that has long-term diachronic continuity and is at the same time multiple. It just gives a succession of selves in a single body, and presumably derives any force it has from the tension (reflected in the dual use of 'I' noted on pages 31–2) that exists between the tendency to think of oneself as, essentially, just a self or mental presence, and the tendency to think of oneself as a human being considered as a whole.

It has strong intuitive appeal for some. In *A la recherche du temps perdu*, it seems clear to Proust's narrator that he is no longer the person who fell in love with Albertine, although he is still living with her, any more than she's the person with whom the person he was fell in love.[89] But this isn't a case in which a (single) persisting self is conceived of as diachronically multiple, and there are various ways in which Proust is wrong even on his own terms, in an arguably self-indulgent way. It is, for one thing, important that he falls in love on the basis of incomplete information, and mere laziness and consequent boredom, which don't entail change of self, can play a part in disaffection. (In fact, Proust never writes about romantic love, and his reflections on what he calls 'love' show that he has no experience of it—a fact of which he is aware.)

—The penultimate paragraph is beside the point. It confuses metaphysics and phenomenology. It may indeed be contradictory to suppose that a (single) persisting self can be diachronically multiple, but that's a point of metaphysics, not phenomenology. To say that a diachronically multiple single self can't exist is not to say that one can't figure or experience or conceive of oneself as being such a thing.

In fact it is to say this. For if the experience is not just experience of oneself* as having radically changed, then it is precisely experience that purports to have a certain non-metaphorical metaphysical content: that one is the same thing and is also not the same thing. If one is unreflective, it may seem to one that one genuinely conceives of oneself in this way. In the same way, some may think that they can conceive of a round

---

[89] One nice consequence of his view is that all marriages are arranged marriages in the longer term: anyone who's been married for any length of time married in accordance with the wishes of someone else.

square. But one can't really conceive of oneself in this way, because one can't really conceive of something inconceivable.

—Phenomenology is a matter of how things are experienced, and a conception can be highly influential in the way things are experienced even if it's not in the end coherent. The notion of radical free will or ultimate moral responsibility is not in the end coherent, but many people believe they have precisely the kind of moral responsibility that is provably impossible, and their experience has in consequence a highly distinctive (phenomenological) character—something that you yourself have discussed. I agree that it's hard to see what phenomenology will be associated with possession of the seemingly incoherent conception of diachronic multiplicity, but we can try. We can try to imagine how those who claim to experience things in this way might reply to certain questions. We ask them 'What do you actually feel? Do you really feel that you're a different self from the self you once were, or do you just feel that you're very different now from how you used to be?' They choose the first option, since the second doesn't describe SELF-experience that figures the self as diachronically multiple. 'What d'you mean?', we ask. 'Do you mean that you were that different self? But then you're really just saying that you are the same self now as you were then, but that you've changed a great deal.' They deny this, insisting that the sentence 'I am a different self—a numerically different self—from the self I once was' exactly describes what they feel (or feel they feel). What do you do then?

I accept the remark as a sincere report of experience purporting to be experience of self as diachronically multiple, noting that it invites the same crucial comment as the claim to have experience of self as synchronically multiple: 'multiple' is a characterization that is being applied to something that must already have been figured as single—diachronically persistent in some fundamental way—in a way that defeats the characterization 'multiple' in order for the characterization to be applied to it at all. Nothing similar is true in the case of experience of radical—incoherent—free will.

—Couldn't the remark express, in diachronic rather than synchronic form, some sense of the self as single in the way a collection of marbles is, rather than single in the way that a single marble is single? Couldn't it express a (diachronic) 'bundle' sense of self, and combine multiplicity with singleness in this way?

I don't know what this experience might be supposed to be like. Thinking back, one would have to be able to say sincerely 'That person really is me, but it is also really not me'. And although, again, I think that someone could find this a natural thing to say, helped on by the natural dual use of 'I', everything still converges on the same crucial, unremarkable, Kantian conclusion: the experience-structuring element SINGLE, and more particularly SINGLE-AS-SUBJECT, is not only part of ordinary human SELF-experience, but is also a necessary part of any SELF-experience. There's a fundamental sense in which the figuring of oneself as a subject of experience in SELF-experience is bound to be the figuring of oneself* as single as subject of experience, whatever theoretical fancies one indulges in: not only in the lived present of experience, but also (and trivially) for as long one takes oneself* to last—whether one takes oneself* to last only as long as the lived present of experience or for a lifetime. To consider the self to be something single at a given time is to be committed to the idea that it (*it*) is the same single thing for as long as it lasts.[90]

The starting assumption in this section is that when human beings figure themselves as selves, they ordinarily conceive the self as something persisting, something that has long-term diachronic continuity. I think this is right, but there are human beings who don't always think of the self in this way, and there may be some who never do. I propose myself. In experiencing myself specifically as a mental presence, a self, I have no sense that *what I am* is something that has long-term diachronic continuity. Nor do I think of the self that I now am as a member of some lineage, in the Proustian way. When I read Proust, imaginative empathy pulls me quite far into his way of seeing things, but I have, otherwise, no trace of any sense of having a significantly extended past—or future—or as belonging to a lineage, in so far as I think of myself as a self.[91]

2.21 AGENT

The self is figured as an agent   Should we add AGENT to the five elements already listed? Surely. The self, as William James says, is ordinarily thought of as 'the *active* element in all consciousness … the source of effort and attention, and the place from which … emanate the fiats of the will'. It is the 'central active self'; 'the very core and nucleus of our self, as we know it, the very sanctuary of our life, is the sense of activity which certain inner states possess' (1890: 1. 297–8, 299; 1892: 163). Activity doesn't entail intentional agency (it may be volcanic, or bacterial), and James is interested in the idea that we may be in error in experiencing ourselves as agent-selves in this way, but he's surely right that ordinary human SELF-experience involves AGENT, and indeed AGENT-as-SUBJECT, and indeed AGENT-as-SUBJECT-as-MENTAL.

He may, however, be insufficiently aware of how much human beings differ in this respect. Some think it obvious that experience of oneself* (oneself considered as a self) as an intentional agent is integral to experience of oneself as a subject of experience, hence integral to SELF-experience. They think it equally obvious that *being* an intentional agent is a necessary part of being a conscious subject of experience. To others this is by no means obvious. Certainly they experience the self as active, but the extent to which they experience it as an intentional agent is much less clear.

The passage from Fichte quoted on page 55, 'the *self posits itself*, and by virtue of this mere self-assertion it *exists*; and conversely, the self *exists* and *posits* its own existence by virtue of merely existing', continues as follows: 'it is at once the agent and the product of action; the active, and what the activity brings about; action and deed are one the same, and hence the "I am" expresses an Act (*Tathandlung*)' (1794–1802: 97). This may be

---

[90]   One can say of a statue that *it* has lasted to this day, but that it is no longer single because it is in pieces, but the case is not relevant here.

[91]   See G. Strawson 2004 and in preparation, *c*. See also 4.8.

thought to suggest not only intentional agency but also an express sense of intentional agency. Here, too, though, there is room for the weaker interpretation in terms of activity and a sense of activity.

I discuss this further in 4.6. For the moment it's enough to say that experience of the self as an agent seems to have a secure place in a general characterization of ordinary human SELF-experience.

2.22 PERSONALITY

The self is figured as having character or personality   Many will think this self-evident, for human beings certainly have personalities, and their personalities are certainly a matter of how they are, mentally speaking; so if the mental being of a human being centrally involves the existence of a self, that self must presumably have the personality that the human being has. It doesn't, however, follow, from the fact that anything that can count as a self in the ordinary human case has a personality, that ordinary human SELF-experience *figures* the self as having a personality, and there appears to be a natural way of experiencing the self that does not—or not clearly—present it as having personality. One can apprehend oneself* as a mental subject or mental presence—a thing of a kind that has thoughts, beliefs, preferences, and so on—without any particular awareness of oneself* as having any particular personality. One can experience oneself* as being in certain moods, subject to certain emotions, without any particular awareness of oneself* as having personality.

—This is certainly not true in the ordinary case. The experience of the self as something that has a specific personality is fundamental to most people's SELF-experience.

Informal research suggests that this is simply not so. I'll argue the point further in 4.5. Until then I'll leave PERSONALITY in place as a candidate for being a base component of ordinary human SELF-experience. It's worth registering a doubt now, because it may help to block a potentially recurrent misunderstanding: what I mean by 'SELF-experience' is not—not at all—what people tend to mean by talking of someone's 'sense of self'. The phrase 'sense of self' is standardly used to refer to something that does essentially involve having a sense of oneself as having a particular personality, a particular identity in the sense of a distinctive—unique—character. Having SELF-experience, by contrast, is simply having a sense of oneself as a mental subject or mental presence or mental someone, and even if this can involve having a sense of oneself as having personality, it need not. It has nothing especially to do with having a sense of 'who one is'.

2.23 DISTINCT

The self is figured as distinct from—in the sense of non-identical with—the whole human being
This is quickly done. It's fundamental to the ordinary human experience/conception of the self that the self is not only not figured as being the same thing as the whole

human being, but is—essentially—figured as not being the same thing as the whole human being. DISTINCT may not be a necessary part of any genuine form of SELF-experience, even when we generalize the definition of DISTINCT by removing the reference to human beings: it seems that we can imagine a case in which the self, although physically embodied in some way, is not experienced in SELF-experience as distinct from, in the sense of non-identical with, any larger organism or entity. I will return to this in 4.2. For the moment it's enough to record the point that DISTINCT is certainly part of ordinary human SELF-experience.

2.24 Summary and conclusion

This completes the answer to the local phenomenological question. In the ordinary human case the self is figured as a *subject of experience*, a *persisting single mental thing* that is an *agent* and is *distinct* from (non-identical with) the whole human being, and also, perhaps, has a certain *personality*. These are the principal thought-elements in ordinary human SELF-experience, although they doubtless occur in different strengths, and with different distributions of emphasis, in different individuals. This phenomenological conclusion can be established prior to and independently of any philosophical theory about whether or not there is such a thing as the self, or about what its nature is.

Many of the proposed elements of SELF-experience interact and form compounds in a way that makes it a little artificial to treat them separately, but they all make separate contributions and are worth separating for that reason. The core element of SELF-experience is 'x-as-SUBJECT-as-MENTAL', as remarked on page 80, for all the other six elements may be put in place of 'x'. I showed how to do this in the case of 'SINGLE' and 'THING', and the procedure is the same for AGENT, PERSONALITY, and DISTINCT.

The next question is whether all the members of the list of elements and their compounds are essential to anything that can count as a genuine form of SELF-experience. I think not, as remarked. I will challenge PERSISTING, AGENT, PERSONALITY, and DISTINCT in Part 4, together with the compounds into which they enter. In doing so, I will proceed on the assumption that the present list captures all the elements that matter, so that one doesn't have to consider additions to it, only subtractions. But anyone who favours further elements—e.g. SELF-CONSCIOUS, considered on page 47—can easily fit them into the present analytical framework.

We have, then, an answer to the local phenomenological question—a description of the cognitive core of ordinary human SELF-experience. Some may say again (45) that affective phenomena must be mentioned in any adequate description of the core of SELF-experience, at least in the human case. They may go further, and propose that a degree of self-concern is necessary to any SELF-experience. Perhaps, perhaps not. Here I've restricted my attention as far as possible to the basic cognitive-experiential structure of SELF-experience. Even if the fuel of self-concern were a necessary source of energy for this structure, it wouldn't follow that it is part of it. Nor is it. Questions about affective phenomena associated with SELF-experience are of enormous interest, but they're not relevant here. The cognitive core of SELF-experience is simply a sense of oneself specifically as a mental presence or mental someone, and this doesn't require any sort of self-concern. There's no logical difficulty in the idea of a fully self-conscious being that has SELF-experience although it is entirely affectless.[92]

—You've argued that ordinary SELF-experience presents the self as a subject of experience that is an agent, a mental, diachronically continuous (persisting) single thing that has a certain personality and is distinct from the whole human being. Maybe you're right, but it's hardly a momentous conclusion, because all except one of the properties that feature in this description of SELF-experience (*subject, thing, mental, single, persisting, agent, personality*) are just as naturally attributed to the whole human being! Human beings, no less than putative selves, are thought of as persisting things that are single in a strong sense, have mental properties and characters or personalities, and are agents and subjects of consciousness. In fact, the only property attributed by the description of SELF-experience that isn't attributed just as naturally to human beings considered as a whole is, trivially, *distinct*—the property of being distinct from the organism considered as a whole, the whole human being.

You say the various elements couple up in certain ways. You claim, for example, that a self is experienced as something that has a distinctively mental form of singleness, a distinctively mental 'principle of unity' (73).[93] Now this may distinguish one's experience / conception of oneself as a self from one's experience / conception of oneself as a whole human being, but talk of a mental principle of unity is really very unclear, and the fact that all the other properties that have been attributed to the self are attributed with exactly equal naturalness to the whole human being (with the trivial—if not question-begging—exception of the property of being distinct from the whole human being) suggests, at the very least, that our SELF-experience is quite profoundly parasitic on our experience of ourselves as human beings considered as a whole.

It suggests, in fact, that SELF-experience is nothing more than a natural but delusory abstraction from that experience. It looks as if the so-called self is really just the living human being illegitimately spiritualized, incompletely grasped, falsely thought of as 'purely mental' (compare the way in which one can hear a note played by an unseen flute—or five unseen flutes playing in unison—and simply not think of it as having any non-sonic underpinning or cause). If one lies in the dark thinking at night one may have no particular sense of one's body, and the idea of the self may seem vivid. But this is possible only because one's SELF-experience is so firmly anchored in one's experience or sense or conception of oneself as embodied.

There are three main suggestions here. The first is that seven of the eight properties that feature in the characterization of SELF-experience fail to distinguish selves from human beings considered as a whole. Granted and intended. It's their various compoundings—in addition to the property *distinct*—that set them right apart from any characterization of human beings. If this doesn't seem enough, there are plenty of other ways of distinguishing selves from human beings. Selves are physical entities on the present terms of discussion, if indeed they exist, and the same goes for human beings considered

---

[92] Note that this claim is wholly compatible with the view that emotion is of primordial importance—both phylogenetically and ontogenetically—in the development of the mental capacities that make SELF-experience possible. See Damasio 1999.

[93] This is not the claim that the self's principle of unity isn't physical, for I take it that the mental—conscious experience, what-it's-likeness and all—is wholly physical.

as a whole, but selves are very much smaller than ordinary human beings, if indeed they exist, and they don't and can't walk or eat or yawn or scratch, although they're wholly part of the natural order (they're brain phenomena).

The second suggestion is that SELF-experience, although indubitably real, may be entirely illusory in so far as it purports to be experience of something correctly called the self. True; the issue has still to be addressed. The ontological question whether selves exist is a matter for Parts 7 and 8.

The third suggestion is that experience of embodiment may be not only a genetic condition of SELF-experience in human beings and other naturally evolved creatures (as it surely is, both ontogenetically and phylogenetically), but also a strictly necessary condition of any sort of SELF-experience. This is a popular suggestion, and I consider it in 3.8–3.11.

Part 3

Phenomenology and metaphysics: SELF-experience and self-consciousness

Everyone is presented to himself in a particular and primitive way in which he is presented to no one else.

(Frege 1918: 25–6)

3.1 SELF-experience and self-consciousness

Where does self-consciousness fit into the present scheme? Presumably it ought to fit in somewhere.

There are four main questions, which I'll discuss in the next five rather dense sections. Those who want to continue with the main line of argument should pick up the definition of 'full' self-consciousness from 3.2 (102–3, 105–6) and go to Part 4.

The questions are: (1) Does a capacity for SELF-experience require self-consciousness (i.e. the capacity for self-conscious experience)? And its converse: (2) Does (the capacity for) self-consciousness require a capacity for SELF-experience? (3) Must selves be self-conscious? And its converse: (4) Is self-consciousness sufficient for being a self? To these one may add: (5) Must one be capable of SELF-experience to be a self? And its converse: (6) Must one be a self if one is capable of SELF-experience?

We may set them out as follows

(1) [x is capable of SELF-experience → x is a self-conscious being]?
(2) [x is a self-conscious being → x is capable of SELF-experience]?
(3) [x is a self → x is a self-conscious being]?
(4) [x is a self-conscious being → x is a self]?

(5) [x is a self → x is capable of SELF-experience]?
(6) [x is capable of SELF-experience → x is a self]?

Dropping the xs, and understanding 'self-conscious' throughout as a capacity term, not a term indicating actual occurrent self-consciousness, we can rewrite them as

(1) [capable of SELF-experience → self-conscious]?
(2) [self-conscious → capable of SELF-experience]?
(3) [self → self-conscious]?
(4) [self-conscious → self]?
(5) [self → capable of SELF-experience]?
(6) [capable of SELF-experience → self]?

   Since it's true by definition (3) that to be capable of having SELF-experience is to possess the experience-structuring element or thought-element SELF, i.e.

[capable of SELF-experience = possession of SELF],

we can rewrite the first and last pairs of questions as

(1) [possession of SELF → self-conscious]?
(2) [self-conscious → possession of SELF]?
(5) [self → possession of SELF]?
(6) [possession of SELF → self]?

   What are the answers? Somewhat surprisingly, perhaps, the materials available don't allow a Yes to (1). I'm going to put the case for answering Yes to (2) in 3.5, aware that this may seem very implausible given the strong notion of self-consciousness which is standard in analytic philosophy, and which I use here (I define it in the next section). I favour No to (3) and (5), and Yes to (4) and (6), where these last two are understood to say not that only things that qualify as selves qualify as self-conscious, or as capable of SELF-experience (for human beings considered as a whole also qualify), but rather that there can be no self-consciousness and no SELF-experience without there being a self.

   The account of ordinary human SELF-experience in Part 2 is likely to raise the *grounds question*

III What are the grounds—the conditions of the possibility—of SELF-experience, possession of the experience-structuring element SELF?

in the philosophical mind, as noted on page 34. I don't need to answer this question, given my main purpose, but it would be nice to be able to put the core of an answer in place.

—It can't be right to attempt anything like this at this stage. The grounds question, taken a priori in this way, is an extremely general question about the necessary grounds of any possible form of SELF-experience. This being so, you can't hope to answer it effectively until you have answered the general phenomenological question about what any genuine form of SELF-experience must be like, and not just the local phenomenological question about ordinary human SELF-experience. This is because one needs to know what something is before one can ask about its necessary grounds.

True. I have, however, already anticipated the answer to the general phenomenological question in claiming that four of the eight elements of ordinary human SELF-experience can be eliminated, to leave SUBJECT, THING, MENTAL, SINGLE, and their associated compound thought-elements—e.g.

SUBJECT-as-MENTAL

SINGLE-as-SUBJECT

SINGLE-as-MENTAL

SINGLE-as-SUBJECT-as-MENTAL

THING-as-SUBJECT

THING-as-MENTAL

THING-as-SUBJECT-as-MENTAL

—and I'm going to assume for the purposes of argument that this is right, although I haven't yet made a detailed case for it, so that I can consider the question of the grounds of SELF-experience (possession of SELF) in the light of it. This is somewhat back to front, but I think it will be useful to have the material of Part 3 in place before attempting to answer the general phenomenological question in detail in Part 4.

A natural first proposal is that self-consciousness is one of the necessary grounds or conditions of possessing SELF, i.e. of being able to have SELF-experience:

(1) [possession of SELF → self-conscious].

If (1) is true, then plainly all the grounds of (the capacity for) self-consciousness are equally grounds of the capacity to have SELF-experience. It follows that one of the things one must ask, when one asks for the grounds or conditions of SELF-experience, is

IV What are the grounds—the conditions of the possibility—of self-consciousness?

—an absorbing and time-honoured question. If it turns out, furthermore, that being a self-conscious creature is not only necessary but also sufficient for possession of SELF, the ability to have at least the minimal form of SELF-experience—

(2) [self-conscious → possession of SELF]

—then to answer question IV will be to answer question III in full. That would be satisfactory.

I don't yet know if self-consciousness is either necessary or sufficient for possessing SELF, but I'm going to try to answer question IV in any case. It seems plausible that the notion of self-consciousness ought to be brought into play in an adequate treatment of the problem of the self even if (2) is false, and even if (1) is false. In fact it seems plausible that it needs to be brought into play even if

(4) [self-conscious → self]

is false, as many suppose it is (since they acknowledge the existence of self-consciousness but don't believe in selves), and even if

(3) [self → self-conscious]

is false, as I think it is (rejecting any definition of 'self' that, like Fichte's, has the consequence that all selves are self-conscious in the strong analytic-philosophy understanding of this term). So too for (5) and (6).

An immediate objection to (1) may be that relatively sophisticated creatures like cats and dogs have *some* sort of SELF-experience even though they're plainly not self-conscious in the way we are, i.e. not fully self-conscious in a way I'm about to define. A commensurate reply is that if SELF-experience requires self-consciousness, then if cats and dogs have SELF-experience, then there must also and equally be some sense in which they're self-conscious, even if—even though—they're not fully or expressly self-conscious in the way we are. This leads on to the much stronger Aristotelian point, picked up by Brentano and stressed in the Phenomenological tradition, that awareness or consciousness or experience of any sort, however primitive, involves some sort of awareness or consciousness *of* that very awareness or consciousness. Husserl infers that 'to be a subject is to be in the mode of being aware of oneself' (1921–8: 151), Heidegger, that 'every consciousness is also self-consciousness'.[1]

The proposal in effect is that

(7) [conscious being → self-conscious being]

which, with

(8) [capable of SELF-experience → conscious being],

which is necessarily true, gives

(1) [capable of SELF-experience → self-conscious being].

But this self-consciousness—Sartre's 'pre-reflective self-consciousness'—is of a kind that must be allowed even to sea snails, if sea snails have any kind of experience, and doesn't concern me here.

I think that the basic Aristotelian idea is sound, but I'm going to put it to one side.[2] I'm going to mean something different and stronger by 'self-consciousness', focusing on the claim that SELF-experience isn't possible without 'full' or 'express' self-consciousness. This is the intended force of (1) [possession of SELF → self-conscious].

---

[1] 1930: 135. He also puts it by saying 'I am always somehow acquainted with myself' (1919–20: 251). See Gallagher and Zahavi 2008: 46.

[2] Harry Frankfurt puts it stylishly:

what would it be like to be conscious of something without being aware of this consciousness? It would mean having an experience with no awareness whatever of its occurrence. This would be, precisely, a case of unconscious experience. It appears, then, that being conscious is identical with self-consciousness. Consciousness *is* self-consciousness. The claim that waking consciousness is self-consciousness does not mean that consciousness is invariably dual in the sense that every instance of it involves both a primary awareness and another instance of consciousness which is somehow distinct and separable from the first and which has the first as its object. That would threaten an intolerably infinite proliferation of instances of consciousness. Rather, the self-consciousness in question is a sort of *immanent reflexivity* by virtue of which every instance of being conscious grasps not only that of which it is an awareness but also the awareness of it. It is like a source of light which, in addition to illuminating whatever other things fall within its scope, renders itself visible as well.   (1987: 162)

See also Gurwitsch 1941, quoted on p. 27.

3.2 Full self-consciousness

What is full or express self-consciousness?[3] It needs to be defined. It isn't just conscious-ness of self—of what is in fact oneself. If it were, a kitten chasing its tail would be self-conscious, for a kitten chasing its tail is conscious of something that is in fact itself. But a kitten that is conscious of something that is in fact itself is not conscious that that thing is itself. It apprehends itself in a certain way, but it doesn't apprehend that what it apprehends is itself. It is itself the *object* of its consciousness, it is itself the thing that it is in fact relating to, perceptually and intentionally and behaviourally, but it isn't cognizant of the fact that it is itself the object of its consciousness. The fact that it is itself the object of its consciousness isn't part of the *content* of its consciousness, as we naturally say. It's *relationally* aware of itself, in the old Quinean terminology, but not *notionally*.[4]

To be fully self-conscious, then, is not merely to have the capacity to be aware of oneself and one's features. The kitten has that, and so does a newborn baby. Is it enough to add that one must also have the capacity, when aware of something, to apprehend or represent in some way that what one is aware of is oneself?[5]

Almost, I think, but 'in some way' is loose. It seems reasonable to say that a dog or cat apprehends its paw as its own in *some* way when it withdraws it, after observation, and in a deliberate, non-reflex manner, from the path of an oncoming object; but we're strongly disinclined to say that cats and dogs are fully self-conscious in the way we are. It's natural to say that a baby in pain is in some way aware that it is itself the thing that is in pain, but the baby isn't self-conscious in the way that we are.

How may we adjust the definition of full self-consciousness? I think it's enough to say that one must be able to figure oneself expressly *as oneself*. To be fully self-conscious is to be able to think of oneself, expressly thought of or grasped *as oneself*, as having some feature or other; or, equivalently, to be able to be expressly aware of one's states or parts or features *as one's own*.[6] I think these italicized phrases fully capture the distinctive content of the specifically self-conscious way of thinking (one needn't be correct in thinking that the parts or features are one's own; it's enough that one can think of things in this way).

Another way to say the same thing (helpful to some, confusing, perhaps, for others) is to say that what is distinctive of self-consciousness is possession/deployment of the concept or thought-element I or MYSELF or ONESELF (I take all these to be the same). It's a familiar point that possession of this thought-element allows one to think about that which is in fact oneself in a way that is unlike any other way: not as *X's daughter*, or *the subject of this report*, or *the person most worried about world water shortages*, or, in Perry's well-known example, *the person leaving a trail of sugar in the supermarket*,[7] but just

---

[3] On the force of 'express', and the distinction of 'express' from the (weaker) 'explicit', see p. 30.

[4] Quine 1955. In this and the next three sections I draw on G. Strawson 1986: ch. 9.

[5] 'Represent' is better than 'apprehend' (a 'success' verb) in so far as one doesn't actually have to be right that the something is oneself. I will ignore this point from now on.

[6] 'Express' can be reduced to the weak sense of 'explicit' (see p. 30) if it's possible to be aware of oneself, somehow apprehended as oneself, in a 'non-thetic' way. I'm inclined to think it is possible.

[7] Perry 1979; see also Castañeda 1966.

as—*oneself*: *I, me, myself*. It's possible to be thinking about oneself when thinking about X's daughter, or the person who is leaving a trail of sugar, while having no idea that the person one is thinking about is oneself, whereas one obviously can't think of oneself *as oneself* and not realize that it is oneself that one is thinking of.

It's a further point that one can't possibly fail to be thinking about oneself when one thinks of something as oneself in the distinctively self-conscious way. One can't possibly fail to be thinking about oneself even if one is in fact making a mistake and taking something that is not oneself to be oneself. For even in this case one is still taking the thing in question to be *oneself*, and this key reference to oneself, this targeting of oneself in thought, can't possibly fail. Fully self-conscious thoughts can be erroneous in all sorts of ways, but they're utterly and absolutely 'immune to error through misidentification' of the subject, in Shoemaker's well-known phrase. (I return to this question in 3.16, and reject Evans's claim that one can fail to be thinking about oneself in circumstances in which all the appearances are that one is thinking about oneself in the distinctively self-conscious way.)

A possible source of confusion: the function of the prefix 'SELF' in 'SELF-experience' is different from the function of the prefix 'self' in 'self-conscious'. The function of 'SELF' in 'SELF-experience' is to identify a certain qualitative type of experience (2–3, 39–40), experience that has the specific cognitive-experiential character of being experience of the self, or a self, and involves at least SUBJECT, MENTAL, THING, SINGLE, and their compounds. The basic function of 'self' in 'self-conscious', by contrast, is the same as its function in 'self-sealing' (as applied to an aeroplane's fuel tank) or 'self-regulating' (as applied to a steam engine). To this extent being self-conscious no more immediately implies consciousness of a *self* than being self-sealing immediately implies sealing of a self. One might put this by saying that 'self-' as it occurs in 'self-conscious' is a merely reflexive term.

In fact, though, this is not accurate, because 'self-consciousness' stands here for 'full self-consciousness'. The 'self-' in 'self-consciousness' is essentially reflexive, but it isn't merely reflexive. What is in question is not just the barely reflexive, merely relational self-consciousness that must be accorded even to the tail-chasing kitten. It's full 'notional' self-consciousness, experience of oneself as oneself, experience that has a certain specific cognitive-experiential character in being experience of oneself as oneself (in involving the thought-element I or ONESELF or MYSELF). The difference between the cognitive-experiential character of SELF-experience and the cognitive-experiential character of self-consciousness remains, for it seems obvious that one can apprehend oneself as *oneself*, or apprehend something as *one's own*, without in any way apprehending oneself specifically as *a self*, i.e. without having SELF-experience: without having any picture of oneself as a special sort of something that is not a human being considered as a whole.

In 3.5 I'm going to question this seemingly obvious fact. I'm going to consider the case for saying that full self-consciousness does, after all, essentially involve possession of some sort of conception of oneself specifically as a self (i.e. SELF). But the point about the conceptual independence of the essentially (even if not merely) reflexive thought-element I or ONESELF or MYSELF from the non-reflexive thought-element SELF remains. The content of I or ONESELF or MYSELF can be completely specified simply by saying that its possession involves being able to think of oneself as oneself, whereas the content of SELF-experience (of SELF) has a much more substantive characterization. I (ONESELF, MYSELF) is the bare thought-element to possess which is to be self-conscious, to be able to think of oneself as oneself; SELF, by contrast, is the concept of a certain sort of concrete entity—a self—that is not a human being considered as a whole.

One may add that the function of the prefix 'self' in 'self-conscious' is not at all the same as the function of the noun 'self' in 'the self', for 'self-' in 'self-conscious' is essentially reflexive, whereas 'self' in 'the self' is akin to 'molecule', 'butterfly', 'chair', 'centre of gravity', 'individual substance'. One proof of the point is that we can know that one of these uses of 'self' is correct even if we don't know that the other is. We know that there are self-conscious beings even if we don't know that there are things that deserve to be called selves. Many philosophers think that one can't properly talk about the self at all; none of them think that one can't properly talk about self-consciousness or self-awareness.

I'm not too worried about the potential confusion of the 'self-' in 'self-conscious' with the 'self' of 'the self', because I'm not going to say much about 'the self' in Part 3. I am, however, going to talk quite a bit about SELF experience, and the typographical resemblances between 'SELF-experience', on the one hand, and 'self-consciousness' and the essentially reflexive 'ONESELF' and 'MYSELF', on the other, may still invite confusion. For this reason I'm going to put the name of the substantive thought-element SELF in boldface—SELF—for the rest of Part 3. I don't want to remove the orthographic connection altogether, for although the thought-element ONESELF or I or MYSELF that is integral to self-consciousness is not at all the same as the thought-element SELF, it may turn out that the latter lies curled up inside the former.

—One thing that has become truly clear in the last half-century is that your last claim, at least, can't be right. Self-conscious thought doesn't depend on any idea of a self or inner mental presence. It can be about one's non-mental being, e.g. one's height or hair colour, just as much as it can be about one's mental being, e.g. one's philosophical puzzlement. There's no difference at all between these two sorts of thoughts so far as their status as fully and distinctively self-conscious thoughts is concerned.[8] Self-conscious thoughts about one's mental being aren't somehow better or purer as examples of self-conscious thought. They have no special status whatever, contrary to what some have supposed. To be fully self-conscious is simply to be such that one can expressly think of or (mentally) grasp oneself as oneself, or take something to be one's own. It makes no difference whether one is focusing on one's mental being or one's non-mental being, so long as it is true that one is indeed thinking of oneself as oneself—

I agree, but this doesn't settle the matter of what is curled up in what. So I'll argue in 3.5.

—and your basic claim about self-consciousness is in fact wholly trivial. Of course self-consciousness involves being able to think of oneself as oneself.

---

[8] Compare G. Evans 1982: 216 ff.

Of course. Triviality—triviality on reflection—is the goal. The fact remains that this way of thinking expressly of oneself is a quite distinct way of thinking. The kitten can't do it, nor can the newborn baby, nor, probably, the 12-month-old. We can, for we're 'fully' self-conscious; this is a real, hard-fact difference about concrete entities and concrete goings on.

—But you haven't really explained why a cat or a dog—or chimpanzee, or elephant—can't be said to do this. The word 'express' is doing a lot of work, and it's vague.

True. For present purposes, I think the central idea can be expanded as follows. If a being is fully self-conscious, it must be capable of grasping itself as itself, when thinking, for example, of itself or one of its parts as having some property, in a way that is fully spelt out or express in something very like the way in which a being's grasp of itself as itself is express when it thinks of itself as itself in a fully comprehending, occurrent, conscious, linguistic form of thought, employing 'I' or 'me' or 'my' or 'mine' or some such term (*My hair's wet*, *I'm hopeful*, *I'm a great ape*, *That book is mine*). What do I mean by 'very like'? Fully self-conscious thought may not require linguistic ability as we know it, but it seems that it must involve thought that is language-like in some fundamental respect, for it requires a medium that permits a conscious, occurrent, express grasp or representation of something as simply *myself* (*oneself*), or *my own* (*one's own*), and this requires representation that is *essentially abstract*: this content (*myself*, *my own*) can't be represented in any way at all in some merely sensory or quasi-pictorial mode. It's abstract in such a way that linguistically articulated thought is our only clear model of what it might be like. Cats and dogs, we suppose, are incapable of such occurrent, express, conscious abstract thought, even if the case of chimpanzees is unclear. It may be said that all genuinely conceptual thought involves contents or apprehensions that are abstract in this sense; it's a familiar point that a capacity to entertain mental images of dogs, however rich, can never amount to possession of the concept or thought-element DOG. Even so, this may help in clarifying the character of full self-consciousness. Certainly the requirement that one be able to grasp oneself as oneself in express conscious thought—that one be able to hold the content I or MYSELF in the focus of attention—marks off full self-consciousness from any form of self-consciousness that is supposed to be attributable just on the basis of overt behaviour.

I think it's an illusion to suppose that one needs to say any more about self-consciousness, but the illusion can be powerful. Self-consciousness can seem very puzzling and mysterious. It's helpful, when this happens, to think of ordinary human beings, and of the fact that they all pass, at a very young age, from a state in which they definitely don't have full self-consciousness into a state in which they definitely do, and of the fact that this transition occurs before the age of 2 and is utterly routine. However remarkable self-consciousness may be or seem, it is a natural, automatic, and early part of human cognitive development.[9]

---

[9] In G. Strawson 1986: 151–4 I attempt to explain in general terms why it's unsurprising. For more detailed hypotheses, see e.g. Bermúdez 1998; Damasio 1999.

'It is noteworthy', according to Kant,

that a child who can already speak fairly fluently does not begin to talk in terms of 'I' until rather late (perhaps a year later); until then he speaks of himself in the third person (Karl wants to eat, to go for a walk, etc.). And when he starts to speak in terms of 'I' a light seems to dawn on him, as it were, and from this day on he never relapses into his former way of speaking. Before, he merely *felt* himself; now he *thinks* himself.   (1798:9)

Kant is wrong if he thinks that mastery of the first-person pronoun is necessary for full self-consciousness, for a being could be fully self-conscious and always refer to itself by a name like 'A' or 'B'. He's wrong to think that no children are fully self-conscious until they start to use 'I' in thought or speech. He's also wrong to think that children always start out by referring to themselves by name. Some use 'I' right from the start—before the age of 2—and never use their own name as a device of self-reference in normal contexts. Kant does, however, capture something important in his idea of the transition from feeling to thinking oneself (arguably, the distinction between cats, dogs, and young babies and ourselves), and one may certainly take competent use of 'I' in genuine thought (and speech) as a sufficient indicator of full self-consciousness.[10]

3.3 Does SELF-experience require self-consciousness?

So much for full self-consciousness.[11] The question now is whether it's presupposed by the capacity for SELF-experience (possession of SELF). Is it true that

(1) [capable of SELF-experience (possession of SELF) → self-conscious]?

–Surely not. Why couldn't a creature figure itself as a self (as SUBJECT, THING, SINGLE-AS-SUBJECT-AS-MENTAL, THING-AS-SUBJECT, etc.) without *ipso facto* figuring itself *figured as itself* as a self? What about Nemo, the character you introduced in your book *Freedom and Belief* and defined as 'being just like a human being in all respects in which it is possible to be like a human being without being [fully] self-conscious'? Why can't Nemo have SELF-experience without being self-conscious?[12]

Your first question may mislead, for we could allow, in line with your suggestion, that

(i) a creature might occurrently figure itself as a self in SELF-experience, at some particular time, without *ipso facto* figuring itself *figured as itself* as a self, at that time[13]

---

[10] Many of the children I've known have at first referred to themselves by their proper names, but three of my recent acquaintance—Joe Schiffer, Harry Strawson, and Ivo Strawson—have used 'I' correctly right from the start, and never 'Joe' or 'Harry' or 'Ivo', except in the following sorts of context: 'Daddy, tell me a story about Mommy and Daddy and Joe Schiffer.' It seems that children's choice of 'I' or their name is simply a matter of how they're spoken to.

[11] From now on I will routinely omit 'full' and 'express'.

[12] G. Strawson 1986: 20. Nemo's function was to be 'the official representative of our intuition that an unselfconscious agent cannot possibly be a free agent'.

[13] It's arguable that some of the 'first-rank' symptoms of schizophrenia show that one can apprehend oneself under SELF—think of oneself as a self—without thinking of that self as oneself.

and at the same time deny that

(ii) a creature can have the general capacity to figure itself as a self without being self-conscious, i.e. without the general capacity for fully self-conscious thought and hence without the capacity to figure itself *figured as itself* as a self.

This is one of the places where the phenomenological term 'SELF-experience' is likely to be misleading in so far as it inclines one to think primarily or only of occurrent goings-on (see 2.8). When we try to establish the content of the experience determining/structuring element SELF, we take our start from the phenomenology of actual occurrent SELF-experience, or so I claim, but what we're really after is simply the content of the element SELF. This too is a matter of phenomenology in the wide sense of the term explained on page 44. It is, in particular, a matter of cognitive phenomenology, which isn't concerned only with occurrent goings-on, but is also, and crucially, concerned with elements like SELF, elements that structure and are exemplarily revealed in the occurrent experiential phenomena they inform but can be considered independently of any particular phenomenological occurrences.

We are, then, concerned with the content of the experience-determining element SELF, and, now, with the conditions of possession of this experience-determining element. The question is whether one can possess SELF, as so far defined, and not be self-conscious, i.e. whether (1) is true. The answer may still be No—as you suggest—but that is the question.

In 3.6–3.19 I'm going to enquire into the conditions of self-consciousness. If (1) turns out to be true (if it turns out that self-consciousness is a necessary ground of the capacity for SELF-experience/possession of SELF), this enquiry will fit neatly into the general project of this book, even if it remains supplementary to the central argument. For if (1) is true, then all the grounds or conditions of self-consciousness are also and *ipso facto* grounds or conditions of SELF-experience. I've raised a doubt about (1), in fact, but I'm going to pursue the enquiry into the conditions of self-consciousness in any case.

There's a natural stronger definition of SELF-experience according to which (1) is certainly true. According to this definition, SELF-experience, true SELF-experience, is not merely experience of oneself as a self; it is also, essentially, experience of oneself *expressly grasped as oneself* as a self. If SELF-experience is understood in this way, one must obviously be self-conscious to have it, and enquiry into the conditions of self-consciousness is certainly a necessary part of a full account of the phenomenon of SELF-experience.

Independently of this definitional proposal, it does seem pretty *unlikely* that a creature might genuinely figure or experience itself as a self or an inner locus of consciousness and yet have no sense that the self that it experienced itself as being was itself. I don't, however, think that this can actually be ruled out, on my terms, so (1) must retain its status as an assumption made temporarily for the purposes of the argument of Part 3.

Can I assume that (1) is true although I reject

(3) [self → self-conscious]?

Yes. I favour a liberal use of 'self' given which you don't have to be self-conscious to be a self (I think that all subjects of experience are selves, and hence that there is a self wherever there is experience), which makes (3) false. But this doesn't involve me in any inconsistency with (1), for (1) can be true even if (3) is false, just so long as

(5) [self → possession of SELF]

is also false—just so long as one doesn't have to be able to have SELF-experience in order to be a self. And this is indeed what I think. (Any view that rejects (3) is likely to reject (5).) I can see why some might favour (3), but one of the consequences of holding it is that a child *becomes* a self (in the Kantian manner) when it becomes self-conscious, and up until that point is not a self at all. That seems implausible to me; or rather—and much as I admire Fichte—it's not how I think it best to use the word 'self'.

3.4 Does self-consciousness require SELF-experience?

I'm preparing to consider the question of the grounds of self-consciousness in a completely general fashion (and thereby—if (1) is true—the grounds of SELF-experience); but before I begin, I want to focus on a particular part of that question. I want to consider the converse of (1)

(2) [self-conscious → possession of SELF].

Is (2) true? Can one be self-conscious without being disposed to have SELF-experience, i.e. without possessing SELF? Or is being self-conscious in fact sufficient for possessing SELF? One reason for considering this question is that it promises to provide part of a more substantive account of the character of self-consciousness of the sort that may have been felt to be lacking in 3.2.

—Stop. (2) is *obviously* false. Being self-conscious doesn't entail possession of the highly complex notion SELF, even in its minimal or core form. To be (fully) self-conscious is simply to be able to think of oneself expressly as oneself, and it's hopelessly implausible to claim that one has to think of oneself as a thing that is a self (deploy the thought-element SELF) in order to do this.

This sounds right, but I'm going to try to make a case for (2). I'll argue that if you're self-conscious, then you must be capable of figuring yourself not only as SUBJECT, but also as SINGLE-as-SUBJECT, and as SINGLE-as-MENTAL, and so on.

This is the first stage of the Building Argument promised on page 63. If it succeeds, then, given (1), a full account of the conditions of self-consciousness is also a full account of the conditions of possession of the core notion of SELF, and we have a major unification of topics and terms (theoretical happiness). For this stage of the Building Argument culminates in

(9) [self-conscious → (possession of) SUBJECT, SINGLE, MENTAL, SINGLE-as-MENTAL, SINGLE-as-SUBJECT-as-MENTAL, etc.]

This then couples with (1) to give

(10) [SELF-experience → (possession of) SUBJECT, SINGLE, MENTAL, SINGLE-as-MENTAL, SINGLE-as-SUBJECT-as-MENTAL, etc.]

and if all goes well, (10), reached here simply by considering the notion—and phenomenology—of self-consciousness, turns out to be identical to the conclusion of the Whittling Argument (62).[14] This is neat, because on the face of it the Whittling Argument proceeds entirely independently of the Building Argument, starting from the elements of ordinary human SELF-experience and trying to whittle them down as far as possible, in pursuit of the minimal case of SELF-experience, without any reference to the notion of full self-consciousness.

If the Building Argument comes off, the right-hand side of (10) contains all the elements of the thought-element SELF that survive the Whittling Argument. Tunnelers start from two sides of a mountain and meet in the middle, their tunnels perfectly aligned. I'm going to start on the Building Argument here, but delay any completion until the Whittling Argument is under way in Part 4. The Building Argument won't formally complement the Whittling Argument if (1) can't be sufficiently defended, but it's interesting in its own right.

3.5 The Building Argument begun: 'single just qua mental'

What would one have to do to show that self-consciousness is sufficient for possessing SELF, and hence for SELF-experience? I'll consider the cognitive phenomenology of self-consciousness, and ask whether it's available to any creature that does not possess SELF. I'll start from the bare fact of self-consciousness, the ability to be fully expressly aware of oneself as oneself. This will be my 'sole text', as Kant might say.

Does self-consciousness entail possession of some grasp or sense of oneself as being, specifically, a mental presence, a mental someone or something? Many philosophers think this highly implausible, for reasons given on page 104, and I don't want to claim that self-consciousness necessarily involves SELF-experience of the ordinary rich human sort described in Part 2—experience of oneself as a (*personalitied*) *agent subject* that is a *persisting single mental thing distinct* from the whole human being. The question is whether it entails anything less that still counts as SELF-experience.

The final answer must wait until the Whittling Argument delivers an account of the minimal case of SELF-experience in Part 4 (the more undemanding the minimal account, the better the chance of a Yes answer), but one can begin by asking the following more specific question:

If one is a fully self-conscious being, and is therefore capable of apprehending oneself expressly as oneself, must one also have some sort of experience/conception of oneself as something that is in some way *single just qua mental* (SINGLE-as-MENTAL)? Must one

---

[14] And (9) turns out to be a version of (2).

have some sort of sense of oneself as something that is possessed of singleness when apprehending oneself specifically or solely in one's mental aspect? Must one have some such sense of oneself even if one also has, and believes oneself to have, singleness considered in some non-mental (or overall both-mental-and-non-mental) aspect?

If the answer to this question is Yes, at least two of the elements of ordinary human SELF-experience described in Part 2, MENTAL and SINGLE, together with their crucial compound SINGLE-AS-MENTAL, are entailed by self-consciousness, and I'll argue that SUBJECT is also entailed. This means that if the Whittling Argument runs to plan, and delivers the verdict that SUBJECT, THING, MENTAL, SINGLE, and their associated compounds are minimally sufficient for SELF-experience, then the Building Argument will only have to add THING (plus associated compounds) to the other three in order to confirm that the Whittling Argument has whittled away everything that can be whittled away.

So let me now try to persuade you that any being that is (fully) self-conscious must have some sense / experience / conception of itself as single just qua mental (SINGLE-AS-MENTAL). I think the argument is useful for exercising thought about self-consciousness, whether or not it is sound. I'll regularly use 'single just qua mental' in this section, rather than 'SINGLE-AS-MENTAL', but I take them to be equivalent in meaning. The 'just qua' is useful because it is more explicit in its force.[15]

—I'd like to stop you before you start. It's true that self-conscious beings like adult human beings possess the fully-fledged concept MENTAL, and the correlative fully-fledged concept NON-MENTAL, and in their case it's easy to see that the phrase 'single just qua mental' can be a correct description of how they sometimes think of themselves, even if (even though) they would never put things this way. Imagine, though, a self-conscious creature C1 that has a conscious mental life, and is therefore familiar with—vividly and directly acquainted with—mental phenomena, but has no conception of the non-mental at all, and so no conception of the-mental-as-contrasted-with-the-non-mental. The claim that C1 thinks of itself as single just qua mental can't then be a literally correct description of the 'notional' content of any thought that it can have, because 'qua' creates an 'intensional' context that requires that one possess the concept MENTAL if one is to be able to think of anything as single just qua mental, and

[P] possession of the concept MENTAL requires possession of the concept NON-MENTAL.

So the claim that C1 thinks of itself as single just qua mental can really only be the claim that it thinks of itself as single and is in fact concerned only with its mental aspects when it does so, although it does not expressly conceptualize them as mental. But this isn't enough for your purposes. So if C1 is possible, self-consciousness doesn't require possession of any conception of oneself as single just qua mental. The Building Argument has failed already.

Some will say that C1 isn't really possible. To be self-conscious at all, they say, one must have experience of objects (real or imagined) of a sort that entails possession of the concept NON-MENTAL. Kant follows many in the German eighteenth-century tradition in arguing for a view of this sort, and many have followed him since, for a variety of

---

[15] This section revises an inadequate discussion of the same question in G. Strawson 1986 (pp. 154–61), in which I use 'single just qua mental'. I'm resigned to the fact that confusions about the notion of mental content, introduced into philosophical discussion of the mental by excessive 'externalism', will prevent some from understanding what I'm saying.

reasons. This response isn't open to me, though, because I'm going to reject all such arguments—some of them very sophisticated—in 3.6–3.15.

A second response is to allow that C1 is possible, while insisting that 'qua' needn't be read as creating an intensional context in a way that opens up this objection. On this view, one thinks of oneself as single just qua mental just so long as one apprehends oneself as single and does so when one is apprehending oneself specifically or solely in one's mental aspect. One can be truly said to figure oneself as mental (mentally propertied) in this case even if it is allowed that [P] is true, and inferred that one does not possess the fully-fledged concept MENTAL (p. 68).

A third reply is to deny [P]. I'll consider this sort of move in the next section. For the moment I'm going to take it that my question remains good: Does self-consciousness entail having some sense of oneself as single just qua mental? The question is not whether one must have some sense or conception of oneself as a *diachronically* single or *persisting* mental thing, just in so far as one is self-conscious; I think the answer to this question is No (4.7). The question is whether one must possess some conception of oneself as something that is single just qua mental synchronically speaking—single just qua mental in the lived present of experience.

—Again, surely not. One can be self-conscious and think of oneself as single in so far as one is a human being—a human being in whom many mental things go on—without in any way conceiving of oneself as somehow single just qua mental.

Suppose one is in the presence of other people, or talking on the telephone, and says 'I admire Otis Rush', or 'I've got three recordings of *The Isle of the Dead*'. One is in such cases highly unlikely to be engaged in any sort of express or thetic figuration of oneself as a *thing of a certain kind*. Our self-conscious thought and speech are standardly completely blank in this respect. Suppose though that one is, unusually, engaged in some sort of express figuration of oneself as a thing of a certain kind, in the situation in question. It may then be that one is thinking of oneself at least partly, and perhaps even primarily, through one's awareness of others' awareness of one as a whole human being, the indissolubly mental-and-non-mental being that one is and is naturally taken by others to be. And some may now want to say that this is the 'default' way of thinking of oneself—simply as a whole human being—and that there is not normally any apprehension of oneself as something that is in some way single just qua mental, even when one is engaged in some sort of express or thetic figuration of oneself as a thing of a certain kind.

I'm not at all sure that this is the default way of thinking of oneself, for reasons given in 2.2–2.3. It seems to be a tribal myth (the tribe of analytic philosophers, steeped in the philosophical logic of 'I', anxious to prove their EEE worldliness and projecting their conclusions falsely on to the everyday phenomenology of the non-philosophical mind). But suppose it is no myth. Suppose one is more likely to think of oneself as single just qua mental, when thinking of oneself as a thing of a certain kind, when one is alone and thinking. What then?

—To concede this is to concede that a self-conscious being need never actually have any express sense of itself as something that is single just qua mental. There may be self-conscious beings who have no tendency to think consciously and silently and who spend their whole lives in public interaction. We can imagine a particular self-conscious creature C2 that is never expressly concerned with its own mental features when engaged in self-conscious thought or speech, but only with its non-mental features. Whenever it thinks consciously of itself, in a way that involves some sort of apprehension of what sort of thing it is, it thinks of itself only in the inclusive way in which we often think of ourselves, especially when we're engaged in communication with others. That is, it thinks of itself only as the single indissolubly both-mental-and-non-mental being that it is, and never actually expressly figures itself as something that is in some sense single just qua mental, single specifically in respect of its mental being. Such a creature is surely possible.

True, but too quick, for the question is not whether one must at the time of occurrent self-conscious thought have some sort of conscious apprehension or experience of oneself as something that is in some sense single just qua mental. It's whether self-consciousness requires possession of some conception or figuration of oneself as something that is single just qua mental. It asks whether this must be a way in which one *can* think of oneself if one is self-conscious.[16] This is the key question at this stage, and the question to which—or so I propose—the answer is Yes. A No answer requires a creature that is fully self-conscious and lacks not only the tendency but even the ability to think of itself as something that is in some sense single just qua mental.[17]

—Well, why not? Why couldn't there be a self-conscious creature C3 that is like C2 in that it is only ever occupied with its own non-mental features, when engaged in self-conscious thought or speech, and is actually *incapable* of being occupied with anything other than its non-mental features in such circumstances?

C3's inability might perhaps be allowed to be the result of some specific block placed on the routes its thoughts can take (perhaps by post-hypnotic command), but I don't think it could stem from an all-out lack of the thought-elemental resources required for thought about its mental features. If you redefine C3 as lacking these resources I think C3 is impossible: one can't be fully self-conscious and incapable of being occupied with any of one's mental features because one lacks the conceptual-experiential resources to do so. Certainly thoughts about one's non-mental features, like 'I've got dark hair', are just as much fully self-conscious thoughts as thoughts wholly expressly about mental features, like 'I'm sad' or 'I don't really understand self-consciousness'. It seems, though, that there's an asymmetry between the two cases, and that while a self-conscious creature can be aware of certain of its mental features as its own without having any awareness

---

[16] It may also be a way in which one is inevitably disposed to think of oneself in certain circumstances.

[17] 'Ability' is ambiguous. Human beings can be said to have the ability to swim either because they can now swim or because they can learn to swim. The corresponding ambiguity here is between (a) having the ability, as one now is, and without acquiring any further skills, to think of oneself as something that is in some sense single just qua mental, and (b) having the ability, given one's overall set-up, to acquire the ability to think of oneself as so single. It is only (a) that is in question.

of having any non-mental features, and even, perhaps, without being capable of any such awareness,[18] the converse is not true. Rather,

[S1] Any being capable of fully self-conscious self-ascription of any feature must be capable of—must have mental resources sufficient for—self-conscious self-ascription of *mental* features: it must have some sort of grasp or awareness of itself as mentally aspected.

It may perhaps be incapable of fully self-conscious self-ascriptions of mental features because a block has been imposed on the possible paths of its thoughts by post-hypnotic command, but it must nevertheless have the general mental resources to engage in self-conscious self-ascription of mental features if it is capable of fully (expressly) self-conscious thought at all.

Furthermore, or so I propose,

[S2] Any fully self-conscious being must not only have some grasp of itself as mentally aspected but must also have some grasp of itself as single just qua mental.

[S2] is the main target conclusion of this section, and a step in the Building Argument for the claim that any fully self-conscious being must have SELF-experience, i.e. (2) [self-conscious → SELF-experience]. Kant (along with many Phenomenologists) may find my progress slow and clumsy. When one is trying to persuade people who disagree with one, one may appear to others to be labouring the obvious.

Consider a self-conscious being, B. It expressly apprehends a part of its body—or an apple—as its own in the distinctively fully self-conscious way. It is, perhaps, only ever concerned with such outer, non-mental things. It must nevertheless—this is [S1]—have access to a conception of itself as mentally aspected, even if it also has a fundamental sense or conception of itself as single qua something that is non-mental or indissolubly both-mental-and-non-mental in nature. This may sound a bit rich to externalist, 'ecological', EEE ears. But what is it, exactly, for B genuinely and fully and expressly to apprehend its hand *as its own*, in the way distinctive of full or express self-consciousness (and so not merely in the way in which a dog may be said to apprehend its paw as its own when it withdraws it from the path of an oncoming object)? It seems that it is, necessarily, for it to apprehend its hand as the hand of the thing that is doing the apprehending. The express content of B's occurrent, conscious self-apprehension may be simply 'My hand hurts', and may be entirely unreflective. The question, though, is 'What is necessarily given in the occurrence of I or MY or any similarly functioning thought-element in express self-conscious thought?'. And the idea is that B's grasp of itself as the thing that is doing the apprehending may be part of what we have to talk about when we try to say what such a thought of something as one's own involves or presupposes.[19]

—Chimpanzees who have red dots painted on their faces without their knowledge raise their hands to the dot when they see themselves in the mirror. We judge that they're self-conscious on

---

[18] I argue for this second claim in 3.12–3.14. Cassam (1997) offers an extended argument against one version of it.

[19] 'Couldn't a self-conscious being lack any conception of apprehending?' It may lack any fully-fledged concept of mental apprehension, but it can't—I propose—lack the basic experience-structuring/determining element.

this basis; we take it that there's a clear and fundamental sense in which they are indeed grasping themselves as themselves. But it's hugely implausible to credit them with a capacity for thoughts about themselves as the things that are grasping what they're grasping.

I agree that it seems implausible to credit chimpanzees with such complicated thoughts, but that's because I take it that they're not fully or expressly self-conscious in the sense defined in 3.2. Self-consciousness of this kind requires, precisely, that one be able to grasp oneself as oneself in express conscious thought—able, for example, to hold the content I or MYSELF in the focus of attention. (Simply put, it requires that one be able to think of oneself as oneself in the way human beings can and do.) If chimpanzees can do this, then it will be right, after all, to attribute such thoughts to them. It is in any case this full self-consciousness, so characteristic of human beings, that is at issue when the question of whether self-consciousness entails SELF-experience is raised.

One might say this: involved, in *some* sense, in any expressly self-conscious self-attribution of a non-mental feature is some sort of apprehension of oneself, apprehended *as* oneself in the distinctively self-conscious way, as the thing that is doing the attributing, and, hence, necessarily, some apprehension of oneself as something that is mentally aspected or propertied—however 'non-thetic' this apprehension is, however far from the focus of attention. (I imagine someone thinking that this is obviously false, and then becoming much less sure.) If B really has a thought like 'My hand is green', or 'I'm in Washington Square', then it seems that the MY or I thought-element must be understood by us to be apprehended by it as in some way involving reference to itself considered as the thinker or haver of the thought, and hence as mentally *aspected*, at least; whether or not it is also understood by it as involving reference to itself considered as the non-mental or indissolubly mental-and-non-mental thing that it also is and doubtless takes itself to be. This claim is stronger than [S1] as it stands, for [S1] states only that one must have access to, be capable of, such an apprehension of oneself as mentally aspected or propertied in order to be truly said to have attributed a feature to oneself in the distinctively self-conscious way. But I leave it for consideration.

What about [S2], the stronger claim that any fully self-conscious being must have some sense/experience/conception of itself as single just qua mental? Perhaps the argument for [S1] already constitutes a sufficient argument for [S2]. It looks as if it's not merely grasp of oneself as mentally aspected or propertied that is in question. What also appears to be necessarily involved in possession of the ability to ascribe features to oneself in a fully and expressly self-conscious manner is—as already remarked—possession of some grasp of oneself as the thinker or apprehender, the mental subject (SUBJECT), and the little word 'the' seems to entail, all by itself, that possession of the ability to ascribe properties to oneself in a fully self-conscious manner must also necessarily involve possession of some grasp of oneself as something that is somehow *single* just qua mental (even if also single in some other respect), and indeed as single qua subject (SINGLE-as-SUBJECT). Many of the points made in 2.19 apply here.

—Not so fast. B's naturally primary conception of itself as a single thing may be a conception of itself simply as non-mentally single, or single qua something indissolubly mental-and-non-mental.

When B thinks of itself as *the* (single) thinker or apprehender or subject of experience, it certainly needn't be thinking of itself solely and specifically as mentally aspected, and so thinking of itself as single just qua mental. It may, precisely, be thinking of itself as single qua non-mental, e.g. single as a body, or at least as single qua indissolubly mental-and-non-mental, single as the *subject of experience* grasped as a mental-and-non-mental whole.

But the following also seems true. When one apprehends oneself as *the* thinker, or apprehender, or subject of experience, and hence apprehends oneself as single, one's apprehension or experience of one's singleness is (so it is argued in 2.19) already sufficiently grounded for one just in the way one experiences oneself as subject of experience (SINGLE-AS-SUBJECT) rather than as, say, a body. More specifically: it is already sufficiently grounded for one just in the way one experiences oneself as subject-considered-just-in-respect-of its-mental-being (SINGLE-AS-SUBJECT-AS-MENTAL). This doesn't essentially involve any sense of or belief in non-mental singularity, although it may well be co-occurrent with and powerfully complemented or underwritten by some such sense or belief.[20] And if one really attributes some feature to oneself grasped as oneself in the distinctively self-conscious way, then one can't fail to have some sort of grasp of oneself as *a* (*the*) thinker, attributer, presenter, etc., that is apprehending something as its own; however unreflective one is. (The content of thought—cognitive experience in general—is rich.) And to have some such apprehension of oneself is necessarily to apprehend oneself not only as singular (SINGLE), and as singular considered specifically as subject (SINGLE-AS-SUBJECT), but also—here is the crucial claim [S2], which I take to be underpinned by the discussion of experience of mental singleness in 2.19 and 2.20—as singular as subject apprehended just in respect of one's mental being (SINGLE-AS-SUBJECT-AS-MENTAL), and hence as singular specifically in respect of one's mental being (SINGLE-AS-MENTAL).

—This is mere assertion, and repetition, not argument.

'I'm falling.' 'I'm here.' 'I'm green.' Who is? I. Who is this I? It is, no doubt, this embodied, conscious, mental-and-non-mental living human being. But it is also *I who am thinking that* I am falling, or here, or green. This is a thought that must be available to one in some form, whether or not it is somehow contained in the simpler thoughts, because it is part of what we have to talk about when we try to say in full what such thoughts involve. It must be available to one in some form that involves not only some figuration of oneself as single as subject, but also (I suggest) an apprehension of oneself as single as subject that is sufficiently founded specifically in one's experience of one's mental being and activity as subject. However body-aware one is, some such grasp of oneself as single as subject in the narrow sense of 'subject', i.e. as single as subject specifically mentally considered, single just qua mental, seems to be built in to full or express self-consciousness.

---

[20] See the cases discussed in 2.19. The fact that ordinary human experience of mental singleness is profoundly (and doubtless necessarily) grounded in experience of non-mental singleness is irrelevant.

Well, I feel sure this is true, but that is not to say that I have proved it. Let me offer one more consideration.

Suppose we grant, backed up by the arguments of 2.18–2.20, that to be fully self-conscious, one must grasp oneself as single in some way, and as subject, and as single as subject. It follows that if one is self-conscious and has no conception at all of oneself as having *non*-mental properties, then one automatically has some grasp of oneself as single as mental, as single just qua mental.[21] A fully self-conscious being may, however, have an intensely vivid conception of itself as non-mentally propertied, and this appears to open up the possibility that one's grasp of oneself as single as subject may be nothing but a grasp of oneself as single as subject considered as a mental-and-non-mental whole, and—again—may not involve any sort of conception of oneself as single just qua mental.[22] Against this, however, it's arguable that all beings that have fully self-conscious experience of having non-mental properties (experience of having a body, say) must, simply by reason of their self-consciousness, be able to understand and entertain the Cartesian doubt about the existence of their non-mental being without automatically prejudicing their (self-consciousness-entailed) sense of their existence and singleness as subjects—assuming of course that they possess the other thought-elements needed for the articulation of the Cartesian doubt.[23] On this view, it's an essential feature of full self-consciousness that it makes the Cartesian doubt possible in any creature that has some sense of itself as having non-mental being and has the requisite concepts;[24] and this, perhaps, sufficiently illustrates the sense in which any grasp that one has of oneself as single, and in particular as single as subject, must already inform one's sense of oneself as a mental phenomenon, whether or not one also has some other—doubtless deeply natural—way of thinking of oneself as single non-mentally considered. When one apprehends oneself (however 'non-thetically') as the apprehender or subject of experience, and in so doing apprehends oneself as single ('the'), and so apprehends oneself as single as subject, one's sense of singularity is sufficiently grounded for one just in the way one experiences oneself mentally, whether or not one has any explicit apprehension of this fact. To entertain the Cartesian doubt ('I might not have a body') is simply to enter into an express appreciation of this fact. This is something one may never do, but the ability to entertain the Cartesian doubt, given that one has experience of having non-mental being at all, and has the requisite concepts, is essential to full self-consciousness.

More assertion, you may say, but Kant at least agrees. He states that 'the proposition *I am simple* [*single*] must be regarded as a direct expression of apperception', and one

---

[21] In a sense of 'grasping oneself as mental' that allows for the possibility that one can lack the full-on general concept NON-MENTAL and also, to that extent, its correlative the full-on general concept MENTAL (68).

[22] It can't be nothing more than a conception of oneself as single just qua non-mental, because it isn't just a conception of oneself as single, but a conception of oneself as single as subject.

[23] Compare Descartes's *Principles*, 1.10: 'when I said that the proposition *I am thinking, therefore I exist* is the first and most certain of all, I did not in saying that deny that one must first know what thought, existence, and certainty are … and so forth' (1644: 1.196). I take it that 2-year-olds don't possess all the required thought-elements in spite of being fully self-conscious.

[24] For a different but interestingly related claim, see P. F. Strawson 1966: 164–5.

of the things he means by apperception here, I take it, is consciousness of oneself specifically as a mental phenomenon.[25] So the conclusion that self-consciousness necessarily involves a sense of oneself as single just qua mental is straightforward on his terms. He is likely to feel that I make heavy weather of the point, but he has a easier time because he pays almost no attention to embodiment and experience of embodiment.

One reason philosophers might have for resisting this conclusion might be their conviction that there is no solid sense in which it is *true* that one is in fact something single just qua mental—so that to grant that self-consciousness necessarily involves some such sense of oneself as single just qua mental is to grant that it involves, and indeed necessarily involves, an illusion (roughly, the illusion of the self). But this is not to the present—phenomenological—point. I don't think that the idea or sense of oneself as single just as mental does involve an illusion, in fact (even if somatosensory experience or possession of some sort of body image is necessary for experience of oneself as single just qua mental, it doesn't follow that the latter experience involves any sort of illusion). I think, and will eventually argue, that it is correct. But even if it does involve an illusion, that doesn't constitute any sort of argument against the claim that self-conscious beings are bound to think of themselves in this way, as Kant would enthusiastically agree.

The claim, in sum, is that self-consciousness has, essentially, a certain phenomenology, in the large sense of cognitive phenomenology described in 2.8, and that it entails possession of some sense or conception of oneself as single as subject (SINGLE-AS-SUBJECT), and as single as subject specifically mentally considered (SINGLE-AS-SUBJECT-AS-MENTAL), and, hence, as single just qua mental (SINGLE-AS-MENTAL). If this is true—the argument is not as tight as I would wish—then I can complete the Building Argument if I can show that self-consciousness essentially involves some sort of conception of oneself as a thing (THING) and then derive the associated compound elements (THING-AS-MENTAL, etc.). Now, however, I'm going to leave the framework of the Building Argument until 4.9, and consider the conditions of self-consciousness in a more general fashion.

This is another point at which readers can turn to Part 4, for the remainder of Part 3 is a fairly complicated set of branchlines off the main track of the argument.

3.6 The grounds of self-consciousness: The core conditions?

What are the grounds of self-consciousness? Answers may be a priori, a posteriori, or both (a posteriori answers are likely to focus on the human case or, more generally, on the case of self-conscious creatures that are the product of evolution by natural selection in a non-magical universe). The two approaches are perfectly compatible. They can

---

[25] A355, B68; see p. 50.

have fruitful exchanges and mount joint operations. Aiming for comprehensiveness, one might start out with highly general requirements of the sort that require a priori philosophical reflection, turn next to general theory of evolution to consider the general conditions of the phylogenesis of the capacity for self-consciousness in naturally evolved species, draw further on evolutionary theory to consider the phylogenesis of this capacity in a given particular species (human beings, say), consult developmental psychology on the question of the ontogenesis of self-consciousness in individual members of the species, and add an account of the neurophysiological bases of their self-consciousness, referring, perhaps, and among other things, to structures of the brain devoted to the monitoring of inputs from the visceral, vestibular, musculoskeletal, and other proprioceptive systems of the body.[26]

Some find it hard to move between a posteriori and a priori approaches; specialization on one side may influence one's thought in such a way that the other seems beside the point. Some think that only the a priori approach can uncover the deep structure of the phenomenon; others, that a posteriori approaches render philosophical speculations about the minimally sufficient conditions of self-consciousness strained and unrealistic. It would, however, be a serious mistake to think that a priori philosophical investigation of the grounds of self-consciousness, of the sort that I hope to engage in here, is in some way less concerned with the nature and structure of reality than empirical, a posteriori investigation. There's no need for confrontation.

What, then, are the grounds of self-consciousness? What are the core conditions? What is necessarily implicated in the ability to think of oneself in the distinctively self-conscious way? What is it to be an actively self-conscious being—one that actually has thoughts like 'I'm five feet tall' or 'I'm sad'? Answering this question may be beyond my powers, but I'll begin by repeating the definition of self-consciousness in one of its versions:

(i) one must possess the reflexive thought-element I or equivalently MYSELF or equivalently ONESELF.

To be self-conscious just is to possess the thought-element I or MYSELF or ONESELF (this doesn't—page 106—require that one have the use of any word like 'I' or 'myself' rather than a proper name) . It's to be able to think of oneself specifically and just *as oneself*, rather than as the person trailing sugar in the shop, or the man with the blue arm seen in the mirror (102). It's to be capable of this entirely distinctive way of thinking about oneself. And if one is actively self-conscious,

(ii) one must deploy the reflexive thought-element I or MYSELF.

To be actively self-conscious just is to deploy this thought-element. The rule for attribution of thought-element deployment parallels the rule for thought-element possession given on page 44: if we judge that we can't give an adequate account of the

---

[26] See e.g. Damasio 1999. 'Ecological' approaches are also likely to be valuable in this connection; see e.g. J. Gibson 1979; E. Gibson 1993; Noë 2005.

overall nature or content of B's experience without making use of κ, then we may judge that B deploys κ.[27]

What else must be true? It seems natural to think that possession of MYSELF requires possession of some conception of that which is not-myself or other than myself—that MYSELF and NOT-MYSELF are essentially correlative in such a way that one can't have either without the other, rather as UP and NOT-UP are essentially correlative.[28] If so,

(iii) one must possess the thought-element NOT-MYSELF.

One may not believe that there *is* anything other than oneself and one's states, but—the idea is—one must have some grasp of the distinction between what is oneself and what is not oneself, for this is constitutive of possession of the thought-element I or MYSELF, and hence of the ability to think 'I am F'.[29]

A less committal claim is available, however, according to which all that follows from the fact that one possesses the thought-element MYSELF is that

(iv) one must be able to come to possess and deploy the thought-element NOT-MYSELF.

Is it also true that

(v) one must deploy the thought-element NOT-MYSELF

if one is actively self-conscious, and if (iii) is true? It may seem that if one deploys MYSELF at all, one makes the fundamental cut between oneself and not-oneself in thought, and must therefore be deploying NOT-MYSELF in some manner. It is, however, hard to be sure that this is the best thing to say. Must a woman who spends eternity trudging uphill, aware that she is doing so, ever actively deploy the thought-element DOWNHILL, or at least NOT-UPHILL? If one thinks 'I'm sad', it's not obvious that one must be grasping anything as not-oneself, however non-thetically (what about God before the creation?). It begins to seem that questions about what thought-elements must actually be deployed in active self-consciousness raise difficulties that are over and above the difficulties inherent in questions about what thought-elements one must possess in order to be self-conscious at all. (This, though, may be merely a reflection of the felt insubstantiality of passing thought, and the vagueness of words like 'deploy'.)

It may be said that there are certain specific thoughts that one must actually have had, if one is to be self-conscious at all, and that they include thoughts involving the idea that something is not-oneself, so that (v) is demonstrably true. I'll consider a number of claims of this form. I'll argue that none are correct, even if (v) is true, and that if (v) is true, then it is true only in a weaker sense than many would wish. In particular,

---

[27] Does the capacity to have 'you' thoughts, 'she' thoughts, and so on, presuppose self-consciousness? Is having such thoughts a form of active self-consciousness even if it never involves any express thought of oneself (any I-thought)? If it is, then it will involve deployment of the thought-element I in a manner sufficient for full self-consciousness.

[28] See e.g. Fichte 1796–9: 123–4; Beiser 2002: 329. UP and DOWN are a more vivid pair, but they're only contraries, not strict contradictories, and one could perhaps possess UP without DOWN.

[29] Bermúdez (1998) discusses the issue of the correlativity of MYSELF and NOT-MYSELF with specific reference to somatic proprioception (ch. 6), points of view (chs. 7–8), and other minds (ch. 9).

I'll argue that (iii) and (v) don't entail that one must have the thought that there are any *things* or *objects* other than oneself. At the limit, it seems, a self-conscious being's experiences may be the only things that fall within the ambit of its disposition to apply the thought-element NOT-MYSELF: it may naturally take its experiences as distinct from itself, the subject of experience (see e.g. 3.12–3.14 below).

What next? I'm going to take it to have been sufficiently established in the last section that a grasp of oneself specifically as a subject of experience is an essential part of the overall grasp of oneself distinctive of full self-consciousness, even if one only ever thinks of oneself as a mental-and-non-mental whole when one grasps oneself as a subject of experience, and so never thinks of oneself as subject just qua mental, and even if one only ever thinks expressly about one's non-mental properties. One must at least be able to think of oneself in this way:

(vi) one must possess the thought-element SUBJECT OF EXPERIENCE.

(vi) invites

(vii) one must in some manner possess (and deploy?) a conception of what is not a subject of experience,

just as (iii) invited (v); but the same doubts arise in the latter case as in the former.

Note that there's a repeating sequence that runs from (a) 'B must possess resources sufficient for it to come to be able to acquire thought-element or conception κ' to (b) 'B must possess κ' to (c) 'B must deploy κ'. This is matched by a similar sequence for NOT-κ, and the question of whether one can weaken a type-(c) claim to a type-(b) claim or a type-(b) claim to a type-(a) claim can always be raised.

It's a small step from (vi) to

(viii) one must have some conception of experience,

and so to

(ix) one must in some manner possess a conception of what is not experience,

both of which are at least candidates for the core, and both of which, being type-(b) theses, invite the question whether they should be weakened to their corresponding type-(a) theses or strengthened to their corresponding type-(c) theses. I won't set all of these out, but it's worth noting that the subject—oneself conceived as subject—may be able to suffice for one as an example (should one need one) of something which is not experience, just as one's experiences may be able to suffice for one as an example of that which is not self—not a subject of experience.

What does all this amount to? Pleasingly little, I think. In effect, the core comes down to the claim that if one is self-conscious,

[1] one must possess the thought-element I or MYSELF or ONESELF,
[2] one must possess the thought-element SUBJECT OF EXPERIENCE,

and

[3] one must have some conception of experience—

if only in possessing some grasp of more particular experiential modalities, like thinking, hearing, and so on. I propose to concertina whatever truths are expressed by (i)–(ix) into [1]–[3] for ease of reference.

—You call this the core, but it's already too rich. Why is possession of a conception of experience included? Why can't one simply have experience without being able to think of it—grasp it—as experience? If a dog can be like this, why should self-consciousness make it impossible?

[1] has a guaranteed place because it merely repeats the definition of self-consciousness. [3] is asserted only in so far as, only in whatever sense in which,[30] it follows from [2]. Many accept [2] without question; but I think it needs argument, when confronted with (say) the objection that a creature could be fully self-conscious, capable of thinking thoughts like *I'm among trees*, and at the same time quite profoundly unreflective. I tried to provide some argument for [2] in 3.5, but if it fails, so be it. If someone can diminish the core, so much the better. My aim is to argue that many have made claims about the conditions of self-consciousness that are too strong, and I can do this starting from this core, even if it is itself too strong.

3.7 The Others Thesis

Many think that self-consciousness—possession of the thought-element MYSELF— doesn't just require (iii) the thought-element NOT-MYSELF and (vi) the thought-element SUBJECT OF EXPERIENCE (or SUBJECT OF EXPERIENCEHOOD); it also requires a fusion of the two—possession of some conception of that which is both not-myself and a subject of experience. If one is self-conscious, on this view,

[4] one must possess some conception of other subjects of experience (Conception of Others Thesis)

This is an old idea, in various guises,[31] and the intuition behind it is clear: to think of oneself as a subject, one must somehow figure oneself as one subject among other actual or possible subjects: the idea of other subjects of experience furnishes a necessary contrast that allows one to emerge for oneself as a subject.

I'll soon challenge this line of thought directly. For the moment it's enough to say that it isn't just obvious that self-consciousness requires actual possession of some conception of other subjects of experience. It's arguable that the most one can say is that

---

[30] I use 'some conception of experience' in [3], rather than 'the thought-element EXPERIENCE', because it seems valuably looser: the latter seems more likely to invite the objection that self-consciousness does not obviously require possession of any *general* concept of experience—any concept of experience-in-general—that goes beyond (a) having visual and auditory experience, say, and (b) being fully self-conscious with all that that entails. But this, perhaps, is, not very satisfactory.
[31] See e.g. Fichte 1796–9: 351 (§16); Beiser 2002: 341–3.

[5] one must have the ability—mental resources—to come to possess and deploy some conception of other subjects of experience (Conceivability of Others Thesis),

and some would say that even this is questionable—though others would hold that it is entailed by (iii) and (vi). I'm inclined to accept [5],[32] but whether it is true or false, it doesn't entail [4]. Nor does it seem as if any stronger version of the Others Thesis can be established. For even if [4] is true, in addition to (iii) and (vi), it doesn't follow that

[6] one must have explicitly had some thought that there might be other subjects of experiences at some time (Thought of Others Thesis)

Still less does it follow that

[7] one must actually believe that there are other subjects of experience (Belief in Others Thesis)[33]

Still less does it follow that

[8] one must have experience that has the character of being experience of interaction with other subjects of experience (Experience as of Others Thesis)

   Still less does it follow that

[9] one must have actual experience of interaction with other subjects of experience (Actual Others Thesis)

I think that [4] and [6]–[9] are all false in their progressively stronger claims, as they move from the *possession of the conception* of others to the *thought* of others to the *belief* in others to the *experience as of* others to the *actual experience* of others. Our own early acquisition of self-consciousness is closely tied in with our coeval (or earlier) and automatic presumption that we're surrounded by other subjects of experience, and there's evidence that this presumption is strongly innate. (Our powerful animistic impulses are also important in this connection.) This, however, is simply a fact about normal human development, not about the essential nature of self-consciousness, and certain cases of abnormal—autistic—human development strongly suggest that [4] and [6]–[9] are false.[34] Whether that's so or not, there's no obvious incoherence in the idea of a subject of experience that thinks of itself in the distinctively self-conscious way, uses a first-person pronoun like 'I', but has (like God before the creation, as Derek Parfit remarked) no belief in other subjects of experience. I'm going to call this subject of experience 'Solo'—'S' for short—and argue that there's no hidden incoherence either.

—S's conception of itself as subject will in this case be peculiarly strengthless, in so far as it exists at all, and will be bound to decay in the absence of any experience animated by belief in the existence of others.

---

[32] The entailment claim relies on the view that if one can exercise concepts at all, then if one has two concepts F (e.g. NOT-MYSELF) and G (e.g. SUBJECT OF EXPERIENCE), one must have the conceptual resources to form the concept [F ∧ G]—the concept of something that is both F and G.

[33] I'll ignore the version of [7] according to which one must at least believe that there were once other subjects of experience although one is now alone.

[34] See e.g. Baron-Cohen 1995.

There seems to be no good reason to believe this, once one puts aside the human frame. Given that S's sense of itself as a subject exists (those who wish to say that S's case is unintelligible have the whole burden of proof and can't rely on EEE considerations), it may continue to be vividly defined for it by its struggle to attain its goals in a recalcitrant and inanimate environment. Nor is struggle—experience of resistance—necessary (again I disagree with Fichte); S's sense of itself as a subject may be clear even if it spends all its time peaceably on logic, or in having, say, smell and sound experiences (see further 3.14).

It does not even seem to be true of human self-consciousness that it depends essentially on some sort of active possession of the idea of other subjects. Human beings ordinarily acquire and possess self-consciousness in a context in which they take it for granted that there are other subjects of experience, but it is hard to see why one couldn't entirely forget this, on a fauna-free desert island, while retaining a robust and ordinarily unreflective form of SELF-experience and use of 'I'. We often have no thought of others when we think. It's hard to see why the belief that other subjects of experience exist would have to continue to be present in the background in some way in order for one to have a normal use of 'I' in thought.

—In this case S's use of 'I' is really just like an unself-conscious being's use of a name to refer to itself. S refers to itself perfectly well, but it doesn't really think of itself as itself, and it can't possibly do so unless it not only has the ability to form and entertain some conception of other subjects of experience (as in [5]), as you've granted, but also believes that there actually are other subjects of experience, or at least one (as in [7]).

I think this reply confuses facts about human development with questions about the essential nature of self-consciousness. I argue generally against this confusion in 3.12–3.16. Here I call Ronald, 'an intelligent young autistic adult', in support of the view that even in the human case self-awareness doesn't require awareness that there are other subjects of experience:

I really didn't know there were people until I was seven years old. I then suddenly realized that there were people. But not like you do. I still have to remind myself that there are people ... . I never could have a friend. I really don't know what to do with other people, really.[35]

No reason is given to think that Ronald didn't have a clear sense of himself as a subject, and research suggests that there is a fundamental respect in which autistic subjects think of themselves in psychological terms as freely as normal subjects. When Lee and Hobson administered Damon and Hart's self-understanding interview to two groups of children and adolescents, an autistic group and a non-autistic mentally retarded group matched

---

[35] Hobson 1993: 257; see also Cohen 1980: 388. Here are three more theses that seem indefensible: (a) certain features of one's actual course of experience must seem to one to provide a basis for supposing that there are or may be other subjects of experience (one may of course firmly believe that there are other subjects of experience without having any basis in experience for such a belief; many people have beliefs for which they have no basis). (b) One must at least believe that one is or could be in a position to identify other subjects of experience, should they exist. (c) One must actually be in such a position to identify other subjects of experience, should they exist.

for age and verbal ability, their prediction was that 'participants with autism would show a relative dearth of … self-concepts … in their talk about themselves'. It was not borne out. Although they found a 'significant group difference in the number and quality of statements that fell into the *social* category of self-concept', they found—contrary to their expectation, but not mine—'no group difference in the *number* of statements that fell into the psychological category'. Nor did participants with autism 'make significantly fewer references to emotional states [although] the quality of such references was restricted'.[36]

P. F. Strawson claims that if one is self-conscious, one must be 'ready and able to ascribe … states of consciousness, or experiences, to other individual entities', and while the import of 'ready and able' is not entirely clear, the quotation as it stands endorses at least [4], which I have rejected: it seems that S—and Ronald—may have no more than [5]. Strawson also claims, with Fichte, that 'the condition of reckoning oneself as a subject of such predicates is that one should also reckon others as subjects of such predicates', and this second, stronger claim appears to endorse all of [4]–[8], although not [9].[37]

Strawson's next proposal is that the second claim entails his thesis of the 'primitiveness' of the concept of a person, according to which entities to which mental predicates are ascribable must also be entities to which non-mental predicates are ascribable. And this appears to commit him to something like the Embodiment Thesis, according to which self-consciousness requires some sense of oneself as being embodied or as having non-mental being, in addition to the Experience as of Others Thesis.[38] His project is ambitious: to build up to the claim that self-consciousness requires some sort of experience of oneself as having (concrete) non-mental being from an extremely simple foundation: from the simple fact that the notions of self and other are essentially correlative.

The Experience as of Others Thesis is too strong, however. So is the Belief in Others Thesis. It isn't even clear that one must have actually had [6] the thought that there might be other subjects of experience, in order to be self-conscious. It isn't even clear that one must have [4] some sort of conception of other subjects of experience. So it doesn't look as if one can establish the Embodiment Thesis by this route. The next question to consider is whether one can do so in some other way.

3.8 The Body Thesis

Many philosophers, including Kant, believe that one can't have certain of the thought-elements and experiences that are necessarily involved in self-conscious thought unless

---

[36] 1998: 1131, 1139. See also Kagan 1982; Lewis and Brooks-Gunn 1979.

[37] 1959: 104. Strawson registers the more cautious position explicitly in a footnote (1959: 99n.). It is, as a thesis about human beings, fully in accord with current views in psychology. See e.g. Hobson 1993: 268: 'in order for a child to adopt a psychological perspective vis-à-vis her own self and her own mental life, she needs to appreciate the potential existence of appropriate kinds of alternative existence'.

[38] See, however, the preceding note.

one also has (or has had) some experience and conception of *body*; or, more generally, some experience and conception of *concrete non-mental being*.[39]

It seems best to state the case in terms of the notion of concrete non-mental being, because it's more general than the notion of body, but I'll often use the familiar word 'body' to refer to concrete non-mental being in general. I'll restrict my concern with non-mental being to concrete non-mental being, and standardly omit or bracket the word 'concrete'. I'll also make the standard assumption that all concrete non-mental phenomena are physical phenomena, but nothing will depend on this: when I talk of body, it won't be obligatory to suppose that the body in question is physical in addition to non-mental, but the ordinary idea of a physical body will always serve for the purposes of assessing what is said.

In its simplest form the *Body Thesis* states that

[*10*] self-consciousness requires experience of body (concrete non-mental being).

It's quickly refuted, for there is no concrete non-mental being in Berkeley's philosophy, which features self-conscious beings and isn't provably incoherent. The Body Thesis can, however, be modified, so that it doesn't claim that self-consciousness requires actual experience of concrete non-mental being, but rather that

[*11*] self-consciousness requires experience that has the character of being experience of body (concrete non-mental being),

whether or not it is veridical. Berkeleyan minds certainly have experience that has the character of being experience of concrete non-mental being, and so constitute no objection to the Body Thesis. The Body Thesis isn't a metaphysically assertive thesis about what there must be in reality, in addition to experience of a certain sort, and about what that experience must be experience of referentially or 'relationally' or causally speaking. It is, rather, a thesis about what sort of structure or character experience must have, considered in itself, and so without reference to its causes, if it is to be the experience of a self-conscious being. [*11*] is the most that can be established by Kant's 'Refutation of Idealism'.[40]

Most philosophers who discuss this question take it that to have experience that has the character of being *experience* of bodies is necessarily to have some *concept* of body, but this is disputable, for even primitive sentient beings presumably have experience

---

[39]   See Kant's 'Refutation of Idealism' (1781–7: B275–9; also A370–1, B417–18, B420). The view is clear in Wolff's *Psychologia empirica* (1732: §§11, 20–2) and is much discussed in Germany in the eighteenth century; see Thiel, forthcoming. For extensions of the Kantian style of reasoning in the analytic tradition see P. F. Strawson 1966; G. Evans 1982; papers in Bermúdez *et al.* 1995; and Cassam 1997. I'll employ the word 'concept' more often than 'thought-element' when discussing views other than my own.

[40]   This in itself is not a problem for Kant, because [*11*] amounts to [*10*] given his doctrine of 'empirical realism' (see e.g. A370–2). His problem is that the 'Refutation of Idealism' argument is unsound.

[*10*] may also trigger a Berkeleyan protest to the effect that the concept of body is incoherent or contradictory (Berkeley 1710: §9), but this objection can be put aside, for Berkeley is wrong, and even if he were right, the force of [*10*] would remain clear enough: it's the thesis that self-consciousness requires possession of a concept of body at least in the sense that it requires possession of a thought-element that is something like the thought-element that we have in so far as we take ourselves to be operating with a concept of body.

that has the character of being experience of body, and presumably do not possess any concept of body. So it is worth distinguishing

[12] self-consciousness requires possession of a concept of body (or concrete non-mental being)

from [11].

3.9 The Embodiment Thesis

Many go further than Kant and endorse a more specific version of the Body Thesis. To the claim that one must have experience of body, they add the claim that one must be aware or conceive of *oneself* as embodied or as having non-mental being, if one is to be self-conscious.[41] I disagree. I take it (as a materialist who is suspending his panpsychist inclinations) that S has non-mental being, but think that S may be self-conscious even if it has no such awareness or conception of itself.

According to the *Embodiment Thesis*, then,

[13] one cannot be self-conscious unless one is aware of oneself as being embodied (or as having concrete non-mental being).[42]

This thesis has been widely endorsed, and has interesting variants. Some claim that

[14] one must have awareness of oneself as embodied by means of external sense organs of some kind.

Others think that

[15] interoceptive experience of oneself as embodied is indispensable, or of primary importance, whether or not one also experiences oneself as embodied by means of external sense organs.

Both variants can be understood to state necessary conditions of the acquisition and persistence of human self-consciousness, but they may also be interpreted more strongly, as stating necessary conditions of any possible self-consciousness (or SELF-experience). In many treatments of this question, it isn't always clear which interpretation is in question. Many take the first as their framework for discussion, and slide silently and unjustifiably from the first to the second. (Kant never makes this sort of mistake.) I think that [14] and [15] are both false on the second interpretation, even if true on the first.

---

[41] Some think that experience of oneself as embodied requires experience of other bodies, and conversely, but both these claims seem false. Arguments for the necessity of bodily experience occur both in the philosophical tradition that passes through Wolff, Knutzen (Kant's teacher), Merian, Fichte, and others, and also in the specifically psychological tradition that subsequently diverges from the philosophical tradition, passing through thinkers like Herbart, Wundt, and James. See James 1890: 1. 303n., which has a fine passage from Wundt (1874), quoted on p. 28 above. See also Bradley 1893: ch. 9.

[42] Maximally general formulations of this sort can be given for each version of the Embodiment Thesis, but I'll omit them here. One can always replace 'embodied' by 'having (concrete) non-mental being'.

It's usually taken for granted that a single body is in question, but it's not clear that this is necessary, and one may therefore distinguish the Embodiment Thesis from the *Single Embodiment* Thesis:

[16] one cannot be self-conscious unless one is aware of oneself as singly embodied.

I doubt that this would be true even if some form of the Embodiment Thesis were true (see page 80), but I'll assume that a single body is in question for purposes of discussion.

The Embodiment Thesis can be weakened in the same way as the Body Thesis, for it isn't strictly speaking true that one must be aware of oneself as embodied. It's enough that one should have experience as of being embodied, whether or not it's veridical. So the Embodiment Thesis becomes

[17] one must have experience that has the character of being experience of (single) embodiment.

Even primitive sentient creatures may be said to have experience that has the character of being experience of being (singly) embodied, experience that is in fact veridical; and although this doesn't show that [17] isn't a necessary condition of self-consciousness, it makes it important to note that many philosophers have understood the word 'experience' as it occurs in [17] in such a way that [17] can be rewritten as

[18] one cannot be self-conscious unless one *conceives* of oneself as (singly) embodied,

where the understanding is that primitive sentient creatures can't properly be said to conceive of themselves in this way or indeed in any way at all. (Cassam (1997) argues, roughly speaking, that [18] is too strong, as an Embodiment Thesis, and that [17] is enough.)

I have no doubt that the Embodiment Thesis is false, in so far as it purports to be a universally valid claim about the conditions of the possibility of self-consciousness, but the basic thought that has motivated many to accept it is (I believe) a good one. At bottom, perhaps, endorsement of the Embodiment Thesis is prompted by the very general thesis that I'll call the *Subject as Thing Thesis*

[19] one cannot think of oneself in the distinctively self-conscious way unless one experiences or figures oneself as a *thing* in some sense.

The Subject as Thing Thesis may look surprisingly substantive, given the minimalist push of this discussion, but I take it to be correct, so long as 'thing' is understood in the way sketched in 2.16 (and elaborated in 4.3). The fundamental point can be sufficiently expressed as before by saying that one experiences oneself as something that can undergo things—e.g. suffer—and do things or, most simply, be in some state or other, in a way that processes, events, states, or properties, as ordinarily conceived, cannot. Those who accept [17] or [18] may make the mistake of supposing that fulfilment of the condition mentioned in [19] requires fulfilment of the condition mentioned in [17] or [18]—supposing, that is, that an ability to think of oneself as a thing or entity in the relevant sense requires possession of some sense or conception of oneself as (singly) embodied (or as having some non-mental being).

It may be objected, against [19], that a self-conscious being might not only experience itself just as a mental subject of experience while lacking any trace of anything like [17] or [18] (as I believe possible), but might also experience itself, so figured, as just a process or property—as a phenomenon that is ultimately 'adjectivally' dependent on some other and more genuinely substantial phenomenon, like a wave on water—rather than as a thing or object of some sort. I take it that Kant answers this objection in his discussion of the first Paralogism when he elaborates on the sense in which the representation of oneself as a thing or indeed a substance of some sort is essentially constitutive of self-conscious experience of oneself as the subject of consciousness: 'everyone must … necessarily regard himself as a substance.'[43]

If the sense of the subject as a thing dissolves in advanced Buddhist meditation, then so does full self-consciousness as here defined, i.e. the ability to think of oneself as oneself. This, perhaps, is what is testified to in Buddhist literature. What is left is a kind of self-translucency of impersonal consciousness that lacks the (experiential-conceptual) structure of self-consciousness as defined. There must still be a subject of experience (however momentary its nature), but its existence may not involve any experience of itself as a thing in the intended sense of the Subject as Thing Thesis. This experience may also fail in certain psychopathological cases.

3.10 The Subjective/Objective Thesis

The Embodiment Thesis is one of the principal tributaries of the Body Thesis. The *Ordered World Thesis* is another. I will state it in a familiar strong way and note some plausible weakenings. First, though, I need to record the *Subjective/Objective Thesis* that

[20] one cannot be self-conscious (and so have a sense of oneself as subject) unless one can distinguish between the way things are subjectively and the way things are objectively—between the way things are and the way one experiences them to be.

It is acceptance of this thesis that leads many to think that some version of the Ordered World Thesis must be true.

The Subjective/Objective Thesis may sound rather plausible, but this formulation of it is misleading—too strong—in so far as it suggests that one must at any given time be able, if one possesses the subjective/objective distinction, to make an actual division of things into the way things are and the way one experiences them to be, for it seems that one may have the resources to grasp the distinction even if one is so constituted or situated that one never has any actual thought like 'This is how things are experienced to be, but how they are experienced to be is (or may be) distinct from how they are'. In this case, one may positively hold that objective reality consists entirely in one's existing and having the experiences one does; one may take it, in other words, that the experiential given is all that there is to reality, other than oneself, and that it is

---

[43] A349; (see p. 51).

not any sort of representation of anything other than itself. Alternatively, perhaps, one may never have given the matter any thought, and may have never had reason to. The possibility may be doubted, but the burden of proof lies with the doubters. I have never seen a convincing argument against it.

In the light of this one may slightly rephrase the Subjective/Objective Thesis, as follows:

[21] one cannot be self-conscious (and so have a sense of oneself as subject) unless one has the resources to grasp the distinction between the way things are and the way one experiences them to be.

Certainly one can have the resources to grasp the distinction even if nothing in one's experience ever invites the thought that how things are experienced either is or might be different from how they are. To judge positively that how things are is in no way different from how one experiences them to be, and perhaps couldn't be, is precisely to exercise grasp of the distinction.

The Subjective/Objective Thesis claims to state a necessary condition of self-consciousness in its own right (i.e. the thesis does not feature only because it leads people to accept the Ordered World Thesis), and the next, much discussed question is whether it is true. I'm not confident of my ability to decide the issue, but I doubt that it is true and will make a few sceptical comments.

The thesis may be argued for as follows: plainly self-consciousness requires possession of (i) the notion of the subject of experience. This in turn requires possession of (ii) the notion of experience. This in turn requires possession of (iii) the notion of what experience is experience *of*: it requires possession of the notion that experience is experience of something other than itself, and hence of (iv) the notion that there is something that is not experience, and hence of (v) the notion that how things are experienced to be is distinct from (is not all there is to) how things are. ...

There are many complexities here, and I won't consider them all. The first thing to say is that the notion of experience is not intrinsically relational in this particular way. Experience necessarily has content—experiential content—but it needn't be experience of something that exists independently of it, and even if it is, the subject of experience needn't suppose that it is.[44] This blocks the argument at stage (iii), and we have, so far, no reason to think that self-consciousness requires grasp of the distinction between things and experience of things—still less of the distinction between how things are and how things are experienced to be.

—But to possess the notion of experience is necessarily to possess the notion of experiential content, and to possess this notion is necessarily to possess the notion of subjective seeming.

Not, I think, if possession of the notion of subjective seeming is thought to carry with it grasp of the subjective/objective distinction. The phrase 'subjective seeming' may be a philosophically natural name for a certain conception of experiential content, but if its

---

[44] Compare P. F. Strawson 1980: 277 ff.

use is allowed, then it must be stressed that one can have the notions of experience and experiential content without any thought that experience involves an appearance or a 'how-it-seems' of something distinct from its content; as already noted. One can think 'Reality might have been different' without thinking 'Things might be different from the way I experience them to be'. One can think 'My experiences went A, B, C, but they might have gone A, C, B' without any grasp of the thought that how things are is or might be different from how they are experienced to be.

Another argument runs as follows:

(a) A being cannot be self-conscious without having a sense of itself, the subject of experience, and a sense of itself *as* the subject of experience (see 3.5).

(b) To have such a sense of oneself as subject is necessarily to have some sort of sense of oneself as distinct from or over and above one's experiences and their content.

(c) The phrase 'the way things are experienced to be' denotes what is given in the content of experience.

(d) A self-conscious subject must understand itself, at least, to be distinct from what is given in the content of experience, i.e. from the way things are experienced to be.

So

(e) self-consciousness requires grasp of the Subjective/Objective distinction.

One problem with this—loose—argument is that it operates with too limited a notion of the content of experience. In the case of self-conscious thought the subject, considered as such, is part of what is presented or given in experience; i.e. in the content of experience. There can be no sense of the subject of experience at all unless this is so. So (d), at least, is false. 'The way things are experienced to be' includes the subject of experience, and we lack, so far, a reason to think that a self-conscious being must grasp the Subjective/Objective distinction. I suspect that (b) is also false, in a way that may be made manifest in meditative states.[45]

—But if the subject of experience (grasped as such) is part of what is presented or given to the subject of experience in experience, and in particular in self-conscious experience, it must then be aware that it is dealing with a representation of a thing that is not the thing itself. So it must after all grasp the distinction between what is and what is experienced—between the way things are and the way it experiences them to be.

Why should the subject be that reflective? S's cousin T—whose possibility, along with S's, has still to be argued for directly—is a minimally self-conscious subject that only ever has sound experience and thoughts of the form 'I am F-ing', 'I am G-ing'.[46] T is

---

[45] For a metaphysical correlate of this idea see 7.4 and 8.8.

[46] These sentences represent its thinking that it is having various types of sound-experience. In his discussion of the 'sound world' (1959: ch. 2), P. F. Strawson argues that the sound world does not provide sufficient resources for acquisition or exercise of the distinctively self-conscious way of thinking, but his case relies on the argument from conceptual need that will be rejected in 3.12 below, and it doesn't show that a being that is simply created already thinking in the distinctively self-conscious way can't think in this way if it inhabits such a world.

very unreflective. It has no thought that its *F*-experiences are or might be experiences of something distinct from itself and its experiences, and it certainly has no thought that it is dealing with a representation of a thing that is not the thing itself, when it thinks about itself or apprehends that it exists (compare our ordinary unreflective encounters with tables and chairs). In general, it's hard to see why one can't be self-present or 'self-intimating' in self-consciousness in such a way that one's apprehension of oneself as subject of experience in the living moment of experience doesn't involve any grasp of any such division into representation and represented. One may simply take it that what is experienced—including oneself as experiencer, and the fact that one is experiencing things—is what is.

—But to be self-conscious is—at the very least—to be able to think *I'm having experience*, and to think *I'm having experience* is already to exercise the concept of objectivity in some manner, for it is in effect to think *It's an objective fact that I am having experience.*

I'm happy to agree that thinking something like *I am thinking* or *I am having experience F* necessarily involves some sort of exercise of the concept of objectivity—of how things actually are. The question, then, is whether such a thought must involve the Subjective/Objective distinction in a way that presupposes ability to grasp the idea that the way things are experienced to be is or might be other than the way they are, rather than merely the essentially correlative idea of how things are not. I can see no reason to think that it must. A second question is whether such a thought must involve the ability to think that objective reality is other than or more than one's own existence as a subject of experience experiencing what one experiences. Again I can see no reason to think that it must. Many believe that it must involve not only the ability to think this but also the actual thinking of it. I think that substantive and interesting transcendental conclusions of this sort—demonstrations that one thing is absolutely impossible without another—are very hard to come by in this area.

It may now be said that to think *I'm having experience F* is to exercise not only the concept of objectivity but also that of subjectivity, inasmuch as the latter is built into the very notion of experience. But even when we grant that there is a sense in which the notion of subjectivity is built into the very notion of experience, it doesn't seem to be built in in such a way that to think a thought like *I'm having experience F* is necessarily to exercise the concept of subjectivity in any way that engages the Subjective/Objective distinction.

3.11 The Ordered World/Wider World Thesis

Whatever the final status of the Subjective/Objective Thesis, the Ordered World Thesis is standardly developed from its stronger form ([20]) as follows: if one is self-conscious, and so has a grasp of the distinction between how things are and how they are experienced to be, then

[22] one must figure oneself as located in, and as tracing a particular experiential route through, a world that exhibits a certain degree of order and regularity of which one is aware (one must have experience that has the character of being experience of tracing such a route).

The notion of the ordered world is initially modelled on the world of persisting bodies in space with which we take ourselves to be familiar, but it is standardly granted that it needn't be just like this. The root idea is considerably more general: one must trace an experiential 'route' through a 'space' or 'dimension' of some kind 'containing' 'entities' of some kind, and these entities must be experienced as possessing an order and variety that are sufficiently similar (what is sufficient invites and resists precise specification) to the order and variety exhibited by objects in space as experienced by us.[47]

There may be argument about whether the Ordered World Thesis is best stated as a requirement that one conceive of things in a certain way or as a requirement that one experience things in a certain way (the conception version is stronger, as before, in so far as it's plausible to say that an animal can have the experience without the conception). I don't think we need to settle this question, however, because the Ordered World Thesis appears to be false either way. Nor is it entailed by the Subjective/Objective Thesis: even if the Subjective/Objective Thesis is true, it is quite unclear why the capacity to make the distinction between the way things are objectively and the way things are subjectively—the seems/is distinction—should be thought to require any sort of large-scale order in experience at all, let alone experience that has the character of being experience of an ordered world or 'world' of things distinct from one's experiences.

Some proponents of the Ordered World Thesis think that it entails [11], the external-sense-organ-requiring version of the Embodiment Thesis. They think that one must have experience of oneself as embodied of the kind that derives from external sense organs, because one must experience oneself as a body among other bodies in order to have experience of an ordered world of bodies in the way they suppose to be necessary for self-consciousness. Others, however, believe that the Ordered World Thesis is separable from all versions of the Embodiment Thesis (all of [10]–[18]), and that its essential idea survives untouched when the body is dwindled to a mere point of view. According to this position, one must experience oneself as tracing a particular experiential route through a reasonably ordered world of objects in space (entities of some kind ordered in some space-like realm), and as standardly occupying a particular position or point of view within that space (or 'space'), but it doesn't follow that one must have experience of oneself (whether exteroceptive or interoceptive) as embodied. Stripped to essentials, the Ordered World Thesis reduces to the *(Mere) Point of View Thesis* that

---

[47]   P. F. Strawson develops a very influential Kantian version of the Ordered World Thesis (1966: 82–112).

[*23*] one must (at least) experience oneself as having a point of view in an ordered world of objects of some sort,

and one may have point-of-view experience without having any experience of oneself as having a body. One may experience—and indeed conceive of—oneself simply as something that has a point of view, without having any further thought about or positive conception of one's nature. One may in this case *have* some sort of physical body, but be incapable of any sensory awareness of it.[48]

I think that the essential idea of the Ordered World Thesis clearly survives intact when it shrinks to the Point of View Thesis, but that it remains incorrect in any case. It seems to me that the considerations sketched in the discussion of the Subjective/Objective Thesis already suffice to show this, but the main argument against the Ordered World Thesis is still to come.

Note, finally, that a being may be so disposed, mentally, that it naturally and automatically construes its experiences as experiences of something other than itself, even though they appear utterly random in character.[49] If so, the Ordered World Thesis needs to be further weakened to become the—highly general—*Wider World Thesis*, according to which

[*24*] one must have experience that has, for one, the character of being experience of a reality or world that is more than or wider than the reality that consists of oneself and one's experiences.

I think, however, that the Ordered World Thesis remains false even when it is improved in this way—even when all order requirements are dropped, and it is turned into the Wider World Thesis.

---

[48] P. F. Strawson (1995: 417; see Cassam 1997: 44 ff.) allows the coherence of [*23*]. It is the pure case of Husserl's 'zero-point of orientation', and seems strikingly consonant with the spirit of Gibsonian 'ecological' models of self-awareness (see e.g. E. Gibson 1993; Butterworth 1995) and some of the reported phenomenology of playing video games. It's arguable that out-of-body experience is experience as of being an unembodied entity occupying a particular spatiotemporal location (although it may be said that coenaesthesia—somatosensory experience of being embodied—still persists in such cases). Dream experience can have this character, as noted on p. 30, and the idea of unembodied experience also features in a common story of what happens to human beings after death: one has a point of view, one perceives, as a ghost or disembodied soul, but one affects nothing; it is as if one has no body at all.

—If a being B has visual experience then it must have some implicit representation of itself as having some sort of body, just in so far as it experiences the visual field as having a left and a right, an up and a down. For it must in this case also have some sort of implicit conception of itself as having some sort of orientation, and hence some real extension, and hence some sort of embodiment.

Both these 'hences' can be challenged—I've just done so. One may also consider the case in which B has 360° vision, or rather wholly spherical vision, its attention being equally distributed over the whole of a visual field in which the only changes are uniform changes of colour. It's not clear that it must then have any sense of its orientation relative to the visual field, or to what it takes to be presented in the visual field. Some say that auditory experience is also essentially spatial in character, but this seems to be a mistake, as listening to music on headphones sufficiently shows. It doesn't seem to be essentially spatial in its overall qualitative character even if we human beings always hear sound as coming from somewhere, or at least as 'in our heads'.

[49] See G. Strawson 1994: 262–3. It's worth noting a much weaker point—that even if human beings experience a total collapse of order in their experiences, they may still think of them as experiences of an external world. They don't have to think 'I've gone mad' rather than 'The world's gone mad'. Their inability to know which hypothesis is true puts in question neither the fact that one or the other is true (if not both) nor the fact that they can grasp this fact.

3.12 The Need Argument

I've considered thirty theses, reduced them to twenty-four, and accepted five. I've suggested that one can be fully self-conscious without any thought of the possibility of other subjects of experience, without any awareness (real or apparent) of body or concrete non-mental being, and even, it seems, without any grasp of the distinction between how things are and how they're experienced to be.

—This can't work, for one will have no *need* or *use* for the thought-element I or MYSELF in such a case, and if one has no need for it—if there is no work for it to do in the articulation of one's experience—then one cannot really be said to have it at all, or a true command of the first-person pronoun. In which case one can't really be said to be self-conscious.

This is the *Need Argument*, to which King Lear gives the first answer: 'O reason not the need.'[50] What need is there for need? We can possess things, including contentful concepts or thought-elements, that we do not need—or use. What reason is there to think otherwise?

Second answer. S (the candidate for minimal self-consciousness) has a *use* for the thought-element MYSELF just in so far as S naturally uses it to think self-conscious thoughts about itself, as we do. And given that S does think in this way, S needs the thought-element. S needs the thought-element to think in the distinctive way that the thought-element's possession makes possible. There's no further external or ante-cedent source of the need, but why should such a source be thought necessary? When philosophers inspired by Kant analyse conditions of thought-element possession, they make a mistake that seems to have its roots (or some of them) in a variety of verification-ism, arguing as follows: S can't really be said to have some fundamental thought-element K—K cannot be legitimately or properly attributed to S—unless S has a need or a use for K *given the character of its experience*. And when they talk of the character of S's experience in this way, they mean S's experience *considered independently of the fact that S possesses K*. It is this second step in the Need Argument that I reject.

Clearly possession of a thought-element can itself make a difference to the character of one's experience. The Kant-inspired philosophers don't want to deny this obvious point. But when they ask about the conditions of possessing K, they take it that there must be something in S's experience antecedent to S's possession of K (or at least considered independently of S's possession of K) that somehow naturally invites application of K, something that creates a need and a use for K that is independent of any need and use for K that derives simply from the fact that K is possessed by S.

But there doesn't seem to be any good reason to accept this as a condition of thought-element possession. We may allow that the argument from conceptual need holds good in the case of ordinary empirical thought-elements: if I'm acquainted with various sorts of animals, but have no knowledge of horses, and for the first time begin to encounter horses, it seems plausible to say that I subsequently have a need and

---

[50] Shakespeare, *King Lear*, II. iv. 259.

a use for the thought-element HORSE in ordering my experience; and (putting aside various complications that tell against the Need Argument) there seems to be a clear sense in which this is so because of the character that my experience has considered independently of the character that it has specifically on account of the fact that I possess the thought-element HORSE. So too for the thought-element RED, and so on. But to say that it holds good of such empirical thought-elements is not to say that it holds good quite generally. Suppose I think up the idea of a centaur. Suppose I think up the idea of a triangle by a stroke of artistic genius, living in a world where everything is and appears smoothly curved. Here I may create a genuine use for CENTAUR or TRIANGLE that doesn't exist antecedently to my thinking it up.

I think it's useful to say that once I have done this, I also have a *need* for the thought-element—call it K. I have a need for it given the space of thought I now inhabit. This use of 'need' may be doubted, because it considers the limiting case in which my need for K isn't independent of the fact that I possess K. It goes against the standard employment of 'need', and some may accordingly prefer to say only that I have a use for K in this case, rather than a need. So be it. I don't need to talk of need. And yet I think it's telling to say that one also creates a need, even if—even though—one doesn't need K to do anything other than think or have experience in the way it makes possible. One is now so disposed, mentally, that certain thoughts or experiences can come to one, and one needs to have K in order to have those thoughts and experiences.

What about the thought-element ONESELF or MYSELF or I, considered as that which lies essentially and sufficiently behind the fully self-conscious use of the pronoun 'I' (102)? It's not at all like the natural-kind thought-element HORSE. Nor is it constructed (like CENTAUR) from thought-elements that are already possessed. But these elements of disanalogy don't matter. Suppose I'm just created thinking in the distinctively self-conscious way. Or suppose I'm a creature that is fully and inexorably innately disposed to come to think in the distinctively self-conscious way even if my experience is very limited. Then I have (or come to have) a genuine use for I or MYSELF even if nothing in the character of my experience considered independently of my possession of the thought-element—e.g. experience that has the character of being experience of interaction with other subjects of experience—has encouraged its deployment. And now that I have it, I need it. I need it to think in the distinctively self-conscious way in which I just do think. I can't think in that way without it. (Smokers don't need to smoke when they take up smoking, then they do.) It's hard to see how it could be a conceptual truth that I can't possibly have this thought-element unless I can be shown to have a natural use for it on account of the character that my experience has considered independently of the character that it has given that I have it. The possession of the thought-element can itself be (and arguably must be—see page 138 below) what makes the experiential difference—the experiential cut—that gives it its function or use.

Does this suggestion beg the question about whether it's possible to have the thought-element MYSELF without any explicit thought that there are or may be other subjects of experience? Anyone who thinks so must say why, or how; they have the burden of proof. We tend to be overimpressed by our own human case when we think about questions of this sort. Very powerful arguments will be needed to show that possession of the idea that one is a subject of experience entails actual belief in the actual existence of other subjects of experience, or at least some explicit thought of the possibility of other subjects of experience, rather than just the capacity (possibly unexercised) to form and entertain the idea of other subjects of experience.[51]

The main present aim, in any case, is to illustrate the sense in which possession of a thought-element κ can itself be a source of use and need for κ without there having to be anything inviting or favouring deployment of κ that stems from the nature of one's experience considered independently of one's possession of κ. Once the thought-element MYSELF is deployed, the world divides for me (let us suppose) into I and not-I. The thought-element has, thenceforth, a use and a proper application, and I have a need for it inasmuch as I think in the distinctively self-conscious way and can't do so without it. One can grant that possession of I requires possession of some conception of what is not-I, given the correlativity of the two concepts, while insisting that possession of NOT-I doesn't require any thought of other subjects of experience, and equally that active deployment of NOT-I doesn't require any thought of other subjects of experience. In the limiting case, as remarked, it seems that my experiences, apprehended by me as phenomena that stand over against me, the subject of experience, can suffice as the not-I.

I've argued that the Need Argument can't be used to defend the Others Thesis ([4], [6]–[9]). I'll now argue that it's no better in defence of the Body Thesis ([10]–[12]) and its main tributaries the Embodiment Thesis ([13]–[18]) and the Ordered or Wider World Thesis ([22]–[25]).

We are human beings, and our experience of single embodiment, and of location in an ordered world, is no doubt integral to our acceding to self-consciousness and SELF-experience (experience of oneself as a mental thing of some sort) in the way we do.[52] But very little follows from this. It doesn't follow, for example, that SELF-experience is mistaken, or is really a distorted image of something else (necessary conditions of the acquisition of some conception aren't *ipso facto* part of the content of the conception; one might as well say that true conclusions reached from false premises aren't really true). And even if human beings can't accede to self-consciousness if they lack experience of being embodied, ± located in a reasonably coherent world, it doesn't follow that nothing can. The Embodiment Thesis is standardly the conclusion of a Need Argument according to which one can't think in a certain way unless one's experience has a certain character considered independently of one's thinking in that way, but all such

---

[51] Even if human infants were raised (as agreeably as possible) in an environment that gave them no sense that there were any other subjects of experience, and even if their powerful innate disposition to assume that other things were minded was not brought into play, it's not clear that this would debar them from acquiring the ability to think of themselves as themselves in the distinctively self-conscious way, given the nature and power and strongly innate character of human intelligence. For the autistic case in which these conditions appear to be fulfilled, see p. 123 above.

[52] When one considers mental capacities like self-consciousness, or the capacity for SELF-experience, it's important to consider phylogeny as well as ontogeny: to consider factors that operate to shape the innate mental constitution of the human species over long periods of time as well as causes that operate in the psychological development of the individual.

arguments, I propose, are unsound. Nor can appeal to the Ordered World Thesis help the Embodiment Thesis, for the Ordered World Thesis can be dwindled down until it becomes the Point of View Thesis. So even if the Ordered World Thesis is true, it doesn't entail any version of the Embodiment Thesis.

What about the Ordered World Thesis? It seems to me that it too is fatally undermined by the foregoing objections to the Need Argument: there are no valid arguments for the claim that one cannot possess the thought-element I or MYSELF unless one's experience has a certain character considered independently of the fact that one possesses the thought-element. If so, a whole further swathe of theses lose their purchase: all those, like the Ordered World Thesis, that make more specific claims about what the character of experience—in particular, the thought-element-MYSELF-independent character of experience—must be like if one is to be self-conscious.

I think they're all false. There's no incoherence in the idea of a self-conscious creature that (1) has all sorts of absorbing experiences, and thinks 'I am happy', 'I am F-ing', 'I am G-ing', although it doesn't take itself to be embodied or located in any sort of ordered or wider world—B-realized for short.[53] Or in the idea of a self-conscious creature that (1) has experiences and (2) naturally thinks of its experiences as experiences, although it does not take itself to be B-realized. Don't ask how it came to be this way. To think that this question is important is to misunderstand the issue.[54] My reply will be that it may just so think of them, and that it may so think of them however disordered they are, so that even [24], the weaker Wider World Thesis, is false. It may be a matter of innate disposition; this is a coherent supposition.

Nor is there any incoherence in the idea of a self-conscious creature that (1) has experiences and not only (2) thinks of its experiences as experiences, but also (3) thinks of them as experiences of something other than itself, although it does not take itself to be B-realized. Nor in the idea of a self-conscious creature that, in addition to (1) and (2), and perhaps (3), also (4) thinks of its experiences *themselves* as something other than itself, the subject of experience considered just as such, although it has no sense that it is B-realized, nor any sense that its experiences have any order or regularity.[55] It may just so think of them, however disordered they are.

How can it? The case is the same as before. Possession of a conception of what is not-myself doesn't depend on possession of any sort of conception of non-mental existence. In the limiting case, my experiences themselves, apprehended as phenomena that are distinct from (not identical with) me, the subject of experience, can suffice as the not-I. It may be added that all claims that stress the necessity of the ability to *reidentify* objects—to think of them as 'the same again' at different times—also fail, on this view.[56]

---

[53] Wittgenstein's 'whatever is going to seem right to me is right. And that only means that here we can't talk about "right" ' line of argument (1953: §258) is irrelevant in this context, and unsound in any case.

[54] As many have observed, from Kant onwards, the question is not how a certain conception may have developed, but what possession of that conception must involve (see e.g. G. Strawson 1994: 261–3).

[55] (4) entails (1) and (2) but not (3). I consider the case in which the subject does not fulfil (3).

[56] See P. F. Strawson 1959: ch. 1; 1966: 142 ff.

If this is right, a whole tradition of argument collapses. All the claims about unobvious incoherence come to nothing, because they depend on the Need Argument, which has no valid form.

A final remark. I've claimed that possession of a thought-element K can be the source of a need for K without anything in experience-considered-independently-of-possession-of-K inviting K's deployment. This is enough to overturn the Need Argument. It is arguable, however, that a much stronger claim can be made. It's not just that possession of K can be the source of a need for K without anything in experience-considered-independently-of-possession-of-K inviting its deployment. It's also arguable that there is a fundamental sense in which *only* the possession of K can be a source of a need for it. Those who argue that self-consciousness requires (e.g.) experience that has the character of being experience of other subjects of experience, or of an ordered external world, are led to talk of experience that invites or favours deployment of the thought-element I or MYSELF, or creates a natural need for it. But there's a more fundamental sense in which it is *only* the possession of the thought-element that gives it a needed use. Not, trivially, because you can't use it unless you possess it, but because only its possession really opens up the scene of thought in which it finds its use; only if you already possess it does it articulate experience in such a way that it has a use. I'm interested in the application of this claim to very fundamental thought elements like I or AND, but it's arguable that there is a respect in which it is a more general truth.

3.13 Empirically applicable criteria of identity

The line of thought started in the last section can be taken further and generalized. One way to do this is to ask whether there is any incoherence in the idea that a creature may be self-conscious (and indeed have SELF-experience) although it entirely lacks any 'empirical criteria of subject-identity'—any empirically applicable criteria of identity for itself and for things of the kind it takes itself to belong to, of the sort that are in our case paradigmatically supplied by our ability to be aware of ourselves as singly embodied and as located in an ordered world of bodies.[57]

I can find no incoherence in this, but many disagree. They endorse the *Empirical Criteria Thesis*, according to which

[25] one cannot have a genuine self-conscious thought about oneself unless one is in possession of empirical criteria of subject identity (of the sort paradigmatically supplied by our experience of ourselves as singly embodied in an ordered world of other bodies).

This is standardly taken to be the thesis that one must be able (or at least must have been able) to apply such criteria of identity in practice, and that one must also be right about what they are. But to claim that the criteria must be possessed and empirically applicable is not to claim that their possessor must have any actual opportunity to

---

[57] See P. F. Strawson 1966: 167. All quotations from P. F. Strawson in this section are from pp. 164–7.

apply them; nor is it clear that it must be right about what they are. [25] is a thesis about the *cognitive resources* and thought-dispositions that one must possess if one is to be a self-conscious being, not about what one's *evidential situation* must be, and a self-conscious being could have the cognitive resources that the Empirical Criteria Thesis holds to be necessary for self-consciousness even if it were circumstantially and indeed constitutionally incapable of any actual application of the criteria. It would, for example, be enough if the being were innately determined to have some conception of itself as a physical object in a spatial order, or as a quasi-object in a quasi-spatial order. It wouldn't matter if it were in fact an immaterial soul with no sensory organs, for it would in this case possess empirically *applicable* criteria of identity in the required sense, even though it was not in a position to apply them correctly itself, and even though they weren't in fact correct. It would have the required cognitive competence or complexity; it would have a picture that involved the right sort of thought-structuring framework although it was mistaken.[58]

I think the Empirical Criteria Thesis is false even when this point has been registered. As always I support S, who thinks of itself as just: a self, a subject, a mental presence, a locus of consciousness, an experiencer. S has no thought of or experience of or as of embodiment, or of spatial or quasi-spatial location, or of bodies in general. It's just a fact that S naturally and automatically thinks of itself as something single, a subject or self. It can't give any account of why this way of thinking is justified. The question has not arisen for it—this is just how things are for it. This is its native disposition. The field of its experience is in fact divided or structured by this habit of thought. It has no empirical criteria of subject identity at all, but it doesn't need any. It's not as if it has to put the way it experiences things to the test, or feels that it has to do this. It's not as if the character of its experience has to make the I/not-I distinction useful for it or needed by it for reasons independent of the fact that it already thinks in this way. For there it always is for itself, the subject of experience, available to be thought about in a way familiar to us all. In apprehending itself as the subject of experience S may apprehend itself as something that is, considered precisely as such, i.e. as the subject of experience, distinguishable from its experiences and their content, whatever their content is. These are available to stand over against it (*gegenständlich*) as what is not-myself, not the subject of experience. It's quite unclear that anything more is required.

We may imagine (it isn't necessary) that S recapitulates part of the *cogito* argument in Descartes's Second Meditation and thinks, in Descartes's words, 'I know that I exist; the question is, what is this *I* that I know? I do not know. But whatever I suppose, and whatever the truth is, for all that I am still something.' (1641: 18). S's reasoning

---

[58] What is the limiting case of such a picture? Can it be wholly abstract or intellectual in nature? Can it exist in the complete absence of anything like sensory experience—so that it doesn't even require possession of a capacity to imagine things in a way that involves sensory content of some kind? If the answer to this question is No, then the notion of empirically applicable criteria of identity retains a connection with sensory phenomena. If the answer is Yes, then (obscurely) it does not, and one is beckoned in the direction of some notion of Fichtean intellectual intuition (very different from Kantian intellectual intuition). As in 2.8 (39) I think it is essential to recognize that there can be and are (wholly naturally evolved) *experiential modalities* that are not sensory modalities.

here is unexceptionable—as unexceptionable as Descartes's at this stage of his Second Meditation. It is, in particular, not open to Lichtenberg's famous but wholly mistaken objection that Descartes should at this stage in his argument have said only 'There is thinking' or 'It is thinking', as in 'It is raining'. The objection is mistaken because 'I', as used by Descartes or S here, is used in such a way that it definitely has a referent whatever the ontological category of what it picks out; even if, for example, it doesn't qualify as a substance in any traditional metaphysical scheme:

What else am I? I will use my imagination. I am not that structure of limbs which is called a human body. I am not even some thin vapour which permeates the limbs—a wind, fire, air, breath, or whatever I depict in my imagination; for these are things which I have supposed to be nothing. Let this supposition stand; for all that I am still something. And yet *may it not perhaps be the case that these very things which I am supposing to be nothing, because they are unknown to me, are in reality identical with the 'I' of which I am aware? I do not know*, and for the moment I shall not argue the point, since I can make judgements only about things which are known to me. I know that I exist; the question is, what is this 'I' that I know? (1641: 18; my emphasis)

Descartes uses 'I' simply because our thought about ourselves naturally and inevitably occurs for us in terms of 'I', and he's quite right to do so. He uses 'I' as a referential term that picks out an undeniable reality, whatever else is true about the nature of that reality. He might for all he knows be something that's more like a process or a property than a self-subsistent substance as ordinarily conceived. He might, as he says, be something that has non-mental being as well as mental being.

   S is by hypothesis a physical being, although it has no experience of embodiment or of body in general. It is therefore something for which empirically applicable criteria of identity of a sort that we can understand are in fact available, although not to it.[59] And the thing that S is thinking of is certainly itself (see pages 103 and 150). Why then insist that S's apparently fully self-conscious thought of itself isn't genuine unless it possesses, in some form, empirically applicable criteria of identity for itself and for things of the kind that it takes itself to be? One reason why this is puzzling is that it's generally agreed that thinking of oneself specifically and simply as a mental presence or subject of experience is a genuine way of thinking of oneself, one that is in fact available to all of us. P. F. Strawson makes the point. When human subjects of experience use the pronoun 'I' to ascribe a state of consciousness to themselves, they typically do so without making any 'use whatever of any … empirically applicable … criteria of identity'. 'It would make no sense [for such a subject] to say: *This* inner experience is occurring, but is it occurring to *me*?' There is in such cases 'nothing that one can … encounter or recall in the field of inner experience such that there can be any question of one's applying [empirically applicable] criteria of subject identity to determine whether the … experience belongs to oneself—or to someone else.'

---

[59]   There is in fact no difficulty in the idea of empirically applicable criteria of identity for immaterial minds; see p. 153 below.

This is exactly right, but Strawson doesn't take it to support the view I'm defending. Instead he identifies it as the 'the fact that lies at the heart of the Cartesian illusion'.[60] When 'I' is used by a subject of experience to ascribe an experience or state of consciousness to itself, he says, there is indeed no 'need or ... possibility of this use being justified by empirical criteria of subject-identity'. How is such a use still possible—valid and properly contentful? Because, he says, 'even in such a use, the links with [empirical] criteria [of subject identity] are not in practice severed'. They're not severed in practice in the human case (with which he is principally concerned) because even when one uses 'I' to refer to oneself in this way, one's use of 'I' is in practice securely underwritten by one's possession of empirically applicable criteria of identity for oneself which are in turn grounded in one's more or less constant experience of oneself as embodied and spatiotemporally located.

Strawson proposes, then, that the experience of criterionless self-ascription of experiences gives rise to an illusion in human beings, 'the illusion of a purely inner and yet subject-referring use for "I" '. But even if the claim that this is an illusion is true in the case of human beings—I don't think it is—it certainly doesn't follow that it's metaphysically impossible for any self-conscious creature to refer to itself (or indeed have SELF-experience) unless it possesses empirically applicable criteria of identity for itself of the sort paradigmatically supplied by experience of embodiment and location in a reasonably ordered world of objects. As it stands, Strawson's observation provides strong support for the view that it is indeed possible for a creature to refer to itself without possessing such criteria. For if we can think about ourselves in such a way that there is 'no question' of our applying empirical criteria of subject-identity when we do so (we may also be in a sensory isolation tank, but it's not important), why can't S always do so?

—It's just that our ability to think of ourselves in this way at any given time depends essentially on the presence, at that time, of the 'somatic field' of awareness, the permanent coenaesthetic background awareness of embodiment that persists even when we are most unconcerned with our bodies.

Even if—even though—this is true of human beings, it doesn't undercut the present suggestion, and it points clearly to another possibility. If a background somatic field of awareness can be so important for self-consciousness and SELF-experience, then presumably a background *psychic* or mental field of awareness, featuring structures of mood, emotion, character, preferences, and knowledge, can serve the same function, and be no less important.[61]

---

[60] Compare Wittgenstein (1958: 69): 'we feel ... that in cases in which "I" is used as subject, we don't use it because we recognize a person by his bodily characteristics; and this creates the illusion that we use this word to refer to something bodiless, which, however, has its seat in our body. In fact, this seems to be the real ego, the one of which it was said "Cogito, ergo sum".'

[61] This may be cognate with C. O. Evans's (1970) suggestion that the self is (or that the sense of the self derives from) 'unprojected consciousness'. See also Bradley 1893: chs. 9 and 10.

—The key point is that one must have prior experience of B-realization (embodiment and location in a reasonably ordered world) in order to come to be such that one can engage in criterionless self-ascription of experiences in the first place.

The reply is the same: if such experience can give rise to the ability to engage in self-ascription of experiences without any concurrent awareness of B-realization, then this ability can exist while lacking this particular aetiology. It can, for example, be supposed to be innately given; the aetiology can't be what matters.

—The fundamental point is that memory of embodiment or awareness of embodiment (or something relevantly equivalent) must always be somehow *actively present*, if only obscurely, when a being engages in what appears to be criterionless self-ascription of experiences.

But how might this (very unclear) claim be proved? The phenomenological facts seem to be as Strawson says: there need be no trace of any thought or experience of oneself as embodied, or as a thing of a kind for which there are empirically applicable criteria of identity, in the experience of oneself as a subject of experience that one may have when ascribing experiences to oneself. One can seem to oneself to have all the solidity of a genuine referent just by virtue of one's experience of oneself as a mental subject of experience, a mental presence with certain properties. And if it can be like this for us on occasion, it can presumably be like this all the time for some other kind of being that is (once again) simply innately disposed to experience things in this way. The habit of self-reference doesn't need any further or external grounding. We may suspect that this being would be or become deranged, or have a deep sense of 'ontological' insecurity, but we base this suspicion on our own ordinary human case, and other self-conscious beings may be quite unlike us.

3.14 Further doubts: 'empirical', 'criteria', 'identity'

Perhaps the fundamental thought behind the Empirical Criteria Thesis is the *Self-Identifiability Thesis*:

[26] if one is genuinely self-conscious, one must be able to identify something as oneself.

I take it that this thesis is trivially true (but none the less important) at one end of the spectrum of readings of the word 'identify', where it amounts to nothing more than the claim that one must (1) be able to fix on oneself in thought in such a way as to be the actual target or object of one's own thoughts, and (2) have the (self-consciousness-defining) property of being able to think of oneself *as* oneself. The puzzling question is why the truth of the Self-Identifiability Thesis should be thought to rest essentially on possession of empirical criteria of subject identity.

The answer, I suspect, lies at the other end of the spectrum of readings of the word 'identify', where 'identify' has powerful connections with the notions of being able to pick something out, establish its identity, reidentify it at a later time, and so on. It's these connections that get activated in the demand for empirical criteria of subject identity. But once they've been activated, the Self-Identifiability Thesis no longer seems true, for it's widely agreed that there can be criterionless self-conscious self-ascription of properties, and I've argued that there are no good grounds for saying that a self-conscious being can't possibly engage in criterionless self-conscious self-ascription of properties unless it also possesses (practically applicable) empirical criteria of subject identity.

A general version of the question that leads people to endorse theses like the Empirical Criteria Thesis can be put like this: What must be true if one is to be able to put a boundary round oneself in thought in such a way that one can really be said to take oneself as an object of thought? Does S really have the resources to do this?[62] It's here that many say—with some confidence—that one has to possess empirically applicable criteria of subject identity of some sort in order to be able to draw this boundary line in thought.

My reply is the same. The line is sufficiently drawn, the boundary sufficiently demarcated, just so long as something is figured as oneself, in self-conscious experience. If this requires that something is always figured as not-oneself, however obscurely, so be it. One's experiences, one's experiences that come upon one, the subject of experience, and that are naturally apprehended as in some way distinct from oneself, are already sufficient to fill this role. What reason is there to think that the delineation or figuration of oneself can't be primitive in the sense that it is just given, unquestioned, built into the structure, the cognitive-experiential character, of one's conscious self-conscious thought, having no further possible expression for one and no independent justification or corroboration? This, in fact, is exactly how it is in our own case, experientially, when we engage in criterionless self-conscious self-ascription of experiences, and there is (once again) no good reason to suppose that the basic structure or cognitive-experiential character that our experience then has depends essentially on its developmental antecedents. The aetiology can't be what matters.

'Experiences that come upon one': sensory experience is typically involuntary and unavoidable, and it's often said, truly enough, that this contributes powerfully to (although it can't fully justify) its being apprehended as experience of something that is not-myself or external to self. But the involuntariness and unavoidability of experience (including much thought-experience) can clearly contribute equally powerfully to *experience itself* being apprehended as not-myself or external to self, quite independently of whether or not it is also taken to be experience of something other than itself. One does not have to think of oneself as having experience of an object, or mind-independent world, in order to categorize something as not-myself.

Apprehension of mathematical truth can also contribute largely to a sense of what is not-myself, in so far as it confronts one as something one can do nothing about. One may have a powerful model for what is not-myself in the content of mental episodes like thoughts about mathematics—or indeed about almost anything—even if one has no experience of sensations and thoughts just coming upon one involuntarily: even if the only thoughts one has are thoughts that one naturally experiences as fully intentionally

---

[62] Quassim Cassam once put this question to me.

produced. (It's arguable that experience of logical or mathematical thought is experience of a quasi-spatial order—one sees, for example, that if p is the case then q is, and then that if q is the case then r and s are too—in addition to being experience that has the character of being experience of a way things are that is distinct from the way one is oneself.)

3.15 The External Figuration Thesis

Perhaps we can re-express the fundamental thought that attracts philosophers to the Empirical Criteria Thesis in the (*External*) *Figuration Thesis*:

[27] if one is self-conscious, then there must be some source or foundation of one's grasp of oneself as an individual something—some image, or model, or experiential corroboration, or figuration of oneself as an individual something—that is external to and independent of any experience of oneself as an individual something that one may have simply in grasping or experiencing oneself as the mental subject of experience.

I can see no reason to accept the Figuration Thesis, however. Why must a self-conscious being be able to figure or put a thought-boundary round itself, in a way that demarcates it as an individual thing, in some experiential-conceptual frame other than the experiential-conceptual frame involved in one's thought and experience of oneself merely as a mental phenomenon or subject of experience? Some think this is necessary because they link thought essentially to language, and hold a mistaken view about the constraints that the role of language in public communication places on the possible content of thought. But this line of thought is bad at the best of times and hopelessly out of place in the present context (2.2).

Others defend the Figuration Thesis by appeal to the Kantian thought that concepts require 'sensible intuitions' and are 'empty' without them (A51/B75). On this view, one can't exercise the concept MYSELF at all unless there is some 'intuition' or sensory experience, or at least some 'non-conceptual' element in one's mental contents, for the concept to lambada with; and this requires that one be figured for—or to—oneself in something like the way proposed by the Figuration thesis characterized above. The way in which a mental subject like S is supposed to apprehend itself when it apprehends itself as present just as the mental subject (we can draw upon our experience of criterionless self-ascription of experiences in forming an idea of this) is thought to be too thin for us to be able to say that the subject can really be said to be thinking of itself as an individual something—unless it is also has some other kind of figuration of itself as back-up.

But why? We may grant that one can't be said to have a concept at all unless the concept in question has some genuine *application occasions*; it doesn't follow that the Figuration Thesis is true. S can have a rich source of experiential application occasions for the concept (MY)SELF, apprehending itself as the mental subject, simply in having fully or expressly self-conscious thoughts in the way that it's innately disposed to do, and without any capacity for any sensory or sense-like self-presentation: without any capacity for any presentation of itself in any mode other than the mode we have experience of when we engage in criterionless self-ascription of experiences.[63] When I consider the way in which S can feature in its own experience when it thinks self-consciously I wonder whether there is any better or more solid way in which anything can ever feature in anything's experience (even if many other ways are just as good). Some think that we're essentially better placed in our thought about tables and chairs or human bodies than S can ever be when it thinks of itself, given its lack of any sense of concrete non-mental being. But this view has no justification. In more or less sophisticated ways, it confuses perceived material solidity, or something like it, with referential solidity. It seems to be misled by a false picture of vividness—thinking, perhaps, that thought about a punch in the stomach has more referential solidity than S's thought about itself.

Am I begging the question? No, I'm just claiming that self-presentation in self-consciousness needn't involve anything as heavy as many suppose. In S's case it needn't involve any self-figuration other than the kind of self-figuration with which we are experientially familiar in criterionless self-ascription of experiences. A subject can be directly experientially given to itself in thought or experience even when it is given just as the mental subject—just as the 'thinking principle' or 'experiencing principle' of the thought or experience it has. It can present as a (single) something and a unity just as the 'experiencing principle' or 'thinking principle'.[64] This way of being available for thought and experience is as solid as any, although it has a profoundly intangible quality when compared with sensory givenness. Granted, self-apprehension must involve some non-conceptual element. The point is then that non-conceptual experience isn't restricted to sensory or sense-like—including proprioceptive or interoceptive—forms of experience (although S's self-apprehension can be allowed to be a form of proprioception, of self-experiencing, if this term is understood sufficiently widely). Certainly S must be given to itself in experience in some way. We may accordingly say that it must be given in some experiential modality or other. But it may be so given (and there is perhaps no way in which it can be more robustly given) in an experiential modality that isn't a sensory modality. It may be so given just by being aware of itself—of its presence—as the mental subject of experience.

What is the minimal form of such givenness? Must any concretely existing object (e.g. the subject of experience) be in some way an object of sense if it is indeed to be an object of thought? Kant discusses this question with exciting subtlety and with specific reference to our experience of the subject of experience. When he says, so famously, that the 'sole

---

[63] One might describe this as the suggestion that there are non-sensory forms of non-conceptual contact with the world (e.g. with oneself: part of the world), and this may be very close to what Kant has in mind at certain points in the Paralogisms; see further below.

[64] It's arguable, as noted in 3.5, that expressly self-conscious episodes constitutively, and so always, involve some such *experienced apprehension* of oneself as the thinking or experiencing principle involved in them, whatever else they involve, and however fleeting and undwelt-on this may be.

text' of rational psychology is 'I experience',[65] he means, at least in part (see page 50) *I experience* as actually comprehendingly entertained or experienced by someone (who in so doing obviously deploys the concept I). Now any such comprehending entertaining of *I experience* is necessarily referentially successful, and indeed, as Descartes observed, necessarily true. It follows that the entertaining of *I experience* records an actual, concrete, and in that sense 'empirical' fact. Kant remarks that it 'expresses the perception of the self' or subject, and 'contains an inner experience' or 'perception'.[66] He goes on to say that 'this inner perception is nothing more than the mere apperception *I experience*', and this, I propose, is the same as what I have in mind when I say that the subject is given to itself 'just by being aware of itself—of its presence—as the mental subject of experience'. The self-apprehending mental occurrence is empirical-experiential in one inescapable sense, and genuinely and successfully referential, but it involves no genuine intuition content, and is in that sense 'empty', so far as its 'I'-content is concerned.

He restates the point forcefully in a note in the second edition of the *Critique of Pure Reason* (B422 n.). 'The *I experience*', he says, 'is ... an empirical proposition, and contains within itself the proposition *I exist*.' As such, it 'expresses an ... empirical intuition, *i.e.* perception (and thus shows that sensation, which as such belongs to sensibility, lies at the basis of this existential proposition)'.[67] However, he says, it only expresses an 'indeterminate empirical ... perception', and 'an indeterminate perception here signifies only something real that is given, and given only for thought as such, and so not as appearance, nor as thing in itself ..., but [simply] as something which does indeed exist'.

[When] I called the proposition *I experience* an empirical proposition, I did not mean to say thereby that the *I* in this proposition is an empirical representation. On the contrary, it is purely intellectual, because belonging to thought in general. Without some empirical representation that supplies the material for thought the act *I experience* would not, indeed, take place; but the empirical is only the condition of the application or [actual] employment of the pure intellectual faculty.

I think that this is a beautiful expression of a point on which Kant could reasonably expect to be endlessly misunderstood: 'the whole difficulty is as to how a subject can inwardly intuit itself'. It is not wrong to say that 'the consciousness of self (apperception) is the simple representation of the *I*', but really 'we cannot even say that ... the simple, and by itself quite empty representation *I* ... is a concept, but only a mere consciousness

---

[65]   A343/B401. As in 2.10 I usually translate Kant's 'Ich denke' by 'I experience' ('I mentate'). We tend to forget the wide Cartesian sense of 'think' when reading Kant. Sometimes he intends the narrower sense, but the wider sense is often very important.

[66]   A342/B400; Kant stresses this point because he wants to make it clear that whatever the failings of rational psychology, its claim to produce fully and genuinely a priori proof of the simplicity, substantiality, etc. of the soul or subject is not put in question *simply* by the fact that it starts from the 'I experience' understood as expressing an actual 'empirical' fact, knowledge of the existence of something. I argue in 2.10 that Kant does see the rational psychologists as starting from an actual episode of reflective self-conscious awareness, although his main 'logico-transcendental' argument against them does not require this

[67]   This is striking (compare B68), and causes William James to intercede and insist that, so far as it is an empirically available phenomenon, 'the "I think" which Kant said must be able to accompany all my objects, is the "I breathe" which actually does accompany them' (1904a: 37). See further 7.6 below, p. 357.

accompanying all concepts' (B68, A346/B404). The sense in which *I experience* is an 'empirical proposition' remains: the subject is successfully referred to and is known to exist as a matter of (empirical) fact.

—Evidently you're enjoying yourself, but the assumption that S has genuine self-conscious experience really does beg the question at this point.

No. The question is whether one can make sense of the idea that S is self-conscious (perhaps innately, and from the first moment of its existence) after having explicitly assumed that it lacks any external figuration of itself in the present sense. Having made this assumption, I offer various descriptions of how things are for S, with its limited experiential resources. The burden of argument is on those who deny that they make sense.

—But when you claim that a subject that has no non-mental figuration of itself (no empirically applicable criteria of identity for itself) can be genuinely self-conscious, you're drawing unconsciously on the non-mental figuration of yourself that you like all human beings possess, and that lies firmly and indispensably behind your capacity to have experience of criterionless self-ascription of experiences.

My reply is the same as before. Even if one's capacity for criterionless self-ascription of experiences were developmentally dependent on one's possession of some non-mental figuration of oneself, it seems that this figuration might be entirely forgotten while the qualitative character of one's experience of oneself as an individual something remained untouched—being as it is for human beings when they engage in criterionless self-ascription of experiences. If so, another being could be created that had self-conscious experience with the same qualitative character although it had never possessed any non-mental figuration of itself. Following (unnecessarily) a human model, one may imagine it spending its life in a sensory isolation tank, in love with algebraic topology, and in no way disposed to fall into hallucination and madness as human beings do in such circumstances.

3.16 'Empirical', 'criteria'

I'll return to this issue in the next section. Here, since the notion of empirical criteria keeps returning, I want to ask about the exact force of the word 'empirical' in the Empirical Criteria Thesis, according to which

[25] a self-conscious being must be in possession of empirical criteria of subject identity.

The problem here is that the use of the word 'empirical' seems to be either redundant or mistaken. Whenever S and I have any experience, and *a fortiori* when we experience ourselves as subjects of experience in self-conscious thought, this is of course a matter of our having empirical experience, experience of some genuinely existing thing in the world (i.e. the subjects of experience that we are). But to say, correctly, that our experience is empirical in this sense is not to say that it's a matter of experience of anything publicly observable. A long tradition of use in which the words 'empirical' and 'publicly observable' have been coextensively applied has led to their confusion. It's a confusion because the private aspects of the content of experience—the qualitative experiential aspects that are directly accessible only to the subject—are, evidently, as much a matter of empirical experience as any other aspects.[68]

If, then, the supporters of the Empirical Criteria Thesis are demanding publicly available criteria of identity, they're misusing the word 'empirical', and should make their thesis plain by distinguishing the Empirical Criteria Thesis from the *Public Criteria Thesis*:

[28] if one is self-conscious, and can genuinely think of oneself as oneself, one must possess public criteria of subject identity.

They must then decide whether they want to endorse this thesis, which I take to be false, and distinguish it in turn from the less specific and more fundamental *Criteria Thesis*:

[29] if one is self-conscious, and can genuinely think of oneself as oneself, one must possess criteria of subject identity.

Is [29] true, at least? I think that there is a sense in which it is certainly true, and belongs in the core of the correct analysis of the conditions of active self-consciousness, along with [1]–[3], [5], [19], and the first, anodyne reading of [26]. But there's also a sense in which it isn't true. It depends on how one understands the rather shifty notion of a criterion. Some may say that the Criteria Thesis and the Public Criteria Thesis are really the same, because all genuine criteria are necessarily public criteria, and if they're right, the Criteria Thesis isn't true.

Are they? Surely not. Confusion arises from the fact that the word 'criterion' can be employed either with an epistemological stress or with a conceptual-logical stress. When the stress is epistemological, the main beat of the Criteria Thesis falls on the idea that a self-conscious being must be in possession of some way of *finding out* or *establishing* that something is a subject of experience within the total field of its experience, some *rule for judgement* (here one is closest to the etymological origin of the word), some *method* for distinguishing that which is a subject of experience from that which is not. And this alone may well be thought to entail that criteria must indeed be public. (One argument for this entailment runs roughly as follows: if X possesses a method or rule, then we must be able to make sense of the idea that there is a procedure for checking whether or not the method or rule is being applied correctly by X, and this requires that the conditions of correct application be publicly accessible.) When the stress is conceptual-logical, by contrast, the beat falls more simply on the idea that a self-conscious being must possess an adequate *conception* of what it is to be a subject of experience: a grasp of what is criterial (as we naturally say, using the word with this stress) for being a subject of experience. The mistake is to think that possession of criteria understood epistemologically in the

---

[68] As in 2.8 (38) I understand the notion of the content of an experience in the crucial internalist way to include its experiential qualitative character in addition to whatever it is experience of in the externalist sense, and take it that experiential qualitative character is as much cognitive as sensory.

above way is necessary for possession of criteria conceptually-logically understood. The mistake goes deep and has old and twisted empiricist roots.[69]

As remarked, I think that [29] is true when the stress is conceptual-logical, and has a place in the core account of the conditions of self-consciousness (it amounts in effect to [2]). One reason why it's distinct from [19], the Subject as Thing Thesis, and [26], the anodyne version of the Self-Identifiability Thesis, is that these allow one to be more seriously mistaken about what it is to be a subject of experience.

It may be said that the Subject as Thing Thesis and the anodyne version of the Self-Identifiability Thesis are right to allow for the possibility that a self-conscious being could be very mistaken about what it is to be a subject of experience, and that the Criteria Thesis is wrong to rule it out. And it's true that there is a sense in which one can think of oneself as oneself in the distinctively self-conscious way and yet be very wrong about what a subject of experience is. But once again two things are confused. One can wrongly think that a subject of experience is an immaterial soul, or whatever, and that being an immaterial soul, or whatever, is essential to—'criterial for'—being a subject of experience, and one may in that sense be spectacularly wrong, metaphysically speaking, about what a subject of experience is. It doesn't follow, however, that one can be fully self-conscious and fail to possess an adequate grasp of what it is to be—what is in fact criterial for being—a subject of experience. A grasp of something may be imperfect inasmuch as it contains a mistaken extra element while being fully adequate inasmuch as it misses out nothing essential (the notion of a subject of experience, like the notions of a person and a self, is in any case a 'functional' notion).

I think in fact that fully self-conscious beings like ourselves not only do have, but inevitably have, a very good idea of what a subject of experience is just in being one and being self-conscious; that fundamental adequacy in one's conception of what it is to be a subject of experience does indeed come automatically with—is inherent to—full self-consciousness (see page 63). In the case of S, the situation is (once again) this: S presents to itself as a unity in a way that even we can grasp, body-soused as we are, if we consider the way we present to ourselves as a unity when we engage in criterionless self-ascription of experiences. S possesses adequate conceptual-logical criteria of subject identity—an adequate conception of what it is to be a subject of experience—simply in experiencing itself as it does, as something that has experiences. The question of how it came to be that way is immaterial (in the sense of irrelevant).

I think, then, that the Criteria Thesis is correct, understood in the conceptual-logical sense, and quite different from both the Empirical Criteria Thesis and the Public Criteria Thesis. (I don't think that the Criteria Thesis is equivalent to the Public Criteria Thesis even when the stress is epistemological, but the—anti-Wittgensteinian—argument for this is for another time.)

---

[69] This difference of stress also affects the words 'identify' and 'identity', as noted on pp. 142–3. The primary force of the noun 'identity' in the phrase 'criteria of identity' seems to be conceptual-logical or constitutive. It has to do with the question of what makes a thing of a certain kind a thing of that kind. The verb 'to identify x', by contrast (which is distinct from 'to identify x with y'), has a primarily epistemological force, suggesting an action of picking out, an 'identification'.

What happens when one gives the Criteria Thesis an epistemological stress? Must S have some method for distinguishing that which is a subject of experience from that which is not, a method for 'picking itself out' in the total field of its experience? No. Nothing can really count as S's possessing—let alone applying—a rule or method for distinguishing, within the total field of its experience, that which is itself (or a subject of experience) from that which is not (its experiences, say, apprehended as distinct from it). This, though, is hardly a problem, for the reason this is so is that the distinction is always already available in the character of its experience in such a way that there's no room for anything that could constitute a rule or method for making the distinction.

The same conclusion follows even if it's allowed that one can't correctly attribute possession or mastery of a rule to a being without being able to make sense of the idea that it might go wrong in application of the rule. For there is no possibility that any being can be wrong about who or what it is thinking about *when all the mental appearances, for it, are that it is thinking about itself.* This is the fundamental sense in which one can't possibly miss one's target, when one thinks in terms of 'I' (i.e. self-consciously), the fundamental sense in which any 'I'-thought that one has is necessarily about oneself and is absolutely 'immune to error through misidentification of the subject' of the thought, even if it involves a major error of some kind.

Suppose (to take a couple of odd but standard philosophical examples) you see an arm painted blue in a mirror in a crowded room, believe wrongly that it's your own arm, and think *I have a blue arm.* Or suppose you have a false 'quasi-memory', i.e. an apparent memory of a past experience that derives directly (by some peculiar mechanism) from someone else's past experience,[70] and think *I fell in the river* or *I was sad.* In all such cases you're wrong about who has the property, but you're not wrong, and can't be wrong, in your (criterionless) latching onto or identification of yourself. Confusion has arisen from the phrase 'immune to error through misidentification of the subject', largely, perhaps, because 'identification' has two uses, one related to the notion of simply identifying or latching onto something, possibly in a criterionless way, the other to the notion of identifying something *with* (or *as*) something. Consider again your thought *I have a blue arm* or *I was sad.* It's false, and it makes sense to say that it's false not because the predicate-term fails to match the right property in the world, but because the subject-term fails to match the right thing in the world (something really does have the property in question; an error has been made about what it is). It doesn't, however, follow that there has been any misidentification of the subject of the thought. For, first, you certainly intend to refer to *yourself* with 'I', and you know this, and you certainly (inevitably) succeed: here there is no possible misidentification of the subject of the thought. Secondly, in so far as you intend to refer to *the person with the blue arm*, you also (if not necessarily) succeed: you do not misidentify (fail to pick out) the person with the blue arm. Your error, of course, is the (mis)identification of yourself *with* the person with the blue arm. Given this misidentification-with, we may say that the error in the thought stems not from the descriptive import of the predicate term but from the referential

---

[70] Shoemaker (1970) coined the term 'quasi-memory' for a phenomenon Locke discusses in 2.27.13 of his *Essay.*

import of the subject-term, since 'I' inevitably refers to you (whether or not there is a sense in which your intention underwrites the claim that it also refers to the person with the blue arm). There is in that indirect sense 'error through misidentification relative to "I" '. But this doesn't touch the fact that your I-thoughts are always about yourself, whatever else they may be about, and are in that fundamental respect absolutely and in all cases immune to error through misidentification of the subject.

3.17 Evans and 'discriminating knowledge'

Some, like Gareth Evans, may still want to insist that a being can't genuinely think about itself as an individual thing unless it possesses empirically applicable criteria of identity for itself analogous to those which we possess for things in space, on the very general grounds (1) that one can't be said to be thinking about any particular thing unless one knows which thing it is that one is thinking about, and (2) that one can't be said to know which thing one is thinking about, in the relevant sense, unless one has 'discriminating knowledge' of that thing, i.e. knowledge that would enable one to pick it out from all other things, i.e. (so it is supposed) empirically applicable criteria of identity for it.[71] Evans calls (1) 'Russell's Principle', endorses it along with (2) as a condition of genuine 'singular thought', i.e. thought about a particular individual thing, and sets about developing the notion of discriminating knowledge introduced in (2).

Russell's Principle seems to be false, however, even in the case of material objects. As so often, Evans himself has thought of the best objection to his own position.[72] One sees two indistinguishable steel balls, one on one day and another on the next day. Years later one has a thought about 'that steel ball'. In this case, it may be that one is thinking about one of them rather than the other, although one has no way of telling which it is (one may remember one of the events and have completely forgotten the other).

Suppose (to take another example) that one is thinking about an ornate clock tower in Zeitburg-am-Sein. One has no idea how one knows about it (one once saw it) or any precise idea of what it looks like. In fact, there is another similar ornate clock tower in Zeitburg, which one has never seen or heard about, and which undercuts any claim one has to discriminating knowledge of the first. Yet it is clear that when one thinks about 'that clock tower' one is thinking about the first clock tower, although one has no way of telling one from the other.[73]

---

[71] G. Evans 1982: ch. 4. Following P. F. Strawson (1964), Evans holds that one has such discriminating knowledge 'for example, when one can perceive ... an object ... at the present time; when one can recognize it if presented with it; and when one knows distinguishing facts about it' (1982: 89). His aim is to give a general theoretical account of what these three things have in common.

[72] See G. Evans 1982: 90.

[73] Reflection can deliver discriminating knowledge in this case: one can think of the clock tower in question as 'the one I saw', where this does in fact pick out just one of them, as one believes (whether or not one knows it). But Evans doesn't want to appeal to this sort of reflective knowledge in arguing his case (see e.g. 1982: 131–2 and 131n.), and there is a clear sense in which it doesn't provide a way of telling one from the other.

It seems, then, that Russell's Principle is false as it stands. So even if it is the case, directly contrary to everything I've been arguing, that no being can be self-conscious without experience of embodiment or location in an ordered world, or something of the sort, this is not because Russell's Principle is true. It isn't because one can't really think of any particular concrete thing unless one has workable, empirically applicable criteria of identity for it. Even if one finds it plausible that one can't think of an everyday thing like a particular table or a chair unless one has empirically applicable criteria of identity for it, the claim seems to be at its least plausible in the present case, in which one is considering a thing thinking of itself, and thinking of itself specifically as the mental subject of experience encountered as an apparent entity in the normal course of thought in the way familiar to us all.

Suppose it is said that one can't possess the general cognitive resources needed for genuine singular thought without possessing empirically applicable criteria of identity for at least some things. I could concede this for the sake of argument, although I don't believe it, because it doesn't entail that S can't be genuinely thinking about itself if it lacks empirically applicable criteria of identity *for itself*. To establish this second claim, one would also need to show that one can't possess the general cognitive resources needed for genuine singular thought unless one is oneself among the things for which one has empirically applicable criteria of identity. (It it could somehow be shown that one can't have empirically applicable criteria of identity for anything at all without also having such criteria of identity for oneself, I would withdraw the concession made earlier in the paragraph, and deny that one must possess empirically applicable criteria of identity for any things at all if one is to be capable of genuine singular thought.)

I continue to hold, then, that S can think of itself in the distinctively self-conscious way without possessing empirically applicable criteria of identity for itself—without possessing discriminating knowledge of itself in Evans's sense. Expanding the sense of 'discriminating knowledge', one might be tempted to say that S has discriminating knowledge for free—and inescapably—simply in so far as its thoughts about itself are absolutely immune to error through misidentification of the subject in the sense described earlier. This expansion, however, offers no support to the claim about the necessity of possessing empirically applicable criteria of identity. Nor is the immunity to error in fact essential to the possibility of S's thinking about itself in the distinctively self-conscious way. Suppose the possibility of error were somehow provided for but never in fact occurred. This wouldn't undermine the claim that S was indeed thinking about itself when it appeared to be. (I'm inclined to add that even if error did somehow actually occur on occasion, that wouldn't undermine the claim that S was thinking about itself when error didn't occur—but it's hard to assess the force of conditionals with impossible antecedents.)

S, then, can think about itself, and can think about itself as itself. When *we* ask what S is thinking about, we may wish to say that S is thinking about the physical thing that it is (unknowingly) considered as a whole—i.e. about the indissolubly mental-and-non-mental thing that it is considered as a whole. For we may be disinclined to say that the apparent *mental self*, considered in isolation, is really a *thing* at all (wrongly, in my view;

see further 4.3 and 6.12). For the moment, though, the point is that S itself doesn't have to be thinking of itself under any description that essentially involves any grasp of itself as having non-mental being—let alone under any description that locates it in an order of things in which empirically applicable criteria of identity of a familiar kind are actually or potentially available (whether to it or to others). Nor does S have to be capable of thinking of itself under any such description.

Perhaps S has some kind of SELF-experience, experiencing itself as a subject of experience (and perhaps as an agent) that is a single, persisting mental thing (2.9). The idea of itself as a particular individual is fully present in this way of thinking even if there are insuperable difficulties with the view that there could actually be a thing with nothing but these features. I've taken it throughout that S has non-mental features as well as mental features, but it doesn't follow from the fact that S is unaware of this that S lacks the resources to think of itself at all, or to think of itself as itself, any more than it follows that we do in having, as we surely do, a partial understanding of our own nature.

If S is philosophically reflective, it may perhaps attain a certain kind of discriminating knowledge of the thing it is thinking about when it thinks about itself in the distinctively self-conscious way and grasps itself as itself: it may, for example, realize that it is in fact the only thing it *can* be thinking about when it thinks in this way. And this thought involves express thought of the possibility that other things (even, perhaps, other similar things) exist. Even so, this discriminating knowledge doesn't consist in its possession of empirically applicable criteria of identity for itself; nor does it have to be philosophically reflective in this way in order for it to be true that it is indeed thinking of itself when it has what appear to be self-conscious thoughts.

—S can't know that it is thinking about a particular thing because it can't know that it is not thinking about ten subjects of experience thinking in unison.

This objection has no force, for, first, even if S can't know that it's thinking about one thing, there may be only one thing, and if there is, then S really is thinking about it. S doesn't need to know, or be able to show, that there is only one thing, in order for this to be the case. Second, even if there are ten subjects of experience, there is no problem, for then each one of them will necessarily be thinking about itself, given self-conscious thought's immunity to error through misidentification of the subject, and will, so far, be quite correct in thinking that it is a single subject of experience (see 2.20). It's sometimes said that we can't meaningfully suppose that there are ten qualitatively identical things—for example—rather than just one thing if we lack empirically applicable criteria of identity for things of the kind in question. But the supposition that things (immaterial souls, subjects of experience, whatever) may be numerically distinct although indistinguishable from each other by embodied human beings is of course fully intelligible. We can give a simple general description of what has to be true if there are to be two qualitatively identical but numerically distinct things X and Y: there must be some dimension or space ('dimension' or 'space') in ('in') which they exist, given which X and Y can differ in some way (e.g. in place or 'place') even while they remain qualitatively identical. We are familiar with spacetime as the dimension that provides for the possibility of numerical distinctness of qualitatively identical things, and we have no reason to think that there aren't any other possibilities.

S's mental life may be rich and diverse in a way already imagined. It may have mathematical thoughts, sound experiences, smell experiences, colour experiences, and so on. It may experience happiness, sadness, anxiety, peace, mental drowsiness. It may take pleasure in proofs, and in certain arrangements of sounds. But it may have no thought that there is or may be anything other than itself and its thoughts and experiences. If it is said that it must at least have experience that has the character of being experience of what is not-myself, it may be replied, once again, that its thoughts and other experiences and their contents may amply fill the role of the not-myself, in being phenomena that it distinguishes from itself considered as the subject of experience. One can take one's experiences to be things distinct from oneself, the subject of experience, without taking them to be experiences *of* things distinct from oneself.

—Sensory experiences like colour or sound experience are already and necessarily experiences that have—essentially—the character of being experience of concrete non-mental being.

I've already rejected this claim on the grounds that they may be apprehended merely as differently qualitied ways of experiencing—in so far as they are reflected on at all.[4] Suppose S is innately mentally disposed in such a way that it automatically and unreflectively takes colour and sound experiences that impinge upon its consciousness to be experiences of something ontologically distinct from itself and its experiences. Even so, it needn't have any further thought about the ontological implications of so doing (it needn't, for example, take them to be experiences of a *single world*, ordered or not, of which it has experience), and it may for all that be fully self-conscious, and indeed have SELF-experience. It need be no more reflective, with regard to questions about the overall ontological nature of the self, than human beings are; and it may be less reflective. It may never sleep, and have no potential problem about what happens when it is asleep or unconscious, or it may sleep and have no knowledge of this, or it may simply never consider the question of what happens when it is asleep. Again, it may think of itself as a 'thinking, active principle' (66) that is somehow constituted by consciousness, and that sometimes sleeps, and simply fail to consider the problem posed by this idea. A proclivity to philosophical speculation isn't a necessary condition of self-consciousness, or indeed SELF-experience.

As for S's sense of the passing of time and of itself as persisting through time, this—in so far as it is necessary to self-consciousness—may simply be intrinsic to its experience of succeeding states of consciousness. To say this is to reject Kant's Refutation of Idealism, but Kant gives us no good reason to believe that a sense that there is a real or 'objective' time-order depends essentially on believing that there is an ordered, external, temporal

---

[4] Even if some version of this objection were sound, it would not yield anything close to a standard Body Thesis. P. F. Strawson considers the possibility that a subject might 'conceive of an objective world of things constituted of colour variously disposed in space' (1980: 278–9). It seems that such a subject might take these colour phenomena to cause its experiences of seeing them without having any thought that they might have other properties.

world of objects, or that there exist objects other than oneself (his argument is in effect a Need Argument of the sort rejected earlier). Even if S is the only thing there is, and the (objective) sequence of events just is the sequence of S's (subjective) experiences, and S doesn't suppose otherwise, it can have thoughts like 'blue-experience has just followed red-experience, but (it is imaginable that) red-experience might have followed blue-experience instead'. In order to think that blue-experience might have followed red-experience instead of vice versa, it certainly doesn't have to think that there exists something other than the colour experiences which is the cause of them.

3.18 Evans, appearance, and reality

I've suggested that if one is self-conscious, then one must [1] possess the thought-element I or MYSELF, [2]–[3] have some conception of experience and of subject-of-experiencehood, [5] possess the conceptual resources (although perhaps not the actual ability) to form and entertain a conception of other subjects of experience, [19] be able to think of oneself as a thing or entity in some sense, [26] be able to identify something as oneself (in the weak sense of 'identify'), and [29] possess criteria of subject identity (when 'criteria' is understood in its conceptual-logical rather than its epistemological sense).

It is not true, I think, that [4] one must possess a conception of other subjects of experience, or that [6] one must have had the thought that there might be other subjects of experiences, or that [7] one must actually believe that there are other subjects of experience, or that [8] one must have (had) experience that has the character of being experience of interaction with other subjects of experience, or that [9] one must have (had) actual experience of interaction with other subjects of experience, or that [10] one must have (had) experience of body or concrete non-mental being, or that [11] one must at least have (had) experience that has the *character* of being experience of body (or concrete non-mental being), or that [12] one must possess a conception of body (or concrete non-mental being), or that [13] one must be aware of oneself as being embodied, or that [14] one must have awareness of oneself as embodied by means of external sense organs of some kind, or that [15] interoceptive experience of oneself as embodied is indispensable or at least extremely important, or that [16] one can't be self-conscious unless one is aware of oneself as being singly embodied, or that [17] one must at least have experience that has the character of being experience of (single) embodiment, or that [18] one must figure oneself as (singly) embodied, or that [20] one must be able to make a distinction between the way things are subjectively and the way things are objectively, or that [21] one must at least have the mental resources to be able to grasp the distinction between the way things are and the way one experiences them to be, or that [22] one must figure oneself as located in, and as tracing a route through, a world that exhibits a certain degree of order of which one is aware, or that [23] one must at least experience oneself as having a point of view in an ordered external world of some sort, or that [24] one must at least have experience that has, for one, the character of being experience of a reality or world, ordered or not, that is more

than or wider than the reality that consists of oneself and one's experiences, or that
[25] one must possess empirical criteria of subject identity (of the sort paradigmatically
supplied by our experience of ourselves as singly embodied in an ordered world of other
bodies), or that [27] one must have some image or corroboration or *figuration* of oneself
as an individual something-or-other that is external to or independent of the experience
of oneself as an individual something that one has simply in experiencing oneself as a
mental subject of experience in self-conscious thought, or that [28] one must possess
public criteria of subject identity. I could add and reject further proposals drawn from
the existing literature: it is not, for example, true that

[30] if one is self-conscious then one must grasp the idea that one's later states causally
depend, at least partially, on one's earlier states, or that
[31] if one is self-conscious then one must grasp the idea that one can function as a
common cause of events around one.[75]

But this is enough for the moment.

I now encounter a new set of opponents.

—It can seem that your minimal subject S is thinking in a fully self-conscious way, even if S
doesn't have many of the features that your original set of opponents believed to be necessary for
self consciousness. But things can't really be as they seem. Suppose S apparently has a thought
with the content (1) 'I'm having an experience of red'. In this situation S has indeed attempted, but
hasn't really achieved, a fully self-conscious thought. S's apparent thought, i.e. (1), is equivalent
to the less determinate and not self-conscious thought (2) 'There is an experience of red'.

Obviously I disagree. The first thing to say, perhaps, is that we can accept that (1) and
(2) are 'empirically equivalent' for S in the sense that (2) is true whenever (1) is, and
conversely, while denying that they are semantically or cognitively equivalent for S.
It may be insisted that (1) and (2) are wholly equivalent for S if they are empirically
equivalent, and that S can't really be said to have a thought with the content of (1), but
only a thought with the content of (2). This argument is odd, though, for if the content
of (1) and (2) are equivalent for S, then there's no asymmetry: for S to have a thought
with the content of (2) just is for S to have a thought with the content of (1). Still, the
idea is clear: (1) and (2) are different for us, and the claim is that in apparently having
(1) S doesn't really have a thought that has a content different from the content that
(2) has for us.

What should we make of this? The starting hypothesis is that S's thought just does
occur in the apparent form of (1), so that the core *phenomenology* of S's conscious
entertaining of apparently self-conscious thoughts is like ours. It is then objected that
even if the phenomenology is as it is, S can't really be said to have such self-conscious
thoughts at all.

Some, of course, may question the coherence of the starting hypothesis. They may
deny that S can even have a thought with the *apparent* content of (1), in the absence

---

[75] Campbell (1994) makes these two proposals.

of experience of embodiment, or belief in an ordered world, or in the existence of other subjects of experience, or ... etc. They may, that is, deny that S can even have the apparent phenomenology of conscious fully self-conscious thought, in the absence of certain of these other beliefs or experiences. This means that they want to return to the arguments of 3.4–3.13 and start again, and that is their right. Here, however, I'm concerned with those, like Evans, who accept the coherence of the hypothesis about the phenomenology of S's putative I-thought while claiming that the content of S's apparent (1)-thought can't really be what it seems—whether or not they go on to say that it's really only something like (2). They accept that things are for S as they can be for us, so far as the basic phenomenology of having the I-thought is concerned, while denying that S can really be said to have a thought with the content of (1). The content of (1) as thought by S is not really the same (in the relevant sense) as the content of (1) as thought by us, they say, even if S's and our experiences of thinking (1) are phenomenologically similar. S's apparent I-thought can't really count as an I-thought at all.

As just remarked, Evans is an example of someone who accepts that the phenomenology of having an I-thought (a fully self-conscious thought) can be fully in place even though the subject isn't really having the apparent I-thought in question.[76] He endorses a form of the Ordered World Thesis as a condition on successful or *genuine* I-thought, claiming that a being can't think of itself as 'I' if it can't think of itself as (or identify itself with) 'an element in the objective order' located at a particular place which it can think of as 'here' (p. 254). He argues that 'one's 'I'-Idea and one's 'here'-Idea are really two sides of a single capacity' (p. 256; see also p. 243). He grants that a being may continue to have *apparent* I-thoughts when it can no longer identify itself with an element in the objective (spatial) order located at a particular place, but holds that in this case 'its "I"—its habitual mode of thought about itself—is simply inadequate for this situation. (It forces the subject to think in ways which are no longer appropriate)' (p. 255).

The case in question, then, is one in which the phenomenology of having a conscious I-thought is preserved intact—there is an apparent I-thought—but the apparent I-thought is held to be really no such thing; the subject simply can't 'think of itself as "I" ' even if—even though—it is indeed the object of its thought (one might try to subtract this element), and even though it is, so far as the phenomenology of the seeming thought is concerned, thinking about itself *as* itself in the distinctively self-conscious way.

Evans doesn't claim that its seeming I-thought is really equivalent to an impersonal thought (this is the suggestion in the case of (1) and (2)). His claim is rather that 'I' as it occurs in its thought fails to refer to anything in the way that it appears to do. It seems to me, however, that this conclusion is a *reductio ad absurdum* of the principle that gives rise to it—Russell's Principle as expounded by Evans.[77]

---

[76] 1982: 249–55; page references in this section are to Evans's book.

[77] If Russell's Principle is differently understood, it seems clear that S—or, equally, the subject Evans is considering—does fulfil the condition that the principle places on thinking about oneself. To put it in terms of Evans's 'discriminating knowledge' requirement: it's unclear why S can't be supposed to fulfil the first of the three sufficient conditions for discriminating knowledge (see n. 71, also Shoemaker 1986), and a case can also be made for saying that it also fulfils—or could fulfil—the second and third.

Developing his argument, Evans writes:

It seems possible to envisage organisms whose control centre is outside the body, and connected to it by communication links. ... An organism of this kind could have an Idea of itself like our own, but if it did it would be unable to cope with the situation that would arise when the control centre survived the destruction of the body it controlled. Thinking like us, the subject would of course have to regard itself as somewhere, but in this case it would not make any sense to identify a particular place in the world it thought of as *here*. The place occupied by the control centre is certainly not the subject's *here*; and even if we counterfactually suppose the control centre re-equipped with a body, there is no particular place where that body would have to be. Because its 'here' picks out no place, there is no bit of matter, no persisting thing, which the subject's Idea of itself permits us to regard as what it identifies as itself. Here, then, we have a very clear situation in which a subject of thought could not think of itself as 'I'; its 'I'—its habitual mode of thought about itself—is simply inadequate for this situation.[78]

This sort of inadequacy can also afflict us in more ordinary situations, according to Evans: 'our ordinary thoughts about ourselves are liable to many different kinds of failings, and ... the Cartesian assumption that such thoughts are always guaranteed to have an object cannot be sustained' (p. 249).

It seems to me, however, that Evans once again provides the best objection to his own view, and that the above passage makes it vivid that 'I' succeeds in hitting its mark—the I, the subject of experience that indubitably exists, whatever its ultimate nature—even when there is no bit of matter or other persisting thing that it can identify as itself. It shows, in effect, that a subject's apparent thoughts about itself—its apparent 'I'-thoughts that lack nothing phenomenologically speaking—always have an object. In fact they always have the object they're thought to have, however many false beliefs the subject has about its own nature. And even if it could somehow be shown that such thoughts don't always have an object, it would still be true that they can have an object in situations in which Evans denies that they can, for a more direct objection to Evans's case runs as follows. Suppose the subject thinks 'I'm in big trouble, wherever I am', or 'I don't know where I am, or how much of me is left intact, but I'm in big trouble, wherever I am, and however much of me is left'. In this case there seems to be no good reason to think that 'the control centre', which I assume to be the locus of the subject's consciousness, 'is certainly not the subject's *here*'.

One important disagreement concerns time. Evans considers another hypothetical case in which one has a false 'quasi-memory', an apparent memory of perceiving a certain past event *e* that derives directly from someone else's perception of that event. One thinks, in the present, 'I perceived *e*', or 'I perceived *e* in 1990'; but in fact it was B, not oneself, who perceived *e*. Evans claims that one's I-thought 'I perceived *e* (in 1990)' actually has no object in this case, because one is bringing 'both present-tense ... and past-tense ... information to bear upon [one's current] self-conscious reflections, and

---

[78] pp. 254–5. Compare Platner (1772: §193): 'we are conscious of ourselves, that is of our existence, if we know the spatial, temporal and other relations of our condition. If we do not know where we are and when we are, then we are not conscious of ourselves.'

there is no one thing from which both kinds of information derive'. He compares this to a case in which one is looking at one cup and feeling another; one falsely supposes that there is just one cup, and thinks 'this cup is well made' (pp. 249–50).

The case of the cups is good, but the comparison is unhelpful. The occurrence of 'I' in the thought 'I perceived *e* (in 1990)' (or, generally, 'I was *F*') is guaranteed a reference because it unfailingly cleaves to one thing, oneself, present at the time of the thought. It concerns oneself thought of as a thing that exists now and that existed in the past. It's false precisely because one did not perceive *e* in the past, in 1990. It isn't a thought that involves any confusion about who or what the subject of the thought is, even though it involves a mistake. (Evans seems to assign the wrong sort of importance to certain causal facts in a way that is surprising given his criticisms of the causal theory of reference earlier in his book.)

Evans claims that 'it is of the essence of an "I"-Idea that it effects an identification that spans past and present' (p. 246), but it's hard to see why this might be thought to be a general truth, for it's hard to see why there could not be a self-conscious being that had no significant sense or conception of the past at all (see 4.7). And even if the claim is granted, it doesn't provide grounds for an objection to the view that one's apparent I-thought has an object, in the case in question, and has, indeed, the object one takes it to have. Even if it is of the essence of an 'I'-Idea to effect an identification that spans past and present, it remains true that one's quasi-memory concerns only oneself—oneself present now and thought of, if only implicitly, as temporally extended and as existing both now and in 1990. This fundamental fact effortlessly trumps any facts about the actual source of the information carried in the quasi-memory.

Here, then, we have another case in which there is an apparent I-thought (i.e. a case in which the phenomenology of thinking an I-thought is not defective in any way) but it's argued that the apparent I-thought is really no such thing. I can see no reason to think that this is the right thing to say, and conclude that when a being appears to have an I-thought—where 'appears' means that the basic phenomenology of I-thought is in place—it really does have an I-thought: always. There is, in other words, no possibility of failure or error through lack of possession of empirically applicable criteria of identity for the subject. By the same token, I hold that S's thought (1) 'I am experiencing red' is not after all equivalent to (2) 'There is an experience of red'. If this makes me a Cartesian, then that is what I am. We may have good reason to reject parts of Descartes's view of the mind—his substance dualism, for example—but he's a lot closer to the truth about mind and experience than most analytic philosophers in the last seventy years.

3.19 Summary and conclusion

I've argued that full self-consciousness requires a capacity for thought with language-like articulation and abstractness, if not for language itself (3.2). I've argued that it requires possession of some sort of conception of oneself as a subject of experience, and, further (more controversially, in the present philosophical climate), access to some conception of oneself as something that is, as such, somehow single just qua mental, considered at any given time (3.5). It isn't clear how much else can be said. Many proposals that have been made about the necessary conditions of self-consciousness seem unconvincing. There seems to be no inexorable logical, conceptual, or metaphysical reason why a fully self-conscious subject (or indeed a subject that has SELF-experience) must have any sense of itself as embodied, or, more generally, as non-mentally aspected. Nor does there seem to be any inexorable reason why it must have any sense of itself as located (either literally or metaphorically) in a domain ontically distinct from it and its experiences, or any belief that its experiences are experiences of things that are ontically distinct from it and its experiences. Nor does it seem to be the case that one can't be self-conscious, or have SELF-experience, unless one possesses empirically applicable criteria of identity for oneself (as ordinarily understood) that one can be in a position to apply. Nor is it the case that one can't really be said to think of oneself at all unless one possesses discriminating knowledge of oneself in the sense discussed in 3.17. There's no incoherence in the idea that a being might be fully self-conscious, and indeed have SELF-experience, and a rich and vivid mental life, without having a mind that had been stocked with or structured by forms of experience that had the character of being experiences of a spatial or 'quasi-spatial' objective order of things distinct from the subject's experiences. In general, it seems that the basic cognitive phenomenology of self-consciousness, and indeed SELF-experience, can exist in the complete absence of anything like our own familiar experiential framework.

Part 4

Phenomenology: the general question

In all thinking … each must necessarily regard himself as a substance … I, whom/that I think, must in thinking always be regarded as a subject.

Kant *Critique* A349, B407.

4.1 The Whittling Argument

In Part 2 I raised the local phenomenological question: How does ordinary human SELF-experience figure the self? My provisional answer was: as a subject of experience, an agent, a single persisting mental thing that is distinct from the human being considered as a whole and possesses a certain personality. In terms of thought-elements, the principal (and variously overlapping) elements of the ordinary human thought-element SELF are: SUBJECT, THING, MENTAL, SINGLE, PERSISTING, AGENT, DISTINCT, and PERSONALITY. One can't leave it at that, however, because it's important that these elements compound in various ways. Ordinary human SELF-experience not only figures the self, considered at any given time, as single, and as a subject of experience, and as mental. It also figures the self as single at any given time considered specifically as a subject of experience (SINGLE-AS-SUBJECT), and as a subject of experience considered specifically as mental (SINGLE-AS-SUBJECT-AS-MENTAL). 'SINGLE' and 'MENTAL' may seem redundant, for of course *a* subject is a single subject, and of course it's mentally propertied; they're listed separately in the interests of full disclosure, and because of the way they compound with other elements.

In Part 3 I moved away from more purely phenomenological matters and addressed the *grounds question*: What are the grounds or conditions of self-consciousness—which are also, perhaps, grounds of SELF-experience? Consideration of this question brought up a mixture of phenomenological and logico-metaphysical considerations, and I ended up with the exiguous answer summarized on page 159–60.

I want now to return to the main phenomenological argument, moving from the local question to the general phenomenological question: What must be true of any genuine form of SELF-experience, any form of SELF-experience worthy of the name? What's the minimal form of SELF-experience?

Some may still wonder whether it's right to spend so much time on phenomenology if one's main concern is to establish whether or not selves exist. I argued in Part 2 that it's a good idea to do this, in order to get a proper sense of what the problem of the self is. It seems the best—although not the only—way to find out what selves are meant to be in such a way as to confer sufficiently determinate content on the question whether they exist.

The phenomenological project issues in two main versions of the question whether selves exist. The content of the first version—Do selves exist as figured in ordinary human SELF-experience?—depends on the answer to the local phenomenological question, and has accordingly become the question:

Are there subjects of experience that are single, persisting mental things, agents that possess a certain personality and are distinct from the organism in which they are located considered as a whole? Are there, in other words, things that have the properties *subject, thing, mental, single, persisting, agent, distinct, personality*, and the associated compound properties, such as *single-as-mental*?[1]

I use 'thing' as before (46) rather than 'object' or 'substance' because it has a valuable openness.

The content of the second version of the question whether selves exist

Do selves exist as figured in the minimal form of SELF-experience?

depends on the answer to the general phenomenological question, which we don't yet have, and I'm now going to try to give it by running the Whittling Argument. This aims to work out the root form of SELF-experience by whittling away as many of the elements of ordinary human SELF-experience as possible. Given that the list of elements of ordinary human SELF-experience omits nothing essential to SELF-experience (46), the only remaining question is whether it includes anything inessential.

—This can't really work. The phenomenological investigation of SELF-experience loses a vital degree of independence when it moves from the local to the general question, because it's no longer based on the human case. Once one goes beyond the human case, metaphysical presuppositions are bound to influence one's judgements about whether or not some thinned-down candidate form of SELF-experience is really genuine SELF-experience. The human case is the only case with which we are or can be genuinely phenomenologically acquainted, and even if we grant that our judgements in the human case can be free of any question-begging metaphysical presuppositions (which I doubt), we can hardly suppose that pursuing

---

[1]   As before (see p. 57) I use italics for names of properties.

the notion of SELF-experience beyond the human case can deliver purely phenomenological, metaphysics-free conclusions that can set the task for metaphysics without in any way prejudging the issue.

This objection was noted on page 54, and it sounds far from unreasonable. So let me say, first, that almost all the thinned-down versions of SELF-experience that I'm going to consider can be related to human possibilities, and indeed to actual human experience. Secondly, I'm happy to allow that metaphysical presuppositions of one sort or another inform all our thoughts, but I think we can keep judgements about whether thinned-down versions of ordinary human SELF-experience are genuine forms of SELF-experience comfortably (or at least sufficiently) independent of any *specifically theoretical* (philosophical) metaphysical views about the self, as opposed to the metaphysical bone–structure of ordinary everyday thought. I hope that the tale will sufficiently prove its independence in the telling, and that it will fail instructively if it fails.

What, then, is the minimal case of SELF-experience? What must any genuine form of SELF-experience be like? If a being has SELF-experience, must it then experience itself* (itself considered as a self) as a single persisting subject of experience, a mental thing that is an agent that possesses a certain personality and is distinct from the entity that it is considered as a whole? Are all seven or eight elements necessary? I'll consider them in turn, beginning with SUBJECT, SINGLE, MENTAL, and DISTINCT.

4.2 SUBJECT, MENTAL, DISTINCT, SINGLE₀

What thought-elements are strictly necessary for SELF-experience? What *must* be the case if one figures oneself as a self in some way? Are

SUBJECT (the self is figured as a subject of experience)

and

MENTAL (the self is figured as mentally propertied or as having mental being)

strictly necessary? Can either of these elements of ordinary human SELF-experience be whittled away?

Evidently not. In the case of SUBJECT a rhetorical question is enough: How could a being have something correctly describable as SELF-experience—experience of itself as a self—and not figure the self it experienced itself to be as a subject of experience?

The 'passivity phenomena' characteristic of schizophrenia, such as 'thought insertion', provide no grounds for doubt.[2] In thought insertion a thought that occurs in one's consciousness is experienced by one as inserted from outside, alien to one, thought or generated by someone else. It follows immediately that there's a fundamental sense in which the experience of subjecthood or ownership isn't lost, for experience of a thought as inserted from outside or alien presupposes some sense of oneself as

[2] See e.g. Nicholi 1999: 246; Stephens and Graham 2000.

a, or the, subject of experience relative to whom the thought is alien or externally originated.

—This doesn't address the possibility that SELF-experience can lapse altogether in psychopathological cases …

True, but this isn't relevant. The question isn't whether there are pathological human cases in which SELF-experience can lapse altogether while experience persists. Perhaps there are. The question is whether anything can qualify as SELF-experience if it involves no sense that the self that there is experienced to be is a subject of experience. No. If meditators retain awareness of their mental being but lose any sense of there being a subject, then they cease to have SELF-experience (see 4.4).

So much for SUBJECT. MENTAL is now equally easy, for one can't experience oneself as a subject of experience without experiencing oneself as mentally propertied or as having mental being: [SUBJECT → MENTAL]. This is obvious whether one adopts the narrow, inner entity reading of 'subject of experience' or the wide, whole creature reading.

—But what is it, exactly, to experience oneself as having mental being, or as mentally propertied, or as a mental phenomenon? What is it, for that matter, to *have* mental being, or to *be* mentally propertied, to *be* a mental phenomenon? I don't see how you can answer the first question without having answered the second.

I'm only concerned with the first, phenomenological question. The second, metaphysical question is important, but I don't need to answer it here. For present phenomenological purposes the meaning of 'mental' is sufficiently and securely grounded in our pre-theoretical understanding of the mental, our ordinary everyday acquaintance with our own mental being, and the experience of apprehending oneself as a subject of experience already contains everything needed, when it comes to experience of oneself as mentally propertied.[3]

So much for MENTAL. What about

DISTINCT (the self is figured as distinct from, in the sense of non-identical with, the whole human being)?

The first thing to do is to adapt it for general use by eliminating the reference to human beings:

DISTINCT The self is figured as distinct from, in the sense of non-identical with, the organism or entity considered as a whole.

Is it in this form a necessary element of SELF-experience?

No. It may hold good in almost every case, including any clearly conceivable human case, but in the minimal case, it seems, a being B may not have any conception of itself

---

[3] See p. 67. Remember also the sense in which a child can be said to have experience that figures the self as mental without this involving possession or exercise of the full-fledged general thought-element MENTAL, with all that that entails (68; see also 110–11).

as anything at all other than the self or mental presence that it experiences itself to be (see 3.14). In this case the question of distinctness—the question whether or not the self that B takes itself to be is distinct from the entity considered as a whole that it takes itself to be—simply doesn't arise for B.

One might try to retain a version of DISTINCT among the core conditions of SELF-experience, on the grounds that it captures something that is very likely to be an important feature of SELF-experience in almost every actual case, but one would have to express it in a doubly conditional form:

DISTINCT$^\circ$ The self is figured in such a way that *if* one does have some sense or conception of oneself as an entity X that permits the question of whether or not oneself considered as a self is identical with X to arise at all for one, then *if* it does arise for one, one figures the self as not identical with X.

It doesn't seem to be true even in this form, however. One might in such a situation take it that the self that one is, is in fact identical with X, that what one's sense or conception of X picks up on is just the non-mental being of the self that one takes oneself to be.

I take it, then, that DISTINCT isn't essential. It's likely to be part of SELF-experience, but it seems that one can experience oneself as a self without in any way figuring oneself as distinct from some entity that one takes oneself to be when one considers oneself as a whole.

What about

SINGLE

and in particular

SINGLE$_S$

the figuring of the self as something that is synchronically single, i.e. single in the lived present of experience? Is this a necessary feature of all genuine SELF-experience?[4]

I believe so. I put the case in 2.18–2.20 (noting that I was answering part of the general phenomenological question in advance), and have nothing to add. I take it to be on firm ground if only because it borders on triviality. It's surrounded by a persistent penumbra of intuitions that a creature that had SELF-experience might somehow experience itself* as multiple, (76) but these intuitions appear to fall apart on reflection. It's not just that attempts to characterize the self as multiple at a given time fail to be anything more than metaphors, and bad metaphors at that—a point of metaphysics. It's also that attempts to characterize SELF-experience as experience of oneself as multiple seem to fail to stand up to inspection—a point of phenomenology.

One way to put the point is to say that the place of SINGLE is guaranteed by SUBJECT: genuinely to grasp or experience oneself as a subject, at a given time, is already and necessarily to grasp or experience oneself as single, at that time, as Kant observed (in so far as his argument has a phenomenological aspect) in his discussion of the Paralogisms. And it isn't just that one must figure oneself as single in some way or other, in SELF-experience, and also figure oneself as subject, in some way or other. One must figure

---

[4] The subscript in SINGLE$_S$ can be dropped, because SINGLE$_D$ has been replaced by PERSISTING, and SINGLE$_S$ entails SINGLE. I retain it sometimes for emphasis.

oneself as something that is single *considered specifically as subject*—as single-as-subject. SINGLE and SUBJECT couple to yield SINGLE-AS-SUBJECT, a further necessary element of SELF-experience—

[SELF → SINGLE-as-SUBJECT]

—and there is a further point, also noted in 2.19 (and 3.5). The term SUBJECT has been given a strictly neutral use, neutral between the wide whole-creature use and the narrow inner-entity use. This being so, the point that SINGLE-AS-SUBJECT is a necessary element of SELF-experience leaves room for the possibility that one might have SELF-experience even if one thought of oneself as single-as-subject only when thinking of oneself as subject of experience in the whole-organism sense of the term. But this isn't a real possibility, or so I claim: one must in SELF-experience figure the self as it is in the lived present of experience not only as single-as-subject but also as single-as-subject-as-mental—however else one does or doesn't figure oneself. It isn't only in ordinary human SELF-experience that SINGLE(s), SUBJECT, and MENTAL link up in this way. They must do so in any genuine SELF-experience:

[SELF → SINGLE(s)-as-SUBJECT-as-MENTAL].

One must figure oneself as single, when figuring oneself as subject, specifically when one is in apprehending oneself as subject apprehending oneself just in one's mental being. This is so however else one may or may not figure oneself as single. It's a fact about any genuine form of SELF-experience even if it isn't a fact about any genuine form of full self-consciousness (i.e. even if the argument in 3.5 fails): SINGLE-AS-SUBJECT-AS-MENTAL is a necessary feature of SELF-experience. The point is at bottom simple. I spell it out in a laborious way so that it can be inspected from all sides. It fits the proposal (80) that the thought-element form '-as-SUBJECT-as-MENTAL' lies at the heart of the whole phenomenon of SELF-experience: that if any thought-element x is a necessary element in SELF-experience, then x-as-SUBJECT-as-MENTAL must also be.

It wouldn't matter if it were shown to be wrong, for that would make the metaphysical task easier. The more elements that are shown to be necessary constituents of any genuine form of SELF-experience, the harder becomes the work of showing that selves exist, given the first part of the Equivalence Thesis (55) according to which

[E1] If there are such things as selves, then they must have the properties attributed to the putative self in any (every) genuine form of SELF-experience.

Thus suppose one concludes that it is only taken singly that SUBJECT, SINGLE(s), MENTAL, and THING are necessary constituents of SELF-experience. In that case one only has to show that there are things that are subjects of experience, single things, and mentally propertied things, in order to show that there are selves. ... But if SINGLE-AS-SUBJECT-as-MENTAL is also partly constitutive of SELF-experience, one's task is much harder. One has to show that there are as a matter of metaphysical fact things that are correctly counted as single things when considered just in respect of their being as subjects of experience, and, furthermore, just in respect of whatever mental properties they have as subjects of experience, i.e. independently of any non-mental properties they may have as subjects of experience. This is a burden I must take up, because I think that SINGLE-AS-SUBJECT-AS-MENTAL is indeed a necessary constituent of any genuine SELF-experience.

It's worth listing its components

SUBJECT-AS-MENTAL

and

SINGLE-AS-MENTAL

separately, although it involves repetition: SELF-experience essentially involves some sense of oneself as being a subject considered just in respect of one's mental being (even if one also thinks of oneself as a subject considered as a mental-and-non-mental whole), and also as being single considered just in respect of one's mental being (even if one also thinks of oneself as single considered as a mental-and-non-mental whole, and indeed as single in one's non-mental being). Both these components are entailed by SINGLE-AS-SUBJECT-AS-MENTAL, given the logic of the 'x-as-y' construction (79), but the intuitive cases for saying that they're part of ordinary human SELF-experience were made independently in 2.19 and carry over directly into the claim that they're necessary parts of any SELF-experience. As for SUBJECT-AS-MENTAL, it is, as remarked, the core element of SELF-experience (SELF). As for SINGLE-AS-MENTAL, it isn't only in ordinary human SELF-experience that the self is apprehended as being single in the lived present of experience in a way that is independent of any singleness it may have considered in its non-mental being. This must also be so in any case of SELF-experience. Given that it's true in general of SELF-experience that there need be no resort to a conception of the self as non-mental as a source of grounds for the conception of it as single, it follows that there is no such resort in the minimal case.[5]

So this is what the Whittling Argument has to say about SUBJECT, MENTAL, SINGLE, and DISTINCT. DISTINCT can be whittled away; SUBJECT, MENTAL, and SINGLE, and their compounds SINGLE-AS-SUBJECT, SUBJECT-AS-MENTAL, SINGLE-AS-MENTAL, and SINGLE-AS-SUBJECT-AS-MENTAL, can't. My hope is that this will seem obvious, either immediately or on reflection, and that I will seem to have made an unnecessary fuss.

It's at this point that the Building Argument attempts to add its support. It assumes that full self-consciousness is a condition of SELF-experience—

(1) [capable of SELF-experience → self-conscious]

—and aims to establish necessary conditions of SELF-experience by establishing necessary conditions of full self-consciousness. Full self-consciousness, it points out, is the ability to think of oneself *as oneself*. However unreflective one is, it continues, the ability to think of oneself as oneself in the distinctive fully self-conscious way not only involves

---

[5] Objection. 'I accept the necessary truth that [1] an experience entails an experiencer, and I'm sure that [2] the existence of an experiencer can't itself be just a matter of experience. So I think that [3] an experiencer can't be conceived as something wholly mental. So I think that [4] it's not my mental being alone which makes me single, that my mental singleness depends essentially on some kind of non-mental singleness.' Reply. This isn't relevant because it's a piece of philosophical reasoning rather than a phenomenological report about the character of SELF-experience. That apart, [3] doesn't follow from [2]—and I'm going to raise doubts about [2] in 7.4 and 8.8.

figuring oneself as subject of experience (SUBJECT); it also (and *ipso facto*) involves some grasp of oneself as something single in the lived present of experience (SINGLE$_s$), and indeed as something that is single in the lived present of experience considered specifically as subject of experience (SINGLE$_s$-as-SUBJECT). The same, therefore, is true of SELF-experience—if SELF-experience of the sort that is at present of concern does indeed require full self-consciousness, so that anything necessary for full self-consciousness is necessary for SELF-experience.

Can the Building Argument provide independent confirmation of the final step in this progress? Can it confirm that full self-consciousness involves figuring oneself not only as SINGLE-as-SUBJECT, but also as SINGLE-as-MENTAL and as SINGLE-as-SUBJECT-as-MENTAL? Can it confirm that full self-consciousness involves figuring the subject as single specifically when figuring the subject as mental?

Certainly it supports MENTAL. It does so by arguing (3.5) that figuring oneself as a subject of experience is a necessary element of being fully self-conscious, even though a being's express self-conscious thoughts may conceivably be wholly restricted to its non-mental properties in the way imagined on page 112. It follows that figuring oneself as mentally propertied is a necessary element of full self-consciousness, because figuring oneself as a subject of experience entails figuring oneself as mentally propertied ([SUBJECT → MENTAL]); as recently remarked.

It may not seem so obvious that full self-consciousness (and hence, given (1), any form of SELF-experience) must also involve experience of oneself as SINGLE-as-MENTAL, or indeed as SINGLE-as-SUBJECT-as-MENTAL—as single specifically in one's mental being, considered as a subject of experience—but I argued for these claims, too, in 3.5 and suggested that the considerations adduced in its favour were persuasive even if they fell short of proof. Here I'm going to take it that this is so.

So this is how things stand. The Whittling Argument and the Building Argument converge on the claim that the following at least are necessary elements of any genuine SELF-experience:

SUBJECT

MENTAL

SINGLE

SINGLE-as-SUBJECT

SINGLE-as-SUBJECT-as-MENTAL

SUBJECT-as-MENTAL

SINGLE-as-MENTAL.

Of the remaining elements—THING, PERSISTING, AGENT, PERSONALITY, and DISTINCT, and their various compounds—I think only THING and its compounds (THING-as-SUBJECT, THING-as-SUBJECT-as-MENTAL, THING-as-MENTAL) can survive the cut, when it comes to the minimal case. DISTINCT has already been knocked out, and I will now take the others one by one.

4.3 THING

Is

THING (the self is figured as a thing of some sort)

a necessary structural element in any form of SELF-experience? Is it true, as Nozick claims, that 'the self has a particular character, that of an entity'?[6] Is Kant right that we're bound to figure / conceive the self as a substance of some sort?[7]

Some may find this claim most peculiar, but I think that THING follows immediately from SUBJECT, so that its inclusion in the core conditions of SELF-experience—its immunity to being whittled away—is already guaranteed. Self-consciousness also requires SUBJECT, according to the Building Argument begun in 3.5, so the Building Argument backs up the Whittling Argument if it can be shown that THING follows from SUBJECT (given, as always, the assumption on which its support for the Whittling Argument rests, the assumption that SELF-experience entails self-consciousness).[8]

It may still seem very odd—to say that one must experience oneself as a *thing*, in SELF-experience, or indeed as an *object* of some sort—for this is what THING comes to in effect, although I prefer to use 'thing' rather than 'object'. Why couldn't a self-conscious creature naturally experience the self or subject of experience as a process of some sort, or as the possession of a property or set of properties by something else that it naturally figured as a thing or entity or object, something non-mental, perhaps, like the whole human being?

It depends, of course, on what one means by the words 'thing', 'property', and 'process', and by 'experience something as a thing ... or property or set or properties ... or process'. I'm still taking 'thing', 'property', and 'process' to have their ordinary, imprecise pre-theoretical force when used phenomenologically to characterize forms of experience, as here, and I'm still deferring (until Part 6) the question of how they're best used in metaphysics. Thus suppose someone holds that the distinction between processes and things is superficial and misleading from the point of view of fundamental metaphysics. It doesn't follow, on the present terms of debate, that experience that is best characterized as figuring the self as a thing is equally well characterized as figuring the self as a process. Or suppose someone claims—puzzlingly, perhaps, but in my view correctly—that the distinction between a thing and its properties is metaphysically superficial. Again it doesn't follow that experience that is best characterized as figuring the self as a thing is equally well characterized as figuring the self as some sort of complex instantiation of properties. Sooner or later questions about the relation between the use of words like 'thing' in phenomenological contexts and their use in theoretical metaphysical contexts

---

[6] 1989: 148. As in Part 1 I take it that the (strictly speaking entirely general) word 'entity' carries some sort of 'thing' connotation in this use. Note that the remark has both phenomenological and metaphysical interpretations (which may not be separate).

[7] As before (51), those who doubt that Kant's argument has a logico-phenomenological aspect over and above its transcendental aspect should take the views I attribute to Kant as my own couched impertinently in Kantian language.

[8] On p. 127 I arrive by a different route at the proposal that self-consciousness requires that one experience oneself as a thing of some sort (the Subject as Thing Thesis).

are going to come to the fore. This is inevitable, given the link between phenomenology and metaphysics proposed by the Equivalence Thesis of 2.12, according to which selves exist, as a matter of ontological fact, just so long as there exist things that have the properties (e.g. 'being a thing of some sort') that turn up in the correct phenomenological account of the minimal form of SELF-experience. For the moment, though, we may continue to take words like 'thing', 'property', and 'process' in their ordinary, loose sense. Kantians may suspect that difference in the usage of such terms, as one moves between metaphysical and phenomenological contexts, may be a source of 'paralogism'. I will try to show that this is not so.

—I can't see why you're so attached to the THING thesis. It seems to me that SELF-experience is better described much more loosely, as 'awareness of oneself as an elusive subjective dimension',[9] or something of that sort. Why do you keep insisting that genuine SELF-experience involve figuring the self as a thing of some kind?

What I have in mind is this. One must figure oneself as a subject of experience in SELF-experience, and Kant (phenomenological Kant) is right that to figure oneself as a subject in 'inner sense ... or empirical apperception' (A107) just is to figure oneself as a thing (a 'substance') in the sense that matters here (he's right that [SUBJECT → THING]). What sense is that? The key point was made in 2.16. The fundamental respect in which the self is apprehended under the category of thing is already manifest in the way in which it's experienced as something that can *have* or *undergo* things like sensations and emotions, something that can have thoughts, something that can *be in some conscious state or other*. No experience that presents X as something that *has experience*, or even just as something that can *be in some conscious state or other*, let alone as something that can *think thoughts*, can figure X merely as a property of something else, or as a mere process or event (here again 'property', 'process', and 'event' have their ordinary pre-theoretical sense, and 'mere' and 'merely' are added to match). Kant puts this by saying that 'everyone must ... necessarily ... regard himself', the conscious subject, 'as a substance' or thing in the present sense, and must regard all episodes of thought or conscious episodes 'as being only accidents of his existence, determinations of his state' (A349). One must apprehend oneself as a thing specifically in so far as one apprehends oneself as a subject. SELF-experience essentially involves the element

THING-as-SUBJECT

and this is so even if one figures the subject of experience in the most passive way imaginable, as something that merely *has* experiences, something that is *subject to* experiences, and not as something that is in any way active, let alone as something that is an intentional agent of any sort.

The reason why one must figure oneself as a thing (or substance) in the relevant sense, in figuring oneself as a subject, isn't that one must have some awareness of oneself as having non-mental being, as a subject, and must figure oneself as a thing

---

[9] Zahavi 1999: 40.

so considered. I don't think that SELF-experience does presuppose having some sort of awareness of oneself as having non-mental being, as a subject, let alone figuring oneself as a thing so considered—as already remarked. If it did, then that might guarantee the place of the thought-element THING-as-SUBJECT. But I don't think it does, and the element THING-as-SUBJECT is in any case independently guaranteed. For what is also true is that one must figure oneself as a subject, and as a thing considered specifically as a subject, specifically when apprehending oneself in one's mental being, and not in any way in one's non-mental being. This must already provide sufficient grounds for one's figuring oneself as thing-as-subject, even if there are other grounds for one's doing so. And to say this is to say that the thought-element

THING-as-SUBJECT-as-MENTAL

is a necessary element of SELF-experience. One is bound to have a sense of oneself as a subject, and a sense of oneself as a thing considered as a subject, when considering oneself simply in so far as one has mental being, and so without any thought of oneself as being a thing (and a subject) in so far as one is or has a body or (more generally) non-mental being.

This is automatic in the Kantian argument, inasmuch as he isn't at this point considering the possibility of figuring the subject as having non-mental being at all. In my scheme it follows from the fact that the thought-element form '-as-SUBJECT-as-MENTAL' is the core of the phenomenon of SELF-experience. I take it to be strongly supported by the fact that (phenomenological) Kant makes a convincing case for the claim that one must think of oneself, as subject, as thing or substance, while simply assuming that it's the subject considered just in respect of its mental being that is in question.

From THING-as-SUBJECT-as-MENTAL we may derive

THING-as-MENTAL

by the logic of the 'x-as-y' construction. It may seem obvious that this is part of SELF-experience, given the present understanding of 'thing', but obviousness is a fine property for a philosophical conclusion to have. SELF-experience is a complex phenomenon, and it seems a good idea to try to take it apart in simple terms, as far as possible, and then try to put it back together again, as far as possible.

This is what I've been doing. So far I claim to have identified eleven elements of the minimal form of SELF-experience:

SUBJECT

MENTAL

SINGLE

THING

SUBJECT-as-MENTAL

SINGLE-as-SUBJECT

SINGLE$_{(s)}$-as-MENTAL

SINGLE$_{(s)}$-as-SUBJECT-as-MENTAL

THING-as-SUBJECT

THING-as-SUBJECT-as-MENTAL

THING-as-MENTAL.

This may already seem rococo—a veritable menagerie—so I hope not to have to add any more. I will in any case simplify my terminology in the final section of Part 4, reducing the seven compound terms to two, and then to one—SUBJECT-as-SINGLE-MENTAL-THING—from which I will form the acronym 'SESMET'. I'm going to claim that SELF-experience is at the very least SESMET-experience; that to have SELF-experience is at the very least to experience oneself as a sesmet—as a subject of experience that is a single **mental** thing—whether or not one also experiences oneself as an agent, as something persisting, and so on. Any obviousness is all to the good.

Let me invoke Kant again. It doesn't follow from the fact that we must regard the conscious self as a thing or substance, he says, that it actually *is* a thing or substance, or that we can know that this is so. We can't even rule out the possibility that the I of thought or consciousness may be just a property of something else, 'a predicate of another being' (B419), i.e. not a substance in the conventional sense of the word. It is (he says) 'quite impossible' for me, given everything I can know about myself as a mental phenomenon, 'to determine the manner in which I exist, whether it be as substance [object] or as accident [property]' (B420). As a theorist one may firmly believe, as I do, that the existence of human selves—if indeed they exist—is 'just' a matter of the existence of processes in or properties of the brain (for the inappropriateness of 'just' see the account of 'adductive' materialism in 6.6). One may also think, as I do not, that this view of selves is incompatible with the view that they're things in any worthwhile sense. And one may go on to conclude that they're definitely not things, in so far as they exist at all. So be it. None of this constitutes an objection to the transcendental-phenomenological claim that one must in one's own case figure or grasp the self as a thing or 'substance' of some kind.

I agree, and have little to add to Kant's arguments understood in this way, or to the point that THING is already sufficiently secured by the evident fact that the self is figured as something that *has* experience, encountered in the act of thinking (in the process of experience) as the *haver* of experience—the experienc*er*. I take the minimal sufficient sense of THING to be very minimal, relative to most ordinary conceptions of what counts as a thing, while insisting that experience of the self as a thing of some sort, in the sense of 'thing' that is of concern, is integral to anything that can count as experience of the self as a subject of experience.

At one point Kant says that we may 'readily accept the proposition *the soul is substance*' (A350). He claims, that is, that we may accept it as true—so long as it's properly understood. It won't help the rational psychologists in any way, for when it's properly understood it doesn't support the claim that the soul or self is indeed a self-subsistent substance rather than an accident or 'mere' property. As used in this proposition, the concept SUBSTANCE 'designates a substance only in idea, not in reality' (A351): so used, it expresses a fact about how the subject of experience must necessarily be thought of, conceived of, or experienced, but not about how it is or must be in itself, so far as its ultimate ontological nature is concerned.

Nor does it support the claim that it's something that can exist apart from matter. Kant's central concern, both in this passage and in the immediately following Second Paralogism, is to show that one can't prove the substantial simplicity of the soul or subject in such a way as to support (let alone guarantee) the claim that it's a non-material thing that may for that reason be supposed to be indivisible, hence immaterial and incorruptible, hence immortal. This is the taken-for-granted and explicit agenda of the time, as remarked in 2.10. Kant took it to be common ground that 'the assertion of the simple nature of the soul is of value only in so far as I can thereby distinguish this subject [i.e. the soul] from all matter, and so can exempt it from the dissolution to which matter is always liable'.[10] It's partly because I have nothing like this on my agenda, when I argue directly for the thinglikeness of the self in Parts 7 and 8, that I like to think that Kant won't judge the argument to be a paralogism, and can agree with its conclusion.

I don't want to suggest that experience of the self as an *agent* is necessary for experience of it as a thing, where experience of the self as an agent is taken to be experience of it as something that engages or can engage in *intentional action*. It may be that figuring the self as an intentional agent is a sufficient condition of figuring it as a thing in the present sense ([AGENT → THING]) but I don't think it is necessary (I don't think that [THING → AGENT]). Nor do I think that experience of the self as a subject requires experience of it as an agent ([SUBJECT → AGENT]).

I'll address this issue directly in 4.6 below. What we have so far is this:

[SELF → SUBJECT]

and

[SUBJECT → THING].

SELF-experience obviously involves figuring the self as a subject of experience, and to figure X as a subject of experience is already to figure it as a thing in a sense sufficient for present purposes. It follows, as remarked, that if the Building Argument secures SUBJECT, then it secures THING. And if the Whittling Argument can't dislodge SUBJECT—which it surely can't—then it can't dislodge THING. On this view, experience of the self as subject of experience is already and necessarily experience of it as thinglike and not merely as a property or process or event (as ordinarily understood) or as an 'elusive dimension'—if experiencing something as an elusive dimension isn't experiencing it as a thing. As before, I think the basic idea is clear and even routine, although the terms aren't precise.

Those familiar with older philosophical usage may find the phrase 'mental principle' or 'thinking active principle' useful when characterizing the experience/conception of the self as a thing, as remarked on page 66. When we take the word 'principle' to

---

[10] A356. Admitting a sense in which we are *right* to conceive the subject to be a simple substance, he points out that it 'cannot yield us ... the everlasting duration of the human soul in all changes and even in death' (A351). But 'this is indeed, strictly speaking, the only use for which the above proposition is intended' (A356): 'apart from such use I could very well dispense with ... the concept of the substantiality of my thinking subject' (A349); this is 'the only case in which this concept can be of service' (A360).

denote a concrete existent in this way, a principle may not seem thinglike in so far as we take tables and chairs to be paradigmatic things. But the term does connect naturally to the category of thing rather than to the category of property or process or event. One might say that it manages to express the claim that something is a thing without triggering a picture of something like a human being or a chair as a paradigm case of a thing and, equally, without automatically inviting the idea that whatever is in question is a 'self-subsistent' entity (i.e. something that can in principle exist independently of anything else in whatever dubious sense things like human beings and chairs can be said to do this).

It may be that the best illustration of the way in which something can seem thinglike without seeming thinglike in the manner of cats and chairs can't be used to throw light on the case of the self, because it's provided by the self itself. And it may be that the self is unique in this respect, so that nothing else can provide a helpful illustration or point of comparison.

—Such uniqueness is hardly a virtue. You suggest that selves may be in some way *sui generis*, as things or objects, but if they're that special, then it's not clear that they should be included in the category of things at all. In fact, it's beginning to sound as if the best metaphysical account of the nature of thinghood would be wise to exclude them. That in turn would mean that you're wrong about at least one component of any genuine form of SELF-experience: THING. And that, given your 'phenomenology determines metaphysics' view, would show that there aren't any selves—because you've made being a thing or object a non-negotiable condition of being a self. You should never have included THING in the first place, in the description of ordinary human SELF-experience.

I'm not claiming that selves are *sui generis* things, metaphysically speaking. I take it that they're regular members of the category of things if they're things at all. My claim is simply that our *experience* of them as thinglike may be *sui generis* relative to other sorts of experience of things as thinglike. That said, I'm inclined to go further and reverse the above objection. I think there may be a deep sense in which the self is the clearest and most instructive—and metaphysically most secure—example of a thing (object, substance) that we have. If so, then any metaphysical account of thinghood that fails to accommodate the self will be mistaken. This, note, is a view one can endorse even if one's final metaphysics doesn't have a place for the category of things or objects at all—as it may well not, especially if the category is meant to allow for the possibility that there be more than one thing or object (as Spinoza's metaphysics, for example, does not).

Note also that one can embrace the idea that SELF-experience may be the fundamental root of our grasp of or commitment to the category of thing, whatever one's metaphysics. Nietzsche takes this line, claiming that 'it is only after the model of the subject that we invented thingness and interpreted it into the hubbub of sensations'.[11] He infers that

---

[11] 1885–8: 154. Nietzsche's claim might be held to be straightforwardly empirically false on the basis of work by Spelke and others, and also on very general evolutionary-psychological grounds, but it can't actually be straightforwardly knocked out in this way (it is in any case a claim about phylogenetic rather than ontogenetic psychological development).

we're mistaken, both in our sense that the self is a thing or substance of some kind and in our general category of thing. One could, however, argue in the other direction, in a way that Nietzsche might also approve, admitting a sense in which the idea of the subject as thinglike is legitimate and exemplary, and arguing on that basis for a huge correction in our general conception of a thing or substance. Such a correction would find support in present-day science and render our notion of a thing or substance immune to whatever objections to the traditional conception Nietzsche had in mind.

These are metaphysical matters that I'll consider in Part 6. For the moment I think we should grant the viability, and great importance, of that sense of the word 'thing' in which SELF-experience certainly figures the self as a thing of some sort, rather than as a ('mere') property, process, state, event, or dimension. We should do this even though the limits on the proper use of the word 'thing' are unclear.

It's worth stopping, now, to think, consciously, in a fully comprehending way, and while considering oneself just in one's mental aspect, an I-thought like 'I'm reading a book' or 'I'm present here now, thinking that I'm present here now'. If one does this, one encounters in a vivid way the insubstantial-seeming but, relative to that seeming insubstantiality, entirely solid respect in which SELF-experience, experience of oneself as a mental subject of experience, involves figuring the self as a thing.[12] Independently of that, I conclude that THING, experience/conception of the self as a thing, in the sense expounded here, is a necessary part of genuine SELF-experience. Some will say that their SELF-experience has no such THING character. I'll reply, perhaps annoyingly, that a good sense of how insubstantial-seeming but robust this THING character can be is available to all those who consider their SELF-experience when they perform this small experiment.

—Even if I concede the point for the human case, how can you possibly rule out a priori the idea that aliens might have SELF-experience that figured the self as 'just a process'?

By the argument just given. If the alien really does have SELF-experience, and really does experience itself, when it apprehends itself as a self, as a (mental) subject of experience that has thoughts and experiences and is in certain mental states, then it experiences the self as a thing in a sense sufficient for my purposes. If someone says that I haven't really given an argument, and have merely presented an intuition in a certain way, I won't take it as a criticism. If someone says that I've taken a very long time to say something obvious that Kant said long ago, I'll accept it as a criticism (bearing in mind the fact that others will deny that Kant said any such thing) but won't mind in the least. If someone says that the whole of Part 4 up to now—the argument that SUBJECT, THING, MENTAL, and SINGLE are ineliminable from any genuine form of SELF-experience—is a laborious statement of the obvious, I'll be pleased.

If someone says that any sense of the self as a thing may dissolve in meditation, I'll reply that in that case SELF-experience of the kind that is at present of concern will also have dissolved: this being, perhaps, and after all, the aim of the meditation. It won't

---

[12] Engaging in this kind of thought tends to produce a distinctive shock, as the loop of expressly self-inspecting self-consciousness closes.

follow that there is no longer a self. The basic metaphysical subject self enquired after in this book isn't some kind of spiritual defect in need of elimination. It's quite different from 'the self' understood as a locus of illusion and selfishness. There are views of the metaphysical self given which it no longer exists in 'pure consciousness experience'. On one such view the self literally consists of SELF-experience, or SELF-experience is at least an essential part of what it consists of. Such a self must disappear—be 'blown out'—in advanced meditative states.[13] There is still a subject of experience in such cases, however, necessarily so, given that there is experience—awareness—at all (6.3); and it follows, on my still to be expounded metaphysical view, that there is still a self.

4.4 Eye and I

When I say that SELF-experience involves figuring oneself* (oneself considered as a self) as a thing of some sort, the kind of self-apprehension I have in mind needn't, and typically doesn't, involve any deliberate targeting of or focusing on oneself as an object of thought, any taking of oneself* as object of attention in a thetic way. It follows, I think, that it needn't, and typically doesn't, involve targeting oneself as an object of thought in a way that invites the ancient objection that the I or self or subject can no more take itself—i.e. itself as it is in the present moment—as the object of its thought than the eye can see itself, and that it is in this sense, and in Ryle's phrase, forever 'systematically elusive' to itself (1949: 186).

   According to Louis Sass,

the most fundamental sense of selfhood involves the experience of self not as an object of awareness but, in some crucial respects, as an unseen point of origin for action, experience, and thought. ... What William James called ... the 'central nucleus of the Self' is not, in fact, experienced as an entity in the focus of our awareness, but, rather, as a kind of medium of awareness, source of activity, or general directedness towards the world.   (1998: 562)

This describes the way in which a sense of the self as a thing can be robust, specifically as a sense of the self as a thing, even when it involves something that seems intuitively very insubstantial or unthinglike. I think that it completely undercuts the ancient eye objection, which seems to rely on the idea that the reason that the subject can never truly grasp itself (as it is in the present moment) in experience is that it must in so doing take itself as an express or thetic object of thought in some way that means that the thing that it is taking as object can't really be the thing that is doing the taking. It shows that the THING thesis doesn't require that experience of self as a thing have the character of experience of 'an entity in the focus of ... awareness'.

   Is the I or subject none the less 'systematically elusive'? Is there some sense in which genuine, immediate self-presence of mind is impossible? It seems to me that Lonergan

---

[13] I'm not sure what Fichte would say about these matters, given his view that the I or subject mentally considered not only can but must apprehend itself as such, and his view that this is what constitutes its existence (see p. 55).

is exactly right, in line with Sass, when he says that 'objects are present by being attended to, but subjects are present [to themselves] as subjects, not by being attended to, but by attending. As the parade of objects marches by, spectators do not have to slip into the parade to be present to themselves' (1967: 226). Deikman makes the same point: 'we know the internal observer not by observing it but by *being* it ... knowing by being that which is known is ... different from perceptual knowledge'.[14] Certainly the eye can't see itself (unless there is a mirror). The knife can't cut itself (unless very flexible), and the fingertip can't touch itself. The idea that the subject of experience can't take itself as it is in the present moment as the object of its thought, that 'my today's self', in Ryle's words, 'perpetually slips out of any hold of it that I try to take' (1949: 187), has many metaphorical expressions. Laycock observes that this is part of 'perennial Buddhist wisdom' (1998: 142), and so it is, considered as a truth about the limitations of a certain particular sort of thetic, object-posing self-apprehension. But it is, so taken, fully compatible with the claim that there's another non-thetic form of self-apprehension in which the I or subject—or just consciousness, if you wish—can be directly or immediately aware of itself in the present moment, in the way just indicated by Lonergan, Sass, and Deikman.[15]

I'm tempted to say that such self-awareness can be *express* (not just explicit in the weak sense of 'explicit' that's equivalent to 'genuinely given in awareness') even though it isn't *thetic*. My own terms rule this out, inasmuch as I've taken 'thetic' and 'express' to be essentially equivalent in meaning, but the idea I'm after is that this self-awareness is or can be a constitutive part of experience in such a way that it's rightly construed as a *foreground aspect* of experience even though there's also a respect in which it normally passes unnoticed, being utterly non-thetic. This way of putting things is also ruled out for me, by the terminological proposal on page 30 to define background awareness as any awareness that is not thetic, but I'm inclined to overrule that proposal, too, if only temporarily, and to propose a sense in which *experiential elements may be constitutive of the nature of the foreground while not being thetic.*

At this point we have five distinct terms. The terminology is threatening to go out of control. But the idea should be discernible to a sympathetic eye. All awareness is *explicit* in the weak sense, since this simply means is that it is genuinely given in awareness. Some explicit awareness is *background*, and not at all thetic or express. Some explicit awareness is *foreground*, but still not thetic or express. And some foreground awareness is in addition *thetic* or *express*.

These matters need careful treatment (a careful terminology), and I won't pursue them further here. Note, though, a parallel with the case of the qualitative character of the sensation of blue when one looks at the sky. There's a clear respect in which it is

---

[14] 1996: 355. Plainly 'knowing by being that which is known', or rather, perhaps, knowing (oneself) by being that which is knowing, does not require knowing everything there is to know about that which is known. On a standard materialist view, one may grant that that which is known, in this sort of self-presence of mind, has non-experiential being whose nature is not then known at all.

[15] Distinguishing between experiencing and 'seeing', understood to stand for any sort of perceptually or otherwise intellectually mediated operation, Deikman says that the 'I' can be experienced, but cannot be 'seen' (1996: 350). There is a philosophically popular, narrow, justification-stressing conception of what knowledge is that makes it hard to see that this kind of thing is a form of knowledge.

in the foreground of experience although it is at the same time wholly 'diaphanous' in G. E. Moore's sense, and to that extent wholly non-thetic, not in the focus of attention considered specifically as the qualitative character of one's sensation.[16]

The form of immediate self-awareness described by Sass and others is, as remarked, non-thetic. This means that it isn't in conflict with the ancient eye objection—if the eye objection can be expressed as the claim that the subject can't take itself as it is in the present moment of experience as the thetic object of its attention. I think, in fact, that immediate (no time lag) self-awareness can also be thetic, or at least express, so that the eye objection is false even in that formulation, and I will shortly say why. First, though, note that the eye objection can't touch the THING thesis even if it succeeds in showing that the subject can't take itself as it is in the present moment of experience as the thetic object of its attention. This is because the THING thesis is a strictly phenomenological thesis about how you *figure* yourself in having SELF-experience, whatever the nature of the thing you're having experience of. The eye objection is, relatively speaking, a non-phenomenological thesis, a thesis about possible objects of thought, and doesn't challenge the phenomenological thesis in any way. It states that the subject of experience that exists in the present moment of experience can't possibly have experience that is relationally (referentially) of itself as it is in the present moment of experience; it says nothing about how the subject of experience experiences itself phenomenologically (notionally) speaking.

—This is hopelessly vague, and you haven't answered the 'systematic elusiveness' objection. You may think *I'm now thinking a puzzling thought*, or *I'm looking down on India*, or just *Here I am*, in an attempt to apprehend yourself as mental self or subject or thinker in the present moment, but in entertaining these contents, you necessarily fail to apprehend the thing that is doing the apprehending—the entertainer of the content, the thinker of the thought, i.e. yourself considered as the mental subject at that moment. Ryle is right. Any mental performance 'can be the concern of a higher-order performance'—one can think about any thought that one has—but it 'cannot be the concern of itself' (1949: 188–9). When one thinks an I-thought, this performance 'is not dealt with in the operation which it itself is. Even if the person is, for special speculative purposes, momentarily concentrating on the Problem of the Self, he has failed and knows that he has failed to catch more than the flying coat-tails of that which he was pursuing. His quarry was the hunter' (1949: 187). William James, whom you favour, quotes Comte's statement of the same point, and agrees with him that 'no subjective state, whilst present, is its own object; its object is always something else' (1890: 1. 190).

I'm not convinced. It's arguable that to think *this very thought is puzzling*, or *I'm now thinking a puzzling thought*, is precisely to engage in a performance that is concerned with itself. In which case a certain kind of immediate self-presence of mind is possible even in an intentional, designedly self-reflexive, and wholly cognitive act—a point quite independent of considerations of the sort adduced by Lonergan, Sass, Deikman, and many others. On this view, *it's only when one tries to apprehend that one has succeeded* that one triggers the regressive step. It may be added that there doesn't seem to be

---

[16] Moore 1903: 450. The place to start, when considering these questions, is with Reid 1764. See also Montague 2009: 501–2.

any obvious reason why hunters can't catch the quarry when the quarry is themselves. A detective with partial amnesia, sitting in her chair and reasoning hard, may identify herself as the person who committed the crime she is investigating. Wandering in the dark, I may get increasingly precise readings regarding the location of my quarry from a Global Positioning System, program my noiseless grabber robot to move to the correct spot, press the Grab button—and get grabbed.[17]

It may be said that concentration on cognitively articulated thoughts like *I'm now thinking a puzzling thought* or *Here I am* can't deliver what is required, or provide a compelling practical route to appreciation of the point that it's possible to have express awareness of oneself apprehended specifically as the mental subject of experience as one is in the present moment of experience. Fine, for the best route to this point is more direct, and doesn't involve any such cognitively—discursively—articulated representations. It's simply a matter of coming to awareness of oneself as a mental presence—or perhaps simply as *mental presence*—in a certain sort of alert but essentially unpointed, global way. My inclination is to say that the awareness of oneself can in this case be fully express, no less express than any awareness of anything is when one's awareness of it is thetic, even though there is in this case no sort of posing or positing or positioning of oneself for inspection of the sort that seems built in (etymologically at least) to the meaning of the word 'thetic'. I think, in fact, that it can be said to be thetic, taking the core meaning of 'thetic' to be just: genuinely in the field of attention, genuinely in attention, and rejecting the idea that attention requires articulation or construction of such a kind that the mental subject is bound to present in such a way that one can't be said to be aware of it as it is at that moment. On this point I think Ryle and others are simply wrong. Their model of awareness is too rigid, in so far as it pushes the subject—the 'now-subject', one might say—into being necessarily distinct from its (attempted) object—itself. It hasn't been shown that there's an insuperable difficulty in the matter of present or immediate self-awareness. It seems I can engage in it with no flying coat-tails time lag.

The case is not like the eye that can't see itself, or the fingertip that can't touch itself. These old images are weak. A mind is rather more than an eye or a finger. If Ryle had spent a little more time on disciplined, unprejudiced introspection, or had tried meditation, even if only briefly, and in an entirely amateur and unsupervised, SCR, way, he might have found that it's really not very difficult—although it's not that easy—for the subject of experience to be aware in the present moment of itself-in-the-present-moment. It's a matter of letting go in a certain way. As far as the level of difficulty is concerned, it's like maintaining one's balance on a parallel bar or a wire in a let go manner that is relatively but not extremely hard to attain. One can easily lose one's balance—one can fall out of the state in question—but one can also keep it, and improve with practice.

The attainment of such self-awareness, for brief periods, in the unpractised (and the incompetent, such as myself), seems to involve a state that has no particular content

---

[17]   There is also the case of Winnie the Pooh, Piglet, and the Heffalump (Milne 1928).

beyond the content that it has in so far as it's correctly described as awareness or consciousness of the awareness or consciousness that it itself is, awareness that incorporates awareness that it is awareness of the awareness that it itself is, but does so without involving anything propositional (contrary to what the word 'that' suggests to many) or thetic in the narrow, distance-introducing, object-of-attention-posing sense. I take it that it is what people have in mind when they speak of 'pure consciousness experience': consciousness that is consciousness of the consciousness that it itself is and that includes consciousness (non-propositional) that it is consciousness of the consciousness that it itself is.[18] It's an early and rather routine step in certain meditative practices, and there's an extremely robust consensus about its reality, precise character and (relative) ease of attainment, as there is also about the more often stressed point that it involves a sense of 'selflessness'.

One mustn't be misled by the fact that it involves a sense of selflessness, or by the fact that I've characterized it with the abstract nouns 'awareness' and 'consciousness', into thinking that it is not after all a genuine case of the phenomenon whose reality I'm trying to establish: awareness on the part of the subject of experience of itself as it is in the present moment of experience. To say that what we have, in the case of such awareness, is awareness on the part of the subject of experience of itself as it is in the present moment of experience is just another way of saying the same thing. In claiming this, though, I'm anticipating a number of points that are still to come, such as the point that if there is awareness or consciousness or experience at all, then there is, necessarily, a subject of experience, in a sense in which no coherent Buddhist would deny (see 6.3), and the point that there is no distinction in fundamental metaphysics between a thing and its propertiedness (see 6.15); and these things must wait their turn.

I've proposed that the mental subject can be immediately relationally aware of itself, both in the non-thetic, everyday Lonergan–Sass–Deikman way, and also, exceptionally, in the express 'pure consciousness experience' way. Evidence? Each must acquire it for himself or herself *in foro interno*. This doesn't mean it isn't empirical; it's wholly empirical. It does mean that it isn't publicly checkable, and it will always be possible for someone to object that the experience of truly present self-awareness is an illusion produced by—say—Rylean flashes of 'swift retrospective heed' (1949: 153).

This notion of 'heed', however, has the flying coat-tails error built into it, and there is another larger mistake that can be decisively blocked—a mistake that may tempt those who carry EEE thinking too far. Suppose that it is in the nature of all naturally evolved forms of consciousness that they are in the usual course of things incessantly (and

[18]   See e.g. Forman 1998; Shear 1998. See also Parfit 1998. I'm tempted to add a 'because', and say that the consciousness in question includes 'consciousness that it is consciousness of the consciousness that it itself is, because there is patently nothing else that it could be consciousness of'. But this could not then be understood to be giving a reason for the consciousness's having the property in question (the property of being consciousness that it is consciousness of the consciousness that it itself is), as if the reason were, as a reason, somehow held in the consciousness in question. It would, rather be an indirect way of expressing the self-evidentness of the situation—its self-evidentness to itself (or equivalently, in the end, its subject).

seemingly constitutively) in the service of the perceptual and agentive survival needs of organisms. It doesn't follow from this that someone like Forman is wrong when he says that 'consciousness should not be defined in terms of perceptions, content, or its other functions' (1998: 197).

The reason Forman gives for holding this view is that in certain meditative states 'awareness itself is experienced as still or silent, perceptions as active or changing', and this leads him to propose that 'instead of defining awareness in terms of its content, we should think about (a) awareness and (b) its mental and sensory *functions* as two independent phenomena or processes that somehow interact' (ibid.). I don't think this is a good proposal: the picture of independent interacting processes is too separatist, and the contentual features of states of awareness (more precisely, the contentual features of states of awareness that involve content other than whatever content is involved in simple awareness of awareness) should be seen rather as forms or modes or types of awareness. I think, nevertheless, that Forman's basic claim about the definition of consciousness is right, and that the idea of pure awareness or consciousness—which is indeed incompatible with the idea that consciousness is to be *defined* in terms of perceptions, content, or other functions—is certainly not in tension with anything in the theory of evolution by natural selection, properly understood.

This is another topic that needs careful and separate discussion. Here it's worth noting that even if consciousness isn't a primordial property of the universe,[19] and even if it came on the scene relatively late, there's no good reason—in fact, it doesn't even make sense—to think that it first came on the scene because it had survival value. Natural selection needs something to work on and can only work on what it finds. Consciousness had to exist before it could be exploited and shaped, just as non-conscious matter did. The task of giving an evolutionary explanation of the existence of consciousness is exactly like the task of giving an evolutionary explanation of the existence of matter: there is no such task. Natural selection moulded the consciousness-involving matter that it found in nature into highly specific adaptive forms in exactly the same general way as the way in which it moulded non-consciousness-involving matter[20] into highly specific adaptive forms. The evolution by natural selection of various finely developed forms of consciousness (visual, olfactory, etc.) is no more surprising than the evolution by natural selection of various finely developed types of bodily organization,[21] and even if evolved forms of consciousness came to be what they were because they had certain kinds of content that gave them survival value and that were (therefore) essentially other than whatever content is involved in simple awareness of awareness, it doesn't follow that pure consciousness experience is some sort of illusion (on the contrary). Even if our knowledge of pure consciousness experience becomes possible only after millions of years of EEE-practical forms of consciousness, it doesn't follow that it isn't uniquely revelatory of the fundamental nature of consciousness.

---

[19] I think it must be; see G. Strawson 2006a.   [20] Panpsychism has been put to one side.

[21] To speak of such forms of consciousness is not to reject the possibility that functional equivalents of e.g. visual and auditory experience could exist in the complete absence of consciousness.

4.5 PERSONALITY

DISTINCT failed to survive the whittling process, and I'm now going to complete the Whittling Argument by arguing that none of the other three remaining proposed elements of ordinary human SELF-experience—AGENT, PERSISTING, and PERSONALITY—survive either, so that only SUBJECT, THING, MENTAL, SINGLE(s), and their various compounds, are left.

I think it's easy to show that PERSONALITY is dispensable. SELF-experience must involve experience of the self as a subject of experience, with all that that entails (SINGLE, MENTAL, THING, and so on), but it needn't involve experience of it as something that has a personality. Most people have at some time, and however temporarily, experienced themselves as a kind of bare locus of consciousness—not just as detached, neutral, and unengaged, but as void of personality, stripped of particularity of character, a mere (cognitive) point of view—and some have experienced this for long periods of time. Such experience may be the result of nothing more unusual than exhaustion, solitude, shock, sex, abstract thought, boredom, or a hot bath. It may just be how one feels when one wakes up. There are many deep and natural ways in which subjecthood transcends—seems entirely detached from—matters of personality, even in normal life. When the blind protagonist of a Henry Green story, listening to a brilliant blackbird, 'lost all sense of personality', so that 'he was just a pair of ears and a brain, absorbent as a sponge' (c.1923:11), his state was not pathological.

Most people, as remarked, have experienced something like this, and Nagel's well-known description of his experience of having or being an 'objective self', which is certainly not something pathological, also seems to involve a loss of a sense of oneself as having anything like the particularity or local colour of personality. Nagel describes his experience of being an 'objective' self as involving lack of any sense of having a particular point of view; but he doesn't mean that there isn't any sense of being a locus of consciousness at all, only that there isn't any sense of being anything as particular—as limited, local, contingent, transient, and lovable—as Thomas Nagel. The objective self, he writes, is 'the self that seems incapable of being anyone in particular'. It's as if 'this thinking subject regards the world through the person TN. ... The real me occupies TN, so to speak; or the publicly identifiable person TN contains the real me. From a purely objective point of view my connection with TN seems arbitrary.' Later he puts it as follows, in a passage already quoted in part on page 17:

The picture is this. Essentially I have no particular point of view at all, but apprehend the world as centerless. As it happens, I ordinarily view the world from a certain vantage point, using the eyes, the person, the daily life of TN as a kind of window. But the experiences and the perspective of TN with which I am directly presented are not the point of view of the true self, for the true self has no point of view. ... Something essential about me has nothing to do with my perspective and position in the world.[22]

---

[22] 1986: 60–2. When I gave a class on the self at New York University in 1997, I asked everyone to read this passage. The following week I asked them if they felt they knew what Nagel was talking about. About a third judged that they had had experience of that kind themselves, and that they knew exactly what he was talking about; a third, including

It seems clear enough, then, that absence of any sense of personality has various non-pathological forms. It also has pathological forms. It's a common feature of severe depression, for example, in which one may experience 'depersonalization'. This is an accurate term, in my experience and in that of others I have talked to, and the crucial point for present purposes is that it doesn't involve any sort of loss of one's sense of oneself as a mental locus of consciousness, however bleak it is in other respects. A friend of mine (not a philosopher) who experienced depersonalization found that the thought 'I don't exist' kept occurring to him; but he was of course well aware that there was a locus of consciousness where the thought 'I don't exist' was occurring, and he continued to have the experience of being a locus of consciousness. One finds the same thing in Meursault, the protagonist of Camus's novel *The Outsider*.

Sustained experience of depersonalization is classified as psychotic relative to normal human experience, but it is of course experientially real, and routine in severe forms of depression—which are by no means uncommon. Depersonalization isn't an all-or-nothing matter—it has degrees—and it adds to the human light that we can throw on the possibility of there being SELF-experience that doesn't involve any sense of personality. One can imagine human beings getting stuck in the condition (some do). Equally, one can imagine aliens for whom it is the normal condition. Such an alien may still have an unimpaired sense of itself as an inner subject, a mental presence, a locus of consciousness, just as we ordinarily do; it may still have clear experience of the self as a mental something.[23]

A very strong form of something that may be lost in depersonalization is recorded by Gerard Manley Hopkins in a passage quoted in part in 1.13:

... my self-being, my consciousness and feeling of myself, that taste of myself, of *I* and *me* above and in all things, which is more distinctive than the taste of ale or alum, more distinctive than the smell of walnut leaf or camphor and is incommunicable by any means to another man (as when I was a child I used to ask myself: What must it be to be someone else?). Nothing else in nature comes near this unspeakable stress of pitch, distinctiveness, and selving, this selfbeing of my own. Nothing explains it or resembles it, except so far as this, that other men to themselves have the same feeling. ... But to me there is no resemblance: searching nature I taste *self* but at one tankard, that of my own being. ... We say that any two things however unlike are in something like. This is the one exception: when I compare my self, my being-myself, with anything else whatever, all things alike, all in the same degree, rebuff me with blank unlikeness. ...[24]

When I first read this, I found it hard to believe that Hopkins could be telling the truth, and all those I asked found his claim as bewildering and implausible as I did. Further enquiries have shown that a few people feel that they know just what he means.

---

myself, felt that they had never had any experience of that kind; and a third were unsure or undecided. It's interesting to compare the passages by Richard Hughes and Elizabeth Bishop on pp 213–16 below.

[23] Experience of 'innerness' isn't a necessary feature of any possible form of SELF-experience; a different species—*Airheads*—might, in figuring the self as something distinct from the Airhead organism considered as a whole, experience it as located somewhere above the organism, rather than as internal to it.

[24] 1880: 123. He adds, rather depressingly: 'above all my shame, my guilt, my fate are the very things in feeling, in tasting, which I most taste that selftaste which nothing in the world can match' (p. 125). This diminishes his dramatic claim, and raises considerable doubt about his certainty that his feeling is unique.

Hopkins compares his experience of his own personality or 'selfbeing' to experience of unusually distinctive sensory phenomena, supercharged objects of the senses. His examples are bitter, acrid, astringent, and ammoniac (he later adds 'the taste of clove, the smell of... hart'shorn'), and although all we should take from the analogy is the idea of qualitative distinctiveness that is radical, salient, and intense,[25] this hardly makes his claim less mysterious to those who have no such experience. For most people, their personality is something that is unnoticed, and in effect undetectable, in the present moment. It's what they look through, or where they look from, not something they look at. It's an automatic and uninspected presupposition, a global and invisible condition of their life, like air, not an object of experience. Ian McEwan speaks of the 'glassy continuum of selfhood' (1997: 187), by which he means, I think, its transparency or invisibility to itself, and Sartre could not be more explicit:

character has no distinct existence except as an object of knowledge to other people. Consciousness does not know its own character—except in so far as it may consider itself reflectively from the point of view of another .... This is why pure introspective description of oneself does not reveal a character.   (1943: 349)

And although John Updike's main point is different, when he says that it isn't our 'selves in our nervous tics and optical flecks that we wish to perpetuate; it is the self [considered simply] as window on the world that we can't bear to think of shutting' (1989: 206), it is interestingly connected (he's considering the desire for immortality or fear of death).

—It's true that one can have SELF-experience without a sense of the self as something that has personality; this is, perhaps, sufficiently shown by the human phenomenon of depersonalization. But one must at some time or other have had such a sense of oneself, and must at least be capable of such a sense of oneself. And in this sense PERSONALITY is, after all, a foundational, constitutive condition of SELF-experience.

It's hard to see why we should accept this. One can imagine a purely cognitive subject of experience. Even if one is human, one can have constant experience of the self as having vivid contentful properties—belief, desire, and mood properties, for example—without having any sense whatever that one has a particular personality. Much more important, though, is the fact that experience of the self as something that has personality doesn't even seem to be the normal human case. It's not something that is only rarely absent, as in cases of depersonalization; its absence doesn't require that one be like Goronwy Rees, who begins his collection of autobiographical sketches as follows:

For as long as I can remember it has always surprised and slightly bewildered me that other people should take it so much for granted that they each possess what is usually called 'a character'; that is to say, a personality with its own continuous history .... I have never been able to find anything of that sort in myself   (1960: 9).

Nor need one be like Iris Murdoch, in the passage from Bayley's memoir quoted in 1.13:

[25] The smell and taste of strawberry, camomile, and banana are as distinctive as any Hopkins mentions, but don't assail the senses in the same way.

Iris once told me that the question of identity had always puzzled her. She thought she herself hardly possessed such a thing, whatever it was. I said that she must know what it was like to be oneself, even to revel in the consciousness of oneself, as a secret and separate person—a person unknown to any other. She smiled, looked amused, uncomprehending. It was not something she bothered about.   (1998: 51–2)

Murdoch's reaction will seem ordinary and accurate to some, and many will feel an affinity with A. J. Ayer, who, questioned in an interview, replied as follows:

I wonder whether I do even have an image of myself? I suppose if you ask me questions about my character, I would have opinions about most of them, I would say: 'Yes, I am X', or 'I'm not Y', [but] I don't think that I have an image of myself in the sense that I am much concerned with my own character. I don't think I'm all that much interested in myself. I'm much more interested in trying to solve philosophical problems, or in what's happening around me, or how my little boy is getting on.   (1971; quoted in Rogers 1999: 286)

Are these extreme cases? I doubt it. Many people go through life without any particular thought of themselves as things that have a character or 'identity'. Even if they do take it for granted that they have such a thing, still they need have no sense of it in the normal course of things. Remember that SELF-experience is experience of *oneself* as a self, and has nothing to do with how one might experience others in so far as one considers them as having or being selves. It seems plausible that PERSONALITY should feature in any account of the notion of self that aims to characterize how we think of others when we think of them as selves; it doesn't follow that we think of ourselves in this way when we think of ourselves as selves. One's personality is the window through which one looks on the world, and one isn't looking at the window. It's part of the mental musculature that one exercises in engaging in the world, and that one doesn't think about in so doing. Most people apprehend it expressly only when thinkingly detachedly about themselves. When one assesses one's actions in retrospect, for example, one may see that one has exhibited consistency of personality. When one thinks of how others think of one, one is likely to be aware of the fact that others take one to have a specific personality, just as one takes them to have a specific personality.

Hopkins may seem horribly self-concerned, but Bayley's version of Hopkinsianism seems very unalarming, and it may be that Hopkins is intensely aware of the unique taste of his self not because he's stewing in it but because he's achieved an unusual degree of spiritual detachment or selflessness. Perhaps this is what has made his self, his unique mental shape—and evidently we all have unique mental shape—come into range for him as a strikingly propertied object of experience rather than persisting as an invisible, all-conditioning, taken-for-granted background of experience. On this view, it may be those who are utterly non-Hopkinsian, like myself, who are the more self-centred. Perhaps we are too drenched in our own personalities to have any felt awareness of them. Perhaps we take our own personality so much for granted that it seems like the null case in spite of the fact that it is intricately peculiar, in both senses of the word. Perhaps there's a sense in which we're bound to feel our outlook to be like clear glass, although it is in fact a thick lens with a complex and highly individual prescription.

Human beings vary hugely in this respect, and I very much doubt that these variations correlate systematically with degrees of selfishness or selflessness. People can be extremely unreflective about themselves without being selfish or self-favouring or self-concerned (contrary to the suggestion in the last paragraph), and certainly self-absorption need have nothing to do with selfishness. It's compatible with great unselfishness, and may merely reflect the fact that one's inner life is very interesting and eventful.

Some may still believe that PERSONALITY is an essential component of ordinary human SELF-experience. I think that they may be confusing (1) the basic unreflective figuring of the self which is actually constitutive of everyday SELF-experience, and which is my main present concern, with (2) a more loaded conception of the self that has the following properties: (i) it's the view that unreflective common sense is likely to come up with when it takes its first step into theory; (ii) it's very likely to be brought to the front of the mind by explicit discussion of the self of the sort I am engaged in at this moment (one of the great difficulties, when it comes discussing SELF-experience, is that the process risks warping the thing that is being discussed out of its normal shape, in so far as it has one); (iii) it does indeed figure the self as something that has personality and does so essentially; (iv) it is essentially richer than (1).

Come to consciousness of yourself now specifically as a self or mental presence aware of whatever is in front of your eyes. Do you immediately and naturally come to consciousness of yourself specifically as something personalitied? No: and this is (1) without (2). If this is not your experience, I think you belong to a small minority. (2) is a kind of reflective accretion on (1) that is likely to be provoked by explicit discussion of the nature of the self, and is much more likely to come to the fore when one is thinking of others as having selves, rather than of oneself*. Does any genuine form of SELF-experience involve commitment to an idea of the self that Buddhism rejects? I take it that the answer is No.

4.6 AGENT

So much for PERSONALITY, what about AGENT? Must SELF-experience involve experience of agency, experience of oneself* as something capable of intentional action? This is not the question whether SELF-experience must involve experience of oneself* as something active in the sense of being something whose existence essentially involves activity; I'm not going to question this, although it may fail in certain pathological cases. It is, to repeat, the more specific question whether SELF-experience essentially involves experience of oneself* as capable of intentional action, i.e. voluntarily and deliberately initiated action. Does SELF-experience essentially involve experience of agency, where by 'agency' is meant specifically intentional agency? I think not.[26]

Many disagree. They not only think, with William James (93), that experience of the self as an agent is essential to any genuine form of SELF-experience. They also think that anything that counts as a self must *be* an agent—an intentional agent in the fullest sense

---

[26] In what follows I draw on G. Strawson 2003a. Those who are already convinced should turn to p. 199.

of the term. Lowe, for example, states that 'the *capacity* for ... agency ... is ... essential to selfhood' (1996: 43); Bruner holds that 'self is a concept one of whose defining properties is agency' (1994: 41).

This is a view that has thousands of expressions, but I can find no incoherence (to go straight to the extreme case) in the idea of a Pure Observer, a motionless, cognitively well-equipped, highly receptive, self-conscious, rational, subtle creature that is well informed about its surroundings and has, perhaps, a full and vivid sense of itself as an observer, although it has no capacity for any sort of intentional action, or even any conception of the possibility of intentional action. It seems excessively unlikely that any such creature could evolve naturally, but that is not material here.[27]

—Your 'Pure Observers' are impossible, because thought of any sort already necessarily involves mental activity, and indeed mental action. Thought evidently involves *mental agency*—i.e. mental activity that is a matter of intentional action. This settles the case even before we ask whether there could be mentally complex creatures that are constitutionally incapable of any large-scale intentional bodily movement.

I disagree. I'll allow, for purposes of argument, that any genuine agency must be accompanied by some sort of experience of agency, but it's a further question whether thought is or must be action, intentional action, action performed for a reason, action in the standard philosophical sense. Obviously thought involves—is—mental activity, but activity, whether mental or volcanic, doesn't always involve intentional action, and if we consider things plainly, we find, I think, that most of our thoughts just happen. They're not actions. Contents simply spring up—the process is largely automatic and largely involuntary. Even when they're most appropriate to our situation and our needs as agents, action and intention need have little or nothing to do with their occurrence.

The case of thought in conversation is striking. One doesn't act to generate material for one's reply, as the other is speaking. It just comes, often before the other has finished speaking, and one often knows—in a flash, it seems—both that the essential content of the reply is ready to hand in the mind, and, in some ineffably compressed manner, what its content is, before one has run through its detail in any way. (As one speaks, one very often elaborates on what had already come to mind, and adds new material that is coming to mind, but that is a further point.)

There's another way of taking cases of this kind. If one drops the assumption that genuine agency must be accompanied by some sort of experience of agency, one can allow that consciously undeliberated but pertinent and responsive thought of the kind just described is in fact a case—indeed, a fundamental case—of human intentional action. The present point remains untouched, because of the dropped assumption; for even if such cases are classified as instances of intentional action, there need be no experience of agency.

---

[27] The Pure Observer's inability to act doesn't mean that it can't experience movement through space of the sort sometimes said to be essential to a grasp of the three-dimensionality of space. Its sister, affixed to a giant drifting lily pad, may have exactly the same mental and bodily equipment and experience movement through space without any ability to act. Its second cousin, one of the 'Weather Watchers' (G. Strawson 1994: ch. 9), may have complicated preferences and desires, a marked personality, and still lack any capacity for, or conception of, intentional action. See also the 'Spectator Subject' and the 'Natural Epictetans' (G. Strawson 1986: chs. 12–13); and, again, Camus's Meursault (Camus 1942).

All I need to establish here is that it's possible for there to be SELF-experience that doesn't involve any sense of the self as an (intentional) agent, because my main present task is simply to describe the minimal case of SELF-experience. This leads naturally to the consideration of extreme cases—imaginary beings like the Pure Observers. But it's also worth considering whether human experience, normal or pathological, can provide insight into the possibility of SELF-experience without any sense of the self as an agent. I think it can, richly.

In putting the case I'll talk mainly about the extent to which mental goings-on are experienced as a matter of action. So let me start by saying something about our experience of ourselves as the authors of bodily actions. To consider bodily action is not to shift the focus away from SELF-experience and on to experience of oneself as a whole human being, because one is just as likely to figure oneself principally as a self or mental presence when experiencing oneself as the initiator and controller of bodily actions as when one is engaged in specifically mental action. One may, for one thing, figure oneself principally as something—a self or mental presence—that *has* a body and acts through it. This is how it is for many people at least some of the time, whatever the richness of their kinaesthetic and somatosensory experience when they engage in bodily action. It isn't something that's more likely to be true of a professor than a peasant.

—Those who figure themselves in this way have a bad and misleading Cartesian picture of the human predicament.

This is an odd remark, for Descartes laid particular stress on the extreme intimacy of the connection between mind and body, and questions about the goodness or badness of metaphysical positions are irrelevant, for the present point is a phenomenological one. It's a point about how something is in fact experienced, not about whether it's metaphysically sound or realistic to experience it in that way.

—The phenomenological claim is also flawed. Ordinary people don't really think in this way. It's an old *philosophical* mistake to think they do. If you think that you sometimes experience yourself in this way, that's because you've been corrupted by your study of philosophy.

You misunderstand me if you think that I'm not taking enough account of the EEE sources of human SELF-experience. I know that SELF-experience, in human beings like us, depends deeply on rich somatosensory experience and rich experience of being engaged as a body in a physical environment. Descartes is right that we're not situated in our bodies like pilots in ships, experientially speaking, and I'm prepared to agree that we often experience ourselves, considered as subjects of experience, as, indissolubly, human beings considered as a whole. Still, none of this gives any reason to doubt the phenomenological claim that we also often experience ourselves as selves that *have* bodies and act through them. We can move almost instantaneously between the two perspectives; they can even coexist at a single time. We're not lodged in our bodies like pilots in ships, phenomenologically speaking, but our experience of ourselves as inner mental subjects is constantly to hand, alongside our experience of ourselves as whole human beings. It's constantly explicit in our experience, in the wide, weak sense of 'explicit' introduced on page 30, according to which something can be fully and genuinely part of the actual, occurrent content of experience, and therefore 'explicit' in the current sense, without being taken as the object of thought in any sort of focused, thetic, attentive fashion. We do readily experience/conceive the body as something distinct from what we most deeply are, even when we think of ourselves as agents and as performers of bodily actions, and a large part of the force of the EEE point lies precisely in this, as remarked in 2.2: the fact that it can seem very surprising, given the nature of SELF-experience, that this innerized sense of what we most deeply are depends essentially, in the human case, on the great array of EEE facts. There is in any case no tension between the EEE position and the view that it is regularly the self, rather than the whole human being, that is felt to be the agent, the agent properly speaking—as much in the case of bodily action as in the case of mental action.

One's experience of oneself* (oneself considered as a self) as an agent has no special roots, then, in one's experience of oneself as the agent of mental actions. It is doubtless grounded in, and most powerfully fed by, one's experience of oneself as the agent of bodily actions—as is one's experience of agency generally considered. But let me now say something specifically about the human experience of mental agency, of intentional action in mental matters. Interest in the minimal case of the human experience of agency supplies one reason for doing this. We need to consider the possible case of a completely paralysed human being who has no experience of bodily agency, has become fully habituated to this condition, yet still has essentially normal experience of mental agency.[28] Even apart from that, the phenomena of mental agency and the experience of mental agency are well worth attention in the present context.

It seems to me that there isn't much intentional action in human mental life, and that what there is has a curiously marginal or merely catalytic role. Certainly I find very little in my own case. Things impinge on me. I remember that I have to do X—it strikes me that Y is true—I hear fire engines. I want some coffee—I wonder where the filter papers are. I know I have to go to Wigan Pier—I find myself thinking about the best way to travel. Thought, it seems, is mostly a matter of things happening, and the passive or non-agentive nature of the ordinary experience of thought is vividly expressed in many of our idioms: 'I realized that p'; 'It struck me that q'; 'I had an idea'; 'I noticed that r'; 'Then I understood'; 'The scales fell from my eyes'; 'The thought crossed my mind'; 'I saw the answer'; 'It suddenly came to me'; 'It occurred to me—it dawned on me'; 'I remembered that s'; 'I realized that t'; 'It hit me that u'; 'I found myself thinking that v'; 'w!—of course—how stupid of me!'

It's started to rain. I think that Harry is going to get wet. We naturally say that this is something I do. But we also say this about sneezing, yawning, dreaming, and tripping over, and my thought about Harry is certainly not a matter of intentional action. And

---

[28] In the milder case of paralysis there will remain something—something mental—which, for the paralysed person, P, constitutes *trying* to perform some bodily action, even though nothing ever comes of the trying. In the more extreme case, in which P has become fully habituated to the condition, there may no longer be anything which, for P, constitutes even trying to perform any bodily action. See G. Strawson 1994: 271–2, 303–4.

yet some seem to think—feel—that having a thought or taking a step in thought is *standardly* a matter of action, something crucially located in the general domain of intentional action, rather than something that simply happens to one.

The cases of judging and reasoning—directed thought in general—are central for those who hold this view, and there are a number of idioms that seem to support the idea that an agentive view of the matter is as natural as a non-agentive view: 'I've worked it out'; 'I judged that p'; 'My considered judgement is that p'; 'After reflection I endorsed the view that q'; 'I reasoned that r'; 'I decided that s'; 'I came to the conclusion that t'; 'I assented to the proposition that u'; 'I speculated, hypothesized, that v, and judged that if v, then w'; 'I accept that x'.

All these more agentive idioms have an easy passive reading, in fact, while the passive idioms don't have an easy agentive reading; but the general issue can't be decided by appeal to idioms, let alone by their relative weight of numbers. What we find is a deep difference of attitude on this question, one of those deep differences among human beings that exist independently of philosophical training or specifically theoretical predilection. Some seem pervasively committed to the idea that entertaining new content—new ideas, making inferential transitions—in thinking, judging, reasoning is a matter of intentional action.[29] Others like myself find this mystifying.

What might explain this difference of opinion? I don't think it stems from a dramatic difference between those who really do routinely operate as conscious intentional agents in major parts of their mental lives and those who don't. The deep difference, I think, is just the difference of opinion, or rather feeling—the difference between those who are inclined to experience themselves primarily as agents in their mental lives and those who aren't. The strength and reach of 'the tendency to attribute control to self is a personality trait', as Wegner says (2002: 330, citing Rotter 1966), and in some the sense of control—or origination—extends further than in others. Some of us are much more likely than others to experience what Wegner calls an 'emotion of authorship' in reason, thought, and judgement.[30] I never experience anything of the sort.

This isn't to say that there's no such thing as mental action, intentional mental action. There's intentional mental action in every sense in which there's intentional bodily action; and there may well be significant differences between people when it comes to the question of how much their mental lives are a matter of intentional action. But those who take it, perhaps very unreflectively, that much or most of their conscious thinking—or conscious mental life in general—is a matter of intentional action are, I believe, deluded. The role of genuine intentional action in thought is at best indirect. It is entirely prefatory, merely catalytic, as remarked. For what actually happens, when one wants to think about something or work something out? If the issue is a difficult one, then there may well be a distinct, and distinctive, phenomenon of setting one's mind in the direction of the problem, a setting of it at the problem, and this phenomenon,

---

[29] For recent examples see McDowell 1998; Burge 1998; Peacocke 1999; discussed in G. Strawson 2003a.

[30] 2002: 318, 325–6. The present line of argument causes a sense of outrage and disbelief in some who have this personality trait.

I think, may well be a matter of intentional action. It may involve rapidly and silently imaging key words or sentences to oneself, or refreshing images of a scene, and these acts of priming, which may be regularly repeated once things are under way, are likely to be fully-fledged intentional actions.

What else is there, in the way of action? Well, sometimes one has to shepherd—or dragoon—one's wandering mind back to the previous thought-content in order for the train of thought to be restarted or continued, and this too may be a matter of action. We talk of concerted thought, and this *concertion*, which is again a catalytic matter, may be (but needn't be) a matter of intentional action. Sometimes thoughts about the answer to a question come so fast and are so rich in content that they have to be, as it were, stopped and piled and then taken up and gone through one by one, and this again can be a matter of action. (I have in mind the speed and wealth of alert, sober, focused thought, not the mental torrent of illness or the drugged or drunken mind, where, typically, little can be done about the content.) Sometimes one has a sense that there's a relevant consideration that isn't in play, although one doesn't know what it is. One initiates a kind of actively receptive blanking of the mind in order to give any missing elements a chance to arise. This too can be a matter of action, a curious, weighted, intentional holding open of the field of thought. Attention, too, can be a matter of intentional action, of maintaining attention. But 'attention *creates* no idea', as James remarks (1890: 1.450). In itself it delivers no new content, and needn't be a matter of action, any more than being keyed up and tensely expectant are. One may be gripped, fascinated, absorbed, swept away, one's attention may be held: all these descriptions correctly imply lack of action.

No doubt there are other such preparatory, ground-setting, tuning, retuning, shepherding active moves or intentional initiations.[31] But intentional action, in thinking, really goes no further than this. The rest is waiting, intellectual receptivity: waiting for something to happen—waiting for content to come to mind, for the 'natural causality of reason'[32] to operate in one. There is, I believe, no action at all in reasoning and judging if these activities are considered, independently of the preparatory, catalytic activity described above, simply in respect of their being a matter of content production or of moves between particular contents.

To this extent Philo was radically understating things when he said that 'a man's thoughts are sometimes not due to himself but come without his will' (20–50 CE: v. 266). The point is not just that 'the faculty of voluntarily bringing back a wandering attention, over and over again, is the very root of judgment'.[33] It's that this catalytic bringing back is all there is in the way of action, in judgement. This, just this, is the true extent of what Descartes called *directio ingenii*, the direction of the mind in thought—'the voluntary ... decision', in Cottingham's words, 'to direct the mind in ways which will allow its natural rational powers to operate properly and productively' (2002: 352).

---

[31] Sophisticated automobile engines retune themselves several thousand times a second. Perhaps something similar to this goes on, at comparatively leisurely speeds, in concentrated thought—something similar to the constant refreshal of a computer monitor.

[32] G. Strawson 1986: 93–4, 105, following Kant.   [33] James 1890: 1. 424. The root is not, I take it, the essence.

Call what goes on mental spontaneity if you like, allow the arising of contents to be a matter of spontaneity; but admit, then, that spontaneity has nothing particularly to do with action, or will. 'The solution of problems', as James remarks, 'is the most characteristic ... sort of voluntary thinking.' In many ways, he says, it is like trying to remember a forgotten name or idea. There's plenty of action—catalytic, priming (and strangely indirect) action—in trying to remember a name; but there's nothing voluntary about what new content comes to mind. Pointers arise as we press the mind, but they *arise independently of the will*, by the spontaneous process we know so well. *All that the will does is to emphasize and linger over those which seem pertinent, and ignore the rest*. ... Even though there be a mental spontaneity, it can certainly not create ideas.'[34]

It's equally clear, I think, that all the *cognitive work* that thought involves, all the computation in the largest and most human sense, all the essential content-work of reasoning and judgement, all the motion and progress of judgement and thought considered in their contentual essence, as it were—the actual confrontations and engagements between contents, the collaborations and competitions between them, the transitions between them, and so on—are not only not a matter of intentional action, but are also non-conscious (sub-experiential). This cognitive work isn't itself a phenomenon of consciousness, however much it's catalysed by conscious primings. Rather, the content outcomes are delivered into consciousness so as to be available in their turn for use by the catalytic machinery that is under intentional control. One knows that P is true and wonders whether [P → Q], holding this content in consciousness. Into consciousness comes 'No; possibly [P ∧ ¬ Q]' ('∧' is the 'and' sign); immediately followed, perhaps, by 'But R, and [[P ∧ R] → Q], so Q.'

This non-consciousness is itself an important fact, I think, and invites reflection. Some may think that it already amounts to the point that the essence of thought (as opposed to the supporting work of catalysis and priming) isn't a matter of intentional action. I'm not sure that this is the right reaction, in fact, but the point remains that no ordinary thinking of a particular thought-content (conscious or otherwise) is ever an intentional action. No actual natural thinking of a thought, no actual having of a particular thought-content, is itself ever an action. Mental action in thinking is restricted to the fostering of conditions hospitable to contents' coming to mind. The coming to mind itself—the actual occurrence of thoughts, conscious or non-conscious—is not a matter of action.

—I'm now going to think that grass is green, and my thinking it is going to be a premeditated intentional action: *grass is green*. And now I'm going to think something—I don't yet know what—and my thinking it is going to be a premeditated intentional action: *swifts live their lives on the wing*. This disproves your last claim.

These are hardly cases of ordinary or natural thought, but let us consider them. In the first case, thinking *grass is green*, it may seem that there is an especially concentrated,

---

[34] 1890: 1. 584, 586, 594. See also James's brilliant discussion of trying to remember something on 1. 251–2.

fully-fledged action of comprehension-involving entertaining of a content. But is this really so? What one finds, I think, if one reflects, does at one stage involve some sort of action, but this is just a matter of a silent mental imaging of words (as sounds or visual marks, say): the actual comprehending thinking of the content is something that just happens thereafter, or perhaps concurrently.

In this case a comprehending entertaining of *grass is green* has already previously occurred—it has already been held in mind as an intended object of thought. Another event of (particularly emphatic) comprehending entertaining is then brought about by one's doing something of the priming or catalytic kind, such as generating a silent acoustic image of 'grass is green' to oneself in some way—something that has already been allowed to be a genuine instance of mental action. But the event of entertaining itself isn't an action, any more than falling is, once one has jumped off a wall.

In the case of *swifts live their lives on the wing*, there is again a certain sort of action—an action of setting oneself to produce some content or other. But what happens then is: a content just comes. Which particular content it is isn't intentionally controlled; it isn't a matter of action. It can't be a matter of action unless the content is already there, available for consideration and adoption for intentional production. But if it is already there to be considered and adopted, it must have previously 'just come' in order to be available. And this takes us back to the first case, while throwing more light on the general respect in which the occurrence of a particular event of entertaining and consciously comprehending a particular thought content neither is nor can be an action, still less an action in which the intention is to entertain, comprehendingly, that very thought-content. One can make such an event occur, but only by doing something else.

—Actions have many true descriptions, and it's a familiar point that they can be redescribed in terms of their consequences, intended or not. I cross the threshold, activate the lighting, illuminate the conservatory, alarm the parrot, wake the burglar. I move my leg, kick the ball, score the goal. So too I aim to think some thought or other, I make millions of neurons fire, I think *swifts live their lives on the wing*; or I aim to work out the truth about some specific matter, and finish up thinking *p*. Why aren't these cases of the same sort? Why can't all intentional mental actions of catalysis and focusing be truly described in terms of their consequences, so that when I focus my mind in order to try to work out what the truth is, and end up thinking *p* (or aim to think some thought or other and end up thinking about swifts), my entertaining this content is correctly said to be an action?

If you think the cases are the same, fine (it won't force you to assimilate either case to the case of alarming the parrot, although it's important that the upshot targeted in intention can be specified only generally, either as just thinking some thought or other, or, in the case of trying to work something out, as thinking whatever is the truth about the question under consideration). Given this way of describing things, perhaps the only error that some people make, when considering these matters, is to conceive of the issuing of a particular thought-content as a 'basic' action: something one does, and does intentionally, and doesn't do by doing anything else. Here as elsewhere I think it's the psychological difference between those who feel thought as action and those who don't that is most interesting—each side finding the other remarkable.

—What about choices and decisions? These are clearly mental actions.

Some are, but the case is far from clear. And we need to consider the mental goings-on that precede choices and decisions. Are these a matter of action, at least in part?

It depends on the case. Very often there's no action at all: none of the activation of relevant considerations is something one does intentionally. It simply happens, driven by the practical need to make a decision. The play of pros and cons is automatic and sometimes unstoppable. At other times there's a deliberate setting of the mind at the problem of what to do, a process of focusing on the problem, a concertion of thought, and this can be a matter of action. But what follows is, again, just a waiting for content to occur. As in the case of theoretical thought, there may well be a process of refocusing and re-refocusing—that curious ballistic launching and relaunching of the mind after it has stalled or stumbled or been distracted, a recasting of it (in the fishing sense) after it has started to settle in one direction, so that it will be receptive to hitherto unengaged relevant considerations. But here again action is the underlabourer, preparatory, catalytic. There's no direct action in the actual issuing of new content, any more than there is in the growth of trees one has planted.

In many situations of practical uncertainty, pressing or not, one believes, often rightly, that there's a straightforwardly right or best answer to the question what to do. And in all cases of this sort reaching a decision needn't—I am inclined to say shouldn't—involve any *agency in decision*, or any *sense* of agency in decision. What happens is that one considers and reconsiders the pros and cons, perhaps involuntarily, perhaps calmly, perhaps frenetically, and what one wants is that it should become clear which is the right choice. One simply wants to come to see what is best (morally or otherwise), and there's nothing in the experience of wanting this, or of actually coming to see what's best, that necessarily or even accurately involves any sense of intentional agency or free decision (compare trying to decide which of a number of melons is ripest, or trying to read the words on a distant sign). Some, no doubt, have such a sense. The movement of the natural causality of reason (practical reason in this case) to its conclusion in choice or decision is lived by some as action when it is in fact a matter of reflex; distinctively rational reflex, to be sure, but not in any case a matter of action.[35] The intentional action of catalysis, combined with openness to, lack of resistance to, harmony with, one's own natural, internal, automatic, non-agentive operations of content processing, comes to seem to extend beyond catalysis. For all that, it seems to me that most deciding what to do is best seen as something that just happens, even if there is also, and crucially, some sort of genuine action of positive commitment to the decision, either at the time it's reached or at the moment of the 'passage à l'acte' (perhaps it was awareness of this point that drove the existentialists into the strenuous artifice of the 'acte gratuit').

---

[35] This isn't any sort of reductive remark, so far as the rationality of the processes (or of the people in whom they take place) is concerned. Here I agree with Brewer (1995).

I think, then, that there's relatively little action in mental life. People may differ considerably—some may train themselves to exercise more agency in their mentation, and engage in a great deal of concerted thought—but any action will be only of the catalytic sort. Once again, the intriguing difference between people is not the difference between those who are regularly agents (catalytic agents) in their thinking and those who aren't. It's the difference between those who *feel* strongly that they're (more than catalytic) agents in their thinking, agents in what they think, and who set great store by this idea, and those who don't—whether they're considering themselves primarily as selves or primarily as whole human beings. My present task, accordingly, is simply to try to make vivid, for those who do experience themselves strongly as agents in their mental lives, the possibility of mental life that lacks this characteristic.

Experimental work by Libet is worth mentioning in this connection, because it's been cited in support of the view that we never really make choices or decisions in the present moment of consciousness in the way we think we do. It doesn't, however, cast any doubt on the reality of the ordinary human *experience* of agency, and of the self in particular as an agent, or on the wider thesis that any genuine form of SELF-experience must involve experience of the self as an agent. On the contrary, it starts from the fact that our experience is that many of our actions do indeed depend essentially on and flow causally from our consciously made choices and decisions (although we may not feel this about typing, say, or shifting position, or taking the next step down the road). We experience ourselves as consciously deciding or resolving what to do, and as consciously deciding or judging that *now* is the time to act, and as then (subsequently) acting. Such experience is routine and often very strong, and in the normal case one has no sense that the time of these choices or resolvings, or the time of their triggering action, is other than the time at which they are consciously experienced as being made and as triggering action. Libet's experiments have been interpreted as showing, against this, that the experience of conscious choice to perform an action occurs about 350 milliseconds after the time at which the brain activity leading to the performance of the intended action (the readiness potential) has got under way. This in turn has been interpreted as revealing a key respect in which the conscious experience of choice occurs some time after the choice has been made, non-consciously, in the mind or brain. On this view, the time of the experience of conscious choice or decision is simply the time at which the content of the choice or decision or resolution first becomes available to consciousness.[36]

Strongly put, the claim is that the neurophysiological evidence shows that the experience of conscious choice is strictly speaking illusory; it occurs only when a choice that has already been made and has already begun to be acted on is (as it were) presented in consciousness. This undermines an intensely natural picture of agency according to

[36] See e.g. Libet 1985, 1987, 1989, 1999; Gazzaniga 1998a; Wegner and Wheatley 1999; Wegner 2002. (In his experimental work Libet concentrates on cases in which the decision isn't simply a decision about what to do, but a decision to do it now, because these cases are more susceptible of experimental test; but if his findings are sound, we may suppose them to apply to all events of decision and choice.)

which it is, essentially, the 'conscious *I*' that is the agent. We take it that in so far as we are deciders and choosers and initiators of action, true exercisers of agency, we are so as conscious beings who are present in the present moment—essentially so. Yet it seems, as Norretranders says, that 'it is not a person's conscious *I* that really initiates an action ... The *I* does not want to accept this. The thinking, conscious *I* insists on being the true player, the active operator, the one in charge. But it cannot be' (1991: 257).

Is this true?[37] There is, it seems, a sense in which it is—although it isn't really an empirical question whether the onset of the readiness potential should count as a choice. If it were true, would it undermine anything that matters? No. Even on their strongest interpretation Libet's results do not in any way threaten the view that we really do make decisions and choices, and are indeed the authors of our actions. For our decisions and choices and actions, mental or bodily, are not in any sense not our own, or in any way less our own, because their original occurrence isn't conscious (the same goes for our thoughts, reasonings, judgements). Libet's results don't threaten any defensible sense in which we can be said to have free will or to be responsible for what we do. The experience one has of being the author or origin of one's decision or choice is mistaken only in so far as it may not be oneself considered narrowly as the 'conscious *I*' present in the moment of the conscious experience of making the choice or decision that actually makes the choice or decision. The choice or decision is, to repeat, no less one's own for occurring outside consciousness (it is certainly no one else's). It flows from oneself, from one's character and outlook, from what one is, mentally. The most that Libet's experiments show is that one doesn't make one's choices and decisions or initiate one's action consciously in quite the way one thinks one does or at exactly the time one thinks one does.[38]

—Quite; and this point has a natural extension. Just as it doesn't follow, from the sense in which the 'conscious *I*' doesn't make choices or decisions, that there's any sense in which one's choices and decisions are not one's own, or in any way less one's own, so too it doesn't follow, from the fact that the processes that lead to the arrival of thought contents in consciousness aren't themselves conscious, that there's any sense in which they're either (a) not truly our own thoughts or (b) not a matter of intentional action on our part.

I agree with (a) but not (b). I agree that our thoughts and judgements are not in any sense not our own, or less our own, for not being direct products of consciousness. The fear that Libet's findings constitute a threat to any remotely defensible account of autonomy, freedom, and responsibility is psychologically telling but superficial. I also agree that the occurrence of our thoughts and choices can be partly caused by genuinely

---

[37] It has been subjected to much criticism. For recent examples see e.g. Dennett 2003: 227–42; Mele 2006: ch. 2; 2007.

[38] See G. Strawson 1994: 172. Libet has also argued that at the time of the conscious experience of making the choice one still has a power to abort or 'veto' the action process that is already under way (see e.g. Libet 1999). The idea is that this can put the 'conscious *I*' back in control in some satisfying sense. The respect in which choices may be non-conscious remains untouched, however, and I don't think Libet succeeds in answering the objection that the veto, too, is presumably under way non-consciously before it becomes conscious.

intentional mental actions on our part (the curious catalytic business discussed earlier, the girding the mind to engage the problem at hand), although these catalytic mental actions too, like bodily actions, will presumably have been decided on, and will have got under way, before they are experienced as being initiated by the conscious I. Even so, I see no reason to say that the operation of the mental system that is catalysed in this way, and that culminates in a thought or judgement, is itself a matter of action, rather than being automatic and standardly involuntary. We return to the fundamental point: human minds are powerfully governed by deep, natural, non-agentive principles of operation, the natural causality of reason, the natural causality of sensation and emotion, the natural causality of the whole huge engine of innate mental equipment, as activated and tuned by experience.

There's much more to be said on this subject, but not here. The last nine pages are an excursion from the principal claim of this section, which is much more general and much more extreme: SELF-experience—experience of mental presence, of self-presence, of being there—doesn't necessarily involve any sense of oneself* as an agent, either in general or in one's mental life in particular. Experience of agency, and in particular of the self as an agent, is not a 'transcendental' or constitutive condition of SELF-experience.

Some may accept this in principle, but insist that human beings, at least, must have some sense of the self as an agent, at least in their mental lives, in having SELF-experience. It seems at first a likely idea, especially if we restrict attention to those who aren't suffering from any major mental pathology. The case of paralysed human beings incapable of any bodily action and fully habituated to their condition has no force to suggest otherwise, for it seems plausible that paralysed human beings ordinarily retain some sense of the self as exercising agency in mental life at least. I think, nevertheless, that human beings need have no sense of the self as an agent in mental life, and needn't be in any way deficient in humanity if they do not. Nor should the possible (non-pathological) effects of spiritual discipline on human mentality be underestimated or discounted. Descriptions of the experiential character of states of spiritual advancement are robust, in the sense that there is a high measure of agreement as to their basic character across different traditions, and Krishnamurti reports an experience which many have had when he claims that 'you do not choose, you do not decide, when you see things very clearly: then you act which [sic] is not the action of will .... Only the unintelligent mind exercises choice in life .... A truly intelligent [spiritually developed] mind ... simply cannot have choice.'[39] To lose a sense of agency may simply be to pass beyond experience of indecision and, equally, beyond any need to push or catalyse one's thinking. It certainly doesn't involve any loss or diminution of responsibility.

It's worth adding that pathological human experience is as real as any other kind, and important in its own right. Experience of oneself as an agent in one's mental life can be lost in depersonalization, for example, while basic awareness of oneself as a locus of consciousness or mental presence remains undiminished. Something like this, pathological or not, afflicted Coleridge. He got up in the morning and put on his

---

[39] Quoted in Lutyens 1983: 33, 204; see G. Strawson 1986: ch. 13.

boots. He lived from day to day. He wrote letters and walked into town. But he felt that he entirely lacked the 'self-directing Principle', and was, 'as an *acting* man, a creature of mere Impact' (quoted in Holmes 1989: 315). Camus's *étranger* comes again to mind.[40]

Experiences of creativity or composition commonly have this form. You do not have to be a poet or a genius to agree with Rimbaud when he writes: 'It's false to say: I think. One ought to say "it thinks [in] me" … for *I* is an other … It's obvious to me that I am a spectator at the unfolding of my thought: I watch it, I listen to it' (1871: 249, 250). This is how it is for me when I think about what to say here. Any action lies in the catalytic prompting of mentation, in the choice of focus as several things strike me when, stuck, I reread the previous sentence or two and wait to see what happens.[41] Apart from that, I find the usual ambient activity, a wide-spectrum scanning that goes on automatically, an apparently empty-headed, purposefully aimless ranging which is not in fact aimless because it has become tuned to a specific subject matter. Then Nietzsche's 'small terse fact that a thought comes when "it" wishes and not when "I" wish', accompanied by Wallas's 'little girl … who, being told to be sure of her meaning before she spoke, said "How can I know what I think till I see what I say?" ' and Hemingway's Federico: 'I never think, and yet when I begin to talk I say the things I have found out in my mind without thinking.'[42]

I conclude that we can get a strong grip on the possibility of SELF-experience without AGENT by reference to human cases, and not just alien—or divine—logical possibilities. Informal research suggests that it is evident to some (perhaps they tend to fall under the heading *melancholic*, in the old, profound fourfold division of human types and tendencies) that a person may have no particular experience of mental agency.

It seems likely that the belief or feeling that judgement is action goes with belief in the possibility of 'self-creation'. Some, for deep reasons of character, have an intuitive sense of themselves as self-making and self-made, or at least as capable of such self-making. They think that Mary McCarthy describes something real and common—and indeed universal—in the following passage, quoted in part in 1.13:

I suppose everyone continues to be interested in the quest for the self, but what you feel when you're older, I think, is that you really must make the self. It is absolutely useless to look for it, you won't find it, but it's possible in some sense to make it. I don't mean in the sense of making a mask, a Yeatsian mask. But you finally begin in some sense to make and choose the self you want. (1963: 37)

People like me, however, find this remote from their experience (unless, perhaps, 'making the self in some sense' can be stretched far enough to cover 'becoming who you are'), and are bewildered by the remarks of Germaine Greer and Thomas Szasz, quoted on page 16.[43] They're amazed by these fantasists—so they find them. They agree with

---

[40] Camus 1942. See also Roquentin's bad moments in *La nausée* (Sartre 1938).

[41] Dennett (1991, 2001) gives some striking descriptions of how contents compete for entry into consciousness.

[42] Nietzsche 1886: §17; Wallas 1926; Hemingway 1929.

[43] See also Glover 1988: Part II: 'Self-Creation'. When Camus says that 'to know oneself, one should assert oneself. Psychology is action, not thinking about oneself. We continue to shape our personality all our life' (1937: 48), he's not describing a planned process of shaping. On the contrary.

Gadamer, also quoted on page 16. They may also know something their opposites may doubt or find hard to understand: that lived awareness of the fact that one is what one is, and can in no way accede to some kind of ultimate responsibility for what one is, doesn't make one in any way irresponsible in outlook, less aware of one's responsibilities.

Here is another deep division between human beings. It may align, if only imperfectly, with another: the division between people who find it natural to think consciously about and consciously work on their overall public persona and people who never do. It never occurs to many people of the second sort that others engage in this sort of shaping, and even if it occurs to them, it's not something they can fully grasp. So too, some people of the first sort find it hard to believe in the existence of people of the second sort.[44]

4.7 PERSISTING

I've argued that four of the base elements of ordinary human SELF-experience—SUBJECT, THING, MENTAL, SINGLE$_{(S)}$, and their various compounds, such as SINGLE-AS-MENTAL—are integral to any genuine form of SELF-experience, and that three—AGENT, PERSONALITY, and DISTINCT—are not.[45] One remains: PERSISTING, a sense of oneself* as something that has relatively long-term diachronic singleness or continuity. I think that this too is unnecessary for SELF-experience, and will now argue the point. 'Long-term' is vague—it can concern an hour or a lifetime, according to context—and it transmits its vagueness to 'persisting' and 'PERSISTING', but it's usefully (not damagingly) vague, given my theoretical purposes.

Many think that to talk of selves is by definition to talk of persisting things, things that continue to exist not only beyond the lived present of experience but also for considerably longer periods of time. This may prompt the view that a sense of oneself* as persisting must feature in anything that can count as genuine SELF-experience, although it certainly doesn't entail it. Others may be more open-minded about the best theoretical use of the word 'self', but still doubt whether one can have genuine SELF-experience without any significant sense of oneself* as persisting. Large questions arise, questions about the general nature of our experience of being in time, some of which I try to answer elsewhere.[46] But the present question is simply this: Is PERSISTING a necessary component of any genuine SELF-experience? Must one have the *Persistence Belief*, belief that one* is something persisting, in order to have SELF-experience? Must one have *Persistence Experience*, experience of oneself* as something persisting, in order to have SELF-experience?

---

[44] People of the second sort may find that they adjust their behaviour—and accent—considerably in the presence of different groups of people, and they may be aware of this; but this is a very different and relatively superficial matter (to behave differently in different company is not to engage in any sort of pretence, or to have more than one 'self').

[45] Those who disapprove of the expulsion of AGENT (the experience of agency) from the minimal case of SELF-experience can factor it back in for their own purposes and read on without any serious hindrance.

[46] See e.g. G. Strawson 2004, 2007.

I think not. It seems that SELF-experience can be vivid and complete at any given time even if it has to do only with the lived present of experience and never involves a sense or conception of the self as something that has any diachronic singleness or continuity. If so, it's not only the relatively capacious experience-structuring element PERSISTING that isn't a necessary part of SELF-experience. Not even SINGLE_D is necessary—not even when it's taken in its original narrow sense (75). On this view, one doesn't have to figure the self as something that has any existence beyond the lived present of experience.

William James makes a crucial point when he says that we have in SELF-experience a sense of something that is 'as fully present at any moment of consciousness in which it *is* present, as in a whole lifetime of such moments'.[47] This, though, is wholly compatible with the view that a sense of the self as persisting is necessary for SELF-experience, and the present claim goes much further: a creature may have experience of itself as a self, an inner subject or mental presence present now in the lived present of experience, without any significant sense or conception of the self as something that exists at other times.

—Perhaps there could be a creature all of whose actual (occurrent) experience of itself* was experience of itself* merely as something present in the lived present of experience, experience that involved no thought of past or future. But it couldn't really have such experience without possessing *some* sort of general sense or conception of itself* as something that had longer-term diachronic continuity. Genuine SELF-experience is impossible without some grasp or sense of the self as something that has some significant degree of extendedness in time.

We disagree; but the disagreement may be less serious than it seems. I'm happy to agree that a being can't exist in time and have genuine SELF-experience without having *some* sort of sense of the self as extended in time, for even the lived present of experience has some sort of temporal or duration-involving or time-is-passing phenomenal character (see 5.9). Even experience of oneself* as synchronically single (SINGLE_S) is experience of oneself* as having temporal extent, in other words; for experience of oneself* as synchronically single is by definition experience of oneself* as something single in the lived present of experience.[48] The present claim isn't that SELF-experience needn't involve any sort of sense of the self as something extended in time. It's simply that genuine SELF-experience doesn't necessarily involve any sense or conception of oneself* as extending beyond the lived present of experience.

I could go further, and allow that no creature can have genuine SELF-experience without experiencing the self as SINGLE_D. I don't believe this, in fact, but it would still be a very small concession, relative to what most people who believe in the self want and assume to be true. This is because figuring the self as SINGLE_D only requires figuring it as something that exists beyond the lived present of experience (before or after or both), and something can be figured as existing beyond the lived present of experience while being figured as enduring for less than a second. Conceding the necessity of

---

[47] James 1890: 1. 301 (this doesn't support the three-dimensionalist in the unhelpfully adversarial debate between three-dimensionalists and four-dimensionalists).

[48] Experiential states are sometimes said to have a quality of 'timelessness', but this, it seems, is experience of a certain sort of stillness or unchangingness that is experienced as such precisely in so far as it is experienced as persisting over time.

SINGLE$_D$ doesn't touch the claim that there can be fully-fledged SELF-experience without PERSISTING, without the Persistence Belief—whether we consider a few seconds, a minute, an hour, a day, or a life.

In fact (switching briefly from phenomenology to metaphysics), I think that the idea that selves are or must be things that persist in this way may be the principal illusion that one has to contend with when one seeks to defend the metaphysical claim that selves exist. I go further than Hume when he expounds a 'bundle' theory of the self, for his central claim is not that there is definitely no persisting self or mind; it's only that we have no empirically respectable evidence for the existence of some sort of persisting self or mind, no evidence of a sort that could underwrite a philosophically respectable use of 'self' or 'mind' to denote such a thing.

I take up the metaphysical suggestion that there's no such thing as a persisting self in Part 7. The present task is still phenomenological, and the first thing to say, in the present phenomenological context, is that when I speak of 'hour' ('day', etc.), I'm not really concerned with an objective measure of time. I mean, rather, a phenomenological unit of measurement—something like 'hour (day, etc.) as typically experienced or experientially conceived of by a typical adult human being, so far as its temporal extent is concerned'. Perhaps this hardly needs to be said, but it is important. It's only the subjective experience of temporal duration that is at issue at the moment. There may be creatures that experience a second in the way we experience a lifetime. Perhaps mayflies grow tired of life.[49]

For the same reason, I'm going to pass over the issue of the nature and reality of time. Some say time doesn't exist. Proponents of the 'block-universe' view say that it exists but doesn't really flow or pass as we think—that it is in some sense already all there, spread out in a spacelike way. None of this matters here, for the present question concerns the temporal character of experience. This is certainly real, and in describing it I'll continue to talk about time in a common-sense realist way.

The question, then, and again, is whether any genuine form of SELF-experience necessarily involves PERSISTING, possession of a sense or conception of oneself* as a persisting thing, something that endures significantly beyond the lived present of experience or consciousness.

—SELF-experience without PERSISTING (or at least some not entirely fleeting version of SINGLE$_D$) may perhaps be a formal possibility, but it is utterly remote from reality and from all our practical and philosophical interests. Life without any significant sense of the diachronic singleness or continuity of the self may be conceivable for self-conscious aliens, but it's hardly possible—or interesting—for human beings.

Aliens are enough for my main argument—it's enough that the possibility of SELF-experience without PERSISTING be admitted—but I think that life without the Persistence

---

[49] James (1890: 1. 639–40) makes this point beautifully, and Ferris (1997: 237) gives it dramatic expression, noting that although 10^{-34}th of a second is a short time by human standards, it 'seems by the standards of early-universe physics as interminable as an indifferent production of *Lohengrin*'.

Belief or Persistence Experience lies within the range of human experience. One can be fully cognizant of the fact that one has long-term continuity as a human being without *ipso facto* having any significant sense or experience-structuring conception of the self as something that has long-term continuity. (It seems to me that this is how it is for me.) Certainly one can have a full and vivid sense of oneself as a self or mental presence, at any given time, and a strong natural tendency to think that that is what one most truly or fundamentally is, while having little or no *interest* in or commitment to the idea that the self—*I who am now thinking*—has any long-term past or future. This idea may have very little emotional importance for one. It may contribute little or nothing to the overall character of one's experience at any given time.

Isn't this bound to be a bad thing, a bad way to live? I don't think so (I'm sure it isn't), but the issue is complex.[50] For the moment it is enough to quote Shaftesbury, who goes to the heart of the matter:

The metaphysicians and notable reasoners about the nice matters of identity, affirm that if memory be taken away, the self is lost. [But] what matter for memory? What have I to do with that part? If, *whilst I am*, I am as I should be, what do I care more? And thus let me lose *self* every hour, and be twenty successive selfs, or new selfs, 'tis all one to me: so I lose not my opinion. If I carry that with me 'tis I; all is well .... — The *now*; the *now*. Mind this: in this is all.[51]

It's likely that Buddhist meditation can induce this attitude to oneself*, oneself considered as a self or locus of consciousness, so long as it doesn't abolish basic SELF-experience in the lived present of experience. A concerted and spiritually motivated attempt to live from day to day or (in a gem-like way) in the moment may do the same,[52] and there are more secular examples. People can retain a strong sense of the self as a mental presence, the present locus of consciousness, when drunk or drugged in such a way that they feel completely out of time and lack any significant sense of the self as having long-term diachronic continuity. They can come round after an accident and be fully self-conscious, aware of themselves as a mental presence, while suffering from complete retrograde amnesia (loss of memories of their life before the accident) and severe anterograde amnesia (inability to retain memories of what happened after the accident).

There are also striking cases of brain lesions that leave intact the basic sense of the self as mental presence while apparently ruling out any lived sense of it as something that has long-term continuity.[53] Squire and Kandel report that when 'EP' returned home from hospital,

his friends and family saw the same high-spirited and friendly man they had always known. He smiled easily and liked to laugh and tell stories. He looked in fine physical health, his walk

---

[50] See e.g. Engler 2003; G. Strawson 2007.

[51] Shaftesbury 1698–1712: 136–7. By 'opinion' he means, roughly, overall outlook, essential character, moral identity.

[52] To do this is not to relapse into what Kierkegaard condemns as the 'aesthetic' (very roughly, the merely sensual) life.

[53] They typically involve damage to the dorsolateral prefrontal cortex, or to the temporal lobes and hippocampus, or all of these.

and manner were as before, and his voice was strong and clear. He was alert and attentive, and he conversed appropriately with visitors. Indeed, testing would later show that his thought processes were intact. But it took only a few moments to sense that something was very wrong with his memory. He repeated the same comments and asked the same questions over and over again, and he could not keep up with conversations …. He could now remember new events or encounters only for a few seconds. The illness … kept him from carrying his thoughts and impressions into the future, and it had broken his connection to the past, to what had happened in his life before. He was now confined, in a manner of speaking, to the present, to the immediate moment.   (1999: 1–2)

'WR' is 'pleasant, … intelligent and articulate', according to Knight and Grabowecky, but his behaviour is 'completely constrained by his current circumstances'. He repeats 'phrases such as "yellow comes to mind" in response to queries of his memory', and is 'lock[ed] … into the immediate space and time' by damage to his dorsolateral prefrontal cortex (1995: 1367–8). The widely discussed 'HM' has since 1953 lived 'in a timeless vacuum …, marooned in the moment …, interacting intelligently minute by minute with whatever stimuli impinge directly upon him …, a favorite with researchers and clinical staff alike … because of his endearing nature, sense of humor, and willingness to be helpful'.[54] 'Right now', he says, 'I'm wondering, have I done or said anything amiss? You see, at this moment everything looks clear to me, but what happened just before? That's what worries me. It's like waking from a dream. I just don't remember.'[55] David, discussed by Damasio, has one of the most severe defects in learning and memory ever recorded, 'more extensive than HM's … his memory loss goes almost all the way to the cradle; he

cannot learn any new fact at all …. He knows very little about himself except his name. He talks to you very charmingly, even intelligently …. Left to his own devices, he sustains purposeful behavior relative to the context he is in for many minutes or hours, provided that what he is doing is engaging …. He can play a whole set of checkers—and win!—although he does not even know the name of the game and would not be able to articulate a single rule for it, … and … the affective modulation of his voice as the game approaches its decision point is a primer of human emotion …. He's a very happy person, jovial, delighted to talk to people …. But he doesn't know the date, why he is talking to you or who you are. He doesn't know who he is in the proper sense of the term. He is a consciousness without an identity.   (1999: 43–7, 113–21; 2000: 48)

These people lack any significant sense of themselves, considered as mental subjects, as PERSISTING, as having long-term diachronic continuity, and their overall experience is radically unlike ours. But they use 'I' as well as any of us, and there is no reason to think that they must lack SELF-experience—that they can't possibly have any sort of sense or conception of themselves as selves, as mental presences, at any given time.

Pathological cases are important, and suffice to make the point. They are also, perhaps, sad, but SELF-experience without any significant sense of long-term diachronic continuity

---

[54]   Ogden 1996: 41–2; see also Scoville and Milner 1957.
[55]   HM: <http://www.brainconnection.com/topics/?main=fa/hm-memory2>.

can also occur naturally—without brain lesions or intoxication—and positively in human beings, and this, I think, is even more important. It's possible to take no thought for the morrow (Matthew 6:34). 'It is possible to live almost without memory,' as Nietzsche remarks.[56]

This completes the Whittling Argument (I'll return to the question of our experience of time in Part 5).

4.8 Sesmets

The Whittling Argument starts out from a set consisting of the eight proposed base elements of ordinary human SELF-experience—SUBJECT, THING, MENTAL, SINGLE(s), PERSISTING, AGENT, DISTINCT ± PERSONALITY—together with their various compounds. It discards the last four and retains the first four, together with their various compounds.[57] It concludes that the minimal form of SELF-experience has four fundamental structural elements: SUBJECT, THING, MENTAL, SINGLE(s). At the very least, SELF-experience figures the self as a subject of experience; as a thing in a sense that has been explained; as something that's mentally propertied, that has mental being; and as something that's single—a unity—at least during the lived present of experience. This is not news, I think.

—Experience of oneself as a whole human being also and equally involves figuring oneself as a subject of experience, and as a thing, and as mentally propertied, and as single. And it also involves figuring oneself as thing-as-subject, for that matter, and as single-as-subject—quite independently of anything that might be called 'SELF-experience'.

True. All of SUBJECT, MENTAL, SINGLE, and THING, not to mention

SINGLE(s)-as-SUBJECT

and

THING-as-SUBJECT,

are components of experience of oneself as a subject of experience considered as a whole organism. There are, however, five more elements on the list of eleven set out on pages 171–2:

SINGLE(s)-as-SUBJECT-as-MENTAL

SUBJECT-as-MENTAL

SINGLE(s)-as-MENTAL

THING-as-SUBJECT-as-MENTAL

THING-as-MENTAL

---

[56] 1874: 62; he adds that it is 'impossible to *live* at all without forgetting'.

[57] Two other possible candidates for membership of the base set—SELF-CONSCIOUS and *has* SELF-EXPERIENCE—are noted in 2.9 (47–8), but put aside.

all of which end in '-as-MENTAL' and do distinguish SELF-experience from any kind of whole-creature-with-non-mental-properties experience of oneself as a subject of experience. One could substitute 'DISTINCT' for 'MENTAL' in all these elements, in describing the human case, but the present list aims to be completely general.[58]

We might build up the description of the minimal form of SELF-experience in a different way, starting from the proposal that SELF-experience has in fact only one truly fundamental element: SUBJECT. On this approach, SELF-experience is simply *a certain way of experiencing oneself as a subject of experience*.[59] More particularly, it's a way of experiencing oneself as being a subject of experience specifically in so far as one has mental being (= is mentally propertied), and not, say, in so far as one is a human being considered as a whole. That is, it's experience of oneself as SUBJECT-as-MENTAL. On this view, SUBJECT-as-MENTAL alone is the fundamental element. I tried to spell this out in 2.17, arguing that it's a matter of figuring oneself as a subject of experience, and hence as something mentally propertied, without any explicit resort to any conception of oneself as non-mentally propertied. It is—at least—a matter of figuring oneself fully as a subject of experience in a context of thought in which the question of whether or not the subject might also have non-mental being isn't in play.[60]

In 4.3 I promised to reduce the seven compound elements listed above to two and then to one, and I will now do so. Since x-as-y-as-z implies or includes all of x-as-y, y-as-z, and x-as-z, given the definition of the '-as' construction on page 71, it suffices to list the four basic elements and the two triple elements:

SUBJECT

MENTAL

SINGLE

THING

SINGLE-as-SUBJECT-as-MENTAL

THING-as-SUBJECT-as-MENTAL.

All the other five (double) elements are comfortably nested inside the two triple elements.

These two compound terms may still seem somewhat *agaçant*, however (especially if one isn't their author, and even perhaps if one is), and a further reduction seems in order. This is what I propose. At its core, SELF-experience is simply a matter of experiencing or figuring oneself as a single thing when experiencing or figuring oneself specifically as a

---

[58]   The reason why one could not generally substitute 'distinct' in place of 'mental' is given on p. 165.

[59]   One might follow Priestley and say that SELF-experience, 'the idea of *self*', is 'the feeling that corresponds to the pronoun I' (1777: 284). Analytic philosophers have been too impressed with the respect in which 'I' refers to the whole human being to appreciate this remark.

[60]   Note that the interaction of the compound elements is thoroughly systematic. If we take MENTAL as the basic term, each of the other three remaining elements attaches to it as a qualifying prefix to give SUBJECT-as-MENTAL, THING-as-MENTAL, and SINGLE$_s$-as-MENTAL. If we take SUBJECT-as-MENTAL as the basic term, both the remaining two thought-elements attach to it to give SINGLE-as-SUBJECT-as-MENTAL and THING-as-SUBJECT-as-MENTAL.

mental subject—whatever else it may or may not involve in any individual case (I use 'single' rather than 'single$_s$' because the temporal qualification needn't be at issue). It's a matter of experiencing oneself as a single thing specifically when one is experiencing oneself as a subject and experiencing oneself experienced as a subject specifically in respect of one's mental being (propertiedness).

In the light of this, I propose, we can compress all the compound elements (and indeed the four basic elements) into one:

SINGLE-THING-as-SUBJECT-as-MENTAL.

This, I expect, is what many supposed the core of SELF-experience to be all along, even before engaging in any philosophy. If so, so much the better. It is also, I think, what Kant supposes it to be in the Paralogisms in so far as he is concerned with SELF-experience ('the representation of myself, as the thinking subject, … in inner sense' (A371)) at all. So much the better again.

At the very least, then, SELF-experience is a matter of figuring oneself as SINGLE-THING-as-SUBJECT-as-MENTAL. Put slightly differently, for acronymic ease, it's a matter of figuring oneself as a subject of experience that is a single mental thing. The single compound thought-element is

SUBJECT OF EXPERIENCE-as-SINGLE-MENTAL-THING

or

SESMET

for short.

The expression 'SUBJECT-as-SINGLE-MENTAL-THING' doesn't in fact display the relations between its component elements in the most perspicuous way, even before it is collapsed into 'SESMET'. But one has only to remember the definition in order to read the term right. To figure oneself as a sesmet is, to repeat, to figure oneself as a single thing or object specifically when one is figuring oneself as a subject and figuring oneself figured as a subject specifically in respect of one's mental being. This is a way of figuring oneself that I take to be fully available to two-year-olds. One need only add that in the minimal case one's sense of oneself as a single thing will extend only to the lived present of experience.

—How can such subjective considerings-*as* be implicated in questions of metaphysical fact?

Easily enough, I think, but that is a matter for Parts 7 and 8. For the moment let me continue to order my language.

I propose to say that there are five core elements in SELF-experience (in SELF): the four simple elements SUBJECT, THING, MENTAL, SINGLE, and their complex product SESMET. These are cognitive-experiential elements. Jointly they constitute the answer to the general phenomenological question: What must be true of any genuine form of SELF-experience? What's the minimal form of SELF-experience? What figurational elements must it contain? It must contain SUBJECT, THING, MENTAL, SINGLE, and SESMET (where SINGLE will in the limiting case be SINGLE$_s$).

If this is the right answer to the general phenomenological question, then the first metaphysical question one has to address, when trying to determine whether or not selves exist, is whether there are in fact any things that have the properties *subject, thing, mental*, and *single*, together with the further property that arises from their combination, *sesmet*: that property which an entity has when it is correctly judged to be a single thing when considered specifically as a subject considered specifically as mental. These properties aren't phenomenological thought-elements, they're (metaphysically) real properties. The proposal is that they're the core properties of anything that can count as a self.

One can treat SESMET alone as the core thought-element, since it contains SUBJECT, THING, MENTAL, and SINGLE. One can then take the Whittling Argument to have shown that all SELF-experience is SESMET-experience,

[SELF-experience → SESMET-experience]

or, equivalently,

[SELF → SESMET]

and—given the assumption that the Whittling Argument has whittled away everything unnecessary from the original, rich set of sufficient conditions of SELF-experience—add the converse claim that all SESMET-experience is SELF-experience

[SESMET-experience → SELF-experience]

or, equivalently,

[SESMET → SELF].

These combine into

[SELF-experience ↔ SESMET-experience]

or, equivalently,

[SELF ↔ SESMET]

—this being the full conclusion of the Whittling Argument, the final summary answer to the general phenomenological question. (If one feels that there is a sense in which the thought-element SESMET fails to contain SUBJECT, THING, MENTAL, and SINGLE as properly independent elements, one can add them explicitly into the definition of 'SESMET'.)

One can do the same with the property *sesmet*, and treat it alone as the core property, on the grounds that its possession entails (incorporates) possession of *subject, thing, mental*, and *single*. I will sometimes do so, but I will also speak of the five properties separately.

Even those who think that anything that is to count as a self must also have the property of relatively long-term diachronic continuity (*persisting*), or the property of being an intentional agent (*agent*), or the property of being fully and expressly self-conscious (pages 47, 101), can agree that the properties *subject, thing, mental*, and *single*, and *sesmet* are at least necessary for being a self. They can agree that these properties are core conditions on being a self, even if they think that there are other core conditions. So even if they think that *subject, thing, mental*, and *single*, and *sesmet* aren't sufficient, they may have an interest in the next task, the task of trying to work out whether sesmets exist.

We now have a straightforwardly metaphysical or ontological question of fact:

Do sesmets exist?

Are there in fact any entities whose nature is such that there are sufficient grounds for judging correctly that they are single things when one is considering them specifically as subjects of experience and is considering them, considered as subjects of experience, specifically in respect of their mental being?

I need to do some preparatory work before answering this question. The main discussion of phenomenological matters is finished, but there are a number of meta-physical preliminaries to consider. I need to say more about the nature of the properties that are compounded in the property *sesmet*—i.e. *subjecthood, mentality, thinghood*, and *singleness*—and about my understanding of what materialism is. I'll do this in Part 6, after saying something about time and our experience of time in Part 5.

It's worth noting straight away that if something is correctly judged to be a thing—a *res*, a *chose*, an object—when considered in one way, then it's correctly considered as a thing (object) *tout court*: there's obviously no way of considering it given which it is correctly judged not to be a thing (object), even if there are ways of considering that don't yield an answer to the question whether or not it's a thing (object).

Note also that the question whether sesmets exist can be treated independently of the question whether selves exist. If, for example, one holds the view that selves must be immaterial entities, one may be able to answer Yes to the question whether sesmets exist, and No (or 'Don't know') to the question whether selves exist. If one thinks that selves must be intentional agents, or last a long time, one may again be able to answer Yes to the question whether something is a sesmet and No to the question whether it is a self.

Some find acronyms off-putting, but I think it's a virtue of the acronym 'sesmet' that it allows one to consider the case for the existence of things of the sort that I have chosen to call by this name while leaving open the question of whether it would also be right or best or comfortable to call these things 'selves'. I favour the Equivalence Thesis in 2.12 (55), from which it follows that sesmets are selves—given that SELF-experience is the same thing as SESMET-experience;[61] but the question whether sesmets exist can be pursued independently of any views about the correct use of 'self'.

4.9 Does SELF-experience require self-consciousness?

The Whittling Argument is finished. Eleven experience-determining/structuring ele-ments remain. These may be reduced, for reasons of terminological convenience, to five (SUBJECT, THING, MENTAL, SINGLE, and their complex compound SESMET), where the five

---

[61] This identity allows the substitution of 'SESMET-experience' for 'SELF-experience' in the Equivalence Thesis: 'selves exist if and only if there is something that has the properties denoted by the thought-elements essentially involved in SESMET-experience'.

are understood to contain all eleven; or to one (SESMET), equally understood to contain all eleven. It's time to move on. In the spirit of dialectical housekeeping, however, I must finally consider how, or whether, the Building Argument fits with the Whittling Argument (the rest of this section is complicated, and may be skipped).

The Building Argument, begun in 3.5, considered the conditions of self-consciousness. It argued, more or less impressionistically, that self-consciousness—full or express self-consciousness—required possession of SINGLE-AS-SUBJECT-AS-MENTAL, and *a fortiori* SINGLE, SUBJECT, and MENTAL. It was completed *en passant* in 4.3, when THING was added to SINGLE, SUBJECT, and MENTAL on the ground that it was already contained in SUBJECT. All the various compounds (e.g. THING-AS-SUBJECT-AS-MENTAL) were presumed, without detailed examination, to drop into place.

The first two propositions put up for inspection in Part 3 (98) were

(1) [capable of SELF-experience → self-conscious]

and its converse,

(2) [self-conscious → capable of SELF-experience],

and the desired conclusion of the Building Argument can be summarized by rewriting (2) as

(2*) [self-conscious → (possession of) SUBJECT, SINGLE, MENTAL, THING, SINGLE-AS-MENTAL, SINGLE-AS-SUBJECT-AS-MENTAL, … etc.].

If we then compress all the elements on the right-hand side of the '→' into 'SESMET', understood as encompassing all eleven elements, we can rewrite this again as

(2*) [self-conscious → (possession of) SESMET],

acknowledging that the best version of the argument may in fact fail to secure all eleven elements on the right-hand side. This is of course a very strong claim (much stronger than the claim that SELF-experience involves SESMET). It hasn't been argued for in detail, and may seem extremely implausible to many analytic philosophers, even though the self-consciousness in question is full self-consciousness as defined in 3.2, i.e. the ability to grasp oneself *as oneself* in the express manner familiar to us all (as before, I often take the qualification 'full' or 'express' for granted). My hope is that the considerations in 3.5 make it seem plausible after all, or at least much less implausible.

—The basic objection is the same as before. One can think a fully and expressly self-conscious thought while thinking of oneself only as truly-indissolubly-both-mentally-and-non-mentally-propertied—while thinking of oneself as a human being, in short, with all that that entails. And we standardly do think in just this way.

At this point I'm inclined to reply (given 3.5, some of the points in 2.2–2.3, and 7.2 below), that the way in which the thought-element I (i.e. any kind of full-self-consciousness-involving thought-element) occurs in our thought is in fact such that it has SESMET at its core whatever else is true of it, e.g. even when it seems phenomenologically accurate to say that it involves thinking of oneself as indissolubly-both-mentally-and-non-mentally-propertied. This may fail to impress—even when it's stressed that SESMET doesn't contain

DISTINCT. So be it. My aim here is simply to summarize the dialectical situation. (It's odd for me to be arguing for necessities in this area after having spent so much time in Part 3 rejecting them.)

The Building Argument was originally designed to provide support for the Whittling Argument's claim to have reached a genuine terminus, i.e. to have whittled away all non-necessary components of SELF-experience; but it can do this directly only given the assumption (in 3.3) that SELF-experience requires full self-consciousness

(1) [capable of SELF-experience → self-conscious]

which couples with (2*) to deliver the conclusion that all the elements listed on the right-hand side of (2*) are indeed necessary components of SELF-experience (SELF)

(3) [capable of SELF-experience → (possession of) SESMET]

as the Whittling Argument affirms. The question, though, is whether assumption (1) can be justified—discharged. If it can, the Building Argument can neatly support the Whittling Argument. If it can't, the Building Argument can contribute to the overall argument only less neatly.

One can certainly make (1) true by definition, as remarked on page 107. One can stipulate that the sort of SELF-experience that is at present in question not only involves figuring oneself as an inner mental subject (etc.), but also essentially involves apprehension of the fact that one is oneself the inner mental subject in question. In this case the Building Argument can function as a tight independent check on the claim of the Whittling Argument to deliver the minimal conditions of SELF-experience (SELF), by showing that the Whittling Argument can't whittle anything else away. And while the Building Argument is confirming (3), the necessity claim that all of SUBJECT, THING, MENTAL, SINGLE(s), and their various compounds are *necessary* for SELF(-experience), via (1), the rest of the discussion of the conditions of self-consciousness in Part 3 can whittlingly support

(4) [(possession of) SESMET → capable of SELF-experience],

the *sufficiency* claim that no other thought-elements are needed—given that no radically new thought-element turns up as necessary for self-consciousness in 3.6–3.19.[62]

Another thing one might try to do, after presenting the Building Argument that self-consciousness entails figuring oneself as a sesmet (i.e. (2*)), would be to argue for its converse, a rewriting of (1): to argue, still travelling in the small circle of analysis, that, in the end, no creature that can be truly said to figure itself as a subject of experience that is a single mental thing (etc.) can fail to be self-conscious in the required way:

(1*) [(possession of) SESMET → self-conscious].

A successful argument along these lines would couple with (3), the conclusion of the Whittling Argument, to justify the claim that

(1) [capable of SELF-experience → self-conscious].

---

[62] 'These supposed relations of mutual support are not nearly as significant as they seem; you're bound to find this confluence of arguments, for in each case you start from the same basic set of intuitions.' Whatever truth there is in this

(1) would then no longer be a mere assumption, and the Building Argument would be fully established as an independent check on the Whittling Argument.

This won't work if we endorse a broad notion of SELF-experience, for we may then want to say with Damasio that all evolved conscious experience incorporates SELF-experience, i.e. a sense 'that there is an individual subject ..., that the images of any given object that are now being processed are formed in our individual perspective, that we are the owners of the thought process' (1999: 125; see p. 89 above). And even if we think it implausible that all evolved conscious experience involves SELF-experience so described, we may want to say that there are or may be non-human, languageless creatures in which it does. Damasio judges that SELF-experience so understood can be said to have this content even though it is (in its simplest form) a wholly non-verbalizable 'feeling-image' that plainly doesn't entail any capacity for full self-consciousness. So if SELF-experience is to entail a capacity for full self-consciousness, it can only be 'high-end' SELF-experience, SELF-experience as it exists in creatures in whom it is capable of being express in the way in which full self-consciousness is express.

I think it's valuable to have the broad Damasian notion of SELF-experience to hand when one thinks about these issues, but I'm going to continue to work with the high-end notion of SELF-experience. Ineliminable vagueness afflicts any such high-end/low-end distinction—connected to the vagueness that afflicts any attribution of genuine concepts to non-human animals, as remarked in 3.2—but it has to be lived with, and can be. We may find the Damasian characterization of low-end SELF-experience compelling even while we think it plainly wrong to say that the creatures that have it have concepts, and we may feel confident that our own SELF-experience is different in being genuinely concept-animated even though we can't say where the dividing line between being genuinely concept-animated and not being genuinely concept-animated falls.

Could there be a true continuum of cases? The question arises forcefully when we consider the cognitive development of children. On the one hand, there is pressure to think that there must be some sort of sudden passage, of the sort imagined by Kant, as young Karl passes from *feeling* himself to *thinking* himself (106). On the other hand, Wittgenstein's remark that 'light dawns gradually over the whole' seems apposite (1950: §141). My sense is that Kant and Wittgenstein both have something right. There is in any case a real question about the character of the internal phenomenology of the developing child.

Seeking a further characterization of the restricted high-end notion of SELF-experience, one might propose, first, that it is *the sort of SELF-experience that can give rise to the problem of the self in those who have it by virtue of having the character it does*, and, secondly, that any SELF-experience that does this must involve full self-consciousness. But this won't really do. It's true that the problem of the self as we confront it doesn't confront creatures that aren't fully self-conscious, concept-exercising creatures like ourselves, and it's true that we confront the problem of the self because we have SELF-experience, but it doesn't follow

(I'm about to abandon the claim to tight formal support), the different angles of approach are instructive; the route through the notion of self-consciousness is not the same as the route through ordinary human SELF-experience.

that SELF-experience necessarily involves self-consciousness. Self-consciousness may allow or even cause SELF-experience to give rise to the problem of the self in minds like ours, even though SELF-experience doesn't itself necessarily involve self-consciousness. Perhaps self-consciousness simply lights up already existing SELF-experience in a certain manner (it's *me*!), making the sense that there is such a thing as the self vivid in such a way as to trigger the philosophical problem of the self, without being a necessary part of SELF-experience. In any event, I don't think it possible to show that SELF-experience as so far defined entails full or express self-consciousness, even after we've ascended from the simple experience of the sea snail *aplysia* (assuming it has some sort of experience) via cats and dolphins to creatures that can plausibly be supposed to have and exercise concepts like SINGLE, MENTAL, THING, and so on. It isn't clear to me that SELF-experience inevitably involves self-consciousness even when it takes an express form. So I can't in the end endorse (1), the assumption that sets up the Building Argument in such a way that it can function as support for the Whittling Argument, and in so doing makes the title 'Building Argument' appropriate for the discussion of the necessary structure of self-consciousness in 3.5.

So be it. The Whittling Argument must stand on its own. If the Building Argument—or at least its perfect execution—establishes the converse of (1), i.e. that self-consciousness entails (minimal) SELF-experience

(2) [self-conscious → capable of SELF-experience],

as I suspect it does, then this is a very important fact in its own right, when it comes to the question of the self, and SELF-experience; but it must stand alongside the Whittling Argument without directly underpinning it.

Appendix 1

Richard Hughes, *A High Wind In Jamaica*, ch. 6.i

THE weeks passed in aimless wandering. For the children, the lapse of time acquired once more the texture of a dream: things ceased happening: every inch of the schooner was now as familiar to them as the *Clorinda* had been, or Ferndale: they settled down quietly to grow, as they had done at Ferndale, and as they would have done, had there been time, on the *Clorinda*.

And then an event did occur, to Emily, of considerable importance. She suddenly realised who she was.

There is little reason that one can see why it should not have happened to her five years earlier, or even five later; and none, why it should have come that particular afternoon.

She had been playing houses in a nook right in the bows, behind the windlass (on which she had hung a devil's-claw as a door-knocker); and tiring of it was walking rather aimlessly aft, thinking vaguely about some bees and a fairy queen, when it suddenly flashed into her mind that she was she.

She stopped dead, and began looking over all of her person which came within the range of eyes. She could not see much, except a fore-shortened view of the front of her frock, and her hands when she lifted them for inspection: but it was enough for her to form a rough idea of the little body she suddenly realised to be hers.

She began to laugh, rather mockingly. 'Well!' she thought, in effect: 'Fancy you, of all people, going and getting caught like this!—You can't get out of it now, not for a very long time: you'll have to go through with being a child, and growing up, and getting old, before you'll be quit of this mad prank!'

Determined to avoid any interruption of this highly important occasion, she began to climb the ratlines, on her way to her favourite perch at the mast head. Each time she moved an arm or a leg in this simple action, however, it struck her with fresh amusement to find them obeying her so readily. Memory told her, of course, that they had always done so before: but before, she had never realised how surprising this was.

Once settled on her perch, she began examining the skin of her hands with the utmost care: for it was hers. She slipped a shoulder out of the top of her frock; and having peeped in to make sure she really was continuous under her clothes, she shrugged it up to touch her cheek. The contact of her face and the warm bare hollow of her shoulder gave her a comfortable thrill, as if it was the caress of some kind friend. But whether the feeling came to her through her cheek or her shoulder, which was the caresser and which the caressed, that no analysis could tell her.

Once fully convinced of this astonishing fact, that she was now Emily Bas–Thornton (why she inserted the 'now' she did not know, for she certainly imagined no transmigrational nonsense of having been any one else before), she began seriously to reckon its implications.

First, what agency had so ordered it that out of all the people in the world who she might have been, she was this particular one, this Emily: born in such-and-such a year out of all the years in Time, and encased in this particular rather pleasing little casket of flesh? Had she chosen herself, or had God done it?

At this, another consideration: who was God? She had heard a terrible lot about Him, always: but the question of His identity had been left vague, as much taken for granted as her own. Wasn't she perhaps God, herself? Was it that she was trying to remember? However, the more she tried, the more it eluded her. (How absurd, to disremember such an important point as whether one was God or not!) So she let it slide: perhaps it would come back to her later.

Secondly, why had all this not occurred to her before? She had been alive for over ten years now, and it had never once entered her head. She felt like a man who suddenly remembers at eleven o'clock at night, sitting in his own arm-chair, that he had accepted an invitation to go out to dinner that night. There is no reason for him to remember it now: but there seems equally little why he should not have remembered it in time to keep his engagement. How could he have sat there all the evening without being disturbed by the slightest misgiving? How could Emily have gone on being Emily for ten years without once noticing this apparently obvious fact?

It must not be supposed that she argued it all out in this ordered, but rather long-winded fashion. Each consideration came to her in a momentary flash, quite innocent of words: and in between her mind lazed along, either thinking of nothing or returning to her bees and the fairy queen. If one added up the total of her periods of conscious thought, it would probably reach something between four and five seconds; nearer five, perhaps; but it was spread out over the best part of an hour.

Well then, granted she was Emily, what were the consequences, besides enclosure in that particular little body (which now began on its own account to be aware of a sort of unlocated itch, most probably somewhere on the right thigh), and lodgement behind a particular pair of eyes?

It implied a whole series of circumstances. In the first place, there was her family, a number of brothers and sisters from whom, before, she had never entirely dissociated herself; but now she got such a sudden feeling of being a discrete person that they seemed as separate from her as the ship itself. However, willy-nilly she was almost as tied to them as she was to her body. And then there was this voyage, this ship, this mast round which she had wound her legs. She began to examine it with almost as vivid an illumination as she had studied the skin of her hands. And when she came down from the mast, what would she find at the bottom? There would be Jonsen, and Otto, and the crew: the whole fabric of a daily life which up to now she had accepted as it came, but which now seemed vaguely disquieting. What was going to happen? Were there disasters running about loose, disasters which her rash marriage to the body of Emily Thornton made her vulnerable to?

A sudden terror struck her: did any one know? (Know, I mean, that she was someone in particular, Emily—perhaps even God—not just any little girl.) She could not tell why, but the idea terrified her. It would be bad enough if they should discover she was a particular person—but if they should discover she was God! At all costs she must hide *that* from them.—But suppose they knew already, had simply been hiding it from her (as guardians might from an infant king)? In that case, as in the other, the only thing to do was to continue to behave as if she did not know, and so outwit them.

But if she was God, why not turn all the sailors into white mice, or strike Margaret blind, or cure somebody, or do some other Godlike act of the kind? Why should she hide it? She never really asked herself why: but instinct prompted her strongly of the necessity. Of course, there was the element of doubt (suppose she had made a mistake, and the miracle missed fire): but more largely it was the feeling that she would be able to deal with the situation so much better when she was a little older. Once she had declared herself there would be no turning back; it was much better to keep her godhead up her sleeve for the present.

Grown-ups embark on a life of deception with considerable misgivings, and generally fail. But not so children. A child can hide the most appalling secret without the least effort, and is practically secure against detection. Parents, finding that they see through their child in so many places the child does not know of, seldom realise that, if there is some point the child really gives his mind to hiding, their chances are nil.

So Emily had no misgivings when she determined to preserve her secret, and needed have none.

Down below on the deck the smaller children were repeatedly crowding themselves into a huge coil of rope, feigning sleep and then suddenly leaping out with yelps of panic and dancing round it in consternation and dismay. Emily watched them with that impersonal attention one gives to a kaleidoscope. Presently Harry spied her, and gave a hail.

'Emilee-ee! Come down and play House-on-fire!'

At that her normal interests momentarily revived. Her stomach as it were leapt within her sympathetically toward the game. But it died in her as suddenly; and not only died, but she did not even feel disposed to waste her noble voice on them. She continued to stare without making any reply whatever.

'Come on!' shouted Edward.

'Come and play!' shouted Laura. 'Don't be a pig!'

Then in the ensuing stillness Rachel's voice floated up:

'Don't call her, Laura, we don't really want her.'

Appendix 2

Elizabeth Bishop, *In The Waiting Room*

I said to myself: three days
and you'll be seven years old.
I was saying it to stop
the sensation of falling off
the round, turning world
into cold, blue-black space.
But I felt: you are an I,
you are an Elizabeth,
you are one of them.
Why should you be one, too?
I scarcely dared to look
to see what it was I was.
I gave a sidelong glance
—I couldn't look any higher—
at shadowy gray knees,
trousers and skirts and boots
and different pairs of hands
lying under the lamps.
I know that nothing stranger
had ever happened, that nothing
stranger could ever happen.

Part 5

Phenomenology and metaphysics: time and the experience of time

The mind is such a new place, last night feels obsolete.

(Emily Dickinson 1870: 211)

5.1 The Persistence Belief—sources

I argued in Part 4 that PERSISTING isn't a necessary part of SELF-experience, even if it's part of ordinary human SELF-experience. I argued that the *Persistence Belief —Persistence Experience*—isn't a necessary part of SELF-experience.

The word 'belief' is slippery in this context. It slides between detached theoretical belief, on the one hand, and lived belief, on the other hand—belief that is built into, active in, the character of experience. One can have the Persistence Belief in a detached theoretical way without having Persistence Experience, and one can have Persistence Experience while rejecting the Persistence Belief on theoretical grounds, as Buddhists do. At the same time, there's a sense in which nothing can really qualify as Persistence Experience, experience of the self as something persisting, without being cognitively structured in such a way that it's right to say that it involves some *conception* of the self as persisting, and to that extent some belief in the self as persisting. In this sense one has the Persistence Belief in having Persistence Experience even if one rejects the Persistence Belief on theoretical grounds.[1] Unless I say otherwise, I'll be concerned with the Persistence Belief considered as lived belief, as foundational of Persistence Experience.

Whether or not the Persistence Belief is a necessary element of SELF-experience, it's a further question whether it's true. I think that there are contexts in which it's highly reasonable, in the human case, but I'm going to argue that it's not metaphysically respectable on the terms of my current brief: that there is in the human case nothing

---

[1] One finds the same structure in the case of belief in free will. See e.g. G. Strawson 1986: 173.

that sufficiently merits the title 'self' and is also a persisting thing in the present sense, i.e. a thing with long-term diachronic continuity. The metaphysical difficulty lies in the requirement that the self qualify as a thing in a sufficiently strong sense, an object; but this is a matter for Part 6. In the next few sections I want to inspect the Persistence Belief, accumulating in no particular order a number of reflections about time and our experience of time that bear on the problem of the self and our attitude to it.

It's not hard to understand why the Persistence Belief is so widespread. It's woven in with, supported (directly or indirectly) by, many things. One could begin with Hume, who notes our deep, innate, automatic, extremely general, and often thoroughly sensible tendency to come to believe in the existence of continuing single things, long-term continuants, when confronted by certain sorts of diachronically sustained patterns of resemblance between phenomena (our successive experiences) that are in fact numerically distinct from each other. Hume argues that this tendency not only leads human beings to come to believe in continuously existing physical objects, and to take them to be the cause (and therefore explanation) of the striking resemblances and coherencies of development that they discern among their successive numerically distinct experiences, but also, and just as surely, leads them to come to believe in a continuing self as the common and persisting locus of these successive experiences, and to take the existence of this self as part of the explanation of some of the resemblances and causal connections among the experiences.[2] Recent work in developmental psychology suggests that one might as well simply say that it is the belief in spatiotemporal continuants that is innate, rather than saying that it is the tendency to come to believe in spatiotemporal continuants.[3] A similar simplification seems no less reasonable in the case of the human belief in a persisting inner subject, although it's not clear, how experimental evidence might be brought to bear on the question.

We have in any case resemblances of content among successive experiences. Fundamental among them, it seems, when it comes to the underpinning of the Persistence Belief, are deep, regularly repeated—constantly revived—EEE similarities of interoceptive, proprioceptive, somatosensory bodily awareness. The point was made by Wundt (see page 28); even 'the most speculative of philosophers is incapable of disjoining his ego from those bodily feelings and images which form the incessant background of his awareness of himself', even as he experiences his ego or self as something 'over against which [his] own body and all the representations connected with it appear as external objects, different from [his] proper self'.

No less important, perhaps, are all the deep similarities and constancies of general mental feeling-tone.[4] To these we may add all the constancies and coherencies of

---

[2] For more detail see Hume, *Treatise*, 133–5/200–4, 165–9/253–9, 169–71/259–62. The first two passages contain general discussions of the process by which we come to believe in continuously existing entities, the third focuses on the particular case of the self.

[3] See e.g. Spelke 1994.

[4] Damasio (1999) observes that mental feeling-tone is a mode of awareness of bodily states, even if it doesn't seem so to us.

development of perceptual and cognitive content from experience to experience as we move around in the world and think our thoughts.[5] 'The objective nucleus of every man's experience, his own body' is, as James says, 'a continuous percept; and equally continuous as a percept (though we may be inattentive to it) is the material environment of that body, changing by gradual transition when the body moves.'[6] All this doubtless contributes to the Persistence Belief, given that a sense of the inner subject is already in place.

Further support pours in from our exteroceptive and cognitive awareness of our evident singleness and continuity as whole human beings. And our thought about ourselves moves extremely freely between our apprehension of ourselves as persisting human beings and our apprehension of ourselves as mental subjects, in such a way that our grasp of ourselves as persisting human beings feeds the Persistence Belief about the self even though conceiving of oneself as a self is precisely conceiving of oneself as something that is *not* the same thing as the whole human being. Tied in with this is the powerful support that the Persistence Belief receives from one's natural apprehension of others as single continuing persons, and one's vivid awareness of others' apprehension of oneself as a continuing single person. All this feeds through to fix the idea of a specifically inner persisting self, which is also centrally funded by the fact that one has a continuing and consistent overall mental form in having a distinctive personality and, more generally, a vast and robustly persisting body of basic beliefs, preferences, mental dispositions and abilities, and so on.[7] Still more support comes from specific forms of persistence-presupposing moral emotions (guilt among them); from the instinct of self-preservation; from our natural self-concern; from the 'narrativity' of much human thought; from fear of death; from religious commitments; from the sense that the process of consciousness is streamlike; from practical planning purposes; from all the backward-looking and forward-looking phenomena of memory and intention; and from the intrinsic continuities of action sequences.[8]

—This is question-begging, to the point of incoherence. A sense of these constancies can't possibly be prior to a sense of oneself as persisting, in such a way that the former supports the latter. The two things are coeval—entangled—as a matter of conceptual necessity. This is part of the point of the Kant–Strawson Ordered World Thesis you unwisely rejected in 3.11, and

[5] 'Constancy' and 'coherence' are Hume's words. He points out that it isn't only (relatively) unchanging constancies in the environment that give rise to belief in a continuously existing external world, but also developmental coherencies of the sort involved, for example, in the progress of a fire from burning coals to embers to ashes, or—shifting from world to experience—in the continuities of change of view when one walks round a chair while looking at it.

[6] James 1904*b*: 65. The way in which the (embodied) self is implicitly defined as a continuing entity by the coherencies of gradual change in one's perception of the environment is a prominent theme in Husserl (who speaks of the 'zero point of orientation') and Gibson. See further pp. 245 below.

[7] See again 2.3. Note that one's personality can make a central contribution although it isn't something that naturally presents as an object of experience (4.5).

[8] In his account of personal identity, which Hume admired, Lord Kames speaks of the '*feeling* of identity, which accompanies me through all my changes' (1751–79: 261), taking it to be integral to our natural self-concern. Dennett gives a striking description of how belief in a persisting self is built into the narrative outlook on life (1991: ch. 11; see also Dennett 1988). The general topic of the causes, conditions, character, and consequences of the way we experience ourselves in time—in particular ourselves considered as selves—is vast.

of Evans's insistence that 'one's "I"-Idea and one's "here"-Idea are really two sides of a single capacity'.   (1982: 256)

There may be misunderstanding here. The first thing to say in reply is that the present question isn't simply about the grounds of one's belief in one's persistence as a whole human being. It's about the grounds of one's belief in one's persistence as an inner self distinct from the whole human being (the fact that one has experience of single embodiedness and so on is taken as given). There are perspectives from which this split seems suspect, but it is what's at issue here. I offer myself as an example of someone who has all the normal human equipment but lacks the Persistence Belief (and Persistence Experience). It may seem artificial that I cite various sorts of constancy and continuity experience as *support* for the Persistence Belief, as if they were independent or developmentally antecedent phenomena, but priorities are not always what they seem,[9] and the point of doing so will, I trust, become clear.

I take it, then, that the Persistence Belief has formidable backing. One of my general aims in this book is to reduce resistance to the *Transience View* of the self (9) which, if true, gives the lie to the Persistence Belief; but I don't for a moment question the existence of the belief or underestimate its force. In what follows I want to consider some smaller-scale temporal matters—the day-to-day and moment-to-moment experience of the process of consciousness, and its possible influence on SELF-experience and contribution to the Persistence Belief. The discussion is involved—dense—in places, and those who want to get on to the metaphysics of the self should skip to the last three sections of Part 5, which are already difficult, or perhaps go straight to Part 6, turning back as necessary to make sense of any references to the skipped material.

—When we take it that there are continuously existing entities like chairs and dogs, we are in fact right, although we go beyond the evidence conceived in a narrow empiricist way. And when we take it that there's a continuing single locus of the experiences of a human being, we're also right—at least in so far as there's a single continuing brain involved. So why aren't we just as right to say that a single *self* is involved (given that we're going to talk of selves at all, and given that there is a continuing single locus of the experiences) as we are to take it that there are such single continuously existing entities as chairs and dogs? I accept the condition you've placed on something's counting as a self—that it must be a *bona fide* physical thing of some sort—but this doesn't mean that I have to identify the self crudely with the brain considered as a whole. I can perfectly well identify it with some complex set of parts of the brain that I can correctly think of as a genuine physical unity, a single physical thing, because it forms a clear unity functionally or operationally considered. I can identity it with what you earlier (9–10) called the 'brain-system self', the 'self-organ', whatever anterior-insula/precuneus/medial-prefrontal-cortex/reticular-activating-system/etc.-involving thing it is in the brain that supports the consciousness and personality—the overall mental being—of a human being and is still there when the human being is in dreamless sleep.

---

[9] In G. Strawson 2007, for example, I argue that emotions that we tend to conceptualize in ways that make it seem analytic that they presuppose and build on the Persistence Belief are in fact better understood as being among its foundations. Replacing 'the Persistence Belief' by 'belief in free will' in the last sentence delivers the central claim of P. F. Strawson's 'Freedom and Resentment' (1962).

I'm inclined to agree with van Inwagen that chairs and brains aren't good enough examples of physical unities to count as objects, when metaphysics gets serious; I think he and Richard Feynman are right that such items come rather low down on the list of candidates for being physical unities that qualify as objects (see 6.12). But this metaphysical intolerance is a matter for later; for the moment I'm happy to grant that there's a lot to be said for the brain-system view of the self—if we're going to talk of selves at all, in a materialist framework, and try to maintain a connection with the common belief that selves are essentially things that persist for relatively long-term periods of time. It's just that the brain-system may not have the degree of unity required for objecthood, incontestable Grade A objecthood.

5.2 Endurantists and Impermanentists, Narratives and Non-Narratives

Before considering connections between the Persistence Belief and smaller-scale features of our experience of the process of consciousness, I want to say something briefly about a larger-scale difference mentioned in 1.12 (14–15): the difference between Endurantist and Impermanentist individuals. Endurantist individuals are those for whom the longer-term Persistence Belief is, as one might say, experientially natural—individuals who in the daily living of their subjecthood, and for any number of the reasons just listed (and quite independently of any particular theoretical or religious beliefs about the matter), intuitively figure the self as something that has long-term diachronic continuity, something that was there in the remoter past and will be there in the further future. Impermanentist individuals, by contrast, are those for whom the Persistence Belief is not experientially natural, in spite of all the possible inducements to it just listed—those whose natural, regular, lived sense of things is that the self that they now experience themselves to be is not something that was there in the remoter past or something that will be there in the further future, although they are of course fully aware of their long-term continuity as human beings considered as a whole.

I suspect that the Endurantist/Impermanentist difference is a fundamental difference between human beings, and that its root lies in brain chemistry and organization, in genetically determined differences in individual temperament or general mental style. But environmental factors can also play a considerable part. Take Endurantist experience as an example: the range, texture, and emphasis of preponderantly Endurantist experience may vary from person to person and change through time in individuals. In some the sense of the presence and persistence of the self may extend effortlessly back to childhood and forward to anticipated old age; in others it may not. In some it may be gappy, in others not. A person may be much more strongly Endurantist with respect to the past than with respect to the future, or vice versa. Predominantly Endurantist individuals may sometimes experience an Impermanentist lack of linkage with well-remembered parts of their past; predominantly Impermanentist individuals may sometimes connect to charged events in their pasts (or anticipate events in their futures) in such a way that they feel that the events happened (are going to happen) to them, even when thinking of themselves specifically as selves. Certain topics of thought may be likely to evoke Endurantist attitudes—however transiently—in the vast majority of people (I consider embarrassment in 5.4). There are many possible variations and exceptions. Nevertheless—I believe—the Endurantist/Impermanentist distinction reflects a fundamental difference between human beings, and not just between the various types of psychological states that they can be in. One way to express it is to say (as in 1.12) that Endurantists are those who tend to experience themselves as things that were there in the remoter past and will be there in the further future specifically when they think of themselves as things whose persistence or existence conditions are not the same as the persistence conditions of a whole human being; while Impermanentists are those who don't.

The distinction between Endurantists and Impermanentists has a complex relation with the distinction between *Narrative* and *non-Narrative* types, the distinction between those who have a generally Narrative outlook on their lives—where the defining feature of having a Narrative outlook is, roughly, having some sort of story-telling, shape-detecting, unity-seeking, form-finding, or form-imposing attitude to one's life—and those who don't. The two distinctions don't line up neatly, however, because while Narratives are likely to be Endurantists, they needn't be; nor need Endurantists be Narratives. So too, *mutatis mutandis*, for Impermanentists and non-Narratives. It seems to me that all combinations are possible, even if some are uncommon.

Although the notion of narrative has been widely utilized and discussed, it is very unclear. It would need careful exposition in any fuller discussion of the Narrative/non-Narrative distinction.[10] All I want to do here is to register these differences, and to note that they may seat deeply different attitudes to the question whether anything that can count as a self must be supposed to have long-term diachronic singleness or continuity.

I turn now to smaller-scale matters.

5.3 The stream of consciousness

Some people believe that conscious experience flows. They think this is a basic phenomenological fact. According to William James:

consciousness ... does not appear to itself chopped up in bits. Such words as 'train' or 'chain' do not describe it fitly as it presents itself in the first instance. It is nothing jointed; it flows. A 'river' or a 'stream' are the metaphors by which it is most naturally described ... *let us call it the stream of consciousness, or of subjective life.*   (1890: 1. 239; see also 1892: 145)

The metaphor stood out happily in 1890 against the dominant atomistic metaphors of 'trains', 'chains', 'collections', 'bundles', 'wads',[11] and 'heaps', and has flourished ever since. Husserl is deeply committed to the image of the stream, the *'flowing cogito'* (1931: 65), and he is one among many. But now, perhaps, we've been misled in the

---

[10] I make a start in G. Strawson 2004 and 2007.   [11] Merian 1793: 186.

opposite direction—into thinking that consciousness has a more truly fluent character than it does. The question is worth considering here, for if consciousness really does feel streamlike, then this may be a further and prominent part of the overall explanation of the Persistence Belief.

In discussing the matter I'll sometimes write with James 'in the first person, leaving my description to be accepted by those to whose introspection it may commend itself as true, and confessing my inability to meet the demands of others, if others there be' (1890: 1. 299). Here James implies (however mildly) that he doesn't really believe that anyone experiences things differently from the way he does, and although I have no doubt that human beings do vary dramatically in the overall way they experience life in time, I feel the same as James about some, at least, of the features of the moment-to-moment experience of the process of consciousness that will be in question in the next few sections. I will, however, have to distinguish between the way people actually experience moment-to-moment consciousness and the way they think they experience it, in order to maintain this stance—a distinction that may be judged to be thoroughly suspect or worse, and may be used against me, especially since I'll give characterizations of the character of experience that seem controversial.

Hume makes a methodological move similar to James's, in one of the most famous passages in philosophy. Having claimed that 'when I enter most intimately into what I call *myself*, I always stumble on some particular perception or other … I never can catch *myself* at any time without a perception, and never can observe any thing but the perception ….' he employs irony, implying that he will not really believe anyone's claim to differ from him in this respect:

If any one upon serious and unprejudic'd reflection, thinks he has a different notion of *himself*, I must confess I can reason no longer with him. All I can allow is, that he may be in the right as well as I, and that we are essentially different in this particular. He may, perhaps, perceive something simple and continu'd, which he calls *himself*; tho' I am certain there is no such principle in me.

But setting aside some metaphysicians of this kind, I may venture to affirm of the rest of mankind, that they are nothing but a bundle or collection of different perceptions …. (*Treatise*, 165/252)

In the same way, I'll be sceptical of anyone who claims to be radically different from me as regards certain aspects of the moment-to-moment character of the process of consciousness, although I won't doubt their sincerity in claiming they're different. I'd better not, for it may be that relatively few will recognize their experience in my description. I'll argue, nevertheless, that many of the features I describe are part of common life and are revealed to be so by open reflection, even if they don't appear so at first.

5.4 James on the stream: continuity across time-gaps

Defending the metaphor of the stream of consciousness, and using the word 'thought' in Descartes's way as a general word 'for every form of consciousness indiscriminately'

(1890: 1. 224), James claims that 'within each personal consciousness thought is sensibly continuous … without breach, crack, or division' (1892: 144). He considers two possible sensible-continuity breakers—'*time*-gaps during which the consciousness [goes] out', as in sleep, or dreamless sleep, and 'breaks in the content of thought, so abrupt' that what follows has 'no connection whatever with what went before'—and rejects both.

'The proposition that consciousness feels continuous', he says, 'means two things':

(a) That even where there is a time-gap the consciousness after it feels as if it belonged together with the consciousness before it, as another part of the same self;

(b) That the changes from one moment to another in the quality of the consciousness are never absolutely abrupt.   (1892: 144–5)

He argues that both are true. I think, and will argue, that both are false. I'll take them literally for purposes of exposition, considering (a) in this section, (b) in the next. First, though, let me record the point that James is explicitly agnostic on the question whether human consciousness is in fact continuous:

Is consciousness really discontinuous, incessantly interrupted and recommencing (from the psychologist's point of view)? And does it only seem continuous to itself by an illusion analogous to that of the zoetrope? Or is it at most times as continuous outwardly as it inwardly seems? It must be confessed that we can give no rigorous answer to this question.   (1890: 1. 200)

He doesn't take the 'inward' feeling of phenomenological continuity to settle the 'outward' question of actual or metaphysical continuity.

If one considers the episodes of consciousness, past and present, of the human being one is, the first thing to say about (a), perhaps, is that one can have

[1] *Connectedness Experience*, experience of temporally separated episodes of consciousness feeling as if they belonged together, as parts of the same self

without having any trace of

[2] *Continuity Experience*, i.e. experience of felt continuity of consciousness from moment to moment or through the waking day

—a point stressed by Locke. I may have [1], when I think about my experience of embarrassment a year ago, without any sense of [2]. So too, one can have Continuity Experience, from moment to moment, without any significant Connectedness Experience, as when one's mind is in spate (84). The two things are distinct. There are, however, many possible connections between them. Connectedness Experience may be cited in support of

[3] the *Continuity Belief*, theoretical belief in the continuity of the process of consciousness,

even when the Continuity Belief is unsupported by Continuity Experience; and the Continuity Belief may in turn fund or encourage Continuity Experience (beliefs condition experience). We may also distinguish

[4] the *Connectedness Belief*, theoretical belief in the belonging-togetherness of episodes of consciousness

as something independent of any actual Connectedness Experience, any experiential feeling of belonging-togetherness. Connectedness Experience strongly supports the Connectedness Belief, but the Connectedness Belief can exist in the absence of Connectedness Experience.

James expounds (a) as follows:

When Peter and Paul wake up in the same bed … each of them mentally reaches back and makes connection with but *one* of the two streams of thought [i.e. experience] which were broken by the sleeping hours. As the current of an electrode buried in the ground unerringly finds its way to its own similarly buried mate, … so Peter's present instantly finds out Peter's past, not Paul's (1892: 145)

and 'appropriates' it. This is an attractive image, but it's metaphorical and certainly not universally true when taken literally. I wake up and I'm conscious and I know I'm very much the same sort of person as I was yesterday, but I don't engage in any such reachings back or reconnections or appropriations, whether these are conceived of as intentional actions of some sort or as entirely involuntary. Constancy of character and general mental set are fixed in the brain and don't require any sort of Connectedness Experience or Continuity Experience. One can suffer complete amnesia and still be the same (kind of) person as one was before. 'HM' (203), famous for having only a very brief memory span after an operation to alleviate his epilepsy, never reconnects with or appropriates his experiences of the previous day, but has none the less strong consistency of personality. The same is true of 'EP', 'WR', and 'David' (202–3), and many people, I think, have no easy access to yesterday's consciousness, let alone to their last waking thoughts. In fact, this may be the normal case. It doesn't occur only on days when one has to spend some time disentangling oneself from one's dreams, although yesterday's waking consciousness can be ancient history after the dramas of sleeping consciousness.

—What about waking in a strange place, wondering where one is, working it out? Isn't that a clear case of reconnection?

When I wake in a strange place and don't know where I am, I don't grope back to my last minutes of waking consciousness; I simply remember where I am, and facts about how I came to be there. I'm rarely able to make any direct or 'from-the-inside' connection to any part of yesterday's consciousness.

If I engage in the philosophical exercise of trying to reach back to some part of yesterday's consciousness in the intimate or from-the-inside way that James has in mind, and manage to come up with something, I will certainly judge that it 'belongs with' today's consciousness in so far as it is consciousness on the part of the same single human being that I am (to that extent, at least, I have the Connectedness Belief). I know, for one thing, that I can't reach back to anyone else's consciousness in that from-the-inside way. But I don't thereby feel that it belongs with my present consciousness in such a way that I think that it was I* who was there yesterday (I have no Connectedness Experience). It feels remote. Nor do I judge, or feel, that it is I* who was there yesterday. On the contrary, I judge—feel—that I* certainly wasn't there (I have no Persistence Belief).

I may be unusual in this respect. Louis may feel that it was he* who was there yesterday, when he engages in this philosophical exercise and makes a from-the-inside connection of this sort. I don't think I'm that unusual, though. In particular, I doubt that many people have the experience of reconnection as described by James.

—If a part of yesterday's consciousness features in your memory with from-the-inside characteristics, then you *must* feel it to be consciousness on your* part—whether or not there is any particular emotion attached to it. This is part of what 'from the inside' means.

Not true. The from-the-inside character of a memory can detach completely from any sense of identification with—any sense of being the same person as—the subject of the remembered experience. My memory of the experience of falling out of a punt last year, for example, has an essentially from-the-inside character, visually (the water rushing up to meet me), kinaesthetically, proprioceptively, and so on, but it doesn't follow, and in my case isn't true, that it carries any sense at all that what is remembered happened to me*: to that which I now apprehend myself to be when apprehending myself specifically as a self.[12]

—This can't be so when emotion figures in the from-the-inside character of the remembered episode of consciousness, at least.

Again not true. Even when emotion does figure in the from-the-inside character of the remembered episode of consciousness, it doesn't follow that I experience the past experience as mine*. The move from (1) 'The remembered episode of consciousness has a from-the-inside character in emotional respects' to (2) 'The remembered episode of consciousness is experienced as something that happened to me*' simply isn't valid, even though (1) and (2) are often true together. For me this is a plain fact of experience. I'm fully aware that my past is mine in so far as I'm a whole human being, and I fully accept that there's a sense in which it has special relevance to me* now, including special emotional and moral relevance, and yet I have no sense that I* was there, and I think that I* was not there, as a matter of metaphysical fact. I think, that is, that what I am, in so far as I am considering myself as a self, was not there.

Times when emotions figure in the from-the-inside character of a remembered episode of consciousness need to be distinguished from times when one is powerfully emotionally affected in the present by such a memory. In the latter case there are at least three possibilities, none of which casts doubt on the present claim. First, there's the situation in which from-the-inside content of the remembered episode of consciousness has no particular emotional character, although it now causes a strong emotional reaction (the emotional neutrality of one's past state of mind can be the main cause of one's present emotion). Second, there's the case in which the from-the-inside content of the remembered episode of consciousness does have an emotional character, but

---

[12] I argue for this in G. Strawson 2004.

it's different from the emotional character of one's present reaction to it: 'even his griefs are a joy long after to one that remembers all that he wrought and endured'.[13] Third, there's the case in which the present emotion is the same as or similar to the emotion that is present in the from-the-inside content of the remembered episode of consciousness, but it's no more true in this case than it is in the others that I need have any sense that the memories are memories of what I* did or experienced—in spite of the fact that they have a possibly powerful present emotional effect on me*. It simply doesn't follow, from the fact that these remembered experiences have this effect, that I now feel that the experiences happened to me*, or indeed that they did happen to me*. This no more follows than it follows, from the fact that events in stories or histories may have a powerful emotional effect on me, either that they're memories of what happened to me or that they're felt to be. Imaginative or empathetic identification with real or fictional personages can be intense, but (pathology aside) it never carries the sense that one[(*)] is in fact the personage, or did the things the personage did, even when all one's feelings appear to be just as they would be if one did believe this. No doubt the effects of memories of my own past are special in some way, but, again, it simply doesn't follow that the memories must involve the sense that what happened happened to me*.

These points will seem clear to some; others may find them hard to accept. Some may find them troubling for ethical reasons. I argue in *Life in Time* that there's no need to worry. For the moment I'll take them for granted.

It may now be said that the episode of consciousness with which I connect is bound to present as mine* because it's bound to be positively or detectably marked by a certain tone or style or 'feeling of familiarity' in something like Hopkins's way, an unmistakable quality of me-ness that is as such distinct from the quality of from-the-inside-ness (183). No. None of my memories of past episodes of consciousness carry any trace of any such feeling of familiarity, and here at least I suspect I'm part of a large majority—the majority that has no feel for what Hopkins is talking about when he talks about his vivid sense of his own personality. The episode of consciousness is certainly apprehended from the inside, and so I take it for granted that it is mine, if I care to reflect: I take it for granted that it is an episode of consciousness of the human being that I am. But there is no sense, affective or otherwise, that it was consciousness on my* part.[14]

Actually, I not only take it that it is mine, if I care to reflect. I also take it that it is mine*, in the sense that it *belongs* to me* now. I take it that everything that belongs to GS is mine* now. Once again, though, I needn't have any sense that it was consciousness

---

[13] Homer *c*.800 BCE: 15.400, quoted by Aristotle in his *Rhetoric* (1.11.1370^{b}5–6).

[14] If other people's past episodes of consciousness somehow began to be accessible to one 'from the inside', in the way imagined in philosophical stories about 'quasi-memory', one might be able to detect that they were not one's own by their 'tone', even if they were very similar to actual or possible episodes of one's own past consciousness. One might, in other words, have a capacity to judge that certain ostensibly remembered episodes of consciousness were not one's own even if one had no positive feeling of familiarity or emotional identification with one's own (genuinely) remembered episodes of consciousness.

on my* part, and in fact I have no sense that it was. My past is mine* in the sense that it belongs to me*, but I don't feel that I* was there in the past.

—The way you've set it up, it's trivially true that I*, the I of the present moment—where the present moment is understood loosely as having a certain short but unclear temporal duration—didn't exist yesterday, or even half an hour ago, and won't exist tomorrow, or even in half an hour: it's simply built into the definition of 'I*' that its temporal duration is limited in this way.

This is a misunderstanding. I introduced 'I*' and its cognates to represent that which one experiences oneself to be in having SELF-experience, i.e. in experiencing oneself specifically as a self or inner subject, and although I've focused on my own case—the case of an Impermanentist who experiences himself* as something with no significant past or future—there's no sense in which short duration is built into the definition of 'I*'. Many people are Endurantist rather than Impermanentist (1.12), and naturally experience/conceive themselves* as things that have long-term continuity and exist at times other than, and more or less remote from, the present. It's true that 'I*' restricts one's focus on oneself not just to oneself considered specifically as a self, but to oneself considered specifically as a self *and present now*, but it doesn't thereby exclude the ontological possibility that the I* one apprehends as present now should exist at other more or less remote times, and it certainly doesn't exclude the phenomenological possibility that one should naturally *experience* this I* as something that existed or will exist at other more or less remote times. One could introduce a new term that explicitly incorporated a specific time limitation. One could talk of 'the-mental-I-of-the-present-moment'—'I°' for short—and make it true by definition that I° can't exist half an hour (five minutes, thirty seconds, one second) later. 'I°' might be useful when trying to convey the character of something that is undoubtedly real, however anyone experiences things: the essential transience of the moment of consciousness in which the living mental subject of experience has its being, the character that consciousness has of being always ongoing, always already falling into the past. But 'I°' would be quite different from 'I*'.

I was saying that I may know a past episode of consciousness to be GS's, and have some from-the-inside acquaintance with it, without any sense that it was consciousness on my* part. I find that this is increasingly so—even in the case of memories of embarrassment, which, otherwise, come close to fitting the Jamesian model. Many find that past embarrassments make a direct lancing connection to the present (evolution has done deep work on this; we see forms of it in species that are our closest living relatives). When I was younger, embarrassing mistakes embarrassed me all over again when I remembered or 'relived' them (the metaphor is exact). Sometimes the mistakes embarrassed me more acutely when I remembered them than they did when I made them. My general capacity to feel embarrassment has since faded, but it used to seem to me that the past mistake still directly concerned me in such a way that I felt, in the moment of remembering it, that it was I* who had made the mistake. (One's skin can thicken with age without coarsening; embarrassment may decline simply because one gains a wider perspective.)

But even if Louis has a continuing and vivid capacity to feel embarrassed about past mistakes in certain circumstances, and to make other searing connections of this sort, this doesn't show that he does really and generally think that it is he* who was there in the past, or that he has, therefore, a generally Endurantist outlook on life, rather than an Impermanentist outlook. It would be a mistake to think that the phenomenon of reliving embarrassments simply lights up a framework that is always solidly there in any human being even when it is hidden in someone like me. The sense that it was one* who made the past embarrassing mistake can be built into one's present particular feeling of embarrassment without it being true that one has any *general* sense that one* was there in the past. An Impermanentist person can be open to these sorts of connections in a variety of circumstances while remaining strongly Impermanentist overall.

Cases of embarrassment seem as good as any, when one is looking for a situation in which it's truly appropriate to say, in James's Lockean phrase, that my past consciousness 'feels as if it belonged together with my present consciousness as another part of the same self'. But even here doubts arise. James's terminology is impressionistic, and potentially misleading. The claim is that one's past consciousness feels as if it belongs together with one's present consciousness, but one's awareness is most unlikely to be directed at one's past state of consciousness. It's almost certain to be directed at what happened at that past time considered independently of one's state of consciousness at that time. It's this, not the memory of one's experience of past embarrassment, that standardly gives rise to a new experience of embarrassment. On the whole, there simply isn't any clearly presented state of past consciousness for the feeling of belonging-with to dock with in such a way as to link past with present consciousness in the Jamesian way.

Suppose one had a good idea yesterday, and today remembers, not just the idea, but the having of it. Even in this case one's attention is likely to be occupied more by the idea than by the having of it. We can choose to focus on a case in which one's attention is occupied mainly by the memory of the having of the idea, rather than the idea itself, but even then one needn't have anything remotely like the Jamesian experience, the feeling that the past conscious episode belongs together with one's present consciousness 'as another part of the same self'. I certainly don't. Even in this case I have no sense that the past having of the idea belongs together with my present consciousness as another part of the same self, any more than I feel that my past breathings are breathings I'm doing now. What is true, again, is that the memory of the having of the idea will standardly present in a special way—'from the inside'—that is explicable by reference to the fact that it is an episode in the mental life of the single continuing human being that I am.

It may be added that memories of embarrassment, or of having good ideas, are relatively unusual occurrences. In themselves they can't give much support to James's view that this is always how things are, and again they provide no support for the idea that there is some kind of Continuity Experience across time-gaps (after sleep, say), even if there is some—possibly very patchy—Connectedness Experience. Even if it were true that consciousness after sleep always felt 'as if it belonged together with the consciousness before it, as another part of the same self' (Connectedness Experience), nothing would follow about continuity or felt continuity (Continuity Experience). In fact, talk of 'belonging-with' fits well with a 'bundle' view of the mind according to which the process of consciousness has many separate parts that may be felt to 'belong together' or be connected together but don't in any way present as a flow. Certainly a sense of responsibility for actions one has performed in the past, a sense of connectedness to those actions, need not bring with it any felt sense of continuity of consciousness, as Locke was well aware. Nor, in fact, and perhaps surprisingly, need it bring any sense that it was one* who performed the actions in question.[15]

Sometimes one wakes up knowing there's something terrible in one's life, although one can't remember what it is. Then one remembers—one's child has disappeared. In this situation one may well have an intense sense that one's consciousness is somehow directly continuous with where it left off the day before—like a paused tape. Once again, though, and fortunately, this distinctive sort of waking experience is relatively rare (it may be characteristic of clinical depression). To this extent it provides no support for the claim that there is always, or even usually or often, Continuity Experience on waking, or indeed Connectedness Experience, a feeling of belonging-with across time-gaps. Indeed, it reinforces the contrary claim that there is in general no such feeling, by contrasting so vividly with normal cases of waking. And although in these terrible cases there may be Continuity Experience—a feeling of seamless recommencement of the consciousness one was experiencing until reprieved by sleep (the misery seems, in fact, impossible to bear, but one can't escape it because one is now awake, and can't go back to sleep), at other times the experience seems to involve no Continuity Experience and to be simply this: there's something bad I have to face (a diagnosis of terminal cancer, someone's death), I'm facing it now, and it's also the case that I, the human being that I am, faced it yesterday. It's interesting that the second reaction is far more likely than the first when one wakes up, not to the knowledge that there is something particularly bad in one's life, but to the knowledge that there is something particularly good, although one can't for the moment remember what it is.

I've made two main observations. First, people like myself never or almost never have Connectedness Experience, reaching back or reconnecting to past consciousness in anything like the manner of James's description. Second, in so far as we do reconnect to past consciousness, we need have no Continuity Experience, no sense of continuity of consciousness in time. Nor need we be drawn into belief in a continuously existing mental self. In reconnecting to past consciousness, we may not have any experience of connectedness of a sort that involves the Persistence Belief or Persistence Experience, the belief/experience that we* who are here now were there in the past. There is, in other words, a kind of reconnection that doesn't involve believing that the past consciousness belongs with the present consciousness 'as part of the same self'.

This is a report of how it seems to some of us outside the study. We may be in the minority, but I doubt whether anyone really fits James's model. I think, in fact, that

---

[15] See again G. Strawson 2007.

belief in the continuity of consciousness, and in the reality of the experience of the continuity of consciousness, may conceal the true character of one's basic experience of consciousness in time, even when the focus is on the moment-to-moment experience of the process of consciousness.

—What do you mean by 'conceal the true character of experience'? If something is concealed, experientially speaking, it isn't there, experientially speaking. What appears to be the case is the case, when it comes to phenomenology. Properly expressed, your claim must be that assumptions about continuity may deeply *condition* the character of the experience of the process of consciousness in time, not that they may *conceal* it. But if they do condition it in such a way as to give it the character of being experience of continuity, then it really does have the character of being experience of continuity, and the most you can mean by the concealment claim is something like this: if people who think their experience of the connection between today's and yesterday's consciousness is different from yours reflect on the matter, rather than merely giving an immediate report, they may well come out with claims about it that sound more like yours. But all that this would show is that the process of reflection had destroyed its intended object—the character of ordinary everyday experience. The process of reflection would have changed the manner in which ordinary experience appears in such a way that the report it prompted was no longer a true report of the character of ordinary experience.

Obviously our beliefs and convictions profoundly influence the character of our experience, and when I talk about our basic experience of consciousness in time, I have in mind something that I take to be already deeply structured by beliefs about or conceptions of self, activity, temporality, and so on. None the less, I think it makes sense to suppose that people may misjudge the general character of their experience of the process of consciousness in their immediate verdicts upon it, and that what may happen, when they reflect, is that they get a more accurate view of its character, not just a different view that has no more claim to validity than the original view, or less validity in being a product of reflection. At the very least, they may get a better idea of the true determinants of its apparent character.

It's hard for us to consider the nature of our experience rather than considering what our experience is of, a point emphasized by Thomas Reid (see page 26). This is the element of truth in the claim that experience is 'diaphanous' or 'transparent', i.e. something we experience through, and rarely take as object of attention. When it comes to the question of the continuity of experience, I think we're almost bound to misjudge it, taking it to have all the continuity of the external scene, reading the evident continuity of the latter almost irresistibly into the former. (Note that the 'evident continuity' of the external scene isn't a bare sensory given, but a product of deep structures of belief.) Inner thought, which makes up such a large part of our existence, even when we're actively employed on other things, markedly lacks the character of experiential continuity supposedly found in experience of the environment, and the hypothesis that the process of consciousness is in fact standardly discontinuous can explain this by pointing out that such inner thought isn't conditioned by the experienced continuity of the external scene.

The present suggestion, then, is that the Continuity Belief—firm belief in the continuity of consciousness—may be principally founded in a natural but strictly speaking illegitimate transfer of the 'evident-continuity' property of the external perceptual scene to the process-of-consciousness scene. It may then further condition experience of the process of consciousness, and block a clear view of whether it does in fact have continuity properties that are independent of any continuity properties it seems to have because of the effect of the presence of the Continuity Belief. Generally, when we consider a form of experience, e.g. Continuity Experience or Persistence Experience, in order to see if it is a genuine source of support for a certain belief (the Continuity Belief or the Persistence Belief), we need to try as far as possible to consider the nature of the experience independently of any respects in which it is a product of the belief whose validity it is invoked to support. In the present case, we need to try to access the Continuity-Belief-independent character of our experience of the process of consciousness, keeping Reid's point always in mind.

I try to show that this is in general a viable project. Even if I fail, it's important to register the point that James's claim (a) isn't universally true. For people like myself, there's no felt continuity of consciousness across time-gaps of the sort he describes, nor any theoretical belief that there is continuity of consciousness across them. One possibility is that the human population contains significant preconception-independent differences of fundamental experiential style, differences that have nothing to do with the force with which the Continuity Belief conditions their experience. Alternatively, it may be that the principal differences between people arise from the different force that the Continuity Belief has for them.[16]

It may be helpful to compare the processes of 'filling-in' that lead us to believe that we see a fully detailed visual scene before us at any given time.[17] One possibility is that something functionally similar operates to convert what is in fact gappy experience into experience of continuity. It's experimentally well established that there's a sense in which we don't in fact see the fully detailed visual scene that we experience ourselves as seeing when we look at the world.[18] The same may be true in the case of our experience of the continuity of the process of consciousness. Continuity Experience may be fully experientially real for those who have it, even though there's a fundamental sense in which it's illusory. Kant's point about the self (81) can be transferred to experience: seemingly continuous experience may consist, as a matter of fact, of a series of experiences (forty a second, say) with temporal gaps between them, each of which comports the sense that it is part of a continuous process of experience.

---

[16] Compare James's diagram (1890: 1. 269) of four different thought-routes to the same conclusion.

[17] See e.g. Pessoa and de Weerd 2003.

[18] I say 'a sense in which' because it's a mistake to think that facts about filling-in show that it's not really true that we experience a fully detailed visual scene. The phenomenological datum from which the experimental work starts, and relative to which its results are striking, is precisely the fact that the character of our experience is that we do. It's not an illusion that this is how things *seem* to us. It's just a remarkable fact about the way in which the apparently fully detailed visual scene arises.

5.5 James on the stream: continuity from moment to moment

This brings me to James's claim (b)—his claim that 'changes from one moment to another in the quality of consciousness are never absolutely abrupt', so that there is never (for example) an experience that is utterly unconnected with its predecessor, in no way coloured or contextually influenced by it. He's very stylish in its defence: 'Does not a loud explosion rend the consciousness upon which it abruptly breaks, in twain?' No, he says, for 'even into our awareness of the thunder the awareness of the previous silence creeps and continues; for what we hear when the thunder crashes is not thunder *pure*, but thunder-breaking-upon-silence-and-contrasting-with-it' (1892: 146; adaptation of 1890: 1. 239–41). And if this is what he means by continuity, his claim looks hard to defeat, for he can grant that consciousness can sometimes seem very unstreamlike, broken, jolted, while denying that there is ever any real discontinuity, phenomenologically speaking. Even in the most spectacular cases of disruption, he will say, there is in fact Continuity Experience.

But this doesn't seem to be true, in so far as it's offered as a universally valid, specifically phenomenological claim. Even if one concedes for argument that there's always some phenomenologically given connection of *content* between any two successive experiential episodes in the human case, some phenomenologically given *contentual connection*, for short, and that this is so however violently disparate they seem, it doesn't follow that there's always some sort of phenomenologically given—experienced—*continuity*. One may concede that James's stylish point is always true in the case of sensations and perceptions like hearing thunder after silence; it doesn't follow that it is true of all aspects of the process of consciousness. When James says that 'it would be difficult to find in the actual concrete consciousness of man a feeling so limited to the present as not to have an inkling of anything that went before' (1890: 1. 241), I'm inclined to say that this happens to me all the time, especially where thoughts are concerned. Even if it's true that an experiential episode always prompts or conditions its successor in some way, it certainly doesn't follow that there's always some sort of experienced sense of connection, conditioning, continuity, or flow. On the contrary. Sometimes the experience is one of a complete break, an inklingless cut.

If one includes the great unremarked *basso continuo* of bodily feeling, interoceptive and somatosensory experience, as part of the content of any particular episode of experience, then—it may be said—James's claim can be upheld even on the phenomenological plane, except in the strangest cases of sensory deprivation. But this idea isn't something he appeals to in this context, and I don't think it's true. It remains an empirical question whether the deep continuo of human interoception really is objectively continuous, and even if it guarantees significant similarities of experiential content from moment to moment, it certainly doesn't follow that the process of consciousness is always experienced as continuous, as a stream.

5.6 Is the 'stream' a stream?

Is the stream of consciousness a stream? I doubt it. My (empirical) bet is that the process of consciousness is pulse-like and discontinuous, neurologically considered, however it ordinarily seems to us.[19] Is it an unbroken stream subjectively or phenomenologically speaking, as James supposes, or is it gappy, full of hiatuses, as I believe? What would happen if we asked people about this? The metaphorical phrase 'the stream of consciousness' is very likeable and widely known, and some may take its validity for granted partly for that reason. Even so, I expect that honest answers would fall along a spectrum from 'Yes' to 'No', via 'Usually', 'Sometimes', and 'Almost never'. I favour 'Almost never' and will present my case. None of the following quotations and descriptions can really be supposed to establish the hiatus view over the stream view, for they can all be interpreted as (more or less eccentric) descriptions of the highly various and often dramatic character of what is, none the less, phenomenologically, a continuous stream of consciousness: descriptions of its continuously pulsating life, its continuous wave motion or peristalsis, of the way in which it features intrusions that by their very intrusive quality confirm its fundamental character of continuity. So I can only assert my own descriptions—experiences—against those of others.

I think the metaphor of the stream is inept, even though streams have pools, falls, whirlpools, weeds, and stones. Human thought has rather little natural phenomenological continuity or experiential flow, if mine is anything to go by. 'Our thought is fluctuating, uncertain, fleeting', as Hume says (1779: 156); it's 'in a perpetual flux' (*Treatise*, 165/252). Kant talks similarly of 'the flux of inner appearances' (A107), 'the constant flux' (B291): 'everything is in continual flux and there is nothing abiding' (A381). It keeps slipping from mere consciousness into self-consciousness and out again. It's always shooting off, fuzzing, shorting out, spurting, and stalling. James himself describes it as 'like a bird's life, ... an alternation of flights and perchings' (1890: 1. 243; the idea is beautifully developed). But this recognition that thought isn't a matter of even flow retains a strong notion of continuity, in so far as a bird traces a spatiotemporally continuous path, and the image fails to take adequate account of the fact that trains of thought are constantly broken by detours—by-blows—fissures—white noise. This is especially so (in my experience) when one is just sitting and thinking. Things usually appear very different when one's attention is engaged by some ordered and continuous process in the world, or by music or a fast and exciting game. In this case thought or experience can appear to take on the ordered continuity of the phenomenon that occupies it. If one turns in a circle, scanning one's surroundings, one's process of consciousness may seem to have the perfect continuity of the continuously changing scene. But even when one is engaged with salient external continuities, one's process of consciousness may still seize up, fly off, or flash with perfectly extraneous

---

[19] See e.g. Damasio 1999: 126. I'm not appealing to the increasingly well supported idea that matter and its operations may be discontinuous at the quantum level, or that spacetime itself has a 'grainy' nature.

matter from time to time, even in a roaring football stand, and reflection reveals gaps and fadings, disappearances and total recommencements, even when there is stable succession of content. It seems to me that the case of solitary speculative thought—in which the mind is left to its own resources and devices—reveals in a relatively dramatic way something that is true to a greater or lesser extent of all thought.

Lying in bed at the end of the day, Molly Bloom, in James Joyce's *Ulysses*, is famous for her unpunctuated streaming consciousness:

let me see if I can doze off 1 2 3 4 5 what kind of flowers are those they invented like the stars the wallpaper in Lombard Street was much nicer the apron he gave me was like that something only I only wore it twice better lower this lamp and try again so as I can get up early Ill go to Lambes there beside Findlaters and get them to send us some flowers to put about the place in case he brings him home tomorrow today I mean no no Fridays an unlucky day first I want to do the place up someway the dust grows in it I think while Im asleep then we can have music and cigarettes I can accompany him first I must clean the keys of the piano with milk whatll I wear a white rose or those fairy cakes in Liptons at 712d a lb or the other ones with the cherries in them and the pinky sugar 11d a couple of lbs of those a nice plant for the middle of the table Id get that cheaper in wait wheres this I saw them not long ago I love flowers ...[20]

But Joyce's rendering of the process of consciousness is no less accurate, and in my experience more accurate, as Stephen Daedalus walks on the beach:

Who watches me here? Who ever anywhere will read these written words? Signs on a white field. Somewhere to someone in your flutiest voice. The good bishop of Cloyne took the veil of the temple out of his shovel hat: veil of space with coloured emblems hatched on its field. Hold hard. Coloured on a flat: yes, that's right.   (Joyce 1922: 40)

It's not clear how one should read the punctuation, however, or the lack of it in Molly Bloom's case. On the one hand, there's no clear indication that Molly's thought is proceeding at a greater speed than Stephen's—he may be jerky but fast. On the other hand, her authentically abrupt shifts of subject show that one doesn't always need to mark breaks and discontinuities with full stops or other forms of punctuation—dashes, slashes, ellipses.

Dorothy Richardson represents thoughts very differently from Joyce. Here is her Miriam Henderson in church:

certainly it was wrong to listen to sermons ... stultifying ... unless they were intellectual ... lectures like Mr Brough's ... that was as bad, because they were not sermons .... Either kind was bad and ought not to be allowed ... a homily ... sermons ... homilies ... a quiet homily might be something rather nice ... and have not *Charity*—sounding brass and tinkling cymbal .... *Caritas* ... I have *none* I am sure ....[21]

---

[20] Joyce 1922: 642. Compare Flora Finching's torrential speech in Dickens's *Little Dorrit*.
[21] Richardson 1915: 73. Virginia Woolf (1928: 367) credited Richardson with having 'invented a sentence we might call a psychological sentence of the feminine gender'. I'm feminine by this count, and suspect that the difference Woolf has in mind cuts right across sex and also across any accurate view of gender (if gender is distinguished from sex).

Richardson is credited with having originated the 'stream of consciousness' technique in English, but she once remarked on the 'perfect imbecility' of the use of the term 'stream of consciousness' to characterize her novels, presumably because she was fully aware of, and tried to convey, the sense in which—the fact that—consciousness is profoundly unstreamlike. If one strips out Miriam's punctuation and renders her Molly-style:

certainly it was wrong to listen to sermons stultifying unless they were intellectual lectures like Mr Broughs that was as bad because they were not sermons either kind was bad and ought not to be allowed a homily sermons homilies a quiet homily might be something rather nice and have not *Charity* sounding brass and tinkling cymbal *Caritas* I have *none* I am sure

one sees, I think, that Molly's uninhibited thought-processes are not necessarily stream-like at all. They do not have to be read that way, and one can equally well rewrite Molly Miriam-style.

Each of these quotations emphasizes different features of the process of consciousness. Miriam Henderson has relatively strong continuity of content across drifting, temporally broken, white-noise ellipses. Molly Bloom has sharp content breaks in what is apparently strong and fast temporal flow, but her transitions are all contentually explicable within the scope of her current concern. Stephen Daedalus's thought-shots occur fully formed; Joyce conveys the familiar sense that the thoughts deploy in an experiential instant, wiping out their predecessors. At the same time, he seems committed to the principle that every moment of experience should always either be intelligibly descended from its predecessors, as far as its content is concerned, and in a way that is always recoverable by a devoted student of the text, or else be explicable by reference to the character's external surroundings. Perhaps he did this for good novelistic reasons, or set himself this constraint as a task, or perhaps it was a failure of experimentalist nerve—or of realism.

Passages like 'I want to do the place up someway the dust grows in it I think while Im asleep then we can have music and cigarettes' are, I think, best taken as renderings of multilayered content. 'The dust grows in it I think while Im asleep' is a small explosive insertion or tmesis—subjectively almost instantaneous—in the enclosing train of thought 'I want to do the place up then we can have music and cigarettes'. But the insertion should not, I think, be seen as an insertion on the same plane, one that interrupts the train of thought and in some way puts it temporarily on hold (it's arguable that this appearance is an inevitable consequence of the linearity of print). It should rather be seen as occurring with and briefly running concurrently with the other thought.[22]

Hume thinks that every experience-transition involves a content connection, although he's open to the idea that a glitch in the brain could disrupt this (*Treatise*, 44/60–1). Freud thinks the same about the apparently chaotic transitions of 'free association' (his claim is relatively plausible, given the psychotherapeutic context). Every thought-jump in Joyce has a contentual explanation, it seems, and James takes it that every experience

---

[22] I attempt a description of the way in which contents can be or seem multilayered in G. Strawson 1994: 18–21, 'An Account of Four Seconds of Thought'.

is at the very least conditioned by the previous one, and to that extent contentually linked to it.[23] Are they right in their various associationisms? I don't know. The question is empirical, and ultimately undecidable, because failure to find a connection can never prove there isn't one. But suppose they're right; suppose there's always a content connection. It doesn't follow, as they would all agree, that every content connection is or can be made available to us, either immediately or after protracted reflection (or brilliant psychoanalysis). There can be radical or absolute discontinuity of subject matter or content phenomenologically speaking, even if there is some deep sense, recorded in God's own *Principles of Psychology* (parts of which are not much different from William James's), in which there's no such thing as absolute discontinuity of content in human experience. Even if the principles that govern the 'pandemonium' of ideas or thought-elements in the mind-brain do conform to certain inflexible principles of content connection, as different words, ideas, thoughts, impulses vie for emergence into consciousness, in Dennett's vivid and plausible model of this process,[24] there may still be experience of radical discontinuity, mental saltation, truly orthogonal intrusions of utterly disparate material. Such experience is, I propose, common, even after James's subtleties have been noted. There are absolute switches of subject matter, phenomenologically speaking, switches that lack any sort of felt internal contentual connection. James is quite wrong, I think, when he speaks of the 'consciousness of the whence and the whither that always accompanies [the] flows' of thought 'strictly and narrowly so called' (1890: 1. 242). Certainly

it is very difficult, introspectively, to see the transitive parts [of thought] for what they really are. If they are but flights to a conclusion, stopping them to look at them before the conclusion is reached is really annihilating them. Whilst if we wait till the conclusion be reached, it so exceeds them in vigor and stability that it quite eclipses and swallows them up in its glare. Let anyone try to cut a thought across in the middle and get a look at its section, and he will see how difficult the introspective observation of the transitive tracts is.   (1890: 1. 243–4)

But James also seems to make a fundamental mistake, the mistake of supposing that all these transitions occur in, or at least have some real representation in, conscious experience. The truth is, rather, that almost all of them occur completely sub-experientially. Nor should one confuse the irruption of content with any slower spelling-out. Conversation, to quote myself,

often provides examples of the presence to mind of lightning, compacted content. As the other person is talking, there is a small, silent, pointlike explosion, and one knows one's answer is there—although it may take some time to speak it out, although the words and syntax in which one does so are not already fixed in the explosion but are to a considerable extent chosen as one goes along, and although people characteristically expand on their initial thought in the act of vocalization.   (1994: 21)

---

[23] The case of undisturbed thinking is very different from cases in which the environment intrudes with an explosion, but I think that James takes the claim to apply quite generally. See his discussion of association (1890: 1. 550–605).

[24] See Dennett 1991: 189, 237–42. The believer in invariable content connection may hold that an item can achieve entry into consciousness only by riding some association with an item already in consciousness.

Switches of subject matter may be phenomenologically absolute and still be phenomenologically *seamless*, in the sense that they involve no experience of a temporal hiatus in the process of consciousness (one might compare phenomenological seamlessness across radical change of content to the dimensionless line that exists between a patch of red and a contiguous patch of green), and some, loyal to the stream, may think that this is how things are in all cases, even those that seem to offer the best support for their opponents' view. They may insist that the process of consciousness always feels phenomenologically seamless, truly continuous and unbroken—even in the most spectacular cases of *contentual* disparateness.

Here, though, human beings may simply differ. The experience of true seamlessness in the flow of consciousness is not a universal feature of normal human waking consciousness. When I'm alone and thinking, I find that my fundamental experience of consciousness is one of *repeated launches of consciousness as if from nothing*, where 'as if from nothing' isn't meant to indicate any sort of positive sense of a preceding temporally extended period of *non*-consciousness (although it isn't meant to rule it out either) but just—a sense of complete beginning. This is a matter of experience, it has phenomenological reality although it is standardly unattended to, far from the focus of attention.

If I'm concentrating on some idea, my background sense is that I'm continually re-seizing it, that it is being continually 'refreshed'. The invariably brief periods of true experiential continuity seem perfectly disjunct from one another, even in cases in which they're not radically disjoined in respect of content—as when one returns to the same scene of thought, or very nearly the same, after a momentary absence. They do not feel seamless or flowing. A positive sense of complete if momentary absence is often part of the phenomenology. Harold Brodkey puts part of it well, although he doesn't explicitly resist the metaphor of the stream: 'our sense of presentness usually proceeds in waves, with our minds tumbling off into wandering. Usually, we return and ride the wave and tumble and resume the ride and tumble … *this falling away and return is what we are*' (1996: 40).

The sense of reprise may be experientially faint, but it's experientially real. It's no less real, experientially, than anything in the focus of attention. (There are no degrees of reality, only of focus and vividness.) The situation is best described, it seems to me, by saying that it is as if consciousness as a whole is continually *starting* or *restarting*. The basic experience of consciousness is not that there is continuous flowing consciousness subject to various small vicissitudes of apparent disconnection, lapses and doglegs and hiatuses. The basic experience, however much it is smoothed out of attentional awareness in everyday life, is, I propose, one of tightly packed but non-seamless series of radically disjunct episodes. The process of consciousness keeps bursting silently out of nothingness, even as it maintains strong contentual continuity from burst to burst, as it so often does (as when one is looking at a painting—but there is also constant newness in the micro detail of the content of the experience). It is a series of comings to, even when its object is a continuous process in the world.[25]

---

[25] This experience has an affinity with the Buddhist theory of the way in which consciousness is an interruption of ongoing, unconscious *bhavanga* mind, although the Buddhist theory has many special further features. See Collins 1982: 238–47.

Certainly this is how it feels to me every time the question of the continuity of the process of consciousness achieves any presence in consciousness. (There's no conflict between this way of experiencing things and SELF-experience. I have strong SELF-experience.) I feel I can catch my consciousness unawares, as it were, without focusing on it in any way, and this is what I find. I don't dwell on the phenomena of disjunction—often nothing more than a flashing sense of hiatus, a silent caesura, a sense that the present moment of experience is a new take, although it has essentially the same content as the preceding one—but whenever they come to attention, however glancingly, it seems clear to me that what I encounter is not some artefact of introspection, but something that is independently the case. I have, however, no reply to the objection that I may just be wrong about this, or that these phenomena of disjunction only ever come to attention when there has actually been a disjunction of a sort that is in fact rare, or that the coming to attention of the process of consciousness, however unpremeditated, always itself produces the experience of disjunction, or that this is just one way in which the passing of time can register in experience, although the experience of the process of consciousness is in fact, otherwise, truly a matter of flow.

Perhaps hiatus-free periods of experience can be extended by conscious effort and training. Perhaps we can extend the amount of time for which we can look fixedly and fully attentively at an object. We can, though, easily deceive ourselves about our capacity for full visual attention or mental fixity.[26] There's a familiar and distinctive experience of realizing retrospectively that one has in fact been briefly absent as one tries to maintain continuous visual attention, and there may be inflexible—and very narrow—neurophysiological constraints on the maximum length of truly hiatus-free periods of experience. My sense is that my own upper bound on full attention without any (however vestigial) sense of return or coming to, when looking at something and trying at the same time to pay some light attention to my experience of looking at it, is (much) less than two seconds. It may be said that this particular sense of return and restart is a product of the flickering back and forth of attention involved in trying both to attend to something and to attend to one's attending, but it's also something that can strike unbidden in normal life. This too invites various explanations of the sort proposed in the last paragraph, though, explanations that make no appeal to the idea that there's a respect in which the ordinary process of consciousness (in so far as it can be considered independently of the smoothing effect—or mask—of the Continuity Belief) is phenomenologically non-streamlike. One can't hope to decide the question by argument. It's a matter for experimental psychology, although it might be hard to test.[27] The present claim is in any case not just a claim about attention. It's the process of consciousness as a whole that is being claimed to have,

---

[26] Perhaps music is unique in its power to engender what seem like long periods of unbroken consciousness in us. And perhaps it is precisely solitary thought that is most susceptible to abrupt saltations. (Clive Wearing, a musician whose memory span was reduced to a matter of seconds by a herpetic infection of the brain, seemed when conducting music to regain access to a larger memory span. See 'The Mind Machine', BBC documentary series, 1988.)

[27] There's no difficulty in the idea that experiencers can be aware of hiatuses in the process of experience that are shorter than the shortest period of time that can have phenomenological reality for them as having that duration. It's

phenomenologically, the character (however little noticed by some) of being constantly interrupted.

5.7   Content breaks, flow breaks, temporal breaks

I've suggested that there may be experience of discontinuity in the process of consciousness even if we're not aware of it in the flow of daily life, and I've tried to cope with the paradoxical nature of this suggestion in a Reidian way. I've also suggested that the process of consciousness may be pulse-like and discontinuous as a matter of neurological fact, even if it doesn't feel that way. Imagine that we have an infallible way of knowing whether or not Louis is having experience at any given time (it might be something to do with the state of his reticular activating system). We can then make judgements about whether or not his process of consciousness is as a matter of fact continuous over a certain period that are completely independent of the best judgements he makes from within his experiential (subjective) perspective. Sometimes we may find continuity where he experiences hiatuses; sometimes we may find hiatuses where he experiences continuity.

Why might the process of consciousness be non-continuous in this way? The hiatuses might be an accidental feature of the neural mechanisms of consciousness, or they might be functional or adaptive in some way, analogous to the constant refreshal of a computer screen. They might be part of a basic process of continually regirding one's attention in such a way as to remain open to the intrusion of new material, whether from the mind or from the world. Such openness or flexibility, one may suppose, requires repeated reprises, new casts of attention, rapid mental saccades or foveations, new bindings of the mental manifold, new syntheses in a Kantian sense, and each may involve a hiatus of some sort. The hiatuses may be very fast, and yet noticeable when attended to, always available in the background as having just happened, informing a constantly renewed sense, always available on reflection, of *coming to*—again and again. Or they may be too brief to be caught individually on the fly, although the fact that they happen is registered in experience in the availability of a general sense of re-beginning which may in many people and for the most part pass wholly unnoticed, although it is in others (myself, and perhaps Hume, Stephen Daedalus, Virginia Woolf, Harold Brodkey, and others), however little attended to, a constant feature of normal consciousness. There may be different kinds of hiatus, hiatuses that are radically undetectable by the subject, occurring 40 or 100 times a second or more as a result of basic features of neural processing, and other, potentially detectable hiatuses with a typical periodicity of, say, 50 ms or more.

The phenomenology of time has been discussed with great subtlety by philosophers—notably Husserl and those influenced by him—and I hesitate to propose any new theoretical terms or devices. It may, though, be helpful for a page or two to distinguish

---

possible that a 0.1 ms discontinuity can be experienced as a discontinuity, although it can't possibly be experienced as being 0.1 ms long.

between content breaks (C), flow breaks (F), and temporal breaks (T). I'll begin by understanding these notions in a phenomenological way and then ask whether they can be taken in another way. The notions of a content break and a flow break are not sharp, and the experience of a temporal break is not of course an (impossible) experience of experiencelessness, it's an experience that has the character of there having just been a complete absence, however brief, of consciousness.

Plunging on into aprioristic empirical psychology, there are *prima facie* seven possible combinations of experiential breaks:

[1] [+T +F +C]

[2] [+T +F −C]

[3] [+T −F +C]

[4] [+T −F −C]

[5] [−T +F +C]

[6] [−T +F −C]

[7] [−T −F +C]

but [3] and [4] are ruled out because a temporal break is necessarily a flow break. The remaining five all seem possible. As for [1], a radical experiential break may be [+T +F +C]; there are certainly no incompatibilities between T, F, and C. As for [2], a temporal break must be a flow break, as remarked, but it needn't be a content break inasmuch as the content of consciousness after the temporal break may be effectively the same as the content of consciousness before the break (the characteristic experience of the reprising or refreshal of thought).

To decide on the remaining three, [5], [6], and [7], one needs to see if there are any other incompatibilities. One suggestion, challenging [5] and [7], is that content breaks must be temporal breaks. I've already suggested that this need not be so: that different contents can seem to succeed each other in a temporally seamless or immediate way. This is one way of reading Molly Bloom's lack of punctuation.

Another suggestion, challenging [7], is that content breaks must be flow breaks. I'm not sure about this. One view is that Molly can experience her consciousness as a matter of flow in spite of all its changes of content, but it seems equally plausible to say that switches of content do inevitably disrupt the experienced flow structure — that content and form are not independent of one another in this case.[28] My inclination is to allow that both cases are possible — that content breaks can amount to flow breaks but don't actually entail them, so that [7] is not ruled out.

Must flow breaks be temporal breaks (this would rule out all of [5]–[7])? Well, if a content break can amount to a flow break, as Gallagher suggests, without *ipso facto* being a temporal break, then flow breaks don't entail temporal breaks, and [5]–[7] survive. If an image of the Triborough Bridge flashes on my mind and runs on top of my thought

---

[28] Shaun Gallagher took this view, in correspondence. See further Gallagher 1998.

that Jerry Fodor's cat is psychologically powerful without displacing it, the episode as a whole may involve experience of break in flow and break in content without any sense of temporal break; this would be a case of [5] (compare Molly's dust tmesis, during her thought about doing her place up). Against this, it may be said that the unbrokenness of the thought that the cat is psychologically powerful means that there isn't any content break, only a flow break stemming from the arrival of new content, so that this is in fact only a case of [6]. But [5] may be possible for all that: a content break and a flow break coupled with a strong sense of complete temporal continuity.

Must flow breaks be content breaks, thereby ruling out [6]? I take it that the answer is No. It seems that one can experience a disruption of flow—a caesura—in the contemplation of a subject matter that need not be experienced either as a content break or a temporal break. This is, for me, a common experience.

These are fine and disputable distinctions, but it seems to me that all of [1], [2], [5], [6], and [7] are possible, and that we can in any case use this scheme to express the stream-of-consciousness position in its purest form. This is the *Strong Stream* Thesis that experience of the process of consciousness is

[8] $[-T -F -C]$.

On this view there are really no experiential breaks in ordinary human waking consciousness. Any inclination to take a radical switch of thought (an *Aha! Erlebnis*, or *Eureka!* experience, a clap of thunder, a sudden horrified realization that one has forgotten something vital) to involve a break in the experienced continuity of the process of consciousness is superficial.

If one takes this view, one must find some way of doing justice to our sense that there can be radical breaks of these sorts. Strong Stream theorists may distinguish in some manner between surface phenomenology and deep phenomenology. They may allow that the experience of the clap of thunder or the horrified realization is $[+F +C]$ at a superficial phenomenological level (although even there it's $[-T]$) while insisting that it is $[-T -F -C]$ at a deeper phenomenological level.

I think the Strong Stream view can deal successfully with sensory-perceptual cases like James's clap of thunder. I don't think it copes so well with all cases of sudden switches of content, especially in the case of thinking. Even if there are in fact always intelligible content-connections between the most disparate-seeming successive experiences, there's no reason to think that these connections are always accessible to consciousness, still less to think that they're always actually explicit in consciousness in some way. And even if we suppose that they're always somehow explicit in consciousness, it doesn't follow that there is no sense of a break in the process of consciousness. Suddenly realizing that *p* after pondering *q* and *r* may be experienced as a content break and a flow break, a true hiatus (whatever sub-experiential processing has gone on). The phenomenological reality of content and flow breaks in the process of consciousness seems undeniable. It can't be resorbed by any distinction between phenomenological levels.

So much for Louis's experience of breaks in the process of consciousness, 'subjective' breaks, as one might call them. What about 'objective' breaks in his process of consciousness that have no experiential aspect? I'll distinguish them from experienced breaks by using italics. The table of combinations has as before seven rows:

[1] [+T +F +C]

[2] [+T +F −C]

[3] [+T −F +C]

[4] [+T −F −C]

[5] [−T +F +C]

[6] [−T +F −C]

[7] [−T −F +C]

but all *temporal* breaks are necessarily *flow* breaks, so that [3] and [4] are, like [3] and [4], ruled out immediately.

Are all *flow* breaks also *temporal* breaks—so that [5] and [6] are ruled out? It's a natural suggestion. It seems that a true *flow* break in the process of consciousness can only be an actual time-gap, an actual absence of consciousness, however momentary. Suppose, though, that there are distinctive neural conditions associated with *content* breaks (radical switches of content), and that they're very different from the neural conditions associated with *temporal* breaks. One might then propose that the notion of a *flow* break in the process of consciousness can connect as easily to the notion of a *content* break as it does to that of a *temporal* break, and that radical *content* breaks may be correctly counted as *flow* breaks even if the process of consciousness is in fact continuous at that time (this knocks out [7]). If one then supposes that there can be a *content* break without a *temporal* break, one has to reject the view that all *flow* breaks must be *temporal* breaks (this restores [5] but not [6]). On this view, one has a *flow* break whenever one has either a *content* break or a *temporal* break, and this allows [1] and [5]. [5] is the case just described, and [1] is unproblematic, a case of a *temporal* (hence *flow*) break in consciousness that is also a *content* break. As for [6], it may now be said in its defence that one can have an objective *flow* break without either a *temporal* break or a *content* break: an objectively seamless reprise of the same content ... but I'll go no further.

If the process of consciousness is in fact objectively continuous throughout the waking day, whatever anyone's experience of breaks, this immediately knocks out [1]–[4] (within any given waking day). A more striking suggestion is that the human process of consciousness is objectively continuous from the first moment of experiential quickening to the moment of death. On this view there's always experience going on in the brain of a normal living human being like Louis, even under anaesthetic and in the deepest sleep.[29] It's an undecided empirical question whether or not this is so. An alternative is that the process of consciousness is in fact constantly gappy, in a way that means that [5]–[7] can concern only very short periods of time. On this view the

---

[29] We may further take it to be experience of such a kind that it's true to say that *Louis* is always experiencing something. The qualification is prompted by the very real possibility that there may be genuine loci of consciousness in Louis of which Louis is not consciously aware. See further 7.4 (348–9), 8.6 (396–7).

process of consciousness consists of discrete packets, or quanta, even if we have no idea that this is so. The breaks or gaps or hiatuses may be like the breaks in the continuity of the image in a film running at 24 frames per second. These continuity breaks are undetectable by us, given our visual 'flicker-fusion' rate. In the same way, gaps in our own process of consciousness may be undetectable by us, given our inner mental 'flicker-fusion' rate.[30]

These are questions of fact that leave a lot of room for speculation and some, perhaps, for experimental test. The answers to them may be material when it comes to straightforwardly ontological questions about the nature and existence of selves. At the moment, though, it's still the experiential breaks that matter most, given the proposal that set this discussion off (the rather specific proposal that Continuity Experience, experience of the process of consciousness as strongly streamlike, may be one significant source of the Persistence Belief about the self), and the claim to which I now return is the claim with which I started: not just that the stream of consciousness may well be no such thing, considered objectively in the present sense of this term, but that it may not even feel like a stream when one becomes a little more aware of it.

This judgement may seem like the product of something impossible and something unacceptable: a priori empirical psychology combined with unwarrantable generalization from my own case. It may seem like an unwitting confession of mild schizophrenia. The fan of human difference is wide. Some have intense powers of concentration or 'single-mindedness', others are scattered and chaotic. There are 'convergers' and 'divergers', hedgehogs and foxes.[31] I think, though, that introspection will reveal the same to everyone, if in different degrees.

—The case wouldn't be settled even if you were (miraculously) right: even if everyone on reflection found that things were as you said. For the experience of disjointedness might be an artefact of introspection—as you've pointed out. Perhaps normal waking consciousness really is a matter of continuous experiencing, phenomenologically speaking, even when it involves radical changes of content. It may be that it has true flow, phenomenologically speaking, and that the facts are invariably distorted—irredeemably altered—by the act of trying to observe what they are.

The issue is undecidable, if settling it requires being able to observe something while it is entirely unobserved. The Reid point (231) applies as much as ever, though, and I think—and have already suggested—that the evidential situation isn't really that bad. A sense of radical disjointedness can surface spontaneously and unlooked for, and isn't then an artefact of directed introspection, whatever else it may be. In such cases we become

---

[30] The breaks may involve neural oscillation frequencies in some way, as James noted: 'Messrs. Payton-Spence ... and M. M. Garver ... argue, the one from speculative, the other from experimental grounds, that, the physical condition of consciousness being neural vibration, the consciousness must itself be incessantly interrupted by unconsciousness—about fifty times a second, according to Garver' (1890: 1. 200n.). On Dennett's view, 'while consciousness appears to be continuous, in fact it is gappy. A self could be just as gappy, lapsing into nothingness as easily as a candle flame is snuffed, only to be rekindled at some later time ...' (1991: 423).
[31] See Hudson 1966; Berlin 1953.

aware—that's the experience—that radical breaks or radical re-beginnings have been occurring; we don't see them only when we look. This is my experience, at any rate.[32]

5.8 The persistence of the self?

I've tried to cast doubt on the idea that the Persistence Belief—the sense of the self as something that has long-term continuity—has some sort of iron phenomenological warrant in the immediate character of our moment-to-moment experience of the process of consciousness. I don't think it's supported at the level of detail by any experiential phenomenon of steady uninterrupted flow, although I grant that people may differ in this respect. At the level of detail, much experience is profoundly scatty, as Hume observes, however much it's smoothed out and 'filled in' by automatic processes of the kind studied by experimental psychologists. Even when one is caught up in some exciting game, all sorts of other contents are to be found flashing at the level of detail. In so far as there's support for the Persistence Belief in the moment-to-moment character of our experience of the process of consciousness, much of it derives indirectly from other sources—the massive constancies and developmental coherencies of content (noted in 5.1) that standardly link up experiences through time, and by courtesy of short-term memory, across all the small radical jumps and breaks of flow. One walks from A to B, looking around, thinking of this and that. One works in a room for an hour. One looks up at the rain on the window and turns back to the page. One holds the same pen throughout. One may be lost in thought, with no salient awareness of one's body. Examined in detail, one's thought may be bitty and saccadic in the way described, a perpetual flux. But one is also experientially in touch with a great pool of constancies and steady processes of change in one's environment including, notably, one's body, of which one is constantly aware, however thoughtlessly, both by proprioception and by external sense; and these constancies and steadinesses of development in the *contents* of one's consciousness may seem like fundamental characteristics of the *operation* of one's consciousness, although they aren't (we employ a great deal of 'stitching software', analogous to the software that 'stitches' a series of overlapping photographs of a scene into a single panoramic view). This in turn may fund a sense of the *self* as uninterrupted and continuous through the waking day, which naturally extends to belief in the long-term persistence of the self across time-gaps like those introduced by sleep.

On the present view, however, belief in the seamless stream of consciousness isn't comfortably grounded in the basic facts of experience. There's an illegal transfer of smoothness from content to process. One is led to overlook the recurrent flicks and micro-crashes of consciousness, the tiny absolute fugues, the thought-blinks like eye-blinks, the interstitial vacancies. We take it unreflectively that the visual system delivers a steady

---

[32] It's arguable that it can claim support from experimental work. See e.g. Dennett 1991: e.g. ch. 11.

and uninterrupted visual flow, although in fact it involves continuous interruptions, some accessible to consciousness, some not: blinks, saccades, new foveations, and so on. I think something similar is true in the case of our experience of the process of consciousness quite generally considered.

A thought-experience may carry with it, or be, a memory of a previous thought-experience (Hume invokes this point as part of his explanation of how we come to believe in a persisting self). It may also involve, or be flashingly accompanied by, an awareness of itself as being the latest member of a particular train of thought that has preceding members, and it may itself be classed as part of such a train in the very next flash of thought. All these things, if and when they happen, may contribute to a sense of the continuity of the self—to the Persistence Belief. But, equally, they needn't, and the experience of the I (I*) as in some sense new each time is, I suggest, fundamental and universally available, in a way disconnected from emotion, even if it's entirely occluded for many, most of the time, by familiar, contrary, valuably simplifying habits of thought.[33]

I have very little sense of flow or continuity in the process of consciousness, whether I'm thinking or having other sorts of experience; but it doesn't follow from this alone that I have no sense of a continuing self. The claim is not that the Continuity Belief (or Continuity Experience) is necessary for the Persistence Belief (or Persistence Experience); for clearly one can experience consciousness as gappy and chaotic and still believe strongly in a persisting long-term self. The Continuity Belief is at most one possible source of support for the Persistence Belief (one possible underlying contributor to Persistence Experience), along with the other sources catalogued in 5.1. Even if one is unusually aware of jumps and hiatuses in consciousness, one may still be profoundly inclined to think of the self as something that *has* all the interrupted and jumping thoughts and experiences but isn't itself a gappy interrupted thing. The various sources of the Persistence Belief listed in 5.1 are, jointly, powerful, and when one first tries to think hard about one's SELF-experience—and to think about it, rather than simply have it, is already a tricky thing to do—one's first reaction may indeed be that the self does in some immediate way present as a single continuing thing, not only throughout the waking day, but also in the longer term.

In my case, however, this first reaction is weak—effectively non-existent—and when I think further about my mental life, I don't find a sensibly continuous process or a sensibly continuous self or mental someone. I'm met by a rapidly and powerfully deepening sense that there simply isn't any 'I' or self that goes on through (let alone beyond) the waking day, even though there's obviously and vividly an 'I' or self at any given time. This is a report of experience, not a statement of a theoretical position—e.g. an endorsement of part of Derek Parfit's 'reductionism' about persons. I feel I have

[33] Compare Damasio's description of 'core consciousness', in which, he says, 'the sense of self arises in the subtle, fleeting feeling of knowing, constructed anew in each pulse ... core consciousness is generated in pulselike fashion, for each content of which we are to be conscious' (1999: 196, 126); 'at each moment the state of self is constructed, from the ground up. It is an evanescent reference state, so continuously and consistently reconstructed that the owner never knows that it is being remade unless something goes wrong with the remaking' (1994: 240; see more generally pp. 236–43).

continuity through the waking day only as an embodied human being. If I consider myself specifically as a mental subject of experience, my deep sense, as remarked, is that I'm continually new. As in the passage from Updike quoted on page 31, I have 'the persistent sensation, in my life …, that I am just beginning' (1989: 239). I think that Updike accurately describes how things are for many people when it comes to their experience of being in time and, in particular, their sense of themselves as selves, although he may have had something else in mind.

I don't mean new or different in respect of personality and outlook. I have a perfectly adequate grasp of the extremely strong mental-and-non-mental similarities that characterize me—GS—from day to day, and when I consider myself in the whole-human-being way I fully endorse the conventional view that there is in my case—that I am—a single subject of experience—a person—with long-term diachronic continuity. But when I experience myself as an inner mental subject and consider the detailed character of conscious experience, my feeling is that I am—that the thing that I most essentially am is—continually completely new.

At this point I meet Hume briefly at a crossroads (we arrive from different directions and depart in different directions). Some people, he observes, take it for granted that the nature of our experience of our mental lives justifies the Persistence Belief. They take it for granted that we have Persistence *Experience* independently of any Persistence *Belief*, direct experience of the presence of a persisting self. They take it for granted that 'we are every moment intimately conscious of what we call our SELF; that we feel its existence *and continuance* in existence' (*Treatise*, 164/251; my emphasis). Are they right? No, he answers: there's no direct experiential evidence for the existence of a continuing or persisting self, let alone a self that is (as his opponents at the time supposed) a perfectly simple, indivisible, unchanging substance.

To think that Hume is right about this, as I do, one certainly doesn't have to agree with what he assumes for the purposes of argument—that only some sort of direct experiential evidence in introspection could warrant or justify belief in the existence of a persisting self. The phenomenological question 'Do we have Persistence *Experience* that is independent of, not a product of, the Persistence *Belief*?' remains the same in any case. In answering No, I take it that I agree with Hume in a way that dissolves differences in the way that the problem of the self is set up in the eighteenth and twenty-first centuries. It's historically important that Hume has in mind the super-strong, religio-philosophical conception of the self as a radically metaphysically simple and unchanging entity, but his general line of thought applies equally against far weaker present-day conceptions of the self as a persisting entity, and the present proposal is in any case simply this: we don't actually find, directly given in experience, a continuing process of consciousness of a sort that might promise to lend a certain sort of immediate support to the idea of a single continuing self.[34] Instead, we find a gappy phenomenon. It's not only when we apply Hume's extremely strong condition on what it would be to find such a

---

[34] It can't possibly establish the existence of such a self, for reasons given in Kant's discussion of the Third Paralogism (see p. 81).

thing that we get this result.[35] We also get it when we apply a far weaker condition, requiring only some sort of untrammelled experience of true continuity in the process of consciousness.

Some may doubt my claims about how I experience consciousness, and those who accept them may think that I am part of a small minority. Experience like mine may be thought to be the unnatural result of philosophy (meditation, youthful drug-taking, excessive introspection, standard non-pathological academic schizotypy, attention deficit disorder, and so on).

Suppose the experience of constant re-beginning turns out to result reliably from philosophically driven psychological reflection. This may be held against it, on the ground that it shows that reflection distorts the data. But this needn't be so. Reflection may not change the data, as already remarked. It may simply uncover facts about the nature of one's already existing form of experience. Even if the experience of constant re-beginning is unnatural or uncommon in human daily life, it doesn't follow that reflection delivers a less accurate picture of how things are. Many natural or common experiences represent things very inaccurately, and even if the experience of re-beginning is uncommon, it may be natural at least in the sense that ordinary human beings who reflect find that they have it.

—Whatever jumps and interruptions there may be in the process of consciousness, human beings engage in sustained and progressive trains of thought and reach points in trains of thought that they couldn't have reached without considerable previous thought. And they experience themselves as doing this. They must therefore feel themselves to be things that have relatively long-term continuity—lived-present-of-experience-transcending continuity, at the very least—even when they're thinking of themselves merely as selves, and not as whole human beings. And surely they should feel this, even if they don't?

No and no. When I consider my own experience of sustained thinking, my feeling that I* have no significant past is untouched. Perhaps I'm at point P in a line of thought that started at A and passed through B, C, D, and so on. Still, A to O might as well have been in a book, for all they have to do with me* as I experience myself* in the lived present of experience. GS may have worked hard for each step, but I* have no presence in the past, nor any emotionally charged proprietorial relation to what happened in the past. This idea has no emotional substance for me—and perhaps it is only emotion, emotional identification or investment, that can give any substance to it. Some may fear for my ethical well-being, but they shouldn't. If something is lost, something else of equal value is gained.[36]

—I agree with Reed that 'our sense of self is intimately related to the subjective awareness of the continuity of life. Any break in personal time [any "time-gap experience"] is alarming, because it suggests some disintegration of psychic synthesis'   (1987: 777).

---

[35] Hume requires an 'impression of the self that continue[s] invariably the same, thro' the whole course of our lives ... constant and invariable' (*Treatise*, 164/251).

[36] I discuss this further in G. Strawson, in preparation, *c*.

I don't know quite how this claim is intended, but one can lack any significant awareness of the continuity of one's life, or of the long-term temporal extendedness of one's life, without any harmful experience of a break in 'personal time'. If the imagined case is one in which one feels that it was oneself* who was there last year, say, and that it is oneself* who is here today, and yet fails to find oneself* at all points in between, that seems, as so far described, entirely harmless. It's the kind of thing an Impermanentist person experiences when afflicted by last year's embarrassment. More importantly, it's a natural everyday reality that lies at the heart of Locke's (almost universally misunderstood) theory of personal identity. It isn't a pathological condition, even if it's a common part of certain pathological conditions. A powerful sense of self and self-unity doesn't depend in any way on a sense of the long-term continuity of the self; a strongly Impermanentist person may have a rocklike sense of self, and be very consistent over time, while a Endurantist person can have a very troubled sense of identity.

The claim that it is actually good to live in the moment, rather than bad, comes at us from two sides—from spiritual experts on the one hand and radical advocates of worldly pleasures on the other, those who pursue the 'aesthetic' life (in Kierkegaard's special sense). The present point is that there lies in between a third, more ordinary form of living in the present that consists in feeling that one* is there only in the lived present of experience. One* was not there in the past, and one* will not be there in the future.

5.9 The lived present of experience

When I introduced the notion of the lived present of experience on page 75, I took its intelligibility and viability for granted. Now it needs further examination. It raises delicate questions about the process of consciousness and our experience of it, some of which I need to consider. It would take a long time to prepare the ground for an attempt at precision, and I'll talk relatively loosely and briefly in a way that will, I trust, be sufficient for my current purposes.[37]

The lived present of experience is, I take it, closely related to Husserl's *lebendige Gegenwart*, or living present, although his notion may have theoretical ties that mine lacks. It's something like the 'conscious Now', the 'experienced Now' (Ruhnau 1995: 168). It's one of the things that is meant by the 'specious present', i.e. what is experienced as the present at any moment, although it is strictly speaking more than the present moment. There's almost universal agreement that we don't experience the present of experience just as a (moving) point or front in time that is itself temporally dimensionless, but as something that has an intrinsically temporally extended phenomenological character. If one counts 1 2 3 4 5 6 7 8 9 10 11 12 … silently or out loud, relatively fast (or even as fast as one can), the occurrence of '3' has a felt quality of absolute pastness by the

---

[37] For a good recent discussion see Dainton 2008a: ch. 3.

time one has reached '12', but the felt quality of pastness isn't yet very decided by the time one has reached '4' or '5'. One knows that the occurrence of '3' is already in the past as '4' or '5' occurs, but it doesn't yet seem to have been radically cast off into the past in the way that it has been by the time '12' occurs. The central idea is well expressed by Lockwood: 'it seems to be a brute fact about experience that events which are contained within a sufficiently small interval can be experienced as a group, encompassed within a single phenomenal perspective, without thereby being experienced as simultaneous' (1989: 263). Augustus Clay, the originator of the term 'specious present', gives as examples the notes of a bar of a song and 'the changes of place' of a shooting star in the summer sky (1882: 165; quoted by James (1890: 1.609), who popularized Clay's term). The notes or changes of place can all seem to be given together in the essentially duration-involving present. James remarks that 'the smallest effective pulse of consciousness, whatever else it may be consciousness of, is also consciousness of passing time. The tiniest feeling that we can possibly have involves for future reflection two sub-feelings, one earlier and the other later, and a sense of their continuous procession' (1895: 1062–3).

Husserl distinguishes three aspects of the *lebendige Gegenwart* in his description of the '*flowing cogito*', the 'flowing conscious life in which the ... ego lives' (1931: 22, 31). Zahavi sets them out as follows: first, the '*primal impression*', that part of our consciousness which is directed at the 'narrow now-phase' of our awareness of whatever is the object of our attention. The primary impression is an element of what Husserl calls the 'streaming system of momentary perceptions' (1925: 154), and is

always embedded in a twofold temporal horizon. On the one hand, it is accompanied by a *retention* which provides us with consciousness of the phase of the object which has just been, i.e. which allows us to be aware of the phase as it sinks into the past, and, on the other hand, by a *protention* which in a more or less indeterminate fashion anticipates the phase of the object yet to come. ... the concrete and full structure of the Living Present is primal-impression-retention-protention.   (Zahavi 1999: 64, 90)

The nature of the protention is of course very different from that of the retention, and one could stress the temporal extent of the lived present of experience while playing down the contribution of the protention as compared with the retention. Zahavi argues for the experiential reality of the protentional element as follows:

That this anticipation is a concrete part of our experience can be seen from the fact that we would be surprised if the figure we took to be a mannequin suddenly moved and spoke, or if the door we opened concealed a stone wall. Our surprise can only occur against the background of an anticipation, and since we can always be surprised, we always have a horizon of anticipation.   (1999: 232)

It's not clear to me that our capacity for surprise shows that the protention, as a 'horizon of anticipation', is strictly part of the content of our experience, rather than a dispositional setting, but the general idea seems a good and important one.

These characterizations of the lived present of experience differ in details but largely coincide in essentials. I am now going to try to clarify my conception of it by introducing some further distinctions.

The example of the shooting star is a beautifully vivid illustration of the way in which an experience can have an intrinsically duration-involving character while at the same time somehow seeming to be all in the present, but it also gives a good indication of something else:

(a) the objective duration of the period of time occupied by the events that can seem to be all given together in the present in this way.

More precisely, it gives a good indication of the typical case, given that this is a case in which one's attention is principally occupied by events in one's external environment, or at least (this qualification allows the inclusion of experience of internal bodily events in the typical case) by events that one experiences as external to the 'place' of one's conscious awareness.

It might be better to call this the case that is typically discussed, rather than the typical case, for we also spend a lot of time thinking, in a manner that can cut us off dramatically from our external environment, not only when lying in bed at night unable to sleep, but also in active waking life; and the objective duration of the events that occupy the typical lived present of experience of such inner thinking (i.e. events of thinking with various contents) may well be different. There seems to be considerable scope for variation. In the case of counting in thought, the number 3 seems to fall into the definite past almost immediately, to be completely gone, if one just imagines the written numerals—their visually apprehended shapes—with accompanying understanding. If instead one imagines the sounds of the words for the numerals with accompanying understanding, this seems to happen more slowly. This is so even though thinking the visual shapes is a much faster process, so that one might expect more of them to be retained. It's as if the imagined sound leaves a more solid or resonant trace of itself than the imagined shape, something that can linger even while the focus of understanding moves on, in a way that the imagined shape cannot. In the case of the shapes it seems that each is somehow immediately obliterated from the lived present of experience by the entertaining of the next (different abilities are required for the two acts of imagination and the accompanying understanding may be easier in the case of the shapes).

This last proposal generalizes powerfully to spontaneous episodes of conscious thinking, which often take place without any images that might leave a retainable trace (although they also often involve silent acoustic word-images). 'The mind thinks with extraordinary rapidity', as Darwin observed (1838: 544), and the immediate past of thought, considered as an experienced event with a certain duration, can be *immediately nothing*, as it were, as conscious thought races ahead. This is not to say that content that has just come to mind isn't present in or influencing the further progress of thought. It's just to say that when one is thinking and conscious of one's thinking, (a), the objective duration of the period of time occupied by the events that can seem to be all given together in the present (which are in this case events of thinking), can be very short indeed. I think it is important to note this fact, but I'm going to stick with the shooting star as the basic example of (a).

The shooting star also illustrates something else, something that needs to be clearly distinguished from (a). This is

(b) the subjective feel of the duration of the lived present of experience, the temporal feel of the temporal 'window' within which one lives as subject of experience.

(b) is, I take it, a wholly non-thetic matter, and hard to pin down. It can be hard, at first, to distinguish it clearly from (a), because there's a respect in which the two things often march in step.

Before I attempt to explain this, let me record a third thing that needs to be distinguished from both (a) and (b): namely,

(c) the actual or objective duration of the psychological phenomenon of the lived present of experience, considered as something happening at the present moment

—i.e. the objective temporal extent of lived-present-of-experience experience[38] as it exists at any given time, e.g. the period of time occupied by the experience of the whole passage of a shooting star seeming to be given in the present. This needs to be considered independently of both (a), the amount of time occupied by the events that lived-present-of-experience experience represents, and (b), how long the lived present of experience feels to its subject as a 'window' or 'temporal space' of experience. The first and most natural supposition is that (c), like (b), typically marches in step with (a).

When Barry Dainton tentatively estimates the typical duration of the specious present to be 'half a second or less' (2000: 171), one thing he's doing, I take it, is making a claim about (a) which I'm going to suppose to be correct: the claim, slightly adapted, that the (perceptual, external-world-directed) lived present of experience normally represents as present events that occupy around a third of a second of objective time.[39] Starting from this benchmark, the first point to make is that (c), the actual or objective duration of the lived present of experience, can't be assumed to match (a), the duration of the period of time occupied by the events it represents. It's not just that (c) and (a) don't occupy exactly the same period of time; there are several reasons why that must be so.[40] It's also that there's no good reason to think that they must occupy effectively the same amount of time (350 ms, say).

I'll say more about this after introducing my second main proposal. This is that the lived present of experience has (b) a subjective, non-thetic 'duration feel' or subjective

---

[38] All experience is lived-present-of-experience experience, and this expression may seem redundant, but it is helpful at various points, e.g. when I discuss the figure on p. 258.

[39] I say 'around a third of a second' because half a second is proposed as a maximum; the 'around' allows that there may be variation depending on which experiential modality is dominant (recall from p. 42 that the experiential modalities include not only the sensory-perceptual modalities, interoceptive and exteroceptive, but also the cognitive-phenomenological modality of inner thinking).

[40] The finite speed of light and sound; the fact that experiential processing involves a time lag; the fact that the experience of the trajectory of the shooting star as fully given in the lived present of experience presumably isn't available until the event is over; and so on.

temporal character—a *subjective duration*, as one might say—that stays relatively fixed at all times independently of (a) the objective duration of the period of time occupied by the events in the world that it represents as present. Some who use the term 'specious present' don't sufficiently distinguish (a) and (b), and perhaps also (c), and this is understandable, because there's often no need to do so. I do, however, want to mark these distinctions, and this is one sufficient reason for me to put aside the term 'specious present' and introduce the new term 'lived present of experience'.

Of the three notions, (b) is perhaps the most difficult to grasp, but the distinction between (a) and (b) is, I think, apparent when one considers moments of life-threatening crisis—as when one flies over the handlebars of one's motorbike. In these circumstances attention goes into overdrive, and time seems to 'slow down'. A first thought may be that this is a case in which (b) varies, in such a way that the temporal space of the lived present of experience is experienced as longer, larger. I think, though, that there is a fundamental sense in which (b) doesn't vary, although (a) and (c) do. On this view the lived present of experience has the same sort of fundamental subjective-duration feel as usual, the same sort of non-thetic, subjective temporal roominess or 'window' size, and this is the *explanation* of the fact that objective time seems to slow down. It seems to slow down because events that occupy a much smaller amount of objective time than usual occupy the whole of the lived present of experience, the relatively unchanging subjective-duration window of the lived present of experience. One may expressly intellectually register the fact that one is experiencing a great deal in a short time (a short time that feels for all that peculiarly calm and leisurely), in moments of crisis, but this does not mean that the basic, subjective experienced temporal extent or 'roominess' of the lived present of experience is not the same as it is in ordinary life.[41]

—How can the lived present of experience feel unusually leisurely and not feel longer than usual?

In the same way that a leisurely trip in a punt needn't seem to take longer than the three hours it takes. These are measures of different things, although they can be confused.

—This is just wrong. It's the lived present of experience itself that feels longer in moments of crisis, it's the window itself that feels larger, and it's clear why this is so. It's because our subjective experience of the duration or size of the lived present of experience is profoundly conditioned by (effectively determined by) our normal experience of the unfolding of things in the world. So when we process information much more rapidly than usual, in such a way that events in the world seem to unfold more slowly (the response is evidently adaptive), the lived present of experience feels longer, because our subjective experience of its extent is calibrated by our deep inbuilt sense of the speed with which events normally unfold in the world and are experienced by us.

We disagree, but not about the key point, for the key point is simply that (a) can vary dramatically relative to (b), and this is acknowledged on both accounts. It's hard

---

[41] It's not clear whether the sense that one is experiencing a great deal in a short time is part of the experience, or whether it's a later judgement about it that is read back into it (if one survives).

to see clearly, because of the respect in which (a), (b), and (c) standardly march in step, or standardly appear to. One thing that's plain, though, is that one shouldn't think that a sense that one is experiencing a great deal in a short time will always make it seem that objective time has slowed, or that the process of experience is leisurely. In the case in which one is thinking extremely rapidly and paying little or no attention to the external environment, one feels that one is experiencing a great deal in a short time, but nothing feels slow or leisurely. On the contrary, everything feels extremely fast and intense.[42]

I maintain, then, that there's a deep sense in which (b), the admittedly elusive but very important subjective-duration phenomenon that I'm trying to describe, is a relatively fixed window. One might put the idea differently by saying that there's a key sense in which the internal, subjective *pace of time* is always about the same. In these terms, the reason why objective time seems to slow when one's processing of data speeds up in response to crisis is precisely that one's fundamental subjective experience of the pace of time doesn't speed up correspondingly, but remains the same. The basic point remains as before: that (a) can vary considerably relative to (b). We can put it dramatically (in a way I'll shortly develop) by saying that the realm of subjective phenomenological time constitutes a different temporal realm from the realm of objective non-phenomenological time.

I don't like metaphorical talk of realms, but the point, as remarked, is not easy to express. The principal obscuring factor is perhaps this. If, having proposed that (a) is normally around a third of a second, one is asked to put a figure on (b), the temporal feel or subjective duration of the lived present of experience, it can seem right to say that it too is around a third of a second, using the *objective* temporal measure 'around a third of a second' to represent the lived present of experience's typical *subjective* temporal 'size' or 'feel' (at considerable risk of being misunderstood). This can give the right general sense of (b), the subjective duration of the lived present of experience, precisely because the lived present of experience typically involves the representation-as-present of the events of around a third of a second's worth of objective time. It is in this sense that (a) and (b) commonly march in step. It is, however, important that (a) and (b) can come apart, and this means that when one proposes to use the (a)-derived characterization 'around a third of a second' as a plausible general characterization of (b), one must sever it sharply from its anchor in (a)-ish facts about how much objective non-phenomenological time is normally represented in the lived present of experience. Only then can it serve as an intuitive characterization of (b), the standard temporal feel of the window of the lived present of experience, a characterization that retains its descriptive accuracy even when things are as they are at times of life-threatening crisis, and much less than a third of

---

[42] Huge temporal distortions can occur under the influence of psychotropic drugs, where a few objective seconds of experience can seem to last, subjectively, an extraordinarily long time, even while the lived present of experience itself retains its familiar dimensions. This can occur even when a marker of normal time is present in experience: one can, for example, grasp that the white lines in the middle of the road are going past at a normal pace, on a car journey, even while feeling that the journey is taking a vast amount of time. 'In hashish-intoxication there is a curious increase in the apparent time-perspective ... we enter a short street, and it is as if we should never get to the end of it' (James 1890: 1.639–40).

a second's worth of objective time is presented in the window of the lived present of experience.

It may be that the distinction between (a) and (b) is not often needed when we discuss our experience of time. It may be that it often passes unnoticed, or is implicitly rejected. It is for all that real, and important for certain purposes, if only because failure to acknowledge it may lead to major error.

Before saying something about (c), it's worth mentioning a recent line of research which claims to have 'clear evidence' not only 'that ... the experienced Now is not a point, but is extended', but also that it 'is—language and culture independent—of the duration of approximately 3 seconds' maximum'.[43] Three seconds is far too long for the lived present of experience (or specious present), and this research is concerned with something quite different, if hardly less important: the phenomenon of the 'time gestalt' or 'temporal gestalt'. The figure of three seconds relates not to (b) the subjectively experienced span of the lived present of experience, or to (a) as so far characterized, but rather to

the time interval within which, *with the aid of memory*, a subject can unify the presented material in the form of an overall pattern or structure that the mind can grasp as a whole. This is the concept of a time gestalt; and the ability to form such gestalts is an essential precondition of appreciating music or sustaining the simplest conversation.[44]

The temporal gestalt, to phrase it slightly differently, is proposed as a measure of

(d) the maximum objective period of time that can be occupied by immediately preceding perceived events that can with the aid of memory be grasped as a whole in a certain way.

This is the notion that the Czech immunologist and poet Miroslav Holub picks up when he cites Pöppel's research in his essay 'The Dimension of the Present Moment' and writes, strikingly, that 'in this sense our ego [or self] lasts three seconds'.[45]

It's plain that (d), the three-second-maximum temporal gestalt, is distinct from (a), the typical around-a-third-of-a-second objective coverage achieved by the lived present of experience, and that (d) must involve some extra mechanism or operation. They are nevertheless both measures of the amount of (objective) time that can be occupied by immediately preceding events apprehended in experience and grasped as a whole in some way.

So far, four different notions are in play in this account of the small-scale temporal character of experience. I'm now going to introduce a fifth.

---

[43] Ruhnau 1995: 168, referring to Pöppel 1988. For a good recent discussion see Lockwood 2005: ch. 15.

[44] Lockwood 2005: 371. It may be that the figure corresponds to the maximum extent of what neurologists call 'working memory', as opposed to other parts of 'short-term memory' and 'long-term memory', but these distinctions are contested in neurology.

[45] 1990: 5. Descartes can call on the notion of a time gestalt in replying to one charge of circularity levelled against his *Meditations*. He can hold that we can grasp the (alleged) proof of the existence of God all in one go and as a whole without the earlier steps of the proof having fallen into the essentially dubitable past by the time we assentingly entertain the conclusion. And this seems plausible.

5.10 The living moment of experience

I've discussed possible differences in the case of (a) and (b). The question of the duration of (c) is an empirical question, like the question of the typical duration of (a), and subdivides into different questions, such as 'What period of time is occupied by all the experience that is part of the experience of the passage of the shooting star?' and 'What period of time is occupied by the experience that has the character of being experience of the full course of the shooting star?' These are perfectly legitimate questions, however hard they are to answer. One reason for thinking that (a) and (c) can diverge is evidence that a stimulus event can be as short as 1–2 ms, although it is not possible for it to be experienced as lasting less than, say 30–50 ms.[46] I don't want to pursue these questions here, however. Instead I propose to pass through (c) as it stands in order to consider something that lies as it were within it, i.e.

(e) the shortest period of time that 'now' can be taken to refer to when one points at an experiencing being (Louis, for example) and says truly 'he is having experience right now'.

I will call this the *living moment of experience*.

What is the duration of the living moment of experience? I take it to be very short indeed. Whatever (b) the subjective duration or felt temporal character of the lived present of experience, and whatever (a) the duration of the objective events represented in the lived present of experience, experience, lived-present-of-experience experience, is itself (c) an objectively occurring psychological phenomenon occurring in time, and it is therefore something about which we can ask, with respect to any particular period of time, 'Is it occurring now?', and, importantly, 'What's the shortest period of time in which it can be said to be occurring?'

One thing I take for granted is that experience takes time: it can't exist or occur at an instant, where an instant is defined as something with no temporal duration at all.[47] So I take 'moment' as it features in the expression 'living moment of experience' to refer essentially to a temporal *interval*, however short.[48] If time is 'dense', however, in the mathematical sense of 'dense' according to which between any two moments there is always a third, and if there are periods of experience that are truly temporally continuous, in the way we assume there to be, then we can't take the term 'living moment of experience' to refer to a discrete entity, for it doesn't carry in its meaning the idea of a neat beginning and end that allows us to say that there are *n* living moments of experience in a given period of time, no more and no less. If time is dense, then, 'living moment of experience' denotes at best a theoretical abstraction from the concrete continuum, not something of which we can say 'This one ends here and this one begins here'. It's irrelevant that living moments of experience are 'countable' in the technical mathematical

---

[46] See Pockett 2003: 59; Dainton 2008a: 93.

[47] Compare Butterfield 1996: 210–11. I take it to be obvious—a necessary truth, underwritten by Russell's 'robust sense of reality' and immune to clever mathematics—that instants with no duration can't add up to duration. Duration can't be 'composed of' or 'constructed out of' durationless instants; for nothing will come of nothing.

[48] *Mo*-ments *move*, as it were; in-*stants stand* still.

sense, for there's a plain sense in which they're not countable: we can't say how many there are. (I assume there are no concrete infinities.)

If, on the other hand, time is not dense, but has a grainy structure at the very small scale, as some suppose, then living moments of experience may indeed be discrete entities. Suppose we call the ultimate units of time 'chronons' (perhaps there are about 10^{43} a second). One proposal may then be that each living moment of experience lasts for one chronon. Another proposal may be that experience has a much coarser-grained discrete temporal structure, for fundamental neurological reasons quite independent of the fundamental character of time, and is made up of what we might call 'neurochronons' (there might be forty a second, perhaps, or 10^3), each of which constitutes—is—a living moment of experience.

—It's ridiculous to propose that experience can go on in a period of time lasting 10^{-43} seconds, or indeed an indefinitely shorter temporal interval. Experience as we have it, with the temporal character that it has, can't possibly exist in the living moment of experience so understood, because there's simply not enough room for it to be what it is.

But if a period of experience is indeed temporally continuous, as we ordinarily suppose, then experience must be going on at all moments in that period.[49] So if we suppose that a particular episode of lived-present-of-experience experience, e.g. experience of the passage of a shooting star, occupies an objective period of say 200 ms (this is a (c)-measure), then we must allow that passage-of-a-shooting-star-experience occupies and is present at each (e)-moment of that 200 ms period, even as the fine details of its content change.

This raises a question about (b): what is the subjective temporal character of passage-of-a-shooting-star-experience at any moment? If I'm right about (b), such an experience must have the subjective character of involving a 'third-of-a-second-ish' window at any moment, even while that moment itself is objectively very short.

How might this be? I need to take a step back, into an area I'm unsure of. I've distinguished between 'real' time, non-phenomenological, experience-independent time, and what one might call 'phenomenological time', experiential-perspective-internal time, and before considering whether and in what way this makes sense, I need to consider, if only briefly, the well-known and troubling fact that the actual nature of the (presumably entirely non-phenomenological) reality that we refer to when we talk about time may be quite unlike what we suppose time to be.[50]

What should we do, faced with this possibility? We may at first want to insist that the reference of our word 'time' must be to a reality whose intrinsic (and non-structural)[51]

---

[49] One can define a notion of temporal continuity whether time is dense or whether it involves quantal discreteness.

[50] It not only seems far from unlikely that this is so; from certain perspectives it is hard to see how it could not be so. Compare James (1890: 1.629–30) and reference there to Ward 1886.

[51] I don't qualify 'intrinsic' by 'and non-structural' because I think that a thing's intrinsic properties don't include its structural properties (this is one common view), but for the opposite reason. I take it that the structure of time is part of its intrinsic nature, just as the structure of an H_2O molecule is part of its intrinsic nature. The point of the qualification is that its structural nature is something that can be fully characterized by a purely mathematical description, and I wish to refer to its intrinsic nature considered as something more than its structural nature so understood.

nature is at least to some extent revealed, known, in experience, a reality with whose distinctive nature we are to some extent truly acquainted in experience. We may want to insist that the meaning of the *referring* expression 'time' can't be entirely cut off from the *descriptive* force it has for us. But we may then have to accept that—roughly—the thing we refer to when we talk about time is quite unlike what we mean when we talk about time. Let '*e*-time' refer to something to whose intrinsic-and-not-merely-structural nature we do have some significant access specifically in experiencing things temporally in the way we do. Let '*n*-time', or plain 'time', refer to that aspect of reality that does indeed exist (whatever its nature, and however wrong we are about it) and is indeed what we refer to when we talk of time and take it to be something entirely objective and experience-independent. In these terms, the possibility we face is that *e*-time is in some stark sense an illusion, a mere mode of experience, 'a mere form of sensibility', in Kant's phrase (A21/B35 and *passim*), relative to objective time or *n*-time—and that *n*-time is really nothing like what we think of as time.

Perhaps things are not that bad. Whether they are or not, Kant (real Kant) can accept that *n*-time exists as defined, for he can allow that *something*—*n*-time as defined—underlies and corresponds to all temporal aspects of our experience, which are appearances of it. Kant can perfectly well allow that there is some sort of homomorphism between the differences that feature in our experiences and the character of noumenal reality—both quite generally, and in the particular case of temporal differences.

That said, a homomorphism between two things permits extraordinary differences between them (the subject matter of what one might call *metaphysical topology*), so that the real structure we can intelligibly take ourselves to refer to when talking about time may not be temporal in any sense we understand. *n*-time may be nothing like what we think of as time, apart from there being some sort of relation of homomorphism between the two things.

With this in place, consider a continuous (uninterrupted) period of experience lasting from time *n*-t_1 to time *n*-t_4 in *n*-time and consider the living moment of experience at *n*-t_3 during that period. One might picture it, impressionistically, as in Figure 5.1. Time

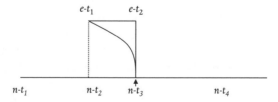

Figure 5.1 The relation between *e*-time and *n*-time.

extends from left to right. The arrowhead on the *n*-time line picks out the living moment of experience, *n*-t_3—the shortest period or interval of time that 'now' can be taken to refer to when I point at Louis and say truly that he is having experience right now. The top horizontal line (the line from *e*-t_1 to *e*-t_2) represents (b), the subjective 'temporal space' of the lived present of experience at $n\text{-}t_3$, the essentially temporally roomy nature of the phenomenological lived present of experience that I've characterized as being 'about a third of a second long', using this expression in the special subjective sense described on page 254. Considered as an event in n-time at any moment, lived-present-of-experience experience is occurring in the possibly very short living moment of experience (= (e)); but it has, phenomenologically speaking, a relatively generous 'third-of-a-second-ish' subjective temporal extent (= (b)). The subjective temporal roominess of (b) is indicated by the length of the e-time line blossoming out of, as contained in, the living moment of experience on the n-time line. The very short n-time living moment of experience can contain the relatively speaking temporally spacious e-time line because n-time and e-time are utterly different things.[52]

As things stand, the expression 'lived present of experience' can be taken to refer to any of (a), (b), and (c): to (a), the objective duration of the events represented in the lived present of experience; (b), the subjective 'temporal space' inhabited by the subject of the lived present of experience; and (c), the lived present of experience considered as an objectively occurring psychological phenomenon in n-time. These distinctions are, I hope, clear enough, and I propose now to introduce a capitalized version of the expression—'Lived Present of Experience'—to refer specifically and only to (b). The Lived Present of Experience, then, is the 'temporal space' represented by the extent of the e-time line. This is the temporal space we inhabit experientially, even as we are located where we are in n-time, and it has a phenomenological character, considered specifically in respect of what we experience as its time-involving character, that may not be any sort of accurate representation of the nature of time (n-time) itself. The reference to temporal extent made by the expression 'Lived Present of Experience' is strictly to (b), then; it's a strictly phenomenological, strictly experiential-perspective-internal, temporal, e-time reference, and has nothing to do with any n-time reference.[53]

The fact that the e-time line representing the Lived Present of Experience is not on the n-time line but parallel to it is intended as a crude representation of two points. The first is that although the domain of e-time isn't to be found anywhere on the plane of n-time, we may nevertheless say that it has a genuine durational character of its own. It has e-temporal duration, and this is represented by its having left-to-right extension in the diagram—although, again, it might be better to represent it as off the plane of the page. The second point is that in having the phenomenological content it does—e.g. the course of a shooting star—the Lived Present of Experience really does represent (a) some non-null portion of n-time, albeit in the e-time mode of sensibility, in representing an n-temporally extended group of events.[54] Finally, the existence of this Lived Present

[52] This view is 'retentionalist', in Dainton's terminology (Dainton 2008b); it might be better to represent the e-time line as off the plane of the page. (Many suppose that reality has more dimensions than the spacetime dimensions we can discern, and Dainton has suggested that the e-time of (b) might possibly be extended in a higher dimension 'attached' to an unextended instant in our spacetime.)

[53] The difference between 'living' and 'lived' is apposite here. The very short living moment of experience is *vivant*, living, as such, but not *vécu*, lived, as such.

[54] The reality of the Husserlian retention can be thought of as being indicated by the backward-stretching character of the line $e\text{-}t_1$ to $e\text{-}t_2$ in the diagram. In so far as the protention has occurrent phenomenological reality, this is not denied or

of Experience phenomenon is itself a concrete phenomenon that exists, like any other concrete phenomenon, in n-time. It's a matter of subjective experience, but it is of course an objective fact that subjective experience occurs, and has the subjective character it does.

I've chosen to convey the size of (a), the portion of n-time that the Lived Present of Experience represents in representing a n-temporally extended group of events, by drawing a dotted line down from the e-time line. In Fig. 5.1 the straight drop of the dotted line is meant to express the fact that (a) is about a third of a second, and so corresponds well with (b), the third-of-a-second-ish subjective temporal feel of the Lived Present of Experience as measured in e-time. In general, and as before, we may suppose that (b) generally marches in step with (a).[55] But there is, once again, no reason why things should always be so neat, if only because the intrinsic metrics of the two horizontal lines are just not the same. (a) can be much 'smaller' than (b) in times of crisis ('smaller' is in scare quotes because of the respect in which e-time and n-time are not commensurable). Figure 5.2 represents one such time of crisis. The amount

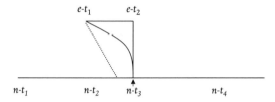

Figure 5.2 The relation between e-time and n-time: a crisis.

of n-time represented in the e-time of the Lived Present of Experience, which is itself occurring in the living moment of experience at n-t_3, is now much less than a third of a second, and the subject of experience accordingly experiences time—n-time—as having slowed down. When one dials a telephone number, briefly takes the telephone away from one's ear to do something else, and then puts it back to one's ear to see if someone has answered, the time until the next ring seems extraordinarily long. It always seems as if the previous ring must have finished only just before one brought the telephone back to one's ear—and even then the waiting time seems strangely distended.

Consider, finally, a sixth notion,

(f) the *experience-pulse*.

downplayed; it's a matter of the overall phenomenological character of the Lived Present of Experience between e-t_1 and e-t_2. I haven't represented the necessary time lag between the occurrence of external events and any experience of them.

[55] We may also suppose that the order in which events in the world are represented (in experience) as occurring generally corresponds very well to the order in which they do occur, for obvious evolutionary reasons. (The neurophysics of this, and of time perception in general, may be thoroughly surprising. We're told that champion tennis players return serve before they can have consciously seen the ball, and so before they can have consciously temporally experienced the ball, but they nevertheless experience themselves as seeing the ball and returning it on the basis of that experience.)

Suppose that temporally continuous periods of human experience consist of discrete neural pulses, seamlessly joined or overlapping, about forty a second, each lasting about 25 ms.[56] A first thought may be that in this case the living moment of experience is 25 ms long. But if experience is continuous within any 25 ms experience-pulse period, then there is, as remarked, experience at any and every moment in that period. Now one may suppose (with William James, and in line with the Transience View of the self—see 7.6), that each experience-pulse has its own subject of experience, so that there are forty numerically distinct subjects of experience in any given second of seemingly continuous experience, each one having experience that has the phenomenological character of being part of a continuous process of experience. Even so, one can't infer that there are only forty living moments of experience. If time is made up of discrete chronons (10^{43} a second, say), we may perhaps frankly identify living moments of experience with chronon-sized periods of experience in the way already suggested. In this case each of the twenty-five-a-second macroscopically discrete experience-pulses is made up of many discrete chronon-sized living moments of experience. It may alternatively be suggested that each 25 ms pulse is made up of twenty-five 1 ms sub-pulses, 'neurochronons', and these too may be be put forward as candidates for being living moments of experience. But any proposed unit of measurement raises the point that if there is continuous experience in the period of time picked out by the unit of measurement, then it is going on at every moment in that period of time.

5.11 Summary and conclusion

With these notions (more or less) in hand, consider again the question 'When does our experience of what we are experiencing at present occur?' The first answer we can give is that it occurs in

(c) the lived present of experience,

where (c) denotes the objective temporal extent of lived-present-of-experience experience as it exists at any given time, taken to be something relatively roomy compared with the living moment of experience.

   The second answer, however, pans down from (c) to

(e) the living moment of experience.

Strictly speaking, we may say, all present experience occurs only in the living moment (the true present) of experience, however short the living moment of experience is. On a strict reading, one may say, (c) is to be identified with (e).

   The third answer, in terms of experience-pulses, is that it occurs in

(f) the present experience-pulse,

---

[56] There's no incompatibility between their being overlapping and their constituting a seemingly smooth and single course of experience. See further 7.6.

which I've assumed for purposes of argument to last about 25 ms (*n*-time). A fourth answer is that it occurs in ('in')

(b) the Lived Present of Experience.

Any (e) living moment of experience is necessarily situated within a given particular (f) experience-pulse, but our experience of what we are experiencing at any moment, measured in *e*-time, i.e. subjectively or phenomenologically, may also be said to occupy a temporal window that is considerably 'larger'[57] than either (e) or (f). I've suggested that this (b) duration is relatively invariant, whatever

(a) the amount of objective time actually occupied by the events that it represents as present,

and have proposed that we can characterize it as being 'around a third of a second long', using the (risky) method of characterization explained on pages 254–5, which appeals to *n*-time duration to characterize the completely different phenomenon of *e*-time duration.

Given that the duration (the *e*-time duration) of the Lived Present of Experience is relatively invariant, any experience of what we are experiencing at present whose content is a product of a

(d) temporal gestalt

will have a subjective or phenomenological temporal span of around a third of a second, like every other experience of what we are experiencing at present, even though the temporal-gestalt mechanism draws on and integrates into an experiential whole material presented in experience up to three seconds before the present moment. Plainly the formation of a temporal gestalt must involve a process of integration additional to whatever process of integration delivers the experience of the whole passage of a shooting star in the Lived Present of Experience. For no experiential content that occurred three seconds ago can be present in the Lived Present of Experience given the operation of the basic Lived-Present-of-Experience mechanism alone, although it can be present in the Lived Present of Experience given the additional operation of the temporal-gestalt mechanism. Presumably the temporal-gestalt mechanism involves some sort of further, larger conceptual integration.[58] There is in any case no conflict between the two mechanisms. To say that the Lived Present of Experience is around a third of a second long is to put an upper bound on (b), the fundamental phenomenological, lived measure of temporally extended experiential unity. To say that a temporal gestalt can integrate up to three seconds of experience is to say that up to three (objective) seconds of immediately past experiential content can in some sense be fully presented inside the relatively invariant around-a-third-of-a-second window of the Lived Present of Experience by the operation of a mechanism supplementary to the basic Lived-Present-of-Experience mechanism.[59]

---

[57] The comparison is between incommensurables and is at best metaphorical.

[58] See Lockwood 2005: 371. On p. 380 he notes that the time-gestalt mechanism is also operative in the processing of sentences; research reveals that 'people tend mentally to segment speech into roughly three-second-portions'.

[59] See e.g. Ruhnau 1995. One can also enquire about the smallest amount of immediately past experiential content that can occupy the Lived Present of Experience.

Note finally that there are experiences of seizing complex content as a whole that seem to comprise far more material than can be presented in three seconds. Lockwood doubts that they are what they seem to be. He takes the example of understanding a long sentence:

Consider … what you have in mind when you say: 'Now I understand what you're saying.' Does this mean that you have the whole picture, in plain view of the mind's eye? … It is more in the nature of an awareness that things have clicked into place than having the whole picture, in all its glory, and all in the same specious present, in plain view of the mind's eye.   (2005: 380)

It may be, though, that there can be all-its-glory content in the Lived Present of Experience, not just clicking-into-place awareness, in the case of understanding long sentences, given the velocity and density of thought, the 'magical rapidity' of the mind (James 1892: 148)—given 'how very quick the actions of the mind are performed', in Locke's words, how 'many of them … seem to require no time … seem to be crowded into an instant' (*Essay*, 2.9.10). Certainly one shouldn't confuse all-its-glory entertaining of content with entertaining of content that involves some sort of experienced linguistic vehicle (e.g. silently entertained inner speech). One shouldn't think that the former requires the latter—that we can't really entertain content in all its glory at all unless we spell it out in some sort of experienced linguistic vehicle in such a way as to have the (higher-order) fact that we understand it plain before us as we do so.[60] Clicking-into-place may well be the best description of what happens in the case of some long sentences, or when one has been listening to someone expounding their new theory to us at some length, but there are many other kinds of experiences of seizing complex content as a whole, and I see no reason to doubt the accuracy of Mozart's description of his apprehension of a whole piece of music all at once, as quoted by James:

Great thinkers have vast premonitory glimpses of schemes of relation between terms, which hardly even as verbal images enter the mind, so rapid is the whole process …. Mozart describes thus his manner of composing: First bits and crumbs of the piece come and gradually join together in his mind; then the soul getting warmed to the work, the thing grows more and more, 'and I spread it out broader and clearer, and at last it gets almost finished in my head, even when it is a long piece, so that I can see the whole of it at a single glance in my mind, as if it were a beautiful painting or a handsome [statue]; in which way I do not hear it in my imagination at all as a succession—the way it must come later—but all at once, as it were. It is a rare feast! All the inventing and making goes on in me as in a beautiful strong dream. But the best of all is the *hearing of it all at once*.'   (1890: i. 255)

I've assembled a number of fairly complicated facts and conjectures about our experience of time. They raise many questions. I favour the idea that selves are short-lived entities, but I don't think the relative brevity of the lived present of experience supports any such claim, any more than the extreme brevity of the living moment of experience does. Nor does this brevity explain the experience of discontinuity—hiatus or continual newness or renewal—in the process of experience, in those who have

---

[60] See again G. Strawson 1994: 18–21, 'An Account of Four Seconds of Thought'.

such experience. Nor does it support any claim about the discontinuous character of the process of experience. One can model the lived present of experience as a puddle of light produced by a spotlight travelling steadily along on the ground. Even if the spotlight's boundary is sharp, so that things come abruptly into the light and leave it just as abruptly, this model provides no support for the view that there is a sense in which the process of experience is in fact continually restarting, or continually new, or for the view that it must be experienced as such. On the contrary, it suggests that the process of experience may have the smoothness of travel of the circle of light along the ground (for purposes of argument we can imagine this being establishable from outside the perspective of the experiencer in the way proposed on page 240, e.g. by reference to activity in the reticular activating system), and that this may be so even when its subject experiences it as broken or jerky. I don't think human consciousness is a matter of flow, in fact, either considered from outside the perspective of the experiencer in the way just described or considered from within it; but these are further issues.[61]

Some may now claim that the true extent of the self is to be measured in e-time, and is the extent of the Lived Present of Experience. As things stand, though, this is like saying that a three-foot by two-foot painting of five miles of countryside can be five miles wide. A subjective, e-time phenomenological measure can't determine the non-phenomenological n-time truth about the actual temporal extent of the self, even though the subjective roominess of the Lived Present of Experience is itself an objective fact (just as it's an objective fact that there is subjective experience and that it has a certain qualitative-experiential character). The following claim by Marcus Aurelius has a certain poetic force, and can be used to convey a certain truth.

Whether you live three thousand years or thirty thousand, remember that the only life you can lose is the one you are living now in the present .... In this sense the longest life and the shortest come to the same thing, for life in the present is the same for all. ... One's loss is limited to that one fleeting instant; one cannot lose either the past or the future, for no one can take from one what one does not have. ... So when the longest- and the shortest-lived among us die their loss is precisely equal, because the only life of which one can be deprived is life in the present, since this is all one has.   (c.170: ii. 14)

So too, the passage from Shaftesbury quoted on page 202. But any claim that selves are short-lived will have to look rather at the proposed objective measures of the living moment of experience and experience-pulses, at least on the present terms of discussion.

---

[61] Another model has three light bulbs in a linear array alight at any time. Every 20 ms, say, the left-hand one goes out, and the first unilluminated bulb on the right lights up. In us this lighting pattern gives rise to experience of a single smoothly moving patch of light, the continuity effect being produced by a series of overlapping discrete events. We can extend the model and have 6 or 25 or 1,000 contiguous bulbs alight at any one time on a three-dimensional array. The switching time can be adjusted up and down; the patch of light can grow and shrink in an amoeba-like fashion as it travels along; the bulbs can grow from dim to bright; a new luminous amoeba can arise as a previous one is declining; the two can overlap temporally, perhaps also spatially, their behaviour analogous, perhaps, to the constant successive activations of neural assemblies that constitute consciousness (although these won't have such simple contiguity relations).

Part 6

Metaphysics: preliminaries

Metaphysics means nothing but an unusually obstinate effort to think clearly.

(James 1890: 1. 164)

6.1 Do sesmets exist?

Do sesmets exist, things that might qualify as selves, subjects of experience that are single mental things in the sense specified in 4.8? Perhaps immaterial minds qualify as sesmets. An immaterial mind seems to possess the property of being correctly judged to be a single thing when considered specifically as a subject of experience that is being considered specifically in its mental being. In fact, immaterial minds seem to conform very well to the rich notion of the self sanctioned by ordinary human SELF-experience: in addition to the properties *subject, single, mental, thing,* and their complex compound *sesmet,* they also possess the properties *persisting, agent,* and *distinct*; although not, perhaps, the property of *personality*.[1] They seem to fit the bill admirably.

There's no reason to think that such things exist, however, and they're ruled out by the assumption that materialism is true. There's also a doubt about whether immaterial minds really possess the property *single-as-mental* (an integral part of the property *sesmet*) in the required way. Cartesian immaterial minds may possess this property, but Cartesian immaterial minds are strikingly different from immaterial minds as standardly conceived of in philosophy (see 7.3), and are in any case ruled out by materialism. The question whether sesmets exist remains to be answered.

In attempting to answer it, I'll continue to appeal to Louis as a representative human being. It will sometimes be convenient to call the portion of reality that consists of Louis the 'L-reality'. The notion of the L-reality is rough: as a physical being Louis is enmeshed in wide-reaching physical interactions and isn't neatly

---

[1] The most common view in religious and philosophical discussion during the last 2,000 years has been that an immaterial soul by itself is not a person. Many hold that personal memory and personality require a body. For a useful survey see Martin and Barresi 2006. See also Sorabji 2006; Thiel, forthcoming.

separable out as a single portion of reality. But it's serviceable and useful none the less.²

As a materialist, I take it that if something exists, and is indeed a *thing*, then it must be a physical thing. It must be a physical *object*, to use the more uncompromising word. I've thought it helpful up to now to use 'thing' rather than 'object', because many people's intuitions about what can legitimately or plausibly count as objects are strongly dominated by everyday applications of the word 'object'. I don't, however, make any philosophical distinction between 'thing' and 'object', and I want now to shift to the harder word.³ My aim is to show not only that

(i) sesmets exist

but also that

(ii) sesmets qualify as physical objects

at least in every sense in which cats and chairs and fundamental particles do. More moderately, I aim to show that sesmets qualify as physical objects if anything does—that there are no better candidates than sesmets for the title 'physical object'.

Some may be prepared to concede that sesmets exist—entities that are subjects of experience that are single mental phenomena in some strong and interesting sense—while denying that these phenomena are really *objects*, physical *objects*. This is not an option for me, given the way I've defined 'sesmet', and my aim to show that sesmets are selves. The strong brief that I've taken on as defence counsel for the self (7) requires that candidates for selfhood must qualify as objects.

The next task (after the task of showing that sesmets are physical objects) will be to argue, precisely, that

(iii) sesmets are (rightly or reasonably called) selves

if indeed they do exist. There's a sense in which this is easy for me, given the present scheme. For if it is true, as I argued in Part 4, both that

[SELF(-experience) → SESMET(-experience)]

and that

[SESMET(-experience) → SELF(-experience)],

i.e. that the answer to the general phenomenological question is that

[SELF ↔ SESMET],

---

² Apart from the arguably irreducible indeterminacy of the spatiotemporal boundaries of Louis, and quantum entanglement, there are at any given time many millions of neutrinos (e.g.) in the spatial volume bounded by the surface of Louis's skin that are not—I take it—part of Louis.

I wouldn't take proof of the irreducible indeterminacy of Louis's spatiotemporal boundaries to show that he is a 'vague object', but rather that (strictly speaking) 'Louis' doesn't denote a fully respectable object in fundamental metaphysics. If this leads to the view that most of the things we ordinarily think of as objects aren't fully metaphysically respectable objects, so be it. If one wishes to be saved from this conclusion, 'penumbral constraints' of the sort discussed by McLaughlin and McGee (2000) can probably do the trick.

³ I planned to shake off some of the constricting associations of 'object' by using a bare circle 'O' as a count noun for things that are objects in the required sense, or by modifying 'object' to 'øbject'—but decided against it.

then I can use the Equivalence Thesis (55), i.e.

[E] If there exist things that have the properties attributed to the putative self in any (every) genuine form of SELF-experience, then those things are selves, and if there are such things as selves, they must have the properties attributed to the self in any (every) genuine form of SELF-experience

to establish the claim

(iii) that sesmets are rightly called selves

together with its converse

(iv) selves are sesmets.

I'll try to give more body to these claims than is given merely by the Equivalence Thesis, however, and will focus more generally on the claim that

(v) sesmets are central to what we are actually thinking or talking about when we say or suppose that selves exist in everyday life

which can be accepted even by someone who rejects the Equivalence Thesis. I believe that (v) is true, although I think that most who believe in the existence of selves would reject it if they knew what I think sesmets are in the human case—short-lived things that are essentially conscious, 'thin subjects', as I will come to call them in 7.1.

I'd like to be able to get on with this straight away, but I need first to say more about the basic components of the property *sesmet*: about what it is to be a *subject of experience*, about what it is to be a *thing* or *object* (or indeed an *individual substance*), and about what *mental being* is. The last of the four central structural notions, *singleness*, is relatively unproblematic in itself, at least logically speaking, but its real-world application is not, and it too will need further discussion.

6.2 A methodological challenge

—Something's gone badly wrong. Your own terms of discussion don't allow you to take key words like 'object' and 'mental' in ways that need special explanation. Your present claim is that a self must possess the five properties *subject, thing/object, mental, single*, and *sesmet* that are adverted to by the five experience-structuring elements (SUBJECT, THING/OBJECT, MENTAL, SINGLE, and SESMET) that jointly characterize the minimal form of SELF-experience. But if metaphysics really has to defer to phenomenology in the way you say, in the case of the self, you can't suddenly start understanding any of these properties, e.g. *thing/object* or *mental*, in ways that need special philosophical explanation. On your own view, the properties that must be possessed by anything that counts as a self must be the same properties as the ones attributed by SELF-experience.

True—but the objection involves a misunderstanding. It appears to assume that we can give a precise account of the way in which things like objecthood, mentality, and subjecthood are figured in any genuine form of SELF-experience. But this isn't so. They're certainly not figured in any precise express manner in human SELF-experience (which is, for one thing, found in the very young). The question one faces, when moving from (cognitive) phenomenology to metaphysics, is not—to take objecthood as an example—'Is there something that exactly fits the very precise condition on selfhood that is set by the cognitive experience-structuring element or thought-element THING/OBJECT?'; for there is no such precise condition. The phenomenological fact one starts from, the cognitive-experiential fact that the self presents in SELF-experience as having features centrally characteristic of being a thing or object of some kind,[4] is certainly solid in some way, get-at-able, but it isn't susceptible of precise and exhaustive specification. The metaphysical or ontological question one faces, when faced with a portion of reality that is a candidate for being a self, is rather—and more vaguely—this:

Is this portion of reality correctly said to be a thing or object of some kind (in which case it fits the fundamental profile of the admittedly unsharp experience-structuring element THING or OBJECT)?

So too for the other experience-structuring elements and their corresponding properties. In the case of the question

Does this portion of reality fit the fundamental profile of the experience-structuring element SINGLE, and in particular the experience-structuring element SINGLE-AS-MENTAL?,

something may be acknowledged to fit the profile, and so be a candidate for being a self, even it is a much shorter-lived thing than any creature can naturally figure itself as being in having SELF-experience. Something in us can qualify as a candidate for being a self, in fitting SINGLE, even if we're very wrong in our natural picture of the duration of selves. This is how the phenomenology and the metaphysics of the self relate, on the present terms of discussion, and this is why I need to do preparatory work on the properties *subject, mental, object,* and *single.*

I'll begin with *subject.* What I say about it may seem overcomplicated, at least at first, and far from what most concerns us when we think about the self, but it is, I think, of central importance.

6.3 *Subject*

Do subjects of experience exist? Of course. Human beings are subjects of experience. So are dogs, dolphins, deer—and dung beetles, for all I know. There are hundreds of billions of subjects of experience on this planet, even when panpsychism has been put aside.

Does anyone disagree? Derek Parfit may be thought to disagree, even though he claims that we say something straightforwardly true, given the nature of our language, when we say that we and other animals are subjects of experience. For although he holds that the conventions governing our language have the consequence that 'subjects

---

[4] The fact that 'the self has a particular character, that of an entity' (Nozick 1989: 148) or 'thinking active principle' (Berkeley 1713: 116); the fact that in apprehending himself as the conscious *I* 'everyone must necessarily regard himself as a substance' (Kant, A349), i.e. as a thing or object in the present terms.

of experience exist' counts as a truth in our language, he claims that experiencing beings may have as good an understanding of themselves as we do even if they entirely lack the concept of a subject of experience and have what he calls an 'impersonal conceptual scheme' (1998: 221, 230). In this case, he says, their impersonal conceptual scheme may be in no way worse, metaphysically or scientifically, than ours. But if their conceptual scheme and their understanding of themselves is in no way worse, metaphysically, than ours, then there can't be any ultimate metaphysical truth registered by us that can't be registered by them. And if this is so, it seems that 'subjects of experience exist' can't be an ultimate metaphysical truth, for it isn't and can't be registered in their scheme. But to say this is presumably to claim that subjects of experience don't really or ultimately exist, even though it is a 'conventional' truth in our language that they do.

Many Buddhists distinguish in the same way between 'conventional' and 'ultimate' truth,[5] and although they don't in fact deny the existence of short-lived subjects of experience, as opposed to persisting selves or persons, the idea that there is some deep sense in which there are no such things as subjects of experience is, in various forms, a view that has a long history. I will now argue that it is demonstrably false.

Frege observes that 'an experience is impossible without an experiencer' (1918: 27). Shoemaker writes that it's 'an obvious conceptual truth that an experiencing is necessarily an experiencing by a subject of experience, and involves that subject as intimately as a branch-bending involves a branch' (1986: 10). Both make the point in a sentence. I'll spread it out a little, drawing on previous work (G. Strawson 1994: 5.10). I'll use the plural-accepting, count-noun form of the word 'experience' to talk about experiences as things (events) that have non-experiential being as well as experiential being,[6] and I'll reserve the phrase 'experiential phenomena', and the plural-lacking, mass-term form of the noun 'experience', to talk specifically and only about the phenomenon of the qualitative character that experiences have for those who have them as they have them, where this qualitative character is considered wholly independently of everything else. This phenomenon of experience, of *experiential qualitative character*, of experiential 'what-it's-like-ness', is part of what exists—it's part of reality, whatever its ontological category—and it's valuable to have some unequivocal way of referring to it and only to it.

—What exactly do you mean by 'experience'?

Standard examples will do—pain, the experience of seeing the colour blue, tasting bananas, finding something funny. Perhaps the best way to convey what it is to be a realist about experience, i.e. a real realist about experience, to philosophers who disingenuously claim not to know, is to say that it's to take experience—colour experience, pain experience, sound experience, whatever—to be what one took it to

---

[5] Parfit's employment of the notion of conventional truth is close to the Buddhist notion as employed, for example, by the *mādhyamika* Buddhists (see Harvey 1990: 98–9).

[6] I continue to put aside my pure panpsychist leanings and to assume that all physical phenomena have non-experiential being in addition to any experiential being they may have.

be (knew it to be) before one did any philosophy. However many new and surprising facts real realists learn about experience from scientists,[7] their fundamental general understanding of what colour (pain, sound, etc.) experience is remains the same as it was before they did any philosophy. In other words, their fundamental general understanding of what it is remains correct.

—How can we know that it exists?

Because the having is the knowing—a point I'll return to in 6.7.

Given these terms, one can distinguish three modes of characterization of the part of reality that concerns us when we're concerned with the existence of mental phenomena. Mode 1 is the *experiential mental* mode of characterization [+E +M]. In this mode we designate and describe experiential phenomena as just defined. I'll call it the *experiential* mode for short, because 'mental' is redundant ([E → M]).

Mode 2 is the *non-experiential mental* mode of characterization [−E +M]. In this mode we designate and describe things that are standardly held to be mental phenomena although they aren't experiential phenomena, using fully mentalistic terms to talk of unconscious (sub-experiential) computational processes or dispositions like beliefs, preferences, character traits, and so on. This mode hardly concerns me here; I mention it for the sake of completeness.

Mode 3 is the *non-experiential non-mental* mode of characterization [−E −M]. In this mode we designate and describe non-experiential, non-mental aspects of that part of reality that concerns us when we're generally concerned with the existence of mental phenomena, e.g. things in the external environment, and the non-experiential being of the brain in so far as it is correctly characterizable by current physics and neurophysiology.

The qualification 'in so far as' is important, for when aspiring materialists discuss the (living) brain, they often slip into supposing that the word 'brain' somehow refers only to the brain non-mentally and non-experientially considered (the brain-as-revealed-by-current-physics-and-neurophysiology), and this is a mistake that can breed other mistakes. It's a mistake because the word 'brain', used to refer to the brain, duly refers to the brain, the living brain considered as a whole, the brain in its total physical existence. And to be a real materialist, a genuine, realistic materialist (5, 283), is to hold that experiential phenomena considered just as such are part of this total physical existence. (The qualification 'considered just as such' is redundant, given the definition of 'experiential phenomena', but I will sometimes include it.) It's to hold that the brain of an ordinary living person is literally constituted, if only in part, by experiential phenomena, in every sense in which it is constituted, in part, by non-experiential phenomena characterizable by physics. It's not as if there's anything still left to say about experiential phenomena once you have said everything there is to say about the physical nature of the brain. You can't think this if you are a real—realistic—materialist

---

[7] Facts about the 'filling-in' that characterizes visual experience, for example, or about 'change blindness' or 'inattentional blindness' (see e.g. Pessoa and de Weerd 2003; Simons and Levin 1997; Chun and Marois 2002).

(see further 6.6–6.9). There is, however, a vast amount left to say about the living experienceful brain once you've said everything that can be said about it using only the terms of physics and neurophysiology. For in that case you've given no descriptive characterization of the experiential being of the brain. There may be no part of the brain to which you have not referred, but there are vast numbers of truths about what its existence consists in which you haven't recorded at all, although they are, according to real materialism, truths about its physical being. (Present-day 'a posteriori physicalists' need to misconstrue this paragraph to maintain their position; I will try to block the misconstrual later.)

So much for the three modes of characterization. Consider, in the framework they provide, Louis's experience *e*: his current experience of looking at St Paul's Cathedral across the River Thames, from the Globe Theatre on the South Bank. If one wants to give a full account of the being of *e*, one must mention many things. One must mention those of *e*'s causes that need to be cited in a full account of its intentional content (St Paul's Cathedral and the River Thames, for example), and any aspects of the brain activity that constitutes the being of *e* that are correctly and sufficiently characterizable in non-mental, non-experiential terms (e.g. the terms of physics and neurophysiology). At this stage one is in mode 3, the non-experiential non-mental mode of description.

Moving to mode 1, the experiential mode, one drops reference to St Paul's and the Thames, to the non-experiential non-mental being of neurons and their activity, and so on. One strips one's account of *e* of any reference to anything that is (a) constitutive of *e*'s existence and (b) non-experiential. One does this in order to focus on one particular and indubitably real aspect of the being of *e*: its experiential being.

Is such exclusive focusing really possible, or legitimate? Is it possible for materialists who take it, as I do, that experience is entirely a matter of brain activity, and who take it, further, that all brain activity has non-experiential being (a point I am assuming for now)? Certainly, for it does not follow, from the fact (if it is a fact) that all experiences have non-experiential being, that we cannot consider experience in isolation, or just as such. We can. We can consider the reality of experience quite independently of the reality of the non-experiential or non-mental causes or being of experiences, restricting ourselves entirely to the experiential mode of characterization of reality.

The claim for consideration, then, is that we're bound to acknowledge the existence of the subject of experience, when considering an experience, and that we're bound to do so even when we restrict ourselves entirely to mode 1, the experiential mode of characterization of reality. An experience is impossible without an experiencer. Many besides Frege have made the point, and many have taken it to be too obvious to mention. I'll call it the Subject Thesis: there can't be experience without a subject of experience, because (this is the whole argument) experience is necessarily experience-*for*: it is necessarily experience for someone or something—an experiencer or subject of experience. Experience necessarily involves experiential 'what-it-is-likeness' and experiential what-it-is-likeness is necessarily what-it-is-likeness *for* someone or something.

Whatever the nature of this experiencing something, its real existence cannot be denied. This Cartesian point (140) is secure even if individual-substance-suggesting noun phrases like 'an experiencer' or 'a subject of experience' are somehow misleading. It's secure whatever one's uncertainty about whether or not it's right or acceptable to call the subject of experience a thing or an object or a substance.

—But what *is* a subject of experience?

The first reply is the same as in 2.15 (63–4): you have a wholly sufficient grasp of what is essential to being a subject of experience just in being one and being self-conscious. This is so whatever the best account of the ontological category of subjects of experience, and however much subjects of experience may differ from each other. It's a key part of the present point that there's a fundamental respect in which this is all I need to (should) say.

Many agree that if an experience occurs, there must be someone or something whose experience it is. They say that there must be a 'physical' thing, by which they mean a non-mental thing, on the present terms (25n, 277), or an indissolubly 'psychophysical' thing, by which they mean an indissolubly both-mental-and-non-mental thing, on the present terms, that is the subject of experience—whether we're concerned with a man or a mouse. The truth of the Subject Thesis, however, is strictly prior to, and wholly independent of, any such claims. It follows immediately from the notion of experience—the fact that experience is essentially experience-*for*. It doesn't depend on a commitment to materialism, or even (more generally) to the view that mental or experiential goings-on must have some non-mental or non-experiential being or other. The truth of the Subject Thesis can be established even when one restricts oneself rigorously to mode 1, and before one makes any kind of reference to, or assumption of, the existence of, non-experiential being.

Consider *e* again—Louis's experience of St Paul's Cathedral. As a conventional materialist, one takes it that *e* has non-experiential and non-mental being, but one can, as remarked, consider its reality while restricting oneself to consideration of its experiential being. One can take this alone as a legitimate object of thought. I'll mark this here by saying that one can restrict oneself to e_e.

One can then ask the following question: Given that e_e exists, what else *must* exist? Call anything non-experiential that must exist if e_e exists 'N'. Some radical mentalists hold that 'N' denotes nothing. They're 'pure experientialists'. Other mentalists hold that 'N' denotes certain immaterial and wholly mental but at least partly non-experiential phenomena. Some immaterialists hold that 'N' denotes certain wholly immaterial but partly non-mental phenomena.[8] Conventional materialists, of course, hold that 'N' denotes various physical non-experiential things or processes. And so on.

Many philosophers will be inclined to refer to their favoured candidate for N—the soul, the body, the brain, a part of the brain—when answering the question of what

---

[8] The supposed difference between these groups is as clear (and as unclear) as the term 'mental'. For a discussion of the differences between mentalists, idealists, and immaterialists see G. Strawson 1994: ch. 5.

the subject of experience is.[9] The Subject Thesis, however, bypasses all these proposed metaphysical differences. It points out that one has to grant that the subject must exist, given that e exists, even when one considers only e_e, and before one has made any other assumptions of any sort about the nature of reality. I take it as a materialist that the existence of e consists in, is literally identical with, the existence of a complex group of neurons in a certain complex state of interaction, a certain sort of *synergy*, as I will say (this claim isn't 'reductive' or experience-denying in any way, given real materialism). I take it, accordingly, that the minimal hypothesis about the existence of the subject that is known to exist given that e exists is that it is literally identical with a part of this synergy, or perhaps the whole of it. In the normal course of things the existence of this synergy depends on the existence of many other physical things, but these other things are not part of what it is. One can put the point by saying that God could conceivably create a synergy of just this sort without creating anything else, and would in so doing create an experience of the same type as e, and also, of course, and necessarily, a subject of experience.

I'll call the subject that can be known to exist given that e exists, and can be known to exist even when one considers e only in its experiential being (e_e), the *synergy subject*. The synergy subject consists of a synergy of neural activity which is either a part of or (somehow) identical with the synergy that constitutes the experience as a whole. Obviously one can't know it to be a physical synergy in knowing it to exist. I'm assuming that it is, in assuming that materialism is true.

—Look, mice presumably have experience, and we're not bound to say that there is anything as grand as a Subject of Experience in their case. A mouse considered as an integral mental-and-non-mental whole may perfectly well be called a subject of experience, but when we give an account of what must exist if a particular mouse experience $e(m)$ exists *while restricting ourselves to the experiential*, and considering only $e_e(m)$, we don't have to talk of a subject of experience at all. And we shouldn't. When we limit ourselves to the experiential, we need and should speak only of experience, or of experiential content. That's all there is to be found, so far as the experiential is concerned, in the case of the mouse. And it doesn't by itself give us grounds for asserting the existence of anything else at all—such as a Subject of Experience.

Yes it does. Let e stand for any individual experience. Even when all one has assumed to exist is e_e, i.e. that which is given when we consider e just in respect of its experiential being, and so without regard to any other being that it may or may not have, one can already know that it involves a subject of experience, simply because experience is essentially experience-*for*. One way to put this, perhaps, is to say that one can already know that what exists given that e_e exists is *complex* in a certain respect. e_e may be complex in virtue of its content; it may be experience as of seeing a complicated array of different colours. But even if it isn't—even if e_e is a wholly uniform and simple experience just of green, or of a pure note[10]—it seems that one is already in

---

[9] 'Content externalists', believers in 'object-dependent modes of presentation', and so on, may include more than the subject of experience—e.g. St Paul's—in their account of N. This shows a misunderstanding of e_e.

[10] I put aside points about brightness/saturation/hue and pitch/timbre/loudness complexity.

a position to assert that what exists, given that e_e exists, is and must be complex in a certain respect. For e_e can't possibly exist without the polarity of experiencer and experiential content, the polarity of subject and content. Where there is experiential content, there is (once again) necessarily experienc*ing*, and where there is experiencing there is necessarily—trivially—an experienc*er*, a subject of experience. To see the sense in which this is trivially true is to understand the present and fundamental use of the term 'subject of experience'.

Some think that Buddhist meditation, or indeed any remotely successful practice of meditation, religious or not, shows the individual-substance-suggesting noun 'subject' to be irredeemably ontologically excessive. They suggest replacing it by the word 'subjectivity', in spite of assurances that the Subject Thesis, in good *Second Meditation* style (140), makes no claims whatever about the ultimate substantial nature of the subject, and certainly doesn't claim that the subject can be known to be something ontologically distinct from e, or indeed e_e. There's no good reason to accept their suggestion, however, because the force of the word 'subject' in its present use, given the Cartesian *Second Meditation* disclaimer, is such that the existence of subjectivity *entails* the existence of a subject (certainly the notion of a subject carries no implication of persistence). So I'm not prepared to allow the replacement of 'subject' by 'subjectivity' in the Subject Thesis unless it's allowed in return that 'subject' can also be correctly used. In so far as this disagreement takes place between those who have a proper grasp of what's involved in the existence of subjectivity, it's simply a matter of terminology, and the heart of the present claim remains untouched: e (or indeed e_e) must still involve *some* sort of irreducible complexity or polarity in involving the phenomenon of subjectivity, on the one hand, and the phenomenon of content, on the other.

Well, perhaps the claim about irreducible polarity is not entirely untouched. Perhaps it doesn't seem quite so luminously evident after the substitution of 'subjectivity' for 'subject' has been allowed. And perhaps this is a good thing. I think it is, and will develop the point in Parts 7 and 8. For the moment it's enough to note that to say that any experience comports some sort of irreducible experiential-content/experiencing-subject *polarity*, and that this can be known to be so even when one restricts oneself to e_e, is not yet to say that one can prove irreducible, full-on ontic *plurality* from the mere existence of e_e. More needs to be said before one can claim to know that the apparently irreducible experiential-content/experiencing-subject polarity of e, and indeed e_e, entails fundamental ontic plurality.

The issue is difficult—it includes, for one thing, ancient problems raised by the distinction between object and property, which I'll consider in 6.15. It may be that one can't in the end prove irreducible ontic plurality, and must in fact give it up. The fact remains that an experience is impossible without an experiencer, and that we can know that this is so even when we restrict attention to e_e.

—I don't know what you mean by 'full-on ontological plurality', and this is all wrong in any case. Experiential *content* (in the key internalist sense—38) is all that can be truly discerned when one is restricted to mode 1, the experiential mode of characterization, and hence to e_e. The subject of experience cannot be discerned. This is what Hume took such pains to show.

Hume did no such thing! But I'll put his views aside.[11] The first point to make in reply is that even it were true that experiential content is all that can be *discerned* when one is restricted to mode 1 and so to e_e, and that nothing of the subject can be discerned, it would still be true that the subject can be known to *exist* if e_e is known to exist. For the same old reason: if there is an experience of pain, say (anything will do), an experienc-ing of pain, a feel-ing of pain (here 'feeling' is a participle, like 'experiencing') then there must be something, however unknown its nature in any further respect, and whatever its ultimate ontological category, that feels—suffers—the pain. There can't be just experiential content, if to say this is in any way to suggest that there is not also an experienc*ing*, and hence, necessarily, a subject of experience. We must discern at least this much structure in the world if it contains an experience. This is the Subject Thesis (never questioned by Hume). It is, once again, completely independent of any particular theoretical opinion about the ontological category of subjects of experience. You don't need to have any such theoretical ontological-categorial opinion in order to understand it, because you have a very good grasp of what is fundamental to being a subject of experience just in being one and in being self-conscious, as remarked in 2.15, a grasp which allows you (contrary to certain Wittgensteinian opinions) to entertain the idea that there may be subjects of experience that are extraordinarily unlike you. The Subject Thesis doesn't depend on the traditional idea that an experience, being a *process* or *event*, necessarily requires some sort of *substance* that is in some way distinct from it, in which it can go on or occur. It's completely independent of any such (superficial) idea. It holds good even on the view that there's nothing but process, 'pure process', indeed pure mental process, in the universe. The fact that one can know that the subject of experience exists even when one restricts oneself strictly to the experiential being of experiences, and doesn't speculate in any way about their non-experiential or non-mental being, is a direct consequence of the necessary 'for-someone-ness' of experience—the necessary 'for-someone-or-something-ness', if you like. That, I think, is all there is to say (it's not the case that the grammatical substantivity of 'something', in the above claim that 'there must be something … that feels—suffers—the pain' contains a step beyond what is metaphysically certain). This won't be enough to strip the view that there could be experience without an experiencer of the excitement it will always carry for some; but I don't think anything can do that.

Suppose we allow that the necessary for-someone-or-something-ness of an experience e isn't any part of the *content* of e—that it isn't something that is necessarily apprehended in some manner by the being whose experience e is, when e occurs. And suppose we also allow that representation of the subject of experience of e isn't part of the experiential content of e.[12] The fact remains that the necessary for-someone-ness of experience

[11] See G. Strawson 2001 and in preparation, *a*.
[12] Both concessions may seem obviously correct at first, but less so on reflection; see 7.4 (346).

requires us to acknowledge the existence of the subject of experience when saying what must exist given that e exists, even when considering e just as e_e, just in its experiential being.

The present point, in other words, is a very low-level point. A subject of experience isn't something grand. It's something of such a kind that it's true to say that there must be a subject of experience wherever there is experience, even in the case of mice or spiders—simply because experience is essentially experience-*for*. One could put the point paradoxically by saying that if *per impossibile* there could be intense pain-experience without a subject of experience, mere experience without an experiencer, as some 'no-ownership' theorists have apparently held, there would be no point in stopping it, because no one would be suffering.[13]

The sense in which the present notion of a subject of experience is not something grand can be expressed in another way. If we consider a number of temporally distinct experiences that occur in a single creature, and confine ourselves to the resources of mode 1, then it doesn't seem that we have any decisive reason to claim that these experiences, or even any two of them, are the experiences of a single (hence diachronically persisting) experiencer—as Hume in effect observed. It may be that the best thing to say, all things considered, is that they are experiences of a single persisting experiencer, but mode 1 doesn't by itself supply any ground for saying this. Most of those who have wanted to insist on the reality of selves or subjects of experience, as distinct from human beings considered as a whole, have been keen to establish their long-term continuity. They've hoped to show that subjects of experience, conceived as distinct things in this way, are rightly thought of as things that persist over long stretches of time, and have many experiences. I don't think this can be shown. I think, in fact, that the best thing to say may be that each distinct experience occurring in the Louis-reality has its own experiencer, that each numerically distinct experience synergy has its own numerically distinct synergy subject (if experience synergies in the L-reality can be sharply distinguished from each other in this way—a problem for Part 8). I also suspect that there's a fundamental way of counting experiences given which they are of short duration, at least in the human case—a view prefigured in Part 5 and returned to in Part 7. The present point is simply that the claim that selves or subjects of experience have long-term continuity receives no support of any kind from the Subject Thesis as elucidated here.

This completes the case for the reality of the subject of experience. There's no sense in which its existence is a 'grammatical illusion', as some have liked to say. It's demonstrable with certainty because it follows directly from the existence of experience, and one can know with certainty that experience exists. It's incoherent to deny the existence of a subject of experience while admitting the existence of experience, even

---

[13] 'Of course there'd be a point: the universe would be a better place, other things being equal, if there were fewer pain sensations. Pains are intrinsically bad, even without owners.' Reply: pains without owners, pains without someone-or-something pained—call them 'pains*'—are pains without pain! Pains* are impossible (apart from not being intrinsically bad). 'All right, *pains* must be pains for someone-or–something, but pain is a special case; not all experience is like that.' Reply: !

if you don't like the term 'subject of experience'; and since any event that constitutes a genuine denial of the existence of experience must itself involve experience, in such a way that the denial is self-refuting, it's incoherent *tout court* to deny the existence of subjects of experience. All 'no-ownership' theses are knowably false, if indeed they assert that experiences have, or need have, no owners or subjects in the current sense.[14] Whatever things exist or do not exist, subjects of experience exist.

If someone wants to say only that subjectivity exists, so be it. As I understand the notion of a subject of experience it's a necessary truth—one that takes no further metaphysical step, involves no further metaphysical commitment—that if subjectivity exists, then a subject exists. Those who prefer to talk of subjectivity rather than subjects will have to find a way of representing the fact—if they allow it as a fact—that subjectivity comes in many discrete patches at given times—yours, mine, and hers, for example. They'll need the use of some sort of count noun to talk of experience ('subjectivities', perhaps, or episodes or patches of experience ...) unless they think there's really only one mind—the World Soul—of which we are all part, in spite of all the appearances of separateness that led William James to remark that 'the breaches between ... thoughts ... belonging to different ... minds ... are the most absolute breaches in nature' (1890: 1. 226).

So much, for the moment, for the *subject* component of the property *sesmet*. I'm now going to consider the *mental* component of *sesmet*, which will require discussion of the notion of the physical. I'll then go on to consider the *thing* or *object* component, which raises questions about unity or *singleness*, before returning again to *subject*. I'll begin somewhat obliquely by raising a question about the way we use the words 'mental', 'physical', and 'object' which seems pertinent, although its precise force—and answer—is not clear to me.

6.4 'Physical object', 'mental object'

In 6.6 I explain further why I think that materialists should use the terms 'mental' and 'non-mental' instead of the terms 'mental' and 'physical' as their key opposed terms when discussing the mind and its place in nature. It is, however, still standard to use 'mental' and 'physical' as the key opposed terms, and since I want in this section to lay out a point about how certain standard phrases strike us, I will temporarily use 'physical' in the standard way to mean 'non-mental'.[15]

The question is this: Why do we talk so freely and easily of *physical objects*, and say that they have *mental properties*, and never talk in this way of *mental objects*, and say that they have *physical properties*? We grant that there are things—e.g. human beings

---

[14] 'No owner' views of this sort don't seem to have much to do with what P. F. Strawson had in mind in *Individuals* (1959: 95–8).

[15] Some self-styled materialists seem to use 'physical' in this way even as they also use it in another incompatible way. For they want to say that the mental *just is* physical, but presumably don't want to say that the mental *just is* non-mental. It seems that they're committed to saying this, in fact, but shy away from saying it outright, causing great and unnecessary confusion.

and cats—that have both mental and physical properties, but for some reason we allow only one of the two highly general predicates 'mental' and 'physical' to qualify the word 'object' directly. We say that these things are physical objects, but not that they're mental objects.

Why? A first reply may be that the phrase 'mental object' has a special use in philosophy. It's used to mean something like: the intentional object of mental attention conceived as something that is not mind-independent (or at least not concrete). But I don't here mean anything like this. For the purposes of the present question I understand the phrase 'mental object' in a more robust way, on the model of the phrase 'physical object' as used in everyday speech. I don't mean anything like an intentional object of mental attention conceived as some sort of non-mind-independent or ontologically abstract mental-content object. I mean a thing that exists, like any cat or chair, whether or not it's the object of anyone's attention, and my perhaps foolish-seeming question is this: Does the phrase 'physical object' as applied in everyday speech to a thing like a human being that has both mental properties and physical properties, and that exists whether or not it is the object of anyone's attention, have some legitimacy that the phrase 'mental object' lacks when it is used in the same way of the same thing?

We certainly seem to think so, but why? Perhaps it has something to do with the fact that we believe that there are billions of things that have physical properties and no mental properties (stones, etc.), and billions of things that have both mental and physical properties (dogs, humans, etc.), but no things at all that have mental properties and no physical properties. Perhaps this fact inclines us to attribute priority to physical properties in such a way that we feel that it is correct to say that objects that have both mental and physical properties are physical objects, and incorrect to say that they're mental objects.

It's not clear that it has much relevance, however. And even if it does help to explain what we do, it certainly doesn't justify it. It doesn't show that it's correct to say that an object that has both mental and physical properties is a physical object, and incorrect to say that it is a mental object. It's arguable that anyone who sympathizes with P. F. Strawson's suggestion (1959: ch. 3) that we should acknowledge the 'primitiveness' of our concept of a person should deny that one can apply the description 'physical object' to a human being in any sense or context in which we cannot also apply the description 'mental object'.[16]

This seems entirely implausible, but why? Perhaps the point is this. When we consider human beings in general, we figure them as single objects, both perceptually and imaginatively, primarily in so far as they are visibly and tangibly extended things.

---

[16] Note that one can repeat the question for a self, materialistically understood as here. Does 'physical object' have some legitimacy, applied to a self that has both mental properties and physical properties and exists whether or not it is the object of anyone's attention, that 'mental object' lacks? (In this case I'm happy to give up the qualification 'exists whether or not it is the object of anyone's attention', in deference to the Fichtean, Nozickian conception of the self (see e.g. p. 350). The qualification 'not a mere mental-content object' covers the case, because Fichte and Nozick don't think that the self is a mere mental-content object.)

Perhaps this is the reason why we naturally say that human beings are physical objects while denying that they are mental objects. The relative primacy or salience of the physical property of extension is naturally reflected in our language.

This may help to explain what we do, but—again—doesn't justify it. And even if it's true of how others strike us, of how we figure others, it doesn't follow that it's true of how we strike or figure ourselves. Ordinary language use reflects the public perspective on things, and gives primacy to the publicly observable physical features of things, but it hardly follows that private thought does, or that sound metaphysics must. It's true that physical properties are what we primarily rely on for the purpose of identifying and reidentifying human beings and many other things, but this too gives no support to the metaphysical claim that one has sufficient grounds for calling Louis an object when considering him merely in his 'physical' (i.e. non-mental) being, and does not have sufficient grounds for calling him a mental object when considering him merely in his mental being. It may sound very queer to call Louis a mental object, and I don't want to do so. I don't think it serves any useful purpose. But that is no reason to think that it's not just as accurate—as true—to think of him as an object when considering his mental being as it is to think of him as an object when considering his physical (i.e. non-mental) being.

—The point is that one's physical properties like one's shape and size are permanently possessed while one's mental properties come and go.

There's no significant asymmetry here. One's dispositional mental properties—beliefs, memories, pro-attitudes, and character traits—are effectively as stable and persistent as one's physical properties, and there's no conclusive evidence that (occurrent) mental activity ever ceases, even in what we think of as dreamless sleep. There isn't even any conclusive evidence that *conscious* mental activity ever ceases, even in what we take to be dreamless sleep. It's true that one's conscious thoughts and experiences are constantly and sometimes tumultuously changing, but so are one's physical states, properties, and dispositions, even when one is in bed asleep. One's blood is circulating, one's digestive system is on active service, one is shifting and breathing, one's electrochemistry is indefatigably at work, one's cells are leading dramatic lives, every atom in one's body is a strictly temporary resident—about 1,000,000,000,000,000 of them are replaced every second[17]—and each of them is in internal uproar. There's no interesting sense in which one retains a stable overall bodily existence in which one does not equally maintain a stable overall mental existence.[18]

—Physical properties are more fundamental than mental properties, because dogs and human beings lose all mental properties when they die, but retain many physical properties.

---

[17] i.e. a trillion every millionth of a second; see Greene 2004: 441 (half of the atoms that constitute one's liver on Sunday are gone by Friday).

[18] When Odysseus came home after twenty years away, his nurse Eurykleia relied on his physical properties (a scar on his thigh) to identify him, while his wife Penelope relied on his mental properties (his memory of how he had built their marriage bed). His old dog, though, was the first to recognize him, reacting as much to his mental presence, perhaps—his psychological signature in the air—as his smell.

Why should this make the difference? How does it show that it's right to say that living human beings are physical objects in some way in which it's wrong to say that they're mental objects? It certainly doesn't show that it's right to classify living human beings as objects under the heading 'non-mental' in some way in which it is wrong to classify them as objects under the heading 'mental'.

—On your own account of materialism, all parts of Louis have physical (non-mental) being, while it's not true that all parts of Louis have mental being. This is why it's correct or legitimate to say that Louis is a physical object in a way in which it's not correct or legitimate to say that he's a mental object. He is everywhere physical in a way in which he is not everywhere mental.

It may be that all the fundamental particles that constitute Louis do have mental being, but even when we put aside this panpsychist idea it's still not clear that this justifies us in classifying Louis as an object under the description 'physical' and not under the description 'mental'.

It still seems overwhelmingly natural to classify him as a physical object, though, and not as something that can be thought of as an object when merely mentally considered. If one tries to clear one's thoughts and adopt a completely neutral stance on the question, a vivid sensory image of Louis and his physical bodily unity is likely to push to the front of one's mind as decisive. It seems that this is built deep into our feelings about the word 'object', justifiably or not: 'Louis is a physically propertied object', the intellect seems to say, 'and he is equally a mentally propertied object. But he is also a physical object and he is not equally a mental object. That's just how it is.'

Imagine, though, that there are creatures that can sense a conspecific's mental presence directly (the other's awareness may feature as a kind of babbling thread of content on the periphery of attention that they can focus on if they wished, or just as a palpable mental force field whose contents are hidden). Imagine, further, that they have no means of sensing the other's physical features directly, although they can sense their own physical features directly. These creatures may be as happy (or more happy) to say that others—and they themselves—are mental things as they are to say that they are physical things. It may be, then, that our bias towards coupling 'object' with 'physical' and not with 'mental' reflects a contingent feature of our exteroceptive equipment. ...

I'm going to leave this line of thought dangling and return to the main argument. I have no particular wish to be able to say that living human beings are mental objects. I do think, though, that the general notion of a mental object understood in the robust sense (a thing that exists, like a cat, whether or not it's the object of anyone's attention) is an entirely legitimate notion for materialists, and I'm already committed to the view that selves, if they exist, must qualify as mental objects robustly understood. It's obvious that SELF-experience must involve MENTAL, a figuring of the self as mentally propertied or as having mental being, and I've also argued that SELF-experience must involve THING-as-MENTAL—it must involve figuring the self as a thing or object of some sort even when considering it merely in its mental being (171). I take it that it follows (given the Equivalence Thesis in 2.12, according to which cognitive-phenomenological analysis of the nature of SELF-experience reveals what selves must be like if they are to exist) that any acceptable positive account of what selves are must deliver a robust sense in which they are indeed mental entities of some sort and are indeed mental things, objects.

This claim still sounds very problematic, given the present terminological climate, not to mention my assumption that materialism is true. It's far from clear what it amounts to. The properties *mental* and *object* both need more discussion. I am, however, going to argue for the claim independently of the Equivalence Thesis, beginning in 6.12. I'll end with a reminder of a point made in 4.8. Suppose we judge that something *x* qualifies as a *unity* in such a way as to qualify as an *object*. Suppose, further, that we judge that it so qualifies mentally considered, and that it so qualifies only mentally considered. Two things are then important. The first is that it certainly doesn't follow that *x* doesn't qualify physically considered, for to qualify mentally considered is to qualify physically considered, for the mental is physical; all that follows is that it doesn't qualify non-mentally considered. The second point is that to say that it doesn't qualify non-mentally considered is certainly not to say that it is correctly judged not to be an object when non-mentally considered. That can't be true, for if there is any way of considering *x* given which it is correctly judged to be an object, then there can't be any way of considering it given which it is correctly judged not to be an object, even if there are ways of considering that do not yield an answer to the question whether or not it is an object.

6.5 *Mental*

The core of our ordinary conception of the mental lies open to view in a list of standard examples, as remarked in 2.17: conscious experience, sensation, emotion; belief, memory, preferences, character traits, moods, hopes, anxieties; activities like thinking, dreaming, calculating, appraising, and inferring. The use and force of the word 'mental' is fiercely disputed in philosophy, however, and more needs to be said. This list, central and important though it is, can't settle the question of how the word 'mental' is supposed to function in science or philosophy. Clarity about the core applications of a concept doesn't determine its borders, and facts about ordinary usage don't settle issues about best or correct usage in philosophical contexts. This is especially so given the assumption that materialism is true, for the first problem with ordinary usage, including ordinary philosophical usage, is that it opposes the mental and the physical in a way that can't possibly be right if materialism is true. This needs explanation. I need to say something more about materialism, and in particular about how the mental is to be conceived in a materialist framework. As before, I take 'materialism' and 'physicalism' to be equivalent in meaning, and use the former.[19]

---

[19] The next section summarizes parts of G. Strawson 2003*b* and 2006*a*, which developed from G. Strawson 1994: 43–104.

6.6 Materialism

The basic function of the word 'materialism' in the philosophy of mind is to name one view among others about the nature of the mental, the view that

(1) everything mental that exists is physical.

Plainly (1) allows for the possibility that there may be non-physical existents. Taken more widely, 'materialism' names the view that

(2) everything concrete that exists is physical.

Some endorse (2) while rejecting *concretism*, the view that

(3) everything that exists is concrete.

They allow that there are or may be non-concrete or ontologically 'abstract' existents (e.g. numbers and propositions) in addition to concrete existents.

In its common strong meaning, however, materialism combines (2) with (3), and is, accordingly, the view that

(4) everything that exists is physical.

I favour (4), which I take to be compatible with the view that there are truths that are not made true by any physical phenomena (mathematical truths, for example, or truths about good and bad), but will make do, here, with (2).[20]

I incline, in fact, to a *panpsychist* form of materialism, which supplements (4) with

(5) everything that exists has experiential/mental being (whether or not it also has non-experiential/non-mental being).

(4) + (5) goes beyond what most people are prepared to call 'materialism', but this restriction is hard to justify.

I'm also intrigued by *pure panpsychism*, which supplements (4) with

(6) everything that exists is experiential/mental.

On this view, nothing has any non-experiential/non-mental being at all, absolutely speaking, although one portion of experiential being may appear or function as non-experiential relative to or from the perspective of another.[21]

(6) seems a particularly difficult view. There is perhaps no great difficulty in agreeing with Russell and Eddington that it is, properly understood, wholly compatible with present-day physics, and with (4), but it seems irresponsible, to say the least, to continue to call it a materialist view, even though it's just a view about what the physical turns out to be (about what 'physical', 'the ultimate natural-kind term', turns out to denote).[22]

---

[20] All four views can be strengthened by replacing 'everything that exists in this universe' with 'everything that exists or could exist in this universe'; see McLaughlin 2002: 146.

[21] See e.g. G. Strawson 2006b: 256–62. Genuinely naturalistic materialists will feel pressure to accept that pure panpsychism is the best supported view, given that experience is the most certainly known natural fact (anyone who thinks that the spatiotemporality of the physical is incompatible with experience's being physical will be forced to agree that the spatiotemporality of the physical is a mere appearance).

[22] G. Strawson 1994: 1. In G. Strawson 2003b and 2006a I discuss the sense in which 'the physical' becomes a term that simply denotes *the concrete real whatever its nature*. In 2006b (228) I mark the point at which I think someone who holds views like mine does best to abandon the words 'physical' and 'material'.

With this in mind, I think it may be better to reject the law of non-contradiction and replace (6), offered as a version of materialism, with the Spinozan-sounding view that

(7) everything that exists is wholly experiential/mental and wholly non-experiential/non-mental,

taking this in an outright ontological way, and not just as a characterization of two ways of conceiving or experiencing something.

This, I suspect, is the true form of materialism. I am nevertheless going to work with a more conventional form, a version of (2) which I'm about to expound in more detail. It doesn't make much sense to take any of (5)–(7) to be materialist views, given present-day terminological sensibilities, but sensibilities have changed before, and may change again. Certainly the pure panpsychist use of the word 'physical' didn't bother Eddington and Russell. McGinn objects that they were 'in flagrant violation of common usage' (2006: 91), but there were very good reasons why they put things in the way they did: they were advancing theses about the intrinsic nature of the phenomena studied by physics.

Materialists, then, hold (2) that every real, concrete phenomenon in this universe is physical.[23] And if they're even remotely realistic, they admit that all *experiential* phenomena (consciousness phenomena, 'what-it's-like-ness' phenomena), considered just as such, are real, concrete phenomena. It follows that they must grant that experiential phenomena, considered just as such, are wholly physical phenomena. They must grant that experiential or what-it's-like-ness phenomena, considered just as such, are as much physical phenomena as the phenomenon of electric current flowing in a wire.

It follows that they express themselves very badly when they talk about the mental and the physical as if they were opposed categories. For this, on their own view, is exactly like saying that cows and animals are opposed categories. For all mental phenomena, including experiential phenomena considered specifically as such, just are physical phenomena, according to them; just as all cows are animals.

So what are materialists doing when they talk, as they so often do, as if the mental and the physical are different? What they presumably mean to do (if they are even remotely realistic) is to distinguish, within the realm of the physical, which is the only realm there is according to them, between the mental and the non-mental, or, more specifically, between the experiential and the non-experiential; to distinguish, that is, between mental (or experiential) aspects of the physical and non-mental (or non-experiential) aspects of the physical.[24] It's this difference that is really in question when it comes to the so-called mind–body problem. Materialists who persist in talking in terms of the difference between the mental and the physical perpetuate the terms of the dualism

---

[23] I use 'phenomenon' as a completely general word for any kind of existent which carries no implication about the existent's ontological category.

[24] All experiential phenomena are mental, but not all mental phenomena are experiential, on the standard view of the mental: dispositional states, for example—beliefs, preferences, and so on—are standardly held to be wholly mental phenomena, although they have no experiential character.

they reject in a way that is flatly inconsistent with their own view. That's why I use the words 'mental' and 'non-mental' and 'experiential' and 'non-experiential' where many use the words 'mental' and 'physical'. I assume in accordance with materialism that every concrete thing and event is physical, and have no choice. (There is still at the time of writing tremendous resistance to abandoning the old mental/physical terminology in favour of the mental/non-mental, experiential/non-experiential terminology, although the latter seems to be exactly what is required.)

Let me rephrase this. When I say that the mental, and in particular the experiential, is physical, and endorse the view that 'experience is really just neurons firing', I mean something completely different from what some materialists have apparently meant by saying such things. I don't mean that all aspects of what is going on in the case of conscious experience can be described by current physics, or even by any non-revolutionary extension of current physics. Such a view amounts to some kind of radical 'eliminativism' with respect to consciousness and is certainly false. It's not a realistic form of materialism at all. My claim is quite different. It is that the experiential considered specifically as such—i.e. the part or portion of reality we have to do with when we consider experiences specifically and solely in respect of the experiential character they have for those who have them as they have them—just is physical. No one who disagrees with this claim is a serious or remotely realistic materialist. One might put the point by saying that real materialism is not reductive but *adductive*. It doesn't claim that experience is anything less than we ordinarily conceive it to be, but that matter is more than we ordinarily conceive it to be.

Thoroughgoing materialists, then, hold that all mental phenomena, including all experiential phenomena, are entirely physical phenomena. But experiential phenomena—together with the subject of experience, assuming that that is something extra—are the only real, concrete phenomena that we can know with certainty to exist. As it stands, then, my terminology leaves open the possibility that a theory according to which mental phenomena are the only real phenomena and have no non-mental being could count as a version of materialism. It would, however, be eccentric to call this materialism. 'The truth about physical objects *must* be strange', as Russell said (1912: 19), but it's reasonable, in the present terminological climate, to take 'materialism' to be the name of a position that is committed to the existence of non-mental, non-experiential being in the universe, in addition to mental experiential being, and in this book I will continue to do so.

It's also reasonable to take materialism to involve the claim that *every* thing or event in the universe essentially has non-mental, non-experiential being, whether or not it also has mental, experiential being. Applied to mental goings-on, then, materialism claims that each particular mental going-on has non-mental being, in addition to mental being. Applied more particularly to experiential goings-on, it claims that each particular experiential going-on has non-experiential being, in addition to experiential being. I say 'going-on', rather than 'phenomenon', because I've defined 'experiential phenomenon' in such a way that it does not refer to anything non-experiential. (A difficulty lurks here for any reasonable definition of materialism that purports to be real materialism, but this is not the place for it.)

To distinguish between mental being and non-mental being is not to claim to know how to draw a sharp line between them. The situation is simply this: we know that there is mental being, if only because we know that there is experiential being, and we assume, as materialists, that this is not all there is. Commitment to materialism of this sort is simply the product of (a) commitment to monism and (b) acceptance of the view that there is non-mental (non-experiential) being, since (c) the existence of mental (in particular, experiential) being is certain. It is, in other terms, an expression of the belief that pure panpsychism is not true—that the seeming existence of non-mental (non-experiential) being is not just a matter of the way one form of mental (experiential) being—which certainly exists—affects another.

The question is then this: How should materialists conceive the relation between the mental and the non-mental; or, more narrowly, between the experiential and the non-experiential? This question—'the mind–body problem'—faces everyone who believes that there is both mental and non-mental being, so it faces nearly all philosophers. My present concern with it is limited to its relevance to the question of the existence of the self; but it may have considerable repercussions. At the end of 6.4 I proposed that there may be no more reason to think that there are physical objects (in the unhelpful but standard use of the word 'physical' to mean 'non-mental') than to think that there are mental objects (in the robust sense of 'mental object' given on page 278). One possibility is that the following discussion of the relation between the mental and the non-mental will provide grounds for thinking that a hospitable attitude to this idea is not just compatible with a realistic and genuinely materialist view of things, but essential to it.

6.7 Imaginative confusion

The first thing one needs to do when addressing the question about the relation between the mental and the non-mental is to recover a proper sense of our ignorance of the non-mental. Many take 'the mind–body problem' to be the problem of how mental or experiential phenomena can be material or physical phenomena *given what we already know about the nature of matter, or the physical*. They've already gone hopelessly wrong, because we have no good reason to think we know anything about matter that gives us any reason to find any problem in the idea that mental or experiential phenomena are physical phenomena. In assuming that we know things about the nature of matter that make this idea fundamentally problematic, we are in Russell's words 'guilty, unconsciously and in spite of explicit disavowals, of a confusion in [our] imaginative picture of matter' (1927a: 382), i.e., in my terms, our picture of the non-mental physical. We tend to think we have a good *general* understanding of what Russell calls the 'intrinsic' nature of matter in spite of all the conundra of current physics and cosmology. But this belief is wholly unjustified, as Arnauld, Regius, Locke, Hume, Priestley, Kant, and many others[25] knew long before matter in the hands of twentieth-century science became, in Russell's words, 'as ghostly as anything in a spiritualist séance', disappearing 'as a "thing"' and being 'replaced by emanations from a locality' (1927b: 78, 84). Russell may exaggerate when he says that 'we know nothing about the intrinsic quality of physical events except when these are mental events that we directly experience' (1956: 153), i.e. that we know nothing about the intrinsic nature of non-mental physical reality, but I don't think he exaggerates much; as I will try to explain.

When it comes to the mental, by contrast, we know quite a lot about its intrinsic nature. We have direct acquaintance with fundamental features of the mental nature of (physical)[26] reality just in having experience in the way we do, a way that has no parallel in the case of any non-mental features of (physical) reality. We don't have to stand back from experiences and take them as objects of knowledge by means of some further mental operation in order for there to be acquaintance—knowledge—of this sort (any such standing back obscures the relation of acquaintance that it seeks to examine). We're acquainted with reality *as it is in itself*,[27] in certain respects, in having experience as we do: the having is the knowing.

The word 'acquaintance' may be thought to introduce too much of an idea of relation. This reveals too narrow a notion of what a relation is. It may be added that the claim that we have having-is-the-knowing acquaintance is fully compatible with acknowledging that there may also be fundamental things we don't know about matter considered in its experiential being. Not only facts about experience in sense modalities we lack, or (e.g.) about the brightness-saturation-hue complexity of seemingly simple colour-experience, but also, perhaps, murkier facts about its composition, and also, perhaps, about the 'hidden nature of consciousness' postulated by McGinn.[28]

—This can't be right. In having experience we only have access to an appearance of how things are and are not—ever—cognizant, in the mere having of the experience, of how anything is in itself.

No. In the case of experience itself, how things appear or seem is how they really are: the reality that is at present in question just is the appearing or seeming. In the case of any experiential episode *e* there may be something X of which it is true to say that in undergoing *e* we only have access to an appearance of X, and not to how X is in itself. But serious materialists must hold that *e* itself, the event of being-appeared-to, with all the qualitative character that it has, is itself part of physical reality. They cannot say that it too is just an appearance, and not part of how things are, on pain of infinite regress.

---

[25] Arnauld 1641: 141–3; Regius 1647: 294–5; Locke, *Essay*, 2.23, 4.3.6; Hume, *Treatise*, 157–64/240–50 (he exits his official system in order to make the point); Priestley 1777–82: 219–20, 244, 303; Kant, A358–60, B427–8 (on his own special terms). There are many other vigorous real materialists in the early eighteenth century, among them Toland and Clarke, all preceded by the very robustly materialist Hobbes (see e.g. Hobbes 1651). See Lockwood (1989: ch. 10) for further discussion of versions of the idea that precede Russell's.

[26] The word 'physical' is bracketed because it is redundant, here as elsewhere, given the assumption of materialism.

[27] Some philosophers think, puzzlingly, that the notion of how things are in themselves is suspect or unintelligible. I take its viability for granted (for a defence see e.g. G. Strawson 2002, 2008a: §2).

[28] McGinn 1991: chs. 3 and 4. I discuss this further in G. Strawson 2006b: 250–3.

They must grant that it is itself a reality, a reality with which we must in plausibility be allowed to have some sort of direct acquaintance in Russell's sense.

—You're forgetting the lesson of Ryle's argument for the 'systematic elusiveness of the "I"' (1949: 186–9): anything that can count as *knowledge* of experience involves an operation of taking experience as an object that necessarily precludes apprehending it in such a way that one can be said to have access to how it is in itself rather than merely to an appearance of it. Even your mentor William James agrees that 'no subjective state, whilst present, is its own object; its object is always something else' (1890: i. 190).

The eye cannot see itself, and the knife cannot cut itself, but I argued in 4.4 that this ancient form of argument is invalid even in its original application, where it's used to demonstrate that the mental subject of experience can never directly apprehend itself. And even if it were valid in its original application, it would have no valid application to the present case—to things like pain and colour-experience, or indeed any experience. The way a colour-experience is experientially for the subject of experience that has it is part of its essential nature, part of its (physical) reality as it is in itself. When we claim with Russell that to have an experience is *eo ipso* to be acquainted with certain of the intrinsic properties or features of reality, we don't have to—mustn't—suppose that this acquaintance involves standing back from the experience reflectively and examining it by means of a further, distinct, 'thetic' experience. It doesn't. This picture is too intellectualist. The having, once again, is the knowing—an old, impregnable truth that has to be carefully stated, given the current orthodoxy in the philosophy of mind, to which it is fatal.[29]

These facts secure the sense in which our general theoretical conception of the mental has clear and substantial positive descriptive content. Whatever the best general account of the mental domain, and however much we don't and can't know about it, it includes experiential phenomena in its scope. And experiential phenomena are not only indubitably real; they're also phenomena whose intrinsic nature just is their experiential character (see the definition on page 269); and their experiential character is something with which we are directly acquainted just in having them, however hard we may find the task of describing it in words.

So much for our general theoretical conception of the mental. What about our general theoretical conception of the non-mental? Is it condemned to remaining, by contrast, a wholly negative concept? Russell thinks so: 'as regards the world in general, both physical (i.e. non-mental, in the present terms) and mental, everything that we know of its intrinsic character is derived from the mental side' (1927a: 402). The science of physics is our fundamental way of attempting to investigate the non-mental being of physical reality, and it cannot help us. 'Physics is mathematical', according to Russell, 'not because we know so much about the physical world, but because we

---

[29] 'The philosophical presumption that, to achieve an objective conception of ... our mentality, we have to find some way of focusing on ourselves from the outside, without the supposed distortions of ... subjective ... appearance, is, I think, more than anything else, what gives materialism its spurious philosophical appeal' (Foster 1991: 235–6). See also Goff 2006.

know so little: it is only its mathematical properties that we can discover. For the rest, our knowledge is negative' (1927b: 125). All that physics can give us is knowledge of structure, without giving us any understanding of the nature of whatever it is—and it must be something—that has the structure. On this view, neither physics nor everyday experience of physical objects gives us any sort of knowledge of the intrinsic nature of non-mental reality.

Is Russell right? Not if physics can give knowledge of structure, because correct structural description of a thing is already description of an aspect of its intrinsic nature, even if the description is purely mathematical in character (257n). This disagreement with Russell is merely terminological, though, and the real question is whether we can go any further than mathematical-structural description when attempting to give a satisfactory characterization of the intrinsic nature of the non-mental. The question is a difficult one, and I won't pursue it here.[30] It's enough to register the point that a currently popular philosophical view of things—according to which the whole domain of the mental is essentially murky and mysterious, while large parts of the domain of the non-mental are, in spite of all the complexities of physics, fundamentally unproblematic and open to view—is a product of 'imaginative ... confusion'. It has things back to front:

the physical [sc. non-mental] world is only known as regards certain abstract features of its spacetime structure—features which, because of their abstractness, do not suffice to show whether the physical world is, or is not, different in intrinsic character from the world of mind   (Russell 1948: 240).

6.8 Real materialism

What is it, then, to be a genuine materialist? The first thing to do is to repeat once again the point that realistic—real—materialism involves full acknowledgement of the reality of experiential phenomena. Experiential phenomena are as real as rocks, hence wholly physical. They are part of reality. So current physics, considered as a general account of the nature of the physical, is like *Hamlet* without the prince—or *Othello* without Desdemona. It contains no predicates for experiential being, so it can't *characterize* experiential phenomena at all, even if it can *refer* to them. So it can't characterize a fundamental feature of (physical) reality at all. It provides no resources for its description, for the positive acknowledgement of its reality.

No one who doubts this is a serious materialist, and I think that materialism, real materialism, the thought that experiential phenomena are physical phenomena—just like extension phenomena or electrical phenomena, as characterized by physics—should at first provoke a feeling of deep bewilderment. I think that some may find it hard to shake off the imaginative confusion.[31] And yet Locke made the crucial move long ago

---

[30] See G. Strawson 2003b, 2008a.

[31] The feeling of bewilderment vanishes as the bad picture of matter loses its grip. I had it until about 1995, but can't recover it.

when he found no insuperable difficulty in the idea that 'some systems of matter, fitly disposed, [could have] a power to perceive and think'.[32] Some may think that modern science has changed the situation since then, and it has, but only in so far as it has reinforced Locke's point.

It may help to perform special acts of concentration—focusing one's thought on one's brain and trying to hold fully in mind the idea that one's experience as one does so is part of the physical being of the brain (part of the physical being of the brain that one may be said to be acquainted with as it is in itself, at least in part, because its being as it is for one as one has it just is part of what it is in itself). It's worth trying to sustain this (it's a philosophical procedure), forcing one's thought back to the confrontation when it slips. At first one may simply encounter the curious phenomenological character of the act of concentration, but it's useful to go on—to engage, for example, in silent, understanding-engaging subvocalizations of such thoughts as 'I'm now thinking about my brain, and I'm thinking that this experience I'm now having of this very thinking (and this subvocalization) is part of the physical activity and being of my brain'. It's useful to look at others—children, say—as they experience the world, and to think of the being-in-time of the common-or-garden matter in their heads (hydrogen, oxygen, carbon, iron, potassium, sodium, etc.), and to think that their having experience is part of the routine being-in-time of this matter. It's useful to listen to music, and focus on the thought that one's auditory experience is a form of matter or energy.

6.9 The radiance of reality

When one considers the metaphysics of the mental in a materialist framework, one has to reflect on one's ignorance of the non-mental, and more particularly of the non-experiential—so I've suggested. One's theoretical attitude to the nature of the non-experiential needs to evolve until any sense that there's an active clash between experiential terms (terms that descriptively characterize experiential phenomena like sensations, emotions, and so on) and non-experiential terms (terms that characterize mass, charge, spatial location, and so on, in physics terms) has disappeared without trace, leaving only the awareness that they fail to connect in a way that brings a sense of intuitive understanding. Achieving this attitude isn't merely a matter of book learning.

At least two paths open up for materialists who reach this point. The first goes deeper into reflection on the nature of understanding in physics, or, more generally, the nature

---

[32] Locke, *Essay*, 4.3.6. The idea was sharpened in the seventeenth-century debate about Descartes's views (it didn't become a difficult idea until the rise of the classical corpuscularian contact-mechanics view of matter). In the same paragraph Locke says that 'matter ... is evidently in its own nature void of sense and thought', and many think that his view is that God could 'superadd' this power to matter, but couldn't make matter have such a power intrinsically or in and of itself, i.e. without any special wizardry. Locke, however, was being cautious; his correspondence with Stillingfleet confirms that his considered view is that our ignorance of the nature of the matter is in the end too great for us to have any good reason to claim that matter could not have the power of thought in and of itself (1696–9: 459–62).

of understanding as it occurs in relation to concrete reality (as opposed to mathematics, say). Proceeding down this path, one encounters a sense that at least some of the terms of physics (both common-sense and scientific) connect up with one another in a way that justifies a feeling of intuitive understanding of at least some of what goes on in the world. The next thought, though, is that a feeling that one understands something is always and necessarily relative to something else that one simply takes for granted. It seems, in fact, that when it comes to concrete reality, understanding is really nothing more than a certain kind of feeling one is disposed to get, either innately or as a result of training, when considering some but not other co-occurrences of properties in the world. I take this to be a familiar point in philosophy of science.[33]

One ought to go down this path at some point, but here I'll take another, which has a sunnier aspect. On this path one confronts the deep puzzlement one feels when one considers experiential properties and non-experiential properties and fails to see how they relate. One then considers whether one can take any positive steps to lessen it. I think one can. Physics can help us—it has already helped us a great deal—by diluting or undermining features of our natural conception of the physical that make non-experiential phenomena appear *toto coelo* different from experiential phenomena. The basic point is simple, and can be elaborated as follows.

At first, perhaps, as a child, one takes it that matter is simply solid stuff, uniform, non-particulate: Scandinavian cheese. Then, perhaps, one learns that it is composed of distinct atoms—particles that cohere more or less closely together to make up objects, but that have 'empty space' between them. Then, perhaps, one learns that these atoms are themselves made up of tiny, separate particles, and full of empty space themselves.[34] One learns that a physical object like the earth, or a person, is almost all empty space. One learns that matter is not at all what one thought.

One may accept this while holding on to the idea that matter is at root solid and dense. For this picture retains the idea that there are particles of matter: minuscule grainy bits of ultimate stuff that are in themselves (in Locke's phrase) 'perfectly solid' or dense. And one may say that only these, strictly speaking, are matter: matter as such. But it is more than 200 years since Priestley (citing Boscovich) observed that there is no positive observational or theoretical reason to suppose that the fundamental constituents of matter have any perfectly solid central part.[35]

In spite of this, a fairly robust conception of truly solid particles survived all the way into pre-1925 quantum mechanics. It suffered its most dramatic blow only in modern (1925 on) quantum mechanics, in which neither the nucleus and its components nor the electrons of an atom are straight-up solid objects, and are much more naturally thought of as fields. It may be said that the basic idea of the grainy particle survives even here, at least inasmuch as the nucleus and its components are still fairly well

---

[33] See e.g. van Fraassen 1980: ch. 5; G. Strawson 1994: 84–93.

[34] As in the old quantum-theory model of the atom, *c.*1910–24 (one standard way to convey the amount of empty space inside an atom is to say that if the nucleus is imagined to be as big as a 1 millimetre pinhead, then the nearest electrons—themselves much smaller than the nucleus—are 100 metres away).

[35] See also Foster 1982: 67–72, and Harré and Madden 1975: ch. 9.

localized within a small central region inside the atom (albeit with little 'tails' that 'go out to infinity'), and inasmuch as the probability of finding one of the (far less localized) electrons is significant only within a volume that is normally considered to be the dimensions of the atom. But this commitment to the localization of particles doesn't in itself amount to any sort of commitment to absolute (mathematically speaking dense) solidity, but only to fields and repulsive forces that grow stronger without any clear limit when one travels in certain directions (i.e. towards the centre of the field associated with a particle). And whatever is left of the picture of ultimate grainy bits is further etiolated in quantum field theory, in which the notion of the field more fully overrides any picture of grainy particles.[36] In this theory it becomes very hard to treat 'bound' systems like atoms at all. As for what I've been calling 'empty space'—the supposed vacuum—it is understood to be simply the lowest energy state of fields like the electron, proton, and photon fields. It turns out to be something which 'has structure and can get squeezed, and can do work'.[37] Descartes was surely right, deep down, in his theory of the plenum.

It may be said that quantum field theory is complicated and ill-understood. Many would deny this—but grainy, inert bits of matter naively conceived are already lost to us independently of quantum field theory, given only the fact that matter is a form of energy, and interconvertible with it. This is a widely known fact, however little it is understood, and it seems to me that it further undermines any understanding of matter that takes it to be in any obvious way irredeemably incompatible with the phenomena of consciousness. To put it dramatically: physics thinks of matter considered in its non-experiential being as a thing of forces, energy, fields, and it can also seem rather natural to conceive of consciousness (i.e. matter apprehended in its experiential being) as a form or manifestation of energy, as a kind of force, and even, perhaps, as a kind of field.[38] We may still think that the two things are deeply heterogeneous, but we have no good reason to believe this. Kant notes that the 'heterogeneity' of mind and body is merely assumed and not known (B427–8). We just don't know enough about the nature of matter considered in its non-experiential being; and doubtless there are things we don't know about matter considered in its experiential being.

Those who think that speculations like this are enjoyable but not really serious haven't really begun on the task of being a materialist. They haven't understood the strangeness of the physical and the extent of our ignorance. It's a long time since Russell argued that 'from the standpoint of philosophy the distinction between physical and mental is superficial and unreal' (1927a: 402), and it seems that physics can back philosophy on this question. In fact—it had to come back to this—we really don't know enough to say that

---

[36] 'In the modern theory of elementary particles known as the Standard Model, a theory that has been well verified experimentally, the fundamental components of nature are a few dozen kinds of field' (Weinberg 1997: 20). We continue to talk in terms of particles because the quantization of the field, whereby each different (normal) mode of vibration of the field is associated with a discrete ladder of energy levels, automatically gives rise to particle-like phenomena so far as observation is concerned.

[37] Harvey Brown, private communication (1989); see Saunders and Brown 1991.

[38] Compare Maxwell 1978: 399; James 1890: 1. 167n. It's arguable that Schopenhauer holds something close to this view.

there is any non-mental being. All the appearances of a non-mental world may just be the way that physical phenomena—in themselves entirely mental phenomena—appear, the appearing being another mental phenomenon.[39]

Whatever you think of this last proposal, lumpish, inert matter, dense or corpuscled, stuff that seems essentially alien to the phenomenon of consciousness, has given way to fields of energy, essentially active diaphanous process-stuff that—intuitively—seems far less unlike the process of consciousness. When Nagel speaks of the 'squishy brain', when McGinn speaks of 'brain "gook"' and asks how 'technicolour phenomenology ... can ... arise from soggy grey matter', when the neurophysiologist Susan Greenfield describes the brain as a 'sludgy mass', they vividly and usefully express part of the 'imaginative ... confusion' in the ordinary idea of matter.[40] But physics comes to our aid, because there's a clear sense in which the best description of the nature of the non-experiential *in non-technical, common-sense terms* comes from physics. For what, expressed in common-sense terms, does physics find in the volume of spacetime occupied by a brain? Not a sludgy mass, but an astonishingly (to us) insubstantial-seeming play of energy, an ethereally radiant vibrancy. It finds, in other words, a physical object which, thus far examined, is like any other, e.g. a stone—a physical object existing in an *n*-dimensional realm that we call spacetime although its nature is bewilderingly different from anything we ordinarily have in mind in thinking in terms of space and time. Examined further, this particular physical object—the brain—turns out to have a vast further set of remarkable properties: all the sweeping sheets and scudding clouds and trains of intraneuronal and interneuronal electrochemical activity which physics (in conjunction with neurophysiology) apprehends as a further level of extraordinarily complex intensities of movement and (non-experiential) organization.

All this being so, do we have any good reason to think we know anything about the non-mental physical (assuming it exists) that licenses surprise at the thought that the experiential is physical? I don't think so. Experiencing brains are special, among physical objects, but their physics is utterly routine. Human experience in all its complexity—the 'ghost in the machine'—may be fairly special, relative to the rest of the physical universe, but it's certainly in the machine, a wholly physical part of the wholly physical machine, and the machine, like the rest of the physical world, is already a bit of a ghost. It's as ghostly, as Russell says, 'as anything in a spiritualist séance' (1927b: 78).

---

[39]   Richard Price is outclassed by Priestley in their *Free Discussion of the Doctrine of Materialism* (1778), but he gets this point exactly right: 'if ... it comes out that [Priestley's] account of matter does not answer to the common ideas of matter, [and] is not *solid* extension, but something *not solid* that exists in space, it agrees so far with spirit', or mind (p. 54; Price held that spirit was not only located in space but might also be extended). This is a rather good description of how things have come out, in physics. The account of matter given by current physics doesn't 'answer to the common ideas of matter'; it doesn't take matter to be 'solid extension', but rather 'something not solid that exists in space'. So far, then, it agrees with our understanding of mind or consciousness (my experience is spatially located where I am), although the agreement can only be negative, given that we have no non-mathematical grasp of the non-experiential being of matter—apart (perhaps) from our grasp of its spacetime structure.

[40]   Nagel 1998: 338; McGinn 1991: 1, 100; Greenfield, BBC, 21 June 1997.

So when David Lewis says that 'the most formidable opposition to any form of mind–body identity comes from the friends of qualia' (1999: 5), there is no reason to agree.[41] The main obstacle to achieving a philosophically serious (sc. minimally realistic, hence wholly ontologically non-reductionist) version of the mind–body identity thesis comes, paradoxically, and most ironically, from those who passionately believe themselves to be the truest defenders of the thesis, those who think that any mind–body identity thesis must be ontologically reductionist (in the mental-to-non-mental direction). Their problem is that they think they know more about the nature of the non-mental physical than they do. Lewis exemplifies this mistake in his well-known summary account of his position in the philosophy of mind: 'Remember', he says, 'that the physical nature of ordinary matter under mild conditions is very well understood' (1994: 412). There is no reason to believe this, and every reason to disbelieve it. 'What knowledge have we of the nature of atoms that renders it at all incongruous that they should constitute a thinking [experiencing] object?', asks Eddington, who took the existence of experiential phenomena—'qualia'—for granted: 'science has nothing to say as to the intrinsic nature of the atom'. The atom, so far as we know anything about it,

is, like everything else in physics, a schedule of pointer readings [on instrument dials]. The schedule is, we agree, attached to some unknown background. Why not then attach it to something of a spiritual nature of which a prominent characteristic is *thought*. It seems rather *silly* to prefer to attach it to something of a so-called 'concrete' nature inconsistent with thought, and then to wonder where the thought comes from. We have dismissed all preconception as to the background of our pointer readings, and for the most part can discover nothing as to its nature. But in one case—namely, for the pointer readings of my own brain—I have an insight which is not limited to the evidence of the pointer readings. That insight shows that they are attached to a background of consciousness.[42]

The point is still negative. It may destroy one common source of puzzlement, but it doesn't offer any sort of positive account of the relation between the play of energy non-experientially conceived and the play of energy experientially apprehended, and some may find it no help at all.

—So long as we grant that we don't know all there is to know about matter, there is no more *logical* difficulty in the thought that the existence of matter naively or classically mechanistically conceived involves the existence of consciousness than there is in the thought that matter quantum-mechanically conceived does so.[43]

Granted. Arnauld, Regius, Locke, Hume, and others illustrate your claim. Nevertheless, many may find the present point useful.[44]

[41] 'Qualia' are experiential phenomena, in my terminology. The term has many odd accretions and is best avoided. For one thing, its use is usually restricted to sense-feeling experiential phenomena (38) to the exclusion of cognitive experiential phenomena.

[42] 1928: 259–60; my emphasis on 'silly'. See also Eddington 1920, 1939 (quoted in Skrbina 2005: 153–5).

[43] See e.g. Regius 1647 (Regius was Descartes's one-time supporter and later opponent).

[44] 'Having realised the abstractness of what physics has to say, we no longer have any difficulty in fitting the visual sensation into the causal series. It used to be thought "mysterious" that purely physical [i.e. non-mental] phenomena

This account of realistic materialism concludes my discussion of the property *mental*, the second basic constituent property of *sesmet*. There is much more to say. There are, for example, reasons for doubting whether physical reality is spatiotemporal at all—if we take 'spatiotemporal' to be anything more than a merely referential term for a form of dimensionality of whose intrinsic nature we have no real understanding. I'll stop here, however. My hope is that when this real materialist account of the property *mental* is combined with the immediately following discussion of the property *object* it will become clear that we can have decisive reason to judge that *subjects of experience* are objects—if any things are—even when we restrict ourselves to the purely experiential mode of characterization (270) of experience and make no other ontological or metaphysical assumptions whatever.

6.10 *Object*

What are objects—concrete objects? What are the best candidates for being objects, given that we wish to retain the category *object* in our fundamental ontology or metaphysics, and are committed to the view (the Plurality Assumption) that there is more than one object in reality?

I assume, in a conventional materialist way, that every candidate for being a concrete object is either itself a 'fundamental particle' or 'field' or 'string' or 'brane' or 'preon' or 'loop' or 'field quantum' or 'simple' or, as I will say, 'ultimate', or is made up of some number of ultimates in a certain relation, a physical, spacetime relation. In line with 5.10 I take 'spacetime' to be a natural-kind term that refers successfully to the actual dimensionality or 'existence-place' of reality however wrong we are about its nature; i.e. even if we might naturally express our scientific conclusions by saying that concrete reality isn't really spatiotemporal at all. I choose 'ultimate' as an unencumbered term, and I'll sometimes also use 'u-field' ('u' for 'ultimate'). I agree with van Inwagen (1990: 72) that Leibniz's term 'simple' is preferable to 'fundamental particle' as a term for the ultimate constituents of reality, first because 'fundamental particle' has potentially misleading descriptive meaning, provoking a picture of tiny grains of solid stuff that has no scientific warrant, and secondly because many of the things currently called 'fundamental particles' may not be genuinely fundamental constituents of reality. I prefer 'ultimate' and 'u-field' to 'simple' because 'simple', too, carries implications—of radical separateness, non-overlappingness, and indivisibility—that are perhaps best dropped. That said, I'm going to take it for purposes of discussion that it's legitimate to speak of individual ultimates or u-fields. The phenomena of quantum entanglement may put great pressure on the idea of radical individuality, but I won't pursue this point

should end in something mental. That was because people thought they knew a lot about physical phenomena, and were sure they differed in quality from mental phenomena. We now realise that we know nothing of the intrinsic quality of physical phenomena except when they happen to be sensations, and that therefore there is no reason to be surprised that some are sensations, or to suppose that the others are totally unlike sensations' (Russell 1956: 153).

here.[45] 'u-field' is plainly less neutral than 'ultimate'—it has a descriptive force that 'ultimate' lacks—but its 'unpunctuality' is potentially helpful.

Sesmets are either single ultimates, then, or made up of a plurality of ultimates in a certain synergetic relation—if they exist. I assume that there is a plurality of ultimates, putting aside for now the important view that spacetime itself may be best thought of as an object (not a mere dimensionality, as it were), and indeed as the only object there is. If this view is correct, spacetime is an object whose existence comports the existence of everything we think of as matter, and we're simply wrong to think of matter, as we normally do, as something whose existence involves something over and above the existence of spacetime. According to one version of this view, the fundamental entities currently recognized in the standard model—leptons and quarks—are not strictly speaking fundamental and are to be explained, in Weinberg's words, as 'various modes of vibration of tiny one-dimensional rips in spacetime known as strings' (1997: 20). All the physical objects ordinarily recognized are made of rips in spacetime, the only object there is. (Spinoza and Parmenides are among those who reject the assumption that there is more than one concrete object in reality, as do a number of present-day physicists. Descartes rejects the assumption that there is more than one physical object.)

6.11 Subjectivism, objectivism, universalism

A physical object is either a single ultimate or a plurality of ultimates in a certain relation. Given that all single ultimates are physical objects, the remaining question is which pluralities of ultimates—if any—are physical objects? What should be our criterion?[46]

I take it that a physical object is, at the least, and first and foremost, and essentially, some kind of *physical unity* or *singularity*. So the question is: Which pluralities of ultimates—if any—constitute physical unities of the right kind?

The phrase 'some kind of physical unity' is as vague as it is crucial, and some philosophers—the *subjectivists*—think that no judgements about which phenomena count as objects are objectively true or false. When we judge something to be an object, they say, we implicitly or explicitly endorse an ultimately subjective principle of counting or individuation relative to which the phenomenon *counts* as a (single) object. We endorse a subjective *principle of objectual unity*; and there are no others.

Can this be right? Many judgements of objecthood—many principles of objectual unity—are so natural for us that the idea that they are in any sense subjective seems preposterous (nearly all of us think that cups, stones, meerkats, jellyfish, fingers, houses, planets, and molecules are individual objects). The subjectivists, however,

---

[45] Post (1963) famously suggested that even if there are ultimate constituents, they may have to be seen as 'non-individuals' in some way. See also Lockwood 1989: 253; French 1998; French and Krause 2006; see also Pullman (1998: 351) on the 'vacuum-matter complementarity'.

[46] van Inwagen (1990*a*) calls this the 'Special Composition' question.

are unimpressed. The fact that some judgements of objecthood are very natural for human beings can hardly entail that those judgements are objectively correct or record metaphysical truths. If we were electron-sized, our natural judgement about a stone might be that it was a mere collection of things, a loose and friable confederacy, and not itself a single object in any interesting sense at all.

It seems uncomfortable at first to think that merely subjective principles of objectual unity underlie our judgements that chairs and stones are objects, but the idea becomes increasingly natural as one moves away from such central cases. Nearly everyone thinks that a chair is a single object, but not everyone does.[47] Many think cities, newspapers, galaxies, and blenders (assembled from parts) can correctly be said to be single things, but quite a few do not. Some think a body of gas is an object, many do not.

Few think that three spoons, one in Hong Kong, one in Athens, and one in Birmingham, constitute a single thing, and yet some philosophers—the *universalists*—claim that the three spoons have as good a claim to be considered an individual object as anything else. According to universalism, any plurality of ultimates in the universe, however scattered, counts as a single object in every sense in which a table does. A lepton in your amygdala, a quark in my left hand, and the ultimates that make up the rings of Saturn jointly constitute a single object just as surely as your pen or pet duck. No plurality of ultimates has a better claim to be an object than any other.

Whatever you think of universalism (a view favoured by Quine, Goodman, and many others since), it has the merit of being a wholly *objectivist* theory of objects. It endorses a principle of objectual unity that delivers a clear principle of counting. It tells you that if there are n ultimates in the universe, then there are exactly $2^n - 1$ objects in the universe. But it also has a highly subjectivist or 'post-modern' aura—it tells you that anything goes and everybody wins, that there is no real issue about whether any particular plurality of ultimates is an object or not—and it's arguable that genuinely objectivist positions emerge clearly only when more specific and limited principles of objectual unity are endorsed, e.g. by common sense, which rules in favour of tables and chairs and against the three spoons, or by Spinoza, who holds that there is only one thing or substance, the universe ('God or nature'), or by van Inwagen, who argues forcefully that only individual ultimates and living beings—and not, say, tables and chairs—are physical objects.[48]

This debate has many mansions, and the mansions have many rooms, but there's no need to enter them now. For present purposes it doesn't matter which side you favour. If you think there are solid, objective principles of objectual unity, and that there are therefore metaphysical facts about which phenomena are genuine objects and which aren't, and reject universalism, as I do, then you can take me to be arguing that sesmets (and thus perhaps selves) are among the genuine objects. If, alternatively, you

---

[47] van Inwagen (1990) doesn't, and his reasons are of considerable interest; the same goes for Nāgārjuna (*c*.150 CE) and perhaps also Chomsky (2000).

[48] For van Inwagen, as for Aristotle (see e.g. *Metaphysics*, Z 7.1032^{a}19, 8.1034^{a}4), animals are the paradigm substances.

think that the subjectivist view is best, and that there are no ultimate metaphysical facts about which phenomena are genuine objects, then you can reinterpret me as trying to convince people who are disposed to think of certain but not all pluralities of ultimates as objects (people, jellyfish, and chairs, but not arbitrarily selected cubic feet of the Pacific Ocean or three newspapers) that it's at least equally reasonable to think of the pluralities of ultimates that I choose to refer to by the expression 'sesmets' (or indeed by the expression 'selves') as objects. Practically speaking, my task is the same either way.[49]

6.12 Principles of unity

A concrete object is a certain kind of physical unity or singularity or singleness. It's an individual ultimate or a plurality of ultimates in a certain relation. I reject 'universalism' and take it that there are at the very least various grades and types of physical unity: some candidates for objecthood have, objectively, a better claim than others. A human being has a better claim than your lepton + my quark + the rings of Saturn, or three spoons. I've assumed that the notion of an object has application to reality in fundamental metaphysics, and indeed plural application: that there are real objective unities that are correctly called 'objects'. There are also vast numbers of merely 'conventional' unities or objects (to use Buddhist terminology—one finds the same idea in Descartes and Leibniz, among others) that aren't correctly judged to be objects in fundamental metaphysics and are not of present concern.[50]

With this in place, consider the following suggestion. As one advances in real materialism in the way outlined in 6.9, deepening one's intuitive grasp of the idea that experiential, mental phenomena are physical phenomena in every sense in which non-experiential, non-mental phenomena are, one of the things that becomes apparent is that, when it comes to deciding which phenomena in the universe count as objects and which do not, there are *no* good grounds for thinking that non-experiential, non-mental criteria or principles of unity—of the sort that we use to pick out a dog or a chair—are more valid than mental or experiential criteria or principles of unity.

It's arguable, in fact, that there is no more indisputable unity in nature, and therefore no more indisputable physical unity or singularity, and therefore no better candidate for the title 'physical object', than the mental and in particular experiential unity that we come upon when we consider a synergy subject (273) in the living moment or lived present of experience,[51] experiencing seeing books and chairs and seeing them as such, say, or consciously comprehending the thought that water is wet—an event that necessarily involves the concretely occurring thought-elements WATER and WET forming

---

[49] I'm concentrating on human sesmets, which I assume to involve many u-fields, although I'm open to the panpsychist idea that individual u-fields are sesmets.

[50] For further discussion see e.g. van Inwagen 1990*a*.

[51] I put the living moment of experience and the lived present of experience together here although they're very different things, as explained in 5.10.

a true unity of some sort, a unity without which the thought *water is wet* can't be said to have occurred at all.[52] I can think of no better candidates for what I'm going to call 'strong' unity, unity that is not just necessary for genuine, irreducible objecthood (if there is such a thing) but also—I'll propose—sufficient. As far as I can see, the only serious (and mutually excluding) competitors for equal first place are

(a) the universe,

to be identified, perhaps, with spacetime considered as a substance, and, lagging somewhat behind,

(b) individual ultimates

—if indeed there are any. Between these two extremes of size, and given the absolute centrality of unity or singularity considerations when it comes to determining objecthood, it's arguable that subjects of experience as just characterized are the best qualified plurality-of-ultimates-involving candidates there are for the status of physical objects.

Here, then, I make a key assumption or rather ruling: to be an object (if objects exist) is simply to be a 'strong unity', in a sense to be further determined. Note that to claim that there is no better candidate for the title 'physical object' than the unity we come upon when we consider a synergy subject in the living moment of experience is not to claim that when we do this we come upon a living-moment-of-experience-sized entity. If time is dense, then living moments of experience are theoretical abstractions from a continuum, infinite in number, not genuinely physically discrete entities. In this case the qualifying phrase 'considered in the living moment of experience' doesn't chop the synergy subject at the boundaries of the living moment of experience in such a way as to deliver a distinct living-moment-of-experience-sized object, because there are no such things as the boundaries of the living moment of experience.[53] It's an empirical question how long synergy subjects last, however they're considered, and if the analytical cut that thought makes in considering the synergy subject in the living moment of experience delivers an infinity of entities, that shows that the cut doesn't correspond to a real division in nature. Questions about the temporal extent of objects—the diachronic identity conditions of objects—are a matter of natural fact, and can't depend on what we can intelligibly isolate as objects of thought (the 'temporal parts' favoured by some metaphysicians are of no ontological interest at all).

I need to say more about diachronic identity conditions, but the first key move has been made: the claim that synergy subjects are strong or true unities, considered synchronically in the living moment of experience, or in the moment of grasping a thought, and are therefore, and so far, unbeatable candidates for being objects. I'll

---

[52] See 2.20 (87–8). There is no implication here that the subject of experience is or must be thought of as an agent that brings about the unity.

[53] The objects in question must be theoretical abstractions, for although they're 'countable' in the mathematical sense they're countably infinite, and a concrete infinity of physical objects can't exist in a finite period of time. To think otherwise is like thinking that infinity is or could be finite (this may be difficult to see clearly after exposure to certain sorts of mathematics).

say more about this in Parts 7 and 8. One product of the discussion will be the claim that phenomenological facts about the character of experience feature among the metaphysical facts about the nature of the self. This will be the key step towards something promised in 2.10 (52): an attempt to produce valid versions of something like Kant's First and Second Paralogisms.

I'll now begin to take things further by considering three doubts about our ordinary notion of an object. The first concerns the fact that we're in danger of being profoundly—hopelessly—misled in our intuitive thinking by an automatic and unexamined picture of objects as somehow essentially static in nature, rather than dynamic. The second is connected to the first: I think we need to acknowledge the respect in which (the fact that) all objects are processes. The third and most troublesome is this: we need to face the ancient philosophical question of the relation between objects and their properties. My brief discussion of these matters may seem naive to those who specialize in them, but I think it will be enough for my purposes.

6.13 Object, process, property

—I'm prepared to grant, at least for now and for the sake of argument, that there may be a real phenomenon picked out by your use of the (potentially question-begging) count noun 'sesmet'. I'm also prepared to accept for the sake of argument that 'sesmets' may be short-lived, at least in the human case, so that there are many of them in the case of the life of a human being. I'm even prepared to allow that one candidate for the title 'sesmet' is the (indubitably real and wholly physical) phenomenon of the *subject of experience as we find it in the living moment of experience or lived present of experience*. I'm prepared to allow that this is a candidate, even an interesting candidate, for being correctly judged to be (here is your definition of 'sesmet') a single object when considered specifically as a subject of experience that is being considered specifically in its mental being, and so without regard to any non-mental being that it may have. What I'm not prepared to do is to accept that it actually passes all the required tests. In particular, I'm not prepared to accept that the right thing to say about an instance of this indubitably real phenomenon (the subject of experience as we find it in the living moment of experience or lived present of experience) is that it is an *object* of some sort. Let's take a case that seems ideally suited to your view, the case of an isolated one-second-long continuous period of experience *e* occurring in a brain and followed and preceded by periods of complete experiencelessness. Let's stipulate that *e* is *experientially unitary* in whatever strong way you require, that it is an *experientially unitary period of experience*. Plainly the existence of *e* at any moment involves a subject of experience, a live-aware subject-of-experience presence, the currently favoured candidate for the title 'sesmet'. But why should I say that this phenomenon is

(a) an *object*, like a rock or a human being or a mayfly, or indeed a *substance*?

Why isn't the correct thing to say simply that

(b) an enduring object of a familiar sort—viz. Louis, a human being—has a certain *property* at a certain time, or is in a certain *state* at a certain time, in having a certain unified, one-second-long, subject-of-experience-involving episode of experience?

Why, alternatively, can't we say that

(c) the occurrence of an experientially unitary period of experience like *e* is just a matter of a certain *event* or *process* occurring in an object (a human being, say) at a certain time, and does not involve the existence of any further distinct *object*?

The canyons of metaphysics open before us. We face the great object/process/property/ state/event conceptual cluster. The distinctions in this cluster seem patently valid. They seem to mark real, irreducible, metaphysically fundamental differences. They're integral to our most basic, discursive, subject–predicate forms of thought, utterly natural, practically indispensable in everyday life (although events and processes may be thought to come down to the same thing, as also states and properties). I think, though, that they're profoundly misleading when taken up in metaphysics as a guide to the fundamental nature of reality, and that it isn't particularly hard to see that this is so, drawing on a mixture of a posteriori and a priori considerations. I think a little thought strips (b) and (c) of any appearance of superiority to (a), whether or not one is a materialist, and I'll now briefly say why, starting with (c).

    The subject of experience currently under consideration, the (human) neural-synergy subject as we find it in the living moment or lived present of experience, is a wholly physical, plurality-of-ultimates-constituted entity. It's only one candidate among others for being a sesmet (an immaterial soul is another), and its claim to be a genuine object, and so a genuine sesmet, is now in question. In order to keep its probationary or candidate status clear, I will in the next two sections call it a 'sysele', short for: **synergy subject of experience** considered as it is in the living/lived process of experience (it falls under a new name— 'thin subject'—in 7.1). The question, then, is whether syseles qualify as sesmets, given that they have to qualify as objects in order to quality as sesmets.

6.14 Object and process

Any claim to the effect that a sysele is best thought of as a process rather than an object (as in (c)) can be sufficiently countered by saying that there is, in the light of physics, no good sense in which a (short-lived) sysele is a process in which a rock or a crow is not also and equally a process. It follows that if a rock or a crow is a paradigm case of an object in spite of being a process, then we have, so far, no good reason not to hold that a sysele is an object even if we're inclined to think of it as a process. To say this is not to say that everything that's naturally thought of as a process—such as the yellowing of a leaf—is helpfully or legitimately thought of as an object. The claim is just that everything that's naturally thought of as an object is legitimately thought of as a process, and that there are things that some may want to think of as processes that are no less properly thought of as objects.

    In making this claim I don't mean to show any partiality to the 'four-dimensionalist' ('4D') conception of objects, as opposed to the 'three-dimensionalist' ('3D') conception.

I think I can overfly this debate, observing in passing that there are contexts in which the 4D conception of objects is more appropriate than the 3D conception and contexts in which the 3D conception of objects is more appropriate than the 4D conception. The 3D/4D debate has its own internal dynamic, and creates contexts in which its disagreements have importance, but it doesn't really matter to the present question about the existence of selves.[54]

—But if there's a process, there must be something—an object or substance—in which it goes on. If something happens, there must be something to which it happens, something which is not just the happening itself. So it can't be true that everything is a matter of process.

This expresses our pre-theoretical conception of things, but things are unimaginably strange relative to our ordinary understanding of them. The general lesson of physics (not to mention a priori reflection) is that our pre-theoretical conceptions of space, time, and matter are in many respects hugely and demonstrably wrong; so we already have one general reason to be cautious about the claim—which is, after all, a very general (universal) claim about the essential nature of *matter-in-spacetime*—that it is a hard metaphysical fact that the existence of a process entails the existence of an object or substance that is in some way ontically distinct from it. Physicists are increasingly content with the view that physical reality is itself a kind of pure process. The view that there is some ultimate stuff to which things happen has increasingly ceded ground to the idea that the existence of anything worthy of the name 'ultimate stuff' consists simply in the existence of fields of energy—consists, one might well say, in the existence of a kind of pure process which is not in any way usefully (or even coherently) thought of as something which is happening to a thing distinct from it.

Physics aside, the object/process distinction lives covertly off a natural, unexamined, massively influential and irredeemably confused picture of objects and matter that presents them statically rather than dynamically, as things whose essential nature at any given time can be fully given in the consideration of them as they are at a fixed instant. This *staticist* picture has deep roots in conventional empiricism, and vice versa, and the entanglement of staticism and empiricism may help to explain one of the larger philosophical mysteries (comedies) of the twentieth century: the spectacle of philosophers endorsing outright realism about physical objects while continuing to adhere to a regularity theory of causation.[55]

Whether or not this explanation is correct, a deep and unremarked staticism constitutes one of the main confusions in what Russell called our 'imaginative picture of matter'. For matter is essentially *dynamic*, essentially in time, and essentially changeful in time.[56] All reality is process, as Whitehead was moved to observe by his study of

---

[54] For an outstanding piece of arbitration see Jackson 1994: 96–103.

[55] There's nothing odd about adopting a regularity theory of causation in the physical world if one is also a phenomenalist about physical objects, as so many were in the early part of the twentieth century; it is, in fact, the right thing to do. See e.g. G. Strawson 1987.

[56] If 'dynamic' is taken to mean nothing more than 'in time', this is true even on the 'block-universe' view, which doesn't of course deny the reality of time. (I'm respectfully putting aside theories that deny the existence of time.)

twentieth-century physics, and as Heraclitus remarked long ago. Matter is best thought of as 'process-stuff'. Perhaps we should always call matter 'time-matter', or at least 'matter-in-time', in contexts like the present one, so that we never for a moment forget its essential temporality and essential changefulness. When we think of matter as essentially extended, we tend to think only of extension in space—something that can, we intuitively feel, be experientially given to us all at once at a single time (hence the pact with old empiricism).[57] But space and time are ontically interdependent, mere aspects of spacetime, and all extension is necessarily extension in spacetime.

There's no need to invoke relativity theory, though, for even if relativity theory is false in its account of the essential non-separateness of space and time, there's no metaphysically defensible conception of a physical object—a 'spatiotemporal continuant', as philosophers say—that allows one to distinguish validly between objects and processes by saying that one is an essentially dynamic or changeful phenomenon in some way in which the other is not. There's nothing in the 3D conception or the 4D conception of objects that supports such a view.[58] The source of the idea that there might be some metaphysically deep distinction between objects and processes which gives the lie to the claim that all objects are processes lies in useful and ordinarily harmless habits of thought that are extraordinarily misleading in certain theoretical contexts.[59]

It seems to me that we continue to be severely hampered by this, even when we have, in the frame of theoretical discussion, fully agreed and, as we think, deeply appreciated, that objects—substances—are entirely creatures of time, process entities, wholly and essentially and constitutively dynamic in nature, essentially active in the basic sense of the word, which doesn't of course imply any sort of capacity for intentional agency, acting for reasons. One illustration of our staticism is that we have no difficulty with the idea of dynamism when we think of electrons, quarks, vibrational 'strings', and so on, but still tend to think of a filing cabinet, say, as a paradigmatically inert thing. In fact, of course, a filing cabinet is wholly made of leptons and quarks, or vibrating strings, or .... It is an inherently dynamic thing whose existence is a matter of furious and unceasing activity.

Leibniz coined the word 'dynamic', and he was surely right in his view that the most important definition of an object or substance is that it is *that which acts*. 'Activity', or *dynamism*, in my non-scientific and possibly un-Leibnizian use of the term, 'is of the essence of substance' (1704: 65). Nothing wholly inert can be a concrete substance, a genuine concrete object. Even if we concede the logical possibility of inert concrete objects, we can still insist that no *physical* object can be inert. A physical object, after all,

---

[57] What is matter, on this view? A dust-covered china doll in a frozen pirouette on a chimney piece, a stone, a boot, something just there, supremely motionless before our eyes, something that proposes itself as—in some fundamental sense—comprehensively given to us in this confrontation alone, wholly given to us in its basic essential quality as matter, whatever the micro details of its composition. And all this is wholly wrong.

[58] Nor is there anything in the 4D view that challenges it, for the fourth dimension is, precisely, that of time—however time is characterized.

[59] P. F. Strawson's remark that 'the category of "process-things" is one that we neither have nor need' (1959: 57) concerns our ordinary everyday conceptual scheme.

is a strong physical unity. It is therefore a strong *spacetime* unity, and the temporal-unity aspect of its spacetime unity is, I propose, essentially a matter of dynamic unity, activity-unity. (If one wants an analogy for the quality—as it were—of the unitariness of the temporal-unity aspect of an object's unity, one may take the spatial unity of an object like a human being as grasped by us at a single time.) It probably doesn't need to be said, but I'm assuming that diachronic strong unity, and hence the temporal persistence of an object, entails temporal continuity. At the same time, I'm not excluding the possibility, considered in 5.10, that what we think of as temporal continuity may turn out to be a matter of discrete chronons (between which there are of course no temporal gaps) rather than something dense.

Could something be (a) a strong physical unity, and (b) essentially dynamic, and yet not be (c) a dynamic unity—a unity specifically in respect of activity? I doubt it, but I won't argue the point here. I think it's sufficiently underwritten by two claims argued for in the next section: that an object is identical with its propertiedness, and that a thing's categorical propertiedness is identical with its dispositional or power propertiedness. With that promissory note let me expressly endorse the view that strong physical unity, strong spacetime unity, essentially involves (c) dynamic unity. It essentially involves being an agentive unity, where 'agentive' carries no trace of any implication of intentional agency. It essentially involves being a locus-of-activity unity, a unity specifically as a locus of activity in spacetime. This, I propose, is the fundamental definition of what a physical object or substance is. If we're going to talk of objects at all, in fundamental metaphysics, then an object is a strong spacetime unity, a strong activity-unity.[60] I'm going to work with this definition without defending it further.

It remains as doubtful as ever that such concrete unities exist in such a way as to fulfil another traditional requirement on substancehood—that they be capable of existing independently of all other things.[61] Individual ultimates ought to be prime candidates for being radically ontically distinct substances in this sense, but it's far from clear that they can really be what they are without other things existing, given the nature of spacetime and the quantum vacuum and quantum entanglement.[62] It may be, as remarked, that spacetime itself or the universe (Spinoza's 'God or nature') is the only thing capable of existing independently of all other things, and that all other candidates for being things are just properties or modifications or local aspects of spacetime; my sense is that physics and cosmology tend this way. But I'll continue to assume that there are a great many distinct and coexistent ultimates, and that they can at least for purposes of argument be treated as ontically distinct substances capable of existing independently of all other things. I'll also continue to assume that plurality-of-ultimates-constituted objects

---

[60] One way to put things is to say that all *genuine* physical unities are *ipso facto* strong unities, and therefore objects, and that there aren't really any non-strong genuine physical unities, only 'conventional' unities, non-objective unities fabricated by discursive thought and language. This makes the word 'strong' redundant, but I'll retain it none the less. For some striking scepticism about objects, see Ladyman *et al.* 2007.

[61] Descartes 1644: 1.210. Descartes qualifies this by saying that they must be capable of existing independently of all other things except God, and one might replace God by spacetime or the universe.

[62] Nāgārjuna, Spinoza, and others seem to be right on this point, independently of current physics.

or substances exist. My prime candidates for being plurality-of-ultimates-constituted objects are as before syseles, neural-synergy subjects, candidate sesmets. I hope the word 'synergy' can do some work against the staticist tendencies of our ordinary conception of objects.

When anti-staticist considerations are applied to the case at hand, the case of syseles, the conclusion, I take it, is that there's no sense in which it's correct to call a sysele a process in which it's not equally correct to call it an object. All objects are legitimately thought of as processes, contrary to (c), even if it's not true that all processes are legitimately or helpfully thought of as objects. (We can treat 'the extinction of the apatosaurus' as the name of a single process while agreeing that it fails to have the right sort of unity to be a good candidate for the title 'object'.) The phenomenon of the existence of a sysele, by contrast, the phenomenon of the existence of a subject of experience as we find it in the living moment of experience—during the thinking of the thought that there is a world shortage of fresh water, say—has a very high degree of unity, on the present terms (in 8.5 I propose, with James and Descartes, that the unity is absolute, absolutely indecomposable or indivisible). So if it's figured as a process, then it's as good a candidate as there can be for being a process that's an object, and in saying that it's well thought of as an object, we're not of course saying that it's not well thought of as a process. There are areas of metaphysics in which it is, I think, crucial to cultivate the intuition of process in thinking about concrete reality.

—So why bother with the solid staticist word 'object'? Why not fall back into a world—or vocabulary—of Russellian 'events' or Whiteheadian 'occasions'?

Good question, but there's no reason why one shouldn't take the word 'object' with one into the processual outlook, realigning it to mean more clearly on its face what it really meant (referentially speaking) all along. I think there are also positive reasons for taking 'object' with one, rather than leaving it behind as a specious rallying point for bad intuitions.

It seems to me that these partly a posteriori, partly a priori points about the superficiality of the object/process distinction find a different, irresistible, and wholly a priori expression when we consider the object/property distinction.

6.15 Object and property, categorical and dispositional

Objects have properties, we say. There are, indisputably, objects, and, indisputably, they have properties. Our habit of thinking in terms of the object/property distinction is ineluctable. And it's perfectly correct, in its everyday way. But ordinary language isn't a good guide to metaphysical truth, and as soon as we repeat the observation portentously in philosophy—OBJECTS HAVE PROPERTIES—we risk error: the error of thinking that there's a fundamental, categorial, metaphysical distinction between objects and their properties. (We compound the error, I believe, if we think that such a categorial distinction is fundamental to ordinary thought.) If millennia of vehement philosophical disagreement about the object/property relation testify to anything, they testify to the fact that this is indeed an error. The debate can't stop until the error is recognized.

I think it's possible to express the truth about the object/property relation. The key is not to say too much (my profound ignorance of the traditional debate may give me a head start). In setting out the issue, I'll restrict attention to concrete phenomena, although the idea has general application. So my concern with properties will be only with concretely existing properties, concrete propertiedness, and only with intrinsic, natural, non-conventional properties of objects.[63] I'll use the word 'property' as it's used with no knowledge of philosophy—I offer this as a definition of my use—although I think this crucial use may have become inaccessible to some philosophers. (I could try to convey the point about being concerned only with concretely existing properties or propertiedness by saying that I'll be concerned only with 'property instantiations', but this term is already problematic inasmuch as it implies a contrast with properties considered as universals considered as abstract objects.)

What is at issue, then, is the relation between a particular concrete object and its properties, i.e. its whole actual qualitative being. The proposal is that one has already gone fatally wrong if one thinks that there's any sort of ontologically weighty distinction to be drawn between the object, on the one concrete ontological hand, and the properties of the object, on the other concrete ontological hand; between the existence or being of the object, at any given time, and its (overall) nature, at that time; between the thatness of the object and the whatness or howness of the object, at any given time. One of the principal agents of confusion in this matter is counterfactual thinking, which I'll consider in due course.

Plainly, objects without properties are impossible. There can no more be objects without properties than there can be closed plane rectilinear figures that have three angles without having three sides. 'Bare particulars'—objects thought of as concretely existing things that do of course *have* properties but are *in themselves* entirely independent of properties—are incoherent. To be, to be at all, is necessarily to be somehow or other, i.e. to be some way or other, to have some nature or other, i.e. to have (actual, concrete) properties.

Rebounding from the obvious incoherence of bare particulars, it may seem that the only other option is to conceive of objects as nothing but collections or 'bundles' of (concretely existing) properties. But this option seems no better. Mere bundles of properties seem as bad as bare particulars. Why accept properties without objects after having rejected objects without properties?

But this is not what we're asked to do, in the second case. The claim isn't that there can be concretely existing properties without objects. It is, rather, and to repeat, that objects are nothing over and above concretely existing properties. However strange this

---

[63] I'm taking the general propriety of such notions for granted. For some helpful discussion, see Lewis and Langton 1998 and the ensuing debate in *Philosophy and Phenomenological Research* 63 (2001). Conventional properties include such properties as the property of meaning *dog*, or the property of being illegal.

claim sounds, it isn't the claim that there can be concretely existing properties without objects. That's no more true than it's true that there can be objects without concretely existing properties.

It still sounds intolerably peculiar, though, to say that objects are nothing but concretely existing properties. Peculiarity of expression can be a vehicle of insight, but it doesn't seem to help much here. What may be helpful (given, as always, the assumption that reference to objects has a place in metaphysics) is to take a longer route. First, compare the point (a) that there can no more be concretely existing properties without objects than there can be objects without concretely existing properties, with the point (b) that there can no more be dispositional (or power) properties without categorical properties than there can be categorical properties without dispositional (or power) properties (the two points are at bottom deeply related). Secondly, go on to consider the case for saying that (a) and (b) can be superseded by vastly stronger identity claims, viz.

[1] that an object is identical with its propertiedness

and

[2] that an object's dispositional propertiedness is identical with its categorical propertiedness.

I think that [1] and [2] are certainly true, properly understood, and that grasping the sense in which they're true sets one well on the way to a plausible metaphysics.

Consider triangularity and trilaterality in a closed plane rectilinear figure. There's obviously a *conceptual* distinction between them. Trilaterality isn't the same thing as triangularity. It's a matter of sides, not angles. But there is, to adapt and extend Descartes's terms, no *real* distinction between them (1644: 1.213–15). Neither, that is, can exist without the other also existing. They can't possibly exist apart. They can't exist apart 'outside our thought', as opposed to merely 'in our thought' (1645/6: 3.280–1). They can be genuinely distinguished or held apart in thought; they can't exist apart in concrete reality. A real distinction isn't a matter of what things actually do exist separately, in reality, at any given time. It's a matter of what things can exist separately, a matter of what is possible as a matter of objective fact. If there's no real distinction between A and B, not even an omnipotent being can get them apart. That's how it is for triangularity and trilaterality in a closed plane rectilinear figure.[64]

What's the ground of this impossibility, this inseparability in reality? I think the answer is simple: identity, identity in the concrete (there can be no better ground). Any actually existing case of triangularity is, I propose, literally identical to the case of trilaterality that it can't exist without; for that in which the real existence of the one wholly consists is the very same thing as that in which the real existence of the other wholly consists. Neither real existence exceeds the other in any way. The (concrete) being of the one is—is identical to—the (concrete) being of the other. (Don't object that the sides could be thicker or thinner.)

---

[64] The restriction to rectilinear figures is not necessary if only angles generate sides—so that a closed 'U', for example, has two sides.

Some may think that the ground of the impossibility could be something other than identity. But what else could it be? The burden of argument lies heavily on those who wish to claim that something other than identity can make it absolutely impossible for two things to come apart. Identity does the trick, because the two things are only one thing, and a thing can't come apart from itself.

Inference to the best explanation looks smilingly upon this view, and I'm not going to argue for it now, although I can imagine objections. 'Look, there can be a one-way necessary metaphysical connection between two properties P_1 and P_2 that doesn't involve identity (if a brain state of type F exists, it may be metaphysically necessary that an experiential state of type G exists, etc.). Why couldn't there be a two-way, no-real-distinction necessary connection between two properties P_1 and P_2 that was the sum of two such one-way connections without involving their identity in the concrete?'[65]

The best reply to this is to ask for an explanation, in a particular case, of how this is possible without identity—an explanation that is furthermore better than the explanation provided by identity. The explanation provided by identity is distinguished by the fact that it leaves nothing 'brute' or unexplained.

I propose, then, and quite generally, that there's no difference 'outside our thought' (no real distinction) between the no-real-distinction inseparability of two things A and B and the identity of A and B (which are then not really two things at all). Plainly

(i) A = B

entails

(ii) there is no real distinction between A and B.

I'm claiming that the converse is also true, that (ii) entails (i), and indeed that

(iii) there is no real distinction between the fact or state of affairs that A = B and the fact or state of affairs that there is no real distinction between A and B,

and indeed that

(iv) the fact or state of affairs that A = B is *identical* to the fact or state of affairs that there is no real distinction between A and B.

I register this claim about the identity of identity and no-real-distinctionhood as an assumption (physics may be thought to provide counterexamples). There is, to be sure, a conceptual distinction between identity and no-real-distinctionhood, and metaphysicians can produce conceptual distinctions without end; but there is, I propose, no real distinction between them.[66]

---

[65] Thanks to Philip Goff.

[66] I'm concerned with concrete particulars: supposed counterexamples that cite abstract objects (e.g. the case of David Lewis and the singleton set—considered as an abstract object—whose only member is David Lewis) are not to the point. So too I'm concerned with concrete particulars considered independently of human intentions and conventions (this is designed to deflect cases of the kind found in Johnston 2003). 'What about a ball and its surface?' Well, either its surface isn't a concrete object and is irrelevant, or it is a concrete object, a collection of ultimate physical constituents that can possibly exist independently of the ball. And so on.

There is perhaps no more valuable tool in metaphysics than the distinction between a real and a conceptual distinction, although it's valuable (needed) only given the weakness—which is perhaps the necessary structure—of our thought.[67] Two important (if ultimately trivial) theses can be formulated in its terms, both of which make use of the term 'property', at least in their initial versions. In formulating them I'll make use of the proposed equivalence of (i) and (ii), and I'll restrict my attention as before to intrinsic, natural, non-conventional properties, although this isn't strictly necessary.

The word 'property', used as a count noun, is harmless enough in some areas of philosophy, but extraordinarily dangerous in others, where it harbours almost irresistible incentives to metaphysical misunderstanding and is to be avoided as far as possible. Whitehead may exaggerate when he says that 'all modern philosophy hinges round the difficulty of describing the world in terms of subject and predicate, substance and quality, particular and universal' (1927–8: 49), or indeed object and property, but I don't think he's far wrong. I think one can avert some of the problems by using the term 'propertiedness', and others by using a categorially neutral term like 'being', in ways I'll illustrate.

With this caveat, the first thesis is that

[1] there is no real distinction between an object considered at any given particular time t and its propertiedness at t.

The (concrete) being of an object at any given time is the (concrete) being of its properties or propertiedness at that time. Neither exceeds the other in any way.

The second thesis is that

[2] there is no real distinction between an object's categorical properties and its dispositional properties or power properties.

There's a perfectly respectable conceptual distinction (it's respectable even if ultimately metaphysically superficial) between an actually existing object O at a time and its propertiedness; using 'C' for 'conceptually', and 'P_O' for O's propertiedness, one may symbolize this as

[3] $C[O \neq P_O]$.

There's also a seemingly respectable conceptual (if ultimately metaphysically superficial) distinction between an object's categorical and dispositional properties; using 'C' for 'categorical', 'D' for 'dispositional', one may symbolize this as

[4] $C[C_O \neq D_O]$.

There is for all that no real distinction between O and P_O: using 'R' for 'in reality' or 'outside our thought', and invoking the assumed equivalence of (i) and (ii), one may symbolize [1] as

[1] $R[O \text{ at } t = P_O \text{ at } t]$,

---

[67] I don't think the weakness is wholly inevitable.

or, taking the time index as read (or inessential), simply as

[1] $R[O = P_O]$.

The whole being of the one, O, is the whole being of the other, P_O. The whole being of O, whatever it actually is, cannot possibly exist apart from (is) the whole being of P_O, whatever it actually is. There's no residue on either side. What—what exactly—is the referent of 'P_O'? It's everything in which the existence of O's being propertied as it is consists.

Nor is there any real distinction between O's categorical and dispositional properties, on the present view, and [2] can be represented as

[2] $R[C_O = D_O]$.

Again, the being of the one is the being of the other. Suppose I want you to be here. All I have to do is to make it the case that you turn up with all your categorical properties. I don't have to do something else—something ontologically extra—to ensure that your dispositional properties are also in place, because that in which the existence of your dispositional properties consists is nothing other than that in which the existence of your categorical properties consists. One can give the fundamental metaphysical point full weight without disturbing the fact that there is a (natural, human) conceptual distinction between the categorical and the dispositional.

I think the truth of [1] and [2] becomes obvious after reflection, although grasping [1] disrupts the standard philosophical understanding of what a property is (the Whitehead point). At bottom they're trivial—and deeply related. [1] is endorsed outright by philosophers like Descartes, Spinoza, Leibniz, Kant, and Nietzsche, and is certainly not undermined by the way in which we speculate counterfactually about objects. Locke, I take it, is a clear and well-known proponent of [2].[68]

I'll take [2] first—the claim that there is no real distinction between an object's categorical properties and its dispositional properties. I'll continue to speak in the traditional way of dispositional properties, rather than of power properties, although I think the second term is better. Actually, 'potential' is the best term, in its old meaning—'potent', 'possessing potency or power'—but this, the first *OED* meaning, has been drowned out by the second meaning, 'possible as opposed to actual', and this is unhelpful, because potential properties in the first meaning are of course actual properties.

Most philosophers agree that

[5] there can no more be dispositional properties without categorical properties than there can be categorical properties without dispositional properties

or, in my preferred terms, that

[5] there can no more be dispositional being without categorical being than there can be categorical being without dispositional being.

---

[68] Other recent defenders of (2) or similar views include C. B. Martin (1997), Mumford (1998), and Heil (2005).

Some reject the first half of [5], claiming that

[6] there are no categorical properties (there is no categorical being), only dispositional properties (dispositional being),

or, more simply, that

[6] all being is dispositional being,

and I'll consider this strange claim later. First, though, consider the addition to [5] of

[7] nothing can possibly have the (total) categorical being that it has and not have the (total) dispositional being that it has, and nothing can possibly have the (total) dispositional being that it has and not have the (total) categorical being that it has.

I think, as remarked, that this is obvious on reflection, even if it needs argument in the current climate of philosophical discussion.

Before I give an argument, note that it's a very short step, if it's a step at all, from [7] to the seemingly stronger claim that

[8] there is no real distinction between an object's categorical being (properties) and its dispositional being (properties),

and from there to the seemingly stronger claim that

[9] an object's categorical being (properties) and its dispositional being (properties) are really (in the Cartesian sense of 'real') identical.

I say 'seemingly stronger' because I don't think [9] is really stronger than [8], any more than [8] is really stronger than [7], for reasons already given. I've already identified [8] and [9], in fact, in ruling that [8] can be written as

[2] $R[C_O = D_O]$,

for [2] is just a different representation of [9].

Routine thoughts about the 'multiple realizability' of certain functional properties may prompt the idea that

[10] two things can be dispositionally identical without being categorically identical,

contrary to the second half of [7]; and this may lead to the idea that

[11] a thing could be changed in respect of its categorical properties without being changed in respect of its dispositional properties.

So too, thoughts about 'possible worlds' (say) may prompt the idea that

[12] a thing could be changed in respect of its dispositional properties without being changed in respect of its categorical properties,

contrary to the first half of [7], and so also that

[13] two things can be categorically identical without being dispositionally identical.

In fact, though, none of these things can be so. As regards [12], many recent philosophical thought-experiments are premised on the assumption that a material thing, say O, can be thought to retain its intrinsic nature or basic categorical being unchanged across different nomic environments while changing its dispositional being on account of its different nomic environment. I doubt that the idea that O can retain its intrinsic nature or basic categorical being unchanged across different nomic environments is even coherent, if laws are understood not as human linguistic or conceptual creations, but as non-linguistic objective principles of working. For I doubt that laws so understood can be properly thought to be in any way independent of, rather than essentially constitutive of, or part of, the (categorical, intrinsic) nature of matter—leptons, quarks, chairs, whatever. Only a bad 'separatist' habit of thought can make this seem initially plausible, and so make it seem that O can retain its nature unchanged across different nomic environments.[69] We can put this point aside, though, and allow for purposes of argument that the assumption is coherent. For even if it is coherent, it doesn't give us any reason (rather the contrary) to think that O's fundamental dispositions will change on change of nomic environment. For these fundamental dispositions include the disposition to behave in way F in nomic environment 1, the disposition to behave in way G in nomic environment 2, and so on. Some students of dispositions will say that this isn't what they have in mind, but the point about fundamental dispositions stands as it is. The same points apply *mutatis mutandis* to [13], where we'd be considering two qualitatively (categorically) identical things X and Y in different environments.

Turning to [10] and [11]: the objection to [7] based on the fact that certain properties may be said to be 'multiply realizable' doesn't deserve serious consideration. Obviously two differently constructed pocket calculators can be functionally identical (mathematically speaking). Equally obviously, their total dispositional being will be different if they're differently constructed (they melt differently, float differently, smell different, etc.). It is in the end a trivial point that if they're in any way categorically different, they'll necessarily be dispositionally different: one atom's difference between them makes a difference between their total dispositions. So too, no less trivially, if you change the categorical being of one of them in any way, you *eo ipso* change its total dispositional being in so doing.[70]

To say more is almost certainly a mistake, but I undertook to consider those who reject the second half of [7] for a different reason, claiming that there are only dispositional properties, or in other words that

[6] all being is dispositional being.

[6] is refreshingly incoherent on my terms, if 'dispositional' is supposed to exclude 'categorical', for all actual concretely existing being is *ipso facto* categorical being—

[14] all being is categorical being

—whatever else it is or isn't; even if (for example) it's correctly said to be nothing but energy in various forms, energy whose nature can be positively characterized by us only in terms of what effects it has. All being is categorical being because that's what it is to be! That's what being is!

---

[69] I criticize separatism in G. Strawson 1987: 393–5.

[70] Many standard moves can be made in protest. Heil (2005: chs. 8–11) deals with them in a tolerant manner.

—This begs the question against [6]—with numbing grossness!

True, but I'm afraid that that's [6]'s own fault. Perhaps we can achieve some reconciliation, though, moving in a very small space, through the cluster [7]/[8]/[9].

[6] raises the question 'What does the real concrete existence—call it "E"—of this dispositional being consist in, metaphysically speaking?' A serious answer to this question exhibits Russell's 'robust sense of reality' (1919: 325). It doesn't for a moment confuse metaphysics with epistemology, and the very least that it can be is 'E can't be nothing (for we are robust)'. But then whatever this non-nothing (something) E is said to be, it is already categorical being—even if it's been somehow forcefully theorized as ('merely') dispositional (or power) being—simply because it's real being: *being*!

—Mere repetition, the same begging of the same question.

The small, supposedly reconciling thought is that when the distinction between categorical and dispositional disappears as a real distinction, as it does if the cluster [7]/[8]/[9] (= [2]) is true, there's no bar to saying [6] that all being is dispositional being, although one is highly likely to be misunderstood, because to say this isn't at all to deny that there's categorical being (identity is a very egalitarian relation) or indeed [14] that all actual being is categorical being. The word 'dispositional' resists the point, and perhaps the best way to weaken its confusing associations is to rephrase [6] as the claim that all being is 'potential' being in the original sense: potent being, power-involving being. Power being is categorical being, like all being. Potency entails actuality, reality. And conversely—for it's not possible to exist without making a difference to reality. It's important to see how undramatic (how boring, as it were) the point is.

So much for

[2] $R[C_O = D_O]$.

Now for

[1] $R[O = P_O]$

—or, in its outwardly milder form, the claim that

[1] there is no real distinction between an object and its properties or propertiedness,

although there is no doubt a useful and workable conceptual distinction between them.

—I accept [2], the thesis of the identity of the categorical and the dispositional, but [1] is off the map. Start from the simple fact that we find it extremely natural to engage in counterfactual thought. We're constantly thinking or hoping or fearing that actual objects may be or could be other than they are, or that they might or could have been other than they were. This way of thinking is clearly legitimate—it's essential to life—and it's equally clear that it depends essentially on the idea that there is after all a real distinction between an object and its properties. Ordinary thought certainly does incorporate this idea, and—equally certainly—it isn't wrong in doing so.

I agree with the first of your claims, but not the second or third. I agree about the legitimacy of counterfactual speculation, but its legitimacy doesn't depend on there being a real distinction between an object and its propertiedness, and ordinary thought isn't in its counterfactual thinking committed to belief in any such thing.

I'll argue for this shortly. First, what's the best way to express the object/property relation? When Kant says that 'in their relation to substance, accidents [or properties] are not really subordinated to it, but are the mode of existing of the substance itself', I think he gets the matter exactly right.[71] Nothing more needs to be said. Put aside philosophy (including Kant's metaphysical framework) and consider an object in front of you in the fullness of its reality. There's no ontological subordination of the object's properties to the object itself. There's no existential inequality or priority of any sort, no ontological dependence of either on the other, no independence of either from the other. (The counterfactuals are coming.) There is, in other terms, no ontological subordination of the total *qualitative* being of the object to the object *an sich*, 'in itself', no ontological subordination of its nature to its existence. It seems just right to put the point by saying again that the distinction between the actual being of a thing or object or particular, considered at any given time, and its overall propertiedness, at that time, is a merely conceptual distinction (like the distinction between triangularity and trilaterality) rather than a real (ontological) distinction. We can, as Armstrong says, '*distinguish* the particularity of a particular from its properties', but 'the two "factors" are too intimately together to speak of a *relation* between them. The thisness and the nature are incapable of existing apart from each other. Bare particulars are vicious abstractions … from what may be called states of affairs: this-of-a-certain-nature.'[72] This seems to me entirely Cartesian (a term of high commendation). We can 'distinguish the particularity of a particular from its properties', we can make this *conceptual* distinction, but we can't really 'speak of a relation', a *real* distinction, 'between them'. Descartes, Spinoza, Leibniz, and Kant agree, and doubtless many others. Nāgārjuna talks in the same vein of the complete codependence of things and their attributes;[73] Nietzsche is admirably brief—'a thing = its qualities' (1885–8: 73); and P. F. Strawson's use of the suggestive phrase 'non-relational tie' can profitably be extended from a logico-linguistic application (to grammatical subject terms and predicate terms) to a straightforwardly metaphysical application (to objects and their properties).[74]

I believe it should be. One should—must—accept the 'non-relational' conception of the relation (!) between an object and its intrinsic properties, if one is going to retain words like 'object' and 'property' in one's metaphysics at all. This is entirely compatible with claiming that an object's properties—including its intrinsic or non-relational properties—may and do change through time, while it remains the same object.

---

[71] A414/B441. Note that 'mode of existing' can't just mean 'the particular way a substance is', where the substance is thought to be somehow independently existent relative to its mode of existing; for that would be to take accidents or properties to be somehow 'subordinate' after all. (I'm assuming that here 'accident' means effectively the same as 'property-instance'.)

[72] 1980: 109–10. Armstrong puts things this way for well-known dialectical reasons to do with stopping 'Bradley's regress', but I take it that there are completely independent metaphysical reasons for saying it.

[73] *c.*150 CE: ch. V, 1995: 14–15 (see commentary on pp. 149–52).

[74] 1959: 167–78. 'Tie', though, is not the best word for this non-relational mutual metaphysical involvement.

—You haven't answered the counterfactual objection. To hold that objects are identical with their properties is to hold that

[15] objects necessarily have all the properties they have

but we naturally say that O, for example, would still have been the object it is, at time *t*, even if its properties had been different, at *t*. We naturally say it would still be the object it is even if (some at least of) its properties were other than they are in fact.

True, but nothing here forbids this way of talking about the non-actual. [1], in particular, allows it. The fact that there are contexts in which we find it natural to say that

[16] O's properties might have been different from what they are while it remained the same object

doesn't provide any support for the mistaken idea that

[17] an object has—must have—some form or mode of being independently of its having the properties it does have.

To think that it does is to build a whole metaphysics of object and property into counterfactual thought, a metaphysics that it doesn't contain or license as it stands, and that is simply incorrect, on the present view.

Putting this aside, one might say that the word 'necessarily' makes [15] ambiguous. In one sense [15] follows directly from [1], because [1] states that an object is identical with its propertiedness, and everything is necessarily identical with itself. But [1] is also compatible with a sense in which [15] is false. We can perfectly well say that

[18] O might not have had the properties it does now have

when supposing that determinism is false, say, for this doesn't put [1] in question. It doesn't challenge the view that whatever happens, everything in which the being of O consists at any time is identical to everything in which the being of O's propertiedness consists at that time. It's possible to read [1] in such a way that it's challenged by [18]; but if one does, one simply misses—chooses to ignore—the fundamental metaphysical truth expressed by [1]. Some philosophers like to distinguish 'compositional' or 'constitutive' identity, on the one hand, from plain identity on the other. This is a well-equipped philosophical playground. But the truth and problem-dissolving power of [1] remain untouched. How can a trivial truth have problem-dissolving power? It can't solve any 'objective' problem, so to speak, but it can solve problems that philosophers make for themselves.

—Look, I'm bald, but my propertiedness is not bald, so I'm not identical to my propertiedness.

Language, not metaphysics (those who wish to invoke 'Leibniz's Law' in this way will have to square it with Whitehead above and Nietzsche and Ramsey below). To understand the present claim, to accept the sense in which it's true that the being of O is identical with the being of the propertiedness of O (that there is such a sense is not in question), is to see that this style of objection has no force. It simply bounces off [1]. It depends on what has been discarded—the standard, language-enshrined object/property distinction that drives the interminable debate. (Discarded, not refuted: it can't be refuted on its own ground, and if it's taken off its own ground, it can protest that the question has been begged.)

—On your view $O = P_{O1}$ at time t_1 and $O = P_{O2}$ at a later time t_2, so $P_{O1} = P_{O2}$ by the transitivity of identity; but O changes from t_1 to t_2, so $P_{O1} \neq P_{O2}$. …

This is really more of the same. One response invokes the four-dimensionalist 'block universe' account of reality and finds a single object and a single propertiedness (no need to speak about 'temporal parts'). A second brackets the block universe and invokes the ancient idea that *strict* identity through time rules out any change at all (or at least any change of parts), so that O at t_1 is not *strictly* identical to O at t_2. On this view, the assumption of the continuing identity of objects under change is a human convenience.

There are contexts in which this last idea is important, but I prefer a third response: to grow familiar with the idea behind [1] is to see that one can retain the ordinary, change-permitting conception of diachronic identity without wavering in one's view that the being of an object is literally identical with the being of its propertiedness, at any given time, and so always. (The two things change together, for they're one thing!) The objection depends on the discarded framework—on linguistic habits and games of discursive thought that can be put aside in order to register the truth in question.

It can take time to acclimatize. There are philosophically habitual ways of understanding the terms 'object' and 'property' that can't survive a proper appreciation of [1]. To object that [1] is just the old 'bundle theory', and has the well-known defects of that theory, is to show that one hasn't understood the point, or (equivalently) is still stuck in an inadequate understanding of 'object' and 'property'. When one sees the sense in which [1] is plainly true, vast regions of the ancient debate about particulars and universals crumble away.

—Whatever the metaphysical facts, it's clear that ordinary thought does incorporate a commitment to [17], i.e. to the negation of [1], in accepting [16] or [18].

If so, so be it. I disagree, but ordinary thought's claim to represent reality correctly is already in the dock in many philosophical courts and already stands condemned on many counts. Some think that conflict with ordinary ways of thinking is always an objection to a philosophical theory, but this is certainly untrue if it's anything more than a recommendation to keep in touch with common-sense conceptions. Philosophy, like science, aims to say how things are in reality, and conflict with ordinary thought and language is no more an objection to a philosophical theory than a scientific one. There are many areas in which we can see clearly that our ordinary concepts and ways of thinking can't be fully adequate to the reality they purport to represent (our ordinary concepts of space, time, and matter). When it comes to [17] in particular, I don't think that ordinary thought makes any error, but ordinary thought's commitment to the general object/process/property/state/event cluster of distinctions may indeed incorporate assumptions about the existence in reality of certain fundamental categorial differences that scientifically informed metaphysics can't underwrite. The object/process/property/state/event cluster, unexceptionable in everyday life, is utterly superficial from the point of view of science and metaphysics.

One of the problems we face is that assumptions of this kind can be active and indeed useful in many parts of philosophy without causing any particular problems (the same is true of the use of Newtonian mechanics in physics). There are, however, areas in metaphysics where their inadequacy to reality is part of the problem at issue, explicitly or not, and then reliance on them in any robust form wreaks havoc, havoc greatly aggravated by their usefulness and unproblematic nature in other areas, which understandably misleads us into thinking that they must be generally viable. I don't think that our ordinary understanding of counterfactuals incorporates the metaphysical error in [17], but there's a related claim that does seem to be true: that when human beings *philosophize* about the object/property relation, certain features of language naturally lead them to think that [17] is true.[75] I don't think Ramsey exaggerates when he says that 'the whole theory of universals is due to mistaking ... a characteristic of language ... for a fundamental characteristic of reality' (1925: 60), agreeing in this with Nietzsche, who writes that

language is built in terms of the most naïve prejudices ... we read disharmonies and problems into things because we *think only* in the form of language—thus believing in the 'eternal truth' of 'reason' (e.g. subject, predicate, etc.)

That we have a right to *distinguish* between subject and predicate—... that is our strongest belief; in fact, at bottom, even the belief in cause and effect itself, in *conditio* and *conditionatum*, is merely an individual case of the first and general belief, our primeval belief in subject and predicate. ... Might not this belief in the concept of subject and predicate be a great stupidity?

The separation of 'doing' from the 'doer', of what happens from a something that makes it happen, of process from something that is not process but is enduring, substance, thing, body, soul, etc.—the attempt to grasp what happens as a kind of displacement and repositioning of what 'is', of what persists: that ancient mythology set down the belief in 'cause and effect' once this belief had found a fixed form in the grammatical functions of language.[76]

These are powerful and dramatic ways to put the point, but perhaps the best thing to do is simply to keep in mind Kant's point that 'in their relation to the object, the properties are not in fact subordinated to it, but are the mode of existing of the object

---

[75] Whether or not they're also led to its converse, the idea that properties have—must have—some form or mode of being independent of the being of the objects that have them.

[76] 1885–8: 110, 104–5, 88. Given that Nietzsche's stress is on causation, it's worth noting that he firmly believes in causation in the sense of natural necessity; what he's objecting to in the last two quotations is the substantivalist separatism of talk of individual causes and effects: 'The unalterable sequence of certain phenomena does not prove a "law" but a power relation between two or several forces. To say: "But precisely this relation remains the same!" means nothing more than: "One and the same force cannot be a different force as well"' (1885–8: 88). Is Nietzsche claiming that metaphysical error is indeed endemic in ordinary thought? It's at least equally plausible that he's simply pointing to the innocent grounds in ordinary thought of the distinctively philosophical error.

itself' (A414/B441, substituting 'object' and 'property' for 'substance' and 'accident'). This is another of those points at which philosophy requires a form of contemplation, something more than theoretical assent, cultivation of a shift in intuitions, acquisition of the ability to sustain a different *continuo* in place in the background of thought at least for a time.

There is in any case no real problem of universals and particulars, as traditionally understood, although there are a number of philosophically habitual ways of understanding the terms 'object' and 'property' that can't survive a proper appreciation of the point. The realization that this is so can be uncomfortable if one has been exposed to the philosophical debate, but it settles out and matures powerfully in time. One looks at any ordinary object, and it is deeply mysterious how there can be thought to be a problem. Its *Sosein* (its being the way it is) is identical to its *Sein* (its being).

So much for the a priori attack on the idea that the standard object/property distinction is metaphysically robust. How does it bear on the objection recorded on page 299? This objection allows that 'syseles' exist, given the way they're defined, but resists the claim that they can be rightly said to be objects, and so qualify as 'sesmets'. It asks why the correct thing to say about the existence of a sysele isn't simply that

(b) an enduring object of a familiar sort—viz. Louis, a human being—has a certain *property* at a certain time, or is in a certain *state* at a certain time, or is the locus of a certain *process* at a certain time, in having a certain unified subject-of-experience-involving episode of experience.

The question seems as good as ever, and the present account of the object/property relation doesn't answer it directly.

It does, however, set up a long-stop. For if some philosophers now try to hold out for the view that the undeniably real phenomenon that I have chosen to denote by the term 'sysele' is really somehow just a matter of the instantiation of a property, something property-like, rather than being a genuine object of any sort, they risk having the whole object/property distinction thrown into doubt. They face the general question, Which among the phenomena are the objects, which the processes, which the events, which the properties of objects, which the states of objects? I've suggested that this question is highly suspect to the extent that it suggests that we have to do with real categorial distinctions rather than with merely conceptual distinctions. I think, in fact, that *all we really have to go on in fundamental metaphysics, when deciding to privilege certain phenomena with the title 'object', are certain sorts of unity considerations* that do not in any way disfavour short-lived syseles, among all the candidates for being objects.

—All very fine. But when one considers a human experience, and hence, on the present terms, an instance of a sysele, it still seems *intensely* natural to say, as in (b), that there is just one object in question—namely, a human being like Louis who is a subject of experience and who has the property of having an experience of a certain kind—rather than saying that there are really two objects in question, a human being, on the one hand, and a sysele on the other.

I think, though, that the two objects claim is just as good—correct—so long as we allow (a plurality of) objects in our fundamental ontology at all. If we consider a sysele, a synergy subject as it is present and alive in the living moment or lived present of experience, a candidate sesmet, then we have in the end no more reason to say that it is really just a property (or state) of some other object, or just a process (or event) occurring in some object, than we have to say that it is itself an object.

—You still haven't given any decided argument against (b). Your general, radical objection to the everyday object/property distinction doesn't bear directly against (b) in the way that your objection to the object/process distinction bears directly against claim (c) on page 300.

I'll try to do so now. Consider Louis, who by the present materialist assumptions is identical with (or is constituted at any time by) a plurality of u-fields in a certain physical, spacetime relation. The same is true of an undetached human hand or cell, or transient blemish. The same is true of a short-lived sysele, the inner mental subject of experience as it is present and alive in a particular episode of experience. Thus far they're all the same.

—I grant the similarity, but it doesn't touch my sense that the best thing to say about the undoubtedly real phenomenon you're choosing to pick out by the term 'sysele' is that it is a process or series of events occurring in a human being, or an aspect of a property of a human being (it's the property of having a certain experience), and not itself a good candidate for the title 'object'.

I know. But as one advances in materialism, in one's conception of the nature of a physical object (assuming that there are such things, and more than one), and in one's intuitive grasp on the point that mental/experiential phenomena and non-mental/non-experiential phenomena are equally physical phenomena, one of the things one comes to see, I believe, is that there are in fact, and as already suggested, no better candidates in the universe for the title 'physical object' ('substance') than syseles as currently understood. Certainly it seems that there is, in nature, as far as we know it, no higher grade of physical unity than the unity of the mental subject present and alive in what James calls the 'indecomposable' unity of a conscious thought.[77]

—Unity proves nothing about ontological category.

Let me re-express the claim. Put negatively, it's the claim that if we consider the phenomenon of the conscious presence of the subject of experience in the living moment or lived present of experience, and agree to speak of this phenomenon by saying that a sysele exists, and make it explicit that we're adopting this (admittedly substantival, count-noun) form of words without prejudice to any final metaphysical conclusion that we may draw regarding its ontological category, then we have no more reason to say that it's really just a property (or state) of some other object, or just a

---

[77] James 1890: 1. 371. The indecomposability of the unities he has in mind is not put in question by his view that their existence involves many neurons and many parts of neurons.

process (or event) occurring in some object, than to say that it is itself an object—a concretely-existing-propertiedness process-entity like any other physical object. That is, in so far it's metaphysically correct to talk of objects at all, it's at least as correct to say that syseles are objects as it is to say that electrons, cats, oak trees, human beings, cars, and stones are objects.

Positively put, the claim is that it's simply correct to say that the sysele phenomenon is an object, a physical object. The point is not only that we have reason to say this, given its intrinsic character as a mental-subject-of-experience unity, and hence as a physical unity in spacetime. It's also hard to see that there are any better candidates for the status of physical objects than syseles. It's hard, in the old language, to see that there are any better candidates (at least so far as this universe is concerned, and as far as our knowledge extends) for the title 'substance'.

—This is charming, but it amounts to very little. You've taken the word 'object' and stripped away the features ordinarily thought to distinguish objects from properties and processes in such a way that it is then easy—not to say empty—for you to call whatever phenomenon you finally identify as the self an 'object'.

The only thing wrong with this objection is that it misdescribes my path and motivation. It's true that I think that the phenomenon I'm proposing to call a 'sysele' (and am putting forward as a candidate for the title 'sesmet', and eventually for the title 'self') qualifies as an object in fundamental metaphysics, if anything so qualifies. I also think there are reasons for saying that there is, in nature, no better example of an object.[78] But I don't start from that point and then adjust the metaphysics until it allows me to say this. The metaphysical moves that destroy the standard demarcations in the object/process/property conceptual cluster seem obligatory in any case. They're as obligatory—irresistible—as they're simple (and initially difficult if one has a conventional training in philosophy). It's in this context that I claim that syseles are objects. If, with dogs and chairs in mind, one continues to find difficulty in the idea that each sysele is a distinct physical thing or object, this may be because one hasn't sufficiently thought through what is involved in first questioning the notion of an object in order to give it a form suitable for use in fundamental metaphysics, and then facing up to the pressure of the claim that it has no legitimate application at all (or no legitimate plural application).

Questions remain, of course, one of which seems particularly difficult. For if syseles are to qualify as objects, and so, possibly, as sesmets, and so, possibly, as selves, then we must presumably be able to say where one begins and another ends. We must in other words be able to specify their 'identity conditions'. I've proposed—and will further argue—that we get a good grip on the requisite synchronic identity conditions when we consider the (necessary) unity of the subject in the living moment or lived present of experience. But a question about diachronic identity conditions remains. It

---

[78] Whatever the value of Nietzsche's speculation on p. 174, which has, I believe, antecedents in the history of philosophy.

may perhaps be quickly solved, if time itself is discrete rather than continuous. But this is still to see.

6.16 *Single*

I'm still considering the nature of sesmets, both in general and in the human case, with a view to considering the proposal that selves (if there are any) are sesmets, and its converse, that sesmets (if there are any) are selves. So far I've discussed three of the four components of the property *sesmet: subject, mental,* and *object. Single* remains, and in particular *single-as-mental.*

Considered in itself, the notion of singleness seems logically and philosophically straightforward, but the property of singleness in question is, crucially, *single-as-mental,* in the sense expounded in 2.18–2.20. This is, in part, a very ordinary property; it's a property possessed by any subject of experience—however the subject of experience is conceived of—at any time that it's conscious. It does, however, raise many questions when considered specifically as a property of sesmets that are being promoted as candidate selves, questions about the synchronic and diachronic identity conditions (the criteria of identity) of sesmets.

6.17 The argument so far

These questions are for Parts 7 and 8. I'm going to end Part 6 by starting a record of the metaphysical argument, expressed in a simple symbolism. As before, the arrow '→' expresses a relation of metaphysical entailment or necessitation (it has strong 'modal' force, in logical terms) and the variables range over concrete reality, concrete existents.[79] At this stage I'll list only the first eight clauses of the interpretation, enough for the first nineteen propositions (many are included merely for the record, not because they serve in the derivation of others). As before, all the properties are assumed to be intrinsic, natural, non-conventional properties or manners of being. I've tried to make sure that one doesn't have to understand the formulae in order to follow the argument.

Interpretation (v1)

Px: x is physical
Ox: x is a concrete object or thing (*res*)
POx: x is a physical object

---

[79] They range over entities in the domain that are *ipso facto* objects in the logical sense, members of a 'universe of discourse' as conceived in model-theoretic semantics, but the symbolism leaves open the question of whether they qualify as objects in fundamental metaphysics.

SUx: x is a strong unity
SAUx: x is a strong activity-unity
Ex: x is experience/experiencing
TCx: x is temporally continuous
Lxy: x is the subject of experience or 'liver' of y

I assumed in 1.2 (4) that materialism is true, that everything that (concretely) exists is physical

{0} [∃xPx ∧ ¬∃x¬Px]

and I assumed in 1.6 (10) that anything that is to count as a self must be a concrete object

{1} [Sx → Ox].[80]

It follows from {0} that all concrete objects are physical objects

{2} [Ox → POx]

and from {1} and {2} that if selves exist, they're physical objects

{3} [Sx → POx].

It's evident that experience exists

{4} ∃xEx

and equally evident (but argued for in 6.3) that experience can't exist without there being a subject of experience

{5} [∃xEx → ∃xSEx],

a subject of experience that is, moreover, the haver or liver of that experience

{6} [∃xEx → [∃ySEy ∧ Lyx]];

and it follows from {4} and {5} that subjects of experience exist

{7} ∃xSEx

—hardly a surprise.

It follows from {0} and {4} that experience is physical

{8} [Ex → Px][81]

and I've assumed for argument (6.10) that objects exist

{9} ∃xOx

---

[80] This is short for '∀x[Sx → Ox]'. I omit explicit statement of the universal quantifier on all propositions of the form [φx → ψx].

[81] There may be 'property dualists' who reject the derivation of {8} from {0} and {4} on the grounds that it doesn't follow from the fact that all objects are physical that all their intrinsic, natural, non-conventional properties are physical. I think, though, that it does follow, for reasons given in 6.15, and that property dualism is incoherent if it supposes otherwise. The derivation is in any case valid as it stands, because the word 'everything' in 'everything that (concretely) exists is physical' isn't restricted to objects, let alone to objects-as-opposed-to-properties or objects conceived of as somehow distinct from their properties. One could put the point (as Barry Dainton pointed out) by saying that the rejection of the standard object/property distinction makes second-order quantification unnecessary.

and also that there is a plurality of objects

{10} $\exists x \exists y[[Ox \wedge Oy] \wedge \neg x = y]$.

I've argued that being a 'strong unity' is necessary for being an object

{11} $[Ox \rightarrow SUx]$

and that a (physical, concrete) strong unity must be conceived in an essentially dynamic way: it must be a strong unity specifically as an activity-unity

{12} $[SUx \rightarrow SAUx]$.[82]

This leads—via the Leibnizian idea that being a strong activity-unity is not only necessary for being a substance or object

{15} $[Ox \rightarrow SAUx]$

but also sufficient

{16} $[SAUx \rightarrow Ox]$

—to the claim that strong unity, strong activity-unity, is not only necessary but also sufficient for objecthood

{17} $[SUx \rightarrow Ox]$.

We may then say that the fact that something is a strong unity (however exactly this is to be established) constitutes sufficient grounds for judging it to be an object whatever other considerations seem to weigh against that judgement; and {11} and {17} add up to

{18} $[SUx \leftrightarrow Ox]$,

the claim that an object just is a strong unity, and conversely. The notion of a strong unity isn't some sharp new analytic tool that allows us to winnow the objects of the world from everything else. It's an intuitive idea to which it is helpful to give first place when one is thinking about what objects are.

Finally for now, I've assumed in 6.14 (303) that diachronic strong unity (and hence objecthood) entails temporal continuity (n-time continuity in the terms of 5.10), whatever account we give of temporal continuity,

{19} $[Ox \rightarrow TCx]$.

So much, for the moment, for the basic metaphysical argument—the barest sketch of a metaphysics. Now for the question of fact: Do selves exist?

---

[82] A strong activity-unity is by definition a strong unity—{13} $[SAUx \rightarrow SUx]$—so we can derive the biconditional {14} $[SUx \leftrightarrow SAUx]$.

Part 7

Metaphysics: the question
of fact, 1

The thinking or the existence of the thought and the existence of my own self are
one and the same.

Kant 1772: 75

7.1 Thin subjects

A sesmet is a subject of experience that is correctly judged to be a single thing or object
when it's considered specifically as a subject of experience that is being considered
specifically in its mental being. What does this amount to in reality, in the human case,
and given that materialism is true?

In 2.15 (64–5) I distinguished two conceptions of the subject: the *thick* conception
according to which

(i) human beings and other sentient creatures considered as a whole are subjects of
experience,

and the *traditional inner* conception, according to which

(ii) a subject of experience is some sort of persisting inner locus of consciousness, an
inner someone, an inner mental presence.

Having made the distinction, I chose to operate with a neutral conception of the subject,
one that neither excluded nor favoured either the thick or the traditional conception.
Now, however, I want to focus on a third conception, the *thin* conception, according to
which

(iii) a subject of experience is something that exists only if experience exists of which it
is the subject.

Both (i) and (ii) build in the standard view that a subject of experience can continue to
exist even when it isn't having any experience—during periods of dreamless sleep, say,

or other possible gaps in the process of experience. (I'm going to assume that such gaps occur.) It's this that creates a need for the third, thin conception of the subject, which can be restated more strongly as

(iii) a subject of experience exists if and only if experience exists of which it is the subject

since a subject of experience exists if experience exists (6.3).

A subject thinly conceived can't possibly have the same duration conditions as a persisting organism like a human being, given that there are gaps in the process of experience, so it will be 'inner', relative to any persisting organism

(iii) a subject of experience is an inner thing of some sort that exists if and only if experience exists of which it is the subject

although it can't have the same duration conditions as a traditional inner subject either, given that there are gaps in the process of consciousness.

As a materialist I take a subject thinly conceived to be literally inner, inner in a straightforwardly spatial sense. A thin subject is a synergy subject (273): the goings on that wholly constitute its existence and experience consist entirely (an 'adductive' point) of activity in the brain. The fundamental property of a thin subject of experience is simply that it can't exist without experiencing, and this is a property that is also possessed by Cartesian minds, so 'inner' can be understood loosely, in a way that allows it to cover such immaterial minds, should they exist.

I've already moved from talking of the thin *conception* of the subject to talking simply of *thin subjects* (I'll consider an objection later), and I'll now expand the interpretation on pages 320–1 in order to continue to display the argument in a simple symbolism.

Interpretation (v2)

Px: x is physical
Ox: x is an object or thing (*res*)
POx: x is a physical object
SUx: x is a strong unity
SAUx x is a strong activity-unity
Ex: x is experience/experiencing
TCx: x is temporally continuous
Lxy: x is the subject of experience or liver of y
TSx: x is a thin subject
Hx: x is human
SLx: x is short-lived
EUPx: x is an experientially unitary period of experience
SES: x is a sesmet
Sx: x is a self
OMx: x has the property *object-as-mental*
SMx: x has the property *single-as-mental*

It's true by definition that thin subjects (TS) exist if experience exists, and conversely

{20} [∃xEx ↔ ∃xTSx],

and since experience certainly exists, so do thin subjects

{21} ∃xTSx.

Whatever their ontological category, they exist: the term 'thin subject' succeeds in referring to some feature of reality, whether or not such a feature can qualify as an object in fundamental metaphysics.

Consider, as in 6.13 (299), an isolated one-second-long experientially unitary episode of experience occurring in a brain, followed and preceded by periods of complete experiencelessness. This experience-existence necessarily involves subjectivity-existence, and this subjectivity-existence necessarily involves subject-of-experience-existence, on the present terms (274). This subject-of-experience-existence is an undeniably actual concrete feature of reality, and it's what is picked out by the term 'thin subject'.

In itself, the definition of 'thin subject' doesn't offer any support to the idea that thin subjects are short-lived or transient entities. I'm assuming that there are as a matter of fact many temporal breaks in the human process of consciousness, and it follows that human (H) thin subjects are as a matter of fact always short-lived (SL),

{22} [[TSx ∧ Hx] → SLx],

for it follows from the definition of 'thin subject' that a temporal break in Louis's process of consciousness is a sufficient condition of there being a new thin subject in the L-reality. Nevertheless the definition of 'thin subject' leaves open the question of duration, and the claim that thin subjects are short-lived in the human case is an independent empirical claim.

I face a problem of exposition, because many are so accustomed to (i) and (ii), and to the idea that they exhaust the options, that they can't take (iii) seriously. But (iii) simply makes a place for a natural use of the term 'subject' according to which it is a necessary truth, no less, that

there can't actually be a *subject of experience*, at any given time, unless some *experience* exists for it to be a subject *of*, at that time.

Given the thin conception of the subject, there can no more be a subject without experience than there can be a surface without extension. The thin conception requires that the subject be *live*, as it were, in order to exist at all.

I think it's very important to have the thin or live conception of the subject in play when taking on the metaphysics of the self. The phenomena I'm calling thin subjects certainly exist, as remarked, whatever their ontological category, for experience certainly exists and to speak of a thin subject is (by definition) just to speak in a certain way of a feature of reality that certainly exists given that experience exists. It's to speak of a feature of reality that is part of what it is for experience to exist. Experience necessarily involves experien*cing* (experience just is experiencing), as observed in 6.3, and the existence of a thin subject is guaranteed by the fact that there is experiencing.

—I agree that there must be *subjectivity* if there is experiencing, but it doesn't follow that there has to be a *subject*.

Subjectivity entails a subject as I understand the term 'subject' (274). This is because of the necessary for-someone-or-something-ness of experience—the Subject Thesis established in 6.3. You can drop the term 'subject' in favour of 'subjectivity' if you like, but only so long as you fully accept the substance of the Subject Thesis.

So far, perhaps, so good.

I've intentionally introduced and defined the notion of a thin subject without any reference to the notion of a sesmet, and my next proposal, unsurprisingly, is that thin subjects are sesmets (SES):

{23} [TSx → SESx].

Sesmets are objects by definition

{24} [SESx → Ox]

(and therefore physical objects, given {2}

{25} [SESx → POx]),

so I'll have to show that thin subjects are objects

{26} [TSx → Ox]

in order to show {23} that thin subjects are sesmets.

{23} and {26}, then, are my main goals. I'm not assuming that the concrete phenomena that I'm picking out by the term 'thin subjects' are objects. I'm taking this as something that needs to be argued for if one wants to claim that thin subjects are sesmets, and can therefore hope to qualify as selves. (The two big remaining questions are: Are thin subjects sesmets? and Are sesmets selves?)

Sesmets are also single-as-mental (SM) and objects-as-mental (OM) by definition (204):

{27} [SESx → SMx]

{28} [SESx → OMx],

so I'll also have to show that thin subjects have the properties *single-as-mental* and *object-as-mental* in order to show that they're sesmets. The last thing will see me home to {26}, for *object-as-mental* entails *object*

{29} [OMx → Ox],

as noted in 4.8 and again in 6.4.

—You're begging the question by using the expression 'thin subject'. It's a substantival, single-object-implying, count-noun neologism like 'sesmet'. You can't move directly from talking of the thin *conception* of the subject to talking simply of the thin subject. I had a related worry earlier (299).

I know I have to argue for the view that thin subjects are objects, and that one can't move straight from the introduction of a thin conception of Xs to the conclusion that thin Xs are a special kind of object. All I've done so far is to point out that human thin subjects as defined certainly exist, whatever their ontological category. As a materialist, I take them to be neural phenomena (adductively understood), synergy subjects, but the claim that these things are strong unities that thereby qualify as *objects* is a further claim that has yet to be established.

—Objects must have criteria of identity, identity conditions.

The question of the synchronic identity conditions of thin subjects—the question of what constitutes a thin subject at a given moment—is relatively easy to deal with. It's already been settled, in effect, in an entirely general manner that doesn't depend in any way on the materialist hypothesis that human thin subjects are synergies of ultimates, for the synchronic identity of a thin subject is inferable from—if it is not simply a matter of—the (trivially) necessary unity of the experiential field at any given moment, a point I discussed in 2.20 and 6.12 and will return to in 8.4–8.5.

The question of the diachronic identity conditions of thin subjects—how long do they last?—may seem considerably more difficult. Every truly experientially unitary period of experience (EUP) has exactly one thin subject

{30} $[EUPx \rightarrow [\exists!yTSy \land Lyx]]$,[1]

because having one thin subject is essentially constitutive of a period of experience's qualifying as an experientially unitary period of experience; but even if we also assert the (as things stand) disputable corresponding claim that every thin subject is the subject of exactly one experientially unitary period of experience,

{31} $[TSx \rightarrow [\exists!yEUPy \land Lxy]]$,

and so endorse the conjunction of {30} and {31}, which (relying on {20}) I will write simply as

{32} $[\exists!xTSx \leftrightarrow \exists!xEUPx]$,

we still need a way of putting clear temporal boundaries on experientially unitary periods of experience if we're going to be able to give clear diachronic identity conditions for thin subjects by reference to them.[2]

I'll call this the *problem of duration*. The final moral of the problem of duration may be that we need to relax our conception of what an object or substance is—or (once again) give up the idea that there is any concrete object or substance other than what Locke calls 'this vast and stupendious universe' (*Essay*, 2.2.3) considered as a whole. Another possibility, mentioned in 5.10 and taken up again in 8.6, is that the problem may have a simple solution.

It helps a little, perhaps, and perhaps a lot more than a little, that we already have it that objects are processes, wholly constituted out of time-matter, process-stuff,

---

[1] '∃!' stands for 'there is exactly one'.

[2] {31} may be contested on the grounds that there can be content breaks and/or flow breaks without temporal breaks (5.7, p. 241). Connectedly, it may be asked why there can't be two distinct experientially unitary periods of experience in a given period of time (e.g. two very different thoughts or experiences) but only one thin subject. I'll consider and reject these suggestions in 8.6.

and that all human thin subjects are entirely constituted out of process-stuff in the brain. The process-stuff of the brain is constantly being recruited—electrochemically corralled or constituted—into one transient thin-subject-involving-and-constituting (and equally experience-constituting) synergy of process-stuff after another, and the proposal, to repeat it, is that these synergies, which are thin-subject-involving-and-constituting occurrences, are intrinsically unified phenomena mentally considered, hence objective physical unities that are candidates for objecthood, and furthermore that they qualify as 'strong' unities mentally considered, and hence as actual physical objects.

—You've added (iii), the thin conception of the subject, to (i) and (ii), the thick and traditional conceptions of the subject. Why stop there? How about the thin conception of an *eater* according to which (iv) an eater doesn't and can't exist at any given time unless it's eating at that time? A (possibly fat) thin eater is just one of those silly putative objects that scholastic metaphysicians like to play with. It's of no real interest or use in philosophy, and your thin subjects seem just as silly.[3]

That remains to be seen. It's true that (iv) is formally similar to (iii), and (iii) can't by itself do the work of showing that the part or portion of reality picked out by the thin conception of the subject is (unlike the thin conception of an eater) philosophically interesting or important.

—All this is hard to follow. It might help a little if you could answer the following direct question. Are thin subjects persons?

You can say so if you wish. In philosophy, the sense of the word 'person' isn't fixed independently of theory. Certainly longevity is not decisive. If a creature qualitatively identical to me during two seconds of my life exists for just two seconds, then that creature is certainly a person and deserves all the consideration due to any of us. There may be natural creatures who live lives that are as complex as ours in two seconds. It's true that thin subjects have been defined as inner things of some sort, but this doesn't decide the issue against their being persons. Some think it obvious that human persons can't be anything other than human beings considered as a whole, but Henry James's (Lockean) phrasing is very natural when he writes of one of his early books, in a passage that I have already quoted, 'I think of ... the masterpiece in question ... as the work of quite another person than myself ... a rich relation, say, who ... suffers me still to claim a shy fourth cousinship' (1915: 562–3). James knows perfectly well that he's the same human being as the author of that book, but rejects the idea that he's the same person as the author of that book.

—This doesn't help. Are we thin subjects?

In one respect, of course, we're thick subjects, human beings considered as a whole. In this respect we are, in being subjects, things that can yawn and scratch. In another

---

[3] Thanks to John Broome, who was more courteous.

respect, though, we are, in being subjects of experience, no more whole human beings than hands or hearts. We are in being subjects of experience inner things (literally, given materialism), neural-synergy subjects; we're no more things that can yawn or scratch than eyebrows or thoughts.

There's nothing anti-materialist about this. One might say that there's a kind of natural and harmless metonymy—a synecdoche—involved in calling Louis-the-whole-human-being a subject of experience. This view is anathema to some, but there's no need for anyone to be put out. The idea is simply that there's a defensible sense in which—indeed, a fundamental respect in which—only a spatiotemporal part of Louis, rather than Louis-the-whole-human-being, is a subject of experience—whether this part is conceived of as a traditional inner subject, or as a thin synergy subject, or even as a gappy diachronically extended plurality or 'bundle' of such thin subjects. There's an immovable sense in which we can call Louis the whole human being a subject of experience only because there are thin subjects in the L-reality; or at least, if such a thing is to be had, a traditional inner subject. There is (once again) nothing in this view that conflicts with anything that is correct in EEE views of the subject of experience, or with any Wittgensteinian wisdom. Nor is there anything that conflicts with ordinary thought or common sense. There is, as just remarked, a straightforward respect in which any truths that involve the idea that there are such things as thick subjects are parasitic on truths about the existence of the features of reality that I'm here calling thin subjects. Whatever the order of language acquisition or thought acquisition, considered either phylogenetically or ontogenetically, this is the metaphysical order. It's not irrelevant that we can imagine a human being reduced by some future surgical *tour de force* to a head, or just a brain, or even something less, without any fundamental disruption of psychological life.

—This sort of example makes bad philosophy and proves nothing. In any case, there's still a human being present after this catastrophic surgery, a person with a passport, rights, property, and so on.

I agree that there's still a person and a human being. This is one way of putting the present point. We seem strongly inclined to say that Louis the person or human being survives in this extreme circumstance, in this grossly shrunken L-reality, just so long as (enough of) his ordinary psychological life survives in the L-reality.[4] Precisely to the extent that we're concerned to stress the point that it's really the human being, the thick subject, that has experiences, we're likely to hold that it will continue to be right to say that it is a *human being* or *person* that has experience (and the vote) under these alarming surgical conditions.

This prompts the thought that we can in principle shrink Louis further, all the way down to a thin subject, so long as there's no fundamental disruption of psychological life. Put otherwise, it suggests that Louis can survive as a human being or person

---

[4] We can debate how much is enough—how far his psychological life can be degraded if he is to remain a human person. Many relevant thought-experiments have been carried out in the recent debate about personal identity.

even when there's nothing left of his brain other than the synergy of ultimates that constitutes—is—the existence of a (necessarily-subject-involving) experience. If you agree that he can survive the originally imagined surgery, it seems that you should accept that he survives even in this case, when we put aside the bistouri, the actual knife, and move on to conceptual surgery, ablation by thought-experiment that pares him down to the thin subject.

On this account, a thin subject does—must—count as a human being and a person. One can't stop at Louis's head (say) and refuse to go further, on the grounds that there's still some physical matter that is the human being in the case in which Louis is down to his head, for the same is true when he's down to a processual synergy of u-fields in the brain. Omnipotent surgical intervention may bring it about that Louis is constituted from moment to moment out of nothing more than the u-fields that would have constituted the thin subject that he would have been at a corresponding moment if his normal fully embodied life, including all its experiential aspects, had been allowed to run on undoctored. (Omnipotence would at each moment have to endow the synergetic structure of u-fields directly with the arrangement that it would normally have as a result of causes outside itself, proximately in Louis's brain and body and less proximately in his environment, but would not find that hard.)

—This is helpful, because now you've clearly gone too far—even putting aside the point that you appear to have two subjects who are Louis in the L-reality at any given time. For even if persons or human beings can survive catastrophic surgery, real or conceptual, thin subjects can't possibly be persons or human beings, because they can't possibly be said to be kind or tactful or know French or algebra.

In an earlier paper on this subject I suggested that a thin subject can be said to know French and algebra 'in every sense in which you can be said to know these things at any given time' (2003c: 157). My idea was that the thin subject that you can rightly be said to be at any given time (whatever else you can rightly be said to be) can be said to know these things in every sense in which you can be said to know these things, at that time, when you're considered as a whole human being, a human animal. It now seems to me misleading or wrong to put the point this way, but what we can say with certainty is that a thin subject can have experience that is just like the experience that thick, whole-human-being subjects have when they have experience that has the character it does because they know French, algebra, and so on. This is immediate, because the being of the thin subject *is* the subjectivity of the thick subject. All experience involves the existence of a thin subject that has the experience that the experience is the having of. This follows from the definition of 'thin subject'. It is, to repeat, a term that picks out a feature of concrete reality that certainly exists, whatever its ontological category. We say that Louis-the-whole-human-being (who knows French and algebra) has these experiences, but Louis's having these experiences is no less truly described by saying that various thin subjects in the L-reality have these experiences. On the present terms the occurrence of the former phenomenon is the same thing as the occurrence of the latter phenomenon.

It was a point much valued in the late twentieth century that a typical, richly conceptually informed human experience can't exist or occur in isolation, and that it's a constitutive fact about such an experience that it is situated in a complex network of other actual and possible experiences, backed by a complex framework of other conceptual and experiential capacities in such a way that it rests on much more than one might initially suppose if one took it to require only possession of the concepts that feature in the foreground of its content. This is a good point, properly handled (not overdone), but it doesn't prevent us from saying that a thin subject can exist and have experience that's just like the experience attributed to a thick human being, although it can't itself be said to have the background network properties. A particular thin-subject synergy occurs in a brain in a human being in an environment, and it can be what it is because it occurs where it does without itself possessing any of the heavy background properties. The idea is similar to Sprigge's when he says that 'each of us, as we are at any one moment, is most essentially a momentary centre of experience or state of consciousness with the duration of the specious present' (2006: 474). Sprigge understands this in a special way, given the particular version of panpsychism he favours, but there's no conflict between my version of the proposal and good orthodox EEE thinking.

—Something is horribly wrong. Nothing is clear enough for me to be sure what it is, but even on your own terms we hit a crux. Suppose I allow your thin subjects, and suppose I grant that they're real concrete phenomena with a very high degree of unity, and that they qualify as objects, and as sesmets (although you haven't shown this). Suppose I grant you all this. And suppose I continue to put aside the troubling point that there seem to be two subjects who are Louis in the L-reality, at any given time at which there is experience in the L-reality. My question is then this. How can thin subjects hope to maintain their bid to be called 'selves' if they're treated as creatures of the surface, as it were, in the way you appear to be doing. How can they possibly deserve the title 'selves' if they're treated as entities that have in themselves no powers or capacities of the sort we want to attribute to selves? Granted, they're real concrete phenomena, but they can't as described be supposed to have dispositional depth, ontic depth, 'modal depth', in David Charles's phrase, of a sort that allows us to say that they in their brief existence know French or algebra. But they have to be treated as things with dispositional depth, things to which unexercised capacities can be attributed, and so on, if they're to have any chance at all of qualifying as selves. ...

I'll call this the *problem of ontic depth*. It's arguable that it arises for Descartes, on one interpretation of his position, and I'll say something about this in 7.3.

7.2 The two—three?—uses of 'I'

—I'm happy to wait, because I have plenty of other problems. I think you're multiplying entities beyond necessity, and I now want an answer to the two-subjects puzzle. Suppose your account of things is in some sense right, or at least possible. My question is then Descartes's question: 'What then am *I*?', at any given time (1641: 18)? What am I if materialism is true, as you're assuming it is, and given that the thin inner subject isn't the same thing as the whole human being? Am I two different sort of things at the same time, a thin inner subject and a thick subject? Are you a thin subject that isn't a whole human being? Is that what you really are? This is *ridiculous*. We may as well add in the traditional inner subject as well, the persisting (fat) inner subject. Then I can be three different things all at once. ...

In sum, what's the relation between GS and a thin subject that exists in the GS-reality? Are you a thin subject? Are you a thin subject that isn't a whole human being? Is that what you really are?

In one sense, No, I'm a human being. In another sense, Yes, this is precisely what I am as I speak and think now—and now—and now. And the same goes for you. As for multiplying entities beyond necessity, I think you'll find in the end that Occam is with me.

—But what then am *I*? Am I two different things, I^H ('H' for human being) and I^s ('s' for self or thin subject or sesmet), at a given time? This is an intolerable conclusion; it's logically and metaphysically intolerable.

Not at all. It's simply a reflection—an accurate reflection—of how the word 'I' or thought-element I works (I'll use *I* in italics to cover both 'I' and I). *I* isn't univocal in ordinary thought and talk, as remarked in 2.4. It tends to refer to two different things at different times in the thought and speech of self-conscious beings like ourselves. Its referential reach varies, so that it refers to more or less according to occasion of use. Locke, who uses the words 'self' and 'person' interchangeably in his discussion of personal identity, notices this when he writes that 'we must here take notice what the word I is applied to; which, in this case, is the man only. And the same man being presumed to be the same [self or] person, I is easily here supposed'—quite wrongly, in his view—'to stand also for the same person' (*Essay*, 2.27.20).

The referring expression *I* is often contrasted with the referring expressions *here* and *now*, which can also vary in their referential reach. But the reference of *I* doesn't expand and contract in a continuous fashion, like that of *now* and *here* (*here* may refer to this room, this town, this country, this planet, ...). Instead, it moves between more or less fixed positions; so I propose. A referring expression like *the castle* provides a better illustration of how *I* functions than *now* and *here*, for *I*, like *the castle*, and unlike *now* and *here*, is ordinarily taken to refer to an object of some sort whether it's taken to refer to the whole human being or the self. Sometimes *the castle* may be used to refer to the castle proper; sometimes it may be used to refer to the ensemble of the castle and the grounds and associated buildings located within its perimeter wall. (Compare 'I'm going to the castle' used by someone twenty miles away and by someone inside the grounds.) Similarly, when I think and talk about myself, sometimes my reference extends to the whole human being that I am, sometimes it extends only to the self that I take myself to be, however the self I take myself to be is best or correctly conceived in fundamental metaphysics. I take the self to be best or correctly conceived as a thin subject, because I think that only a thin subject is going to qualify as an object in the way I require, and accordingly take the actual reference of the inner use of *I* to be to this thing (or perhaps loosely to a series of thin subjects), although this has the consequence that almost all the things we say about it are false,[5] and although most take the inner reference of *I* to pick

---

[5] Horgan and Potrč have a useful way of dealing with this old issue (2008: ch. 3).

out a persisting inner self, and would never suppose it to be a reference to a thin subject (or a series of them).

The castle proper isn't the same thing as the castle in the broad sense, but it is a (proper) part of the castle in the broad sense. Exactly the same is true in the case of an individual thin synergy subject in the L-reality and Louis considered as a whole human being: they stand in a completely straightforward, spatiotemporal, part–whole relation to each other. The same is true of Louis the whole human being and Louis conceived of as a traditional persisting inner self, e.g. a brain-system self (10). If there is a defensible conception of a traditional inner persisting self, then *I* may equally well be supposed to refer to this entity, giving three possible notches or positions on the referential scale, three nested objects to which *I* may refer (if *ātman* is *brahman*, in some nesting sense that allows that *ātman* is none the less a distinct object of reference from *brahman*, there may be four—a new take on the 'extended mind'). And there's no reason why *I* can't occupy more than one position in any actual use in thought or speech. It's arguable that it often does so, in fact, given the extreme fluency of our semantic intentions for *I*. They can flicker between two positions, and my sense is that they can comport both at the same time, or be indeterminate with respect to them.

Having left open the possibility that the inner reference of *I* may legitimately be supposed to be to a persisting self (e.g. a brain-system self), rather than a thin synergy subject, I'm now going to restrict attention to a thin synergy subject, s. s is a spatiotemporally bounded piece of physical process-stuff which one may call p^s; Louis considered as a whole is a spatiotemporally bounded piece of physical process-stuff which one may call p^l. The two things stand in a wholly straightforward spatiotemporal, part–whole relation. p^s is ontically distinct from p^l in the way in which any (proper) part of an object that is itself correctly thought of as an object (a cell, a heart, a finger) is ontically distinct from the larger object of which it is a part. s is also not ontically distinct from Louis in any sense in which such a part of Louis is not ontically distinct from Louis.

I take '$[s = p^s]$' to be a simple identity claim, not a 'constitutive' identity claim—if, that is, a constitutive identity claim is one that allows that the constituter can possibly exist in the absence of the constitutee, or conversely. p^s and s are defined in an essentially temporal-dynamic way, as the very same process/object. Neither can exist without the other. s could not possibly have consisted of anything other than the particular synergy of process-stuff p^s, and p^s could not possibly have existed without s existing. This is not like the much discussed case of a statue and the lump of bronze out of which it is made, given that the latter can exist without the former existing, and that the former can survive change in the latter (these cases offer scholastic pleasures but are of little metaphysical interest). The identity conditions of subject-constituting synergies of process-stuff are a strict function of their parts, in whatever sense they have parts. If one adds or subtracts a single constituent ultimate to or from p^s, one no longer has the same synergy or the same subject s. This decision offends some common intuitions about the conditions under which something can be correctly said to remain the same thing, and I will consider and reject some counterfactual-based objections in 8.8.

Some may refuse to accept that *I* isn't univocal, appealing to the 'tribunal' of ordinary language, or simply to language considered as an essentially public phenomenon or activity. The non-univocality of *I* is, however, plainly marked in the ordinary public use of language, as remarked in 2.2. Even Wittgenstein once proposed that there are two legitimate uses of *I* in thought and talk: the use 'as object' and the use 'as subject' (1958: 66–9)—although it doesn't follow that he thought that the two uses had different references. I think Wittgenstein's distinction is mistaken, or at least unhelpful, for reasons given earlier (23, 150), and my proposal is unlike his. For, first, I have no doubt that all uses of *I* are—necessarily—uses 'as subject', and that there's really no such thing as the use 'as object', although I grant that the phrase has been used in a way that allows one to say that there is such a thing (150). Second, I take it that the two uses I distinguish reflect a real ontological difference between two things that are correctly referred to by *I*.

The present proposal, then, is that there are (at least) two uses of *I* 'as subject', the whole-creature use and the inner-mental-self use. Both are fully metaphysically legitimate, because there really are two objects in question, in at least the sense in which there really are two objects in question when we talk about Tom and Tom's hand, or of Tom and a molecule of water in his body. I think we can acknowledge as materialists, without any hedging reference to *façons de parler*, that an outright truth can be expressed by the claim (so deeply backed by intuition) that I'm not the same thing as my living body considered as a whole; we can acknowledge that there are cases in which what I mean by *I* is not the same thing as the whole human being. At the same time, we can insist that an outright truth is expressed by the claim that I'm a human being. There's no sound argument from the nature of the word or thought-element *I* to the conclusion that this commits us to saying that two things with different identity conditions are in fact the same thing.[6]

This distinction between the two uses of *I* will seem immediately plausible to non-philosophers, but philosophers may still balk. They may doubt its propriety as a way of representing what is the case even if they accept it as an accurate report of how we sometimes think and talk.

—I'm not going to accept any such thing. Even if *I* is used with the semantic intention of referring only to I^s (the putative 'self'), its referential force automatically flows on out to encompass I^H (the whole human being), even in the case you consider in 2.2 (22), in which someone says 'I was floating out of my body and looking down on it from above', and even when it's used in this way in solitary thought. This is a straightforward, non-negotiable fact about the essentially public, essentially intersubjective phenomenon of language. It simply overrides any alleged facts about variations in semantic intention. I'm tempted to go further and argue that such semantic intentions aren't really possible, because the possible content of thought is a strict function of the possible content of language conceived as an essentially public institution with essentially public objects of reference.

---

[6] We're prepared for this point as soon as we allow that dualism isn't provably incoherent. For when dualists say 'I'm distinct from my body', they manage to refer by the use of 'I' and to say something true, if dualism is true. It doesn't, however, follow that 'I' can't in that case also be used to refer to the whole human being.

I don't agree, but let it so flow. However language works, what matters now is the claim that I^s and I^H are different things, at least as different as the castle and the castle proper, as different as Tom and Tom's hand. The argument about the nature of language is irrelevant to the ontological question of fact. What matters—what needs further discussion—is simply the factual claim that we do indeed have to do with two different physical objects (which stand in a part–whole relation). As before, I hope that the discussion of real materialism and of objects in Part 6 will have made it easier to see how this can be so than it might otherwise have been.

—It can't work! If you distinguish I^s and I^H, then you must equally distinguish Louis^s and Louis^H. This shows up the fundamental implausibility of the proposal, because Louis is Louis is Louis^H. Period.

It's true that what goes for 'I' goes for 'Louis', but all that follows is that a truth can be expressed both by saying that Louis is Louis^H and by saying that Louis is Louis^s, even though Louis^H and Louis^s are different objects (I rejected the objection from the transitivity of identity in 1.3). I agree with you, in fact, that Louis is and can only be Louis^H, in so far as the name 'Louis' is assumed to refer to an object with relatively long-term diachronic continuity, because I doubt that there's any other object (such as a traditional inner self) that can be rightly called 'Louis' and that has long-term diachronic continuity. For the moment, though, I'm leaving in play the popular view that Louis^s may reasonably be thought of as something that has long-term continuity, the traditional inner (non-thin) view of Louis^s as something that persists through periods of experiencelessness. On this view, the claim that Louis^H and Louis^s are two different objects is as simple as the claim that Tom's hand isn't the same object as Tom.[7] My claim is somewhat more complicated, not only because I believe that thin subjects are always short-lived in the human case, but also because I take it that there aren't any thin subjects at all in the L-reality when Louis isn't conscious. One can distinguish Louis^s from Louis^H at any time when Louis is conscious, on my view, just as one can distinguish Tom and Tom's hand; but when Louis isn't conscious, there is nothing—no object—that is Louis^s (Louis^s is more like a goose pimple than a hand).

Note that I'm assuming that there's only one subject of experience in the L-reality at any given time when there's experience in the L-reality. It seems increasingly likely that this assumption is false, even when one has put panpsychism aside (the study of cerebral commissurotomies is one disputed source of evidence). I am, however, going to continue to make this assumption for the moment, for the sake of simplicity of exposition (see, though, 348–9 below).

—I'm not sure you can simply help yourself to this, but I have another problem in any case. I may produce a long sentence, lasting half a minute or so, and in which I use the word 'I' several times. Am I to suppose that it has a different reference each time?

---

[7] Note a sense in which to pick out Tom is to pick out Tom's hand, and equally a sense in which to pick out Tom's (undetached) hand is to pick out Tom.

unreflectively intended referent	actual referent
1 = a-d whole human being	= **1** whole human being
2i = a-c persisting mental self traditionally conceived	= **2a** at best, persisting neural basis of self-phenomena
3 = a-b self of the present of experience (thin subject, sesmet)	= **3** self of the present of experience (thin subject, sesmet)

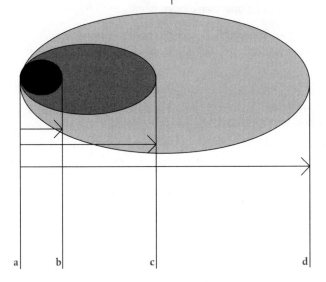

a   b   c   d

Claim: the **actual** reference of 'I' shifts between **1** [whole human being] and **3** [self of the present of experience]. Most reject this. They say that *if* the actual reference ever shifts from the whole human being (if we ever do refer to ourselves as an inner mental subject rather than as a whole human being) then it doesn't shift to **3** but to **2i** the persisting inner self traditionally conceived. I don't think it's helpful to think that there's an object that's the persisting inner self; I think that if you want a persisting thing you should stick to the whole human being. So I think that the *actual* reference, when we take ourselves to be referring to the persisting inner self, is at best to **2a**, the persisting neural basis of self-phenomena, or to **3**, or to **3** + **2a**. The trouble with **2a**, on my view, is that it doesn't sufficiently qualify for being a subject of experience, or indeed an object, although it does fulfil the condition of being something inner that is not the same thing as the whole human being.

What about the **completely unreflective intended** reference, i.e. the thing one unthinkingly takes oneself to be referring to when one says 'I'? Again, it seems that the unreflectively intended reference is either to **1**, the whole human being, or to **2i**, a persisting inner self as traditionally conceived. Some (including committed materialists) feel it is more often, or virtually always, or always, or at least most fundamentally, to **2i**; others think the same about **1**. Some, though, think of the inner self as **3**, and it's arguable that many people sometimes naturally 'speak out of' the self of the present moment—in which case the unthinkingly intended reference is to **3**. Compare Nozick: 'The self which is reflexively referred to is synthesized in that very act of reflexive self-reference' (1981: 91).

Figure 7.1 The two—three?—uses of 'I' (the referential behaviour of 'I').

Not in so far as you take your 'I' to refer to you considered as a whole human being. If, however, you take it to refer to you considered specifically as a self or inner mental presence, and if traditional persisting selves are unavailable as *bona fide* objects, if (as I propose) selves are short-lived thin subjects in so far as they exist at all, then this is indeed what you must suppose (although you can if you like take 'I' to refer to a set or bundle of such selves). You don't have to worry about this, or even believe it, but this succession of thin subjects is, I suggest, the reality that underlies any experience of being a persisting inner self—any experience, in the case in question, of being the same self throughout the having of the thought. This is my proposal about how things are—or at least about what it's best to say if one takes on the strong brief (10) and so takes on the view that selves must qualify as objects in fundamental metaphysics, and not just 'conventionally' speaking, if they're to defend themselves against the charge of non-existence.

—But who, or what, actually *speaks* when Louis says 'I'?

Louis does. The reference of 'I' is fluid in his thought and talk in the way just described. We move naturally between conceiving of ourselves primarily as a human being and primarily as some sort of inner subject. Sometimes we mean to refer to the one, sometimes to the other, sometimes our semantic intention hovers between both, sometimes it embraces both.

—This semantic intention stuff isn't going to work, because you think that inner subjects are thin, and human beings certainly don't conceive of themselves as thin subjects when they conceive of themselves as inner subjects. They conceive of themselves as 'traditional' persisting inner subjects. So they never refer to thin subjects, so far as their semantic intentions go. I don't think you do either, in daily life. You face the question Merian put to Hume: 'What is the meaning in your mind and your mouth of these personal pronouns which you cannot prevent yourself from continually using, and without which you would not know either to think or to express your thoughts, *me, I, we*, etc.?'[8]

I've already granted that most (not all) people think of themselves as traditional persisting inner subjects when they think of themselves as inner subjects, but my reply to your previous question stands. If in the end the best thing to say is that there's no such thing (object) as the persisting inner subject, then we obviously fail to refer to any such object when we think of ourselves as things (objects) that are inner subjects. Instead we refer to **3** the current thin/live subject as specified in Figure 7.1, or to the recent series of thin subjects (although these don't together constitute a single object), or to **2**, the persisting 'brain-system self' phenomena, although they don't in fact constitute an object, let alone an object that could be a subject or self, or to **2** and **3** together, or …

—Scholastic fiddlesticks. The persisting neural basis of self-phenomena is a *bona fide* object. It's something that qualifies as a subject of experience and as an object in a way that suffices for it to

---

[8] Merian 1793: 190; but see n. 36 below.

qualify as a self even given your insistence that a self must be an object. You still haven't said anything to discourage me from this view.

This is the 'brain-system view' of the self. It's a perfectly reasonable view, seaworthy for many purposes of thought, and I don't expect to be able to argue you or anyone else out of it. My best hope is that you'll eventually find that you no longer hold it.

7.3 Thin subjects: Descartes

The central feature of the thin conception of the subject is that it takes subjects of experience to be things that don't and can't exist in the absence of experience. It's hardly new in philosophy. Descartes, for one, endorses it. It's fundamental to his conception of the I or mind or soul or self or subject that it doesn't and can't exist in the absence of experience or consciousness or—in his terminology—'thinking' or 'thought' (*cogitatio*). A subject of experience that exists without experience existing—conscious mental process of which it is the subject—is as impossible for Descartes as a physical object existing without extension. So Cartesian minds are thin subjects, although they're far from transient, being possibly immortal. Leibniz also endorses thin subjects, taking them to be long-lived—naturally indestructible, and so does Spinoza, as I understand him, even as he holds that there is at bottom only one. So do Kant, and William James, and also, perhaps, Fichte and Nozick. Hume, as a genuine sceptic, doesn't commit himself, but he certainly doesn't think that any other positively contentful conception of the subject is available to an empiricist.

—Descartes is certainly committed to the view that the mind is always thinking, but he isn't committed to the extremely problematic view that all thinking is conscious or consciousness-involving, a matter of experience.

So some say, but they're surely wrong. Descartes says that the term 'thinking' applies 'to all that exists within us in such a way that we are immediately aware of it. Thus all the operations of the will, the intellect, the imagination, and the sense are thoughts (thinkings)' (1641: 2.113). 'We cannot', he says, 'have any thought of which we are not aware at the very moment when it is in us' (1641: 2.181). 'By the term "thinking"', he says, 'I understand everything which we are aware of as happening within us [i.e. in the mind], insofar as we have awareness of it. Hence, *thinking* is to be identified here not merely with understanding, willing and imagining, but also with sensory awareness' (1644: 1.195) and emotion (see e.g. 1644: 2.281). 'Understanding, willing, imagining, having sensory perceptions ... all fall under the common concept of thinking or perception or consciousness' (1641: 2.124).

I think such quotations sufficiently show that Descartes does identify thinking with conscious experience, i.e. with experience, in my terms (5). He uses 'thinking' as an entirely general word for all experience—although he also uses it more narrowly at certain points.[9] The clearest modern translation of 'cogito, ergo sum' is 'I experience, therefore I am'. I'll continue to use Descartes's 'thinking', but it can always be replaced by 'experiencing'.

Descartes, then, holds that the mind is always thinking—a view summarily rejected by Locke ('every drowsy nod shakes their doctrine, who teach, that the soul is always thinking' (*Essay*, 2.1.13)). But this is not the most striking feature of his position. By far the most striking and difficult feature of Descartes's position is that he holds that there is nothing more to the mind, ontologically speaking, than experiencing, actual conscious mental process. Underlying his conviction about this is his most fundamental metaphysical view, which I mentioned in 6.15 and will now set out in more detail: the view that there's no real distinction between a thing or object and its attributes or properties. The distinction between the notions of attributes like thinking/experiencing or extension 'and the notion of substance itself is', as he says in *Principles*, 1.63, 'a merely conceptual distinction' (1644: 1.215). It's a distinction that can be made in thought (a 'distinction of reason'), not a 'real' distinction, where to say that there's a real distinction between two things is simply to say that each can exist in reality without the other existing. For Descartes, there is, as Clarke says, 'no real distinction … between a thing and its properties' (2003: 215). Nadler concurs: Descartes's 'considered position … is that while there is a conceptual distinction between substance and attribute … there is not a real distinction between them. Substance and attribute are in reality one and the same' (2006: 57).

I think Descartes is right about this. It's a point that appears to render vast tracts of recent analytic philosophy otiose, but the naturalness and availability of counterfactual speculations about how objects could be different from how they actually are give us no reason to doubt it, or so I argued in 6.15. I also argued that the ground of the lack of real distinction between a substance or object and its attributes or properties is identity. Descartes agrees: the attributes of a substance 'are indeed identical with the substance' (1648b: 15).

Some feel that the Cartesian notion of a 'real distinction' is musty or obscure, accompanied as it is by the notions of substance, attribute, and mode (or modification). But this isn't so. The *real* in 'real distinction' simply means 'in reality', 'in concrete reality', 'outside our thought', as opposed to merely 'in our thought'.[10] An *attribute* is a fundamental or general property; a *mode* is a particular way of possessing such a general property. Extension is an attribute, and being spherical or triangular is a specific mode of extension, a particular way of being extended. Experience or thinking is an attribute, and seeing Paris or hoping it will rain is a specific mode of experience or thinking. The fact that an attribute can't possibly exist without existing in a certain mode (you can't have

---

[9] See e.g. 1644: 2.209. It would be perverse to treat his use of 'thought' as evidence that he's some sort of early eliminativist about sense-feeling experience.

[10] 1645/6: 3.280. I'm putting aside the fact that Descartes deeply mistrusted and had no real use for the notion of 'substance' (see especially Clarke 2003: esp. chs. 1, 8, 9.) and preferred to use the word 'thing' (*res* and *chose* in Latin and French respectively) to indicate the properties of existence and individuality.

extension without some particular mode of extension, e.g. triangularity or squareness or horse-shapedness) means that there is no more a real distinction between the existence of an object or substance considered at a given time and the existence of the particular modes that its attributes exemplify at that time—i.e. its properties considered as a whole—than there is between a substance and its attributes *tout court*. Its being, if I may permit myself the trope, is its being.

Consider the particular case of the self or mind or 'thinking thing'. According to Descartes, there's no real distinction between a thinking thing and its attribute of thinking. Neither can exist without the other, any more than a thing can exist without itself. The being of the one at any given time (and so always) is the being of the other. So when he states that the mind ('soul') or subject neither does nor can exist in the absence of actually occurring thinking—when he holds that thinking is an essential property of mind in this sense, a property it can never lack—this is not some sort of extra stipulation on his part, a special condition added to an already existing conception of the nature of the mind. The reason why a mind or self or subject in which no thinking is going on is as impossible as a physical object without extension is that mind or self or subject *is* thinking; it's wholly and literally constituted of occurrent thinking. That is what *res cogitans*—a mind or self—is. It's just—it just is—thinking, consciousness, experiencing. There is no real distinction between (i) the concrete existence of the attribute of thinking and (ii) the concrete existence of thinking 'substance'. They're identical. The point is already secured by Descartes's commitment to the identity of substance and attribute, whatever problems it raises. (It's not hard to understand why Leibniz feels the need to postulate 'petites perceptions', tiny little conscious states that one doesn't notice, in order to try to defend it.)

A Cartesian immaterial mind is quite unlike an immaterial mind as traditionally conceived, because an immaterial soul is traditionally conceived of as some sort of locus of experiencing that isn't itself wholly constituted of experiencing.[11] The existence of a Cartesian mind, by contrast, is wholly a matter of occurrent experiencing, conceived of as some sort of inherently active phenomenon, and so obviously can't exist when there isn't any experiencing going on. In the *Principles* Descartes talks of 'our soul or our thinking' as if the two terms were strictly interchangeable (1644: 1.184). Later he writes, seemingly unequivocally, that 'thinking', in being the essential attribute of thinking substance, 'must be considered as nothing else than thinking substance itself … , that is, as mind' (1644: 1.215). In his *Notes against a Certain Broadsheet*, in which he reiterates his official doctrine that there's a real distinction between mind and body in the face of

---

[11] It isn't wholly constituted of experiencing even if it is always host to experiencing—even if experiencing is one of its essential properties. In fact, this conception of the immaterial mind is about as traditional as Christmas. It's common now, but among modern philosophers, Descartes, Spinoza, and Leibniz all reject it. So does Berkeley, for his own special reasons (see *Principles*, § 139). So does Hume, for his, in a passage (*Treatise*, 165/252) quite wrongly thought to involve the denial of the existence even of short-lived subjects (see G. Strawson 2001: 70, 78–80, and in preparation, *a*). Of the members of the two great rationalist and empiricist triumvirates, only Locke makes use of it, and he himself is, at bottom, a materialist who has no difficulty with the idea that the material mind can continue to exist in the absence of occurrent experience.

Regius's most unwelcome exposure of his baseline view,[12] he treats being a thing (*res*) and being an attribute as effectively the same, saying of the attributes of extension and thinking 'that the one is not a mode of the other but is a *thing, or attribute of a thing*, which can subsist without the other'.[13] Questioned on the point by Burman, he confirms that his view is that 'the attributes [of a substance], when considered collectively, are indeed identical with the substance'.[14]

Contrary quotations can be found—at one point in his conversations with Burman Descartes speaks of substance as a 'substrate'—but his basic commitment is quite clear.[15] When Descartes seems equivocal, or says things that seem incompatible with his view as stated here, it's important to remember that he is anxious not to rouse the Church and the philosophers of the Schools by expressly denying the existence of entities to whose existence they are committed ('I do not deny that ...' is a recurring phrase). 'I wish above all that you would never propose any new opinions', he wrote to Regius in 1642,

but, while retaining all the old ones in name, only offer new arguments. No one could object to that, and anyone who understands your new arguments properly will conclude immediately from them what you mean. Thus, why did you need to reject substantial forms and real qualities explicitly?[16]

Leibniz makes the same move thirty years later:

a metaphysics should be written with accurate definitions and demonstrations, but nothing should be demonstrated in it apart from that which does not clash too much with received opinions. For in that way this metaphysics can be accepted; and once it has been approved, then, if people examine it more deeply later, they themselves will draw the necessary consequences.[17]

The trick, for Descartes, as for Leibniz, is to do one's philosophy using the conventional terminology as far as possible, without making any real substantive appeal to any dubious entities it recognizes, trusting that one's intelligent readers will see that this is what one has done.

It's plain, in any case, that Descartes doesn't endorse one standard (Lockean) picture of the immaterial mind or self, for according to this picture, P1 in Figure 7.2, there is

---

[12] His true baseline view, taken up by Spinoza, is agnosticism on the question of whether there is, knowably, a real distinction between thinking and extendedness. See n. 21 below.

[13] 1648a: 1.299; my emphasis picks out two expressions that are offered as equivalent.

[14] 1648b: 15. Kant's elastic balls example (81) succeeds against the 'rational psychologists', but has no force against Descartes himself because it utterly misrepresents his fundamental metaphysics. It posits unbroken continuity of the attribute of consciousness carried successively by many different substances. On Descartes's view, however, unbroken continuity of consciousness is already a sufficient condition of there being a single continuing mental substance, because it's the same thing as there being a single continuing mental substance. (How this point interacts with Descartes's identification of continuity of existence with continual 'creation afresh'—see p. 402 below—I leave to be considered.)

[15] Descartes 1648b: 17; the matter is usefully adjudicated by Cottingham (1976: 17, 77–9).

[16] Quoted by Clarke 2006: 224, who has an excellent discussion of the matter; see also Descartes 1619–50: 205. Descartes had particular reason to ask Regius to be more circumspect because Regius was publicly identified with the Cartesian cause.

[17] Leibniz 1676: 95. Most strikingly, Leibniz writes these words after breaking off in mid-sentence—in fact mid-word—a train of thought that is leading him into a Spinozism he can't possibly officially endorse. See Stewart 2006: 193. See also Mercer and Sleigh 1995: 71; Rutherford 1995: 155–9, 163.

(i) some sort of immaterial mind-substance or mind-stuff that is (ii) the *ground* or *bearer* of conscious mental process, and that (iii) can continue to exist even when there isn't any conscious mental process going on, and that therefore (iv) has some nature other than conscious mental process.[18] Everyone agrees that Descartes rejects (iii), in holding that

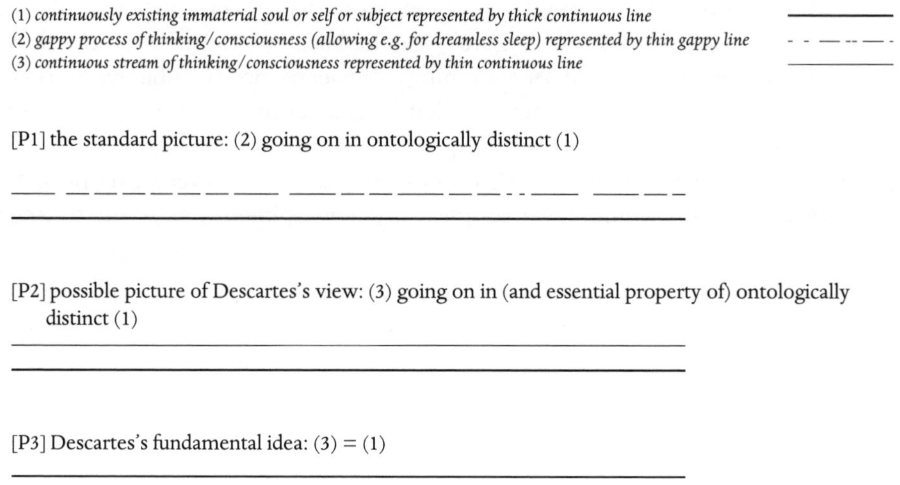

---

(1) *continuously existing immaterial soul or self or subject represented by thick continuous line*   ─────────

(2) *gappy process of thinking/consciousness (allowing e.g. for dreamless sleep) represented by thin gappy line*   - - ── -- ── -

(3) *continuous stream of thinking/consciousness represented by thin continuous line*   ─────────

[P1] the standard picture: (2) going on in ontologically distinct (1)

── ── ── ── ── ── ── ── ── ── ── ── ── -- ──   ── ── ──

[P2] possible picture of Descartes's view: (3) going on in (and essential property of) ontologically
distinct (1)

[P3] Descartes's fundamental idea: (3) = (1)

Figure 7.2 Three pictures of the immaterial self

---

a mind or subject must always be thinking, but his claim that 'each substance has one principal property which constitutes its nature or essence … and thinking constitutes the nature of thinking substance' (1644: 1.210) is often read as if it allowed, as in P2, (iv) that the mind has *some* other necessary manner of being that is not occurrent thinking (experience). This reading is extremely problematic, however, because to claim that something Y constitutes the nature of something X is to claim that nothing else does.[19]

---

[18] If we suppose, rather, that the standard picture is P2, and incorporate the view that experiencing is an essential property of immaterial mind-stuff, we drop (iii) while retaining (iv). Note that it's (iv) that raises the doubt mentioned earlier (265) about whether immaterial minds as ordinarily understood, as opposed to Cartesian immaterial minds, can properly possess the property *single-as-mental*. The problem is that it seems that their singleness is fundamentally secured, both synchronically and diachronically, by the singleness of their substance, where this, so far, is something that is not itself guaranteed to be intrinsically mental in nature. In philosophy we habituate to the purely negative word 'immaterial' in such a way that we tend to take it that anything called 'immaterial' is guaranteed to be something (wholly?) intrinsically mental in nature, but the word simply doesn't warrant this (see G. Strawson 1994: 114–20). I'm not going to press the point, though; most will be inclined to think that an immaterial mind as ordinarily understood (or equally a neural 'brain system', put forward as a candidate for being the self) does indeed possess the property *single-as-mental* in the required way, just in being the 'seat' of memory, character, conscious experience, and so on.
[19] The point is not undermined by the fact that X may be said to have other essential but non-qualitative, non-nature-constituting attributes like duration and existence, or ultimate dependence on God (see Descartes 1644: 1.200, 211–12).

It is also, of course, very problematic to reject (iv). For the moment, though, it seems plain that Descartes rejects all of (ii)–(iv). What's more, he accepts (i), which employs a word—'substance'—of which he has, as already noted, an extremely low opinion, only inasmuch as he takes it that there is no real distinction between 'the thing … we call … a substance' (1641: 2.166) and its attributes. His picture is P3: the continuously existing immaterial mind or self or subject just is the continuous stream of thinking/consciousness.

—Impossible. Replying to Arnauld, Descartes agrees that episodes of thinking like 'understanding, willing, doubting etc. are … attributes which must inhere in something if they are to exist; and we call the thing in which they inhere a substance' (1641: 2.166). Replying to Hobbes, he notes that 'a thought cannot exist without a thinking thing', and that if confusion has arisen in the interpretation of his position, it's because ' "thought" is sometimes taken to refer to the act, sometimes to the faculty of thought, and sometimes to the thing which possesses the faculty'. The implication of this last quotation seems clear: all these three references are references to distinct things, so that there is a *thing* or *substance* which possesses certain *faculties* and accordingly performs certain sorts of *acts*; and Descartes further insists that he does not 'deny that I, who am thinking, am distinct from my thought, in the way in which a thing is distinct from a mode'   (1641: 2.143–5).

The last quotation doesn't support your claim; if anything it supports mine. The other two seem more promising at first, but they don't undermine the attribution of P3 to Descartes, who for reasons of caution, and as just remarked, makes a point of continuing to use accepted terminology even though it plays no active role in his position. P3 can't be understood to incorporate any standard substance/property distinction, for while Descartes grants, as you note, that 'we *call* the thing in which [mental attributes] inhere a substance', he doesn't think that the notion of substance has any meaning or intelligible reference or explanatory force whatever, in so far as a substance is supposed to be something that is in any way distinct from its attributes or properties.[20] It's just a 'dummy' word, a peace-keeping word. He says that 'the attributes [of a substance], when considered collectively, are indeed identical with the substance' (1648*b*: 15). The *res cogitans* is just the *cogitans*; the force of the *res* is to indicate the *real existence* of the *cogitans*. It's only in so far as we accept to employ the language of 'inherence' and 'substance', and therefore accept to speak of thought and extension as 'inhering in a substance', that we must—given the way in which the properties of thought and extension are on his official view *essentially* mutually repellent—say that there are two substances. But the word 'substance', again, is doing no work, and towards the end of his life Descartes—the indefatigable dissector of brains, in every other pore of his philosophy a materialist—admits in effect, and as he should, that he doesn't know enough about the nature of matter to be sure of this repulsion.[21]

---

[20] See again Clarke 2003: chs. 1, 8, 9. Descartes rightly rejects a widespread (but not universal) assumption of his times and ours.

[21] In 1648 Descartes conceded to Burman, contrary to his official position, that (in Clarke's words) 'we cannot claim to have adequate knowledge of anything, including even bodies, and … are obliged to work within the limitations of our concepts even if we recognize those limits' (Clarke 2006: 385). It follows from this that we can't definitively rule out the possible

There is of course an extremely serious difficulty in the radical position as so far characterized.[22] This is the difficulty of finding a ground or 'place of residence', a manner of real existence, for mental faculties or capacities like will and understanding, for innate ideas, and for what Descartes calls 'intellectual memory'.[23] Where can they be lodged, given the rejection of (iv)—the idea that the thinking subject is, metaphysically, nothing other than experiential process? Descartes doesn't really believe in faculties as entities, holding that 'the term "faculty" denotes nothing but a potency' (1648a: 1.305), but potencies or powers also seem to need a place of residence (a manner of real existence) of a sort that seems hard—impossible—to supply if all one has to hand at any time is experiential process with the particular content that it has at that time.

The difficulty seems somewhat less serious for those who believe that Descartes's use of 'thinking' extends to non-experiential goings-on; but Cartesian thinking can't be non-conscious or non-experiential in any way. It's true that an individual *cogitans*—an individual, persisting, uninterrupted, thinking-process—is something inherently active and powerful in some manner; it's not in any sense a mere streaming of passive content (the passive-content conception of experiential goings-on may be the first that comes to the present-day philosophical mind). But to say that the process involves powers is not to say much, because anything that exists at all, and that therefore has categorical properties, *ipso facto* has powers, according to the argument in 6.15, and there still appears to be a very difficult question about how any conscious-experience *cogitans* process can possibly involve the sorts of powers we associate with a human mind—will, understanding, memory, possession of concepts, innate or not, and so on. How can this categorical being—this conscious-experience process with the content that it has—constitute what one might call the *power being* of a mind? This is the problem of ontic depth signalled on page 331. Somehow or other, Descartes has to find room for a mind or self or subject with sufficient ontic depth while denying that it consists of anything other than conscious mental process whose whole being is manifest in consciousness.

This last requirement seems to sink his position, unless Leibniz can help.[24] And even if it doesn't sink Descartes's position, it seems to sink mine. For if I want to argue that selves are thin subjects, I must either find room for a subject or self with sufficient ontic depth given only the resources of thin subjects, transient synergies of neural process-stuff, or

---

corporeality of mind, a view that was of course in circulation at the time (see also Clarke 2003: 258; G. Strawson 2006b: 214). For a great discussion of 'adequate' as opposed to 'inadequate' knowledge, and the associated but different distinction between 'complete' and 'incomplete' knowledge, see Yablo 1990: 158–77. The same distinctions and claims are in play, in a muddier form, in current discussion of the mind–body problem (e.g. in the debate about 'a posteriori physicalism'), which is condemned by historical ignorance to spend a great deal of time laboriously retreading ancient ground.

[22] I discuss it in G. Strawson 1994: 136–44. On the attribution to Descartes, compare Priestley, who, discussing Mamertus, finds 'in some of his expressions the peculiar opinions of Descartes. For he says, the soul is not different from the *thoughts*, that the soul is never without *thought*, because it is all *thought*' (1777–82: 362; Mamertus died *c.* 475). Compare also Dainton's 'minimal subject', whose existence, in what Dainton terms the 'Cartesian nightmare', consists of absolutely nothing but a stream of consciousness (2008a: 249–51).

[23] Intellectual memory is memory that can't on Descartes's official theory be stored in the brain along with autobiographical memory, memory of contingent facts, memory of particular mathematical truths that one has worked out, and so on (see e.g. Descartes 1640: 146).

[24] Its difficulty helps to explain why Descartes's position has been so consistently misunderstood.

else agree that selves are indeed 'creatures of the surface', entities with no great ontic depth who can't possibly be said to know French or algebra in any rich dispositional sense, although they have experience indistinguishable from the experience that thick, whole-human-being subjects are correctly said to have when they have experience that has the character it does because they know French or algebra.

For the moment I'll say only that I take the creatures-of-the-surface view to be a real option. Note that the word 'self' may drive the demand for ontic depth more strongly than the word 'subject'. 'Subject' is a great deal less exigent, to my ear, and it may be that some of the associations of the word 'self' are putting an unnecessary drag on the discussion. My concern with the self is simply a concern with the subject of experience conceived as something that isn't the same thing as the whole human being, and I can do without the word 'self', which one can always read as short for 'subject of experience conceived as something that is not the same thing as the whole human being'. I could have called this book *Subjects* rather than *Selves*.

7.4 $[e = s = c]$ (1)

What is to be done? Consider the distinction between

(i) a particular individual experience e, a clearly temporally bounded experientially unitary period of experience lasting from t_1 to t_2,

(ii) the thin subject s of e,

and

(iii) the experiential content c of e conceived of as something concrete and occurrent, as the 'what-it's-likeness' that actually occurs between t_1 and t_2.[25]

Here we seem to have three really distinct (in Descartes's technical sense) things. It appears, though, that Descartes thinks that the thin-subject *res cogitans* just is the process of consciousness itself, that the *res cogitans*, the thin-subject self, is not really distinct from its experience at any given time, i.e. that

[1] $[s = e]$.

And that's not all, for the experience is on his view nothing ontically over and above its experiential character or being. It contains nothing hidden, i.e. nothing over and above what is manifest, i.e. nothing over and above its total experiential content; this is its whole being. In which case

[2] $[e = c]$.

[1] and [2] deliver the seemingly extraordinary conclusion that the (thin-subject) self is nothing other than the experiential content

[3] $[s = c]$

---

[25] By 'content' I mean, as usual, 'narrow' content, purely 'internal' content, 'experiential' content, 'phenomenological' content—whatever you want to call the thing whose existence is the most certain of all things and which includes cognitive experience—conscious entertainings of thoughts—as much as sensory experience (2.8).

—that, in sum,

[4] $[e = s = c]$.

I'll call this the *Experience/Subject/Content Identity Thesis*—the $[e = s = c]$ *thesis* for short. It seems a strange view, at least at first; but it does appear that Descartes holds it in some form, given that he holds that substance and attribute are one and the same. I'm not surprised by this, because I think it may be right (see 8.8–8.10), and Descartes is usually right on fundamentals. Kant also endorses [1], whatever his position on [2], when he writes that 'the thinking or the existence of the thought and the existence of my own self are one and the same', subscribing thereby to the thin conception of the subject, which is entailed by [1].[26]

Two points before the $[e = s = c]$ thesis is dismissed as ridiculous, both in itself and as an account of Descartes's conception of the nature of mind. The first is small and oblique, but may be useful for some. It's still commonly held in present-day analytic philosophy that in the case of any given particular experience e, neither e's subject, s, nor e itself is part of the experiential content of e (whether the content is construed internalistically or externalistically). This may be thought to show that [4] can't possibly be true even if all the other difficulties that it raises can be somehow overcome. This view about the content of experience is, however, thoroughly disputable. As for e, there's a crucial sense, recorded notably by Aristotle, in which e is itself essentially, constitutively, and unparadoxically, part of its own content.[27] So too, there's a crucial sense in which s is essentially, constitutively, part of the experiential content of e, part of what is given to s in the having of e, even when s's attention is wholly focused on the external environment (a tree, say) and not at all on itself.[28] Both these claims need careful exposition, though. They lie at the heart of the answer to the question of what consciousness or experience is, but they don't in themselves get us any closer to the bluntly metaphysical triple identity claim, and may even be thought to hinder an approach. At the same time, they may help to remove one kind of bad basis for thinking that it can't possibly be true.

The second and much more important point is that Descartes's conception of the nature of mind bears a deep resemblance to his conception of the nature of matter. Everyone agrees that Descartes holds that matter is literally nothing other than extension

---

[26] 1772: 75. The quotation is from Kant's famous letter to Herz. There's no reason to think that he abandons this view in his critical philosophy, no reason to think that he takes the as-it-is-in-itself being of the self or subject of experience to be different from the as-it-is-in-itself being of experience itself.

[27] On Aristotle, see Caston 2002; see also the quotation from Gurwitsch on p. 27 above. 'The initial experience [thought] by means of which we become aware of something does not differ from the second experience by means of which we become aware that we were aware of it' (Descartes 1641: 2.382). 'Consciousness … is inseparable from thinking, and, as it seems to me, essential to it: it being impossible for any one to perceive without perceiving that he does perceive' (Locke, *Essay* 2.27.9, using 'think' in the all-inclusive Cartesian fashion). What many philosophers have in mind, in making this sort of claim, is really nothing more than the subjective qualitative character or 'what-it's-likeness' of experience. The root idea is simply that experience is in some key sense 'self-intimating' or 'self-luminous'—to use phrases Ryle employed with disparaging intent (1949: 158–9).

[28] 'Whatever it is that I know, I know that I know by an implicit reflection that accompanies all my thoughts. Thus I know myself in knowing other things' (Arnauld 1683: 53). See also the quotations from Gurwitsch, Frankfurt, Lonergan, and Deikman (101, 176–7, 27), and Zahavi 2006: chs. 1–4.

(*res extensa*). To that extent it's hardly surprising that he holds that mind is literally nothing other than thinking or experiencing. What's surprising, perhaps, is that there has not been more discussion of what this amounts to.

Descartes's view about matter is often derided. One common objection is that there can be no difference, for him, between a cubic metre of deep space and a cubic metre of lead or cheese. What such objections show, though, is that Descartes doesn't conceive of extension in anything remotely like the way we do. He conceives of it more in the way Weinberg does when he proposes that all physical objects of the sort we take ourselves to have to do with are made of rips in spacetime, spacetime being itself a physical object, an essentially substantial something that is itself, in some immovable sense, the only thing there is (295). One might say that Descartes conceives of extension as something inherently powerful, an idea seemingly mirrored in the current conception of the 'quantum vacuum', and perhaps also in the idea that the 'dark energy' posited in current physical theory is identical with the existence of space (it is that which makes or keeps it 'roomy', so to speak).

Certainly Descartes agrees that there is, strictly speaking, only one material thing or substance, the spatially extended universe. It's a 'plenum', that is, it contains no vacuum (the definitional opposite of plenum), no place that isn't occupied by 'matter'. How could there be, given that extension is matter? Extension is itself something concrete, substantial. The universe is one big extended thing 'with different nubbly gradients of texture'[29] at different places that amount to trees, people, railway lines, and so on—an idea which, once again, seems profoundly in accord with the spirit of present-day physics and cosmology.

Descartes never claims in parallel fashion that there is really only one *res cogitans*. Here there is a major structural difference between his notions of mind and matter. He assumes without argument that there are many irreducibly numerically distinct individual minds, as required by conventional Christian eschatology, without offering any sort of account of their identity and individuation conditions, claiming that 'each of us understands himself to be a thinking being and is capable in thought of excluding from himself every other substance'.[30] The deep similarity between his view of mind and his view of matter is simply that he holds that thinking—experiential process—is literally all there is to the former, just as he holds that extension is literally all there is to the former, and the present point is this. It's plain that we need to adjust our conception of extension quite radically if we want to acquire any sense of what Descartes thinks matter is; we need to adjust it to the point where it allows us to accommodate

---

[29] Catherine Wilson, in correspondence. If, as some physicists believe, our spacetime is just one 'sheet' or 'brane' in a higher-dimensional space containing a plurality of branes which occasionally collide to produce a 'big bang', then we may as Barry Dainton points out (in correspondence) allow that there is a plurality of objects—the branes—while continuing to maintain that our universe is a single object. Alternatively, of course, we can stand further back, and continue to maintain that there is only one object.

[30] 1644: 1.213. Spinoza removed the structural difference between the notions of mind and matter when he systematized Descartes's philosophy without worrying about the local religious orthodoxy in his *Principles of Cartesian Philosophy* (1663). He restored the idea—recurrent in the Western Greek-Judaic-Christian-Islamic tradition—that our minds are all aspects of one single universal mind.

the fact that Descartes is fully realist about ordinary physical objects in every sense in which we are (although he denies that they're strictly speaking numerically distinct entities) while at the same time holding that the existence of matter is simply the existence of extension. The present and parallel suggestion is that if we want to approach a sense of what Descartes thinks a subject of experience is, we shouldn't be in the least surprised, but should rather expect, that we will need to adjust our conception of mind/experience/consciousness/thinking no less radically, to the point where it can accommodate the fact that Descartes is as realist about the existence of subjects of experience as we are, although he holds that there is nothing more to their existence than the existence of experience/consciousness/thinking, experiential process.

It seems, then, that we shouldn't quickly dismiss the attribution of the $[e = s = c]$ thesis to Descartes. Given that he holds that experience/consciousness/thinking (*res cogitans*) is all there is to the existence of mind, and hence to the existence of subject-of-experience-hood, his conception of experience/consciousness/thinking must be at least as rich as his conception of extension (*res extensa*) must be if it is to cover all the phenomena of the non-mental physical world in the way he thinks it does.

Does this help with the problem of ontic depth that arises for my account of Descartes's position and also for my own view? It's hard to see how; for whatever the nature of these riches, the mind or self or subject is still held to consist of nothing other than mental process, conscious mental process whose whole being is manifest in consciousness. And when we contemplate a given mind at a given time, it seems obvious that there just isn't any room, in the being of the conscious mental process we find at that time, for all the things we want attribute to the mind at that time—faculties or capacities of reason, will and imagination, concepts, innate or not, and so on. The very least we can do, it seems, is reject the thesis that the whole being of the mental process is manifest in consciousness, and allow that the *cogitans* that constitutes one's mind can include non-conscious mental process. But this is ruled out on Descartes's view.

Perhaps there is another way. Perhaps one can hold that although all mental process is necessarily conscious (and therefore subject-involving), there is mental process which is part of what constitutes one's mind, and constitutes in particular its needed ontic depth, although—how to put it?—the conscious subject that one experiences oneself to be, and experiences as having the experiences one has, isn't conscious of it.

Does this idea make sense? One way to try to make sense of it is to suppose that one's mind (soul, subject, self) consists of more than one 'locus' of awareness. Suppose one uses 'top subject' as a name for the putative entity picked out at the end of the last paragraph—the conscious-subject-that-one-experiences-oneself-to-be-and-experiences-as-having-the-experiences-one-has, as it were. One can then express the idea by saying that there may be more to the full metaphysical reality of the subject of experience that one is than the top-subject-that-one-experiences-oneself-to-be. One can allow that experience whose whole being is fully manifest in consciousness occurs in loci of awareness, in the subject of experience that one is considered as a whole, other than the top-subject locus of awareness. One can also allow, if one likes, that the top subject always has some sort of dim awareness of all the awareness that is, outside the top subject locus, fully manifest. (It must be fully manifest somewhere, for that is what constitutes its existence.)

This, I take it, is Leibniz's principal thought when he postulates tiny experiences or conscious mental goings-on (*petites perceptions*) that are partly constitutive of one's mind and whose whole being is by definition fully manifest in consciousness (hence fully manifest to some subject), although one, i.e. the 'top' subject, is not conscious, or is only dimly conscious, of their content. Some have said that Leibniz's 'petites perceptions' are wholly unconscious goings-on, but Leibniz doesn't believe in mental occurrences that involve no consciousness any more than Descartes does.

If this makes sense, it provides a means of greatly expanding the c, and hence the e, and hence the s—a vast increase in the categorical being, and hence the power being, of the human thin subject.[31] On one version, though, it requires one to hold that a human thin subject is somehow or other partly constituted by many subjects (perhaps along panpsychist lines), and it isn't enough to quieten doubts about how anything that consists of absolutely nothing but conscious mental process can have the whole mental power being of subjects of experience like ourselves. This isn't a problem for conventional (real) materialists, of course, because they take the mind—the mind-brain—to have non-experiential being in addition to experiential being, non-experiential being that provides all the ontic depth anyone could possibly want.

I think some such Leibnizian line of thought is the best option if one is attempting to solve Descartes's problem while retaining as many of his commitments as possible. It needs careful development, however—if it is to succeed, it mustn't disrupt the doctrine of the simplicity of the mind, to which both Descartes and Leibniz are committed—and this is not the place for it. Having put the $[e = s = c]$ kite up in the air, I'm going to let go of the string until 8.8.

7.5 Thin subjects: Fichte, Husserl, and Nozick

I want now to consider William James, and, more briefly, Hume, but let me first briefly interpolate two other philosophers whom I have already quoted. Fichte can be read as adopting the thin-subject view, and as taking thin subjects to be relatively short-lived, when he writes, in a passage already quoted in part:

What was I before I came to self-consciousness? The natural answer to this question is: I did not exist at all, for I was not an I. The I exists only in so far as it is conscious of itself ... *The self posits itself*, and by virtue of this mere self-assertion it *exists*; and conversely, the self *exists* and *posits* its own existence by virtue of merely existing. It is at once the agent and the product of action. (1794–1802: 98, 97)

---

[31] On one account, the human thin subject turns out to consist of a great deal more than the synergy of ultimates that directly constitutes the experience of the 'top' subject.

His view seems to be, in Neuhouser's words, that 'to be aware of oneself as thinking is already to exist as an I, and to be an I consists in nothing beyond such self-awareness' (1990: 109). Husserl endorses a similar view: 'the ego continuously constitutes itself as existing' (1931: 66); 'my consciousness of myself and I myself are, concretely considered, identical. To be a subject is to be in the mode of being aware of oneself' (c. 1922: 151); and Nozick makes a similar suggestion, with express reference to Fichte, in his book *Philosophical Explanations*:

There is no preexisting I; rather the I is delineated, is synthesized around the reflexive act. An entity is synthesized around the reflexive act and it is the "I" of that act ... the self which is reflexively referred to is synthesized in that very act of reflexive self-reference ... an entity coagulates.   (1981: 87, 91, 88)

In a later work Nozick puts the point by saying that 'it is reflexive self-consciousness that constitutes ... the self' (1989: 14).

   I'm unsure of Nozick's exact meaning and metaphysical commitments, and very unsure of Fichte's, but it would be superficial to think that Fichte is open to the objection Butler put to Locke's theory of personal identity when he wrote that

one should really think it self-evident, that consciousness of personal identity presupposes, and therefore cannot constitute, personal identity, any more than knowledge in any other case, can constitute truth, which it presupposes.[32]

It's clear, too, that Fichte and Nozick have 'full' or 'express' self-consciousness (102) in mind, and that their focus is to that extent narrower than Husserl's, whose claim allows the possibility that a subject can (and must) have consciousness of itself just in being conscious at all, without necessarily being fully or expressly self-conscious. Some, I think, take Fichte's view to be not that

(i) a self or I arises only when there is an episode of self-conscious thought,

but rather that

(ii) the I or self exists permanently, in the case of a human being, from the first moment of self-consciousness on.[33]

The case for thinking that he subscribes to (i) seems more strongly supported by the text, however. Neuhouser remarks that Fichte is committed to the view that 'the subject ... ceases to exist in the absence of its own self-awareness'; 'the cessation of the I's immediate self-awareness leaves no trace or residue behind itself; in the absence of that intellectual intuition there is in fact no conscious subject "still there"' (1990: 112, 108).

   A compromise between (i) and (ii) is that

(iii) the self or I arises—and in some sense re-arises—each time there is an episode of self-conscious thought.

---

[32] 1736: 302. Butler's objection was in fact wholly mistaken (and unoriginal—see Strawson, in preparation, *b*). He thought it 'wonderful', i.e. extraordinary, that Locke should have made such a mistake, and so it was, because he didn't.
[33] Compare the quotation from Kant's *Anthropology* on p. 106.

On this view, one's self isn't really present or existent except in these conscious (self-conscious) episodes, but it is none the less somehow numerically the same self from t_1 to t_2, from one occasion to the next. Must it have some lesser form of continuous existence in between the conscious episodes? I don't know what Fichte's view would have been (it would depend, for one thing, on his view about time). Perhaps he would have judged it to be enough that there be some sort of causal basis for saying that I or self at t_1 is the same I or self as the I or self at t_2, while denying that there is any real sense in which the t_1 I, the I of the t_1 *Tathandlung*, persists across a period of non-consciousness in such a way as to be for that reason numerically the same as the t_2 I, the I of the t_2 *Tathandlung*.

I can't be sure that Fichte and Nozick adhere to the Transience View of the self (the drift of Nozick's 1989 book suggests that he wouldn't welcome this consequence), but they can be read as giving striking expression to the idea that the self is, most fundamentally, just the thin subject, the mental someone or mental presence alive in any given episode of consciousness, the indubitably real mental presence that (whatever else is true of it) doesn't and can't exist at all when there's no experience or consciousness. Both, however, endorse this idea in a significantly restricted form according to which a self exists only during an episode of expressly self-conscious thought. My view, by contrast, is that a self exists during any conscious episode, not just during a fully self-conscious experiential episode, for a self is just a subject of experience. The basic thought—no experience, no self—remains the same, and Buddhists also accept short-lived thin subjects of experience, in spite of the fact that they're sometimes supposed to deny the existence of subjects of experience altogether. They subscribe to the Transience View, as does William James.

7.6 Thin subjects: James and Hume

William James explicitly endorses Descartes's wide use of the word 'thought' to cover all types of conscious experiential episodes (1890: 1.186, 224). He then appoints 'Thought ... with a capital T' as a name for 'the present mental state', and argues, radically, that 'the *I*' or self 'is a *Thought*' (1890: 1.338, 400–1). He puts it very plainly: 'the thoughts themselves are the thinkers' (1892: 191). Each '"perishing" ... pulse of thought [or] "section" of consciousness' is a (short-lived) thinker or self or subject of experience (1890: 1.371, 337)—a thin subject, in my terms. He takes it, as I do, that these thinker pulses are occurrences in the brain.

'[T]he thoughts themselves are the thinkers.' It sounds hopelessly odd, at first. One can replace 'thought' by 'experience' and recast it as

(i) the experiential episodes themselves are the subjects of experience

(the most ingenuous modern translation of Descartes's 'cogito, ergo sum' is as remarked earlier 'I experience, therefore I am', or 'I am conscious, therefore I am'). But this hardly improves matters. Slightly less indigestible, perhaps, is

(ii) the existence of each experiential episode consists in the existence of a subject of experience entertaining a certain experiential content

—this episode being, of course, in all its experiential qualitative complexity, a wholly physical event.

Picking up the numbering and terminology of 7.4 one might propose to write (ii) as

[5] $[e = s{:}c]$,

'e', 's', and 'c' standing as before for, respectively, an individual experience, its thin subject, and its experiential qualitative content, the new term '$:$' representing some intensely intimate relation that needn't be specified further here except to say that it doesn't entail the irreducible ontic distinctness of s and c (see page 274) and so doesn't rule out the seemingly preposterous

[4] $[e = s = c]$

although it makes a much weaker claim.

If the colon in [5] seems too appositional, and too separatist, and perhaps also too egalitarian—suggesting full equality of ontological status across the double dots, so that there is no difference between $s{:}c$ and $c{:}s$—one graphic alternative is to replace [5] by

[6] $[e = s(c)]$,

the curved brackets indicating some kind of qualification or modification of s by c, the fact that c is essentially something *for* s and essentially *belongs* to s (experiences being, as one used to say, 'logically private').

I find these symbolic pictures helpful (apologies to those who don't). Putting them aside for now, the suggestion is that there's a way of reading (ii) which doesn't obviously dilute James's claim and which may sound just a little less unpalatable to some. This formulation may have a slightly better chance of delivering the odd mental shock that comes from grasping (however briefly) truths that have no non-counterintuitive expression.

One can only go so far with such rephrasings, however, and the idea remains very difficult on first acquaintance, given the ordinary background of thought. I believe that it's correct, given that one is operating with the thin conception of the subject, and that it's the best thing to say overall, given that one is seeking to give an account of the subject considered as inner mental presence. It does, though, have to grow on one.

A little more fully, James proposes that the self or subject or

> I ... is a *Thought* [present mental state], at each moment different from that of the last moment, but *appropriative* of the latter, together with all that the latter called its own. All the experiential facts find their place in this description, unencumbered with any hypothesis save that of the existence of passing thoughts or states of mind.   (1890: 1.400–1; see also ibid. 338–42)

There are many subjects, on this view, many successive 'top subjects', in the life of a human being like Louis. Each one, each 'pulse of thought', each *Louis*°—where 'Louis°' names whatever short-lived top subject is having experience at the moment—is an 'indecomposable unity' (1890: 1.371) in every sense in which it needs to be for distinct thought-elements like *grass* and *green* to be able to be genuinely combined in whatever way they must be if a thought unity like the thought *the grass is green* is genuinely to occur, or if a single pulse of experience is to be (for example) both experience of hearing part of Beethoven's song cycle 'An die ferne Geliebte' and experience of swimming.

What is the metaphysical status of these pulse subjects relative to each other? James seems clear on the point. He agrees with Hume that they are, as far as we know, entirely numerically distinct substances, albeit short-lived ones. A brain, no doubt, is a single continuing object, on his view, but 'the same brain may subserve many conscious selves, either alternate or coexisting', that have 'no *substantial* identity' (1890: 1.401; 1892: 181). Each self is an upsurging of a Thought/subject, an experience/subject, a Louis°, a transient pattern of synergetic activity in the brain.

At one point James says that the self or subject consists in 'a remembering and appropriating Thought incessantly renewed' (1890: 1.338; 362–3). Does this mean that he thinks selves do have some sort of long-term continuity? Only in a loose 'bundle theory' sense. He knows that it's extremely natural for us to think of the self as something that has long-term continuity, and he's happy to speak in sympathy with that tendency, but his proposal is that the actual metaphysics involves many distinct selves:

Successive thinkers, *numerically distinct*, but all aware of the past in the same way, form an adequate vehicle for all the experience of personal unity and sameness which we actually have. ... My present Thought stands ... in the plenitude of ownership of the train of my past selves, is owner not only *de facto*, but *de jure*, the most real owner there can be ... .   (1892: 181; 1890: 1.360; first emphasis mine)

How does this fit with James's doctrine of the 'stream of consciousness'? How does it fit with the fact that Louis—or rather Louis°, the short-lived (top) subject of any moment—has no sense that there is a series of numerically distinct subjects and naturally thinks of himself (himself°) as being, in so far as he is a self, a single, persisting, continuously existing entity?

The first thing to recall is that James doesn't claim to know that the stream of consciousness is continuous (224). Second, he has a ready explanation of the appearance of continuity: each subject 'appropriates'—makes its own, takes to itself, inherits, has access to—the content of the experiences of its numerically and substantially distinct predecessors. The notion of appropriation is loose and metaphorical, but it's clear enough what James has in mind, and it supplies all the apparent experienced continuity and developmental coherence of experience.[34] A further reason why the appearance of continuity is unsurprising, on his view as on mine, is that the subjects—subjects/experiences—in question arise successively, in a single person's brain, from brain conditions that have considerable similarity from moment to moment even as they change. (They're similar for more than one reason. First, given short-term or

---

[34] See further James 1890: 1.340–2. Compare Kant's famous footnote in the Third Paralogism (A363–4). Plainly, the notion of appropriation would too strong if it were interpreted to mean that no content is ever lost.

'working' memory, the content of the immediately preceding experience standardly forms part of the overall experiential context in which the new experience arises in every sense in which features of the external environment do; this is true both of content in the focus of attention and background content, somatosensory content, mood-tone content, and so on. Second, independently of memory, somatosensory and mood-tone contents are in any case continually refreshed from sources that usually undergo only slow change—from pulse to pulse, subject to subject—even as salient contents may turn over rapidly; and salient contents show developmental coherence in Hume's sense (*Treatise*, 195) even when they change rapidly, as when one happens on a lively tiger. Third, all the features of the brain that constitute a human being's character, beliefs, general epistemic and cognitive outlook, general conative and emotional outlook, and so on, also generally remain highly stable from moment to moment. It's a bit like the view from a train, close things streaming past, a line of trees a field away moving more slowly, the hills or mountains in the distance more slowly still, or indiscernibly.)

—None of this can be right, because James doesn't really believe in numerically distinct short-lived metaphysical subjects. His 'pulses of thought' are really just convenient theoretical abstractions from the fundamental given fact, a metaphysically single flow. At one point he writes that 'as the brain-changes are continuous, so all these consciousnesses melt into each other like dissolving views. Properly they are but one protracted consciousness, one unbroken stream'.[35]

Here there are various possibilities. One is that Louis's numerically distinct pulses of experience, riding on continuous brain changes, succeed each other in a seamlessly joined fashion to form what is experienced by Louis (more strictly, by each Louis°) as an unbroken stream of experience (**b** in Figure 7.3). Another possibility that James might favour is that the pulses succeed each other in a possibly partly temporally overlapping way, 'coexisting' during the time in which one is fading out and the next is gathering strength (**c** in Figure 7.3). A third possibility is that there are in fact temporal gaps between the experience pulses, although there's no experience of gappiness, and although brain activity is continuous (**a** in Figure 7.3). James has already denied that we can know there to be an unbroken stream of *experience*, even if we assume (as he does in the passage just quoted) that there's an unbroken stream of *brain changes*, and this passage gives no reason to doubt that his proposal is what it seems to be: that the subject-constituting pulses of thought are genuinely metaphysically distinct entities rather than mere theoretical abstractions from a single flow that is single in some way that goes beyond the singleness or uninterruptedness of seamlessness or overlappingness.

—Won't there be two subjects in the L-reality if there's temporal overlap? And isn't this consequence completely unacceptable?

Yes to the first question. If there can be overlapping of the sort represented by experience-pulses ep3 and ep4 in Figure 7.3, then there will for a time be two

---

[35] 1890: 1.247–8. Mark Sacks put this to me.

experiences-with-subjects in the L-reality, one rapidly waning and the other rapidly waxing. No to the second. The idea that there may be two subjects or loci of experience

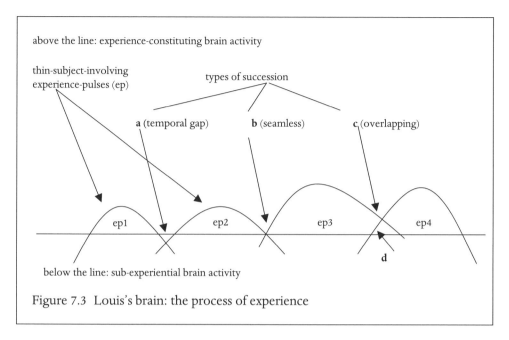

Figure 7.3 Louis's brain: the process of experience

coexisting in a single brain at a single time may offend our ordinary intuitions, emotions, and sense of identity, but there's no theoretical difficulty in it, and a great deal of more or less indirect experimental evidence for it. It may be a routine occurrence, in fact, something that has evolved to maintain the (useful) character of continuity that Louis's (Louis°'s) experience has for him without ever giving rise to any sense on his (his°) part that there is more than one subject present in the L-reality.

If there is such temporal overlapping at a given time, neither of the two experience-pulse-constituted thin subjects that will then be numerically distinguishable at that time will be aware of there being two subjects in the L-reality at that time, any more than Louis the whole human being considered as a (thick) subject of experience will be. This will be so whether or not there are grounds for saying, at any point in the overlapping, that one of them, say the ep4 subject, is the 'top' subject, the best candidate for being the conscious-Louis-subject of the moment, while the other, the ep3 subject, is, relative to that, subsidiary. (In this case we will take it that the section of ep3 that coincides with a section of ep4 and is marked **d** in Figure 7.3 does still represent the existence of experience on the part of ep3, as the figure requires, but that it represents experience that is nothing to the 'top' subject.) However we count or rank subjects, the experience of each one of them will have, for that subject, the character of being part of a single process of experience had by a single subject. The 'stitching software' that underwrites our sense of being a single persisting subject—and delivers a sense of the flowing continuity of experience (for those who have such experience)—is as remarked extremely powerful.

Obviously the 'our' of 'our sense of being a single persisting subject' suggests a single continuing subject of experience, and the experience-pulse theory accordingly translates this into 'the sense that each successive short-lived experience-pulse thin subject has of being a single persisting self': it converts 'our' to 'our°'. It's important that such translations are always possible and entirely perspicuous.[36]

A further proposal (the proposals are empirical, testable or not) is that the experientiality of the waxing pulse ep4 occludes that of the waning pulse ep3 in such a way that it is no longer correct to say that the section of ep3 marked **d** represents the existence of any experience at all—so that the situation is, strictly speaking, better represented as

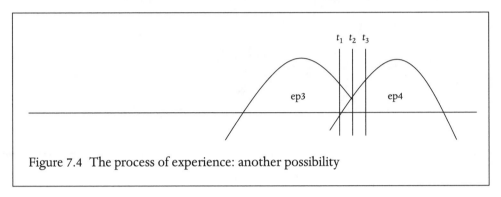

Figure 7.4 The process of experience: another possibility

in Figure 7.4. In the previous case there were two subjects of experience in the L-reality between t_1 and t_3. In this case there are two subjects only between t_1 and t_2 (we may again suppose that ep4 is the top subject in this case). A further possibility is that the beginning of ep4 is the immediate end of ep3, as in Figure 7.5, so that there is no

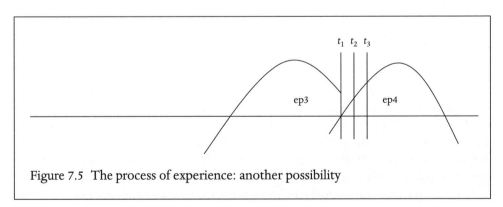

Figure 7.5 The process of experience: another possibility

[36] It's worth noting that they're equally available to Hume when he is faced with the objection that his use of 'our', in phrases like 'our several perceptions' (*Treatise*, 169/259) or 'our successive perceptions' (*Treatise*, 400/636), presupposes the reality of a continuing self—the very thing he is aiming to put in doubt. The objection has no force against Hume; he's speaking loosely, relative to the bundle hypothesis, just as I have done in speaking of 'our sense of being a single persisting subject'. We can either take him to be considering us as continuing whole human beings, when he speaks in this way, or to be representing the way things seem to the—as far as we know very short-lived—subject of any given experience from the perspective of that experience. See G. Strawson, in preparation, *a*.

overlapping of subjects, whatever the correct description of the nature of the further career of ep3 in completing its natural neural arc.

This is unconstrained speculation, but the details don't matter. The basic claim is simply that a one-subject-per-pulse experience-pulse theory of the human process of consciousness is wholly coherent and far from implausible. Whichever picture of pulse succession is most accurate, the stitching software will ensure that things will seem to Louis° —the thin subject in the L-reality that embodies Louis's subjectivity at any given time—just as they do to us (us°) in everyday life.

According to James's proposal, then, we have a large number of successive, numerically distinct selves—numerically distinct capital-T 'Thoughts'. These are physical unities, on James's (1890) view. In 6.12 I proposed that they have the seemingly unique distinction of being physical unities that we can know to exist and to be true unities (given, as always, that materialism is true and that there is indeed a plurality of objects). This is something I'll return to.

I'm inclined to think that James's proposal is correct in the case of human beings, as remarked. More moderately, I think that this is the best thing to say about the notion of the subject of experience once one has put aside the thick, whole-creature use of 'subject of experience' and gone 'inner'. James is motivated partly by an unacceptably radical form of empiricism, but that is no objection to the substance of his conclusion. I think that his thought on this matter goes deeper than anything demanded merely by radical empiricist principles.

Some think that James holds the self to 'consist mainly of peculiar (muscular) motions in the head or between the head and throat' (1890: 1.301). But this ostensibly ontological remark tends to be lifted out of context and misunderstood. It's not a claim about what selves are. It is, rather, a claim about what gives rise to our sense or feeling of the self. The question James has here asked himself is 'Can we tell more precisely in what the **feeling** of this central active self consists,—not necessarily as yet what the active self is, as a being or principle, but what we feel when we become aware of its existence?' (1. 299; my emphasis in bold). His final, somewhat tentative reply is that it may be that 'our entire **feeling** of spiritual activity, or what commonly passes by that name, is really a feeling of bodily activities [the peculiar motions in the head or between the head and throat] whose exact nature is by most men overlooked'.[37]

What about Hume? There is a lot of confusion about his views on the mind or self, and three principal errors, of which I'll briefly mention two.[38] The first and almost universal error is to think that Hume claims that he doesn't come upon any subject of experience at all when he famously decides to examine the nature of his

---

[37] 1890: 1. 301–02, my emphasis in bold. James makes essentially the same point in his *Essays in Radical Empiricism*—although he talks of 'consciousness', conceived of as some sort of entity in a way that is highly likely to mislead, rather than of the self—when he proposes provocatively (and perhaps completely misunderstanding Kant) that 'the "I think" which Kant said must be able to accompany all my objects, is the "I breathe" which actually does accompany them …' (1904a: 37).

[38] The third is a mistake about Hume's reasons for saying, in his 1740 Appendix to the *Treatise*, that his hopes for his theory of personal identity vanish (*Treatise*, 400/635). See G. Strawson, in preparation, *a*: Part 3.

mind by 'entering intimately' into himself and announces that all he comes upon is some individual particular perception or experience (*Treatise*, 165/252). The point is sufficiently established by a passage already quoted—'when my perceptions are remov'd for any time, as by sound sleep ... I ... may truly be said not to exist' (*Treatise* 165/252)—for here 'I' refers to Hume in so far as he is considering himself as mind or subject. Some may find it impossible to read this passage as saying what it says, given the weight of the traditional mistaken interpretation of Hume, but it would be no less certain without it, for it is after all a necessary truth, aired in 6.3, that there can't be experience without a subject of experience, an experiencer, simply in so far as experience is essentially experience-*for*-someone-or-something, and Hume doesn't go in for denying necessary truths. What he does deny, in expounding the 'bundle' theory of the self, is something much more specific: the idea that we have any good evidence for the existence of a *persisting* self or subject, let alone an invariable, unchanging self or subject of the sort whose existence is taken for granted by almost all philosophers in his time. He makes it sparklingly clear that this is his target in the first two paragraphs of his discussion of personal identity. Obviously experiences can't exist without having subjects, subjects for whom they are experiences. So far as the empirical data are concerned, though, we find, Hume says, only transient experiences or perceptions, hence only transient selves or subjects; and there is, he says, no 'I' or self or subject at all when there is no experience.

The second principal error is to think that he not only presents a 'bundle' theory of the mind or self as the only empiricistically acceptable account of the mind or self, but also commits himself to its truth as an account of the actual nature of the human mind or self (considered as something that has some sort of long-term existence). In fact, his claim is simply that we have no empirically respectable evidence for the existence of anything more than a series or collection of separate experiences or 'perceptions'. It follows from this, given his empiricist theory of ideas or theory of meaning, that 'the true idea of the human mind', i.e. the empirically warranted idea of the human mind or self, hence the only idea of the mind or self *that we can legitimately deploy when doing philosophy*, is that of a bundle or series or collection of numerically distinct experiences (each of course, with its own short-lived subject, for an experience is an experienc*ing*, and an experienc*ing* necessarily involves an experienc*er*). But in making this claim, in speaking of the 'true idea of the human mind', Hume doesn't claim to know that this is all there is to the human self or mind. He doesn't convert his epistemological claim ('this is all we can know of the human mind or self, given empiricist principles, so this is the only philosophically legitimate idea we can have of it') into an all-out ontological claim ('this is all there is to the human mind or self').

We can be certain that Hume isn't doing this, because the most certain thing about him is that he's a sceptic, a true if moderate sceptic, and sceptics don't make outright ontological claims of this kind. They don't—ever—claim to have certain knowledge of the ultimate nature of reality (other than that part of reality which consists of their experiences considered just as such). Hume's basic view—unsurprisingly, given that he's a sceptic—is that the essence of the mind is unknown. He puts this rather clearly,

I think, when he writes that 'the essence of the mind [is] unknown' (*Treatise*, 5/xvii). His powerful empiricist point against his contemporaries is simply that they're wrong to claim knowledge or experience of a simple persisting self or mind, because the most careful inspection delivers only a bundle of successive and distinct experiencings or perceivings, nothing more. (Another way to see that Hume doesn't claim that (1) the mind is definitely just a bundle of perceptions is to conjoin (1) with two other claims in the *Treatise*: (2) 'the essence of the mind (is) unknown', just quoted, and (3) 'the perceptions of the mind are perfectly known' (*Treatise*, 237/366).)

Hume and James are close in their views, but not identical. Hume says that a series of fleeting ontically distinct experiences or perceptions (which are of course, and necessarily, subject-involving experiences or perceptions) is all we can have as the referent of the word 'self' or 'mind' if we want an idea of the self or mind that counts as clear and distinct by empiricist principles, an idea cleared for use in philosophy: this is the only philosophically respectable positive conception of the human self or mind that the experiential data warrant. James is somewhat more mild: a series of ontically distinct subject-involving experiences is all we need to account for the experiential data: 'all the experiential facts find their place in this description, unencumbered with any hypothesis save that of the existence of passing thoughts or states of mind' (1890: 1.401). But James also proposes that the Transience View of the self—according to which a series of ontically distinct subject-involving experiences is all there is, when it comes to the self or subject—is correct. Perhaps, though, the Transience View is best expressed as a conditional: *if* you want to speak of selves at all, then the best thing to say about them, on certain assumptions (such as the assumption that they must qualify as objects in fundamental metaphysics in order to be said to exist), is that they're short-lived entities, essentially-subject-involving-experiences, briefly flaring neural synergies—thin subjects.

7.7 Still to do

I must now try to give identity conditions for thin subjects of a sort that will allow me to claim that they qualify as objects

{26} [TSx → Ox]

and therefore have a chance of qualifying as sesmets

{23} [TSx → SESx]

given that sesmets are objects by definition:

{24} [SESx → Ox].

I will also have to show that thin subjects fulfil the other conditions on being sesmets, e.g.

{27} [SESx → SMx]

and

{28} [SESx → OMx],

and, finally, say some more about why I think that sesmets are reasonably or rightly called selves—about why I think they're the best candidates for the title 'self' given the strong brief of 1.4, which commits us to showing that selves are objects if they exist at all, and therefore commits us to showing that they're physical objects, given the assumption that materialism—real, realistic materialism—is true.

Part 8

Metaphysics: the question of fact, 2

The span of a thinking being is the span of a single thought.

Buddhaghosa.

8.1 The weak brief

In 4.8 I introduced the notion of a sesmet, as a step towards a well-formed notion of the self. In 7.1 I introduced the notion of a thin subject, as a step back from the notion of a sesmet. I stressed the point that to introduce the notion of a thin subject is simply to introduce a certain way of talking about a concrete phenomenon whose existence isn't in question, whatever its ontological category. It's to draw a theoretical line around a certain spatiotemporal portion or feature of concrete reality and to choose to give it a certain name. This way of talking may be disliked or thought unhelpful, but the phenomenon referred to is indisputably real and extremely commonplace. Consider Louis—the L-reality—at a particular time. The expression 'thin subject' picks out that portion or feature of the L-reality which constitutes the existence of a subject of experience at that time, given that a subject of experience is defined as something that isn't the same thing as a whole human being and exists (if and) only if experience exists, experience of which it is the subject or 'haver'. A thin subject is a concretely existing 'subjectivity phenomenon' that may or may not be in good standing as an object, something that can be known to exist even when all that is known to exist is experience. I take the existence of a thin subject in the L-reality to consist wholly of goings-on in Louis's brain, but that is a further materialist supposition. I'm going to argue that thin subjects qualify as objects, and accordingly have a chance of qualifying as sesmets, and indeed as selves. The expression 'thin subject' may be thought to give illegitimate support to the idea that thin subjects are objects simply by being a count noun, but I think I've sufficiently warded off that danger.

In Part 6 I argued that anything that has a chance of qualifying as an object must constitute a 'strong unity' (298). I went on to endorse the view that strong unity is not only necessary for objecthood but also sufficient, and suggested that thin subjects, considered at any particular time, are unbeatable candidates for strong unity (6.12). For the moment, though, I'm going to return to the position Kant takes up when engaging the 'rational psychologists' on their own metaphysical ground in the Paralogisms section of the *Critique of Pure Reason*, and allow that I don't yet have decisive reason to think of the subject as an object rather than as a property or 'accident' or (mere) 'predicate of another being' (B419–20).

Some may find the thin use of 'subject of experience' unnatural and strained. I think it's valuable to get used to it. The sense of strain is a product of verbal habituation (the thin use was once philosophically standard and felt natural), and it's precisely this undoubtedly real phenomenon—the phenomenon of the subject of experience considered as something that is essentially present and alive in conscious experience and that can't be said to exist at all when there is no conscious experience—that concerns me at present, because I'm taking it to be a leading candidate for the title 'sesmet' and, in the longer term, for the title 'self'. The traditional inner conception of the subject assumes that subjects of experience are things that can exist and persist in the absence of any experience, and one result of this is that the property of having long-term diachronic continuity tends to get a free pass as integral to the notion of the self. But perhaps we shouldn't issue this pass. Perhaps the best candidates for being selves, given that selves (if they exist) are objects, are thin-subject sesmets, things that can't be said to exist at all in the absence of any experience.

Can thin subjects qualify as objects? On the assumption that we have to provide both synchronic and diachronic identity conditions for things that we want to call objects, we face the problem of duration (327): How long do thin subjects last? We also face the problem of ontic depth (331): Do thin subjects have enough solidity, as it were, to be good candidates for selves, or are they creatures of the surface in a way that rules them out? Such 'superficiality' doesn't worry Fichte or Nozick, on the face of it, but it threatens to create huge difficulties for some very basic assumptions about selves, e.g. that they are morally responsible agents, or at the very least intentional agents.

These are powerful concerns, so let me now briefly fill the 'weak brief' (13), offering a way out of the present line of argument for those—surely many—who want to say that there is such a thing as the self, a subject of experience that isn't the same thing as the whole human being, but who take it that nothing can count as a self unless it has some sort of long-term persistence.

I think that their best bet—assuming they're materialists who take the self to be a physical object—is to adopt some version of the 'brain-system' view introduced in 1.6, according to which the self is 'whatever supports the consciousness and personality of a human being and is still there when the human being is in dreamless sleep' (10; cf. Dainton 2008a). A more restricted version of this view has it that Louis's self is simply whatever part of Louis's brain physically constitutes his having the character, temperament, or personality he does.[1] Another version adds in that part of Louis's brain which constitutes the whole neural part of his capacities for experience. Another, perhaps, adds that part of Louis which constitutes his actually having experience at any given time.[2] Another adds the neuronal structures that constitute Louis's memory traces, taking these too to be part of the whole neural entity that is his self.

There are many possibilities, when it comes to detail. On all accounts, the thing in question, the brain-system self, is some highly complex, persisting set of physical structures whose right to be considered a *single* structure or system, in such a way as to be able to qualify as 'the self', derives from certain functional connections between its various physiologically distinguishable parts. Materialists who accept that selves must qualify as objects (it's not clear what other sorts of things can be morally responsible), and who feel that brain systems aren't enough, should give up the quest for the self. They should agree with Kenny and van Inwagen that Louis's self is just Louis the human being, in so far as it exists at all (a way of saying that there's no such thing as the self, given that the self is defined as an object that isn't the same object as the human being). They should agree with Dennett that Louis's self is on any other account a 'fiction', an intensely natural and useful posit that has no more real, substantial physical existence than Louis's centre of gravity.[3] If they dislike Kenny's appeals to ordinary language (20–1), they may prefer van Inwagen's argument, which I adapt here from private correspondence:

Let us suppose for the sake of argument that I am a 'self', whatever else I am. As a materialist (at least as regards human beings and their mental processes) I think that every real thing is material. Since I think that I exist, I therefore think that I am material. That is, I think that I am a material object (I don't see how I could fail to be an object). Now this living animal is the only available material object for me to be, so that's what I think I am .... If I thought that there were such things as my brain or my left cerebral hemisphere or my cerebral cortex, I suppose I'd have to regard these as serious candidates for the office of myself. But my general position on the ontology of material objects entails that there are no such things as these.

This is all I have to say, when it comes to the weak brief. Brain-system selves have plenty of ontic depth and duration. They may even qualify as objects, if we speak loosely enough. I don't, however, think that they qualify as objects if we speak more strictly, because I believe they fail to fulfil the 'strong unity' condition on being an object.[4] And even if it's allowed that they're objects, I think they fail to be objects of the right kind, on the present terms, for reasons to come (one doubt concerns whether they can sufficiently qualify as single-as-mental—see page 342n.).

---

[1] A variant of this view drops the restriction to the brain on the ground that a persistent character trait may depend on the production of some chemical in almost any part of the body, while a subvariant allows that Louis's whole body is part of what constitutes his having the character he has. Here, however, I'm sticking to the brain.

[2] 'Whatever physical thing the activity of which constitutes Louis's experience' cuts much more finely than 'whatever must be active in the L-reality if Louis is having experience', for there may be many concurrent physically necessary conditions of experience which are no part of the neural synergy that directly constitutes the experience.

[3] Dennett 1991: ch. 13.

[4] There are also van Inwagen's powerful and related objections to the idea that things of this sort can really be said to be objects—or even, in his 'reist' scheme, to exist. See e.g. van Inwagen 1990b.

Can it be right to maintain the requirement that selves must qualify as objects in fundamental metaphysics, if this is the consequence? If it is right, can my account of what it takes to qualify as an object in fundamental metaphysics be correct? These questions remain for consideration. Those who are weary of the idea that what I'm after has any interesting claim to be called a self can treat what follows as a reflection on certain aspects of the metaphysics of experience, and on the notion of an object.

8.2 The plan

Back now to the strong brief. The plan is to argue that thin subjects are sesmets

{23} [TSx → SESx]

and in particular that human thin subjects are sesmets (I'll take this qualification for granted unless I expressly cancel it). To qualify as sesmets they must qualify as objects

{26} [TSx → Ox]

and must also possess the further sesmet-defining properties *single-as-mental* and *object-as-mental* ({27}, {24}).

If we can establish {23}, that thin subjects are sesmets, we can conclude that sesmets exist

{33} ∃xSESx

for we know {21} that thin subjects exist. If we can then consolidate the case for the claim that sesmets are (rightly or reasonably called) selves

{34} [SESx → Sx],

we can conclude, first, given {23}, that thin subjects are selves

{36} [TSx → Sx]

and, second, given {21}, and finally, and in fulfilment of my original brief, that selves exist

{37} ∃xSx.

Some, I think, may be prepared to accept the converse of {34}, that all selves are sesmets

{38} [Sx → SESx]

while rejecting {34} itself. They may be prepared to accept that anything that is to count as a self must have the property *sesmet* (the property of being correctly judged to be a single thing when considered specifically as a subject of experience that is being considered specifically in its mental being) while rejecting {34}, the converse, on one ground or another. They may for example hold that selves must not only be sesmets but must also have property ϕ

{35} [[SESx ∧ φx] → Sx]

for some property φ such as the property of being a relatively persisting thing, or immaterial, or immortal, and so on.

I take the considerations set out in Parts 2–4 to provide strong general support for {38},[5] and I think that many, perhaps most, will be able to accept {38}. But I don't think they'll be prepared to do so unless the further claim that all true or genuine sesmets are thin subjects

{39} [SESx → TSx]

is firmly rejected: unless it's allowed that traditional inner subjects (subjects that continue to exist even in the absence of experience) can possibly be sesmets and therefore (given {34}) selves. The option of rejecting {39} remains open at this point, because there's nothing in the notion of a sesmet as so far characterized that rules out the possibility that traditional inner subjects can qualify as sesmets, whether they're conceived of as physical brain systems or as standard, non-Cartesian immaterial minds, immaterial minds that (unlike Cartesian minds) are not wholly constituted of consciousness/experience/thinking.

It isn't clear, however, that brain systems can qualify as strong unities in such a way as to qualify as objects that can, as objects, be candidates for being sesmets. Furthermore, and as remarked, sesmets possess the property *single-as-mental* by definition ({27}) and it isn't clear that brain systems can properly or sufficiently qualify as single-as-mental even if they can somehow manage to qualify as strong unities. A sesmet, furthermore, has the property *object-as-mental* by definition ({28}), and it isn't clear that either brain systems or non-Cartesian immaterial minds can properly or sufficiently possess the property *object-as-mental*.

Their ability to do so must be in question, in fact, if their ability to possess *single-as-mental* is in question, because nothing can qualify as object-as-mental without qualifying as single-as-mental

{44} [OMx → SMx].

This is because one must qualify as a strong-unity-as-mental ('SUM') to qualify as an object-as-mental

{40} [OMx → SUMx],

but to qualify as a strong-unity-as-mental is necessarily to qualify as single-as-mental

{43} [SUMx → SMx]

---

[5] {38} and its converse {34} follow from the Equivalence Thesis together with the answer to the general phenomenological question in 4.8 (207), i.e. [SELF ↔ SESMET]. I hope, though, that the present discussion will give some further general support to {38}. As before, one can reject the Equivalence Thesis as a substantive philosophical claim and treat it instead as a discussion-structuring proposal that transmits that status to {38}. The question is then: Do selves exist if (on the assumption that) selves are sesmets?—a question one can pose for discussion without reliance on the phenomenological reflections in Parts 2–4.

Interpretation

Px:	x is physical
O:	x is an object or 'substance'
POx:	x is a physical object
SUx:	x is a strong unity
SAUx:	x is a strong activity-unity
Ex:	x is experience/experiencing
TCx:	x is temporally continuous
Lxy:	x is the subject of experience or 'liver' of y
TSx:	x is a thin subject
Hx:	x is human
SLx:	x is short-lived
EUPx:	x is an experientially unitary period of experience
SES:	x is a sesmet
Sx:	x is a self
OMx:	x has the property *object-as-mental*
SMx:	x has the property *single-as-mental*
SUMx:	x is a strong-unity-as-mental
Mx:	x is mentally propertied
SEx:	x is a subject of experience
CPEx:	x is a continuous period of experience
ESx:	x is an experience-constituting neural synergy (E-synergy)
Cxy:	x constitutes y

The three main propositions that occur in the list before they've been derived from assumptions and definitions, or propositions that have been argued for, are marked in bold as *demonstranda*. When they are derived they are repeated in italics (the reference numbers of propositions that depend on the *demonstranda* for their derivation are also in bold)

Argument

{0} [∃xPx & ¬∃x¬Px]	assumption of physicalism (1.2)	**Part 6**
{1} [Sx → Ox]	(constraint on) definition of 'S' (1.7)	
{2} [Ox → POx]	{0}	
{3} [Sx → POx]	{1}, {2}	
{4} ∃xEx	evident (1.4)	
{5} [∃xEx → ∃xSEx]	evident, argued in 6.3	
{6} [∃xEx → [∃ySEy ∧ Lyx]]	evident, argued in 6.3	
{7} ∃xSEx	{4}, {5}	
{8} [Ex → Px]	{0}, {4}	
{9} ∃xOx	assumption (6.10)	
{10} ∃x∃y[[Ox & Oy] & ¬x = y]	assumption (6.10)	
{11} [Ox → SUx]	assumption/definition (glossed 6.11–6.12)	
{12} [SUx → SAUx]	assumption (glossed 6.14)	
{13} [SAUx → SUx]	evident	
{14} [SUx ↔ SAUx]	{12}, {13}	
{15} [Ox → SAUx]	{11}, {12}	
{16} [SAUx → Ox]	assumption (6.14)	
{17} [SUx → Ox]	{12}, {16}	
{18} [SUx ↔ Ox]	{11}, {17}	
{19} [Ox → TCx]	assumption (6.14)	
{20} [∃xEx ↔ ∃xTSx]	definition of 'TS' (7.1)	**Part 7**
{21} ∃xTSx	{4}, {20}	
{22} [[Hx & TSx] → SLx]	assumption (6.3)	

{23} [TSx → SESx]	**to be shown** ({49}, {53})
{24} [SESx → Ox]	definition of 'SES' (4.8)
{25} [SESx → POx]	{2}, {24}
{26} [TSx → Ox]	**to be shown** ({23}, {24} or {29}, {52})
{27} [SESx → SMx]	definition of 'SES' (4.8)
{28} [SESx → OMx]	definition of 'SES' (4.8)
{29} [OMx → Ox]	evident (argued in 4.8)
{30} [EUPx → [∃!yTSy ∧ Lyx]]	assumption / definition (supported in 7.1, 8.6)
{31} [TSx → [∃!yEUPy ∧ Lxy]]	assumption (supported in 8.6)
{32} [∃!xTSx ↔ ∃!xEUPx]	{30}, {31} ('Inseparability Thesis')
{33} ∃xSESx	{21}, **{23}** Part 8
{34} [SESx → Sx]	assumption (articulated in Parts 2 and 4)
{35} [SES+Fx → Sx]	hypothetical position
{36} [TSx → Sx]	**{23}**, {34}
{37} ∃xSx	**{33}**, {34} (also {21}, **{36}**)
{38} [Sx → SESx]	assumption (articulated in Parts 2 and 4)
{39} **[SESx → TSx]**	**to be shown** ({64}, {65})
{40} [OMx → SUMx]	definition (special case of {11})
{41} [SUMx → OMx]	definition (special case of {17})
{42} [SUMx → Ox]	{29}, {41}
{43} [SUMx → SMx]	evident
{44} [OMx → SMx]	{40}, {43}
{45} [TSx → SMx]	**{23}**, {27}
{46} [Sx ↔ SESx]	{34}, {38} (articulated in Parts 2 and 4)
[A] [S = SES]	best explanation of {46}
{47} [SESx ↔ TSx]	**{23}**, **{39}**
[B] [SES = TS]	best explanation of {47}
[C] [S = TS]	[A], [B]
{48} [SESx → SEx & Mx]]	definition of 'SES' (4.8)
{49} [SESx ↔ [SEx & Ox & Mx & SMx & OMx]]	{24}, {27}, {28}, {48} (df. of 'SES')
{50} [TSx → [SEx & Mx]]	definition of 'TS' (7.1)
{51} [TSx → SUMx]	argued in 8.3–8.6
{52} [TSx → OMx]	{41}, {51}
{26} *[TSx → Ox]* **QED**	{29}, {52}
{53} [TSx → [SEx & Ox & Mx & SMx & OMx]]	{26}, {44}, {50}, {52}
{23} *[TSx → SESx]* **QED**	{49}, {53}
{54} [EUPx → SUMx]	definition of 'EUP'
{55} [EUPx → Ox]	{42}, {54}
{56} [EUPx → CPEx]	definition of 'EUP'
{57} [TSx → CPEx]	{19}, {26} depends on {63}, (endorsed on p 398)
{58} [NISx → CPEx]	definition of 'NIS'
{59} [EUPx → [∃!yNISy & Cyx]]	?
{60} [TSx → [∃!yNISy & Cyx]]	?
{61} [CPEx → EUPx]	hypothesis (perspective-relative)
{62} [EUPx ↔ CPEx]	{56}, {61}
{63} [TSx ↔ EUPx]	proposal
[D] [TS = EUP]	best explanation of {65}
{64} [SUMx → TSx]	assumption (supported in 8.4–8.5)
{65} [SESx → SUMx]	{28}, {40}
{39} *[SESx → TSx]* **QED**	{64}, {65}
{66} ¬[SESx → SCSx]	{49}
{67} ¬[Sx → SCSx]	{34}, {49}

and {40} and {43} entail {44}. So any doubt about single-as-mental is already a doubt about object-as-mental.[6]

How do traditional inner subjects measure up to these demands? I'll consider brain systems first. The problem with Louis's brain system is not that it's a scattered entity neurophysiologically considered, for we're considering its claim to be single-as-mental, and we may allow it an interesting and considerable degree of unity, mentally considered, precisely to the extent that we suppose that it constitutes a functional unity, mentally considered, in being the persisting locus of Louis's experience and character, his overall mental being (putting aside any difficulties with this notion). The problem is rather that the functional unity that is revealed to us when we restrict attention to the brain system mentally considered seems to be far from qualifying as an objective strong unity of the sort that we're taking (with scientific reservations) to be paradigmatically exemplified by ultimates. It seems, rather, to be a merely conventional unity, in the Buddhist sense, the product of a natural human way of partitioning reality for purposes of thought.[7] Thin subjects considered in the living moment of experience certainly qualify as objective strong unities if any things do, as strong-unities-as-mental, as single-as-mental

{45} ⌜TSx → SMx⌝,

but none of the grounds we have for saying this about thin subjects apply in the case of brain systems. It's true that I've set the threshold for objecthood very high, for it's not just tables and brain systems that count as merely conventional unities, on the present account. The same goes for human beings. But that, I think, is as it should be. (I expect human selves to qualify as objects even if whole human beings don't.)

What about immaterial minds as standardly conceived, non-Cartesian immaterial minds? They qualify as strong unities by definition, and hence as objects. Unfortunately, they're ruled out by materialism. And even if we don't hold that against them, it's far from clear that they can properly or sufficiently qualify as single-as-mental or, therefore, as objects-as-mental, because the foundation of a standard non-Cartesian immaterial mind's single objecthood seems to be simply the definitional strong unity of its indivisible immateriality, and there is, so far, nothing intrinsically mental about that.[8] Cartesian immaterial minds, by contrast, are thin subjects, and may indeed qualify as single-as-mental and hence as object-as-mental.

The burden of the last few paragraphs is to support {39}, the suggestion that all sesmets are thin subjects, by raising doubts about the other standard candidates for being sesmets, i.e. traditional inner subjects. {39} is a pretty strong claim, given that we're

---

[6] {40} is a special case of {11}, and its converse, {41} [SUMx → OMx], the claim that to be a strong-unity-as-mental is to be an object-as-mental, is a special case of {42} [SUMx → Ox]; which is in turn a special case of {17}. I hope that the fact that some of the terms I use to articulate the problem of the self turn out to overlap in this sort of way won't be judged to be a defect of exposition. I find it rather encouraging, although it falls short of *mos geometricus*.

[7] If in the end the same is true of ultimates, so be it.

[8] Supporters of the standard immaterial mind's candidacy for selfhood may be prepared to renounce the single-as-mental and object-as-mental requirements, but they're more likely to insist that both requirements are simply built into the definition of immaterial substance. This, though, raises the questions noted on p. 340, and needs argument.

pleading the case of the self, for on the present terms it entails that all sesmets—our prime candidates for selves—are essentially conscious entities, entities that can't exist at all in a state of non-consciousness.

Many will immediately conclude that sesmets can't be what they take selves to be, since it's integral to most people's picture of selves that they can exist when not conscious. The question for them continues to be whether there can be legitimately supposed to be something—a thing of some sort, a genuine object, a physical object—that is

(a) a subject of experience,

(b) not a human being considered as a whole,

(c) present in the L-reality when there's no conscious experience in the L-reality.

There's certainly a subject of experience in the L-reality in the thick whole-creature sense when Louis is in dreamless sleep ([+a, −b, +c]): namely, Louis the whole human being. There's certainly—by definition—a subject of experience in the L-reality in the thin sense when Louis is having conscious experience ([+a, +b, −c]). And there are objects of one sort or another that satisfy every combination of (a), (b), and (c).[9] The crucial question is whether there's a genuine object that sufficiently satisfies [+a, +b, +c]—a subject of experience in the traditional inner-entity sense. Does the traditional inner-entity self exist, the self that seems to feature in the *Oxford English Dictionary* definition:

self … *sb* … 3. Chiefly *Philos* … the ego (often identified with the soul or mind as opposed to the body); a permanent subject of successive and varying states of consciousness?[10]

Many will answer Yes. They'll be happy with the brain-system self, or the standard-issue immaterial soul. For me, though, the question continues to be whether {26} is true—whether real, material, human thin subjects qualify as objects.

—Everything, perhaps, is going according more or less to plan; but you've rigged the discussion. You've set up your standard for objecthood in such a way that brain systems can't qualify. Let's suppose that the persisting brain system that is a candidate for being the self is deeply unified dispositionally and functionally speaking; let's suppose that it's a deep functional-dispositional unity, a DFDU, for short, in some superlative way that remains to be specified in detail. Why isn't DFDU a genuine form of strong unity, object-constituting unity, and indeed strong-unity-as-mental unity? The suggestion is hardly more radical than many you've made yourself, and you can't plausibly reply that a DFDU isn't a real concrete unity, a genuine matter-in-spacetime unity, on the ground that functional unity is wholly a matter of dispositional unity, for you yourself have argued that the dispositional/categorical distinction is superficial—that there's no real distinction between a thing's categorical properties and its dispositional properties.

This is a good objection. It strengthens the account of why we should think of the brain system as a unity, and brings forward the idea that it might be metaphysically superficial

---

[9] If you allow, for [−a, −b, +c], that a human being can be a corpse.

[10] This definition doesn't explicitly include [+c], and is therefore compatible with the Cartesian view; but most will take it to allow that the self, being something 'permanent', may continue to exist at times when there is no experience.

to think that functional unity of a sort that is reasonably attributed to the brain system is somehow essentially inferior, as a principle of unity, to any other kind of supposedly absolute, intrinsic metaphysical unity. The question it raises is whether the brain-system DFDU can indeed be supposed to be an objective unity in fundamental metaphysics, considered independently of human interests, or whether it is at best a conventional unity, a unity that we find it very natural to discern.

Unsurprisingly, I think that the answer to the first part of this question is No, and the answer to the second part Yes. But one needs to look carefully at what grounds the judgement of unity. One proposal may be that a brain-system DFDU can pass a version of van Inwagen's test for being an object (an object that is not a single ultimate), even though his test rules out almost all the kinds of things that are usually taken to be objects. On this view, a brain-system DFDU has as good a claim to be an object as a living thing like a human being, or a cell. It is, in fact, a living thing in its own right, a mental life, a candidate for being a person, indeed, although it's only a part of a human being and isn't a natural biological unity according to standard conceptions of biological unity.[11]

It may for all that fall short of the required standard of objectual unity, as I think it does; but it may in falling short suggest that the standard is too high, when it comes to the requirement that the self be an object. Most of those who want a materialistically respectable persisting self will find their needs met here.

I think, in fact, that the brain-system view faces another insuperable difficulty, the difficulty of supposing that anything that is delineated as an entity in the way in which the brain system is—i.e. in a functional-dispositional way—can be truly identified with any entity that is correctly called a subject of experience in fundamental metaphysics. But then, I hold that the whole human being is no better off than the brain system in this respect, as already remarked—at bottom the objection is that simply *the term 'subject of experience' has no proper use as a dispositional term in fundamental metaphysics*—so I don't expect many people to be worried by my doubt, even though (or perhaps all the more because) I have Buddhists, Descartes, Spinoza, Leibniz, Hume, Kant, and many distinguished others on my side. Here my position stands in stark contrast to Dainton's position in his book *The Phenomenal Self*, for he defines the self or subject of experience wholly dispositionally, as a collection of potentialities. His view accords with the idea that an entity that was a subject of experience could exist without ever actually having any experience. My focus on the thin conception of the subject leads me to say (less naturally to most present-day philosophical ears) that no actual subject of experience ever exists in a universe in which millions of Daintonian subjects of experience exist but never have any experience. There's a sense in which our disagreement is terminological; each of us can say to the other that he agrees, given the other's use of the expression 'subject of experience'. But it is also, of course, substantial,

---

[11] If this is allowed, then (given that a brain-system DFDU can be wholly contained in a human brain) a brain transplant may involve the transfer of an object even if a brain is—as on van Inwagen's view—not itself allowed to count as an object.

in that we disagree about the best use of the expression. I think, in fact, that a collection of potentialities can't be a subject of experience; it can't properly be said to have experience at all.[12]

I'll now summarize the argument to come. If {26}, the claim that thin subjects are objects—single-as-mental, object-as-mental objects—can be established in such a way as to remove what I take to be the only remaining objection to {23}, the claim that thin subjects are sesmets, then we can, as remarked, know {33} that sesmets exist, because we know {21} that thin subjects exist. So if we can also establish {34}, that sesmets are rightly taken to be selves, selves will be ontologically home and dry—as thin subjects.

Many who favour the self will find this conclusion no better than the conclusion that there are no such things as selves, and they won't be mollified by the information that {34} and {38} amount to

{46} [Sx ↔ SESx],

with its intimation that selves just are sesmets—a claim which I propose to represent simply as

[A] [S = SES]

—or by the observation that {23} and {39} amount to

{47} [SESx ↔ TSx],

with its strong suggestion that sesmets just are thin subjects—a claim which I propose to represent simply as

[B] [SES = TS],

—or by the consequence of [A] and [B], that selves—selves strictly speaking, the things that can be allowed to qualify as selves given the strong brief (12)—just are thin subjects

[C] [S = TS].

They should, though, remember that it doesn't follow from the claim that sesmets/selves are thin subjects that they're short-lived. Thinness in the present sense implies nothing about temporal extent (325). I've proposed that the human process of consciousness is gappy, disjointed, constantly broken, even within the waking day, and accordingly that human thin subjects are always short-lived, but I don't claim to know this (questions about the 'top' subject—page 348—complicate the issue), and the possibility is left open that human selves may last for considerable periods of time even if they're thin subjects. It may be, as remarked, that the human process of consciousness is uninterrupted throughout life, even throughout the night and under the deepest anaesthetic, and this, so far, leaves open the possibility of saying that human selves may last for life even if they're thin subjects. That said, it doesn't follow, from the fact that there's continuous conscious experience in the L-reality, that there is a single thin subject in the

---

[12] In correspondence Dainton agrees that to speak of selves or subjects ' "having experience" isn't quite right', on his view; 'it has to be construed as "selves or subjects *have the capacity to produce* experience"—the latter is what the "having" involves'; see also Dainton 2008a: 134.

L-reality, for numerically distinct thin subjects may succeed each other seamlessly or in an overlapping manner.

This, then, is how things stand. Putting aside assumptions, definitions, and evident truths, I have to support {18}, {23}, {26}, {31}, {34}, {38}, and {39}.

I take {18}, the claim that strong unity is both necessary and sufficient for objecthood, to have been sufficiently established (defined into place) in 6.11–6.12.

I've expounded my commitment to {34} and {38}, the view that all selves are sesmets and all sesmets selves, in Parts 2 and 4 (bearing in mind that some might accept {34} more easily than {38}).

{31} doesn't lie in the main present line of argument, but will need to be considered in 8.6.

That leaves {23}, {26}, and {39}. I need to establish that thin subjects are objects

{26} [TSx → Ox],

in order to establish that thin subjects are sesmets

{23} [TSx → SESx],

and if I want everything to come out as I think it should, I also need to establish the converse of {23}, i.e. that all sesmets are thin subjects

{39} [SESx → TSx].

If I can do this, the rest will sufficiently follow. The argument could be more succinct, but the general idea should be plain.

For the sake of completeness let me introduce 'M' to stand for 'mentally propertied' and 'SE' to stand for 'subject of experience'. We can then add the definitional point that a sesmet is a subject of experience and mentally propertied

{48} [SESx → [SEx ∧ Mx]]

to the defining conditions of 'SES' and gather them all together in

{49} [SESx ↔ [SEx ∧ Mx ∧ Ox ∧ SMx ∧ OMx]].[13]

Thin subjects, too, are by definition subjects of experience and mentally propertied

{50} [TSx → [SEx ∧ Mx]],

and if something is correctly considered as an object when considered in its mental being, then it is correctly considered as an object *tout court*,

{29} [OMx → Ox],

as observed in 4.8 and at the end of 6.4. All that remains to be done, then, to establish {23} that thin subjects are sesmets, is to show that a thin subject has the property *single-as-mental*

{45} [TSx → SMx],

---

[13] I'm omitting some brackets and taking the singleness condition to be sufficiently contained in the SM and OM conditions.

i.e. the property of being correctly judged to be a single thing when considered only in its mental being, and also the property *object-as-mental*

{52} [TSx → OMx],

i.e. the property of being correctly judged to be an object when considered only in its mental being. But {52} entails {45}, given {44} that being an object-as-mental entails being single-as-mental—

{44} [OMx → SMx]

—so it's enough to establish {52}. And to do this it's enough, given {18} that being a strong unity is equivalent to being an object—

{18} [SUx ↔ Ox],

—to show {51} that a thin subject has the property strong-unity-as-mental (the property of being correctly judged to be a strong unity when considered only in its mental being)

{51} [TSx → SUMx].

So all that needs to be established is {51}. For it follows as a special case of

{17} [SUx → Ox],

the principle that if something is a strong unity, then it is an object, that {41} if something is a strong-unity-as-mental, then it is an object-as-mental

{41} [SUMx → OMx],

as already remarked; and {41} and {51} together entail

{52} [TSx → OMx],

the claim that thin subjects are objects-as-mental; and {52} and

{29} [OMx → Ox],

the fact that if something is an object-as-mental, then it is *a fortiori* an object, deliver the crucial proposition that thin subjects are objects

{26} [TSx → Ox].

The conjunction of {26}, {45}, {52}, and {51} then yield, with comfortable redundancy, the claim that thin subjects fulfil all the conditions needed to qualify as sesmets

{53} [TSx → [SEx ∧ Ox ∧ Mx ∧ SMx ∧ OMx]]

and {53} joined with {49}, i.e. the fully spelt-out definition of 'sesmet', accordingly delivers the second crucial proposition that thin subjects are sesmets

{23} [TSx → SESx],

which then joins with {34}, the claim that sesmets are selves

{34} [SESx → Sx]

to yield the conclusion {36} that thin subjects are selves

{36} [TSx → Sx].

Finally, {23} couples with {21}, the claim that thin subjects exist

{21} ∃xTSx

to yield {33}, the conclusion that sesmets exist

{33} ∃xSESx

and {33} couples in turn with {34} to yield the conclusion that selves exist

{37} ∃xSx

which was what was to be established, on the terms of the strong brief specified on page 12.[14]

It isn't necessary to establish that all sesmets are thin subjects

{39} [SESx → TSx]

in order to reach this conclusion; but I think, and will argue, that there is a good case to be made for {39}. It remains to say that {34} is still disputable even if its converse

{38} [Sx → SESx]

is plausible. But the essential wideness of the word 'self' requires that {34} remains disputable.

The deduction need not be so laborious or contain such redundancy, but there it is. Even those who are prepared to concede that the intuitions I pursue have some degree of initial attractiveness are likely to think that I pursue them past the point where it becomes clear that they're hopelessly misguided. But perhaps the intuitions are sound, and drive us into ways of thinking of things that are far from our ordinary ways, and reveal things about the structure of reality that we might not otherwise have suspected.

Perhaps. We still have to establish that thin subjects are strong unities-as-mental

{51} [TSx → SUMx]

in order to trigger the required cascade of consequences: in order to establish {26} that thin subjects are objects and can therefore {23} be sesmets and therefore {36} selves. The work is already done, in effect, but I want to go over it again.

8.3 Strong unity

The three uses of the term 'subject of experience'—the thick whole-creature use, the traditional inner-entity use, and the thin/live inner-entity use—present us with three candidates for objecthood: the human being, the subject conceived as some sort of persisting inner entity that can exist in the absence of any experience, and the subject considered as something that is live and present in the lived present of experience and that can't exist in the absence of any experience.

How do they compare in their claims to objecthood? I'm still allowing that thick subjects—human beings—have a good claim to be genuine physical objects, if there are such things (and if, in particular, there is a plurality of them). I've proposed that

---

[14] {21} and {36} also produce {37}.

thin subjects have at least as good a claim, and I'm now going to say more about this. I've given up on the immaterial mind, the persisting inner (or 'inner') inhabitant postulated by so many discussions of the mind or self or subject in the history of philosophy and human thought in general, for the case of the self, the philosophical trial of the self, has long since transferred to the court of materialism.[15] As a very junior and very late-arriving counsel for the defence who claims to have a relatively well-developed general conception of what it is to be a materialist, by which I mean a real or realistic materialist, I'm extremely impressed by the thought that a physical object is, if anything, and essentially, a certain kind of strong physical unity, and I still worry that the best remaining candidate for being the traditional inner subject—the brain system—isn't going to make the grade, in spite of being a 'deep functional-dispositional unity' (369). A thin subject, by contrast, a thin subject considered at any given time, seems unbeatable as an example of mental unity, and therefore of physical unity, and therefore as a candidate for physical objecthood. Questions remain, questions about the diachronic identity conditions of such supposed objects, but this point at least seems secure.

—I think these questions are going to prove fatally difficult; and before we get to them, I'd like you to consider a sharply delimited, uninterrupted one-second-long experience of uniform red that occupies the whole visual field. Consider the concrete phenomenon of the existence for one second—between t_1 and t_2—of this experiential content, which we may call C. C seems as unbeatable as an example of mental and hence physical unity as your thin subject, but it doesn't seem to have any very good claim to be an object rather than, say, a state or property of some object, or indeed a property of a state of an object. So it seems that the transition from the claim that a thin subject considered at any given time is a beautiful example of a 'strong' physical unity to the claim that it is as good a candidate as any for the title 'physical object' is simply unwarranted. Mental unity entails physical unity, given realistic materialism, and physical objecthood entails physical unity, as you have claimed, but physical unity doesn't entail physical objecthood, as the case of C shows.

I have three connected replies. The first stops the objection in its tracks by rejecting the way it uses the state/property/object distinction, on grounds set out in 6.13–6.15.

The second reply concedes for argument that strong physical unity alone doesn't entail physical objecthood, and also allows that strong physical unity doesn't essentially involve dynamic unity, activity-unity (both concessions are contrary to the position endorsed in 6.14). It then calls Leibniz in support on the point that the fundamental essential property of substance is activity, to act,[16] in this universe, at least, and adds to the unity requirement the requirement that an object be something that is an activity-unity in this sense:

---

[15] For an informative survey of this process see Martin and Barresi 2006. There have always been materialist accounts of the self.

[16] I leave this claim undefended in this book. Leibniz, as I understand him, takes activity to be essentially a matter of mindedness. Real materialism may reach the same (panpychist) conclusion by inference to the best explanation, starting from the existence of experience.

{15} [Ox → SAUx].

In this way it rules out C as presented here. That is, it rules out C in so far as C is conceived as something that is in itself intrinsically passive. C is not, however, conceived of in this way by Descartes and others, for whom C is a segment of *res cogitans*, literally part (if not all) of what constitutes the subject, the active substance or object, between t_1 and t_2. I agree with Descartes about this, for when we focus on thin subjects, I think we find (as in 7.4) that the distinction between an experience, the subject of the experience, and the content of the experience is in the end only a conceptual distinction, not a real distinction; but I will put this aside until 8.8.

The third reply begins by reaffirming {15}, the intensely plausible suggestion that a genuine object or substance must be a single agent, in the fundamental Leibnizian sense, an activity-unity, a dynamic unity, a single spacetime player. It then takes back the concessions of the second reply, insisting that a genuine strong physical unity is *ipso facto* a strong activity-unity, i.e. that the terms 'strong unity' (SU) and 'strong activity-unity' (SAU) are interchangeable

{14} [SUx ↔ SAUx].

This done, it moves on from the claim that strong unity is necessary for objecthood

{11} [Ox → SUx],

which you allow, to the view that any true physical unity is, *ipso facto*, and whatever your preferred conception of true unity, a physical object

{17} [SUx → Ox]

(given, as always, that we're still allowing that the term 'object' has a reference in our metaphysics) and asserts the conjunction of {11} and {17}

{18} [SUx ↔ Ox].

I think this is the right move to make, both in general and in the particular case of C—the concrete physical unity C. And (reverting to the first reply) the object/property point made in 6.15 also comes into play. It's no longer enough to say that C is evidently 'just' a property or a state of an object, evidently not in the category of objects, for there is no real distinction between the existence of an object, considered at any time, and the existence of its properties or propertiedness, considered at that time.

I haven't claimed that a thin subject is the only good example of strong mental and hence strong physical unity, only that it is as good an example as can be found. I'm prepared to give up, for the sake of argument, the second 'therefore' in 'a thin subject is unbeatable as an example of mental unity, and therefore of physical unity, and therefore of physical objecthood', and argue independently for the idea that when we survey the class of physical unities, and ask which ones are good candidates for being objects (having agreed to continue to allow ourselves the use of the thought-element OBJECT in our metaphysics, and having granted that a physical object is a certain kind of physical unity, whatever else it is or isn't), subjects of experience must on any good account of things be first, or at the very least equal first, in the queue.

—The price of strong unity, of the sort you attribute it to thin subjects, is lack of ontic depth. Their claim to be superlative objects is bought at the cost of their claim to be selves. You say your aim is to represent the self, but you're representing it out of existence. Some counsel! Even if you can throw off the problem of ontic depth, you'll be no further forward. If selves exist at all, they must be things that can exist when not conscious.

Many will agree with you, but let me finish my case.

—I trust this is a No Win No Fee arrangement.

8.4 Thin subjects as objects—synchronic identity conditions

We have to show that thin subjects are objects—and objects-as-mental. This presumably requires being able to give a satisfactory account of their identity conditions, synchronic and diachronic. We need to be able to draw a line round thin subjects in analytic thought, while restricting our attention to their mental/experiential being, in such a way as to be able to say, at a given moment of time t_1, 'Here is one thin subject, and here is another'. Moving on to consider thin subjects as things that last longer than the living moment of experience (focusing for convenience on a single brain, and allowing for the possibility that a human life involves breaks in experience of a kind that entail a diachronic plurality of thin subjects), we presumably also need to be able to draw a line round thin subjects, while restricting attention to their mental/experiential being, in such a way as to be able to say 'This is one thin subject, existing for the period of time t_1–t_2, and this, now, is another different one, existing from t_2 to t_3, or from t_7 to t_8' (I say 'presumably' because I'll raise a crucial doubt, later, about whether we really do have to be able to give an account of the diachronic identity conditions of something, even in principle, in order to have sufficient reason to say that it is an object). I'll begin with synchronic identity conditions, the identity conditions of a thin subject as we find it in the living moment of experience, and I'll take it for granted that we're considering identity conditions that can be discerned by reference to nothing other than mental/experiential being. I've already made the central point, e.g. in 4.2, but it invites restatement, and expansion.

Consider an experiencing subject at a given moment, and consider the totality of its experience at that moment. Consider, that is, the total content of its experiential field at that moment, its total-experiential-field-with-the-content-that-it-has—its 'total experiential field', for short. Ask whether it could fail to be experientially single or unified, single-as-mental (SM), a strong-unity-as-mental (SUM), in being what it is (here content is internalistically understood).

To ask the question is to see the fundamental sense in which the answer is No. The total experiential field involves many things. It involves interoceptive and exteroceptive sensation, mood-and-affect tone, deep conceptual animation, and so on. It has, standardly, a particular focus, and correspondingly dim peripheral areas, and it is, overall, quite extraordinarily complex in content. But it is, for all that, a unity, and essentially so. It is fundamentally unified, utterly indivisible as the particular concrete phenomenon it is, simply in being, indeed, *a* total experiential field; or, equivalently, simply in being *the* content of the experience of a single subject at that moment.[17] Equivalently: the unity or singleness of the (thin) subject of the total experiential field in the living moment of experience and the unity or singleness of the total experiential field are aspects of the same thing. They're necessarily dependent on each other even if they aren't the same thing.

I think, in fact, that there is only a conceptual distinction between them, not a real distinction, in Descartes's sense. Neither can possibly exist without the other, but there's no dependence of a sort that requires two really (real-ly) distinct entities. The present point, however, is independent of any dramatic metaphysical claim about the ultimate metaphysical identity of the unity of the (thin-subject) experiencer and the unity of the experiential field. It's simply the point—the simple point—that *a* field, a single field, entails *a* subject, a single subject, and conversely. If you bring a single thin subject into existence at t_1, then you necessarily bring a single, unified experiential field into existence at t_1, and conversely. The singleness of the (thin) subject at t_1 entails, and is essentially constitutive of, the singleness of the total experiential field at t_1. So too the singleness of the total experiential field at t_1 entails (and is arguably constitutive of—see 8.8) the singleness of its subject at t_1, for the material that is experienced is necessarily experienced in a single or unified experiential perspective. The point is a 'logical' one, as trivial as it is important, and no problem of vagueness arises, of the sort that is thought to arise when one considers the spatial boundaries of objects like Mount Everest, for experience is an absolute, all-or-nothing matter.

I'll call this *Fundamental Singleness*. It applies to all necessarily-subject-of-experience-involving experiential-field unities, whatever their duration, and it applies to all possible subjects of experience, however primitive. To this extent it's independent of Kant's relatively high-level claim that when we consider ourselves as subjects, we must necessarily apprehend ourselves as single—his claim that 'the proposition *I am simple* [i.e. single] must be regarded as a direct expression of apperception' (A355). For one thing, his claim is about expressly self-conscious creatures like ourselves, whereas the present Fundamental Singleness claim doesn't depend on the subject's having any sort of express or thetic experience of itself as subject, let alone any such experience of itself as single as subject. If worms have experience, their experience has Fundamental Singleness, at any given time, and not just by being simple, if indeed it is. So does experience that seems utterly chaotic; the experience of chaos at any given time depends on the singleness, as noted in 2.20.

There's a further respect in which the Fundamental Singleness point is more basic than the claims for which Kant is famous. For what is in question is a necessary unity of experience (of experiential field) that we can know to exist before we have had any distinctively Kantian thoughts about the 'necessary unity of consciousness'

---

[17] I leave open the possibility that there can be more than one total experiential field in a human being at a given time (335). If there can be, the point about necessary singleness applies to each one of them taken individually.

and 'necessary synthesis of the manifold'.[18] It is, in other words, a necessary unity of experience that we can know to exist before we come to any aspect of the unity of experience that we can know to exist because it's a necessary condition of the possibility of other relatively complicated things that we know to exist—e.g. articulated thoughts like *grass is green*, or experiences that involve 'co-consciousness' in being at once and indissolubly both visual and auditory, or what Kant simply calls 'experience', by which he means experience that has, for the experiencer, the character of being experience of a world of objects (or at least an ordered world) existing independently of the experiencer. What is in question is a still more basic necessary unity of experience or experiential field we know to exist not by running any kind of transcendental argument but simply by considering what it is for a subject to be having any experience at all—by considering what it is for there to be an experiential point of view at all.[19]

8.5 Fundamental singleness—Descartes, Kant, and James

The Fundamental Singleness point is secure, but let me call Kant and James as witnesses, and record a point about Descartes. When Descartes claims that the indivisibility of the mind or soul or subject is something certain (1641: 2.79), Fundamental Singleness is a key part of what he has in mind. He's been widely condemned—even mocked—for the indivisibility claim, but it's certainly correct as a metaphysical thesis, given the central tenet of his metaphysics of mind, i.e. that the mind, or *res cogitans*, just is experience/consciousness/thinking, necessarily subject-of-experience-involving experience/consciousness/thinking, and indeed subject-of-experience-constituting experience/consciousness/thinking, and has no other mode of being. For, given this tenet, the indivisibility thesis is nothing more than the assertion of Fundamental Singleness, at least so far as the synchronic case is concerned. Kant doesn't criticize this view in the Paralogisms section of the *Critique of Pure Reason*; he simply criticizes a certain metaphysical (and in particular religious) use to which it is put.

Turning to Kant's own views, and focusing on experiential unities that are the thinking of thoughts in the narrower, cognitive, non-Cartesian sense, particular events of proposition comprehension, e.g. judgements, we can, I propose, extract the following unity argument, and give it a materialist bedding.[20] We know, to begin, that

(1) particular thoughts exist.

We also know that

---

[18] '… the necessary unity of consciousness, and therefore also of the synthesis of the manifold' (A109; this is the only occurrence in the first *Critique* of the phrase 'necessary unity of consciousness').

[19] I take it as given that things just are a certain way for one, experientially, at any given moment of experience, and that it is entirely determinate how they are, even if—even though—we cannot specify in exhaustive detail how they are (for a brief defence see G. Strawson 2002: § 3).

[20] The main argument occurs in Kant's Transcendental Analytic, but can be easily integrated with his discussion of the 'I' or self in the Paralogisms section of the Transcendental Dialectic, and I move freely between the two.

(2) such thoughts must have distinguishable elements, or at least a certain complexity, in order to be genuine thoughts at all, discursively articulated thoughts like *grass is green*.

We also know that

(3) these distinguishable elements, or this complexity, must form a unity, the (mental) unity that is the phenomenon of the comprehension of the proposition by a subject, if there is to be a genuine thought at all.

On the present materialist view

(4) such unities are wholly physical unities, in being mental unities, although they may not present as intuitively unitary entities when non-experientially considered (e.g. when examined by neurologists; cf. A355).

We know, then, that there are actually existing physical entities that concretely realize a certain sort of unity. This interim conclusion is not very exciting, because the same can be said of cars or bananas. The further point, though, is that the concrete unity in question is a unity of a very strong sort, a 'logical' unity, on Kant's view. It's what he calls the 'logical unity of every thought'.[21] Cars and bananas can lose car parts or banana parts and retain their identity as the cars or bananas they are, so long as we're reasonably relaxed about the identity conditions of things. A thought, by contrast, can't lose any thought-part and retain its identity as the particular thought it is, and the same goes for a total experiential field. They are indivisible (and in that sense simple) unities.

If we accept this, we can infer that

(5) there are actually existing physical entities—thoughts—that concretely realize a certain sort of extremely strong and indeed 'logical' unity.

What is this logical unity? It's the unity specified in (3), nothing more; the unity that must exist if a thought is to occur at all. It is, on the one hand, a very ordinary everyday thing, but it is also, on the other hand, something exceptional, because it is an absolute or 'logical' and yet fully concretely existing unity.

There's a further reason why it's exceptional. If we ask generally what logical or absolute unity or indivisibility might be, a first thought is that it involves perfect simplicity. On this view, if something is an absolute unity, then [U] it has no true description that furnishes any sense in which it can be said to involve complexity, or parts. The unity of a thought such as *grass is green* is not like this, however, for [¬U] it has a true fundamental description that displays it to have a certain sort of complexity. (The same goes for any actually existing total experiential field, whether or not it is a thought.) If this is right, then even if [U] is sufficient for absolute unity or indivisibility, it isn't necessary. One might call absolute unities/indivisibilities which fail to satisfy [U] 'complex absolute unities', and one might then wonder whether there can be such things. I am at present supposing that there are many of them, but one might also suppose that there is only one—the

---

[21] A398. I'm translating 'denken' by 'thought', here, although I take it (as in 2.10) that it can in most contexts be equally well translated by 'experience'.

universe. This, though, raises the question of the one and the many, which I don't want to consider. The best answer to the question, perhaps, given discursive thought's limited capacity to represent the nature of reality, is that it is true that there is only one thing, and true that there are many things,[22] or at least that it is true that there is diversity but also true that it is, somehow, all one. I think, though, that we must take Locke's advice and 'sit down in a quiet ignorance of those things which, upon examination, are found to be beyond the reach of our capacities' (*Essay*, 1.1.4).

However this may be, the heart of Kant's notion of logical unity is simple. One can re-express it by saying that it is one half of

(6) Fundamental Singleness

adjusted, here, to the particular case of propositional thought. It's the simple point that if a thought is had, if a proposition is genuinely entertained, then it's necessarily had or entertained by a single subject. In Kant's words,

(7) the 'logical unity of every thought' is inseparable from the 'absolute ... logical unity of the subject' (A356) of the thought.

What about the other half? It's not only true that concretely occurring thoughts realize a certain sort of unsurpassable concrete unity. It's equally true that

(8) the (thin) subjects of thoughts—concretely realize a certain sort of 'absolute ... logical' unity,

as Kant observes in a passage already quoted on page 87: 'That ... the *I* in every act of thought is *one*, and cannot be resolved into a plurality of subjects, ... is something that lies already in the concept of thought, and is therefore an analytic proposition' (B407). I believe that these two unities are in fact and at bottom the same unity, and take it again that Kant agrees, in another passage already quoted, when he says that 'the thinking or the existence of the thought and the existence of my own self are one and the same' (1772: 75); but this is a further, difficult idea. For the moment we may take it that when we have to do with these actual concrete logical or absolute unities, we have to do with unities of an absolute or unsurpassable sort, unities that must count as strong unities on any account of what strong unity is.

How do things stand? In knowing that such thoughts really exist, as I take it we do, and in knowing that any thought must have a certain sort of absolute unity if it is to exist at all (even though there is also a respect in which it must involve difference and complexity), we know—to put it in terms that may seem provocative to some Kantians, but should not seem so to Kant, just so long as he grants, as he surely does, that thoughts really concretely exist—that there exist entities that are genuine, *concrete metaphysical* unities or indivisibilities of an unsurpassable sort.

The same degree of unity exists in the case of complex sensory experiences involving different sensory modalities, and a parallel argument establishes the necessary singleness

---

[22] I hear the voices of the Nyāya-Vaiśeṣika and the Advaita Vedānta, rising behind me in debate.

of the subject of any such experience. Such unity also exists, of course, in the case of experiences that are absolutely simple in content.[23] The simple content cases are less interesting than the complex content cases, because they don't supply the unity claim with the power it derives from the point that there is absolute unity in spite of complexity, but the unity point is established by the mere existence of experience.[24]

Here, then, I propose, we move validly (i.e. without paralogism) from a 'logical' or 'logico-phenomenological' point to a substantive metaphysical conclusion, in the way anticipated on page 52. There may be neurological or cognitive-science accounts of what is going on that find astonishing complexity in these cases, many disparate and discrete events. None of this matters, given that there are genuine *experiential* unities, e.g. actual comprehending entertainings of propositions (generally, experiences of any kind that are as they are at any given time). For, crucially, each of these experiential unities is itself a concretely existing metaphysical unity or indivisibility of an unsurpassable sort. The phrase 'experiential unity' mustn't be misunderstood. There's no requirement that the subject have any express experience of itself or its thought *as* a unity. The requirement is only that it have a genuine thought—that a genuine thought (experience) occur. This is the experiential unity in question, which is itself an unsurpassable, concrete metaphysical unity.

It may be granted that Kant is committed to the existence of thoughts and judgements, by his moral views if by nothing else, but objected that he can't and won't claim to know that these existent thoughts are metaphysically unsurpassable unities, if only on the grounds that they have an irreducibly temporal character, so far as we know anything about them, and so can't be known by us as they are in themselves, but only in so far as they appear to us. Against this we must bring his own claim that they—and their subjects—involve 'absolute', 'logical' unity. I think that Kant would—must—on this ground be prepared to agree that they're unsurpassable unities that we can know to exist and to be such. My present aim, though, is to put forward a suggestive proposal, not to attempt detailed Kantian exegesis.

—I really don't think you can expect Kant's blessing. On page 88 you quote approvingly the passage in which Kant speaks of the 'merely logical qualitative unity of self-consciousness in thought in general, which has to be present whether the subject be composite or not' (B413). But his point here is precisely that there may be no real substantial metaphysical unity at all, although there may be and indeed must be this 'qualitative unity' (compare, also, the use of 'qualitative' in the Transcendental Deduction on B114).

Kant has a specific *ad hominem* purpose in the Paralogisms, as remarked in 4.3: to stop the simple/single → indivisible → immaterial → incorruptible → immortal chain of

---

[23] If such cases are possible. As in 6.3, we might allow a sense in which experience of a single pure note is simple, although it involves pitch, timbre, and loudness, and there seems no reason in principle why a sensory state-space could not be strictly one-dimensional. 'Pure awareness', of the sort that Buddhists claim to attain, is another possible example of absolute simplicity of content.

[24] It's irrelevant that there are cases in which it's natural to say that someone has had or has entertained *a* thought, but in which what we mean by 'a thought' is such that having or entertaining it involves more than one unity of the sort I have at present in mind.

argument that was so popular in his time.[25] In this traditional sense of 'metaphysical' his claim is indeed, quite unequivocally, that we have no good grounds for believing that there is a real metaphysical singularity or unity. This is his correct (although not original) objection to the use that the 'rational psychologists' seek to make of Fundamental Singleness. The present proposal, though, is that there's another wider sense of 'metaphysical' that Kant not only can but seemingly must allow, which yields a real, known metaphysical unity after all,[26] and doesn't disrupt his argument against the rational psychologists. In this way we legitimize the Second Paralogism argument by removing the equivocation that renders it paralogistic (51 n. 51): the subject that is knowably single is also knowably a metaphysically real concretely existing entity.

The proposal depends, as before, on the claim that Kant agrees that thoughts— experiences, judgements—really, concretely exist (I avoid the expressly temporal word 'occur'). It goes from there to the point that he must then agree that the unity that their existence requires must truly exist and be real, a genuine metaphysical unity of some sort, although it licenses no conclusions about immortality and so forth.

Michael Ayers attributes to Locke the view that life in an organism is 'a non-substantial principle of substantial unity, and that consciousness is just like life' (1991: 2.263); from which it follows, given Locke's claim that 'consciousness makes personal identity',[27] that the notion of a self or person, too, is the notion of a 'non-substantial principle of substantial unity'. The phrase is suggestive. Thoughts exist, they're metaphysically real, and they necessarily have single subjects. We can't know that the subjects that we can know to exist are metaphysically single or simple substances in the immortality- underwriting sense. Perhaps, though, we can say that a subject of a thought is at least a real 'non-substantial principle of substantial unity'; non-substantial relative to the traditional understanding of 'substance', but a fully metaphysically real concrete unity none the less, a metaphysically real unity phenomenon that has, on the fundamental metaphysical stage, every right to count as a true or absolute unity.[28] Kant's view, once again, is that the fact that 'the *I* in every act of thought is *one* ... lies already in the very concept of thought, and is therefore an analytic proposition'.[29] So if he agrees that thoughts concretely exist in any manner at all, as he certainly does, he must agree that this oneness concretely exists, in some crucial, metaphysically solid (but not conventionally metaphysical or immortality-supporting) sense.

It may be objected that these unities (unity of subject, unity of thought or experience) are 'merely functional' unities; but it's not clear what this 'merely' means, as applied

---

[25] On this see 4.3, esp. p. 173n. 10.

[26] It is known that it exists, and that it is a unity, whatever the sense in which its nature remains unknown.

[27] Locke, *Essay*, 2. 27.10. Locke uses the word 'consciousness' in a special sense that needs no comment here. Note that one might take the first occurrence of 'substantial' in Ayers's phrase to be a conventional modern use—common to Locke, the rational psychologists, and Kant in his debate with them, and so on—while the second opens up an importantly wider metaphysical view (apart from being Aristotelian).

[28] An activity unity and hence, on the present terms, an object or 'individual substance' (in so far as there are allowed to be such things).

[29] B407. Kant's logical point about oneness is additional to his point that there is no intuition of the subject involved in apperception, that the bare representation 'I' is in this sense 'completely empty' (B404/A345).

to concretely actualized entities. In particular, it's not clear that it detracts in any way from these unities' claim to be true metaphysical unities. Even if we can find a sense in which they are 'merely' functional unities, this won't touch the fact that they're concretely existing unities, genuine metaphysical unities. And by the time we've revised and processualized the notions of object and substance in the way we have to if they're to retain any place in fundamental metaphysics, and stripped them, with Kant's blessing (313), of their claim to stand in fundamental ontological contrast with properties and attributes, we'll be in no position to hold on to any view that has the consequence that these unsurpassable thought unities or experience unities, these thinker unities and experiencer unities, have less claim to be objects or substances than paradigmatic examples of ultimates (or indeed, good old-fashioned immaterial minds).

We may as materialists suppose that the existence of these unsurpassable mental unities involves the existence of a large number of neurons (and *a fortiori* ultimates) acting in concert. In this case we may say that it essentially involves a plurality of 'different substances acting together', to use Kant's general formulation in his discussion of the Second Paralogism (A353). Kant is right that we can't ground any claims about the non-materiality and hence possible long-term simplicity or indivisibility and hence incorruptibility and hence immortality of the soul on the knowable existence of these 'absolute' concrete unities.[30] This, again, is the line of thought he demolishes in his discussion of the Paralogisms. This demolition is, however, wholly compatible with, and, crucially, derives its principal force from, the fact that it succeeds *even though we can know that these fundamental and unsurpassable unities exist*. We can know they exist even though they're of no use in establishing the existence of a persisting immaterial subject. It's Kant himself, as remarked, who makes it most vivid that the fact that 'the I in every act of thought is *one* … lies already in the very concept of thought'. He's prepared to '*allow full objective validity*' to the '*proposition … everything which thinks is a simple substance*', at least for the sake of argument, for his point is that even if we do this, 'we still cannot make *the least use* of this proposition in regard to the question of [the mind's or soul's] dissimilarity from or relation to matter' in such a way as to hope to establish immateriality and thence incorruptibility and immortality (A357; my emphasis). We can know the necessary singleness or simplicity of the subject of experience in the having of experience, but to know this is not to have 'knowledge of the simple nature of the self as subject, *such as* might enable us to distinguish it from matter, as from a composite being' (A360; my emphasis).

It may next be said that Fundamental Singleness is a 'merely experiential unity' and so not a real metaphysical unity. The first target of this objection is likely to be the claim that the total experiential field of an experience is a metaphysical unity—the objection being that this unity is only an appearance, that it is only from a certain point of view that the total experiential field presents as unified. But the objection may also be aimed at the claim about the unsurpassable unity of the (thin) subject of the experience, the objection being that this too is somehow 'merely experiential'.

---

[30] Kant does, however, take his arguments in the Paralogisms to show that materialists can't give an adequate explanation of the existence of the subject, given its 'logical' simplicity property. See B419–20.

There's a lot to say to this, but the basic reply is simple: what's 'merely' about it? It's true that the unity of the total experiential field of an experience is essentially, and if you like merely, an internal experiential (*IE*) unity, whatever else it is or isn't. It's true that it's a unity considered just in respect of its internal experiential character, a unity considered from the point of view of its subject, a unity constituted as such by the existence of the point of view of its subject.[31] And it's true that there is a crucial sense in which its fundamental-unity characteristic is a matter of its experiential being (when we consider the existence of the experience non-experientially, we find millions of u-fields in a certain state of synergetic interaction). But it is at the same time an objective fact that subjective experience exists, and it's an objective fact that it has the character it does for the experiencer. The subjective or experiential fact that one of these IE unities exists is itself an objective metaphysical fact, a fact about the world. That is, it's a fact that stands as a fact from a perspective external to the perspective internal to the IE unity.

The reason why we're right to judge an IE unity to be a fully metaphysically real unity when considering it *externally*, from the outside, objective point of view, is nothing other than the fact that it is indeed a strong *internal* experiential unity, a unity from the internal subjective point of view. But there's nothing odd about the sense in which subjective phenomena can be objective facts. This is part of any minimally sensible realism about the subjective. All that's added here is the slightly more specific point that the existence of an IE unity, in the objectively real process of the subjective experience of a human being, is itself an objectively existing real unity (experience is real!), both in its single-subject aspect and in its single total-experiential-field aspect (which may at bottom be the same thing). The statement that this unity exists and is wholly metaphysically real holds true outside the perspective of the subject in question, although the unity in question consists wholly of the phenomenon of the existence of that subject having that experience, with the content that it has, at the time in question.[32]

When William James speaks of the 'indecomposable unity of every pulse of thought',[33] he's well aware both of the Kantian points and the Fundamental Singleness point. His main discussion of the matter is in chapter 9 of *The Principles of Psychology*, and I'll quote it at some length because of the interest of the passage:

the object of every thought … is neither more nor less than all that the thought thinks, exactly as thought thinks it, however complicated the matter, and however symbolic the manner of the thinking may be. [And] *however complex the object may be, the thought of it is one undivided state of consciousness*. As Thomas Brown says:

---

[31] However unreflective the subject, however little 'thetic' apprehension it has of the fact that the unity in question is a unity.

[32] The qualification that one then needs to enter is that there need be no distinctive *experience of unity* on the part of the subject of the IE unity, inasmuch as the necessary unity in question is simply the fact already mentioned: the trivial fact that any subject necessarily experiences all the material it experiences at any given time in a single experiential perspective. Some Phenomenologists may hold that there must in every case, however lowly, be some sort of experience of unity *experienced as such*. I think I can agree to this, in any sense in which it is true, without disturbing the point of this qualification.

[33] 1890: 1.371. As previously noted, James uses 'thought' in the broad Cartesian way to denote all experiential episodes.

I have already spoken too often to require again to caution you against the mistake into which, I confess, the terms which the poverty of our language obliges us to use might of themselves very naturally lead you; the mistake of supposing that the most complex states of mind are not truly, in their very essence, as much one and indivisible as those which we term simple—the complexity and seeming coexistence which they involve being relative to our feeling[34] only, not to their own absolute nature ....[35]

The ordinary associationist-psychology supposes, in contrast with this, that whenever an object of thought contains many elements, the thought itself must be made up of just as many ideas, one idea for each element, and all fused together in appearance, but really separate. ... The enemies of this psychology find (as we have already seen) little trouble in showing that such a bundle of separate ideas would never form one thought at all, and they contend that an Ego must be added to the bundle to give it unity, and bring the various ideas into relation with each other. ... We will not discuss the ego just yet, but it is obvious that if things are to be thought in relation, they must be thought together, and in one *something*, be that something ego, psychosis, state of consciousness, or whatever you please.[36] If not thought with each other, things are not thought in relation at all. Now most believers in the ego make the same mistake as the associationists and sensationists whom they oppose. Both agree that the elements of the subjective stream are discrete and separate and constitute what Kant calls a 'manifold'. But while the associationists think that a 'manifold' can form a single knowledge, the egoists deny this, and say that the knowledge comes only when the manifold is subjected to the synthetizing activity of an ego. Both make an identical initial hypothesis; but the egoist, finding it won't express the facts, adds another hypothesis to correct it. Now I do not wish just yet to 'commit myself' about the existence or non-existence of the ego, but I do contend that we need not invoke it for this particular reason—namely, because the manifold of ideas has to be reduced to unity. *There is no manifold of coexisting ideas*; the notion of such a thing is a chimera. *Whatever things are thought in relation are thought from the outset in a unity, in a single pulse of subjectivity, a single psychosis, feeling, or state of mind.*

The reason why this fact is so strangely garbled in the books seems to be what on an earlier page ... I called the psychologist's fallacy. We have the inveterate habit, whenever we try introspectively to describe one of our thoughts, of dropping the thought as it is in itself and talking of something else. We describe the things that appear to the thought, and we describe other thoughts *about* those things—as if these and the original thought were the same. If, for example, the thought be 'the pack of cards is on the table,' we say, 'Well, isn't it a thought of the pack of cards? Isn't it of the cards as included in the pack? Isn't it of the table? And of the legs of the table as well? The table has legs—how can you think the table without virtually thinking its legs? Hasn't our thought then, all these parts—one part for the pack and another for the table? And within the pack-part a part for each card, as within the table-part a part for each leg? And isn't each of these parts an idea? And can our thought, then, be anything but an assemblage or pack of ideas, each answering to some element of what it knows.'

---

[34] Instead of saying *to our feeling only*, he should have said, to the *object* only (James's footnote).

[35] *Lectures on the Philosophy of the Human Mind*, Lecture 45 (James's footnote).

[36] A 'psychosis', in James's terms, is simply a concrete psychological occurrence, just as a neurosis is a neural occurrence. 'No psychosis without neurosis' (1890: 1.129); 'as the total neurosis changes, so does the total psychosis change' (1890: 1.243).

Now not one of these assumptions is true. ...[37]

James then draws a nice diagram depicting the structure of the thinking of the thought *the pack of cards is on the table.*

One can dispute all sorts of details, but the Fundamental Singleness point and Kantian points remain as secure as they are (happily) trivial. The unity of the thin subject and the experiential unity of its experience are two aspects of the same unity. The unity in question is by present hypothesis a physical unity, and I've argued that it is an exemplary strong unity, and therefore qualifies a physical object (if indeed there are such things—and more than one). More moderately, I've argued that there are no better candidates in nature for the title 'strong unity' than the unity of the subject of an experience. This remains the case, of course, even if we give up the struggle to maintain that there is a plurality of objects, and revert to the lovely Spinozan position that there is only one, 'Nature', i.e. the universe.

—Suppose I were prepared to contemplate, for your sake, the possibility that a thin subject is a unity that qualifies as an object. Why would I have any reason to say the same about a unified experiential field? Even if it's a strong unity, why should I think it's an object?

The radical Cartesian proposal in 7.4, to be revived in 8.8, is that there isn't a real distinction between the thin-subject unity and the experiential-field unity, only a conceptual distinction. If I were forced to give up that difficult idea, I'd be prepared to give up the inference from strong unity to objecthood in the case of the total experiential field while maintaining it in the case of the subject, on the ground that a subject is a strong activity-unity even if a total experiential field isn't, and that strong activity-unity is necessary (and sufficient) for objecthood. That, though, would be a retreat to a pack of metaphysical ideas that I take to be ultimately untenable, although they will always be popular in philosophy.

In this section I've backed the idea that we can give synchronic criteria of identity for thin subjects, and that thin subjects are so far on track to {26} qualify as objects and so {23} qualify as sesmets, and so, on my assumptions, {36} qualify as selves. A thin subject as we find it in the living moment of experience necessarily constitutes a strong activity-unity (whatever it's made of). Its existence necessarily involves the strong (and necessary) unity of the total experiential field that its existence involves. We can if we like *argue* from the knowable strong and necessary unity of the total experiential field as we find it in the living moment of experience to the strong unity of the thin subject that the existence of that total-experiential-field-with-the-content-that-it-has necessarily involves; but it's a pretty small move.

As we find them in the living moment of experience, then, thin subjects appear to be strong unities that have as such the look of objects; and they have this look specifically

---

[37] James 1890: 1.276–8. I suspect that Thomas Brown may be led to the point that 'the most complex states of mind are ... one and indivisible' principally by a pre-existing conviction that the mind is a simple substance, an assumption that James, of course, does not share.

in so far as they are considered as subjects of experience and only as subjects of experience, and so independently of any other mode of being they may have. They have in other terms the properties *single-as-mental* and *strong-unity-as-mental*, and they can be seen to have these properties when considered specifically as subjects of experience rather than as synergies of neurons or ultimates as they appear to neurophysiologists or physicists. It's tempting to conclude straight away that we can know that they're objects (if there is more than one object), even if we don't yet know how to count them, or—therefore—how many there are. The more moderate conclusion is that we're at least half way to establishing the crucial proposition that thin subjects are strong-unities-as-mental

{51} [TSx → SUMx],

i.e. the proposition on which everything else hangs (according to the argument on pages 372–4), by having established that thin subjects have the property *strong-unity-as-mental* when synchronically considered. We're at least half way even if we have to do more work to show that they have this property diachronically considered.

8.6 Experientially unitary periods of experience

—Now the real problems begin. Things may be metaphysically comfortable for you inside the living moment of experience, but now you must step outside. You have to tell me how long your 'thin subjects' last. If they're going to qualify as objects, and in particular as objects-as-mental, you have to show how to give clear diachronic identity conditions for them, while restricting attention to their mental/experiential characteristics alone. The problem of duration is upon you, even as the problem of ontic depth, the problem you can't possibly solve, darkens the horizon.

The first thing to do is to recall that I'm using 'synchronic' in a stretched sense. The synchronic unity of a thin subject is its unity in the living moment of experience, and the living moment of experience is by definition a temporal interval, a period of time, however brief, not a durationless instant. So the synchronic unity of the thin subject in the living moment of experience is already a diachronic unity strictly speaking. Thin subjects, like all concrete existents, necessarily have temporal duration.

This provides one possible answer to the question of duration. If time is discrete and living moments of experience are chronon-sized, one possibility is that the diachronic identity conditions of thin subjects are the same as their synchronic identity conditions. One need only suppose that thin subjects last no longer than the living moment of experience (if time is dense, this answer isn't possible, for living moments of experience are in this case theoretical abstractions from a continuum, and are not the kinds of things that can be said to have diachronic identity conditions). This said, I accept that the present question is whether we can give clear diachronic identity conditions for thin subjects given the assumption that they do last longer than the living moment of experience, in the way we naturally suppose. If we give 'diachronic' an asterisk in this section to mark the fact that it's being used (in specific apposition to the stretched sense of 'synchronic') to mean 'lasting longer than the living moment of experience', the question is whether we can give clear diachronic* identity conditions for thin subjects ('diachronic*' entails 'diachronic', but not conversely). I've argued that the unity of the thin subject and the unity of its total experiential field are inseparable when we consider things synchronically in the living moment of experience. What happens when we go beyond the living moment of experience? This argument of this section is involved, probably unnecessarily so, and those who wish can skip to page 403, where I propose that it's unnecessary, because we don't need to show how one might establish sharp diachronic identity conditions for thin subjects in order to assert that they qualify as objects.

I'll begin by assuming that the unity of the thin subject and the unity of its total experiential field, which are—I've just argued—inseparable in the living moment of experience, are no less inseparable when we go beyond the living moment of experience and consider things diachronically*. The word 'field' has a static air, though, which suits the synchronic case better than the diachronic* case, so I'll replace it by the expressly durational term 'experientially unitary period of experience'. The claim, then, is, first, that a truly experientially unitary period of experience can't last longer than its (thin) subject, however long it lasts, and, second, that a thin subject can't last longer than the (single) experientially unitary period of experience of which it is the subject, however long it can last. In other words: every experientially unitary period of experience has just one thin subject or 'liver'

{30} $[EUPx \rightarrow [\exists!yTSy \wedge Lyx]]$

(it can't of course exist at any time without a subject), and every subject of experience is the subject or 'liver' of just one experientially unitary period of experience

{31} $[TSx \rightarrow [\exists!yEUPy \wedge Lxy]].$

This is the Inseparability Thesis, which can be sufficiently expressed in the present symbolism, given {20}, by saying that one experientially unitary period of experience means just one thin subject, and conversely

{32} $[\exists!xTSx \leftrightarrow \exists!xEUPx].$

—Why should I believe {31}? I accept that a single experientially unitary period of experience can't last longer than its subject (in so far as I accept your terms at all), but why should I accept the converse? Why can't a single thin subject last longer than a single experientially unitary period of experience, once it's broken the bounds of the living moment of experience? Why can't it be the subject first of one experientially unitary period of experience and then of another completely different one? A thin subject can't by definition survive a temporal break in the process of experience, but the second experientially unitary period of experience could succeed seamlessly upon the first.

{31} is, so far, a substantive metaphysical thesis, as noted in 7.1. Having a single thin subject is provably integral to the unity of an experientially unitary period of experience as it is in the living moment of experience, and the idea behind {31}, evidently, is that it is no less integral in the diachronic* case—so that it can't be right to count two of them while counting only one thin subject. I'm *assuming* the general validity of the Inseparability Thesis in order to see if I can specify what it involves in the diachronic* case. If I can't, you may win by default.

An experientially unitary period of experience is by definition a strong unity, and it's a specifically experiential strong unity, i.e. something that is correctly judged to be a strong unity on the basis of its experiential character alone. It is therefore a strong-unity-as-mental (experiential entails mental)

{54} [EUPx → SUMx],

whether or not there are other (non-experiential) bases for judging it to be a strong unity; and it therefore qualifies as an object

{55} [EUPx → Ox],

given {42}. The term 'experientially unitary period of experience' leaves open the possibility that the living moment of experience is itself an experientially unitary period of experience, since the living moment of experience is by definition a temporal interval, a period of experience, but the question, again, is whether there are diachronically* extended experientially unitary periods of experience, and whether there is any hope of specifying clear diachronic* identity conditions for them if there are.

'Experiential unitary period of experience' can be given a wide application in everyday speech, and applied to things that aren't absolutely unbroken periods of experience—to a day or a game of chess. Here, though, I'm only interested in a narrow sense of the term that requires that experientially unitary periods of experience be truly uninterrupted, truly continuous periods of experience (CPE)

{56} [EUPx → CPEx].

Two periods of experience separated by a gap in which no experience is going on can't possibly constitute an experientially unitary period of experience, however else they're related, and equally can't possibly have the same thin subject (a thin subject can't survive a break in experience because it can't exist at any moment unless there is experience for it to be the subject of). I propose to represent this imprecisely by

{57} [TSx → CPEx],

although this presupposes something that still has to be argued for (8.8)—that a thin subject can be (identical to) a period of experience.

An experientially unitary period of experience is, as remarked, a strong unity, and it follows that the neural synergy with which it is identical is also a strong unity, even if its strong unity characteristic is not discernible when it's examined neurophysiologically. Neurophysiology might come up with its own, non-experiential criteria of identity for individuating experience-constituting neural synergies, however, and we can imagine finding out that the two principles of individuation slice reality differently. A single experientially unitary period of experience might turn out to consist of several *neurophysiologically individuated* experience-constituting neural synergies, 'ni-synergies' for short. We can stipulate that a *ni*-synergy (NIS) is always a continuous period of experience

{58} [NISx → CPEx]

and still allow that a single experientially unitary period of experience may be constituted (C) of many such (seamlessly joined or overlapping) neural synergies, i.e. that

{59} [EUPx → [∃!yNISy ∧ Cyx]]

is false. Given {32}, the Inseparability Thesis, the same goes for thin subjects as goes for experientially unitary periods of experience. The possibility is left open that

{60} [TSx → [∃!yNISy ∧ Cyx]]

is false: there can't be more than one thin subject involved in any *ni*-synergy, but it doesn't follow from the fact that we have a whole *ni*-synergy that we have a whole thin subject/experientially unitary period of experience.[38]

It follows from {32}—one subject per experientially unitary period of experience, and conversely—that no actually existing experientially unitary period of experience can be divided into parts, even in thought, in such a way that it's right to say that the division yields more than one subject of experience. Equally, there's no possible division of an actually existing experientially unitary period of experience, even in thought, into parts that yields more than one experientially unitary period of experience. These things are indecomposable. A slice of an *actually existing* experientially unitary period of experience is not an experientially unitary period of experience, any more than a slice of cake is a cake (the emphasis on 'actually existing' is important). One can, in thought, divide an actually existing experientially unitary period of experience into distinct temporal sections, and one can happily consider the seamless set of its successive temporally non-overlapping segments, but one can't do this is in such a way as to yield, even in thought, a plurality of subjects of experience. One can imagine a thousand very small and mutually qualitatively coherent (and necessarily subject-involving) experientially unitary periods of experiences existing in seamless succession in a brain, and one can then try to imagine them fused together to make one experientially unitary period of experience with one subject. But one is bound to fail. One hasn't thought of a thousand subjects becoming one, or a thousand experientially unitary periods of experience becoming one. One's thought has simply jumped from the thought of a thousand subjects or experientially unitary periods of experience to the thought of a single, longer, numerically distinct subject or experientially unitary period of experience that has nothing to do with the originally imagined thousand. So too the other way round, *mutatis mutandis*. The unities

---

[38] The hypothetical notion of a *ni*-synergy is therefore quite unlike that of a Jamesian thought-pulse or experience-pulse, for this is something that is taken to be a whole experientially considered, something which comes by definition with its own experiencer, and is indeed identical with its experiencer.

in question are indeed indecomposable unities. No amount of counterfactual reflection or philosophical play can break them up (333, 409).

—Fine, maybe, but the question remains unanswered. How long can experientially unitary periods of experience last, in the case of any given species of thin subject?

The first proposal, again, is that they may last no longer than the living moment of experience. On this account time is quantally discrete, made up of chronons, and there is one thin subject and one experientially unitary period of experience per chronon. That in virtue of which it is true to say that chronons are discrete entities constitutes a form of temporal boundedness that delivers chronon-sized experientially unitary periods of experience and thin subjects. Thin subjects are fabulously short-lived even as they successively host experience that has the character of being continuous and uninterrupted at any given time. This should not surprise us. Physics takes us to the extremely small in its account of the fundamental nature of non-experiential reality (what we take to be irreducibly non-experiential reality). According to one currently influential theory, this is true of space itself, not just of the ultimates that we take to be something other than space. Why should we expect things to be different when it comes to the nature of experiential reality, which is also a wholly natural (and according to materialism wholly physical) phenomenon? We take it that we detect a straightforwardly objective, theory-independent feature of physical reality when we judge that it comes in very small units spatially speaking. Why should we think that this is unlikely to be true temporally speaking? Are we going to quantize everything else in nature and leave selves and experience—the real physical phenomenon of consciousness—as densely continuous?

The first proposal, then, offers a straightforward solution to the problem of duration, one which sits well with Buddhist doctrine and is also, arguably, Descartes's view, although he takes it in such a way that thin subjects may also be said to last sempiternally (see the quotation on page 402 below). No human being can have experience that has the character of being 1 chronon long, or even 1 ms or 10 ms long, but this is no objection to the present proposal, for reasons set out in 5.10 and illustrated in Figure 5.1 on page 258, where $n\text{-}t_3$ represents the living moment of experience in n-time, i.e. the shortest period or interval of time that 'now' can be taken to refer to when I point at someone and say truly, 'he is having experience right now', while the $e\text{-}t_1 - e\text{-}t_2$ line represents the (subjective) temporal character of the experience that is being had at $n\text{-}t_3$.

If time is not quantally discrete but densely continuous, this solution is not available, for in this case (once again) the living moment of experience is not a neatly bounded entity but a theoretical abstraction from a continuum. Still, other sharp solutions are possible. It may be, for example …

—I don't understand what's going on. Your transitions between experiential facts and 'n-time' facts don't make sense. There's an irresoluble tension between your claims that experientially unitary periods of experience (and so thin subjects) may possibly be chronon-sized, or 1 ms or 10 ms long, and your use of essentially experiential/phenomenological criteria of unity. You seem to be saying that our experience involves access to—is the living of—experientially unitary periods of experience, and that these very things, these very unities, may be a chronon long, or a millisecond long—in which case they're utterly unexperienceable by us. This can't be right. We have no access to these tiny things. This isn't what we're acquainted with when we consciously comprehend thoughts like *grass is green*, or have experience that has the character of being simultaneous experience of yellow, salt, and a blackbird's alarm call. The experientially unitary period of experience (if such it is) that consists in the conscious comprehending entertaining of the thought *grass is green* can't exist in such a tiny space. If there's something that you want to call an experientially unitary period of experience in that tiny space, it must be a different strong unity from the one we experience. But then how do the two relate to each other?

I tried to address these issues in Part 5. Suppose I consciously and fully comprehendingly entertain a proposition Q, and that the period of experience that consists in my fully comprehending conscious entertaining of Q, call it q, lasts for 100 ms of n-time, say from $n\text{-}t_2$ to $n\text{-}t_3$. I take it that-q is much longer than the (n-time) duration of the living moment of experience, and accordingly that q is a prime candidate for being a diachronically* extended experientially unitary period of experience. (If I'm asked how long I think q lasted, I may wrongly judge that it lasted about 400 ms of n-time or more, but it doesn't matter if I'm wrong.) The question is whether it can be true that I am, during any tiny portion of the period q, in an experiential state that is a state of consciously and fully comprehendingly entertaining Q, or even a part of such a state; the suspicion is that there just isn't enough 'room' for this to be possible.

I've no other answer to this than the one I gave in 5.10 (257). If such comprehension ever really takes place, it must be a mistake, however natural, to think that it can't be taking place in a tiny part of q.

You've also raised another issue. When I say that we have direct experience of—live—experientially unitary periods of experience, am I saying that we have experiential access to chronon-sized things, or millisecond-sized things? Well, we don't experience them as such, but the experience we have when we live an experientially unitary period of experience is something that must be there even in these very short temporal intervals.

—This doesn't really answer my question. My problem is that you appeal at various points to the idea that we have direct acquaintance with these experiential strong unities and experience them as such, but are now proposing that they may be far too small to be directly experienced as such.

We experience experientially unitary periods of experience as such, in having the e-time experience we do, whatever the n-time truth about the temporality of experience. Note that although I've said that there may possibly be experientially unitary periods of experience that are very small indeed, I don't know if there are any. It's a question of fact to which I don't know the answer. If time is quantally discrete, one possible view, again, is that experientially unitary periods of experience, and hence (given {30}) thin subjects, are chronon-sized; but I don't know whether time is this way, and even if it is, it certainly doesn't follow that experientially unitary periods of experience are chronon-sized. Experientially unitary periods of experience require continuity, but time may be (non-densely) continuous even if it's made of chronons (there aren't any temporal gaps between chronons!). I've claimed that it must be right to say that experience is going on in extremely small periods of time, on certain natural assumptions, but this isn't to say that a whole experientially unitary period of experience can be found in extremely small periods of time, rather than a segment of one that isn't itself an experientially unitary period of experience. I argued in the last section that we can know a priori that there is unity of experience, unity of an unsurpassable kind—Fundamental Singleness—in the living moment of experience. But this, again, is not to say that we find a whole (diachronically* complete) experientially unitary period of experience in the living moment of experience. For all that has been said so far, there aren't any extremely small experientially unitary periods of experience. There may be very small neurophysiologically individuable *ni*-synergies, but the notion of an *ni*-synergy is quite different from the notion of an experientially unitary period of experience, and although the neurophysiologists' *ni*-synergies could turn out to be experientially unitary periods of experience, it could also turn out that they're only ever small parts of experientially unitary periods of experience.

This brings us back, more or less, to the point of interruption. I'd proposed that experientially unitary periods of experience, and hence (given {30}) thin subjects, might conceivably last for 1 chronon, and I was about to observe that there are other possibilities, whether time is quantally discrete or dense. One such possibility is that the *ni*-synergies that make up human experience occur at a rate of about forty a second, as suggested in 5.10, and so last much longer than the living moment of experience on any plausible account of it. Each one is a continuous period of experience ({58}), and it may also be that each one is itself an experientially unitary period of experience with its own numerically distinct thin subject, rather than just a component of a longer-lasting experientially unitary period of experience.[39]

Another possibility is that these 25 ms synergies aren't truly continuous periods of experience but are made up of much smaller discrete *ni*-synergies, 'neurochronons' (in the language of 5.10) that occur at a rate of about 1,000 a second and are truly continuous periods of experience. Perhaps these 1 ms *ni*-synergies are experientially unitary periods of experience, in which case thin subjects, too, last no longer than about 1 ms. In this case the 25 ms pulses aren't true experientially unitary periods of experience, and don't have a single thin subject: If my conscious comprehending entertaining of Q lasts for 100 ms then it involves 100 thin subjects entertaining Q.

The present point is that the problem of duration has a straightforward solution in these cases, and there are other more generous proposals. Perhaps experience comes in truly continuous periods of up to 500 ms (possibly constituted of seamlessly joined or overlapping *ni*-synergies) that have short, absolute, experiential gaps between

---

[39] Note that 'continuous' in 'continuous period of experience' always qualifies objective or non-phenomenological time, '*n*-time' in the terminology of 5.10, and has nothing essentially to do with any experience of continuity, '*e*-time' continuity. 'Presontists' have their own reasons for favouring a very short-lived self.

them, relative to a single brain, gaps that may or may not be subjectively detectable. Perhaps experientially unitary periods of experience also come in this size and have the structure shown in Figure 8.1. Perhaps continuous periods of experience, if not

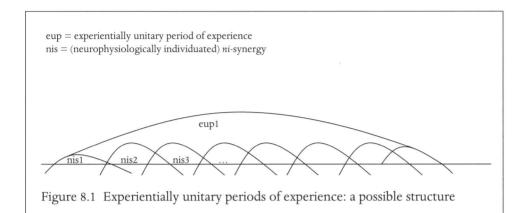

eup = experientially unitary period of experience
nis = (neurophysiologically individuated) *ni*-synergy

eup1

nis1   nis2   nis3   ...

Figure 8.1 Experientially unitary periods of experience: a possible structure

experientially unitary periods of experience, can be 3 seconds long. Perhaps conscious experience never ceases in Louis, from his experiential quickening in the womb to his death, or is broken only in sleep, and perhaps the problem of duration has a straightforward solution even in these cases. Perhaps it can be argued that

{61} [CPEx → EUPx]

that every truly unbroken period of experience is *ipso facto* an experientially unitary period of experience, and hence involves a single thin subject. Perhaps there's a single thin subject throughout the existence of a human mind, as Descartes supposes. Perhaps we can conjoin {61} with its converse {56} to get

{62} [EUPx ↔ CPEx].

It's not that simple, though, because there seems, so far, to be no difficulty in the idea that {61} is false, as observed in 5.7. It seems that there could very well be a temporally continuous period of experience that isn't an experientially unitary period of experience. The notion of continuity, however, raises a question about the perspective from which we detect and judge continuity. Suppose we take Louis the whole human being as our unit of study, and find continuous experience in the L-reality between times t_1 and t_3. In that case we can know that there's always a thin subject in the L-reality between t_1 and t_3, but not that there's only one. One possibility, noted in 7.6, is that numerically distinct thin-subject-involving synergies succeed each other seamlessly in the L-reality in such a way that there is only ever one at any given time. Another possibility, also noted in 7.6, is that they succeed each other overlappingly, so that there are sometimes two at a given time although there's only a single sequence of neural synergies. A third possibility, noted in 7.4, is that there are two or more at a given time, not because there's overlapping in a single sequence but because it's completely normal for there to be more than one sequence going on at any given time in a human being, and so normal for there to be more than one thin subject/locus of experience at any given time in a human being, in spite of the fact that (pathology aside) it always seems to each of us in our experience of our subjecthood that there's only one. It's a question of fact whether …

—What do you mean by 'us'? Surely it's …

there can be only one thin subject in a human being for so long as experience occurs unbrokenly in that human being, and there are respectable experimental reasons for thinking that the answer is No.

The first two possibilities are represented in Figure 7.3 on page 355, which shows

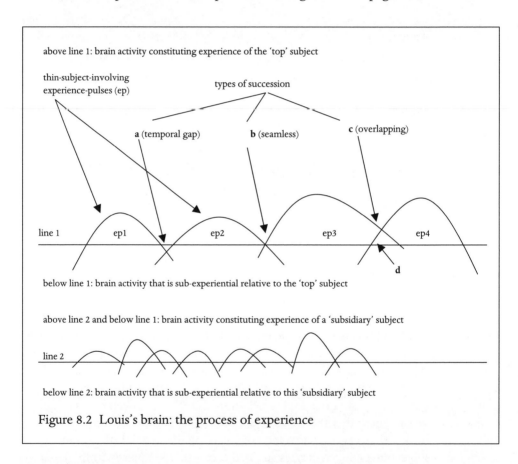

Figure 8.2 Louis's brain: the process of experience

neural synergies gathering momentum in sub-experiential processes of brain activity before maturing into experience-constituting brain activity. The third can be represented by an addition to Figure 7.3, as shown in Figure 8.2. It would be unwise to claim that a theory that allows that two thin subjects may be simultaneously present in the L-reality must be less plausible than one that doesn't. Under empirical, scientific-psychological investigation the facts of our psychological existence turn out to be extremely surprising, relative to what we naturally suppose, and it may be that there is always more than one macroscopic-brain-activity-constituted subject-of-experience-involving neural synergy present in the L-reality, even while the human being Louis always experiences himself to be a mentally single subject, and to be the only one that exists in the L-reality.[40]

—But who is this 'human being Louis', this 'himself'? This is the question I tried to ask earlier. Who are the 'we' who always (pathology aside) feel that we are the only subject of experience in the human being that we are?

Louis is Louis°, we are we°—the 'top' subjects introduced in 7.6, 'top' relative to other 'subsidiary' subjects (348, 353). I'm assuming for argument that there's only one 'top' subject at any given time in the L-reality, and this is who I mean when I take it that there is a (thin) subject of experience whom I can call 'Louis'. It may be that there's sometimes more than one plausible candidate for the position of 'top' subject in the L-reality (one of them may have control of large-scale bodily behaviour to the exclusion of the other(s)), but this isn't a difficulty for the present position. It's just a complication, put aside by an assumption.

   Some of our beliefs about our subjecthood are under great pressure here, even as our basic conception of a subject of experience remains secure (63), but this is as it should be. I've argued that we shouldn't take brains considered as a whole to be the relevant locations when we ask questions about continuity of experience of the sort that concern us now. We should instead consider much smaller things, neural synergies that constitute strong experiential continuities.

—I'm lost. Your account of the synchronic identity conditions of thin subjects incorporates the claim that {30} there can only be one thin subject per experientially unitary period of experience, and you're hardly less committed to the claim {31} that there can only be one experientially unitary period of experience per thin subject. But you haven't actually made any progress in saying this, because to say that one has a single experientially unitary period of experience if and only if one has a single thin subject is simply to restate the problem about the diachronic(*) identity conditions of thin subjects as a problem about the diachronic identity conditions of experientially unitary periods of experience, which remains unanswered; and {31} still seems less secure than {30}.

The restatement is meant to be helpful—I think it helps our thought to move around in the problem area. I think we can get some further purchase on the problem by shifting

---

[40] Figure 8.2 is crude, and can be developed in many ways. Should we allow for the possibility that (i), the brain activity that constitutes a subsidiary thin subject having the experience it has, can in some way constitute part of (ii), the activity that constitutes the 'top' thin subject having the experience it has? A very difficult question, similar to the question addressed by James when considering the prospects for panpsychism (1890: ch. 6, 1909: lecture 5) and discussed by many since, recently by Coleman (2006), Goff (2006), Sprigge (2006), G. Strawson (2006b). The proposal can't be represented on this two-dimensional diagram, because (ii) is represented by the above-the-line sections of the arcs on line 1, and can't be somehow partly constituted by (i), given that (i) is represented by the spatially distinct above-the-line sections of the arcs on line 2.

focus in this way, and I'm going to continue by reviving my suspicion (aired in 7.4, developed in 8.8) that there is at bottom no real distinction between any individual experientially unitary period of experience e and its thin subject s, and that they are in fact identical: that, picking up the numbering from 7.4

[1] $[s = e]$.

The closest we can get to [1], given the resources of the curly bracket scheme, is the much weaker

{63} $[TSx \leftrightarrow EUPx]$,[41]

but we can perhaps take this, as I do (argument is to come), as a strong intimation that

[D] $[TS = EUP]$,

which is the same as [1], following the pattern of [A]–[C] on page 371. Together the four claims [A]–[D] make the following fine chain

a self = a sesmet = a thin subject = an experientially unitary period of experience

and if (again following 7.4 and anticipating 8.8) we add

[2] $[e = c]$

we also have it that an experientially unitary period of experience consists entirely of experiential content, living (Cartesian) experiential content, experiential content properly understood, i.e. not understood as some sort of passive content patch.[42] Life, after all, is simple.

Identity claims from 7.4 and 8.2

[1] $[s = e]$
[2] $[e = c]$
[3] $[s = c]$
[4] $[e = s = c]$

[A] $[S = SES]$
[B] $[SES = TS]$
[C] $[S = TS]$
[D] $[EUP = TS]$

[1] = [D]

—I hope so. But it's still difficult. And we still don't know how long thin subjects last.

True, but I've noted various possible suggestions—maybe $1/1.855 \times 10^{-43}$ seconds (the Planck time), or 1 ms, 25 ms, 500 ms, 2–3 seconds, a lifetime, sempiternity. Perhaps one of these answers is correct.

[41] Note that this addition renders {57} legitimate.   [42] We have it, in the terms of 6.3, that $[e = e_e]$.

The larger answers return us to the matter that arose in 5.7, and again three pages ago. We have, so far, no reason to reject the possibility that continuous periods of experience may not be experientially unitary periods of experience. An experientially unitary period of experience entails a continuous period of experience

{56} [EUPx → CPEx],

but the possibility is left open that there might be radical changes of topic or subject matter in a continuous period of experience of such a kind that it can't be an experientially unitary period of experience, so that the converse of {56},

{61} [CPEx → EUPx],

is false. What reason is there to think that a single thin subject couldn't possibly be the subject of a continuous period of experience that involved two experientially unitary periods of experience with very different content—so that

{31} [TSx → [∃!yEUPy ∧ Lxy]]

is after all false, along with the Inseparability Thesis (389) of which it is part?[43]

I've assumed the truth of the Inseparability Thesis. I've taken it that the unity of an experientially unitary period of experience and the unity of the thin subject of that experience are aspects of the same thing not only in the synchronic case (where it's provable a priori) but also in the diachronic* case. It may now be said that there isn't any one true way to individuate subjects, even when we restrict attention to thin subjects, and that different ways serve different purposes (ecological, emotional, eschatological, etc.).

This point has its place. I think, though, that when we get down to what we can still (in spite of all interest-relativity) call the fundamental metaphysics of experience, and ask about the nature of the thing that constitutes a single human thin subject (a neural synergy, on my view, adductively understood), we can take ourselves to face an objective, non-interest-relative question of fact. And perfect science (which harbours all such facts) will, I venture, show that a radical change of subject matter requires a new thin subject, given that a thin subject is a neural synergy of a certain particular sort. On this view, it's a fact about our brains that new content of a sort that amounts to a strong content break necessarily involves a new seizing, a new synergism, and hence, *eo ipso*, a new thin subject. To think otherwise is perhaps like thinking that a high-speed guided missile can turn on a pin.

So this, I think, is how things are. And I take it that these experientially unitary periods of experience/thin subjects are as a matter of fact always short in the human case. I propose, in the terms of 5.7, that a radical content break or flow break always involves a new experientially unitary period of experience and a new thin subject, although Louis's

---

[43] —Synergy-subjects, thin subjects, experience-pulses, experientially unitary periods of experience—this multiplication of terms is wasteful, unnecessary, and intensely confusing.

The different terms arise in different contexts of discussion with different currents of thought behind them. I think it can be illuminating for it to turn out that they're terms for the same thing, given their different points of origin. But people have very different intellectual styles.

experience (i.e. the experience of each of the post-break Louis° subjects) will be that he continues to exist as the same subject as a sudden thought, car, or thunderclap hits him. There is in fact a clear sense in which he can't experience the rupture as a rupture unless he experiences himself as continuing to exist as the same single subject. But this fact about the character of his experience has no weight (Kant's elastic balls) when it comes to answering the metaphysical question about the actual continuity of the thin subject that he is at any given (n-)time.

I have no idea how to specify what kind of content change requires a new thin subject, but the general conclusion of this stretch of argument is that there's no difficulty in the idea that experientially unitary periods of experience, and hence thin subjects, can last longer than the living moment of experience and can be neatly (non-vaguely) diachronically* bounded in one way or another, the actual way being a matter of fact we don't need to establish. There is, in other words, no difficulty in the idea that diachronic(*) identity conditions of thin subjects/experientially unitary periods of experience are specifiable in principle. And since the synchronic identity conditions are already in place, there's no remaining block to the idea that experientially-unitary-period-of-experience-inhabiting thin subjects are strong-unities-as-mental, with fully respectable synchronic and diachronic identity conditions:

{51} [TSx → SUMx].

This means that we can now at last run the argument set out on pages 372–4. Starting from {51}, we can go, via {42}, to the claim that thin subjects are objects

{26} [TSx → Ox]

and from there, via {49} and {53}, to the claim that they qualify as sesmets

{23} [TSx] → SESx]

and so to the conclusion that they are selves

{36} [TSx → Sx]

via the claim that all sesmets are selves

{34} [SESx → Sx],

i.e., more verbosely, the claim that anything that has the complex property *being a subject of experience that is correctly judged to be a single thing or object when considered specifically as a subject of experience that is being considered specifically in its mental being* is rightly counted as a self. In this book this claim is grounded in the arguments and commitments set out in Parts 2 and 4, but it doesn't depend on them. In particular, it doesn't depend on acceptance of the Equivalence Thesis on page 51. It stands as a metaphysical proposal independently of the 'phenomenological deduction' of the content of the thought-element SELF.

The final move is from the fact that thin subjects exist

{21} ∃xTSx

which I take to be evident, given the way thin subjects are defined in 7.1, to the claim, via {36}, that selves exist

{37} ∃xSx.

I conclude that selves exist, although I don't know how long they last.[44]

Being a sesmet doesn't require being fully self-conscious, i.e. having the capacity for expressly self-conscious thought:

{66} ¬[SESx → SCSx],

so being a self doesn't either:

{67} ¬[Sx → SCSx].

It follows from the present view that there are selves wherever there is experience—even in sea snails—because selves are just subjects of experience. It is, however, open to anyone who wishes to take selfhood to be something over and above subjecthood, and to add full self-consciousness to the basic requirements I've worked with: the requirements that a self must qualify (a) as an object, given that there are allowed to be such things

{1} [Sx → Ox],

(b) as a physical object

{3} [Sx → POx],

given that materialism is assumed to be true, and (c) as a certain specific sort of physical object, a sesmet

{38} [Sx → SESx].[45]

Have I left no place for Descartes, for his view that selves last a very long time—perhaps for ever? As things stand, it's ruled out by the assumption of materialism. But if we waive that difficulty, and imagine Descartes accepting some sort of monism—he was too honest, intellectually, too passionate about truth, and far too intelligent, to think that he could finally rule it out—then there's room for his view in the present scheme, for a Cartesian mind is a thin subject, considered at any given moment, and is also, therefore, a self.

—You *can't* recruit Descartes. It's true that Cartesian minds fit the definition of a thin subject given on page 324. Since then, however, you've identified thin subjects with experientially unitary periods of experience, and it's hopelessly unrealistic, given the way you've developed the notion of an experientially unitary period of experience, to claim that a human being's lifelong course of experience constitutes a single experientially unitary period of experience. To achieve that result one would have to introduce some special mystical sense of 'experientially unitary period of experience' that would simply beg the question.

Perhaps—but one needs to bear in mind Descartes's view of what it is to continue to exist:

---

[44] What about {39} [SESx → TSx]? The case for it is implicit in the foregoing. The idea is that only a thin subject can be enough of a strong unity-as-mental to qualify as a sesmet, i.e. {64} [SUMx → TSx]. From {28} [SESx → OMx] and {40} [OMx → SUMx] we have {65} [SESx → SUMx], which couples with {64} to give the missing {39}.

[45] The case for adding self-consciousness might be pursued in the current framework by arguing that a sesmet can't be truly SM, truly SUM, without being self-conscious. In so far as it's hard to see what an occurrent, short-lived *e*-synergy's *capacity* for self-consciousness can consist in if the occurrent *e*-synergy isn't an expressly self-conscious experience, to reject {67} is to unite with Fichte and Nozick in the view that the self exists only in expressly self-conscious thought. I'm not inclined to make this move, although there is something attractive about it.

a lifespan can be divided into innumerably many parts, each completely independent of the others, so that it does not follow from the fact that I existed a little while ago that I must exist now, unless there is some cause that as it were creates me afresh at this moment—that is, which preserves me. It is quite clear to anyone who attentively considers the nature of time that the same power and action are needed to preserve anything at each individual moment of its duration as would be required to create that thing anew if it were not yet in existence. Hence the distinction between preservation and creation is only a conceptual one ...'   (1641: 1.33)

from the fact that we now exist it does not follow that we shall exist a moment from now, unless there is some cause—the same cause which originally produced us—which continually reproduces us, as it were, that is to say, which keeps us in existence'.[46]

If Descartes were brought up to date, I think he'd reject the old move from the apparently infinite mathematical divisibility of time (or space) to its concrete infinite divisibility. He might endorse chronons (and hodons), and embrace the view that experientially unitary periods of experience, and hence subjects, are chronon-sized. He might at the same time abandon the idea of time as mere passive dimensionality and endorse its absorption into spacetime, understanding spacetime in the way that he already understands physical reality, i.e. as a single *res* (the universe, no less).

It's a question of fact whether the process of consciousness is segmented in anything like the ways I've suggested. We know that experientially unitary periods of experience and thin subjects exist, because we find both in the present in the living moment of experience. But we don't know whether the living moment of experience contains a whole or complete experientially unitary period of experience or thin subject, and it seems highly unlikely, except on certain special assumptions. So the question how long these things last, the question of their diachronic identity conditions, remains unsettled. We have it, as before, that {56} all experientially unitary periods of experience are continuous periods of experience, but we don't know whether {61} all continuous periods of experience are experientially unitary periods of experience, and {61} seems very likely to be false when we consider the question at the level of a whole human being. I've proposed that it may be true when we consider the question at the level of thin subjects. We can't, however, hope to determine precise boundaries for experientially unitary periods of experience by mental self-examination, and although any such boundaries must be detectable under perfect neurophysiological inspection, if materialism is true, we can't attain a perfect science of these things, a science that will tell us—to the attosecond and beyond—whether a particular continuous process of consciousness is still under way or has stopped to be succeeded by another (whose subject, like its predecessor, will doubtless experience itself as a persisting presence riding the wave of a long-term continuous process of consciousness). This perfect science will also have to be able to tell us, on the basis of neurophysiological inspection alone, what the experiential content of a process of consciousness is at any given moment, and even then a problem will remain. For we will have to settle the question of what sorts of

---

[46] 1644: 2.190. One old Buddhist estimate has it that this happens 16,000,000 times a second, although we may be better off looking in the region of 10^{43}.

changes of content are compatible with diachronic experiential unity. What sorts of *experiential* or *contentual becoming* can occur within a single experientially unitary period of experience?

We can't hope to do this—a poor ending to the search for the diachronic identity conditions of experientially unitary periods of experience, and hence of thin subjects. The main aim of the search, though, is simply to articulate certain thoughts about these matters, and now—more importantly—a doubt recorded on page 389 comes into its own. It's arguable that the synchronic strong-unity considerations are enough to deliver the conclusion that thin-subject selves are objects, if any things are, before one has given any thought at all to the claim that objects must have respectable sharp temporal boundaries in order to qualify as objects *in bona fide*. If so, the conclusion that thin-subject selves are A-grade metaphysical objects can't be undermined by doubts about the task of specifying neat temporal boundaries for them. If one's philosophical conception of objecthood requires one to withhold the title of object from anything that lacks nice temporal boundaries, so much the worse, perhaps, for one's philosophical conception of what an object is (given that one is retaining the category of object in one's fundamental metaphysics). Subjects have, knowably, the strong activity-unity sufficient for objecthood, and they have temporal extent (given that time is real), because nothing can exist only at an instant. We don't need to think further, on this account, for we already have it that objects exist, objects that are thin subjects—selves. The key point is that we can judge a phenomenon to be an object on the basis of inspection at a given moment, merely on the basis of the quality—the unity quality—of its mode of being at that moment. An object is a *unity mode of being*, a node in the great universal process, and the straightening out of the Second Paralogism in 8.5 is at the same time the straightening out of the First Paralogism.

Something like this must be right, I think, if we're going to allow a plurality of objects at all. Nothing else in nature, except perhaps—but questionably—certain ultimates, conventionally (non-panpsychistically) conceived, can match the strong unity property of the subject of experience in the living moment of experience. Living animals certainly can't, although one can, following van Inwagen and others, endorse a less stringent unity requirement that admits them as objects in fundamental metaphysics.

8.7 The problem of ontic depth

—You've had a good run. Sometimes, though, you've survived only by throwing out almost everything that's actually in question when it comes to the existence and nature of the self. Now it's over. Your selves are flimsy nothings. Even if selves can be very short-lived (which I don't for a moment believe), they can't be creatures of the surface in the way you suppose, transient neural synergies with no further ontic keel or bottom. These transient synergies may indeed exist. They may be active, experience-involving phenomena. They may, as you say, be forms of energy. But they're not *selves*, for heaven's sake. They're not selves even if they can be allowed to qualify as physical objects. Selves are necessarily more than that. The problem of ontic depth has closed over your head.

The problem of ontic depth. What problem is that? We're human beings, to be sure, but we may with equal justice be said to be selves, and in so far as we're selves, the fundamental fact, I think, and as Sprigge says, is that each one of us is 'at any one moment … most essentially a momentary centre of experience or state of consciousness' (2006: 474), i.e. a thin subject. Some may find this a difficult or frightening (or ridiculous) claim, but it's a way of expressing a truth about a core aspect of our being. It's wholly compatible with thoughtful, non-polemical EEE thinking, and it stands as a truth even if one is disinclined to say that this is what being a *self* consists in, because one wishes to reserve the word 'self' for something larger and longer.[47]

—It's not just that your selves can't breathe or sit or run; we allow that as soon as we go along with you so far as to say that selves, if they exist, are inner subjects of experience, subjects of experience that aren't the same thing as human beings. The problem is that they can't even have the most basic mental properties. They can't reason or think in any concerted way; they don't have time. Then there's the point that thoughts don't make sense in isolation, but only when situated in a network of other possible thoughts and applications of the terms they deploy. You mention this point in 7.1, and it's also your principal objection in *Mental Reality* (pp. 136–44) to what you call the 'pure process idealist' theory of the nature of the mind; but it applies with equal force to your selves. There just isn't enough to them for them to have the kind of dispositional richness they need to be mental beings that could possibly qualify as selves. They can't believe anything or have any preferences; we can't make sense of the attribution of such dispositions to them. Nor can they love or have duties, or be faithful or moral, or anything else that matters.

All the appearances—some of which I value as much as you do—remain as they are. The passions of life (some of which we could do without) remain as they are. I agree with James, who, after proposing that the self or 'I' is nothing but 'a *Thought*' or experience 'at each moment different from that of the last moment', observes, correctly, that 'all the experiential facts find their place in this description, unencumbered with any hypothesis save that of the existence of passing thoughts or states of mind' (1890: 1.400–1).

Human beings have brains, and brains are extremely important when it comes to the existence of human selves. The passing thoughts or experiences or thin-subject selves are wholly neural phenomena, neural synergy phenomena, and the brain also provides a place of residence for everything that is needed for Louis's experience to be exactly as it is compatibly with the fact that Louis's existence as a subject of experience (a subject of experience understood as something that is not the same thing as the human being considered as a whole) consists in nothing other than the existence of the short-lived thin-subject selves I have described.

—After hundreds of pages, all you have is a wearisomely elaborate and profoundly counterintuitive terminological claim: the claim that the portions of reality you've delineated and chosen to

---

[47] 'Holographic' conceptions of the nature of reality of the sort advanced by cosmologists should give serious pause to anyone who believes that the problem of ontic depth is fatal—anyone who thinks that the 'creature of the surface' objection to thin-subject selves is decisive. See Greene 2004: 482–5.

call 'thin subjects' have a good claim to be called 'selves', as good a claim as anything else, and perhaps a better claim than anything else.

I'd be happy if I managed to convince anyone of this. You say it's only a terminological claim, but it's enough for me, and the word 'selves' can always be replaced by the word 'subjects'. The claim is simply that this is all that subjects of experience are, strictly speaking, and as a matter of fundamental metaphysics. Once this has been acknowledged, all our conventional conceptions of what subjects of experience are can retain their variously useful places.

There is, to put it differently, a correct use of 'we' given which this is all we are, a use of 'we' that is no less correct than the use that is correct because we are human beings that are not identical with thin subjects.

There's still a question about what exactly we are, considered as thin subjects, and I turn now, and finally, to the triple identity claim floated in 7.4.

8.8 $[e = s = c]\,(2)$

Consider, as before, an individual experience e, e.g. one occurring in the L-reality. Suppose, for simplicity, and generously, that it's a sharply delimited, uninterrupted, one-second-long experientially unitary period of experience lasting from t_1 to t_2 and preceded and followed by a period of complete unconsciousness on Louis's part. Call this event of *experience* 'e', call the thin/live *subject* of this experience 's', and call the overall phenomenon of the occurrent, concretely existing, experiential *content* of this experience 'c' (here again mental content is internalistically understood). The question is: What is the relation between e, s, and c?

In 7.4 I considered the hypothesis that the relation is identity. On this view, it's not only true that

$[1]\;s = e$

but also that

$[2]\;[e = c]$

and hence that

$[3]\;[s = c]\,(!)$

and in sum that

$[4]\;[e = s = c]$.

I'm now going to defend [4]. It goes far beyond the claim that an experience *consists of* a (thin) subject entertaining (having, living) a content, i.e. the claim represented in 7.6 (352) first by

$[5]\;[e = s{:}c]$

and then by

$[6]\;[e = s(c)]$.

I'll first propose that

[7] $[e \leftrightarrow s \leftrightarrow c]$,

taking this to be a strong modal claim stating a necessary truth, and then argue that [7] is true because [4] is.

Let me begin with the identity claim made in 7.2 (333), the materialist claim that that s is identical with a spatiotemporally bounded piece of physical process-stuff p^s, a collection of ultimates in a certain state of (synergetic) interaction:

[8] $s = p^s$.

This was put forward as, and remains, a 'simple' identity claim. That is, it's not a 'constitutive' identity claim, if a constitutive identity claim is understood to allow that the constituter can possibly exist in the absence of the constitutee, or conversely. s couldn't possibly have consisted of anything other than the particular synergy of process-stuff p^s, and p^s couldn't possibly have existed without s existing (7.2). The use of the word 'synergy' is designed as before to counter the staticist tendencies of our ordinary conception of objects. It is the *synergy* of process-stuff p^s, virtual particles and all, that constitutes—is—s. One isn't thinking accurately about the piece of process-stuff (involving 10^{12} ultimates, say) that wholly constitutes the entity $|s = p^s|$[48] if one is thinking of it in any way that allows it to be some sort of further fact about it that it's synergetic in the way that it is. The word 'ultimate' also invites an incorrectly staticist reading, and it needs to be borne in mind that each ultimate or u-field (in so far as they can be individuated) is itself a portion of synergetic process-stuff.

May we also say that

[9] $e = p^e$

and

[10] $c = p^c$?

Yes, for e and c are real concrete existents, like s, and are therefore, by the present materialist hypothesis, identical to some (dynamic, spatiotemporal) portion of process-stuff in the brain. [9] and [10] are also 'simple' identity claims, in the sense just explained, for neither e nor c could possibly have consisted of any ultimates (including virtual particles) other than the ones of which it does consist, or indeed of the same ultimates in any other sort of relation. Doubts based on counterfactuals are to come; note for now that it's very unclear that we can make sense of the idea that exactly the same synergy of ultimates might exist at any other time, given the massive involvement of the quantum vacuum in the existence of the synergy, if only because the actual temporal position of the quantum vacuum ultimates may be essential to their identity.

Many think that c is best understood as a property and not as an object. They may think the same about e, and indeed about s, the thin subject—at least when s is considered relative to Louis the human being. The distinction between object and property has no leverage against the triple identity claim, however, if there is anything

---

[48] I introduce '$|s = p^s|$' as the name of an entity. '$s = p^s$' states that **s** is identical with **p^s**.

to the argument of 6.15. I've argued for the respectability of thinking of s and e as objects, and c's candidacy for being thought of as an object—c being, recall, occurrent experiential content—is also in good shape, at least prima facie, in as much as we can legitimately think of c's existence as consisting wholly (like the existence of any other concrete entity) in the existence of a certain unified portion of process-stuff.

I'll return to these issues. For the moment consider again the claim that

[7] $[e \leftrightarrow s \leftrightarrow c]$,

and for good measure the claim that

[11] $[p^e \leftrightarrow p^s \leftrightarrow p^c]$,

which is derivable from [7] given [8]–[10]. The double arrow '$\leftrightarrow$' expresses a relation of metaphysical necessitation, as before; it has strong modal force. It is, however, not very informative. If [7] (or [11]) is true, it would be good to know more about what makes it true. It would be nice to know more about the metaphysics of the situation. I've suggested that [7] may be true because

[4] $[e = s = c]$,

but [4] seems as absurd as ever, and it may now be wondered whether even the much weaker

[7] $[e \leftrightarrow s \leftrightarrow c]$

has been sufficiently established. So let me now take a step back and consider the components of [7]—

[7.1] $[e \rightarrow s]$

[7.2] $[s \rightarrow e]$

[7.3] $[s \rightarrow c]$

[7.4] $[c \rightarrow s]$

[7.5] $[e \rightarrow c]$

[7.6] $[c \rightarrow e]$.

This will involve going over some points already discussed, but in a somewhat different light.

The old slogan 'ideas are logically private' (ideas being contents or experiences) secures both

[7.1] $[e \rightarrow s]$

and

[7.4] $[c \rightarrow s]$.

If e did *per impossibile* have a different subject, it couldn't be e—it couldn't be the experience it is. There's a simple and immovable sense in which the identity of a particular experience is essentially tied to the subject whose experience it is, as remarked on page 87. I can't—logically—have your experience, nor can you have mine. Suppose you and I are live 'consciousness functions' in a single brain, and suppose we're having qualitatively identical experiences because we're both somehow related to the same portion of brain activity. Even in this case there are two experiences numerically speaking—yours and mine.

The same holds for [7.4]. This particular bit of occurrent, living, experiential content couldn't have had a different subject from the subject for whom it is experiential content. You and I may again be live 'consciousness functions' in a single brain that are having qualitatively identical experiences because we are related to the same bit of brain activity. Even so, there are two distinct occurrences of experiential content, numerically speaking, if you and I are indeed two distinct subjects. There is yours, and there is mine. One of us could conceivably exist without the other, if you and I are indeed two distinct subjects.[49]

Given the similarity of the points I've made about [7.1] and [7.4], it may seem odd to distinguish e and c at all. True—but one has to do so as soon as one allows that the total existence of an experience involves the existence of a subject and an experiential content, and holds (so very naturally) that the subject is distinct from the content. For then one has to grant that the occurrent content is not identical with the experience. The only way to reject the distinction between e and c is to reject the distinction between them and s, and that is to accept [4].

With [7.1] and [7.4] secure, we can add

[7.6] $[c \rightarrow e]$.

This particular event of actually occurring experiential content, this particular bit of synergetic process-stuff p^c, couldn't have been the content of some patch of experience other than e. Perhaps the very same ultimates that are caught up in p^c could have been caught up in some other content occurrence at some time other than $t_1 - t_2$ (although this doesn't seem to be possible, given that p^c is essentially partly constituted by virtual ultimates). Perhaps they could have been caught up in a content occurrence qualitatively identical to p^c, every one of them in the same relative position in the new synergy. Even so, this synergetic process wouldn't have been c—or e; it would have been a completely different entity.

The next component of [7]

[7.5] $[e \rightarrow c]$

may seem no less secure. Plainly this very experience couldn't have had a different content and still have been the experience it is.

—Yes it could. e occurred, and it actually had content c, and it's true that it couldn't have come into existence at all without its existence involving the existence of content right from the start. Still, as soon as e has come into existence (in a necessarily content-involving way) we can get a referential grip on it that allows us to consider the possibility that its content might have been different from what it actually was without its actually ceasing to exist.

The same goes for the other two remaining components of [7], i.e. [7.2] $[s \rightarrow e]$ and [7.3] $[s \rightarrow c]$. s existed, and it actually had experience e, and it couldn't have come into existence at all

---

[49] Could we both be not only related to but partly constituted of the same bit of brain activity? I would need to be convinced that we could not.

(by definition of a thin subject) without its existence involving the existence of experience from the start. But once it has come into existence, necessarily already having experience of some sort, we can get an identifying fix on it which allows us to suppose that its experience might thereafter have been different from what it was in fact, so that [7.2] is false—which is to suppose that the actual occurrent content of its experience might thereafter have been different from what it was, so that [7.3] is also false.

Suppose s and c begin to exist together at time t_1, in the L-reality, as of course they do and must, only for c to be cut short after 10 ms, at $t_{1.1}$ and seamlessly replaced by content $c^* \neq c$, which lasts until t_2? Surely in this case s continues with c^* and without c? President Mandela would have continued to exist throughout 27 April, 1994 if he'd eaten a different breakfast from the one he did eat. So too s would have continued to exist—apart from c—in the case just described. Essentially the same sort of point holds even when we allow [5] that $[e = s{:}c]$, or, if you prefer, [6] that $[e = s(c)]$. We can suppose that the $|s : c|$ or $|s(c)|$ entity begins to exist, but that c is then cut short—after a millisecond—to be seamlessly replaced by $c^* \neq c$. In this case s continues without c.

In sum, an experience could possibly have had a content other than the content it does have, a thin subject could have had an experience different from the experience it actually does have—experience with occurrent content different from the content it actually does have.

It's precisely these sorts of counterfactual proposals that are blocked on the present view. This isn't the same objection to the use of counterfactuals as the objection made in 6.15 (314). The point there is that the naturalness and legitimacy of counterfactual speculation don't touch the fact that there is no real distinction between an object and its properties. This is the specific claim that e, s, and c are *counterfactually invariable relative to each other*—that

[7] $[e \leftrightarrow s \leftrightarrow c]$.

We can speculate counterfactually about e, s, and c as much as we like, so long as we don't try to hold any one of them constant while varying any of the others. Their mutual counterfactual invariability is guaranteed, given the way I've introduced the terms, although they're clearly terms for conceptually distinct things. The identity of a piece of process-stuff is a strict function of its constituent ultimate process-parts. If one meddles in any way with any constituent ultimate process-part of $|e = p^e|$ or $|s = p^s|$ or $|c = p^c|$, one no longer has $|e = p^e|$ or $|s = p^s|$ or $|c = p^c|$. e, s, and c can't survive any such change under counterfactual speculation, let alone change relative to each other. The sense in which [7] is secure is clear. It stands against a tide of contrary philosophical speculative habits, but the present task is not to defend a factual claim that stands in need of argument. It is, rather, to try to work out what must be the case *given* that [7] is correct.

What, then, is the relation between the three portions of process-stuff $|e = p^e|$, $|s = p^s|$, and $|c = p^c|$? It would be extremely surprising if the referential terms 'e', 's', and 'c' all picked out portions of process-stuff with no overlapping parts at all. They must surely overlap to some extent. But how much?

The target suggestion is that there is perfect overlap. On this view, both the '$\leftrightarrow$' signs in [7] can be replaced by the identity sign, giving

[4] $[e = s = c]$.

Without yet going this far, I've proposed that we can and should take one large step away from [7] and towards [4] by endorsing the thesis (favoured by James and many august others) that an experience *consists* of a (thin) subject entertaining—having, living—a content. We can represent this as before (352) by

[5] $[e = s{:}c]$.

Here the first '↔' in [7] is replaced by the identity sign, this being an explanatory move, relative to [7]. The second is replaced by the colon ':' introduced in 7.6, which has some kind of strong intimacy-intimating function whose precise metaphysical force, over and above the strong modal '↔', remains to be determined, so that this is only a potentially explanatory move.

The colon seems to serve a valuable purpose in representing an apparently irreducible respect in which experience involves a polarity—a polarity of subject and content. Is it certain, though, that we can know that this polarity involves some sort of genuine ontic plurality? This is the question raised on page 274. There is (again in Descartes's terms, as adapted and extended in 6.15) no more evident *conceptual* distinction than the distinction between the (thin) subject of an experience and the content of that experience, but it's already clear that there is no *real* distinction between them, i.e. a distinction of such a kind that they can possibly exist apart, and this raises the question of what, other than identity, could be the ground of the absence of any real distinctness.

—Stop now. The subject can't be the content. Even if there's some sense in which it's best to say that the subject of the experience is just the (necessary) subjectivity, the necessary subjectivity characteristic, of the experience, still the subjectivity can't, can't, surely, obviously, *be* the content.

That remains to be seen. In the meantime, it may be said, as in 7.6, that the colon in [5] is too appositional and egalitarian, and that we should rewrite [5] as

[6] $[e = s(c)]$

the curved brackets introducing a clear asymmetry between *s* and *c* and also representing the fact that *c* is essentially something *for s* and essentially *belongs* to *s*. Perhaps we can go further, and take the brackets' embrace to represent the idea that *c* is somehow involved in *s* in such a way that its being is at least partly *constitutive* of the being of *s*. On this view *c* is, as it were, the body or flesh of *s*, without which *s* (the thin subject) cannot exist, and is nothing. *s*, we still feel, can't be the same as *c*, but it is as a thin subject nothing without *c*—not just utterly empty, but non-existent. The existence of *s* is the existence of p^s, a synergy of process-stuff, whatever else it is or is not; the existence of *c*, too, is, given materialism, nothing over and above the existence of some process-stuff, p^c. The question is this: What is the relation between p^s and p^c? What is the relation between the process-stuff that is (wholly constitutive of) the being of *s* and the process-stuff that is (wholly constitutive of) the being of *c*?

—This is very hard to follow. The only achievement of the colon and the curly brackets is to dramatize our uncertainty about the metaphysics of the relation between *s* and *c*. At the very least, it would be better to use a neutral symbol, say 'R', to signify relation and rewrite [5] and [6] as '$e = sRc$'. The meaning of ' $=$ ', by contrast, is very clear.

True. '$=$' has an agreeable clarity. It would be nice to have more of it—and perhaps [4], the triple identity, is not as crazy as it sounds. Obviously the neutral symbol 'R' doesn't rule out identity, and if [4] is in the end incoherent, it's worth examining where and how it hits incoherence.

The central strangeness is the identification of s and c. How can the subject be the content? How indeed? But perhaps the intense intuition that s can't be the same as c feeds off some elision or (all too common) blurring of the difference between contents considered as abstract particulars and contents considered as concrete, occurrent particulars; or perhaps it's fuelled by the false picture of the relation between an object and its properties. I think one needs to bring the question 'What is it, actually, for concrete, occurrent, live, experiential content to exist?' before one's mind again and again.

The polarity and non-identity of s and c is fundamental to our thought, but I've just proposed that c is in some way constitutive of the very existence of s, and now the converse proposal also seems apt. For what is c? c is (so to say) *living content*. It is an actual occurrence of content that is (necessarily) an actual *entertaining* of content, an episode that necessarily involves there being 'what-it's-like-ness' in the world, and its very life and reality—its being something concrete and particular, rather than being an uninstantiated what-it's-like-ness type—just is its being lived, had, animated, by a subject. It's impossible for c—this very occurrence of experiential content—to exist without s—this very (thin) subject existing and being its 'animating principle', and as for s ...

—Repetition.

... as for s (we won't move if all you can hear is a wordy restatement of an abstract proposition you've already registered), s doesn't exist at all when e doesn't exist, the experience of which it is the subject, and e doesn't exist at all without c, its content, which is its very matter. If one reflects, it can begin to seem that there is after all no obvious asymmetry between s and c as regards their mutual dependence. The egalitarian implication of the colon symbol in '$s{:}c$'—the suggestion of (ontological) parity, commutativity, relational symmetry—may begin to look less problematic.

Suppose this is so. What remains to favour '$:$' over ' $=$ '? Well, the colon, unlike the identity sign, continues to stand up for the apparently adamantine fact that s and c must be *somehow* distinct, however intimate their relation of mutual dependence. They're plainly conceptually distinct, even if they're not really distinct in the technical sense, because they can't possibly exist apart, and it still seems that they can't possibly be the same single thing.

—It's obvious that you're going to go on to say that concrete particulars can't be absolutely unable to exist apart from each other unless they're the same thing. The trouble is that you're not extracting anything you haven't already put in. What's more, you've simply defined your favoured entities s and c (and e) into this intense degree of metaphysical intimacy, and although you may not have meddled much with the notion of an *experience*, or the (already peculiar) notion of *occurrent content* in doing so, you've had to bend the notion of a *subject of experience* way out of shape to get anywhere near where you think you are now.

Out of shape? I think that's terminological prejudice, for reasons given earlier. Why should the term 'subject of experience' have a dispositional reading, i.e. a reading that allows there to be a subject of experience when there's no experience? What's the *evidence* that a subject of experience continues to exist when there is no experience?

This is a silly question, because the matter under discussion isn't a matter of fact. That's the point of the question. It makes it vivid that it is indeed just a terminological decision—to say that subjects of experience are things that can continue to exist when there's no experience. Human beings do so continue, of course, and brains, and parts of brains that are capable of being recruited into experience-constituting and subject-constituting synergies; but I don't think subjects of experience do. That's my terminological decision. You don't disagree with me, on my terms. You simply choose to put things differently.

—I'll grant this, because [4] [$e = s = c$] remains as absurd as ever. The experience *is* the subject? The subject *is* the content? Contents have *experience*? *Experiences* have experience? Experiences experience *themselves*? [5], the claim that [$e = s{:}c$], may come to seem relatively tolerable once one has acclimatized to your odd thin use of 'subject'. It simply states that a particular experience occurrence is a particular subject-entertaining-a-content-occurrence, and that is certainly true, on the present terms. But why go on to the triple identity?

I sometimes feel the same. But I suspect that [$e = s = c$] is a deep truth. I think that the point that s and c stand in an intensely intimate relation given which they can't possibly exist apart—so that there is (in my augmented Cartesian terms) at most a conceptual distinction and no real distinction between them—is solid. As for the claim that if two concrete particulars aren't really distinct, and can't possibly exist apart, then they must be numerically identical—I take it, as in 6.15, that the burden of argument lies heavily on those who seek to deny it. This 'can't possibly' is very strong—so strong that it seems that only identity can guarantee it. And if this is right, then unless one can show a real distinction—a more than merely conceptual distinction—between s and c one will be driven to

[3] [$s = c$]

even if [3], like [4], seems as crazy as ever.

So let me now formally re-endorse the principle first endorsed in 6.15—that if there is at most a conceptual distinction between two apparently distinct (concrete) particulars, if there's no real distinction between them, if they can't possibly exist apart, then they're not really two but only one. There's only one thing that is—of course—identical with itself. Caution suggests that we should ask one more time whether

[7.3] [$s \rightarrow c$]

and

[7.4] [$c \rightarrow s$]

are true, or whether s and c can possibly exist apart after all. But the answer No is contained in what has gone before. Certainly c can't possibly exist without s; no actual, concrete, occurrent content, occurring at some particular place at some particular time, can possibly have any subject other than the subject it does have, whatever the subject's girth (thick, traditional inner, thin inner). This is [7.4], a point covered by the slogan that ideas are logically private. You want to reject the converse, [7.3], arguing that s and c can begin to exist together at time t_1, c being cut short after 10 ms, at $t_{1.1}$ and seamlessly replaced by $c^* \neq c$, which lasts until t_2, while s continues to exist. I reply that this is not so on my view, that c is the very body of s without which s cannot exist. In this story, s ceases to exist at $t_{1.1}$ and a completely new subject comes into existence. One experience/subject-upsurging is cut short, another crosses the line into existence at the same moment, as depicted in Figure 8.3.

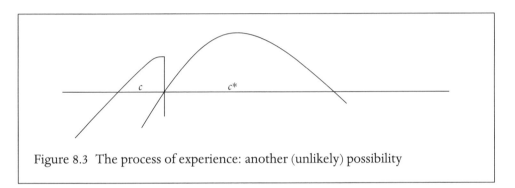

Figure 8.3 The process of experience: another (unlikely) possibility

Again the fact that certain sorts of counterfactual speculation run smoothly in everyday thought has no force. To appeal to this fact is simply to presuppose that s is substantially distinct from c in some way. It begs the question. One needs some independent reason to think that s is substantially distinct from c. But what gives one an independent fix on the identity of s that allows one to say such a thing?

—Fine. Just give me a reason for saying that s can't possibly exist without c that doesn't equally beg the question. It isn't enough for you to appeal to your definition of 'subject' according to which a subject exists in the L-reality only if experience exists in the L-reality. My proposal blocks that move with the phrase 'seamlessly replaced': there is no time between t_1 and t_2 at which there is no experience in the L-reality.

I'll take back 'begs the question', but this reply fails, because it doesn't follow, from the fact that there is temporally seamless experience in the L-reality between t_1 and t_2, that there's a single thin subject (371–2). My empirical bet about the human case remains the same as before: new experiences—and so new subjects—arise constantly as old ones die away, each such experience-and-subject being a primitive unity, a matter of a certain sort of upsurging of activity in and across neurons, each such upsurging effectively numerically distinct from the next (the identification of experience with neuronal activity is as always 'adductive'). I think that this is what the phenomenon of there being a subject of experience actually consists in, in the human case. This is the reality that underlies all the subjective phenomena of continuity and flow in experience, such as they are, and the whole natural picture of the persisting inner self or subject.

What more can be said? I argued in 6.14 that we need to cultivate a realistically processual understanding of the nature of physical objects. This point combines with the account of the relation between an object and its properties given in 6.15 to remove (so I hope) any remaining felt strangeness in the claim that subjects—even thin subjects—are well thought of as objects, or are at least as well thought of as objects as any other things.

This may be one of those points at which it's helpful to put 'subjectivity' in place of 'subject', taking it as a constituent of a count noun such as 'an event or episode of subjectivity'. [7.3] is then the claim that the existence of s (this particular episode of subjectivity) is really nothing over and above the existence of c (this particular episode of occurrent living content). The existence of this subjectivity entails—indeed is—the existence of this occurrent content; the existence of this occurrent content entails—indeed is—the existence of this subjectivity. Neither is in any way ontologically distinct from the other.

Many, I think, will find this talk of 'subjectivity' far less unacceptable than talk of 'the subject'. But it's only the tremendous inertial force of the ordinary notion of what an object is, and so of what a subject-considered-as-an-object is, that makes many want to deny the existence of any such thing as the subject, even when the subject is supposed to be something fleeting, as here, and to throw up their hands at the further idea that the subject might have as much claim to be called an object as anything else in reality. In certain theoretical frames, the idea that the correct thing to say is that there is no subject, and certainly no *object*, only occurrent subjectivity or occurrent consciousness, seems an early, easy lesson of reflection, or meditation. An experience many find it natural to characterize as experience of the non-existence of the self or subject can seem inescapable in the present moment of meditation if it is practised with any success at all (the experience is reliable, even banal, as remarked in 4.4; it's entirely robust in the sense of experimental psychology, and occurs without delivering any particular spiritual benefits). In the present frame, however, this fact doesn't give any reason to think that the notion of the subject is in any way inappropriate in the description of reality, either in general or in the description of certain meditative states, for in the present frame it's a trivial (definitional) point that it is appropriate to speak of a subject whenever it is appropriate to speak of subjectivity: whenever there is experience, with its necessary *for*-ness. It is, more bluntly, a necessary truth that there is a subject whenever there is subjectivity.[50]

It's equally trivial, on the present terms, that there's an *object* that is a subject of experience whenever there's subjectivity. To think that the idea that subjects of experience are objects can be put in question by what meditation (say) reveals is simply to have an excessively *lumpen* and scientifically absurd picture of what objects are.

---

[50] This would be my—I take it conciliatory—reply to the doubts raised by Jim Stone (2005).

8.9 The purple pulse

I suppose I'm offering the triple identity as some sort of necessary truth. But let me now try briefly to present it quasi-empirically—'quempirically'—as if it were an empirical claim. Experience e, then, is (by materialist hypothesis) identical with a one-second-long synergy of process-stuff p^e ($[e = p^e]$); s is identical with a one-second-long synergy of process-stuff ps ($[s = p^s]$); and c is identical with a one-second-long synergy of process-stuff pc ($[c = p^c]$); and the proposal is that as a matter of fact

[12] $[p^e = p^s = p^c]$

—that in any and all cases of experience the process-stuff that is the experience just is the process-stuff that is the subject, which in turn just is the process-stuff that is the content. We cannot section p^e into regions, a p^s region and a p^c region. In which case [4] $[e = s = c]$.

How might we establish this? Suppose that the art of mapping the neural direct constituters (not correlates) of consciousness has been perfected, and that we've picked out the synergy of process-stuff p^e that constitutes (is identical with) e. And suppose we find that we can somehow independently identify the subject synergy p^s that must exist given that e exists, and the content synergy p^c that must exist given that e exists. The present claim is that in this case we will find that p^s and p^c are the same, and that both are the same as p^e.

If we suppose instead that we can corral out a subject sub-synergy p^s of p^e, or a content sub-synergy p^c of p^e, neither p^c nor p^s being identical with p^e, then the claim is that p^s and p^c will still always be the same. This last supposition—about a subject/content sub-synergy—is directly contrary to [12], and so to [4], but it's worth pursuing a little for that reason.

Consider, then, the following quempirical challenge to the claim that if we could identify a subject sub-synergy p^s or a content sub-synergy p^c within an experience synergy p^e existing from t_1 to t_2, then p^s and p^c would have to turn out to be the same thing. Suppose that there seem at first to be good intuitive reasons—simple spatial reasons, say—for distinguishing p^s from p^c. At t_0, say, one is considering the collection of ultimates, K, that will participate in the constituting of p^e from t_1 to t_2. K, modelled in colour in two dimensions, has the shape of a blue crescent moon curled tightly to the side of an orange ball. There are little nodes on the crescent/ball boundary, and pathways for sensory inputs lead to the ball and only to the ball. At t_0 sensory inputs flow into the ball. A flush of red suffuses rapidly across the ball and through the nodes into the crescent. Pulses of blue shoot out from the crescent through the nodes, and at t_1 the whole crescent/ball complex pulses purple for two seconds—this is the existence of p^e—until t_2, when K precipitately loses its purple colour as neurons (or ultimates) constitutive of p^e become inactive with respect to s's experience, or are rapidly recruited into other transient experience synergies.

The idea is that one might think it right to say that the purple-pulsing crescent is $|s = p^s|$ while the purple-pulsing ball is $|c = p^c|$. But nothing in this story gives one good reason to suppose that $|s = p^s|$ is ontologically distinct from $|c = p^c|$. For e, in this quempirical story, is purple-pulsing p^e. No (thin) subject exists in the K-reality before t_1, although there is a crescent formation; nor is there any occurrent experiential content in the K-reality before t_1, although there is an orange ball formation that has been suffused with red. Neither s nor c exists at all before the onset of purple at t_1. They begin together. The occurrent content c is the body of s without which s can't exist at all, and the subject s is the animation of c without which c can't exist at all. The crescent ball story supplies no reason to think that the crescent formation between t_1 and t_2 is s while the ball formation is c.

How might we express the suggestion rejected on page 409—that s could continue to exist even if c were replaced by $c^* \neq c$? It won't do to imagine that the red flush in the ball (material for an F-type experience, say) is annihilated and seamlessly replaced at $t_{0.9}$ by a differently caused darker red flush (material for a G-type experience) before any empurplement occurs, for s does not yet exist at all in this story, and nor does c; experience has not yet begun. We have to suppose instead that empurplement has taken place at t_1 (experience has begun, s exists) and that the ball part of the purple process-stuff is then annihilated and seamlessly replaced by different (darker) process-stuff at $t_{1.1}$[51] while the crescent part of the process-stuff remains the same.

Suppose we admit this as a quempirical possibility. Is it a case in which s continues while c doesn't? No. For that in virtue of which e is a (thin) subject-involving entity is no more located in the crescent than in the ball. The subjectivity of the experience is undisentanglably distributed across p^e. So s does not continue to exist with this replacement. This highly distributed conception of the location of subjectivity ('consciousness') is, I believe, the present consensus among the neurophysiologically informed about how experiences exist in the brain, both among those who are genuine or real realists about consciousness, and those, like Dennett, who aren't. On this view, there's simply no locus in the brain, however scattered, that is (a) the locus of the subject of experience and (b) distinct from the place where the neuronal activity in virtue of which the experience has the content it does is located.

8.10 $[e = s = c]$ (3)

I think this is enough. When we try to approach this part of reality, our categories of thought seem close to breaking point. The standard conception of the relation between

---

[51] We can allow for argument that the same ultimates may be involved: to constitute a numerically distinct portion of synergetic process-stuff, they need only be in a different state of activation.

a thing and its properties is locked into the terms 'experience', 'subject of experience', and 'content' in a way that makes it hard for us to grasp, let alone endorse, the proposed identity, even if the best current neurophysiology seems to support something like it. We can, it seems, pull c into line with e to get

[2] $[e = c]$

as in William the traditional misunderstanding of Hume (an experience is just content). And, jumping off from [5], the $[e = s{:}c]$ picture, or [6], the $[e = s(c)]$ picture, we can perhaps pull s into line with e to get

[1] $[e = s]$.

as in William James's 'the thoughts themselves are the thinkers', Kant's 'the thinking or the existence of the thought and the existence of my own self are one and the same', Hume's 'when my perceptions are remov'd for any time, as by sound sleep … I … may truly be said not to exist', or Descartes's 'thinking must be considered as nothing else than thinking substance itself …, that is, as mind'.[52] And when we have [1] and [2] we have

[4] $[e = s = c]$.

But as soon as we've pulled one of s or c into line—as soon as we've achieved some sort of grip on the proposal that one of s or c is identical with e—the other seems to pop out of line, deliquescing and recrystallizing as propertyish or aspectish. Suppose we've managed to set things out in such a way as to give some plausibility to the claim that the existence of the experience just is—is just—the existence of the subject, the thin subject that exists if and only if (not only *if*, but also *only if*) experience exists. In this case the content of the experience seems left out, and it seems we can get it back in only by thinking of it as an aspect or property or 'modification' of the subject—a retreat to [5] $[e = s{:}c]$ or [6] $[e = s(c)]$. Suppose, alternatively, that we've drawn our intuitions closer to the thought that the experience just is—is just—the occurrent content, as in the old misunderstanding of Hume. In this case the subject of the experience seems left out, and it seems we can get it back in only by thinking of it as the necessary subjec*tivity* of occurrent content:

[13] $[e = c_s]$

as it were. It seems that we need to push either or s or c down in some way, because we can't face [3] $[s = c]$.

But the subjectivity just is the subject—or so I have proposed. And the subject has the strong unity characteristic. It is (at the least) something whose claim to objecthood can't be less than the claim of the episode of experience or the patch of occurrent experientially unified content. So [13] $[e = c_s]$ won't do if it accords lesser status to s.

---

[52] James 1892: 191/83; Kant 1772: 75; Hume, *Treatise*, 165/252; Descartes 1644: 1.215.

Identities and equivalences

[1] $[s = e]$

[2] $[e = c]$

[3] $[s = c]$

[4] $[e = s = c]$

[5] $[e = s{:}c]$

[6] $[e = s(c)]$

[7] $[e \leftrightarrow s \leftrightarrow c]$ [7.1] $[e \rightarrow s]$

                                [7.2] $[s \rightarrow e]$

                                [7.3] $[s \rightarrow c]$

                                [7.4] $[c \rightarrow s]$

                                [7.5] $[e \rightarrow c]$

                                [7.6] $[c \rightarrow e]$

[8] $[s = p^s]$

[9] $[e = p^e]$

[10] $[c = p^c]$

[11] $[p^e \leftrightarrow p^s \leftrightarrow p^c]$

[12] $[p^e = p^s = p^c]$

[13] $[e = c_s]$

I don't think we can reach [3] by any conventional way of thought. Even if we can reach either [1] or [2] individually, the way in which we reach it seems to block the way to the other. And yet I suspect that [4] $[e = s = c]$ is true, and that similar wonders of identity apply in the case of all other physical objects, masked by the bad old picture of objects and their properties to which our minds keep defaulting. I think, in fact, that the case of the relation between an experience, the subject of the experience, and the content of the experience—the sheer difficulty of the triple identity—may be exemplary. We can perhaps get closer to apprehending the identity of a thing and its properties (the identity of its being and its being, the identity of its existence and its qualitative nature) in this case than in any other. Perhaps $[e = s = c]$ gives us a glimmering of an extremely general metaphysical truth. It opens a small frosted window on to the nature of things in a way that nothing else can (the frosting is in the mind, not the glass, given that intellectual insight can bring us, however transiently, to transparency).

—All this time you've been avoiding an obvious, fatal objection. It's true on your terms that s can't exist without c and that c can't exist without s, but this fact is no more difficult than the fact that no object that has an essential property can exist without having that property. c is really just a *property* of s, and is on your terms (your thin conception of the subject) an essential property of s. That's why s and c are unbreakably locked. And this doesn't force us into any strange identity claim. You should stick to [5] $[e = s{:}c]$.

I used to think that [5] was the most that could be said. Now, though, I think that this objection draws any force it has from the reality-fogging inadequacy of the standard account of the relation between an object and its properties.

—I'll grant this for argument's sake (and because I'm worn out). I'll even grant that 's' and 'c' name things that have as good a claim to be physical objects as anything else, so that the question of their identity can be posed. But an identity claim entails that the 'two' things that are said to be identical have all their properties in common (because they are, after all, only one thing). And *s* and *c* do not have all their properties in common. If one thing is certain, subjects experience things, and contents don't.

The triple identity claim is in flagrant conflict with ordinary thought and talk. If you're content to rely on them, they will secure your case (like baldness on page 314). My aim is to begin to reach beyond this sort of objection. *s* isn't a subject as conceived in your objection; *c* isn't a content as you conceive it. What we have is an experience *e*, a living content, a content-bodied subject *s/c*, a subject-animated content *c/s*: what we have is $[e = s = c]$. A closer approach to $[e = s = c]$ requires a certain sort of intellectual discipline, or at least time.

   This is really the end. The selective summary in the two closing sections twists certain main themes together, but it's not designed to show the whole thing in an easy glance.

8.11 Summary

Plainly

[1] experience exists.

It follows that

[2] subjectivity exists.

This can be put equally well by saying that

[3] subject-of-experience-hood exists,

because [3] doesn't add anything to [2]. Subjectivity is sufficient for, can't be less than, subject-of-experience-hood.

   One can gloss the point by introducing a mediating term: [2] entails that

[4] *for*-someone-or-something-ness exists,

as indeed does [1], and [4] entails [3]. (In fact [2] = [3] = [4].)

   Does it follow from the fact that subject-of-experience-hood exists that

[5] *a* subject of experience exists

—in which case it follows equally from the fact that experience and subjectivity exist? In considering this question, I'll take it as before that

[6] the count noun '(a) subject of experience' has a legitimate use only if subjects of experience are correctly said to be objects—genuine concrete individuals of some sort.

What are the consequences of [6]? In 6.10 I asked 'What are the best candidates for being objects given that we're committed to retaining—indeed, finding application for—the category *object* in our fundamental ontology or metaphysics?' (294). We can take this commitment to amount to the assumption that

[7] at least one object exists.

I claimed that

[8] unity considerations are paramount in deciding questions of objecthood,

and, having acquired and adopted the *thin* conception of the subject of experience in 7.1, argued that

[9] a subject of experience qualifies for objecthood if anything does,

on the grounds that

[10] a thin subject of experience is unsurpassable when it comes to possession of the unity characteristic.

At the end of 8.6 (403) I argued that we can know that a thin subject is an object, given [8], and given that there is at least one object, simply on the basis of being able to specify its synchronic identity conditions, and even if we don't know how to give diachronic(*) identity conditions for it.

On these terms my conclusion is plain. [5] does follow from [1] (or [2] or [3]) even given [6]—even if a subject of experience can't be said to exist unless it's correctly said to be an object. For we're assuming [7] that something qualifies as an object, and [9] a subject of experience qualifies as an object if anything does.

In fact I think that [5] follows from [1] even when we drop [7] and put aside all questions about the ontological category of subjects of experience, such as whether they're objects or not.[53] When I assert that a subject of experience exists, I'm not asserting anything that those who like to say that only subjectivity exists can properly deny. Those who favour the nothing-but-subjectivity view are wrong if they think that it can be true that subjectivity exists without a subject of experience existing. One way to put this is to say that if they deny [4], they have an inadequate understanding of the nature of subjectivity. If, on the other hand, they accept that [2] entails [4], then they accept that the existence of [2], subjectivity, entails the existence of [5], a subject of experience, as I understand the term 'subject of experience'. I think Derek Parfit can agree.[54]

So much, for the moment, for [5]. Consider now the proposal that

[11] experience is distributed more or less as we think

in at least one fundamental respect, i.e. I have it, you have it, he and she have it, and so on. Does it follow from [11] that

[12] a plurality of subjects of experience exists?

---

[53] To take it that a subject exists isn't of course to take it that a persisting subject exists.
[54] In spite of his arguments in Parfit 1998.

Does it follow that [12] is a truth of fundamental metaphysics, not just a 'conventional' truth, in Buddhist terms, and hence, given [6], that

[13] a plurality of objects exists?

I don't know. It all depends on what you mean by 'object'. I'm not yet ready to divest myself of the opinion that a fundamental truth about reality—a truth about plurality or

---

Proposals

[1] experience exists

[2] subjectivity exists

[3] subject-of-experience-hood exists

[4] *for*-someone-or-something-ness exists

[5] *a* subject of experience exists

[6] the count noun '(a) subject of experience' has a legitimate use, singular or plural, only if subjects of experience are correctly said to be *objects*

[7] at least one object exists

[8] concrete-unity considerations are paramount in deciding questions of concrete objecthood

[9] a subject of experience qualifies for objecthood if anything does

[10] a (thin) subject of experience is unsurpassable when it comes to possession of the concrete-unity characteristic

[11] experience is distributed more or less as we think (I have it, you have it, etc.)

[12] a plurality of subjects of experience exists

[13] a plurality of objects exists

---

diversity—is well expressed by [12], given [11], and that we may take [12] to be true even after we've put aside all the considerations I've adduced in favour of the idea that we find many short-lived subjects of experience even when we consider a single human being. And [12], with [7] and [9], entails [13].

8.12 The one and the many

Spinoza rejects [13] while retaining [7], and if we follow him in this, we must follow him further in rejecting [12] (given [9]). If, however, we reject [6] and [9], we can agree with Spinoza that there is a sufficient sense in which [12] is true after all—even in fundamental metaphysics. We simply have to accept that finite human subjects of experience—selves—like ourselves are not in the final ontological analysis individual objects but rather features—'modes' or 'modifications'—of the only object there is, the universe. In Russell's words, 'individual souls and separate pieces of matter are, for Spinoza, adjectival; they are not *things*, but mere aspects of the divine Being', i.e. the universe (1961: 554). This is a view of a kind that finds considerable support in present-day physic, (7.4) although it can very well seem to encounter a special obstacle in the case of subjects of experience, given the appeal of James's remark that 'the breaches between ... thoughts ... belonging to different ... minds ... are the most absolute breaches in nature' (1890: 1.226).

Spinozan monism in some form may in the end be the best position in fundamental metaphysics. My conclusion—assertion—so far is simply this. Given that experience exists more or less as we think it does ([1] and [11]), and given that a plurality of objects exists ([13]), and even if subjects of experience can't be said to exist unless they qualify as objects ([6]), we can assert both [5], that a subject of experience exists, and indeed [12] that subjects of experience exist. I distanced myself from the traditional notion of substance in 1.7 and again in 2.16, and in arguing in 6.12 that selves qualify as objects, if any existents do, because they're unsurpassable strong unities, I didn't intend to imply that they fulfil the traditional requirement on individual substances of existing independently of everything else.[55]

Should we retain the notion of an object in fundamental metaphysics? There can, I think, be no reasonable objection to it in the case in which we hold with Spinoza and others that there is only one object—the universe, spacetime, *deus sive natura*. It may be said that we need evidence that the universe possesses the strong-unity characteristic in a sufficient degree, and does not possess it merely trivially, being necessarily single simply by being everything. It is, however, a question whether this way of possessing concrete unity could be merely trivial. My sense is that the answer is No.

Here, perhaps, I part company with Nāgārjuna, in thinking that a term like 'object' can have a fully respectable (count-noun) use when applied to reality as a whole—even if I'm prepared to agree with him (and again Spinoza) that the category of object has, at bottom, no respectable application *within* the totality of reality, or, in other words, no respectable plural application.[56]

What if I do agree with him about this second thing? Does that jeopardize my claim that subjects of experience exist—subjects of experience that are selves?

No. I take the requirement that selves must qualify as objects if they are to exist to hold only to the extent that objects exist at all. The requirement is that selves must qualify as objects if there are objects, but needn't if there aren't. The strong brief for the self (12) can hardly require one to prove that selves are objects if it is given that objects don't exist, for to prove that would be to prove that selves don't exist.

One could argue as follows: if selves exist, they must be objects, but there aren't any objects, so there aren't any selves. The argument is valid, but it doesn't have any force

---

[55] Or, in the traditional framework, everything other than God. (If, like Spinoza, one identifies God and nature, this qualification is redundant.)

[56] The count-noun and mass-term use of 'substance' use merge on Spinoza's view.

against my position. I have the same reasons as ever for asserting that selves exist, even if I allow that the term 'object' has no legitimate application, or at least no legitimate plural application, to concrete reality, and I can argue back as follows. First, selves as I have defined them certainly exist, however short-lived they are, and whatever their ontological category:

(a) selves (as defined) certainly exist.

Secondly, they have the fundamental metaphysical characteristic of objects, the strong activity-unity characteristic (where activity has, as always, no implication of intentional agency):

(b) selves are strong unities, strong activity-unities.

(b) is the case, I propose, whatever difficulties we may encounter in giving them clear boundaries as objects (e.g. in specifying their diachronic identity conditions—8.6). It follows that if we allow that

(c) strong activity-unities are rightly called 'objects'

then we may say that

(d) selves are objects

and also of course that

(e) objects exist.

This said, I'm no longer particularly anxious to secure (c)–(e). The assumption that the term 'object' has plural application may be more trouble than it's worth in fundamental metaphysics, given some of the traditional associations of the terms 'object' (and 'substance') and the bent of present-day physics. Increasingly it seems enough to say that a thin-subject sesmet self is an unsurpassable example of a strong activity-unity, and is, as such, an unsurpassable revealer of the nature of substance (in the mass-term use), of what there is, of the *res*—whether or not it counts as an irreducibly ontically distinct substance (in the count-noun use) relative to something else that exists. One can agree that the breaches between experiences belonging to different minds are the most absolute breaches in nature while observing that 'most absolute' does not imply 'absolutely absolute'.

The conditional claim remains: if there are any true unities in nature other than the unity of the universe, if there is an irreducible plurality of true unities in nature, then there are no better candidates for being such unities than thin-subject ses-met selves, whatever we want to do with the word 'object'. Their existence is certain, given the existence of experience, which is certain, and their strong—object-grade—unity is also certain, given Fundamental Singleness, even if there is some sense in which they are, ultimately, just modes, aspects or features of the only thing there is.

It remains hard to grasp this last proposal, given Fundamental Singleness. The existence of a thin subject in the living moment of experience appears to be a *unum per se*, in Leibniz's terminology, a unity in and of itself, independently of any unity-discerning perspective on it. It's true that it involves, constitutes, is partly constituted by, a perspective, but it's not a unity only in so far as it is discerned to be a unity by or in or from that perspective. The existence of the perspective constitutes the unity in question, but not because it represents it as a unity.

Even as I insist on the unsurpassable or absolute unity of the thin subject in the living moment of experience, I want to hold on to the idea that it is in some way ontically composite, or complex, or diversity-involving—that the multiplicity we discern, when examining a thin-subject synergy with the tools of physics and neurophysiology, corresponds to some real complexity in nature.

—If one thing is certain, it's that an absolute unity can't be composite.

So it may seem—but I find no conceptual impossibility in the idea that something ontically composite, or at least complex, can be an absolute unity, a 'complex absolute unity', in the terms of 8.5, although I don't have an argument (the word 'absolute' is open to discussion). The proposal is the product of the confluence of two ideas that I'm still inclined to favour: the idea that the physical is irreducibly plural, or at least complex, diversity-involving, and the idea that we have respectable metaphysical reason to hold that thin-subject selves are absolute unities even when their existence consists in the existence of a plurality of u-fields in synergetic interaction—or at least of something structurally complex.

This is not to say that we can know how many there are. Spinoza, it seems, finds a fundamental sense in which there is only one subject of experience, the universe—even as he fully acknowledges the reality of human subjectivity. I've proposed that there are many more, and a great many more than most people suppose, given that most people understand the notion of a sentient being in the conventional way, think that there's one subject of experience per sentient being, and decline to endorse the thin conception of the subject according to which subjects of experience are thin subjects. Once again, though, I don't see how to rule out the possibility that there may be a fundamental sense in which Spinoza is right. So too, there may be compelling reason in physics to think of a field as composed of many fields, although there is also a clear sense in which there is only one field. This is the problem of the one and the many, to which the best answer seems to be, contrary to conventional reason, and as remarked on page 000, that it is true that there is only one thing and true that there are many things; or at least, somewhat less alarmingly, that it is true that there is diversity but also true that it is, somehow, all one.[57]

Subject to the Spinozan thought, the conclusion remains. Selves exist—sesmets or thin subjects exist. Thin subject sesmets are central to what we're actually thinking or talking about when we say or suppose that selves exist in everyday life, whatever we think we're talking about. They exist whatever their duration, and whatever the

---

[57] It's arguable that the full transparency assumption delivers irreducible distinctness for Descartes, and no less arguable that it causes him insuperable problems, given his endorsement of the radical $[e = s = c]$ thesis, problems for whose solution he needs, at least, the help of Leibniz's *petites perceptions*.

bottom truth about their seemingly irreducible complexity of being. If they are indeed irreducible individuals, then they may be called objects. If not, not; but it no longer matters. They are as they are, and as we know them to be, at least in part, in experiencing things as we do from moment to moment and from day to day.

REFERENCES

ARISTOTLE (*c*.340 BCE/1936) *De Anima*, trans. W. S. Hett (Cambridge, MA: Harvard University Press).

—— (*c*.340 BCE/1963) *Categories* and *de Interpretatione*, trans. with notes by J. L. Ackrill (Oxford: Clarendon Press).

—— (*c*.340 BCE/1924) *Metaphysics*, trans. with commentary by W. D. Ross (Oxford: Oxford University Press).

—— (*c*.340 BCE/1963) *Rhetoric*, ed. W. D. Ross (Oxford: Clarendon Press).

ARMSTRONG, D. M. (1980/1997) 'Against "Ostrich Nominalism"', in *Properties*, ed. D. H. Mellor and Alex Oliver (Oxford: Oxford University Press).

ARNAULD, A. (1641/1985) 'Fourth Set of Objections', in Descartes, (1985), vol. 2, 138–53.

—— (1683/1990) *On True and False Ideas*, trans. with introduction by S. Gaukroger (Manchester: Manchester University Press).

AUGUSTINE (*c*.410/2002) *On the Trinity Books 8–15*, ed. G. B. Matthews (Cambridge: Cambridge University Press).

AYER, A. J. (1971) 'A Profile of Sir A. J. Ayer', Eurotelevision.

AYERS, M. R. (1991) *Locke*, 2 vols. (London: Routledge).

BAARS, B. (1996) *In the Theater of Consciousness: The Workspace of the Mind* (New York: Oxford University Press).

BARON-COHEN, S. (1995) *Mindblindness: Essay on Autism and Theory of Mind* (Cambridge, MA: MIT Press).

BAYLEY, J. (1998) *Iris: A Memoir* (London: Duckworth).

BEISER, F. (2002) *German Idealism: The Struggle Against Subjectivism 1781–1801* (Cambridge, MA: Harvard University Press).

BERKELEY, G. (1710/1998) *Principles of Human Knowledge*, ed. J. Dancy (Oxford: Oxford University Press).

—— (1713/1998) *Three Dialogues between Hylas and Philonous*, ed. J. Dancy (Oxford: Oxford University Press).

BERLIN, I. (1953) *The Hedgehog and the Fox* (London: Weidenfeld & Nicholson).

BERMÚDEZ, J. L. (1998) *The Paradox of Self-Consciousness* (Cambridge, MA: MIT Press).

—— MARCEL, A., and EILAN, N. (eds.) (1995) *The Body and the Self* (Cambridge, MA: MIT Press).

BISHOP, E. (1971/1983) *The Complete Poems 1927–1979* (New York: Noonday).

BRADLEY, F. (1893/1897) *Appearance and Reality*, 2nd edn. (Oxford: Oxford University Press).

—— (1897) Letter in *The Correspondence of William James*, vol. 8, ed. I. K. Skrvpckelis and E. M. Berkeley (Charlottesville: University of Virginia Press).

BREWER, M. W. (1995) 'Compulsion by Reason', *Proceedings of the Aristotelian Society*, suppl. vol. 69.

BRODKEY, H. (1996) *This Wild Darkness* (London: Fourth Estate).

BROWN, H., and SAUNDERS, S. (eds.) (1991) *The Philosophy of Vacuum* (Oxford: Clarendon Press).

BROWN, T. (1820) *Lectures on the Philosophy of the Human Mind* (Edinburgh).

BRUNER, J. (1994) 'The "Remembered" Self', in Neisser and Fivush (1994).

BURGE, T. (1998) 'Reason and the First Person', in Wright, Smith, and MacDonald (1998).

BUTLER, J. (1736/1975) 'Of Personal Identity', in *Personal Identity*, ed. J. Perry (Berkeley: University of California Press).

BUTTERFIELD, J. (1996) 'Whither the Minds?', *British Journal of the Philosophy of Science* 47, 200–21.

BUTTERWORTH, G. (1995) 'An Ecological Perspective on the Origins of Self', in Bermúdez, Marcel, and Eilan (1995).

—— (1998) 'A Developmental-Ecological Perspective on Strawson's "The Self"', *Journal of Consciousness Studies* 5, 132–40.

CAMPBELL, J. (1994) *Past, Space, and Self* (Cambridge, MA: MIT Press).

CAMUS, A. (1937/1963) entry for May 1937, in *Notebooks 1935–42*, trans. Philip Thody (New York: Knopf).

—— (1942/1982) *The Outsider*, trans. Joseph Laredo (London: Hamish Hamilton).

CASSAM, A.-Q. A. (ed.) (1994) *Self-Knowledge* (Oxford: Oxford University Press).

—— (1997) *Self and World* (Oxford: Clarendon Press).

CASTAÑEDA, H.-N. (1966/1994) 'On the Phenomeno-Logic of the I', in Cassam (1994).

CASTON, V. (2002) 'Aristotle on Consciousness', *Mind* 111, 751–815.

CHOMSKY, N. (2000) *New Horizons in the Study of Language* (Cambridge: Cambridge University Press).

CHUN, M., and MAROIS, R. (2002) 'The Dark Side of Visual Attention', *Current Opinion in Neurobiology* 12, 184–9.

CICERO (54–51 BCE/1929) *De Republica*, trans. G. Sabine and S. Smith (Columbus, OH: Ohio State University Press).

CLARKE, D. (2003) *Descartes's Theory of Mind* (Cambridge: Cambridge University Press).

—— (2006) *Descartes* (Oxford: Oxford University Press).

CLAY, E. R. (1882) *The Alternative: A Study in Psychology* (London: Macmillan).

CLOUGH, A. H. (1862/1974) 'The Mystery of the Fall', in *Poems* (Oxford: Oxford University Press).

COHEN, D. J. (1980) 'The Pathology of the Self in Primary Childhood Autism and Gilles de la Tourette Syndrome', *Psychiatric Clinics of North America* 3, 383–403.

COLE, J. (1997), 'On "Being Faceless": Selfhood and Facial Embodiment', *Journal of Consciousness Studies*, 4 (5–6) 467–84.

COLEMAN, S. (2006) 'Being Realistic: Why Physicalism May Entail Panexperientialism', *Journal of Consciousness Studies* 13 (10–11), 40–52.

COLLINS, S. (1982) *Selfless Persons* (Cambridge: Cambridge University Press).

COTTINGHAM, J. (1976) 'Commentary' on Descartes's *Conversations with Burman*, trans. J. Cottingham (Oxford: Clarendon Press).

—— (2002) 'Descartes and the Voluntariness of Belief', *Monist* 85, 343–60.

CRABBE, J. (ed.) (1999) *From Soul to Self* (London: Routledge).

DAINTON, B. (2000) *Stream of Consciousness: Unity and Continuity in Conscious Experience* (London: Routledge).

—— (2008a) *The Phenomenal Self* (Oxford: Oxford University Press).

—— (2008b) 'Sensing Change', *Philosophical Issues* 18, 362–84.

DAMASIO, A. (1994) *Descartes's Error: Emotion, Reason, and the Human Brain* (New York: Avon).

DAMASIO, A. (1999) *The Feeling of What Happens: Body and Emotion in the Making of Consciousness* (New York: Harcourt Brace).

——— (2000) Interview, *New Scientist* 165, 46–9.

DAMON, W., and HART, D. (1988) *Self-understanding in Childhood and Adolescence* (New York: Cambridge University Press).

DARWIN, C. (1838/1987) 'Notebook M', in Charles *Darwin's Notebooks, 1836–44* (Cambridge: Cambridge University Press).

DAWKINS, R. (1998) *Unweaving the Rainbow* (London: Penguin).

DEIKMAN, A. J (1996) ' "I" = Awareness', *Journal of Consciousness Studies* 3, 350–6.

DENNETT, D. (1988) 'Why Everyone is a Novelist', *Times Literary Supplement*, 16–22 September.

——— (1991) *Consciousness Explained* (Boston: Little, Brown).

——— (2001) 'Are We Explaining Consciousness Yet?', *Cognition* 79, 221–37.

——— (2003) *Freedom Evolves* (New York: Viking Press).

DESCARTES, R. (1618–28/1985) *Rules for the Direction of the Mind*, in Descartes (1985), vol. 1.

——— (1619–50/1991) in *The Philosophical Writings of Descartes*, vol. 3: *The Correspondence*, trans. J. Cottingham et al. (Cambridge: Cambridge University Press).

——— (1637/1985) *Discourse on the Method*, in Descartes (1985), vol. 1.

——— (1637/2001) *Meteorology*, in *Discourse on Method, Optics, Geometry, and Meteorology*, trans. P. J. Olscamp (Indianapolis: Hackett).

——— (1640/1991) letter to Mersenne, 1 April 1640, in Descartes (1991), vol. 3.

——— (1641/1985) *Meditations* and *Replies*, in Descartes (1985), vol. 2.

——— (1642/1985) *Letter to Father Dinet*, in Descartes (1985), vol. 2.

——— (1644/1985) *The Principles of Philosophy*, in Descartes (1985), vol. 1.

——— (1645–6/1991) letter to an unknown recipient in Descartes (1991), vol. 3.

——— (1648a/1985) *Comments on a Certain Broadsheet*, in Descartes (1985), vol. 1.

——— (1648b/1976) *Conversations with Burman*, trans. with a philosophical introduction and commentary by J. Cottingham (Oxford: Clarendon Press).

——— (1649/1985) *The Passions of the Soul*, in Descartes (1985), vol. 1.

——— (1985) *The Philosophical Writings of Descartes*, vols. 1 and 2, trans. J. Cottingham et al. (Cambridge: Cambridge University Press).

DEWEY, J. (1929) *The Question for Certainty* (New York: Minton, Balch and Co).

EDDINGTON, A. (1920) *Space, Time, and Gravitation* (Cambridge: Cambridge University Press).

——— (1928) *The Nature of the Physical World* (New York: Macmillan).

——— (1939) *The Philosophy of Physical Science* (Cambridge: Cambridge University Press).

ENGLER, J. (2003) 'Being Somebody and Being Nobody: A Reexamination of the Understanding of Self in Psychoanalysis and Buddhism', in *Psychoanalysis and Buddhism: An Unfolding Dialogue*, ed. J. Safran (Boston: Wisdom Publications).

ERIKSON, E. (1968) *Identity: Youth and Crisis* (New York: Norton).

EVANS, C. O. (1970) *The Subject of Consciousness* (London: Allen & Unwin).

EVANS, G. (1982) *The Varieties of Reference* (Oxford: Oxford University Press).

FENTON, J. (1972/1983) 'The Wild Ones', in *The Memory of War and Children in Exile* (London: Penguin).

FERRIS, T. (1997) *The Whole Shebang* (London: Wiedenfeld & Nicolson).

FEUERBACH, L. (1843/1986) *Principles of the Philosophy of the Future*, trans. M. H. Vogel, with an introduction by T. E. Wartenberg (Indianapolis: Hackett).

FICHTE, J. G. (1792–1810/1971) *Johann Gottlieb Fichtes sämmtliche Werke* (Berlin: de Gruyter).

—— (1794–1802/1982) *The Science of Knowledge*, ed. and trans. P. Heath and J. Lachs (Cambridge: Cambridge University Press).

—— (1796–9/1992) *Foundations of Transcendental Philosophy (Wissenschaftslehre) novo methodo*, ed. and trans. D. Brezeale (Ithaca, NY: Cornell University Press).

FLANAGAN, O. (2003) *The Problem of the Soul* (New York: Basic Books).

FODOR, J. (1984) 'Observation Reconsidered', *Philosophy of Science* 51(1), 23–43.

FORMAN, R. (1998) 'What Does Mysticism Have to Teach us about Consciousness?, *Journal of Consciousness Studies* 5, 185–201.

FOSTER, J. (1982) *The Case for Idealism* (London: Routledge).

—— (1991) *The Immaterial Self: A Defence of the Cartesian Dualist Conception of the Mind* (London: Routledge).

FRANK, R. (1988) *Passions within Reason: The Strategic Role of the Emotions* (New York: Norton).

FRANKFURT, H. (1987/1988) 'Identification and Wholeheartedness', in *The Importance of What We Care About* (Cambridge: Cambridge University Press).

FREGE, G. (1918/1967) 'The Thought: A Logical Inquiry', in *Philosophical Logic*, ed. P. F. Strawson (Oxford: Oxford University Press).

FRENCH, S. (1998) 'Withering Away Physical Objects', in *Interpreting Bodies: Classical and Quantum Objects in Modern Physics*, ed. E. Castellani (Princeton: Princeton University Press).

—— and Krause, D. (2006) *Identity in Physics: A Historical, Philosophical and Formal Analysis* (Oxford: Oxford University Press).

GADAMER, G. (1962/1976) 'On the Problem of Self-Understanding', in *Philosophical Hermeneutics*, trans. and ed. D. E. Linge (Berkeley: University of California Press).

GALLAGHER S. (1998) *The Inordinance of Time* (Evanston, IL: Northwestern University Press).

—— and Marcel, A. (1999) 'The Self in Contextualized Action', *Journal of Consciousness Studies* 6, 4–30.

—— and Shear, J. (eds.) (1999) *Models of the Self* (Thorverton: Imprint Academic).

—— and Zahavi, D., (2008) *The Phenomenological Mind: An Introduction to Philosophy of Mind and Cognitive Science* (London: Routledge).

GALLUP, G., ANDERSON, J., and SHILLITO, D. (2002) 'The Mirror Test', in *The Cognitive Animal*, ed. M. Bekoff, C. Allen, and G. Burghardt (Cambridge, MA: MIT Press).

GAZZANIGA, M. (1998a) *The Mind's Past* (Berkeley: University of California Press).

—— (1998b) 'The Neural Platonist', *Journal of Consciousness Studies* 5, 706–17; also at <http://www.imprint.co.uk/gazza_iv.htm>

GEERTZ, C. (1974/1984) 'From the Natives' Point of View: On the Nature of Anthropological Understanding', in *Culture Theory*, ed. R. A. Shweder and R. A. Levine (Cambridge: Cambridge University Press).

GIBSON, E. (1993) 'Ontogenesis of the Perceived Self', in Neisser (1993).

GIBSON, J. (1979) *The Ecological Approach to Visual Perception* (Boston: Houghton Mifflin).

GLOVER, J. (1988) *I: The Philosophy and Psychology of Personal Identity* (Harmondsworth: Penguin).

GOFF, P. (2006) 'Experiences Don't Sum', *Journal of Consciousness Studies* 13 (10–11), 53–61.

GREEN, H. (*c*.1923/1993) 'Adventure in a Room', in *Surviving* (New York: Viking).

GREENE, B. (2004) *The Fabric of the Cosmos* (New York: Knopf).

GREER, G. (1986) article in *The Times*, 1 February 1986.

GURWITSCH, A. (1941) 'A Non-egological Conception of Consciousness', *Philosophy and Phenomenological Research*, 1, 325–38.

HALLIDAY, S. (1973) 'Poems' (unpublished).

HAMILTON, S. (2001) *A Very Short Introduction to Indian Philosophy* (Oxford: Oxford University Press).

HARE, R. M. (1981) *Moral Thinking* (Oxford: Clarendon Press).

HARRÉ, R., and MADDEN, E. H. (1975) *Causal Powers: A Theory of Natural Necessity* (Oxford: Blackwell).

HARVEY, P. (1990) *An Introduction to Buddhism* (Cambridge: Cambridge University Press).

HEIDEGGER, M. (1919–20/1962) *Grundprobleme der Phänomenologie* (Frankfurt: Vittorio Klostermann).

——(1927/1962) *Being and Time*, trans. J. Macquarrie and E. Robinson (Oxford: Blackwell).

——(1930/2001) *Einleitung in die Philosophie* (Frankfurt: Vittorio Klostermann).

HEIL, J. (2005) *From an Ontological Point of View* (Oxford: Oxford University Press).

HEMINGWAY, E. (1929) *A Farewell to Arms* (London: Cape).

HERBART, J. F. (1816/1891) *Textbook of Psychology*, trans. M. K. Smith (New York: D. Appleton).

——(1824–5/1850–2) *Psychology as a Science*, in *Sämmtliche Werke* (Leipzig: G. Hartenstein).

HOBBES, T. (1651/1996) *Leviathan*, ed. Richard Tuck (Cambridge: Cambridge University Press).

HOBSON, R. P. (1993) 'Through Feeling and Sight to Self and Symbol', in Neisser (1993).

——and Lee, A. (1998) 'On Developing Self-Concepts: A Controlled Study of Children and Adolescents with Autism', *Journal of Child Psychology and Psychiatry* 39, 1131–44.

HOLMES, R. (1989) *Coleridge—Early Visions* (London: HarperCollins).

HOLUB, M. (1990) *The Dimension of the Present Moment* (London: Faber).

HOMER (*c*.800BCE/2006) *Odyssey*, trans. E. V. Rieu (London: Penguin).

HOPKINS, G. M. (1880/1959) 'Commentary on the Spiritual Exercises of St Ignatius Loyola', in *Sermons and Devotional Writings*, ed. C. J. Devlin (London: Oxford University Press).

HORGAN, T., and POTRČ, M. (2008) *Austere Realism: Contextual Semantics Meets Minimal Ontology* (Cambridge, MA: MIT Press).

HUDSON, L. (1966) *Contrary Imaginations: A Psychological Study of the English Schoolboy* (London: Methuen).

HUGHES, R. (1929) *A High Wind in Jamaica* (London: Chatto & Windus).

HUME, D. (1739–40/1978) *A Treatise of Human Nature*, ed. L. A. Selby-Bigge and P. H. Nidditch (Oxford: Oxford University Press).

——*A Treatise of Human Nature* (1739–40/2000), ed. D. F. Norton and M. J. Norton (Oxford: Oxford University Press).

——(1748–51/1999) *An Enquiry Concerning Human Understanding*, ed. T. L. Beauchamp (Oxford: Oxford University Press).

——(1779/1947) *Dialogues Concerning Natural Religion*, ed. N. Kemp Smith (Edinburgh: Nelson).

HURLBURT, R., and SCHWITZGEBEL, E. (2007) *Describing Inner Experience?* (Cambridge, MA: Bradford Books).

——Happé, F., and Frith, U. (1994) 'Sampling the Form of Inner Experience in Three Adults with Asperger Syndrome', *Psychological Medicine*, 24, 385–95.

HUSSERL, E. (*c*.1922/1973) *Zur Phänomenologie der Intersubjektivität, Texte aus dem Nachlass. Zweiter Teil: 1921–8* (The Hague: Martinus Nijhoff).

——(1925/1977) *Phenomenological Psychology: Lectures, Summer Semester, 1925*, trans. J. Scanlon (The Hague: Martinus Nijhoff).

——(1931/1973) *Cartesian Meditations*, trans. D. Cairns (The Hague: Nijhoff).

JACKSON, F. (1994) 'Metaphysics by Possible Cases', *Monist* 77(1), 93–110.

JAMES, H. (1915/1999) *Henry James: A Life in Letters*, ed. Philip Horne (London: Penguin).

James, W. (1890/1950) *The Principles of Psychology*, 2 vols. (New York: Dover).

—— (1892/1984) *Psychology: Briefer Course* (Cambridge, MA: Harvard University Press).

—— (1895/1992) 'The Knowing of Things Together', in *William James: Writings, 1878–1899*, ed. Gerald E. Myers (New York: The Library of America).

—— (1904*a*/1996) 'Does Consciousness Exist?', in *Essays in Radical Empiricism* (Lincoln, NE: University of Nebraska Press).

—— (1904*b*/1996) 'A World of Pure Experience', in *Essays in Radical Empiricism* (Lincoln, NE: University of Nebraska Press).

—— (1909/1987) *A Pluralistic Universe*, in *William James: Writings 1902–1910* (New York: The Library of America).

Johnston, M. (2003) 'Parts and Principles of Unity', in *Handbook of Contemporary Philosophy*, ed. F. Jackson (Oxford: Oxford University Press).

Jolley, N. (ed.) (1995) *The Cambridge Companion to Leibniz* (Cambridge: Cambridge University Press).

Joyce, J. (1922/1986) *Ulysses* (Harmondsworth: Penguin).

Kagan, J. (1982) 'The Emergence of Self', *Journal of Child Psychiatry and Psychology* 23, 363–81.

Kames, Lord (Henry Home) (1751–79/2005) *Essays on the Principles of Morality and Natural Religion* (Indianapolis: Liberty Fund Classics).

Kant, I. (1772/1967) Letter to Marcus Herz, February 21, 1772, in *Kant: Philosophical Correspondence 1759–99*, ed. and trans. Arnulf Zweig (Chicago: University of Chicago Press).

—— (1781–7/1889) *Kritik der reinen Vernunft*, ed. E. Adickes (Berlin: Mayer and Müller).

—— (1781–7/1933) *Critique of Pure Reason*, trans. N. Kemp Smith (London: Macmillan).

—— (1781–7/1996) *Critique of Pure Reason*, trans. W. S. Pluhar (Indianapolis: Hackett).

—— (1781–7/1998) *Critique of Pure Reason*, trans. P. Guyer and A. Wood (Cambridge: Cambridge University Press).

—— (1783/1953) *Prolegomena*, trans. P. G. Lucas (Manchester: Manchester University Press).

—— (1798/1974) *Anthropology from A Pragmatic Point of View*, trans. Mary J. Gregor (The Hague: Nijhoff).

Kenny, A. (1988) *The Self* (Milwaukee, WI: Marquette University Press).

—— (1989) *The Metaphysics of Mind* (Oxford: Clarendon Press).

—— (1999) 'Body, Soul, and Intellect in Aquinas', in Crabbe (1999).

Kierkegaard, S. (1843/1974) *Either/Or*, trans. W. Lowrie (Princeton: Princeton University Press).

Kircher, T., and David, A. (eds.) (2003) *The Self in Neuroscience and Psychiatry* (Cambridge: Cambridge University Press).

Knight, R. T., and Grabowecky, M. (1995) 'Escape from Linear Time: Prefrontal Cortex and Conscious Experience', in *The Cognitive Neurosciences*, ed. M. Gazzaniga (Cambridge, MA: MIT Press).

Ladyman, J., and Ross, D., with Spurrett, D., and Collier, J. (2007) *Every Thing Must Go: Metaphysics Naturalized* (Oxford: Oxford University Press).

Lakoff, G. (1997) 'The Internal Structure of the Self', in Neisser and Fivush (1997).

Laycock, S. (1998) 'Consciousness It/Self', *Journal of Consciousness Studies* 5, 141–52.

Lee, A., and Hobson, R. P. (1998) 'On Developing Self-Concepts: A Controlled Study of Children and Adolescents with Autism', *Journal of Child Psychiatry and Psychology* 39, 1131–44.

Legerstee, M. (1998) 'Mental and Bodily Awareness in Infancy: Consciousness of Self-existence', *Journal of Consciousness Studies*, 5 (5–6), 627–44.

LEIBNIZ, G. (1676) *De summa rerum: Metaphysical Papers 1675–1676*, ed. and trans. G. H. R. Parkinson (New Haven: Yale University Press).

—— (1704/1981) *New Essays on Human Understanding*, ed. and trans. P. Remnant and J. Bennett (Cambridge: Cambridge University Press).

—— (1720/1965) *Monadology and Other Philosophical Essays*, trans. P. and A. M. Schrecker (Indianapolis: Bobbs-Merrill).

LEWIS, D. (1994) 'Reduction of Mind', in *A Companion to the Philosophy of Mind*, ed. S. Guttenplan (Oxford: Blackwell).

—— (1999) 'Introduction', in D. Lewis, *Papers in Metaphysics and Epistemology* (Cambridge: Cambridge University Press).

LEWIS, D. and LANGTON, R. (1998/1999) 'Defining "Intrinsic" ', in D. Lewis, *Papers in Metaphysics and Epistemology* (Cambridge: Cambridge University Press).

LEWIS, M., and BROOKS-GUNN, J. (1979) *Social Cognition and the Acquisition of Self* (New York: Plenum).

LIBET, B. (1985) 'Unconscious Cerebral Initiative and the Role of Conscious Will in Voluntary Action', *Behavioral and Brain Sciences* 8, 529–66.

—— (1987) 'Are the Mental Experiences of Will and Self-Control Significant for the Performance of a Voluntary Act?', *Behavioral and Brain Sciences* 10, 783–6.

—— (1989) 'The Timing of a Subjective Experience', *Behavioral and Brain Sciences* 12, 183–5.

—— (1999) 'Do We Have Free Will?', in *The Volitional Brain: Towards a Neuroscience of Free Will*, ed. B. Libet, A. Freeman, and K. Sutherland (Thorverton: Imprint Academic).

LOCKE, J. (1689–1700/1975) *An Essay Concerning Human Understanding*, ed. P. Nidditch (Oxford: Clarendon Press).

—— (1696–9/1964) 'The Correspondence with Stillingfleet', in *An Essay Concerning Human Understanding*, ed. and abridged by A. D. Woozley (London: Collins).

LOCKWOOD, M. (1981) 'What *Was* Russell's Neutral Monism?', *Midwest Studies in Philosophy* 6, 143–58.

—— (1989) *Mind, Brain, and the Quantum* (Oxford: Blackwell).

—— (2005) *The Labyrinth of Time* (Oxford: Oxford University Press).

LONERGAN, B. (1967) *Collection*, ed. F. Crowe (New York: Herder & Herder).

LOWE, E. J. (1996) *The Subject of Experience* (Cambridge: Cambridge University Press).

LUTYENS, M. (1983) *Krishnamurti: The Years of Fulfilment* (London: John Murray).

MARCUS AURELIUS (c.170/1964) *Meditations*, trans. with an introduction by M. Staniforth (Harmondsworth: Penguin).

MARKUS, H. R., and KITAYAMA, S. (1991) 'Culture and the Self: Implications for Cognition, Emotion, and Motivation', *Psychological Review* 98, 224–53.

MARTIN, C. B. (1997) 'On the Need for Properties: The Road to Pythagoreanism and Back', *Synthese* 112, 193–231.

MARTIN, R., and BARRESI, J. (2006) *The Rise and Fall of Soul and Self: An Intellectual History of Personal Identity* (New York: Columbia University Press).

MAXWELL, G. (1978) 'Rigid Designators and Mind–Brain Identity', in *Perception and Cognition: Issues in the Foundations of Psychology*, ed. C. Wade Savage (Minneapolis: University of Minnesota Press).

McCARTHY, M. (1963) Interview, in *Writers at Work: the Paris Review Interviews, Second Series*, ed. George Plimpton (New York: The Viking Press).

McDOWELL, J. (1994) *Mind and World* (Cambridge, MA: Harvard University Press).

McDowell, J. (1998) 'Having the World in View: Lecture One', *Journal of Philosophy* 95, 431–50.

McEwan, I. (1997) *Enduring Love* (London: Cape).

McGinn, C. (1989) 'Can We Solve the Mind–Body Problem?', *Mind* 98, 349–66.

——(1991) *The Problem of Consciousness* (Oxford: Blackwell).

——(1995) 'Consciousness and Space', *Journal of Consciousness Studies* 2, 221–30.

——(1999) *The Mysterious Flame* (New York: Basic Books).

——(2006) 'Hard Questions', in *Consciousness and its Place in Nature*, ed. A. Freeman (Thorverton: Imprint Academic), 90–9.

McLaughlin, B. (2002) 'Colour, Consciousness, and Colour Consciousness', in *Consciousness: New Essays*, ed. Quentin Smith (Oxford: Oxford University Press).

——and McGee, V. (2000) 'Lessons of the Many', *Philosophical Topics* 28, 129–51.

Mbiti, J. (1969/1990) *African Religions and Philosophy* (London: Heinemann).

Mele, A. (2006) *Free Will and Luck* (Oxford: Oxford University Press).

——(2007) 'Decisions, Intentions, Urges, and Free Will: Why Libet Has Not Shown What He Says He Has', in *Explanation and Causation: Topics in Contemporary Philosophy*, ed. J. Campbell, M. O'Rourke, and D. Shier (Cambridge, MA: MIT Press).

Mercer, C., and Sleigh, R. (1995) 'Metaphysics: The early period to the *Discourse on Metaphysics*', in Jolley (1995).

Merian, J. (1793/1997) 'On the Phenomenalism of David Hume', *Hume Studies* 23, 178–91 (from *Mémoires de l'Académie Royale des Sciences et Belles-Lettres depuis l'avènement de Frédéric Guillaume II au trône* (Berlin: G. Decker)).

Merleau-Ponty, M. (1945/1962) *The Phenomenology of Perception*, trans. Colin Smith (London: Routledge & Kegan Paul).

Midgley, M. (1984) *Wickedness: A Philosophical Essay* (London: Ark).

Milne, A. A. (1928) *The House at Pooh Corner* (London: Methuen).

Montague, M. (2009) 'Perceptual Experience', in *Oxford Handbook of Philosophy of Mind*, ed. B. McLaughlin, A. Beckermann, and S. Walter (Oxford: Oxford University Press).

Moore, G. E. (1903) 'The Refutation of Idealism', *Mind* 12, 433–53.

Mumford, S. (1998) *Dispositions* (Oxford: Oxford University Press).

Nadler, S. (2006) *Spinoza's Ethics: An Introduction* (Cambridge: Cambridge University Press).

Nāgārjuna (c.150/1995) *The Fundamental Wisdom of the Middle Way*, trans. with a commentary by Jay Garfield (Albany, NY: SUNY Press).

Nagel, T. (1986) *The View from Nowhere* (New York: Oxford University Press).

——(1998) 'Conceiving the Impossible and the Mind–Body Problem', *Philosophy* 73, 337–52.

Neisser, U. (1988) 'Five Kinds of Self-Knowledge', *Philosophical Psychology* 1, 35–9.

——(1993) *The Perceived Self: Ecological and Interpersonal Sources of Self-knowledge* (Cambridge: Cambridge University Press).

——(1999) 'The Ecological Self and its Metaphors', *Philosophical Topics* 27, 201–16.

——and Fivush, R. (1994) *The Remembering Self: Construction and Accuracy in the Self-narrative* (Cambridge: Cambridge University Press).

——(1997) *The Conceptual Self in Context: Culture, Experience, Self-understanding* (Cambridge: Cambridge University Press).

——and Winograd, E. (1988) *Remembering Reconsidered: Ecological and Traditional Approaches to the Study of Memory* (Cambridge: Cambridge University Press).

Neuhouser, F. (1990) *Fichte's Theory of Subjectivity* (Cambridge: Cambridge University Press).

NICHOLI, A. M. (1999) *The Harvard Guide to Psychiatry* (Cambridge, MA: Harvard University Press).

NIETZSCHE, F. (1874/1983) *Untimely Meditations*, trans. R. J. Hollingdale (Cambridge: Cambridge University Press).

—— (1883–5/1961) *Thus Spoke Zarathustra: A Book for All and None*, translated by R. J. Hollingdale (London: Penguin).

—— (1885–8/2003) *Writings from the Last Notebooks*, trans. Kate Sturge, ed. Rüdiger Bittner (Cambridge: Cambridge University Press).

—— (1886) *Beyond Good and Evil (Jenseits von Gut und Böse)* (Leipzig: Naumann).

NISBETT, R. E. (2003) *The Geography of Thought: How Asians and Westerners Think Differently ... and Why* (New York: Free Press).

NOË, A. (2005) *Action in Perception* (Cambridge, MA: MIT Press).

NORRETRANDERS, T (1991/1998) *The User Illusion: Cutting Consciousness Down To Size* (London: Penguin).

NOZICK, R. (1981) *Philosophical Explanations* (Oxford: Clarendon Press).

—— (1989/1990) *The Examined Life: Philosophical Meditations* (New York: Touchstone).

OGDEN, J. A. (1996) *Fractured Minds: A Case Study Approach to Clinical Neuropsychology* (Oxford: Oxford University Press).

OLSON, E. (1998) 'There is No Problem of the Self', *Journal of Consciousness Studies* 5, 645–57.

PARFIT, D. (1984) *Reasons and Persons* (Oxford: Clarendon Press).

—— (1995) 'The Unimportance of Identity', in *Identity*, ed. H. Harris (Oxford: Clarendon Press).

—— (1998) 'Experiences, Subjects, and Conceptual Schemes', *Philosophical Topics* 26, 217–70.

PEACOCKE, C. (1999) *Being Known* (Oxford: Clarendon Press).

PERRY, J. (1979) 'The Problem of the Essential Indexical', in Cassam (1994).

PESSOA, L., and DE WEERD, P. (2003) *Filling-In: From Perceptual Completion to Cortical Reorganization* (Oxford: Oxford University Press).

PHILO OF ALEXANDRIA (*c*.20–50/1929–62) *Collected Works*, trans. F. H. Colson and G. H. Whitaker (Cambridge, MA: Harvard University Press).

PICKERING, J. (1999), 'The Self is a Semiotic Process', *Journal of Consciousness Studies* 6, 31–47.

PITT, D. (2004) 'The Phenomenology of Cognition, or What is it Like to Think that *p*?', *Philosophy and Phenomenological Research* 69, 1–36.

PLATNER, E. (1772) *Anthropologie für Ärzte und Weltweise* (Leipzig: Dyck).

—— (1793) *Philosophische Aphorismen nebst einigen Anleitungen zur Philosophischen Geschichte*, 3rd edn. (Leipzig: Schwickert).

PLIMPTON, G. (1963) *Writers at Work,* 2nd series (New York: Viking).

POCKETT, S. (2003) 'How long is "now"? Phenomenology and the Specious Present', *Phenomenology and the Cognitive Sciences* 2, 55–68.

PÖPPEL, E. (1978) 'Time Perception', in *Handbook of Sensory Physiology*, viii, ed. R. Held, H. W. Leibovitz, and H. L. Teuber (New York: Springer).

POST, H. (1963) 'Individuality and Physics', *Listener* 70, 534–7.

PRIESTLEY, J. (1777–82/1999) *Disquisitions Relating to Matter and Spirit*, in *The Theological and Miscellaneous Works of Joseph Priestley*, vol. 3, ed. J. T. Rutt (Bristol: Thoemmes Press).

—— and Price, R. (1778/1999) *A Free Discussion of the Doctrines of Materialism, and Philosophical Necessity*, in *The Theological and Miscellaneous Works of Joseph Priestley*, vol. 4, ed. J. T. Rutt (Bristol: Thoemmes Press).

PULLMAN, B. (1998) *The Atom in the History of Human Thought* (New York: Oxford University Press).

QUINE, W. V. (1955/1966) 'Quantifiers and Propositional Attitudes', in Quine (1966).

QUINE, W. V. (1966) *The Ways of Paradox* (New York: Random House).

RAMSEY, F. (1925/1997) 'Universals', in *Properties*, ed. D. H. Mellor and Alex Oliver (Oxford: Oxford University Press).

REED, G. (1987) 'Time-Gap Experience', in *The Oxford Companion to the Mind*, ed. R. Gregory (Oxford: Oxford University Press).

REES, G. (1960) *A Bundle of Sensations* (London: Chatto & Windus).

REGIUS, H. (1647/1985) *An Account of the Human Mind, or Rational Soul, which explains what it is and what it can be*, in *The Philosophical Writings of Descartes*, vol. 1, trans. J. Cottingham et al. (Cambridge: Cambridge University Press).

REID, T. (1764/1969) *An Inquiry into the Human Mind* (Chicago: University of Chicago Press).

—— (1785/2002) *Essays on the Intellectual Powers of Man* (Edinburgh: Edinburgh University Press).

RICHARDSON, D. (1915) *Pointed Roofs, Pilgrimage*, 1 (London: Virago Press).

RIMBAUD, A. (1871/1972) *Oeuvres complètes* (Paris: Gallimard).

ROGERS, B. (1999) *A. J. Ayer* (London: Chatto & Windus).

ROSENTHAL, D. (2005) 'Sensory Qualities, Consciousness, and Perception', in *Consciousness and Mind* (Oxford: Oxford University Press).

ROTTER, J. B. (1966) *Generalized Expectancies for Internal versus External Control of Reinforcement*, in *Psychological Monographs* 80.

RUHNAU, E. (1995) 'Time Gestalt and the Observer', in *Conscious Experience*, ed. T. Metzinger (Thorverton: Imprint Academic).

RUSSELL, B. (1912/1959) *The Problems of Philosophy* (Oxford: Oxford University Press).

—— (1919) *Introduction to Mathematical Philosophy* (London: George Allen & Unwin).

—— (1927a/1992a) *The Analysis of Matter* (London: Routledge).

—— (1927b/1992b) *An Outline of Philosophy* (London: Routledge).

—— (1948/1992) *Human Knowledge: Its Scope and Limits* (London: Routledge).

—— (1956/1995) 'Mind and Matter', in *Portraits from Memory* (Nottingham: Spokesman).

—— (1961/1979) *A History of Western Philosophy*, 2nd edn. (London: Unwin).

RUTHERFORD, D. (1995) 'Metaphysics: the late period', in Jolley (1995).

RYLE, G. (1949) *The Concept of Mind* (New York: Barnes & Noble).

SACKS, O. (1984) *A Leg to Stand On* (London: Picador).

SARTRE, J.-P. (1936–7/2004) *Transcendence of the Ego*, trans. A. Brown, introduced by S. Richmond (London: Routledge).

—— (1938/1996) *La nausée* (Paris: Gallimard).

SASS, L. (1998) 'Schizophrenia, Self-Consciousness and the Modern Mind', *Journal of Consciousness Studies* 5, 543–65.

SAUNDERS, S., and BROWN, H. (1991) *The Philosophy of Vacuum* (Oxford: Clarendon Press).

SCHOPENHAUER, A. (1819–1844/1969) *The World as Will and Representation*, trans. E. F. J. Payne (New York: Dover).

SCOVILLE, W. B., and MILNER, B. (1957) 'Loss of Recent Memory after Bilateral Hippocampal Lesions', *Journal of Neurology, Neurosurgery, and Psychiatry* 20, 11–21.

SENGHOR, L. S. (1964) *On African Socialism* (New York: Praeger).

SHAFTESBURY, EARL OF (1698–1712/1900) 'Philosophical Regimen', in *The Life, Unpublished Letters, and Philosophical Regimen of Anthony, Earl of Shaftesbury*, ed. B. Rand (New York: Macmillan).

SHEAR, J. (1998) 'Experiential Clarification of the Problem of Self', *Journal of Consciousness Studies* 5, 673–86.

SHEETS-JOHNSTONE, M. (1999) 'Phenomenology and Agency', *Journal of Consciousness Studies* 6, 48–69.

SHOEMAKER, S. (1968/1994) 'Self-Reference and Self-Awareness', in *Identity, Cause, and Mind* (Cambridge: Cambridge University Press) and in Cassam (1994).

—— (1970) 'Persons and their Pasts', *American Philosophical Quarterly* 7, 269–85.

—— (1984) *Identity, Cause, and Mind* (Cambridge: Cambridge University Press).

—— (1986/1996) 'Introspection and the Self', in Shoemaker (1996).

—— (1996) *The First-Person Perspective and Other Essays* (Cambridge: Cambridge University Press).

—— and SWINBURNE, R. (1984) 'Personal Identity: A Materialist's Account', in *Personal Identity* (Oxford: Blackwell).

SIMONS, D. J., and LEVIN, D. T. (1997) 'Change Blindness', *Trends in Cognitive Sciences* 1, 261–7.

SKRBINA, D. (2005) *Panpsychism in the West* (Cambridge, MA: MIT Press).

SORABJI, R. (2006) *Self: Ancient and Modern Insights about Individuality, Life and Death* (Oxford: Clarendon Press).

SPELKE, E. (1994) 'Initial Knowledge: Six Suggestions', *Cognition* 50, 431–45.

SPENSER, Edmund (c.1594/1989) 'Amoretti', in *Shorter Poems* (New Haven: Yale University Press).

SPINOZA, B. de (1663/1985) *Principles of Cartesian Philosophy*, in *The Collected Works of Spinoza*, ed. and trans. E. Curley (Princeton: Princeton University Press).

—— (1677/1985) *Ethics*, in *The Collected Works of Spinoza*, ed. and trans. E. Curley (Princeton: Princeton University Press).

SPIRO, M. (1993) 'Is the Western Conception of the Self "Peculiar" within the Context of the World Cultures?', *Ethos* 21, 107–53.

SPRIGGE, T. L. S. (2006) *The God of Metaphysics* (Oxford: Oxford University Press).

SQUIRE, R., and KANDEL, E. (1999) *Memory: From Mind to Molecules* (New York: Scientific American Library).

STEPHENS, G. L., and GRAHAM, G. (2000) *When Self-consciousness Breaks* (Cambridge, MA: MIT Press).

STERN, D. (1985) *The Interpersonal World of the Infant* (New York: Basic Books).

STEWART, M. (2006) *The Courtier and the Heretic: Leibniz, Spinoza, and the Fate of God in the Modern World* (New York: Norton).

STONE, J. (1988) 'Parfit and the Buddha: Why There Are No People', *Philosophy and Phenomenological Research* 48, 519–32.

—— (2005) 'Why There Still Are No People', *Philosophy and Phenomenological Research* 70, 174–92.

STRAWSON, G. (1983) 'Freedom and Belief and Belief in Freedom' (D.Phil. thesis, University of Oxford).

—— (1986/1991) *Freedom and Belief* (Oxford: Clarendon Press).

—— (1987/2008) 'Realism and Causation', in Strawson (2008d).

—— (1989; repr. with corrections 1992, 1996, 2003) *The Secret Connexion* (Oxford: Clarendon Press).

—— (1994) *Mental Reality* (Cambridge, MA: MIT Press).

—— (1997/1999) ' "The Self" ', in *Models of the Self* ed. S. Gallagher and Shear (1999).

—— (1999a), 'The Self and the Sesmet', *Journal of Consciousness Studies* 6, 99–135.

—— (1999b) 'Self, Body, and Experience', *Proceedings of the Aristotelian Society*, suppl. vol. 73, 307–32.

——(1999c) 'The Sense of the Self', in Crabbe (1999).

STRAWSON, G. (2001) 'Hume on Himself', in *Essays in Practical Philosophy: From Action to Values*, ed. D. Egonsson, J. Josefsson, B. Petersson, and T. Rønnow-Rasmussen (Aldershot: Ashgate Press).

——(2002) 'Knowledge of the World', *Philosophical Issues* 12, 146–75; revised version see 2008a.

——(2003a) 'Mental Ballistics: The Involuntariness of Spontaneity', *Proceedings of the Aristotelian Society* 20, 227–56.

——(2003b) 'Real Materialism', in *Chomsky and his Critics*, ed. L. Antony and N. Hornstein (Oxford: Blackwell).

——(2003c) 'What is the Relation between an Experience, the Subject of the Experience, and the Content of the Experience?', *Philosophical Issues* 13, 279–315; revised version see 2008e.

——(2004/2008a) 'Against Narrativity', in *Real Materialism and Other Essays* (Oxford: Clarendon Press).

——(2005/2008) 'Intentionality and Experience: Terminological Preliminaries', in Strawson (2008d).

——(2006a) 'Realistic Monism: Why Physicalism Entails Panpsychism', in *Consciousness and its Place in Nature*, ed. A. Freeman (Thorverton: Imprint Academic).

——(2006b) 'Reply to Commentators, with a Celebration of Descartes', in *Consciousness and its Place in Nature*, ed. A. Freeman (Thorverton: Imprint Academic).

——(2007/2008) 'Episodic Ethics', in *Real Materialism and Other Essays* (Oxford: Clarendon Press).

——(2008a) 'Can we Know the Nature of Reality as it is in Itself?', revised version of Strawson (2002), in Strawson (2008d).

——(2008b) 'The Identity of the Categorical and the Dispositional', *Analysis* 68/4, 271–82.

——(2008c) 'Real Intentionality 3', *Theorema* 27, 35–69, and in Strawson (2008d).

——(2008d) *Real Materialism and Other Essays* (Oxford: Clarendon Press).

——(2008e) 'What is the Relation between an Experience, the Subject of the Experience, and the Content of the Experience?', revised version of Strawson (2003c), in Strawson (2008d).

——(in preparation, *a*) *The Evident Connexion: Mind, Self and David Hume* (Oxford: Oxford University Press).

——(in preparation, *b*) *Locke on Personal Identity* (Princeton: Princeton University Press).

——(in preparation, *c*) *Life in Time* (Oxford: Oxford University Press).

STRAWSON, P. F. (1959) *Individuals* (London: Methuen).

——(1962/1974) 'Freedom and Resentment', in *Freedom and Resentment* (London: Methuen).

——(1964/1971) 'Identifying Reference and Truth-Values', in *Logico-Linguistic Papers* (London: Methuen).

——(1966) *The Bounds of Sense* (London: Methuen).

——(1980) 'Reply to Evans', in *Philosophical Subjects*, ed. Z. van Straaten (Oxford: Clarendon Press).

——(1995) 'Reply to Cassam', in *The Philosophy of P. F. Strawson*, ed. P. K. Sen and R. R. Verma (Delhi: Indian Council of Philosophical Research).

SZASZ, T. (1973) 'Personal Conduct', in *The Second Sin* (London: Routledge & Kegan Paul).

THIEL, U. (2001) 'Kant's Notion of Self-Consciousness in Context', in *Kant und die Berliner Aufklärung*, ed. V. Gerhardt, R. Horstmann, and R. Schumacher (Berlin: de Gruyter).

——(2006) 'Self-Consciousness and Personal Identity', in *The Cambridge History of Eighteenth-Century Philosophy*, ed. K. Haakonssen (Cambridge: Cambridge University Press).

THIEL, U. (in preparation) *Self-Consciousness and Personal Identity in Eighteenth-Century Philosophy* (Oxford: Oxford University Press).

TRAHERNE, T. (*c*.1660/1903) *Poetical Works* (London: Bertram Dobell).

TREFIL, J. (1997) *Are We Unique? A Scientist Explores the Unparalleled Intelligence of the Human Mind* (New York: Wiley).

TRIVERS, R. (1988) *Social Evolution* (Menlo Park, CA: Benjamin/Cummings).

UPDIKE, J. (1989) *Self-Consciousness* (London: Deutsch).

—— (2000) *Gertrude and Claudius* (London: Deutsch).

VAN FRAASSEN, B. (1980) *The Scientific Image* (Oxford: Clarendon Press).

—— (2004/2005) 'Transcendence of the Ego (The Non-Existent Knight)', in *The Self?* ed. G. Strawson (Oxford: Blackwell), 87–110.

VAN INWAGEN, P. (1990*a*) *Material Beings* (Ithaca, NY: Cornell University Press).

—— (1990*b*) 'Symposium on *Material Beings*', *Philosophy and Phenomenological Research* 53, 683–719.

WALLAS, G. (1926) *The Art of Thought* (London: Cape).

WALSH, W. (1975) *Kant's Criticism of Metaphysics* (Edinburgh: Edinburgh University Press).

WARD, J. (1886) 'Psychology', in *Encyclopaedia Britannica*, 9th edn.

WEGNER, D. M. (2002) *The Illusion of Conscious Will* (Cambridge, MA: MIT Press).

—— and WHEATLEY, T. (1999) 'Apparent Mental Causation: Sources of the Experience of Will', *American Psychologist* 54, 480–92.

WEINBERG, S. (1997) 'Before the Big Bang', *New York Review of Books* 44(10), 12 June.

WHITEHEAD, A. (1927–8/1979) *Process and Reality*, rev. edn. (New York: Macmillan).

WIREDU, K. (1998) 'Anglophone African Philosophy', in *The Routledge Encyclopaedia of Philosophy*, ed. E. J. Craig (London: Routledge).

WITTGENSTEIN, L. (1916/1986) *Notebooks 1914–1916*, trans. G. E. M. Anscombe, 2nd edn. (Oxford: Blackwell).

—— (1950/1969) *On Certainty* (Oxford: Blackwell).

—— (1953) *Philosophical Investigations*, trans. G. E. M. Anscombe (Oxford: Blackwell).

—— (1958) *The Blue and Brown Books* (Oxford: Blackwell).

WOLFF, C. (1732) *Psychologia empirica* (Frankfurt).

WOOLF, V. (1923/1988) 'A Romance of the Heart', in *The Essays of Virginia Woolf*, vol. 3: *1919–1924*, in ed. A. McNeillie (London: Hogarth Press).

—— (1941) *Between the Acts* (London: Hogarth Press).

—— (1985) *Moments of Being*, ed. Jeanne Schulkind (London: Grafton).

WRIGHT, C., SMITH, B. C., and MACDONALD, C. (1998) *Knowing Our Own Minds* (Oxford: Oxford University Press).

WUNDT, W. (1874/1911) *Principles of Physiological Psychology,* trans. E. B. Titchener (New York: Macmillan).

YABLO, S. (1990) 'The Real Distinction between Mind and Body', *Canadian Journal of Philosophy*, supp. vol. 16, 149–201.

ZAHAVI, D. (1999) *Self-Awareness and Alterity: A Phenomenological Investigation* (Evanston, IL: Northwestern University Press).

—— (2006) *Subjectivity and Selfhood: Investigating the First-Person Perspective* (Cambridge, MA: MIT Press).

INDEX

This index does not cite every occurrence of every listed term or topic. Page numbers in bold indicate the place at which an entry is introduced or defined, or the main place at which it is discussed.